NEW REVISED EDITION

Webster's

Classic
Reference
Library

Over
6 million
in print!

DICTIONARY

NEW ENCYCLOPEDIC EDITION

Mc Graw Hill **Children's Publishing**

Copyright © 2001 McGraw-Hill Children's Publishing.
Published by Landoll, an imprint of McGraw-Hill Children's Publishing, a division of The
McGraw-Hill Companies.

Send all inquiries to:
McGraw-Hill Children's Publishing
8787 Orion Place
Columbus, Ohio 43240-4027

 2 3 4 5 6 7 8 9 PHXBK 07 06 05 04 03 02

The McGraw-Hill Companies

Table of Contents

This is an abridged dictionary, containing a selection of the many words and definitions that make up the English language. In the interest of convenience, we have made this volume as comprehensive as space permits, choosing words and definitions for both reliability and versatility.

In this manner, we have excluded place names, proper names, and historical events, which are best researched in more expansive dictionaries. An abridged dictionary like this one offers the reader a reliable listing of everyday words in a compact, convenient format.

ABBREVIATIONS

abbr.—abbreviation

adj.—adjective

adv.—adverb

coll. n.—collective noun

conj.—conjunction

contr.—contraction

ind. art.—indefinite article

interj.—interjection

meta.—metaphor

n.—noun

pl.—plural

prep.—preposition

pron.—pronoun

var.—variant

v.—verb

A, a The first letter of the English alphabet; the highest grade, meaning excellent or best; in music, the sixth note of the C major scale. *art.* A singular unspecified referent; one, any.

aard•vark *n.* A large burrowing insect-eating mammal resembling the anteater, native to sub-Saharan Africa.

a•back *adv.* Unexpectedly; by surprise; startled.

a•bac•te•ri•al *adj.* Not being caused by bacteria.

a•ba•cus *n.* A frame holding parallel rods with beads, used for manual computation, especially by the Chinese.

a•baft *adv.* On or toward the stern, aft, or hind part of a ship.

ab•a•lo•ne *n.* A member of the genus of gastropod mollusks that cling to rocks and have a flat shell lined with mother of pearl.

a•ban•don *vt.* To yield utterly; to desert, forsake, or withdraw protection, support, or help from. **abandonment** *n.*

a•ban•doned *adj.* Deserted; forsaken.

a•base *v.* To lower in rank, prestige, position, or estimation; to cast down, to humble.

a•base•ment *n.* A state of depression, degradation, or humiliation.

a•bash *v.* To embarrass; to disconcert; to make ashamed or uneasy. **abashment** *n.*

a•bate *v.* To diminish or decrease in strength, value, or intensity; to wane or ebb. **abater** *n.*, **abated** *adj.*

a•bate•ment *n.* The process of abating something; the amount which is abated.

ab•a•tis *n.* A collection of felled trees with the smaller branches already cut off.

ab•bess *n.* The female superior of a convent of nuns, possessing the same authority as an abbot.

ab•bey *n.* An abbey church, monastery, or convent, run by an abbot or abbess.

ab•bot *n.* The male superior of the monastery.

ab•bre•vi•ate *v.* To make briefer; to abridge; to shorten; to reduce to a briefer form, as a word or phrase.

ab•bre•vi•a•tion *n.* A shortened form of a word or phrase, used to represent the full form.

ab•di•cate *v.* To relinquish power or responsibility formally; to renounce. **abdication** *n.*

ab•do•men *n.* That part of the human body that lies between the thorax and the pelvis and contains the stomach, spleen, liver, kidneys, bladder, pancreas, and intestines. **abdominal** *adj.*, **abdominally** *adv.*

ab•duct *v.* To carry away wrongfully, as by force or fraud; to kidnap; to draw aside or away. **abductor, abduction** *n.*

a•beam *adv.* At right angles to the keel of a ship.

a•bed *adv.* In bed; to bed; restricted to bed.

ab•er•rant *adj.* Straying from the right way or usual course; not being proper or truthful; abnormal or exceptional. **aberrantly** *adv.*

ab•er•ra•tion *n.* A disorder of the mind; deviation from a type of standard. **aberrational** *adj.*

a•bet *v.* To incite, encourage, or assist by countenance, aid, or approval.

ab•hor *v.* To dislike intensely; to loathe. **abhorrence** *n.* **abhorrent** *adj.*

abide *v.* To tolerate; to bear; to remain; to last; [with *by*] to conform to; to comply with.

a•bid•ing *adj.* Enduring, long-lasting, deep-rooted.

a•bil•i•ty *n.* State of being able; possession of necessary qualities; competence; skill; talent; physical or mental prerequisite.

ab•i•o•log•i•cal *adj.* Not made or produced by organisms.

ab•ject *adj.* Sunk to a low condition; groveling; mean; despicable; worthless. *n.* A person who is an outcast. **abjectness, abjection** *n.*

ab·ju·ra·tion *n.* The process of abjuring.

ab·jure *v.* To renounce solemnly or on oath; to repudiate; to forswear.

ab·late *v.* To remove something by cutting or erosion.

ab·la·tion *n.* A removal of a part; a process of ablating.

a·blaze *adv.* On fire; brilliantly lighted up; *meta.* Very excited; angry.

a·ble *adj.* Having sufficient ability; capable or talented. **ableness** *n.*

a·ble-bod·ied *adj.* Having a sound, strong body; competent for physical service.

a·bloom *adj.* In the state of flowering, especially of plants with multiple flowers; blooming; *meta.* Opening, as a flower.

ab·lu·tion *n.* The act of washing, cleansing, or purification by a liquid, usually water; specifically, a washing of the body as a part of religious rites. **ablutionary** *adj.*

ab·ly *adv.* Done in an able manner; capably.

ab·ne·gate *v.* To deny; to refuse or renounce; to relinquish or surrender.

ab·nor·mal *adj.* Not normal; irregular; unnatural. **abnormality** *n.*, **abnormally** *adv.*

a·board *adv.* On board a ship or other vehicle.

a·bode *n.* Dwelling place; home; place of residence; habitation.

a·boil *adj.* Boiling; heated to the point where a fluid turns into a gas; *meta.* Angry, fuming, about to erupt.

a·bol·ish *v.* To put an end to; to annul, especially a tenet or law. **abolition** *n.*

ab·o·li·tion *n.* The principle or belief that a political policy should be abandoned; specifically, the effort to end slavery; the state of being abolished. **abolitionary** *adj.*

a·bom·i·na·ble *adj.* Detestable; loathsome, extremely disagreeable. **abominably** *adv.*

a·bom·i·na·ble snow·man *n.* A type of animal reported to exist in the Himalayas, having features similar to those of man; a

yeti.

a·bom·i·nate *v.* To loathe intensely; to detest; to hate extremely; to abhor.

a·bom·i·na·tion *n.* An extreme hatred; the act of abominating; detestation; hateful vice.

a·born·ing *adv.* While being produced or made.

ab·or·ig·i·nal *adj.* The first in a region; primitive when compared with a more advanced type.

ab·o·rig·i·ne *n.* Earliest inhabitant of a region, especially after invasion and colonization by others; *cap.* One of an indigenous people of Australia.

a·bort *v.* To terminate or cause to terminate an operation or procedure before completion; to miscarry in giving birth; to cancel a mission or flight before completion of its goal.

a·bor·tion *n.* Induced termination of pregnancy before the fetus can survive; something malformed.

a·bound *v.* To have plenty; to exist in large numbers; to multiply and expand to or past bounds.

a·bout *adv.* Approximately; near to; out, here and there. *prep.* Regarding; pertaining to; throughout.

a·bout-face *n.* In military, a marching maneuver reversing the direction of the troops; *meta.* The abrupt reversal of one's point of view or attitude.

a·bove *adv.* Higher or greater than; in or at a higher place.

a·bove all *adv.* Before all other considerations.

a·bove·board *adv.* In a straightforward manner; open, fully revealed to all parties.

a·bove·ground *adj.* Located or positioned above the level or surface of the ground; legitimate.

ab·ra·ca·dab·ra *n.* A word believed by some to have magical powers, used in casting spells; nonsense, foolish talk.

a·brade *v.* To wear or rub off; to grate off.

a·bra·sion *n.* The act of grinding, as a surface, with the use of friction; a shallow skin injury caused by abrading.

a•bra•sive *adj.* Abrading; capable of increasing abrasion; of behavior, coarse or offensive, causing irritation and friction.

ab•re•act *v.* To release an emotion that is forgotten in psychoanalysis.

ab•re•ac•tion *n.* The elimination of a bad experience by reliving it.

a•breast *adv.* or *adj.* Side by side, as bodies in line; up to date on current trends and events.

a•bridge *v.* To make smaller, fewer, or shorter while maintaining essential contents. **abridgment** or **abridgement** *n.*

a•broad *adv.* Widely; in many places; outside one's country; at large; in the open air.

ab•ro•gate *v.* To cancel; to put an end to; to repeal. **abrogation** *n.*, **abrogable**, **abrogative** *adj.*

a•brupt *adj.* Happening or coming suddenly without warning; terse or short of patience in discourse; rudely brief. **abruptness** *n.*, **abruptly** *adv.*

ab•scess *n.* A locally infected place in the body, characterized by pus surrounded by sore and swollen inflamed tissue. **abscessed** *adj.*

ab•scind *v.* To cut off; to sever; to pare away; to separate.

ab•sinthe *n.* A type of green liqueur flavored by wormwood.

ab•scond *v.* To remove oneself, as to flee from justice. **absconder** *n.*

ab•sence *n.* Failure to attend; not present; time not in attendance; the state of being not in one's presence; inattention, lack of mental focus; not in existence, as in a diagnostic analysis. **absent** *adj.*, **absently** *adv.*

ab•sen•tee *n.* An absent person.

ab•sen•tee bal•lot *n.* A type of ballot submitted to an election by a voter who is not able to be at the polls.

ab•sen•tee•ism *n.* The chronic absence from something, such as school.

ab•sen•tee vot•er *n.* A person who is allowed to vote in an election with an absentee ballot.

ab•sent-mind•ed *adj.* Forgetful; preoccupied with thoughts other than the present; tending to forget or lose concentration.

ab•sent with•out leave *adj.* In military, absent without permission from the place of duty.

ab•so•lute *adj.* Unconditional; without restraint or qualification; perfect. **absoluteness** *n.*, **absolutely** *adv.*

ab•so•lu•tion *n.* An act of absolving.

ab•solve *v.* To free or release from responsibility, guilt, or penalty; to perform absolution. **absolver** *n.*, **absolvable** *adj.*

ab•sorb *v.* To take in; to incorporate into an existing form; to engage one's whole attention; in physics, to transform energy or store one substance inside another. **absorbability** *n.*

ab•sor•ben•cy *n.* The act or state of being absorbent; a measure of capacity to absorb.

ab•sor•bent *adj.* Able to absorb something.

ab•stain *v.* To refrain; to avoid on principle; to deny by self-discipline; to choose neither side, as in a vote. **abstainer** *n.*

ab•ste•mi•ous *adj.* Showing moderation in the use of drink and food. **abstemiousness** *n.*, **abstemiously** *adv.*

ab•sten•tion *n.* The act of holding off from using or doing something.

ab•stract *v.* To remove from, reduce, or summarize; to separate from the specific instance. **abstractedness** *n.*

ab•stract *adj.* Nonrepresentational; theoretical or nonpractical; not based in pragmatism or reality; apart from applicability or practicality.

ab•stract *n.* A summary of a larger document; a painting or other work of art based on nonrepresentational principles.

ab•strac•tion *n.* The process or product of abstract thinking or creating. **abstractive** *adj.*

ab•strac•tion•ism *n.* The practice of making abstract art.

ab•struse *adj.* Hard or difficult to

understand. **abstruseness** *n.*, **abstrusely** *adv.*

ab•surd *adj.* Contrary to reason; unreasonable beyond consideration; logically contradictory; meaningless. **absurdity**, **absurdness** *n.*

ab•surd•ism *n.* A philosophy based on the idea that humanity has been thrown into a meaningless universe where order is an illusion, and any search for purpose will conflict with the irrationality of the universe itself. **absurdist** *adj.* or *n.*

a•bun•dance *n.* Ample supply; plenty; amount more than enough. **abundant** *adj.*, **abundantly** *adv.*

a•buse *v.* To use in an improper or wrong way; to mistreat, especially physically. *n.* Improper treatment; injury or damage resulting from mistreatment.

a•bu•sive *adj.* Injurious or damaging to another. **abusiveness** *n.*

a•but *v.* To border; to touch at one end.

a•but•ment *n.* Support at the end of an arch or bridge.

a•but•ting *adj.* To abut or to serve as an abutment of something.

a•buzz *adj.* Filled with a buzzing.

a•bys•mal *adj.* Immeasurably deep or low; extremely poor; fathomless.

a•byss *n.* A deep crack or gap; in mythology, a bottomless cavern to the center of the earth; any unbridgeable distance, especially in space.

ac•a•dem•ic *adj.* Pertaining to or related to an academy.

a•cad•e•my *n.* A private school for special training, as in music, dance, or art; a military or law enforcement training school.

a•cap•pel•la *adj.* Singing without instrumental accompaniment.

a•cat•a•lec•tic *adj.* Not stopping short; having the complete number or syllables, in a line of verse.

ac•cede *v.* To consent; to agree; to arrive at a certain condition or state; to give in to.

ac•cel•er•ate *v.* To make run or work faster; to increase the speed.

ac•cel•er•a•tion *n.* The process of accelerating something.

ac•cel•er•a•tor *n.* Something that accelerates something else; in engineering, the machine part allowing the operator to increase speed.

ac•cent *n.* In linguistics, a pronunciation that gives one syllable more prominence than the others; the mark indicating such prominence; emphasis; area of concentration; focus of attention.

ac•cept *v.* To take what is offered or given; to believe to be true; to agree; to embrace, as a concept or belief. **accepter, acceptor** *n.*

ac•cept•able *adj.* Satisfactory; proper; good enough; agreeable.

ac•cep•tance *n.* Approval or belief; a condition of being accepted; the receipt of agreed-upon terms or conditions.

ac•cess *n.* Admission, entrance; permission or power to enter; opportunity to communicate or influence. **accessibility** *n.*, **accessible** *adj.*

ac•cess *v.* In computers, to open files and obtain data from electronic storage.

ac•ces•so•rize *v.* To wear with accessories.

ac•ces•so•ry *n.* Aid or contributor to an action or state; a detail accompanying a visual display, especially a wardrobe. **accessories** *pl.*

ac•ci•dent *n.* An unplanned or unexpected event; a collision of vehicles; injury or damage to persons or property caused by unavoidable circumstances; an unintentional variation in a work of art. **accidental** *adj.*, **accidentally** *adv.*

ac•claim *v.* To greet with strong approval or loud applause; to hail or cheer. *n.* Strong regard, recognition; public acknowledgment of accomplishment.

ac•cla•ma•tion *n.* An expression of approval, especially quite loud.

ac•cli•mate *v.* To get used to a different climate or new surroundings. **acclimatization** *n.*

ac•cli•ma•tize *v.* To change to or to adapt to a change in altitude, climate, or temperature.

ac•cliv•i•ty *n.* An ascending slope.

ac•co•lade *n.* Award; praise; ceremony used in conferring knighthood.

ac•com•mo•date *v.* To give room or lodging; to make fit; to adjust to new conditions. **accommodation** *n.*

ac•com•mo•dat•ing *adj.* Ready to help; willing to please; obliging.

ac•com•pa•ni•ment *n.* Something that shares or supports; a companion dish to the main course; in music, the instrumental support to singing or recitation; the harmonic addition to melody.

ac•com•pa•nist *n.* A person who plays a musical accompaniment.

ac•com•pa•ny *v.* To be together with; to go along with on a journey.

ac•com•plice *n.* Companion who helps another, especially in an illegal act.

ac•com•plish *v.* To perform; to carry out; to complete through effort; to do. **accomplisher** *n.*, **accomplishable** *adj.*

ac•com•plish•ment *n.* A finished task; completion of effort, especially admirable or noteworthy.

ac•cord *n.* Harmony; agreement; formal treaty between opposing factions. *v.* To grant or award. **accordance** *n.*

ac•cord•ing•ly *adv.* In a way that is proper and fitting.

ac•cor•di•on *n.* A musical instrument fitted with bellows and button keyboards, played by pulling out and pressing together the bellows to force air through reeds; a shape or configuration folded like an accordion.

ac•cor•di•on•ist *n.* An accordion player.

ac•cost *v.* To come close to and to speak first in an unfriendly manner.

ac•count *n.* A description of an event or experience; a statement of debts and credits in money transactions; a record; a report. **accounts** *pl.* The bookkeeping records of a company or enterprise.

ac•count *v.* [with *for*] To explain; to justify, especially amounts or actions.

ac•count•a•ble *adj.* Liable to be held responsible; able to be explained. **accountableness** *n.*, **accountably** *adv.*

ac•count•ant *n.* One who keeps accounts; the position of responsibility in public or private accounting.

ac•count•ing *n.* A report on how accounts have been balanced; the system of keeping business records or accounts.

ac•cou•tre *v.* To give or to provide with furnishings.

ac•cred•it *v.* To authorize someone; to give official power. **accreditation** *n.*

ac•crete *v.* To grow together or join. **accretive** *adj.*

ac•cre•tion *n.* The process of enlargement of something. **accretionary** *adj.*

ac•crue *v.* To result naturally; to increase at certain times.

ac•cul•tur•a•tion *n.* The modification of one's culture with a prolonged interaction involving another culture.

ac•cu•mu•la•tion *n.* A process of accumulating.

ac•cu•ra•cy *n.* Exactness; precision; the fact of being accurate or without mistakes. **accuracies** *pl.*

ac•cu•rate *adj.* Without mistakes or errors; careful and exact; correct; precise in detail; true.

ac•cursed *adj.* Sure to end badly; under a curse; unpleasant or annoying; very bad. **accursedness** *n.*, **accursedly** *adv.*

ac•cu•sa•tion *n.* A charge that a person is guilty, especially of breaking the law.

ac•cu•sa•tive *adj.* Relating to the direct object of a preposition or a verb;

ac•cu•sa•to•ry *adj.* Expressing accusation.

ac•cuse *v.* To find fault with; to blame; to charge someone with doing wrong or breaking the law. **accuser** *n.*

ac•cus•tom *v.* To familiarize by habit.

ac•cus•tomed *adj.* Customary; usual.

ace *n.* The face of a playing card, die, or domino marked with one spot; an expert in an event, especially flight combat; in tennis, a score made by an unreturned serve.

a•cer•bic *adj.* Acid in one's mood.

ac•et•a•min•o•phen *n.* A compound used for relieving pain and fever.

ac•e•tate *n.* Salt formed by the union of acetic acid with a base, used in making rayon and plastics.

a•ce•tic *adj.* Pertaining to or related to vinegar or acetic acid.

a•ce•tic acid *n.* The main ingredient of vinegar; a sour, colorless liquid with a sharp smell.

a•ce•ti•fy *v.* To change or to turn into acetic acid. **acetification** *n.*

a•ce•to•phe•net•i•din *n.* A type of compound used for relief of pain and fever.

a•cet•y•lene *n.* A highly inflammable, poisonous, colorless gas that burns brightly with a hot flame, used in blowtorches for cutting metal, welding, and soldering.

ache *v.* To give or have a dull, steady pain; to want very much; to experience longing or yearning; to long for. **achy** *adj.*, **achiness** *n.*

ache *n.* A dull, continuous pain.

a•chieve *v.* To set or reach by trying hard; to do; to succeed in doing; to accomplish. **achiever** *n.*, **achievable** *adj.*

a•chieve•ment *n.* Something achieved by work, courage, or skill.

ach•y *adj.* Having aches; mildly painful, especially in the bones and joints. **achiness** *n.*

ac•id *n.* A chemical compound containing hydrogen that forms a salt when combined with a base; a substance with less than pH 7. *slang* The drug LSD. **acid** *adj.*

a•cid•i•ty *n.* Condition or quality of being acid.

a•cid rain *n.* Acid precipitation that falls as rain.

a•cid•u•late *v.* To become or make somewhat acid.

ac•knowl•edge *v.* To admit the truth, existence or reality of; to publicly credit; to respond to a gesture. **acknowledgment** *n.*, **acknowledgeable** *adj.*

ac•ne *n.* A common skin disorder of young people in which minor inflammation of glands and follicles continue to appear on the body, especially the face.

ac•o•lyte *n.* An altar boy or someone who assists a priest at Mass.

ac•o•nite *n.* A poisonous plant with flowers resembling hoods.

a•corn *n.* The nut of an oak; the distinctive shape of an acorn.

a•cous•tic *adj.* Pertaining to sound or the sense of hearing; the sense of sound; absorbing sound. **acoustical** *adj.*, **acoustically** *adv.*

ac•quaint *v.* To make familiar; to let know; to make aware; to inform.

ac•quain•tance *n.* A person known casually or briefly but not as a close friend; [with *with*] a superficial knowledge of a subject or topic. **acquaintanceship** *n.*

ac•qui•esce *v.* To agree without arguing; to comply without protest. **acquiescent** *adj.*

ac•quire *v.* To secure control or possession; to become the owner; to get.

ac•qui•si•tion *n.* Something acquired; the act of acquiring; a purchase.

ac•quis•i•tive *adj.* Eager to gain and possess things; greedy.

ac•quit *v.* To rule that a person accused of something is not guilty; to conduct oneself in a manner that removes doubts or reservations in others. **acquittal** *n.*

a•cre *n.* A measurement of land that, in U.S. and England, equals 43,560 square feet. **acres** *pl.*

a•cre•age *n.* The total number of acres in a section of land.

ac•rid *adj.* Having a sharp, bitter, pungent, or irritating taste or smell. **acridity**, **acridness** *n.*, **acridly** *adv.*

ac•ri•mo•ni•ous *adj.* Sharp or bitter in speech or manner. **acrimoniously** *adv.*

ac•ro•bat *n.* One skilled in gymnastic feats; a physically nimble or flexible performer. **acrobatic** *adj.*

ac•ro•bat•ics *n.* The art, sport, or performance of an acrobat.

ac•ro•pho•bi•a *n.* Unusual fear of heights.

a•cross *prep.* From side to side; to one side from the other; on the other side of.

a•cryl•ic *adj.* Relating to or of acrylic acid or its derivatives.

act *n.* A thing done; deed; an action; one of the main parts of a play or opera; a law; decree. **actability** *n.*, **actable** *adj.*

act *v.* To perform in a play or mimesis; to feign an emotion or reaction that is not real or true; to take action; [with *on*] to produce an effect or result.

act•ing *adj.* In the temporary state of performing the duties, services, or functions of another person. *n.* The art or practice of mimesis.

ac•tion *n.* The process of doing or acting; an effect produced by something; a lawsuit.

ac•tion•a•ble *adj.* Affording grounds for a suit at law.

ac•tion paint•ing *n.* A style of painting where paint is often smeared or dribbled to give a thickly textured surface.

ac•ti•vate *v.* To put into action; to begin or make active; to bring into motion. **activation** *n.*

ac•tive *adj.* Working; full of action; busy; lively; quick. **activeness** *n.*, **actively** *adv.*

ac•tiv•ism *n.* A practice based on direct action to affect changes in government and social conditions.

ac•tiv•i•ty *n.* An event or action, with a series of steps, usually ordered and benign; the normal process of a living being.

ac•tor *n.* A person of either gender who acts in films, plays, television shows, and other media, usually in fictive, mimetic roles.

ac•tress *n.* [Obsolete] A female actor.

ac•tu•al *adj.* Acting or existing in fact or reality; as it really is; true; real; not theoretical. **actuality** *n.*

ac•tu•al•ly *adv.* In truth.

ac•tu•ar•y *n.* A person who figures or calculates insurance.

ac•tu•ate *v.* To put into motion or action.

actuation *n.*

act up *v.* To behave in a manner that is capricious or unruly.

a•cu•i•ty *n.* A sharp perception of something.

ac•u•punc•ture *n.* A traditional Chinese means of treating some illnesses or lessening pain by inserting thin needles into certain parts of the body.

a•cute *adj.* Extremely sensitive; sharp and quick, as pain; shrewd; serious; pivotal to result. **acuteness** *n.*, **acutely** *adv.*

a•cute ac•cent *n.* A mark to indicate heavy stress on a syllable.

ad•age *n.* A proverb; a wise or true saying; a metaphor or analogy embracing a universal observation.

a•da•gio *adj.* At rest; term used in music to tell how slowly a piece should be played.

ad•a•mant *adj.* Standing firm; not giving in easily; unyielding. **adamantly** *adv.*

a•dapt *v.* To fit or suit; to change oneself as to adjust to new conditions; to alter one's behavior to surroundings; in biology, to alter genetic makeup by natural selection in response to environment. **adaptability** *n.*, **adaptable** *adj.*

ad•ap•ta•tion *n.* Variation from original; an act of changing so as to fit or become suitable; a creative work restructured from the original genre or source.

add *v.* To join or put together with another; to cause an increase; to perform mathematical addition; to include into a group.

ad•den•dum *n.* An addition to a formal document, usually at the end; supplement attached to the main body of a discourse. **addenda** *pl.*

ad•der *n.* A common venomous viper found in North America and Europe.

ad•dict *n.* A person with a habit so strong that it cannot easily be broken; one with chemical or psychological dependency on a substance. **addiction** *n.*, **addicted** *v.*

ad•di•tion *n.* An adding of numbers to find their total; the act of joining one thing to another; the mathematical

additional

process of combining numbers; a part of a house or building attached to the original structure.

ad·di·tion·al *adj.* Extra; added onto; more than the original amount; supplemental. **additionally** *adv.*

ad·di·tive *n.* A substance added to another in small amounts to alter or improve its performance or properties.

ad·dress *v.* To direct or aim; to speak to; to give attention to; *n.* The location to which mail or goods can be sent to a person; in computers, one's identifying electronic code allowing access to an internet.

ad·dress·ee *n.* The person to whom a letter or package is addressed.

ad·duce *v.* To offer as proof or give as a reason. **adducer** *n.*, **adducible** *adj.*

ad·e·noids *n.* Lymphoid tissue growths in the upper part of the throat behind the nose, that may need to be removed surgically.

a·dept *adj.* Highly skilled; expert; proficient. **adeptly** *adv.*, **adeptness** *n.*

a·dept *n.* A person learned in the arts, especially of magic or alchemy.

ad·e·qua·cy *n.* The state of being good enough; sufficiency; acceptability.

ad·e·quate *adj.* Sufficient; good enough for what is needed; meeting the minimum requirements; capable. **adequateness** *n.*, **adequately** *adv.*

ad·here *v.* To stay attached; to stick and not come loose; to stay firm in support.

ad·her·ent *n.* A person who follows a leader, party, or belief; a believer or supporter.

ad·he·sion *n.* The act or state of sticking to something or of being stuck together.

ad·he·sive *adj.* Tending to stick and not come loose; clinging; having a sticky surface. **adhesively** *adv.*

ad·he·sive tape *n.* A type of tape that has an adhesive on one side.

ad·i·pose tis·sue *n.* A type of connective tissue where fat is stored in the body.

ad·ja·cent *adj.* Close or nearby; touching;

next to each other. **adjacency** *n.*

ad·jec·tive *n.* A descriptive word used to modify a noun or pronoun, denoting quality, quantity, extent, and the like.

ad·join *v.* To be next to; to be in or nearly in contact with. **adjoining** *adj.*

ad·journ *v.* To close a meeting or session for a time. **adjournment** *n.*

ad·ju·di·cate *v.* To settle a dispute judicially. **adjudicator** *n.*

ad·junct *n.* Something less important added to something with more importance.

ad·just *v.* To arrange or change; to make work correctly; to regulate; to change settings for best result. **adjustability** *n.*

ad·just·a·ble *adj.* Capable of adjustment; variable by choice.

ad·just·ed *adj.* Altered to attain or achieve a harmonious relationship; regulated; changed to suit a particular circumstance or environment.

ad·just·ment *n.* The act or process of changing; a settlement of a suit or claim.

ad·ju·tant *n.* An administrative staff officer who serves as a secretary to the commanding officer.

ad lib *v.* To improvise; to compose or make up spontaneously. **ad lib** *n.*

ad·min·is·ter *v.* To direct or manage; to give or carry out instruction. **administrable** *adj.*

ad·min·is·tra·tion *n.* The organizational structure of a school, company, or bureau; collectively, the persons who operate the structure.

ad·min·is·tra·tor *n.* A person who administers or directs; an executive; a manager.

ad·mi·ra·ble *adj.* Worthy of being admired or praised; excellent.

ad·mi·ral *n.* The highest rank for a naval officer; the commanding officer of a navy.

ad·mi·ral·ty *n.* The department of the British navy; the court and law dealing with ships and shipping.

ad·mire *v.* To hold a high opinion; to regard with wonder, delight, and pleased approval. **admiringly** *adv.*

ad•mir•er *n.* One who admires; a romantic suitor in the early stage of courtship.

ad•mis•si•ble *adj.* Capable of being admitted, accepted or allowed.

ad•mis•sion *n.* The right or act of being admitted; an admitting of the truth of something; a confession.

ad•mit *v.* To take or accept as being the truth; to permit or give the right to enter. **admittedly** *adv.*

ad•mit•tance *n.* Permission to enter; successful entry.

ad•mit•ted•ly *adv.* By one's own admission or confession.

ad•mix•ture *n.* Blend; mingling.

ad•mon•ish *v.* To warn a person to correct a fault; to criticize in a gentle way. **admonition** *n.*

a•do•be *n.* A brick or building material made from clay and straw and then dried in the sun.

ad•o•les•cence *n.* The period of physical and psychological development between childhood and adulthood; also known as youth.

ad•o•les•cent *n.* A person in the transitional period between childhood and adulthood.

a•dopt *v.* To take into one's family legally and raise as one's own; to accept as a process; to take up formally; to choose as a source or method. **adoption** *n.*

a•dor•a•ble *adj.* Very likable; charming; worthy of deep admiration. **adorably** *adv.*, **adorableness** *n.*

a•dore *v.* To love greatly; to worship or honor highly; to like very much; to venerate as a deity. **adoration** *n.*

a•dorn *v.* To add splendor or beauty; to embellish; to wear as decoration.

a•dorn•ment *n.* Something that adorns; decoration; ornament; the act of adorning.

a•drift *adv.* Drifting; floating freely without being steered; having no clear purpose or aim; lost or directionless.

a•droit *adj.* Skillful and clever in difficult circumstances. **adroitly** *adv.*

ad•u•late *v.* To give greater praise or flattery than is proper or deserved. **adulation** *n.*

a•dult *n.* A fully grown man or woman; a mature person. *adj.* Having reached full size and strength; appropriate for grown persons. **adulthood** *n.*

a•dul•ter•ate *v.* To make impure or of less quality by adding improper ingredients.

a•dul•ter•y *n.* The act of sexual intercourse between a married person and someone other than the husband or wife.

ad•vance *v.* To move ahead; to make or become higher; to increase in value or price.

ad•vance *n.* An improvement or progression; payment of wages or compensation before completion of a task; proposition or suggestion, especially romantic.

ad•vanced *adj.* Ahead in time; beyond beginning status; precocious or educated past one's age.

ad•vance•ment *n.* A promotion in position; progression; money ahead of time.

ad•van•tage *n.* A better chance or more forcible position; a condition, thing or event that can help or benefit; in tennis, the first point after deuce.

ad•van•ta•geous *adj.* Giving advantage; favorable.

ad•vent *n.* A coming or arrival; the four Sundays before Christmas.

ad•ven•ture *n.* An exciting, dangerous or unusual experience; a series of events offering new experiences. **adventure** *v.*

ad•ven•tur•er *n.* A person who engages in unusual or experiential activities; one who seeks wealth and social position. **adventurous** *adj.*

ad•verb *n.* A word which modifies a verb, adjective, or another adverb signifying condition or manner, as when, where, how, what kind, or how much. **adverbial** *adj.*, **adverbially** *adv.*

ad•verse *adj.* Opposed; not helpful; against someone or something. **adverseness** *n.*, **adversely** *adv.*

ad•ver•si•ty *n.* Bad luck or misfortune.

advertise

ad•ver•tise *v.* To draw public attention to a product for sale; to disseminate information about, as a job or opportunity. **advertiser** *n.*

ad•ver•tise•ment *n.* A public notice stating the qualities of a commodity, conditions of sale, and methods for purchase.

ad•ver•tis•ing *n.* The profession of preparing advertisements for publication or broadcast; the act of promoting for sale.

ad•vice *n.* Suggestion or recommendation regarding a course of action or decision; expert opinion, especially legal, used in decision making.

ad•vis•a•ble *adj.* Fit to be done or advised; recommended; capable of being suggested as a course of action. **advisability** *n.*

ad•vis•ed•ly *adv.* Deliberately; with consideration; carefully.

ad•vis•er *n.* A person who gives an opinion or advises; one who helps prepare academic schedules.

ad•vis•o•ry *adj.* Exercising or having the power to advise; giving or containing advice, without actual legislative power.

ad•vo•cate *v.* To write or speak in favor of or support. **advocate** *n.*

ae•gis *n.* Protection; support or sponsorship.

aer•i•al *adj.* Of or in the air; pertaining to aircraft. *n.* An antenna for television or radio. **aerially** *adv.*

aer•i•al•ist *n.* An acrobat who does stunts high above the ground on a wire or trapeze.

aer•ie *n.* The nest of a predatory bird, built on a cliff or other high places.

aer•o•bics *n.* Strenuous exercise that increases oxygen to the heart and lungs, therefore strengthening them.

aer•o•plane *n.* British word for airplane.

aes•thet•ics *n.* The study of the nature of beauty. **aesthetically** *adv.*

a•far *adv.* Far off; far away.

af•fa•ble *adj.* Good-natured; easy to talk to; friendly. **affably** *adv.*

af•fair *n.* An event or occurrence; matters of business or public concern; a romantic relationship outside marriage.

af•fect *v.* To move emotionally; to feel sympathetic or sad; to bring about a change in. **affecting, affected** *adj.*

af•fect *n.* Emotional element; subjective response aside from physical or logical conditions.

af•fec•ta•tion *n.* Artificial behavior meant to impress others.

af•fec•tion *n.* A tender or fond feeling toward another.

af•fec•tion•ate *adj.* Loving and gentle; feeling deeply. **affectionately** *adv.*

af•firm *v.* To declare positively; to stand by the truth; to state in positive terms. **affirmation** *n.*

af•flict *v.* To cause suffering or pain; to cause mental suffering. **affliction** *n.*

af•fi•da•vit *n.* A written statement by a person swearing that something is the truth.

af•fil•i•ate *v.* To join in, connect, or associate with. **affiliation** *n.*

af•fin•i•ty *n.* A special attraction with kinship; a natural attraction or liking.

af•firm•a•tive *adj.* Asserting the fact is true. **affirmative** *n.*

af•fix *v.* To attach; to fasten; to add at the end. *n.* A prefix or suffix added to a word.

af•ford *v.* To be able to provide; to have enough money to spare.

af•flu•ent *adj.* Prosperous; rich; having all the wealth or money needed. **affluently** *adv.*

af•fray *n.* Brawl or noisy fight.

af•front *v.* To insult one to one's face; to confront. *n.* An insult.

af•ghan *n.* A crocheted or knitted cover in colorful designs.

a•fire *adv.* Burning; on fire; full of energy and purpose.

a•flame *adj.* Burning; in flames; glowing.

a•float *adv.* Floating on the surface of water; circulating or moving freely.

a•fraid *adj.* Hesitant; filled with fear; reluctant.

a•fresh *adj.* Once more; again; begun

anew.

aft *adv.* At, close to, near, or toward the rear of an aircraft or stern of a ship.

af•ter *adv.* In the rear; behind. *prep.* Following spatially or temporally; subsequent in order to.

af•ter•ef•fect *n.* An effect coming after.

af•ter•math *n.* State or condition after an event; consequence; result; subsequent environment.

af•ter•thought *n.* An idea occurring later; idea added after.

a•gain *adv.* Moreover; another time; once more; on the other hand; yet; in addition.

a•gainst *prep.* In opposition to or in combat with; in contrast with; in exchange for; in preparation for; counter to.

a•gape *adv.* With expectation; in wonder; open-mouthed.

a•ga•pe *n.* Universal, spiritual love; overwhelming compassion and understanding; affection without criticism or limitation.

ag•ate *n.* Quartz chalcedony containing bands or patterns of colors; a playing marble made of agate; in typesetting, a type size of about 5 1/2 points.

a•ga•ve *n.* Fleshy-leaved tropical American plant.

age *n.* The length of time from beginning to a certain date; [with *of*] the time of life when a person has full legal rights; *v.* To grow or become old; to mature; to rest until fruition, as wine or cheese. **aged** *adj.*, **agedness** *n.*, **agedly** *adv.*

ag•ed *n.* Very old; venerably advanced in years; ancient.

age•ism *n.* In law, discrimination, prejudice, or bias based on age.

age•less *adj.* Existing forever; never seems to grow old.

a•gen•cy *n.* A business or service that acts for others; a subdivision of a bureaucratic structure; action; active influence; power.

a•gen•da *n.* Program or list of things to be done; formal order of discussion topics; aim or goal.

a•gent *n.* One who acts as the representative of another; that which acts or exerts power; the active or precipitating ingredient in a reaction.

ag•glom•er•ate *v.* To collect; to form into a mass. **agglomerate** *n.*

ag•gran•dize *v.* To enlarge, to extend; to increase. **aggrandizement** *n.*

ag•gra•vate *v.* To annoy; to make worse; to reinjure or damage again; to cause a reaction to.

ag•gre•gate *v.* To gather together into a mass or whole. **aggregate** *adj.*

ag•gres•sion *n.* Hostile action or behavior; an unprovoked assault; anger manifested in attack or confrontation.

ag•gres•sive *adj.* Offensively and combatively active; tending to initiate confrontation; pushy; proactive and deliberate. **aggressiveness** *n.*

a•ghast *adj.* Appalled; struck with amazement; taken aback; momentarily breathless.

ag•ile *adj.* Marked by the ability to move quickly and easily; nimble or flexible; capable of complex movement. **agility** *n.*

ag•i•tate *v.* To disturb; to upset; to stir or move with violence; to try to arouse the public interest. **agitation**, **agitator** *n.*

a•glit•ter *adj.* Glittering.

a•glow *adj.* Glowing.

ag•nos•tic *n.* One who doubts that there is a God or life hereafter.

a•go *adj* or *adv.* In the past; gone by; earlier than now.

ag•o•nize *v.* To afflict with great anguish or suffering; [with *over* or *about*] to worry excessively; to fret painfully; to suffer regarding a decision or course of action. **agonized**, **agonizing** *adj.*

ag•o•ny *n.* Intense mental distress or physical pain; anguish; suffering caused by internal conflict. **agonies**, *pl.*

ag•o•ra•pho•bi•a *n.* Fear of open spaces.

a•grar•i•an *adj.* Pertaining to or of land and its ownership; pertaining to farming; agricultural.

a•gree *v.* To give assent; to consent; to share an understanding or opinion; to be beneficial or suitable; to correspond.

a•gree•a•ble *adj.* Pleasant; pleasing; willing; ready to consent. **agreeableness** *n.*, **agreeably** *adv.*

a•gree•ment *n.* Harmony; concord; state or act of agreeing; coincidence of mathematical or scientific results.

ag•ri•busi•ness *n.* Big business farming, embracing the product, distribution, and processing of farm products and the manufacture of farm equipment.

ag•ri•cul•ture *n.* The science and occupation of raising livestock, crops, or other consumable products grown on land. **agriculturalist**, **agriculturist** *n.*

a•ground *adv.* or *adj.* Stranded; on the ground; stopped by contact with the floor of a body of water; run ashore; beached.

a•gue *n.* Fever accompanied by chills or shivering and sweating.

a•head *adv.* Before; in advance; to or at the front; successfully or progressively.

a•hoy *interj.* A nautical call or greeting.

aid *v.* To give help or assistance.

AIDS *abbr.* Acquired Immune Deficiency Syndrome; a disease in men and women, transmitted by exchange of bodily fluids, that destroys the body's immunological system, especially the ability to produce helper T cells.

ail *v.* To feel sick; to make ill or uneasy.

ai•ler•on *n.* Movable control flap on the trailing edge of an airplane wing.

ail•ment *n.* Mild illness; chronic disorder.

aim *v.* To direct a weapon; to direct purpose. *n.* Intention; goal.

aim•less *adj.* Lacking of purpose; without direction or motive.

ain't *contr.* [Lit.] Are not; *slang* am not, is not, has not, or have not; do not, does not, did not.

air *n.* An odorless, tasteless, colorless, gaseous mixture, primarily composed of nitrogen (78%) and oxygen (21%); the sky; a breeze; [with *on the*] broadcast medium; a melody.

air•borne *adj.* Borne by or carried through or by the air.

air•brush *n.* Machine using compressed air to spray paint and other liquids on a surface.

air con•di•tion•er *n.* Equipment used to lower the temperature and humidity of an enclosure.

air•craft *n.* A machine that flies, such as a helicopter, airplane, or glider.

air•craft car•ri•er *n.* A large ship on which airplanes can be transported, stored, launched, and landed.

air•field *n.* Paved runways at an airport; landing strip.

air•foil *n.* Part of an airplane which controls stability, lift, thrust, etc.

air•frame *n.* The structure of a rocket or airplane without an engine.

air•ing *n.* Exposing something in the open air.

air•line *n.* An air transportation company.

air•lin•er *n.* A large passenger aircraft.

air•mail or **air mail** *n.* Mail sent by means of air.

air•plane *n.* A fixed-wing vehicle capable of flight, heavier than air, commonly propelled by jet engine or propeller.

air•port *n.* A terminal station where aircraft take off, land, board and discharge passengers; usually attached to storage and maintenance facilities.

air raid *n.* Bombing attack by military aircraft.

air•ship *n.* Dirigible; a self-propelled lighter-than-air aircraft.

air•sick•ness *n.* Nausea resulting from flight in an aircraft. **airsick** *adj.*

air•strip *n.* Concrete runway on an airfield; minimally equipped airfield.

air•y *adj.* Open to the air; breezy; light as air; graceful. **airiness** *n.*, **airily** *adv.*

aisle *n.* Passageway between rows of seats, as in a church, auditorium, or airplane. **aisled** *adj.*

a•jar *adv.* or *adj.* Partially opened; not tightly closed.

a•kim•bo *adv.* Bent; with a crook.

a•kin *adj.* Related, as in family; similar in quality or character.

al•a•bas•ter *n.* A dense, translucent,

tinted or white, fine-grained gypsum.

a la carte *n.* Separate price for each item on the menu.

a•lack *interj.* An exclamation expressive of sorrow.

a•lac•ri•ty *n.* Readiness; cheerfulness; eagerness; briskness.

a la mode *adv.* Served with ice cream, as pie; in the fashion.

a•larm *n.* A warning of danger; sudden feeling of fear; the bell or buzzer of a clock. *v.* To frighten or warn by an alarm. **alarming** *adj.*, **alarmingly** *adv.*

a•larm•ist *n.* Someone who needlessly alarms others.

a•las *interj.* Expressive of anxiety or regret.

al•ba•tross *n.* Large, web-footed, long-winged sea bird.

al•bum *n.* A bound book with pages or receptacles for photographs, autographs, stamps, or other small flat items; a book of collections; a collection of songs, music, or other recordings marketed in one package.

al•bu•min *n.* Several proteins found in the white of eggs, blood serum, milk, and plant and animal tissue.

al•che•my *n.* Traditional chemical philosophy concerned primarily with changing base metals into gold.

al•co•hol *n.* Hydroxyl derivatives of hydrocarbons; a series of related organic compounds; intoxicating liquor containing alcohol; ethanol

al•co•hol•ic *adj.* Resulting from alcohol; containing or preserved in alcohol; suffering from alcoholism. **alcoholic** *n.*

al•co•hol•ism *n.* Excessive alcohol consumption; a habit or addiction.

al•cove *n.* Recess or partly enclosed extension of a room.

al•der *n.* Tree of the birch family, grows in marshy soil.

al•der•man *n.* Member of a municipal legislative body.

ale *n.* Beverage similar to, but more bitter than beer, made from malt by fermentation.

a•lert *adj.* Vigilant; brisk; watchful; active.

n. A signal by siren of air attack. *v.* Bring attention to, make noticeable. **alertly** *adv.*, **alertness** *n.*

al•fal•fa *n.* Plant with purple flowers resembling the clover, widely grown for forage.

al•fres•co *adv.* In the fresh air; outside.

al•gae *pl. n.* Various primitive, chiefly aquatic, one-celled or multicellular plants, as the seaweed.

al•ge•bra *n.* A procedure of mathematics in which symbols, especially letters, represent members of a specified set of numbers and are related by operations that hold for all numbers in the set. **algebraic** *adj.* **algebraically** *adv.*

a•li•as *n.* Fictitious or assumed name. *adv.* Otherwise known as.

al•i•bi *n.* In law, a form of defense by which the accused shows the physical impossibility of having committed a crime; an attempt by a defendant to prove absence from a crime scene; an excuse.

a•li•en *adj.* Unfamiliar; outside of one's natural environment; not in residence at the place of one's allegiance; *n.* A member of another region or country; a stranger; a foreigner; a non-native.

a•li•en•ate *v.* To cause to become indifferent or unfriendly. **alienation** *n.*

a•light *v.* To settle; to come down; to dismount. *adj.* or *adv.* Burning. lighted.

a•lign *v.* To arrange in a line; to position in a straight line; to take one side of an argument or cause. **aline** *v.*

a•like *adj.* Similar in all essentials; parallel and equal; having very close resemblance. *adv.* In the same manner, way, or degree.

al•i•ment *n.* Nourishment; food. **alimentation** *n.*, **alimental** *adj.*

al•i•mo•ny *n.* Court ordered allowance for support, usually given by a man to his former wife following a divorce or legal separation.

a•live *adj.* Living; having life; able to sustain life processes; in existence or effect; viable; full of life. **aliveness** *n.*

al•ka•li *n.* A hydroxide or carbonate of an

alkali metal, whose aqueous solution is slippery, bitter, caustic, and basic in reactions.

al·ka·line *adj.* Of, relating to, or containing alkali; not acidic. **alkalinity** *n.*

all *adj.* Total extent or total entity; being a whole number, amount, or quantity; every.

all-a·round or **all-round** *adj.* Total; in full spectrum; comprehensive; in every aspect.

al·lay *v.* To relieve; to lessen; to calm; to pacify. **allayer** *n.*

al·le·ga·tion *n.* The act or result of alleging.

al·lege *v.* To affirm; to assert to be true; to declare before or without proof.

al·le·giance *n.* Loyalty to one's nation, cause, or sovereign; faithfulness and commitment to an ideology; obligations of a vassal to an overlord. **allegiant** *adj.*

al·le·go·ry *n.* A dramatic, literary, or pictorial device in which each object, character, and event symbolically illustrates a moral or religious principle. **allegorical** *adj.*, **allegorically** *adv.*

al·le·gro *adv.* In music, faster than allegretto but slower than presto.

al·le·lu·ia *interj.* Expressing praise to God or of thanksgiving.

al·ler·gen *n.* Substance which causes an allergy. **allergenic** *adj.*

al·ler·gic *adj.* Causing a reaction; hypersensitive, especially to a substance; responsive or reactive to an allergen.

al·ler·gist *n.* A doctor specializing in allergies.

al·ler·gy *n.* Pathological or abnormal reaction to environmental substances, as foods, dust, pollens, or microorganisms. **allergic** *adj.*, **allergies** *pl.*

al·le·vi·ate *v.* To make more bearable. **alleviation, alleviator** *n.*

al·ley *n.* Narrow roadway, lane, or passageway between or behind buildings; a bowling lane. **alleys** *pl.*

al·li·ance *n.* A union, relationship, or connection by kinship, marriage, or common interest; a confederation of nations by a formal treaty; an affinity.

al·li·ga·tor *n.* Large amphibious reptile with very sharp teeth, powerful jaws, and a shorter snout than the related crocodile.

al·lit·er·a·tion *n.* Occurrence of two or more words having the same initial sound. **alliterative** *adj.*

al·lo·cate *v.* To assign; to allot. **allocation** *n.*

al·lot *v.* To distribute or set aside as a share of something. **allotment, allotter** *n.*

all out *adv.* With every possible effort or resource; leaving no reserve.

al·low *v.* To make a provision for, to permit; to permit to have; to admit; to concede. **allowable** *adj.*, **allowably** *adv.*

al·low·ance *n.* The amount allowed or set aside; the permissible degree of refinement or calibration; the act of allowing something; a periodic payment for regular duties or compliances; a price discount.

al·loy *n.* Something added to; an item reduced in purity or value; a mixture or combination of two or more pure elements, especially in metallurgy.

all right *adj.* Meets satisfaction, certainly. *adv.* Satisfactory; correct; unhurt. *adj.*, *slang* Good; of sound character.

all-round *adj.* Total; versatile; including all aspects.

all·spice *n.* Tropical American tree bearing aromatic berries, used as a spice.

all-star *n.* An exemplary player or performer; one chosen to perform among other superior players; composed entirely of star performers.

al·lude *v.* To refer to something indirectly. **allusive** *adj.*, **allusively** *adv.*

al·lu·sion *n.* The act of referring to something indirectly; a hint; a reference to a source not in evidence.

al·ly *v.* To connect or unite in a formal or close relationship or bond; to claim an affinity for or agreement with. *n.* One united with another in a formal or personal relationship; one who agrees; a force or power on the same side in a conflict.

al·ma·nac *n.* Annual publication of meteorological, agricultural, astronomical, and geological cyclic information, containing calendars with weather forecasts, natural phenomenal information, and other facts.

al•might•y *adj.* Having absolute power; possessing the highest authority. **almighty** *n.* [cap., with *the*] Almighty God.

al•mond *n.* An oval, edible nut with a soft, light-brown shell; tree bearing such nuts; the wood from this plant.

al•most *adv.* Not quite; slightly short of; nearly.

alms *n.* Goods or money given to the poor in charity.

al•oe *n.* Any of various mostly African plants having fleshy, spiny-toothed leaves; a cathartic drug made from the juice of the leaves of this plant.

a•loft *adv.* Toward the upper rigging of a ship; in or into a high place; in the air.

a•lo•ha *interj.* Hawaiian expression of greeting or farewell.

a•lone *adj. or adv.* Away from other people; single; solitary; excluding anyone or anything else; with nothing further; sole; by oneself; only. **alone** *adv.*

a•long *adv.* In a line with; on the length or path; in association; together; as a companion; following shortly.

a•long•side *adv.* Along, at, near, or to the side of; side by side with; nautically; touching at the beam.

a•loof *adj.* Indifferent; distant; haughty; above in class or quality; uninvolved. **aloofness** *n.*, **aloofly** *adv.*

a•loud *adv.* Orally; audibly; with the result of making a sound.

al•pha *n.* First letter of the Greek alphabet.

al•pha•bet *n.* The letters of a language, arranged in an order fixed by custom.

al•pha•bet•i•cal *adj.* Arranged in the traditional order of the letters of a language. **alphabetically** *adv.*

al•pha•bet•ize *v.* To arrange in alphabetical order.

al•read•y *adv.* By this or a specified time; previously to now.

al•so *adv.* Likewise; besides; in addition.

al•tar *n.* An elevated structure for raising or isolating a religious or sacrificial ceremony.

al•ter *v.* To make change or become different; to modify; to castrate or spay, as an animal. **alterability** *n.*

al•ter•a•tion *n.* A change in structure or specification after manufacture. *pl.* Cutting and sewing done to a garment for improved fit, after manufacture.

al•ter•ca•tion *n.* Noisy and heated quarrel.

al•ter•nate *v.* To happen or follow in turn; to occur in successive turns. **alternately** *adv.*, **alternation** *n.*

al•ter•nate *n.* Substitute; second choice; deputy; person selected to replace first choice.

al•ter•na•tive *n.* A choice between to or more possiblities; one of the possibilities to be chosen. **alternatively** *adv.* **alternative** *adj.*

al•ter•na•tor *n.* Electric generator producing alternating current.

al•though *conj.* Even though; despite the fact that.

al•tim•e•ter *n.* Instrument for measuring and indicating altitude.

al•ti•tude *n.* The height of a thing above a reference level; distance above the earth's surface, usually in feet; flying space; distance above sea level.

al•to *n.* [Italian] High. Lower of two female singing voices in a four-part chorus; the range between soprano and tenor.

al•to•geth•er *adv.* Entirely; with all included or counted; taken as a whole.

al•tru•ism *n.* Selfless concern for the welfare of others. **altruist** *n.*, **altruistic** *adj.*, **altruistically** *adv.*

alu•mi•num *n.* A silvery-white, ductile metallic element used to form many hard, light, corrosion-resistant alloys.

a•lum•na *n.* Female graduate or former student of a school, college, or university. **alumnae** *pl.*

a•lum•nus *n.* A male graduate or former student of a school, college, or university.

alumni *pl.*

al•ways *adv.* Continuously; forever; on every occasion; at all times.

am *v.* First person, singular, present tense of *be*.

a•mal•gam *n.* An alloy of mercury with other metals, as with tine or silver; a blend of diverse elements.

a•mal•ga•mate *v.* To mix so as to make a unified whole; to blend.

am•a•teur *n.* One who engages in an activity for enjoyment rather than profit; one outside the profession; one who lacks expertise; dilettante. *adj.* Not up to professional standards; not engaged in as a profession. **amateurish** *adj.*, **amateurism** *n.*

am•a•to•ry *adj.* Of or expressive of sexual love.

a•maze *v.* To astound; to affect with surprise or wonder; to confound as in a maze. **amazingly** *adv.*, **amazedness**, **amaze** *n.*, **amazing** *adj.*

am•bass•a•dor *n.* Official representative of the highest rank, accredited by one government to another; chief executive of an embassy; an envoy or courier, especially of good will. **ambassadorial** *adj.*, **ambassadorship** *n.*

am•ber *n.* A hard, translucent, yellow, brownish-yellow, or orange fossil resin, used for jewelry and ornament. *adj.* Medium to dark orange yellow in color.

am•bi•ance *n.* Environment; atmosphere.

am•bi•dex•trous *adj.* Able to use both hands with equal facility.

am•bi•ent *adj.* Surrounding.

am•big•u•ous *adj.* Doubtful; uncertain. **ambiguousness** *n.*, **ambiguously** *adv.*

am•bi•tion *n.* Strong desire to achieve; will to succeed; the goal or object desired.

am•bi•tious *adj.* Challenging; complex and demanding; desirous of achievement or advancement. **ambitiousness** *n.*, **ambitiously** *adv.*

am•biv•a•lence *n.* Existence of mutually different feelings abut a person or thing.

am•ble *v.* To move at a leisurely pace; to walk with a leisurely gait; to stroll aimlessly; to saunter.

am•bro•sia *n.* Food of the Greek Gods and immortals; food having exquisite flavor or fragrance.

am•bu•lance *n.* Vehicle equipped to transport the injured or sick.

am•bu•la•to•ry *adj.* Moving about; movable; of or to do with walking.

am•bus•cade *n.* Ambush.

am•bush *n.* Surprise attack made from a hidden position.

a•mel•io•rate *v.* To become or make better. **amelioration** *n.*, **ameliorative** *adj.*

a•men *interj.* Used at the end of a prayer to express solemn approval; so be it; expression of agreement.

a•me•na•ble *adj.* Responsive; tractable; accountable. **amenability** *n.*

a•mend *v.* To correct; to improve; to rectify; to add to or change, as a statute or law. **amendable** *adj.*

a•mend•ment *n.* Correction, reformation or improvement; added alteration or refinement; the parliamentary procedure where such alteration is made.

a•mends *pl. n.* Compensation for insult or injury, usually informal; a balancing gesture or action to rectify an earlier wrong.

a•men•i•ty *n.* Agreeableness; means of comfort or convenience. **amenities** *pl.*

a•mi•a•ble *adj.* Friendly and pleasant; likeable; willing to treat hospitably. **amiability** *n.*, **amiably** *adv.*

am•i•ca•ble *adj.* Harmonious; friendly. **amicability** *n.*, **amicably** *adv.*

a•mid *prep.* In the middle of; surrounded by; during.

a•miss *adj.* Out of order or place; in an improper or wrong way; not right; suspiciously different.

am•i•ty *n.* Friendly relationships, as between two states.

am•mo•nia *n.* Colorless, pungent gas.

am•mu•ni•tion *coll. n.* A supply of projectiles containing explosive material, propelled or discharged from guns; bullets;

any means of offense. *meta.* Fact or evidence in support of an argument.

am•ne•sia *n.* The loss of memory; a mental disorder preventing recollection of past events.

am•nes•ty *n.* Pardon for political offenders; a general policy of nonreprisal or forgiveness.

a•moe•ba *n.* Any of various minute one-celled organisms having an indefinite, changeable form, and lacking structural stability. **ameba** *var.,* **amoebas** or **amoebae** *pl.*

a•mong *prep.* In or through the midst of; with others; considered as a group.

a•mor•al *adj.* Neither moral nor immoral. **amorality** *n.,* **amorally** *adv.*

am•o•rous *adj.* Inclined to or indicative of sexual love; romantic; receptive to or inviting love. **amorousness** *n.*

a•mor•phous *adj.* Lacking definite form; shapeless; general; vague.

am•or•tize *v.* To liquidate a loan by installment payments; a loan. **amortization** *n.*

a•mount *n.* Aggregate, sum, or total quantity; the measurable equivalency; a measure of mass or collectives.

a•mour *n.* A forbidden love affair; a sweetheart or partner in affection.

am•per•age *n.* Strength of an electric current, expressed in amperes.

am•pere *n.* Unit of electric current equal to a flow of one amp per second.

am•per•sand *n.* The character or sign that represents and (&).

am•phib•i•an *n.* An organism, as a frog or toad, developing from an aquatic state into an air-breathing state; vehicle, especially an aircraft, that can take off and land on land or water.

am•phi•the•a•ter *n.* A round or oval building having tiers of seats rising around an arena.

am•ple *adj.* Sufficient; abundant; large; full past need. **ampleness** *n.,* **amply** *adv.*

am•pli•tude *n.* Maximum value of a periodically varying quantity; greatness of size; fullness.

am•pule *n.* A small, sealed vial containing a hypodermic injection solution.

am•pu•tate *v.* To cut off; to remove, as a limb from one's body. **amputation** *n.*

am•pu•tee *n.* A person who has had one or more limbs amputated.

a•muck *adv.* In an uncontrolled manner; in a murderous frenzy; out of control.

am•u•let *n.* A charm worn as protection against evil or injury.

a•muse *v.* To entertain in an agreeable, pleasing way; to make mildly or temporarily happy. **amusable, amused** *adj.*

a•muse•ment *n.* A diversion; a pleasant activity; a diverting event holding one's temporary attention.

an *art.* One; a (used before words beginning with a vowel or with an unpronounced *h*); one sort of; each.

a•na•chro•nism *n.* Connection of a thing, of a person or happening with another that came after in history; anything that seems to be out of place in history; event or object out of time sequence.

an•a•gram *n.* Word formed by transposing the letters of another word. **anagrammatical, anagrammatic** *adj.*

a•nal•o•gous *adj.* Similar; corresponding in certain ways. **analogously** *adv.*

an•a•logue *n.* Something that bears resemblance to something else.

a•nal•o•gy *n.* Connection between things that are otherwise dissimilar; an illustration of an abstract principle or idea by concrete parallel example; a conclusion or opinion that if two things are alike in some respects they must be alike in others.

a•nal•y•sis *n.* The disassembly or separation of elements for identification; an examination of relationships among parts of a whole; a detailed inventory of interconnected elements. **analytical** *adj.*

an•a•lyst *n.* A person who analyzes or who is skilled in analysis.

an•a•lyze *v.* To make an analysis of; to examine for cause.

an•a•pest *n.* Metrical foot made up of two short syllables followed by one long one. **anapestic** *adj.*

an•ar•chy *n.* The absence of recognized political authority; the dissolution of order, purpose, or standard; the absence of external or artificial constraints.

a•nath•e•ma *n.* Curse; ban; or excommunication. **anathematize** *v.*

a•nat•o•mize *v.* To examine in great detail; to analyze; in biology, to dissect.

a•nat•o•my *n.* Structure of an organ or organism; a detailed analysis of such a structure; analysis of the interrelationship among living parts. **anatomical**, **anatomic** *adj.*

an•ces•tor *n.* A person who comes before one in a family line; someone earlier than a grandparent; forefather or foremother. **ancestral** *adj.*

an•ces•try *n.* Line of descent; lineage; ancestors collectively. **ancestries** *pl.*

an•chor *n.* Heavy metal device lowered into the water by a chain or line, whose weight and configuration prevent stopped ships from drifting relative to the bottom. *v.* To attach or fix firmly.

an•chor•age *n.* A shallow protected place for anchoring a ship; a strong support that keeps something steady; a harbor offering moorage rather than dockage.

an•cho•rite *n.* A religious hermit.

an•cho•vy *n.* A very small fish of the herring family; usually salted, canned in oil, and used for making sauces and relishes.

an•cient *adj.* Very old; from a time long past; belonging to the early history of people. *n.* An extremely elderly person in a position of wisdom or authority. **ancientness** *n.*, **anciently** *adv.*

and *conj.* Together with; along with; as well as; added to; as a result; plus; also.

an•dan•te *adv.* In music, rather slow in tempo.

and•i•ron *n.* Heavy metal support for logs or wood in a fireplace.

an•drog•y•nous *adj.* Having the characteristics or nature of both male and female; having both staminate and pistillate flowers in the same cluster with the male flowers uppermost. **androgyny** *n.*

an•droid *n.* In science fiction, a synthetic man made to look like a human being.

an•ec•dote *n.* Story; brief fictive or factual account, usually illustrative of an argumentative point. **anecdotal** *adj.*

a•ne•mic *adj.* Of or having anemia.

a•nent *prep.* Regarding; concerning.

an•es•the•si•a *n.* Condition in which one has no feeling of heat, touch, or pain in all or part of the body.

an•es•thet•ic *adj.* Taking away the feeling of pain. *n.* Drug, gas, etc. used to bring on anesthesia before surgery. **anesthetically** *adv.*

a•new *adv.* Over again; with a fresh start.

an•gel *n.* An immortal being attendant upon God; a very kind and lovable person; a helping or guiding spirit; one lacking inclination or ability to do evil; a backer or supporter of a creative enterprise. **angelic** *adj.*

an•ger *n.* Feeling of extreme hostility; rage; intense emotional displeasure; aggressive reaction to wrongdoing or injustice.

an•gle *n.* A shape made by two straight lines meeting in a point, or two surfaces meeting along a line; a sharp change in planar configuration. *v.* To make an angle; to move in an angular path; to persuade by distorting argument.

an•gler *n.* A fisherman; one who fishes, especially by casting with pole and hook. **angling** *n.*

an•gle•worm *n.* Earthworm, used as fishing bait.

an•gling *n.* The act of fishing with a hook and line.

an•go•ra *n.* The long silky hair of the Angora rabbit or Angora goat; yarn or fabric made from the hair of an Angora goat or rabbit.

an•gry *adj.* Feeling or showing anger; having a menacing aspect; inflamed.

an•guish *n.* Great suffering, from worry,

grief, or pain; agony.

an•gu•lar *adj.* Having angles or sharp corners; measured by an angle or degrees of an arc; gaunt; bony; lean. **angularity** *n.*, **angularly** *adv.*

an•i•mad•vert *v.* To comment with disapproval. **animadversion** *n.*

an•i•mal *n.* Any being other than a human being; any four-footed creature; beast.

an•i•mate *v.* To give liveliness, life or spirit to; to cause to act; to inspire. **animatedly** *adv.*

an•i•ma•tion *n.* The process of bringing to life; an art form in which movement is simulated by a rapidly visualized series of subtly changing still figures.

an•i•mism *n.* A belief in primitive tribes that natural objects and forces have souls. **animist** *n.*, **animistic** *adj.*

an•i•mos•i•ty *n.* Hostility; bitterness; hatred.

an•i•mus *n.* Feeling of animosity.

an•ise *n.* A plant with yellowish-white flower clusters and licorice-flavored seeds; aniseed.

an•kle *n.* Joint that connects the foot with the leg; slender section of the leg immediately above this joint.

an•klet *n.* A short sock, an ornament worn around the ankle.

an•nals *pl. n.* Descriptive record; history. **annalist** *n.*

an•neal *v.* To heat and then cool glass slowly to make it less brittle.

an•nex *v.* To add or join a smaller thing to a larger one; *n.* a structure added to another. **annexation** *n.*

an•ni•hi•late *v.* To destroy completely; to raze to the ground; to cause to cease to exist; to bring into nothingness.

an•ni•ver•sa•ry *n., pl.* **-ries** The date on which something happened at an earlier time; this event, especially a marriage, celebrated on this date each year.

an•no•tate *v.* To use notes to give one's opinions. **annotation** *n.*

an•nounce *v.* To proclaim; to give notice; to state publicly. **announcement** *n.*

an•nounc•er *n.* A performer on radio or television who provides program continuity and gives commercial and other points of interest.

an•noy *v.* To bother; to irritate; to make slightly angry. **annoying** *adj.*, **annoyingly** *adv.*

an•noy•ance *n.* A nuisance; irritation; act of annoying.

an•nu•al *adj.* Yearly; recurring or done at the same time each year. *n.* A yearly publication, as a yearbook. **annually** *adv.*

an•nu•i•ty *n.* Annual payment of an income or allowance.

an•nul *v.* To cancel a marriage or a law; to do away with; to put an end to. **annullable** *adj.*, **annulment** *n.*

an•nu•lar *adj.* Shaped like or forming a ring. **annularity** *n.*, **annularly** *adv.*

an•nun•ci•ate *v.* To proclaim; to announce.

an•nun•ci•a•tion *n.* An announcement; the act of announcing.

an•ode *n.* Positively charged electrode. **anodic** *adj.*, **anodically** *adv.*

a•noint *v.* To apply oil in a religious ceremony. **anointer** *n.*

a•nom•a•ly *n.* Anything irregular or abnormal. **anomalistic** *adj.*

a•non *adv.* Soon; in a short period of time.

a•non•y•mous *adj.* Unknown; without a name; not identified or credited; of unknown origin or authorship. **anonymity** *n.*, **anonymously** *adv.*

an•oth•er *adj.* Additional; one more; different, but of the same character; the other.

an•swer *n.* A written or spoken reply, as to a question; a result or solution, as to a problem; a response. *v.* To respond; to be responsible for.

ant *n.* A small insect, usually without wings, which lives in or on the ground, or in wood in large colonies.

ant•ac•id *n.* A substance that neutralizes or weakens acids.

an•tag•o•nism *n.* Hostility; condition of being against; the feeling of unfriendliness toward.

an•tag•o•nize *v.* To arouse hostility; to make an enemy of someone.

ant•eat•er *n.* Mammal with a long snout and a long, sticky tongue, indigenous to the New World, feeding mainly on ants and termites; aardvark.

an•te•ce•dent *n.* An event that precedes another; *adj.* previous.

an•te•date *v.* To precede in time; to give an earlier date than the actual date.

an•te•me•rid•i•en *n.* Time before noon, abbreviated as A.M.

an•ten•na *n.* Slender feelers on the head of an insect, lobster, crab, and other crustaceans; wire or other device used in radio and television to send and receive signals.

an•te•ri•or *adj.* Toward or at the front; coming before; earlier.

an•te•room *n.* Waiting room; a room leading to a larger, more important room.

an•them *n.* Hymn of praise or loyalty; an official song of a country, school, or other organization.

an•ther *n.* The part of the flower where the pollen is located at the end of a stamen.

an•thol•o•gy *n.* A collection of stories, poems, or other writings.

an•thra•cite *n.* Coal with a high carbon content and low volatile matter; hard coal.

an•thrax *n.* An infectious, usually fatal disease found in animals such as cattle and sheep, but transmittable to man.

an•thro•po•cen•tric *adj.* Interpretive of reality in terms of human experience and values.

an•thro•poid *adj.* Resembling man, as gorillas or chimpanzees.

an•thro•pol•o•gy *n.* The science that studies the origin, culture, and development of man. **anthropological** *adj.*, **anthropologist** *n.*

an•ti•ba•lis•tic mis•sile *n.* A missile designed to destroy a ballistic missile.

an•ti•bi•ot•ic *n.* A substance, as streptomycin or penicillin, produced by organisms, as fungi and bacteria, effective in the destruction of microorganisms and used widely to prevent or treat diseases.

an•ti•bod•y *n.* Proteins generated in the blood that react to foreign proteins or carbohydrates of certain types, neutralizing them and producing immunity against certain microorganisms or their toxins.

an•tic *n.* Mischievous caper or act; a clownish acrobat. *pl.* Misbehavior, erratic actions.

an•tic•i•pate *v.* To look forward to; to act in advance of; to foresee; to act as a preventive to. **anticipation, anticipator** *n.*

an•ti•cli•max *n.* A letdown or decline, a commonplace conclusion; a series of significant events or happenings. **anticlimactic** *adj.*

an•ti•dote *n.* A substance that counteracts an injury or poison.

an•ti•freeze *n.* Substance, as ethylene glycol, mixed with water or other liquid to lower the freezing point.

an•ti•ma•cas•sar *n.* A protective covering for the backs and arms of chairs and sofas, used to prevent soiling.

an•ti•mat•ter *n.* A form of matter composed of antiparticles.

an•tin•o•my *n.* An opposition or contradiction.

an•ti•par•ti•cle *n.* Identically matched atomic particles, but with exactly opposite electrically charged magnetic properties and spin.

an•ti•pas•to *n.* Appetizer including cheese, fish, vegetables, and smoked meat served with oil and vinegar.

an•tip•a•thy *n.* Feeling of repugnance or opposition. **antipathetic** *adj.*

an•ti•per•spi•rant *n.* Substance applied to the underarm to reduce excessive perspiration.

an•tiph•o•ny *n.* A sound that echoes or answers another; responsive chanting or singing.

an•ti•pode *n.* A direct opposite.

an•tique *adj.* Belonging to or of ancient times; very old.

an·tique *n.* An object, customarily over 100 years old, whose value lies in its rarity and example of lost skills and crafts; collectibles of a certain age. *v.* To seek antiques; to shop for or trade in old and rare items, especially furniture, artwork, and household objects.

an·ti·qui·ties *coll. n.* Objects from ancient times, especially other cultures; movable items of cultural value to a country, classified as not exportable without special license.

an·ti·qui·ty *n.* Quality of being ancient or old.

an·ti·sep·tic *adj.* Pertaining to or capable of producing antisepsis; thoroughly clean. **antiseptically** *adv.*

an·ti·so·cial *adj.* Unsociable; opposed to society.

an·tith·e·sis *n.* Direct opposition or contrast. **antithetical, antithetic** *adj.*

an·ti·trust *adj.* Having to do with the regulation of trusts, monopolies, and cartels.

ant·ler *n.* One of a pair of bony growths on the head of a member of the deer family.

an·to·nym *n.* A word opposite in meaning to another word.

an·vil *n.* A heavy block of steel or iron on which metal is formed.

anx·i·e·ty *n.* A state of uncertainty; disturbance of the mind regarding uncertain events; uneasiness caused by indecision or the failure of events to reconcile themselves.

anx·ious *adj.* Troubled in mind or worried about some uncertain matter or event. **anxiousness** *n.*, **anxiously** *adv.*

an·y *adj.* One of some; no matter which; some; every; an unqualified quantity or part.

an·y·bod·y *pron.* Anyone; any person.

an·y·how *adv.* By any means; in any way; whatever.

an·y·more *adv.* At present and from now on.

an·y·one *pron.* Any person; anybody.

an·y·place *adv.* Anywhere.

an·y·thing *pron.* Any occurrence, object or matter.

an·y·time *adv.* At any time whatever.

an·y·way *adv.* Nevertheless; anyhow; in any manner; regardless of outcome.

an·y·where *adv.* In, at, or to any place, regardless of location; to any extent.

a·or·ta *n.* The main artery that carries blood away from the heart and distributes blood to all of the body except the lungs. **aortal, aortic** *adj.*

a·pace *adv.* Rapid in pace; quickly.

a·part *adv.* Separate or at a distance; in pieces; to pieces; set aside.

a·part·heid *n.* In the Republic of South Africa, an abandoned official policy of political, social, and economic discrimination and segregation against nonwhites.

a·part·ment *n.* A suite or room in a building, sharing walls, floor, or ceiling with others, equipped for individual living.

ap·a·thy *n.* The lack of emotions or feelings; indifference; absence of emotional involvement or reaction.

ape *n.* A large mammal of the hominid group, such as a gorilla, chimpanzee, or monkey; a very clumsy, coarse person.

ape *v.* To mimic or copy; to imitate in a comic way; to follow faithfully in action or behavior.

ap·er·ture *n.* An opening, especially of a camera lens or similar optic device.

a·pex *n.* The highest point; tip; top.

a·pha·sia *n.* Any partial or total loss of the ability to express ideas, resulting from brain damage. **aphasiac** *n.*, **aphasic** *adj.*

a·phid *n.* Small insects that suck sap from plants.

aph·o·rism *n.* Brief statement of truth or principle. **aphorist** *n.*, **aphoristic** *adj.*

aph·ro·dis·i·ac *n.* Something that increases or arouses sexual desire or potency.

a·pi·ar·y *n.* Place where bees are kept and raised for their honey.

a·piece *adv.* For or to each one; each; singly.

a·plomb *n.* Assurance; poise; self-confidence.

a•poc•ry•pha *n.* Fourteen books not included in the Old Testament by Protestants, considered uncanonical because they are not part of the Hebrew scriptures; eleven of the books are accepted in the Roman Catholic Church.

ap•o•gee *n.* The point most distant from earth in the moon's orbit.

a•pol•o•get•ic *adj.* Making an expression of apology. **apologetically** *adv.*

a•pol•o•gize *v.* To make an apology.

a•pol•o•gy *n.* A statement expressing regret for an action or fault; a formal justification or defense; a protracted explanation in response to criticism.

a•pos•ta•sy *n.* Desertion of one's political party, religious faith, or cause.

a•pos•tle *n.* A person sent on a mission; the first Christian missionary to go into a new area or group; the person who first initiates a moral reform or introduces an important system or belief; a member of a Mormon council of twelve men. **apostleship** *n.*

a•pos•tol•ic *adj.* Relating to an apostle; living by the teachings of the New Testament and the apostles.

a•pos•tro•phe *n.* The mark used to indicate the removal of letters or figures, the plural of letters or figures, and the possessive case; the act of turning away; addressing the usually absent person or a usually personified thing rhetorically.

a•poth•e•car•y *n.* A person who prepares drugs for medical uses.

a•po•the•o•sis *n.* The elevation of something or someone to the rank of a god; the ideal example.

ap•pall *v.* To overcome by shock or dismay; to weaken; to fail; to become pale.

ap•pall•ing *adj.* Dismay or disgust caused by an event or a circumstance.

ap•pa•nage *n.* A rightful adjunct; provision for a younger offspring or child; a section of property or privilege appropriated by or to a person as a proper share.

ap•pa•ra•tus *n.* Appliance or instrument designed and used for a specific operation. **apparatus** or **apparatuses** *pl.*

ap•par•el *v.* To dress or put on clothing; to adorn or embellish. *n.* Clothing; decoration or ornament, especially of fabric.

ap•par•ent *adj.* Clear and opened to the eye and mind; open to view, visible; on the surface; according to the immediate evidence of the senses. **apparently** *adv.*

ap•pa•ri•tion *n.* An unusual or unexpected appearance; the act of being visible; a ghostly figure.

ap•peal *n.* Power to arouse a sympathetic response; an earnest plea; a legal proceeding where a case is brought from a lower court to a higher court for a rehearing. *v.* To make a request; to ask another person for corroboration, vindication, or decision on a matter of importance; to beg or ask formally but vigorously. **appealable** *adj.*

ap•peal•ing *adj.* Attractive, personable, desirable, or pleasant; having acceptable or agreeable properties; having elements in favor of adoption. **appealingly** *adv.*

ap•pear *v.* To come into sight or existence; to come into public view; to come formally before an authorized person; to give ocular evidence; to seem; to be apparent.

ap•pear•ance *n.* The action or process of appearing; an outward indication or showing; presence at an event.

ap•pease *v.* To give peace; to cause to stop or subside; to calm; to pacify. **appeasement** *n.*

ap•pel•late *adj.* Having the power to hear and review the decisions of the lower courts.

ap•pel•la•tion *n.* Identifying by a name or title.

ap•pend *v.* To add an appendix or supplement, as to a book; to attach.

ap•pend•age *n.* Something added to something more important or larger; a subordinate or a dependent person; a part attached but clearly outlined; a partially detached but still connected section of a body, as an arm.

ap•pen•dec•to•my *n.* The surgical

removal of the appendix.

ap•pen•dix *n.* Supplementary material usually found at the end of a written work; any addition after the main body; in medicine, the vermiform appendix, a vestigial organ attached to the large intestine and abdominal wall by mesenteries.

ap•per•cep•tion *n.* The mental understanding of something perceived in terms of previous experience.

ap•per•tain *v.* To belong to or connect with, as a rightful part.

ap•pe•tite *n.* The craving or desire for food or other need; a desire to consume.

ap•pe•tiz•er *n.* Food or drink served before a meal to stimulate the appetite; an aperitif.

ap•plaud *v.* To express or show approval by clapping the hands; to congratulate, as an accomplishment; to encourage by acknowledging previous effort.

ap•plause *n.* The expression of public approval. **applausive** *adj.*

ap•ple *n.* The round, red, yellow, or green edible fruit of a tree.

ap•plet *n.* A task-specific small program in Java computer language.

ap•pli•ance *n.* A piece of equipment or device designed for a particular use; a kitchen or household device, usually electrical or gas-powered, to ameliorate housework.

ap•pli•ca•ble *adj.* Appropriate; suitable; capable of being applied; germane to the task at hand. **applicability** *n.*

ap•pli•cant *n.* A person applying for a job, position, membership, or other entry.

ap•pli•ca•tion *n.* The act of putting something to use; the act of superposing or administering; request or petition; a form used to make a request.

ap•pli•ca•tor *n.* A device used to apply a substance; one who applies.

ap•plied *adj.* Put to practical use to solve definite problems.

ap•ply *v.* To make a request in the form of a written application; to put into use for a practical purpose or reason; to put into

operation or to bring into action; to employ with close attention.

ap•point *v.* To arrange something; to fix or set officially; to place into office or position without election. **appointable** *adj.*, **appointer** *n.*

ap•point•ment *n.* The act of appointing or designating; arrangement for or time of a meeting; a nonelective position or office; engagement or meeting.

ap•por•tion *v.* To divide and share according to a plan. **apportionment** *n.*

ap•po•si•tion *n.* A grammatical construction in which a noun or noun phrase is followed by another with the same referent and syntactical relationship to the sentence. **appositional** *adj.*

ap•pos•i•tive *adj.* Relating to or standing in apposition.

ap•prais•al *n.* The evaluation of property by an authorized person; the act of placing value on an action or plan.

ap•praise *v.* To estimate the value, worth, or status of a particular item or action. **appraiser** *n.*, **appraising** *adj.*

ap•pre•ci•a•ble *adj.* Measurable; able to be perceived, noticed, or estimated; considerable. **appreciably** *adv.*

ap•pre•ci•ate *v.* To recognize the worth, quality, or significance; to value very highly; to realize; to acknowledge the value of; to increase in price or value over time. **appreciation** *n.*, **appreciative** *adj.*

ap•pre•hend *v.* To anticipate with anxiety, dread or fear; to recognize the meaning of; to grasp, as a prisoner; to understand. **apprehensible** *adj.*

ap•pre•hen•sion *n.* The act of or comprehending power to comprehend; suspicion or fear of future events.

ap•pre•hen•sive *adj.* Viewing the future with anxiety or fear.

ap•pren•tice *n.* A person learning a trade, art, or occupation under a skilled worker for a prescribed period of time; someone learning a task by performing its simpler aspects. *v.* To work as an apprentice under the supervision of a skilled worker. **apprenticeship** *n.*

ap•prise *v.* To inform; to give notice.

ap•proach *v.* To come near to or draw closer; to be close in appearance. *n.* Access or entrance to a place; a method for analysis; the first stage of an act, especially landing an aircraft. **approachable** *adj.*

ap•pro•ba•tion *n.* A formal approval.

ap•pro•pri•ate *v.* To take possession of; to take by authority, with or without permission; to attach by bonds of ownership.

ap•pro•pri•ate *adj.* Suitable for a use or occasion; fitting; measured in a like manner or amount. **appropriately** *adv.*, **appropriateness** *n.*

ap•pro•pri•a•tion *n.* Money set apart for a particular use; the act or instance of appropriating.

ap•prov•al *n.* The act of approving; the right of acceptance or refusal; blessing or permission from higher authority.

ap•prove *v.* To regard or express a favorable opinion; to give formal or official permission; to acknowledge as satisfactory; to warrant the meeting of standards. **approvingly** *adv.*

ap•prox•i•mate *adj.* Located close together; almost accurate or exact; near. *v.* To bring close or near to; to approach; to estimate; to be near the same. **approximately** *adv.*

ap•pur•te•nance *n.* Something that belongs with another more important thing; an accessory that is passed along with the main issue.

a pri•o•ri *adj.* Deductive; reasoned from a self-evident basis; based on theory rather than personal experience.

ap•ron *n.* A garment, easily worn and removed, used to protect clothing; the area of a proscenium stage in front of the curtain line; paved area around an airport terminal building or airport hangar; waterfront edge of a wharf or pier.

ap•ro•pos *adv.* At a good time; by the way.

apse *n.* A semicircular or polygonal projection of a building or church.

apt *adj.* Unusually qualified or fitting; appropriate; having a tendency; suitable; capable, intelligent, or quick to understand. **aptly** *adv.*, **aptness** *n.*

ap•ti•tude *n.* A natural talent, skill, or ability; a tendency to excel; quickness in learning or understanding.

a•qua *n.* Water; aquamarine.

a•qua•ma•rine *n.* A color of pale blue to light green; a mineral that is blue, blue-green, or green in color.

a•qua•relle *n.* A transparent watercolor drawing.

a•quar•i•um *n.* An artificial pond where living plants and aquatic animals are maintained and exhibited.

a•quat•ic *adj.* Occurring on or in the water; viable in water; related to water.

a•qua vi•tae *n.* A very strong liquor; alcohol.

a•que•duct *n.* A conduit for carrying a large quantity of flowing water; a bridge-like structure supporting a canal over a river.

a•que•ous *adj.* Like or resembling water; dissolved in water; watery.

a•qui•fer *n.* The layer of underground gravel, sand, or rocks where water collects.

a•qui•line *adj.* Resembling or related to an eagle; hooked or curved like the beak on an eagle.

a•quiv•er *adj.* Trembling or quivering.

ar•a•besque *n.* An intricate style or design of interwoven leaves, flowers, and geometric forms.

ar•a•ble *adj.* Suitable for cultivation by plowing.

a•rach•nid *n.* Arthropods, including spiders, scorpions, and ticks, that are mostly air-breathing, with two major body segments, having four pairs of legs but no antennae.

ar•bi•ter *n.* A person chosen to decide a dispute, having absolute power of determining and judging.

ar•bi•trar•y *adj.* Based on a whim or

impulse; ungoverned or unregulated by law or tradition; illogical; coming about at random; not predictable. **arbitrarily** *adv.*, **arbitrariness** *n.*

ar·bor *n.* A garden shelter from the sun or weather, covered with or made of broad-leafed climbing plants; an axle or rotating shaft on a tooling machine. **arborous** *adj.*

ar·bo·re·al *adj.* Resembling or related to a tree; living in trees.

ar·bo·re·tum *n.* A place for studying and exhibiting trees, shrubs, and plants culti-vated for educational and scientific pur-poses.

ar·bor·ist *n.* A specialist in the mainte-nance and care of trees.

arc *n.* A shape or structure that is curved or arched; a continuous curved line, especial-ly part of a circle; the measurement of such a curve; the luminous discharge of electric current across a gap of two elec-trodes.

ar·cade *n.* An arched covered passageway supported by columns; a long arched gallery or building, sometimes having shops and stores; a shopping mall; an amusement facility, usually indoors, offer-ing coin-operated games of chance and skill. **arcaded** *adj.*

arch *n.* A structure that spans over an open area and gives support. **archly** *adv.*, **archness** *n.*

ar·chae·ol·o·gy *n.* Scientific study of ancient times and ancient peoples by analysis of artifacts, remains, gravesites, monuments, and antiquities. **archaeo-logical** *adj.*, **archaeologist** *n.*

ar·cha·ic *adj.* Belonging to an earlier time; old past value or currency; characteristic of an earlier language or expression, now used only in special cases. **archaist** *n.*

ar·cha·ism *n.* Something outdated or old fashioned, as an expression or word.

arch·an·gel *n.* The highest in order of angels in the celestial spheres. **angelic** *adj.*

arch·di·o·cese *n.* The territory or district of an archbishop.

arch·en·e·my *n.* One who is a chief enemy.

arch·er *n.* A person trained in the skills of the bow and arrow.

ar·cher·y *n.* The practice or art of shoot-ing with a bow and arrow; the equipment used by an archer.

ar·che·type *n.* An original from which copies are patterned; the prototype; origi-nal manifestation of a subsequently prolif-erating phenomenon.

arch·fiend *n.* A chief or principal fiend; a person of great wickedness, especially Satan.

ar·chi·tect *n.* A person who designs and supervises the preparation for and con-struction of large structures, especially those requiring knowledge of physical principles.

ar·chi·tec·ture *n.* The art or science of designing and building structures; the method or style of construction or build-ing; architectonics. **architectural** *adj.*

ar·chive *n.* To catalog, taxonomize, store, and retrieve documents or objects for study or long-term preservation. *pl. n.* Public documents or records; the place where archives are kept.

arch·way *n.* A passage or way under an arch; an arch over a passage.

arc·tic *adj.* Extremely cold or frigid; relat-ing to the territory north of the Arctic Circle. *n.* A waterproof boot that covers or comes just above the ankle.

ar·dor *n.* Extreme warmth or passion; emotion; intense heat of expression or feeling.

ar·du·ous *adj.* Taking much effort to bring forth; difficult; hard, as a task. **arduously** *adv.*

are *v.* First, second, and third person plural and second person singular of the verb *to be.*

ar·e·a *n.* A flat or level piece of ground; the product of length and width; field of study; the scope of a concept, activity or operation; region, especially geographical.

ar·e·a code *n.* The three-digit number

assigned to each telephone area, and used to call another area, in the U.S. or Canada.

a•re•na *n.* Enclosed area for public entertainment, such as football games, or concerts; a place of combat or confrontation; area of concentration or attention.

a•re•na the•a•ter *n.* A theater with the stage located in the center and the audience seated around the stage.

ar•go•sy *n.* A fleet of ships; a large merchant ship.

ar•got *n.* A secret, specialized vocabulary.

ar•gu•a•ble *adj.* Open to argument; questionable; capable of being supported by evidence; separable by point of view. **arguably** *adv.*

ar•gue *v.* To debate, to offer reason for or against; to dispute or quarrel; to persuade or influence; to state evidence for in a court or deliberative body. **arguer** *n.*

ar•gu•ment *n.* A quarrel or dispute; a reasoned statement of a point of view or opinion; the body or summary plot of a literary work; a formal presentation of evidence.

ar•gu•men•ta•tion *n.* The process or act of arguing; debating.

ar•gu•men•ta•tive *adj.* Given to argument; debating or disputing; verbally combative.

ar•gyle *n.* A pattern knitted with varicolored, diamond-shaped designs.

a•ri•a *n.* A vocal piece with accompaniment sung in solo; part of an opera.

ar•id *adj.* Experiencing little or insufficient rain; dry; climatologically low in total rainfall; lacking in interest or feeling; dull; aloof and unemotional in demeanor.

a•right *adv.* Correctly; rightly; in a right way or form.

a•rise *v.* To come up; to rise; to come to one's attention; to come into view; to mount; to move to a higher place; to get out of bed.

ar•is•toc•ra•cy *n.* A government by a small privileged class of hereditarily superior individuals or families; class or group viewed as superior; the hereditary privileged ruling nobility or class. **aristocrat** *n.*, **aristocratic** *adj.*

a•rith•me•tic *adj.* Branch of mathematics dealing with addition, subtraction, multiplication, division.

ark *n.* Any large vessel whose cargo provides the means for survival and proliferation; the ship Noah built during the Great Flood; the chest containing the Ten Commandments or covenant on stone tables, carried by the Jews; something that gives protection.

arm *n.* The body part between the shoulder and the wrist; upper limb of the human body. *v.* To furnish with protection against danger; to provide weapons to; to load or activate in preparation for use.

ar•ma•da *n.* A fleet of warships; a large force of moving military vehicles; a flotilla.

ar•ma•dil•lo *n.* A burrowing nocturnal animal with an armor-like covering of jointed, bony plates.

ar•ma•ment *n.* Military supplies and weapons; the process of preparing for battle.

ar•ma•ture *n.* The main moving part of an electric device or machine; a piece of soft iron that connects the poles of a magnet.

arm•chair *n.* A chair with armrests or supports.

arm•ful *n.* As much as the arm can hold. **armfuls** *pl.*

ar•mi•stice *n.* The temporary suspension of combat by mutual agreement; truce between warring factions; the document declaring such an agreement.

ar•mor *n.* Covering used in combat to protect the body or a piece of machinery, made of metal or other impenetrable material; fleet of vehicles with such covering, as tanks and heavy transports. **armor** *v.*, **armored** *adj.*

ar•mor•er *n.* A person who makes armor; one who assembles, repairs, and tests firearms.

ar•mor•y *n.* The supply of arms for attack or defense; the place where military equipment is stored.

arm•pit *n.* The hollow area under the arm where it joins the shoulder.

arm•rest *n.* The support for the arm, as on a chair.

ar•my *n.* A group of persons organized for a country's protection; the land forces of a country. **armies** *pl.*

a•ro•ma *n.* A distinctive fragrance or pleasant odor; pleasing smell, especially of food. **aromatical, aromatic** *adj.*

a•round *adv.* To or on all sides; in succession or rotation; from one place to another; in a circle or circular movement; near; in the vicinity of; occasionally seen.

a•rouse *v.* To wake up from a sleep; to stir; to excite. **arousal** *n.*

ar•raign *v.* To call before a court to answer a charge or indictment; to accuse of imperfection, inadequacy, or of wrongdoing. **arraignment** *n.*

ar•range *v.* To put in correct order or proper sequence; to prepare for something; to take steps to organize something; to bring about an understanding or an agreement.

ar•range•ment *n.* The state of being arranged; something made by arranging things or parts together.

ar•ras *n.* A screen or wall hanging of tapestry, used to trap air for insulation in stone structures.

ar•ray *v.* To place or set in order; to draw up; to decorate or dress in an impressive attire.

ar•rears *pl. n.* The state of being behind something, as an obligation or payment; an unfinished duty.

ar•rest *v.* To stop or to bring an end to; to capture; to seize; to hold in custody by the authority of law. *n.* The act of bringing into custody; the legal recording of such acts.

ar•rest•ing *adj.* Very impressive or striking; catching the attention.

ar•riv•al *n.* The act of arriving.

ar•rive *v.* To reach or get to a destination; to succeed into public attention; to attain

a sum or answer.

ar•ro•gance *n.* An overbearing manner, intolerable presumption; an insolent pride. **arrogant, arrogantly** *adv.*

ar•row *n.* The shaft shot as a weapon or projectile from a bow; a sign or mark to show direction; a pointed missile designed to penetrate the target.

ar•row•head *n.* The striking end of an arrow, usually shaped like a wedge; the archeological remains of primitive projectile weaponry, especially those found in open spaces.

ar•se•nal *n.* A collection of weapons; a place where arms and military equipment are manufactured or stored.

ar•se•nic *n.* A solid, poisonous element, steel-gray in color, used to make insecticide or weed killer.

ar•son *n.* The fraudulent burning of property; the crime of destruction by fire. **arsonist** *n.*, **arsonous** *adj.*

art *n.* A human skill of expression of other objects by painting, drawing, sculpture, etc.; a branch of learning.

ar•ter•y *n.* A blood vessel that carries blood from the heart to the other parts of the body; a major means for transportation or transport. **arterial** *adj.*

ar•te•sian well *n.* A well that produces water without a pump.

art•ful *adj.* Showing or performed with skill or art. **artfully** *adv.*

ar•thri•tis *n.* Inflammation of joints due to infectious or metabolic causes.

ar•thro•pod *n.* Member of phylum Arthropoda; invertebrate animal with jointed limbs and segmented body, including insects, crustaceans, and arachnids.

ar•ti•choke *n.* A plant with a thistle-like head, which can be cooked and eaten as a vegetable.

ar•ti•cle *n.* A term or clause in a contract; a paragraph or section; a condition or rule; an object, item or commodity; a grammatical signifier of the presence of a noun.

ar•tic•u•late *adj.* Able to express oneself

clearly, effectively, or readily; speaking in distinct words or syllables. **articulation** *n.*

ar•ti•fact *n.* Something made by man showing human modification or workmanship.

ar•ti•fice *n.* An artful or clever skill; ingenuity.

ar•ti•fi•cial *adj.* Not genuine; made by man; not found in nature; following the design of, but without the genuineness of, a natural occurrence. **artificially** *adv.*

ar•til•ler•y *n.* Weapons, especially cannons; troops trained in the use of guns and other means of defense and attack.

ar•ti•san *n.* A mechanic or a craftsman.

art•ist *n.* A person practicing the fine arts of painting, sculpture, architecture, literature, music, dance, or theater.

ar•tis•tic *adj.* Relating to the characteristic of an artist or art; creative; answering to aesthetic rather than practical criteria. **artistically** *adv.*

art•ist•ry *n.* Artistic ability, or quality of workmanship or effect.

art•less *adj.* Lacking knowledge, art, or skill; crude; natural; simple. **artlessly** *adv.*, **artlessness** *n.*

art•work *n.* The artistic work of an artist; the product, usually collective, of the graphic element in a print layout.

as *adv.* In the manner like; of the same degree or amount; similar to. *conj.* At the same time when; since; given the fact that.

as•bes•tos *n.* A noncombustible, fibrous, mineral form of magnesium silicate once used in fireproofing, but since linked to some forms of cancer.

as•cend *v.* To rise up from a lower level; to climb; to mount; to walk up.

as•cen•dant *adj.* Rising; moving up.

as•cent *n.* A way up; a slope; the act of rising; a journey to the summit.

as•cer•tain *v.* To find out for certain; to make sure; verify by evidence.

as•cet•i•cism *n.* The practice of strict self-denial through personal and spiritual discipline.

ASCII *abbr.* American Standard Code for Information Interchange; type of text file without binary characters.

as•cot *n.* A scarf or broad tie placed under the chin.

as•cribe *v.* To assign or attribute to something. **ascribable** *adj.*

a•sex•u•al *adj.* Lacking sexual reproductive organs; without sex; absent of sexual intent or implication. **asexuality** *n.*

ash *n.* A type of tree with a hard, tough elastic wood; the grayish dust remaining after something has burned.

a•shamed *adj.* Feeling guilt, disgrace, or shame; feeling unworthy or inferior; emotionally acknowledging wrongdoing, sin, or guilt.

a•shore *adv.* On or to the shore.

a•side *adv.* Out of the way; to a side; to one side. *n.* Something said in an undertone and not meant to be heard by someone; a theatrical device for informing the audience of a character's thoughts or reactions without revealing them to other characters on stage.

as if *conj.* As it would be if; like; that; acting despite the unlikelihood that.

ask *v.* To request permission; to require or seek information; to pose a question or request. **asker** *n.*

a•skance *adv.* With a side glance, with suspicion or distrust.

a•skew *adj.* Out of line, not straight.

a•slant *adv.* In a slanting direction.

a•sleep *adv.* In a state of sleep; lacking sensation; numb; not alert.

a•slope *adv.* In a slanting or sloping position or direction.

a•so•cial *adj.* Selfish, not social.

as•par•a•gus *n.* A vegetable with tender shoots, very succulent when cooked.

as•pect *n.* The situation, position, view, or appearance; an area of interest in a study or problem.

as•pen *n.* A tree known as the trembling poplar, having leaves that flutter even in a very light breeze.

as•per•i•ty *n.* Roughness in manner.

as•per•sion *n.* False charges or slander; defamation; maligning.

as•phalt *n.* A sticky, thick, blackish-brown residue of petroleum manufacture, used in paving roads and roofing buildings.

as•phyx•i•ate *v.* To suffocate, to prevent from breathing; to close off or reduce air to. **asphyxiation** *n.*

as•pic *n.* A savory jelly made from fish, meat, or vegetable juices.

as•pi•rate *v.* To give pronunciation with a full breathing sound; to draw out using suction. **aspiration** *n.*

as•pire *v.* To desire with ambition; to strive towards something that is higher. **aspiringly** *adv.*, **aspirer**, **aspiration** *n.*

as•pi•rin *n.* Medication containing a derivative of salicylic acid, used for the relief of pain and fever.

ass *n.* A hoofed animal; a donkey; a stupid or foolish person.

as•sail *v.* To attack violently with words or blows. **assailant** *n.*

as•sas•sin *n.* Murderer, especially of a politically or ideologically important person, either from fanatical beliefs or for hire; a hired killer used by others to change the course of events.

as•sas•si•nate *v.* To murder a prominent person by secret or sudden attack. **assassination** *n.*

as•sault *n.* A violent physical or verbal attack on a person; a valiant attempt at conquering or completing something.

as•say *v.* To evaluate or to assess; to try; to attempt. **assayer** *n.*

as•sem•blage *n.* A collection of things or people; artistic composition made from junk, scraps, and miscellaneous materials.

as•sem•ble *v.* To put together the parts of something; to come together as a group. **assembly** *n.*

as•sent *v.* To give approval; to agree on something.

as•sent *n.* The act of giving permission; acceptance of terms or conditions.

as•sert *v.* To declare or state positively, to maintain; to defend.

as•sess *v.* To fix or assign a value to something. **assessor** *n.*

as•sess•ment *n.* Appraisal, opinion, evaluation; the official determination of value for tax purposes.

as•set *n.* A valuable quality or possession; all of the property of a business or a person that can be used to cover liabilities

as•sign *v.* To designate as to duty; to give or allot; to attribute. **assignable** *adj.*

as•sign•ment *n.* A given amount of work or task to undertake, allotted by a superior; a post, position, or office to which one is assigned.

as•sim•i•late *v.* To take in, to understand; to make similar; to digest or to absorb into the system. **assimilator**, **assimilation** *n.*

as•sist *v.* To give support, to aid, to give help. **assistance**, **assistant** *n.*

as•size *n.* An edict, ordinance, or enactment made at a session of legislative assembly.

as•so•ci•ate *v.* To connect or join together; to accompany socially; to find relationships between. *n.* A partner, colleague, or companion; one with whom another works or does business.

as•so•ci•a•tion *n.* An organized body of persons or professions having a common interest; a society; the act of making mental connections among disparate ideas or facts. **associational** *adj.*

as•so•nance *n.* The repetition of sound in words or syllables.

as•sort *v.* To distribute into groups of a classification or kind. **assorter** *n.*

as•sort•ed *adj.* Made up of different or various kinds; intentionally mixed as a sample of possibilities; miscellaneous.

as•sort•ment *n.* The act or state of being assorted; a collection of different things.

as•suage *v.* To quiet, pacify; to put an end to by satisfying.

as•sume *v.* To accept as fact; to take upon oneself to complete a job or duty; to take responsibility for; to take for granted.

as•sump•tion *n.* An idea or statement

believed to be true without proof; the taking on of, laying claim to, or otherwise possessing by authority.

as•sur•ance *n.* A statement made to inspire confidence of mind or manner; freedom from uncertainty; guarantee.

as•sure *v.* To give the feeling of confidence; to make sure or certain; to guarantee by self-reputation. **assurer** *n.*

as•sured *adj.* Satisfied as to the truth or certainty; confident; sure of. **assuredly** *adv.*

as•ter *n.* A plant having white, bluish, purple, or pink daisy-like flowers.

as•ter•isk *n.* The character used to indicate letters omitted or as a reference to a footnote.

a•stern *adv.* Toward the rear or back of an aircraft or ship.

as•ter•oid *n.* One of thousands of small planetary fragments in solar orbit between Jupiter and Mars.

asth•ma *n.* A respiratory disease marked by labored breathing, accompanied by wheezing, coughing, and gasping. **asthmatic** *adj., n.*

as though *conj.* As it may be; acting on the likelihood that.

a•stig•ma•tism *n.* A defect of the lens of an eye resulting in blurred or imperfect images.

a•stir *adv.* Out of bed, awake; in motion.

as•ton•ish *v.* To strike with sudden fear, wonder, or surprise; to amaze, confound, or momentarily disorient. **astonishing** *adj.* **astonishingly** *adv.* **astonishment** *n.*

as•tound *v.* To fill with wonder and bewilderment. **astounding** *adj.*, **astoundingly** *adv.*

as•tral *adj.* Resembling, or related to the stars.

a•stray *adv.* Away from a desirable or proper path or development.

a•stride *prep.* One leg on either side of something; placed or lying on both sides of; extending across or over.

as•trin•gent *adj.* Able to draw together or to constrict tissue.

as•tro•dome *n.* A large stadium covered by a dome.

as•trol•o•gy *n.* The study of the supposed influences of the planets and stars, and their movements and positions, on human affairs. **astrologer** *n.*

as•tro•naut *n.* A person who travels in a spacecraft beyond the earth's atmosphere.

as•tro•nom•i•cal *adj.* Relating to astronomy; something inconceivable or enormously large. **astronomically** *adv.*

as•tron•o•my *n.* The science of the celestial bodies and their motion, magnitudes, and constitution. **astronomer** *n.*

as•tro•phys•ics *n.* Branch of astronomy dealing with the chemical and physical constitution of the celestial bodies. **astrophysicist** *n.*

as•tute *adj.* Sharp in discernment; very shrewd. **astutely** *adv.*, **astuteness** *n.*

a•sun•der *adv.* Separate into parts or positions apart from each other.

a•sy•lum *n.* A refuge or institution for the care of the needy or sick; a place of security and retreat; the granting of political protection to a noncitizen; an institution providing care for the destitute or insane.

a•sym•met•ric *adj.* Not symmetrical; lacking balance, evenness, or fairness. **asymmetry** *n.*

at *prep.* Next to; in the same place as; indicative of presence, occurrence, or condition; in congruence with the time of.

at•a•vism *n.* The reappearance of a hereditary characteristic that skipped several generations; the return or retreat to earlier and less civilized or complex conditions. **atavistic** *adj.*

at•el•ier *n.* An artist's workshop; a garret or studio where the artist works and lives.

a•the•ist *n.* A person who does not believe in God. **atheistic** *adj.*, **atheism** *n.*

a•thirst *adj.* Having a strong, eager desire for something; thirsty.

ath•lete *n.* A physically skilled and trained person who participates in competitions and sports.

ath•let•ic *adj.* Relating to athletes; physically strong and active.

a•thwart *adv.* Opposition to the expected or right; from one side to another.

a•tilt *adj.* Inclined upward or tilted in some way.

at•las *n.* A collection or book of maps; *cap.* Greek titan said to hold up the world on his shoulders.

at•mos•phere *n.* A gaseous mass that surrounds a celestial body, as the earth; a predominant mood or feeling.

at•oll *n.* An island of coral that encircles a lagoon either partially or completely.

at•om *n.* A tiny particle; the smallest unit of an element; the basic building block of matter, consisting of a nucleus and electrons in erratic orbit.

at•om bomb or **a•tom•ic bomb** *n.* A bomb that explodes violently due to the sudden release of atomic energy, occurring from the splitting of nuclei of a heavy chemical element.

at•om•ic en•er•gy *n.* Energy released by changes in the nucleus of an atom.

a•ton•al *adj.* Marked by the deliberate avoidance of a traditional key or tonal center. **atonality** *n.*

a•tone *v.* To give satisfaction; to make amends; to pay an emotional, moral, or ethical debt.

a•tone•ment *n.* Amends for an injury or a wrongdoing; the reconciliation between God and man.

a•top *prep.* On the top of something.

a•tri•um *n.* One of the heart chambers; the main hall of a Roman house. **atrial** *adj.*

a•tro•cious *adj.* Exceedingly cruel or evil. **atrocity** *n.*

a•tro•phy *v.* To decrease in size; to waste away from disuse.

at•tach *v.* To bring together; to fasten or become fastened; to bind by personal attachments. **attachable**, **attached** *adj.*

at•ta•ché *n.* An expert on the diplomatic staff of an embassy.

at•tach•ment *n.* The state of being attached; a tie of affection or loyalty; the supplementary part of something; a document added to a direct communication.

at•tack *v.* To initiate the offensive; to apply force, to assault; to work on with vigor.

at•tain *v.* To arrive at or reach a goal; to achieve by effort. **attainable** *adj.*

at•tain•ment *n.* Accomplishment; an achievement.

at•tar *n.* The fragrant oil from flowers.

at•tempt *v.* To make an effort to do something; to try.

at•tend *v.* To be present; to take charge of or to look after; to listen with attention.

at•ten•dance *n.* The fact or act of attending; the number of times a person attends; the number of persons present at an event.

at•ten•dant *n.* One who provides a service for another; a helper or assistant in a specific act; one who accompanies the main participant in a ceremony.

at•ten•tion *n.* Observation, notice, or mental concentration; a military condition or command of extreme readiness.

at•ten•u•ate *v.* To lessen the force, amount or value; to become thin; to weaken. **attenuation** *n.*

at•test *v.* To give testimony or to sign one's name as a witness. **attestation** *n.*

at•tic *n.* The space directly below the roof of a building.

at•tire *n.* A person's dress or clothing. *v.* To clothe; to dress.

at•ti•tude *n.* A mental position; a predisposition or assumption at the start of a communication; the feeling one has for oneself; the position, especially regarding levelness, of a vessel.

at•tor•ney *n.* A person with legal training appointed to transact business or represent another in litigation; a lawyer. **attorneys** *pl.*

at•tract *v.* To draw by appeal; to cause to draw near.

at•trac•tion *n.* The capability of attracting; something that attracts or is meant to attract; a popular site or event.

at•trac•tive *adj.* Having the power of charming, or quality of attracting.

attractively *adv.*, **attractiveness** *n.*

at·trib·ute *v.* To explain by showing a cause. *n.* A characteristic, especially favorable, of a thing or person. **attributable** *adj.*

at·tune *v.* To bring something into harmony; to put in tune; to adjust.

a·twit·ter *adj.* Very excited; or nervously concerned about something.

a·typ·i·cal *adj.* Not confirming to the typical type. **atypically** *adv.*

au·bade *n.* A poem or song for lovers who part at dawn; a love song in the morning.

au·burn *adj.* A reddish brown color, used in describing the color of a person's hair.

auc·tion *n.* A public sale of merchandise, property, or rights to the highest bidder. *v.* To offer for sale by the auction process.

auc·tion·eer *n.* One who conducts an auction, describing the item and regulating the bidding.

au·da·cious *adj.* Bold, daring, or fearless; insolent. **audacity** *n.*

au·di·ble *adj.* Capable of being heard; within the range of human auditory perception.

au·di·ence *n.* A group of listeners; those in attendance at an event or performance; the opportunity to express views; a formal hearing or conference.

au·di·o *adj.* Of or relating to sound or its high-fidelity reproduction.

au·dit *n.* Verification or examination of financial accounts or records.

au·di·tion *n.* A trial performance given by an entertainer to demonstrate ability or suitability; a tryout.

au·di·tor *n.* A person who listens or hears; one who audits accounts.

au·di·to·ri·um *n.* A hearing place; a large room in a public building or a school that holds many people.

au·di·to·ry *adj.* Related to the organs or sense of hearing.

au·ger *n.* The tool used for the purpose of putting holes in the ground or wood.

aught *n.* Zero (0).

aug·ment *v.* To add to or increase; to enlarge. **augmentation**, **augmenter** *n.*, **augmentative**, **augmentable** *adj.*

aunt *n.* A sister of one's father or mother; the wife of one's uncle; a close, older female family friend not literally an aunt.

au·ra *n.* An emanation said to come from a person's or animal's body.

au·ral *adj.* Relating to the ear or the sense of hearing.

au·re·ole *n.* A halo; a circle around a point.

au·ri·cle *n.* The two upper chambers of the heart.

au·ric·u·lar *adj.* Dealing with the sense of hearing or of being in the shape of the ear.

au·ro·ra *n.* The brilliant display of moving and flashing lights in the night sky, believed to be caused by electrically charged particles.

aus·tere *adj.* Stern in manner and appearance; thrifty; plain and unadorned. **austerity** *n.*

au·then·tic *adj.* Real; genuine; worthy of acceptance.

au·thor *n.* A person who writes an original literary work; the creator of anything; the source or fountain. **author** *v.*

au·thor·i·ty *n.* A group or person with power; a government; an expert. **authorities** *pl.*

au·thor·i·za·tion *n.* Authorizing something; permission; legal right; the process of gaining authority. **au·thor·ize** *v.*

au·tism *n.* Absorption in a self-centered mental state, such as fantasies, daydreams or hallucinations in order to escape from reality; a mental disorder marked by silence and isolation. **autistic** *adj.*

au·to·bi·og·ra·phy *n.* The life story of a person, written by that person. **autobiographer** *n.*

au·toc·ra·cy *n.* Government by one person who has unlimited power. **autocrat** *n.*, **autocratic** *adj.*

au·to·graph *n.* A handwritten signature. *v.* To sign with one's signature.

au·to·mate *v.* To operate by automation; to convert something to automation.

au·to·mat·ic *adj.* Operating with little control; self-regulating; without thought or premeditation. **automatically** *adv.*

au·to·ma·tion *n.* The equipment and techniques used to acquire automation.

au·to·mo·bile *n.* A four-wheeled passenger vehicle commonly propelled by an internal combustion engine; a car.

au·to·mo·tive *adj.* Relating to self-propelled vehicles.

au·ton·o·my *n.* Independence; self-government.

au·to·pi·lot *n.* A device for automatically steering aircraft and ships.

au·top·sy *n.* Postmortem examination; the examination of a body after death to find the cause of death.

au·tumn *n.* The season between summer and winter; the fall; the waning years of a cycle. **autumnal** *adj.*

aux·il·ia·ry *adj.* Providing help or assistance to someone; giving support; additional or extra; acting as an emergency replacement or supplement to.

aux·il·ia·ry verb *n.* A verb that accompanies a main verb and expresses mood, voice, or tense.

a·vail *v.* To be of advantage or use; to use. *n.* The advantage toward attaining a purpose or goal.

a·vail·a·bil·i·ty *n.* The state of being available; handiness or readiness to use; the state of being accessible or attainable.

a·vail·a·ble *adj.* Ready for immediate use.

av·a·lanche *n.* A large amount of rock, snow, or other mass that slides down a mountainside; any overwhelming amount suddenly present.

a·vant garde *n.* Advance guard; the innovative and risk-taking contingent of an artistic or stylistic movement.

av·a·rice *n.* The desire to have wealth and riches without regard to ethics or values.

a·vast *interj.* A nautical command to stop or cease.

a·venge *v.* To take revenge for something. **avenger** *n.*

av·e·nue *n.* A street lined with trees; a wide thoroughfare in a city or residential area; a strategy for achieving something.

a·ver *v.* To state positively and firmly, without reservation; to attest as the truth.

av·er·age *adj.* Typical or usual; not exceptional; common; expressive of the normal. *n.* The number that summarizes a set of unequalities; the expression of the arithmetic mean; the expected or previously determined or experienced amount.

a·verse *adj.* Having a feeling of distaste or repugnance. **aversely** *adv.*

a·ver·sion *n.* A feeling of strong dislike, or distaste for something.

a·vert *v.* To prevent or keep from happening; to turn aside or away from.

a·vi·ar·y *n.* A place where birds are kept.

a·vi·a·tion *n.* The operation of planes and other crafts of flight.

a·vi·a·tor *n.* Operator or navigator of an aircraft; a pilot.

av·id *adj.* Eager; enthusiastic; vigorously or inordinately desirous.

av·o·ca·do *n.* The pear-shaped edible fruit from the avocado tree, having a large seed and yellowish-green pulp.

av·o·ca·tion *n.* A pleasurable activity that is in addition to the regular work a person must do; a hobby.

a·void *v.* To stay away from; to shun; to prevent or keep from happening. **avoidable** *adj.*, **avoidably** *adv.*

a·void·ance *n.* The act of avoiding something.

a·vouch *v.* To assert; to guarantee.

a·vow *v.* To state openly on a subject. **avowal** *n.*

a·wait *v.* To wait for something; to watch in anticipation.

a·wake *v.* To wake up; to be or make alert or watchful. **awaken** *v.*

a·ward *v.* To give or confer as being needed or merited; to give in favorable judgment of. *n.* A judgment or decision; a prize; a recognition of accomplishment.

a·ware *adj.* Being conscious or mindful of something. **awareness** *n.*

a·wash *adj.* Flooded; afloat; washed by water.

a·way *adv.* At a distance; apart from; gone; not available for communication.

awe *n.* A feeling of wonder mixed with reverence; astonishment in response to splendor or excellence. *v.* To give such a feeling to another.

a·weigh *adj.* To hang just clear of a ship's anchor.

awe·some *adj.* Impressive, outstanding; causing astonishment or wonder; expressive of awe. **awesomely** *adv.*, **awesomeness** *n.*

aw·ful *adj.* Very unpleasant or dreadful; very poor; below the lowest minimum standard; so powerful as to be frightening.

a·while *adv.* For a short time; some time past; since.

awk·ward *adj.* Lacking grace or felicity; clumsy; uncoordinated; socially slightly embarrassing. **awkwardly** *adv.*, **awkwardness** *n.*

awl *n.* Tool used to make holes in leather.

awn·ing *n.* Roof-like structure, often of canvas, that serves as a shelter over a window.

a·wry *adv.* In a twisted or turned position.

ax or **axe** *n.* Tool consisting of a head and handle, used to split wood.

ax·i·om *n.* Statement recognized as being true, from which corollary statements can be deduced; something assumed to be true without proof. **axiomatic** *adj.*

ax·is *n.* The line around an object or body that rotates or may be thought to rotate. **axes** *pl.*

ax·le *n.* A spindle or shaft around which a wheel or pair of wheels revolve; a rotating weight-bearing bar or beam.

az·ure *n.* The blue color of the sky.

B

B, b The second letter of the English alphabet; a student's grade rating of good, but not excellent.

bab·ble *v.* To reveal secrets; to chatter senselessly; to talk foolishly.

babe *n.* A very young child or infant; a baby.

ba·boon *n.* A species of primate of Africa and southwestern Asia, with large canine teeth and distinctive muzzle features.

ba·bush·ka *n.* A kerchief folded into a triangle and worn as a covering on the head.

ba·by *n.* A young child; infant. **babyish** *adj.*, **babies** *pl.*

ba·by boom *n.* A statistically measurable rise in the U.S. birth rate immediately after the end of World War II.

bac·ca·lau·re·ate *n.* A bachelor's degree given by universities and colleges; the address given at a graduation ceremony.

bac·cha·na·lia *n.* A Roman festival celebrated with dancing and song.

bach·e·lor *n.* An unmarried male; the first degree from a four-year university.

ba·cil·lus *n.* A rod-like microscopic organism which can cause certain diseases. **bacilli** *pl.*

back *n.* The rear part of a structure or object; the human body from the neck to the end of the spine; the rear part of an animal; a position in the game of football. *adv.* At the rear of, to or toward the rear; in the direction of return.

back·ache *n.* A pain in the back.

back·board *n.* A board that supports when placed under or behind something.

back·bone *n.* The spinal column or spine of the vertebrates; the strongest support, or strength; emotional or moral strength.

back·drop *n.* A flat, curtain, or scene at the back of a stage set.

back·er *n.* One who gives support to a cause.

back·field *n.* Football players who are positioned behind the line of scrimmage.

back·fire *n.* Premature explosion of unburned exhaust gases or ignited fuel of an internal-combustion engine; a fire deliberately set to check an advancing forest or prairie fire.

back·gam·mon *n.* A game played by two

people wherein each player tries to move counters on the board, at the same time trying to block the opponent.

back•ground *n.* The area or surface behind which objects are represented; conditions leading up to an event; the collection of a person's complete experience.

back•hand *n.* A stroke in the game of tennis, made with the back of the hand facing outward.

back•hand•ed *adj.* Indirect; accomplished by a circuitous route; slightly unfair in tactic.

back•hoe *n.* An excavating machine used to dig ditches, foundations, and graves.

back•ing *n.* Support or aid; a supply in reserve; support material behind a portrait or picture.

back•lash *n.* A violent backward movement or reaction in response to reform; a snarl in a fishing line.

back•log *n.* An accumulation of unfinished work; a reserve supply.

back•pack *n.* A piece of hiking or walking equipment used to carry items on the back, mounted on a lightweight frame, and constructed of nylon or canvas. **backpacker** *n.*

back•rest *n.* A support given to the back.

back•saw *n.* Saw with metal ribs on its back side.

back•seat *n.* The seat in the back of an automobile, etc.; an inferior position.

back•side *n.* The buttocks.

back•slide *v.* To lapse back into a less desirable condition, as in a religious practice or improvement program. **backslider** *n.*

back•spin *n.* A spin which rotates in the reverse direction.

back•stage *n.* The area behind the visible performing area in a theater.

back•stop *n.* A wall that prevents a ball from being hit out of play.

back•stretch *n.* The opposite of the homestretch on a racecourse.

back•stroke *n.* A swimming stroke performed while on the back.

back•swept *adj.* Slanting or swept backward.

back•talk *n.* A smart or insolent reply; retort; argument against authority.

back•track *v.* To reverse a policy; to retrace previous steps

back•up *n.* One that serves as an alternative or substitute; an alternative plan of action.

back•ward *adv.* Toward the back; to or at the back. **backwardness** *n.*

back•wash *n.* A backward flow of water.

back•wa•ter *n.* A body of water turned back by an obstruction.

back•woods *pl. n.* A sparsely populated, heavily wooded area. **backwoodsman** *n.*

back•yard *n.* An area to the rear of a house, usually fenced or enclosed, for recreation or storage.

ba•con *n.* Side and back of a pig, salted and smoked; a breakfast preparation of pork in strips.

bac•ter•i•a *pl. n.* The plural of bacterium.

bac•te•ri•ol•o•gy *n.* Scientific study of bacteria and its relationship to medicine, etc.

bac•te•ri•um *n.* Any of various forms of numerous unicellular microorganisms that cause disease. **bacterial** *adj.*

bad *adj.* Not good; naughty or disobedient; unfavorable; inferior; poor; spoiled; invalid. **badly** *adv.*, **badness** *n.*

badge *n.* An emblem worn for identification or proof of jurisdiction, especially by enforcement authorities.

bad•ger *n.* A sturdy burrowing mammal. *v.* To harass or trouble persistently.

bad•lands *pl. n.* Area with sparse life, peaks, and eroded ridges.

bad•min•ton *n.* A court game played with long-handled rackets and a shuttlecock.

bad•mouth *v.* To criticize someone.

baf•fle *v.* To puzzle; to perplex or confuse; to impede the progress of. *n.* A device that checks or regulates the flow of gases, liquids, or sound. **baffled, baffling** *adj.*, **bafflingly** adv.

bag *n.* A flexible container used for holding, storing, or carrying; a white canvas square used to mark bases in baseball. *v.* To contain in a bag; to win or capture; to take and keep game, as in hunting. **baggy** *adj.*

ba·gasse *n.* Plant residue.

bag·a·telle *n.* A game played with a cue and balls on an oblong table.

ba·gel *n.* A hard, glazed, round doughy roll with a chewy texture and a hole in the middle to augment thorough baking.

bag·gage *n.* The personal belongings of a traveler, usually in canvas or cloth carriers with handles; any excess burden impeding free movement.

bag·gy *adj.* Loose; loose-fitting; containing more than necessary material.

bag·man *n.* A person who collects illicit payments for another.

bag·pipe *n.* A musical wind instrument with a leather bag allowing the controlled express of air through a variety of melody pipes, some of which can be fingered to vary notes, and some of which are drones. **bagpiper** *n.*

ba·guette *n.* A gem in the shape of a long, narrow rectangle.

bail *n.* Security or money given to guarantee the appearance of a person for trial after arraignment. *v.* To remove water from a vessel by dipping and emptying the water overboard.

bail·iff *n.* The officer who guards prisoners and keeps order in a courtroom.

bail·i·wick *n.* The office or district of a bailiff.

bails·man *n.* The person who puts up the bail for another.

bait *v.* To lure; to entice; to set a trap with a desirable offering. *n.* Food used to catch or trap an animal, especially in fishing.

baize *n.* A coarse woolen or cotton cloth.

bake *v.* To cook in an oven until chemical changes are completed; to harden or dry. **baked** *adj.*, **baker**, **baking** *n.*

bak·er·y *n.* A store where baked goods are made and sold.

bak·sheesh *n.* A tip or gratuity.

bal·a·lai·ka *n.* A three-stringed musical instrument.

bal·ance *n.* Physical equilibrium; device for determining the weight of something; the agreement of totals in the debit and credit of an account.

bal·ance beam *n.* A narrow wooden beam approximately four feet off the ground used in gymnastics.

bal·co·ny *n.* Gallery or platform projecting from the wall of a building; the high seating area in a theatre or arena.

bald *adj.* Lacking hair on the head; void of growth, as mountaintops above the treeline; bare; obvious; unadorned by artifice. **baldness** *n.*

bald ea·gle *n.* The eagle of North America, dark when young but with a white head and neck feathers when mature.

bal·der·dash *n.* Nonsense.

bale *n.* A large, bound package or bundle, especially of stalks.

balk *v.* To refuse to go on; to stop short of something; in baseball, a pitcher's false move toward home plate.

ball *n.* A round body or mass; a sphere; a pitched baseball delivered outside of the strike zone.

bal·lad *n.* A narrative story or poem of folk origin; a romantic song of moderate beat.

bal·lade *n.* A verse form, consisting of three stanzas with recurrent rhymes and a refrain for each part.

bal·lad·eer *n.* A person who sings ballads.

bal·last *n.* Heavy material, usually of no intrinsic value, placed in a vehicle, especially a water vessel, to give stability.

ball bear·ing *n.* A sphere or series of spheres of hard material, encased in a metal sheath, to reduce friction by separating the stationary parts from the moving parts of a mechanism.

bal·le·ri·na *n.* A female ballet dancer in a company.

bal·let *n.* An artistic expression of dance by formal choreographic design.

bal·lis·tic mis·sile *n.* A self-powered projectile that is guided during ascent, and has a free fall trajectory at descent.

bal·lis·tics *n.* The science of motion in flight; the firing characteristics of a firearm.

bal·loon *n.* A thin membrane bag or shaped container, inflated with air or a gas lighter than air, which floats in the atmosphere, used as a child's toy; a large air vessel relying on the properties of gases to stay aloft.

bal·lot *n.* A slip of paper used in secret voting; one's right to vote.

ball·park *n.* A stadium where ball games are played.

ball·point *n.* A pen with a small self-inking writing point.

bal·ly·hoo *n.* Exaggerated advertising.

balm *n.* A fragrant ointment that soothes, comforts, and heals.

ba·lo·ney *n.* Nonsense; var. of bologna.

bal·sa *n.* American tree whose wood is very light in weight; the wood of the tree, used in model making.

bal·sam *n.* A fragrant ointment from different trees; a plant cultivated for its colorful flowers.

bal·us·ter *n.* The upright post that supports a handrail.

bam·boo *n.* Tropical, tall grass with hollow, pointed stems; the stalky wood-like material from the plant.

ban *v.* To prohibit; to forbid; to proscribe by formal decree. **ban** *n.*, **banned** *adj.*

ba·nal *adj.* Trite; lacking freshness.

ba·nan·a *n.* The crescent-shaped usually yellow, edible fruit of a tropical plant.

band *n.* A strip used to trim, finish, encircle, or bind; the range of a radio wave length; a group of musicians who join together to play their instruments. *v.* To wrap or encircle; to mark with a band.

band·age *n.* A strip of cloth used to protect an injury; any material or activity designed to repair or aid in healing.

band·age *v.* To bind or cover, as a wound, to prevent bleeding and infection.

ban·dan·na *n.* A brightly colored cotton or silk handkerchief, often worn around the neck.

ban·deau *n.* A narrow band worn in the hair; a narrow brassiere.

ban·di·coot *n.* A very large rat of India, destructive to the rice fields and gardens.

ban·dit *n.* A gangster or robber, especially a member of a marauding or plundering gang. **banditry** *n.*

ban·do·lier *n.* A belt worn over the shoulder with pockets for cartridges.

band·stand *n.* A raised platform on which an orchestra or band performs.

band·width *n.* Measurement of information-carrying capacity, in bits per second.

ban·dy *adv.* Bent; crooked; curved outward.

bane *n.* A cause of destruction; an ill omen or negative force or influence. **baneful** *adj.*, **banefully** *adv.*

bang *n.* A sudden loud noise, as a gunshot; short hair cut across the forehead.

ban·gle *n.* A bracelet worn around the wrist or ankle; an inexpensive ornament or decoration, often pendant from a bracelet or necklace.

ban·ish *v.* To leave; to drive away; to refuse entry by official declaration. **banished** *adj.*, **banishment** *n.*

ban·is·ter *n.* The handrail on a staircase with its upright supports.

ban·jo *n.* A stringed instrument similar to a guitar. **banjoist** *n.*

bank *n.* A slope of land adjoining water; a slant or obtuse angle, especially to a movement; an establishment that performs financial transactions. **banking** *n.*, **bankable** *adj.*

bank·rupt *adj.* Legally insolvent; in a condition in which remaining property is divided among creditors. **bankrupt** *v.*, **bankruptcy** *n.*

ban·ner *n.* A piece of cloth, such as a flag, used as a standard by a commander or monarch.

banns *pl. n.* The announcement of a forthcoming marriage.

ban·quet *n.* An elaborate dinner or feast; a ceremonial meal held for many persons, usually to mark an occasion or honor a prestigious guest.

ban·yan *n.* A tree from the tropics whose aerial roots grow downward to form additional roots.

bap·tism *n.* A Christian sacrament of spiritual rebirth through the application of water. **baptismal** *adj.*

bar *n.* A rigid piece of material used as a support; an obscured or invisible sedimentary collection of sand or gravel that impedes the progress of a vessel into and out of harbor; a counter where a person can receive drinks. *v.* To prohibit or exclude; to keep out.

barb *n.* A sharp projection that extends backward making it difficult to remove; a breed of horses from Africa noted for their speed and endurance.

bar·bar·i·an *n.* A person or culture thought to be primitive and therefore inferior. **barbarous, barbaric** *adj.*

bar·be·cue *n.* An outdoor fireplace or pit for roasting meat. **barbecue** *v.* To cook on a barbecue pit.

barbed wire *n.* Wire twisted with sharp points, to prevent passage or damage.

bar·bell *n.* A bar with weights at both ends, used for exercise.

bar·ber *n.* A person whose business is cutting and dressing hair and shaving and trimming beards. **barbershop** *n.*

bar·ca·role *n.* A Venetian boat song with a strong and weak beat which suggests a rowing rhythm.

bard *n.* A poet or oral storyteller, often moving from place to place; a piece of armor for a horse's neck.

bare *adj.* Exposed to view; without coloring or ornament; naked. *v.* To make obvious or self-evident; to expose; to make naked.

bare·back *adv.* or *adj.* Riding a horse without a saddle.

bare·ly *adv.* Sparsely; by a very little amount.

bar·gain *n.* A contract or agreement on the purchase or sale of an item; a purchase made at a favorable or good price. **bargainer** *n.*

barge *n.* A flat-bottomed boat, used for transport of cargo, especially in bulk.

bar·i·at·rics *n.* The branch of medicine that treats obesity.

bar·i·tone *n.* The male voice in the range between tenor and bass.

bark *n.* The outer covering of a tree; the abrupt, harsh sound made by a dog; a sailing vessel of three or more masts.

bar·ken·tine *n.* A three-masted ship with fore-and-aft rigging.

bark·er *n.* A person in a circus who stands at the entrance and advertises the show.

bar·ley *n.* A type of grain used for food and malt products, and for making whiskey and beer.

bar·low *n.* A sturdy jackknife.

barm *n.* A yeast that forms on fermenting malt liquors.

bar mitz·vah *n.* A Jewish rite of passage for boys who, having reached the age of 13, assume the moral and religious duties of an adult.

barn *n.* A farm building used to shelter animals, house equipment, and store products.

bar·na·cle *n.* A marine crustacean with a hard shell at maturity that remains attached to an underwater surface, especially the hulls of ships; a European goose which breeds in the Arctic.

barn dance *n.* A dance gathering, usually in a barn or other large structure, featuring square dancing and a rustic atmosphere.

barn·storm *n.* A tour through rural areas to obtain votes during a political campaign.

ba·rom·e·ter *n.* An instrument that records the weight and pressure of the atmosphere. **barometric** *adj.*

bar·on *n.* The lowest rank of nobility in Great Britain. **baroness** *n.*, **baronial** *adj.*

ba·roque *adj.* An artistic style

characterized by elaborate and ornate forms.

ba•rouche *n.* A four-wheeled carriage.

bar•racks *coll. n.* Buildings for housing soldiers; residential area of a military base.

bar•ra•cu•da *n.* A fish with a large, narrow body, found in the Atlantic Ocean.

bar•rage *n.* A concentrated outpouring or discharge of missiles from small arms; an artificial dam to increase the depth of water for use in irrigation or navigation.

bar•ra•try *n.* The unlawful breach of duty by a ship's crew that results in injury to the ship's owner.

bar•rel *n.* A cylindrical container, often of wood, with round, flat ends of equal size and sides that bulge; the elongated hollowed section of a firearm that focuses the force of the explosive and gives direction and rotation to the projectile.

bar•ren *adj.* Lacking vegetation; sterile; infertile; absent of life.

bar•rette *n.* A clasp or small bar used to hold hair in place.

bar•ri•cade *n.* Barrier, especially mobile, that inhibits passage or prevents trespass.

bar•ri•er *n.* A structure that restricts or bars entrance; an impediment to progress.

bar•ri•er reef *n.* A coral reef parallel to shore but separated by a lagoon, which prevents passage from sea to land.

bar•room *n.* A building or room where a person can purchase alcoholic beverages sold at a counter; a tavern; a pub.

bar•row *n.* A rectangular, flat frame with handles; a wheelbarrow.

bar•tend•er *n.* A person who serves alcoholic drinks at a bar.

bar•ter *v.* To trade something for something else without the exchange of money.

ba•salt *n.* A greenish-black volcanic rock.

base *n.* The fundamental part; the foundation of an object or process; the bottom; a chemical solution having a pH greater than 7; one of four corners of a baseball infield. **baseless** *adj.*, **basely** *adv.*, **baseness** *n.*

base *v.* To begin with; to build from; to

initiate; to establish before continued research or inquiry.

base•ball *n.* A game played with a ball and bat, in which players occupy bases around a diamond; the ball used in a baseball game.

base•board *n.* A molding at the base of a vertical construction that covers the area where the wall meets the floor.

base•ment *n.* The foundation of a building or home; the cellar formed by the space between the ground and the first floor.

bash *v.* To smash with a heavy blow; to crush flat; to strike, especially with an object. *slang* An informal party or gathering of some energy and noise. **bashed** *adj.*

bash•ful *adj.* Socially shy; reclusive or nonassertive. **bashfully** *adv.*

ba•sic *adj.* Forming the basis; fundamental. **basically** *adv.*

BASIC *n.* A common computer programming language.

bas•il *n.* An herb used as seasoning in cooking.

ba•sil•i•ca *n.* An early Christian church building.

ba•sin *n.* A sink; a washbowl; a round open container used for washing; an area that has been drained by a river system.

ba•sis *n.* The main part; foundation; the initial action or observation from which subsequent activity grows. **bases** *pl.*

bask *v.* To relax in the warmth of the sun; to enjoy a state of stillness; to savor an accomplishment or acknowledgement.

bas•ket *n.* A container made of woven material, as straw, cane, or other flexible items, open at the top, for carrying goods; in basketball, the hoop with woven strings used as a goal, or the scoring of a point. **basketry** *n.*

bas•ket•ball *n.* A team sport played on a court, each team trying to throw the ball through the hoop at the opponent's end of the court.

bas mitz•vah *n.* A Jewish rite for girls

43

who, having reached the age of 13, assume the moral and religious duties of an adult.

bass *n.* A fresh water fish, one of the perch family; the lowest male voice in a quartet; a large stringed musical instrument with a deep range.

bass drum *n.* A large drum with a low booming sound.

bas·si·net *n.* A basket on legs used as an infant's crib.

bas·soon *n.* A woodwind instrument with a low-pitched sound.

bas·tard *n.* An illegitimate child; a disagreeable, nasty, or mean person. **bastardize** *v.*

baste *v.* To run a loose stitch to hold a piece of material in place for a short time; to moisten a roast or fowl with its own juices. **basted** *adj.*

bat *n.* A wooden stick made from strong wood; a nocturnal flying mammal. **batter** *n.*

bat boy *n.* A boy who takes care of the equipment of a baseball team.

batch *n.* A quantity (as of cookies) baked or prepared at one time; the total output for a given period of time. *v.* To submit or make available in groups.

bath *n.* The act of washing the body by immersion; hot water or other liquid that is part of an immersion process.

bathe *v.* To take a bath.

bath·y·scaphe *n.* A submersible ship for deep sea exploration.

ba·tik *n.* A soft sheer fabric.

bat·tal·ion *n.* A military unit consisting of a headquarters and three or more companies.

bat·ten *v.* To secure; to fasten together; *n.* a stiff board used to shape sails.

bat·ter *v.* To beat or strike continuously; to assault. *n.* A cricket or baseball player at bat. **battered** *adj.*

bat·ter·y *n.* A chemical device for generating and storing electrical energy; a group of heavy guns.

bat·tle *n.* A struggle; combat between opposing forces; a prolonged strategic engagement of troops and weapons in warfare. *v.* To engage in a war or battle.

bawl *v.* To cry very loudly; to weep convulsively and somewhat out of proportion to the cause. **bawling** *n.*

bay *n.* The inlet of a body of water; an inwardly curved portion of the shoreline, allowing some protection from the sea; one of several workstations in a garage or other repair or assembly area.

bay·ber·ry *n.* Evergreen shrub used for decorations and making candles.

bay·o·net *n.* A spear-like weapon, often attached to the barrel of a rifle.

ba·zaar *n.* A fair where a variety of items are sold as a money-making project for charity, clubs, churches, or other such organizations.

ba·zoo·ka *n.* A hand-held weapon for firing rockets.

BBS *abbr.* Bulletin board system; a computer system for leaving and retrieving messages and other files.

be *v.* To exist; used with the present participle of a verb to show action; to occupy a position in space; to occur.

beach *n.* Pebbly or sandy shore of a lake, ocean, sea, or river.

bea·con *n.* A coastal guiding or signaling device.

bead *n.* A small round piece of material with a hole for threading. **beading** *n.*

bea·gle *n.* A small breed of hunting dog with short legs.

beak *n.* The bill of a bird; the horizontally protruding front edge of a cap. **beaked** *adj.*

beak·er *n.* Large, widemouthed cup for drinking; a cylindrical, glass laboratory vessel with a lip for pouring.

beam *n.* Large, oblong piece of wood or metal used as a support element in construction; a ray, especially of light. *v.* To shine or glow.

bean *n.* An edible seed or seed pod of a legume. *v.* To hit on the head.

bear *n.* A large mammal of America and Europe, with shaggy fur and short tail. *v.*

To endure; to carry. **bearable** *adj.*

beard *n.* Hair growing on the chin and cheeks.

beast *n.* A four-legged animal.

beast•ly *adj.* In the manner of a beast; uncouth or uncivilized.

beast of bur•den *n.* An animal used to perform heavy work or transport heavy materials.

beat *v.* To strike repeatedly; to defeat; to stir a mix rapidly.

beat *adj.* Exhausted. **beaten** *adj.*

beat *n.* A measure of time in music; a route, territory, or regular path of activity.

be•a•tif•ic *adj.* Giving or showing extreme bliss or joy; blessed; gracious in spirit; like a saint.

beau *n.* Sweetheart; dandy.

beau•ty *n.* Pleasing to the eye; felicity, especially of appearance; graceful or balanced structure; aesthetic perfection. **beautiful** *adj.*, **beautifully** *adv.*

bea•ver *n.* A large semiaquatic rodent with webbed feet and flat tail, whose fur is valuable for coats, hats, and other items.

be•calm *v.* To make quiet. **becalming** *adj.*

be•cause *conj.* For a reason; since; from the cause that.

beck *n.* A summons, a call.

beck•on *v.* To summon someone with a nod or wave.

be•come *v.* To come, to be, or to grow into existence.

bed *n.* Furniture for sleeping; a piece of planted or cultivated ground; the horizontal base of a truck. **bedding** *n.*

be•daz•zle *v.* To confuse with bright lights. **bedazzling, bedazzled** *adj.*

bed•bug *n.* A wingless insect that sucks blood and infests human homes, especially beds.

bed•fast *adj.* Confined to a bed; bedridden.

bed•lam *n.* A state or situation of confusion; chaos.

be•drag•gled *adj.* Limp and wet; soiled as though pulled through mud.

bee *n.* A hairy-bodied flying insect, often living in hives, with structures for gathering pollen and nectar from flowers.

beech *n.* A tree of light-colored bark, with edible nuts.

beef *n.* A cow, steer, or bull that has been fattened for consumption; the flesh of a bovine; a contention or argument. **beefy** *adj.*, **beefs, beeves** *pl.*

bee•keep•er *n.* One who raises bees for their honey.

beep *n.* A warning sound from a horn.

beer *n.* An alcoholic beverage made from malt, hops, and other fermented grains.

bees•wax *n.* The wax from bees used for their honeycombs.

beet *n.* The root from a cultivated plant that can be used as a vegetable or a source of sugar.

bee•tle *n.* An insect with modified, horny front wings that cover the membranous back wings when not in flight.

be•fit *v.* To be suitable. **befitting** *adj.*

be•fore *adv.* Earlier; previously. *prep.* In front of.

be•friend *v.* To make a friend of someone.

beg *v.* To make a living by asking for charity; to ask for fervently. **beggar** *n.*

be•gan *v.* The past tense of *begin*.

be•gin *v.* To start; to come into being; to commence. **beginner, beginning** *n.*

be•gone *v.* Imperative meaning go away; depart.

be•go•nia *n.* A tropical plant with waxy flowers and showy leaves.

be•grudge *v.* To envy someone's possessions or enjoyment; to wish ill to one who possesses.

be•guile *v.* To deceive; to delight; to charm. **beguiling** *adj.*

be•gun *v.* The past participle of *begin*.

be•half *n.* The support or interest of another person; in the name of another.

be•have *v.* To function in a certain manner; to act according to set laws, especially physical; to conduct oneself in a proper manner. **behavior, behaviorism** *n.*

be•head *v.* To remove the head from the

body; to decapitate.

be•held v. Past participle of behold.

be•hind adv. To or at the back; late or slow in arriving.

be•hold v. To look at; to see; to view with awe.

be•hoove v. To benefit or give advantage.

beige adj. Light brown-grey in color.

be•ing n. One's existence; the physical presence.

be•la•bor v. To work on or to discuss beyond the point where it is necessary; to carry to absurd lengths; to emphasize past need.

be•lat•ed adj. Tardy; late. **belatedly** adv.

bel•fry n. A tower housing the bells of a church.

be•lief n. Something trusted or believed; a creed or set of axioms by which one makes moral and ethical decisions.

be•lieve v. To accept as true or real; to declare as considered subjectively true in hypothesis; to hold onto religious beliefs. **believable** adj., **believer** n.

be•lit•tle v. To think or speak in a slighting manner of someone or something; to make small or trivial.

bell n. A metal instrument that gives a metallic sound when struck; any object shaped like a bell; a mechanical or electrical device for announcing one's presence.

bel•la•don•na n. A poisonous plant with black berries; a medicine extracted from the belladonna plant.

belles-let•tres pl. n. Literature regarded not for its value, but for its artistic quality.

bel•lig•er•ent adj. Hostile and inclined to be aggressive. **belligerence** n., **belligerently** adv.

bel•low v. To make a deep, powerful roar like a bull.

bel•lows n. An instrument that produces air in a chamber and expels it through a short tube.

bel•ly The abdomen or the stomach; the innermost chamber.

be•long v. To be a part of; to be owned by.

be•long•ings n. Articles of ownership; personal effects; one's material goods, especially portable.

be•lov•ed adj. Dearly loved; held in deep affection.

be•low adv. At a lower level or place; in the lower levels of a vessel. prep. In an inferior position to; under.

belt n. A band worn around the waist; a zone or region distinctive in a special way; an encircling shape.

belt•way n. A highway that encircles an urban area.

be•lu•ga n. A large white whale whose roe is used to make caviar.

be•muse v. To bewilder or confuse; to be lost in thought. **bemused** adj.

bench n. A long seat for more than two people; the seat of the judge in a court.

bend v. To arch; to change the direct course; to deflect; to form into a curve or angle.

be•neath prep. To or in a lower position; below; underneath.

ben•e•dic•tion n. A blessing given at the end of a religious service.

ben•e•fac•tion n. A charitable donation; a gift. **benefactor** n.

ben•e•fice n. Fixed capital assets that provide a living for a church.

be•nef•i•cence n. The quality of being kind or charitable; goodness; generosity.

ben•e•fi•ci•ar•y n. The person or institution named to receive the estate of another in case of death.

ben•e•fit n. Aid; help; an act of kindness; a social event or entertainment to raise money for a person or cause. v. To help or ameliorate; to gain advantage.

be•nev•o•lence n. The inclination to be charitable; overwhelming goodness and goodwill. **benevolent** adj.

be•night•ed adj. Overtaken by night.

be•nign adj. Having a gentle and kind disposition; gracious; not malignant; entirely curable. **benignly** adv.

ben•i•son n. A blessing; benediction.

bent adj. Curved, not straight; past tense of bend.

be•numb *v.* To dull; to make numb.

ben•zene *n.* A flammable toxic liquid used as a motor fuel.

be•queath *v.* To give or leave to someone by legal will; to hand down; to teach to the next generation.

be•quest *n.* Something that is bequeathed.

be•rate *v.* To scold severely; to chastise by finding fault; to criticize by listing short-comings.

be•reave *v.* To deprive; to suffer the loss of a loved one. **bereft** *adj.*, **bereavement** *n.*

be•ret *n.* A round, woolen cap that has no brim.

berg *n.* A large mass of ice; iceberg.

ber•i•ber•i *n.* Nervous disorder from the deficiency of vitamin B, producing partial paralysis of the extremities.

ber•ry *n.* An edible fruit, such as a straw-berry or blackberry, grown on bushes; the fruit of certain flowering plants.

ber•serk *adj.* Destructively violent.

berth *n.* Space at a wharf for a ship or boat to dock; a built-in bunk or bed on a train or ship; space between moving objects.

ber•yl *n.* A mineral composed of silicon, oxygen, and beryllium that is the major source of beryllium.

be•seech *v.* To ask or request earnestly. beseechingly adv.

be•side *prep.* At the side of; next to.

be•sides *adv.* In addition to; as an extra; preempting or counterindicating a previous statement or argument.

be•siege *v.* To surround with troops; to harass with requests.

be•speak *v.* To indicate; to speak.

be•spoke *adj.* Spoken for; ordered in advance; custom tailored.

best *adj.* Exceeding all others in quality or excellence; most suitable, desirable, or use-ful; of the highest degree.

bes•tial *adj.*, *pl.* **–ties** Of or relating to an animal; brutish. **bestiality** *n.*

bes•ti•ar•y *n.* A medieval collection of fables about imaginary and real animals, each with a moral; any zoological exhibi-tion.

be•stir *v.* To rouse into action.

be•stow *v.* To present or to give honor.

be•stride *v.* To step over or to straddle.

bet *n.* An amount risked on a stake or wager. *v.* To place a wager.

be•take *v.* To cause oneself to make one's way; to move or go; to take oneself else-where.

be•think *v.* To remember or to remind oneself.

be•tide *v.* To happen to; to take place.

be•to•ken *v.* To show by a visible sign.

be•tray *v.* To be disloyal or unfaithful; to indicate or give an outward sign of; to deceive. **betrayal** *n.*

be•trothed *n.* A person to whom one is engaged to marry.

bet•ter *adj.* More suitable, useful, desir-able, or higher in quality; the comparative of *good*. *v.* To improve oneself. **better-ment** *n.*

be•tween *prep.* In the position or time that separates; in the middle or shared by two; in a place limited by two edges or forms.

be•twixt *prep.* Not knowing which way one should go; between.

bev•el *n.* The angle at which one surface meets another when not at right angles.

bev•er•age *n.* A refreshing liquid for drinking other than water.

bev•y *n.* A collection or group; a flock of birds. **bevies** *pl.*

be•wail *v.* To express regret or sorrow with loud lamentation and displays of grief.

be•ware *v.* To be cautious; to be on guard; to warn.

be•wil•der *v.* To confuse; to perplex or puzzle; to confound, as in a maze. **bewilderment** *n.*

be•witch *v.* To fascinate or captivate com-pletely; to enchant. **bewitchment** *n.*

be•yond *prep.* Outside the reach or scope of; at a farther distance. *n.* Something past or to the far side; the vague place of the afterlife.

bez•el *n.* A flange or groove that holds the beveled edge of an object such as a gem in a ring mounting.

bi•an•nu•al *adj.* Taking place twice a year; semiannual.

bi•as *n.* Prejudice or reaction based on previous impressions without fairness. *v.* To act prejudicially; to slant or weigh rhetorically in one direction. **biased** *adj.*

bib *n.* A cloth tied under the chin of small children to protect their clothing; a napkin which ties at the back.

bib•li•og•ra•phy *n.* A list of works by one writer or publisher; a list of sources of information, especially on a specific subject; the reference sources of a study, listed alphabetically by authors' last name. **bibliographer** *n.*

bib•li•o•phile *n.* A person who collects books.

bib•li•ot•ics *n.* The study of handwriting to determine authorship.

bi•cen•ten•ni•al *adj.* Happening once every 200 years. *n.* Anniversary or celebration of 200 years.

bi•ceps *n.* Large muscle in the front of the upper arm and at the back of the thigh. **bicipital** *adj.*

bick•er *v.* To quarrel or argue in a small-minded way; to exchange insults in place of sound argument.

bi•cul•tur•al *adj.* Having, containing, or influenced by two distinct cultures; relating to cross-cultural influences or effects.

bi•cus•pid *n.* A tooth with two roots.

bi•cy•cle *n.* A two-wheeled vehicle propelled by pedals, balanced in motion by centripetal inertia, designed for one rider. **bicyclist** *n.*

bid *v.* To request something; to offer to pay a certain price; to offer to buy at auction. *n.* The amount offered in an auction. **bidder** *n.*

bid•dy *n.* A young chicken; hen; a fussy woman.

bide *v.* To remain; to wait.

bi•en•ni•al *adj.* Occurring every two years; lasting for two years. *n.* The celebration

or observance of a two-year event. **biennially** *adv.*

bier *n.* A stand on which a coffin is placed before burial.

bi•fo•cals *n.* Eyeglasses having two focal lengths ground into one lens, to correct both close and distant vision.

bi•fur•cate *v.* To divide into two parts. **bifurcation** *n.*

big *adj.* Very large in dimensions, intensity, and extent; grown-up; bountiful; generous in size or effect.

big•a•my *n.* The act of marrying one person while still married to another. **bigamist** *n.*

big-heart•ed *adj.* Habitually generous and kind; open and accessible.

big•horn *n.* A wild game sheep from the mountainous western part of North America, with heavy curled horns.

bight *n.* The slack in a rope; a bend in the shoreline.

big•ot *n.* One fanatically devoted to one's own group, religion, politics, or race; a hypocrite or intolerant, prejudiced person. **bigoted** *adj.*, **bigotry** *n.*

big•wig *n.* *slang* A person of authority; a superior; an influential person, outside one's own social and economic range.

bike *n.* A bicycle. **bike** *v.*, **biker** *n.*

bi•lat•er•al *adj.* Having or relating to two sides; on both sides of a division. **bilaterally** *adv.*

bile *n.* A brownish-yellow alkaline liquid secreted by the liver.

bi•lev•el *adj.* Divided into two floor levels.

bilge *n.* Lowest inside part of the hull of a ship.

bi•lin•gual *adj.* Able to speak two languages with equal ability.

bil•ious *adj.* Undergoing gastric distress from a sluggish gallbladder or liver.

bilk *v.* To cheat or swindle.

bill *n.* Itemized list of fees for services rendered; a document presented containing a formal statement of a case complaint or petition; a government document proposed to a lawmaking body for consideration into law; the beak of a bird.

bill•board *n.* A place for displaying advertisements, usually outdoors.

bill•fold *n.* Pocket-sized wallet for holding money and personal information.

bil•liards *n.* Game played on a table with cushioned edges.

bil•lion *n.* A thousand million.

bil•lion•aire *n.* A person whose wealth equals at least one billion dollars.

bil•low *n.* Large swell of water or smoke; wave. *v.* To puff out or fill with wind. **billowy** *adj.*

bil•ly goat *n.* A male goat.

bi•met•al•lism *n.* The use of two metals, gold and silver, as legal tenders. **bimetallist** *n.*

bi•month•ly *adj.* Occurring every two months.

bin *n.* An enclosed place, sometimes closed at the top, for storage of bulk items.

bi•na•ry *adj.* Made of two different components or parts.

bind *v.* To hold with a belt or rope; to bandage; to fasten and enclose pages of a book between covers. **binding** *n.*

bind•er *n.* A notebook for holding paper; payment or written statement legally binding an agreement.

binge *n.* Uncontrollable self-indulgence; a spree; excessive consumption, especially liquor or food.

bin•go *n.* A game of chance in which markers are placed on numbered cards in accordance with numbers drawn by a caller.

bin•na•cle *n.* A place where a ship's compass is contained.

bin•oc•u•lars *pl. n.* An optical magnifying device for both eyes at once.

bi•o•chem•is•try *n.* Chemistry of substances and biological processes.

bi•o•de•grad•a•ble *adj.* Decomposable by natural processes. **biodegradability**, **biodegradation** *n.*

bi•o•feed•back *n.* The technique of controlling involuntary bodily functions.

bi•og•ra•pher *n.* A researcher and writer of another person's life story.

bi•og•ra•phy *n.* A researched and accurate report of the life and accomplishments of a prominent or important person, usually chronological, written by another.

bi•o•haz•ard *n.* Biological material that threatens humans or their environment if infective.

bi•o•log•i•cal war•fare *n.* Warfare using organic biocides or disease-producing micro-organisms to destroy crops, livestock, or human life.

bi•ol•o•gy *n.* Science of living organisms and the study of their structure, reproduction, and growth. **biological** *adj.*, **biologist** *n.*

bi•o•med•i•cine *n.* Medicine that has to do with human response to environmental stress.

bi•on•ics *n.* Application of biological principles to the study and design of engineering systems, as electronic systems.

bi•o•phys•ics *n.* The physics of living organisms. **biophysical** *adj.*

bi•op•sy *n.* The examination for the detection of a disease in tissues removed from a living organism.

bi•ot•ic *adj.* Related to specific life conditions or to life itself.

bi•par•ti•san *adj.* Support by two political parties. **bipartisanship** *n.*

bi•ped *n.* An animal having two feet.

bi•plane *n.* A glider or airplane with wings on two levels.

bi•pol•ar *adj.* Having or related to two poles; concerning the earth's North and South Poles.

bi•rac•ial *adj.* Composed of or for members of two races.

birch *n.* A tree providing hard, close-grained wood.

bird *n.* A warm-blooded, egg-laying animal, usually capable of flight, whose body is covered by feathers.

bird bath *n.* A shallow basin of water set out for birds.

bird•ie *n.* A stroke under par in the game of golf; a shuttlecock.

birl•ing *n.* A game of skill in which two lumberjacks try to balance on a floating log while spinning the log with their feet.

birth *n.* The beginning of existence; the moment of extraction of an offspring from the womb.

birth con•trol *n.* Any of several techniques used to control or prevent the number of children born by lessening the chances of conception; the practice of controlling the birth rate in a society.

birth•day *n.* The day a person is born and the anniversary of that day.

birth•mark *n.* A blemish or mark on the skin present at birth.

birth•place *n.* The city, state, and/or country of one's birth.

birth•rate *n.* The ratio of the number of births to a given population over a specified period of time.

birth•right *n.* Privilege granted by virtue of birth, especially to the first-born.

birth•stone *n.* A gemstone that represents the month in which one was born.

bis•cuit *n.* Small baked quick bread made with baking soda or baking powder; a cookie.

bi•sect *v.* To divide or cut into two equal parts. **bisection** *n.*

bi•sex•u•al *adj.* Relating to both sexes; attracted to persons of either sex. **bisexuality** *n.*

bish•op *n.* A Christian clergyman with high rank. **bishopric** *n.*

bis•muth *n.* A white, crystalline metallic element.

bi•son *n.* A large buffalo of northwestern America, with a dark-brown coat and short, curved horns.

bisque *n.* A creamy soup, made from fish or vegetables; unglazed clay.

bis•tro *n.* A bar or small nightclub.

bit *n.* A tiny piece or amount of something; the rotating cutting element of a tool designed for boring or drilling; in computer science, either of two characters, as the binary digits zero and one, of a language that has only two characters; a unit of information; storage capacity, as of computer memory.

bitch *n.* A female dog.

bite *v.* To cut, tear, or crush with the teeth. **bite** *n.*, **bitingly** *adv.*

bit•stock *n.* A brace that secures a drilling bit.

bit•ter *adj.* Having a sharp, unpleasant taste; not sweet; angry or negative after a defeat or reversal of fortune. **bitterly** *adv.*, **bitterness** *n.*

bit•ter•sweet *n.* A woody vine whose root, when chewed, has first a bitter, then a sweet taste.

bi•tu•mi•nous coal *n.* Coal that contains a high ratio of bituminous material and burns with a smoky flame.

bi•valve *n.* A mollusk that has a hinged two-part shell; a clam or oyster.

biv•ou•ac *n.* A temporary military camp in the open air. *v.* To camp overnight in the open air.

bi•week•ly *n.* Occurring every two weeks.

bi•year•ly *n.* Occurring every two years.

bi•zarre *adj.* Extremely strange or odd. **bizarrely** *adv.*

blab *v.* To reveal a secret by indiscreet talking; to gossip; to talk incessantly without focus.

blab•ber *v.* To chatter. **blabber** *n.*

black *adj.* Very dark in color; reflecting or transmitting no light; dark and serious in theme.

black•ball *n.* A vote that prevents a person's admission to an organization or club.

black belt *n.* The rank of expert in karate.

black•ber•ry *n.* A thorny plant with black edible berries that have small seeds.

black•bird *n.* A small bird, the males of the species having mostly all black feathers.

black•board *n.* Hard, slate-like board written on with chalk.

black box *n.* The damage-proof container protecting the tape recordings of airline pilots from water and fire, normally recoverable in the event of an accident.

black eye *n.* A bruise or discoloration

around the eye.

black•head *n.* A small mass of dirt that clogs the pore of the skin.

black•jack *n.* A card game in which each player tries to accumulate cards with points higher than that of the dealer, but not more than 21 points.

black•light *n.* Ultraviolet or invisible infrared light.

black•list *v.* To make or add a name to a list containing the names of people to be privately and unofficially boycotted.

black•mail *n.* The threat of exposing a past discreditable act or crime; money paid to avoid exposure.

black•smith *n.* One who shapes iron with heat and a hammer, or manufactures beaten metal items; a smithy.

black-tie *adj.* The wearing of semiformal evening wear by men.

black•top *n.* Asphalt, used to pave or surface roads; a road surfaced with a mixture of asphalt, tar, stone, and other binding materials, poured in a semisolid state and hardening upon cooling and pressing with rollers.

black wid•ow *n.* A poisonous spider of North America, with a distinctive hourglass shape on the female's abdomen.

blad•der *n.* The expandable sac in the pelvis that holds urine; any expandable bag for holding liquids.

blade *n.* The cutting part of a knife; the leaf of a plant or a piece of grass; the runner of an ice skate.

blame *v.* To hold someone guilty for something; to find fault; to attribute to as a cause. *n.* The cause of; guilt.

blame•less *adj.* Without blame; not guilty; innocent of effect.

blanch *v.* To remove the color from something, as to bleach; to pour scalding hot water over fresh vegetables; to pale in fear or apprehension.

bland *adj.* Lacking taste or style; dull; neutral. **blandly** *adv.*, **blandness** *n.*

blan•dish *v.* To coax by flattery. **blandishment** *n.*

blank *adj.* Having no markings or writing; empty; confused; at a loss for thought or word. **blankly** *adv.*, **blankness** *n.*

blan•ket *n.* A woven covering used on a bed for warmth. *v.* To cover completely.

blank verse *n.* A poem whose lines adhere to all the conditions of poetry except end rhyme.

blare *v.* To make or cause a loud sound; to shout; to broadcast loudly.

blar•ney *n.* Talk that is deceptive or nonsense; exaggerated excuses or explanations.

blas•pheme *v.* To speak with irreverence. **blasphemously** *adv.*, **blasphemy** *n.*

blast *n.* An explosion; a strong gust of air; the sound produced when a horn is blown. *slang* An exciting, active, or unusually enjoyable event. **blasted** *adj.*

bla•tant *adj.* Unpleasant; offensively loud; shameless. **blatancy** *n.*

blath•er *v.* To talk without making sense. **blather, blatherer** *n.*

blaze *n.* A fire, especially sudden; a sudden outburst of anger; a trail marker; a white mark on an animal's face. *v.* To flare up suddenly; to become full of light.

blaz•er *n.* A jacket with notched collar and patch pockets.

bla•zon *v.* To make known; to proclaim by emblem or insignia. **blazoner** *n.*

bleach *v.* To remove the color from a fabric; to become white. *n.* A chemical solution that whitens fabric or cleans stains.

bleach•ers *pl. n.* Rows of plank seating for spectators in a stadium; the cheapest section of seats in an arena.

bleak *adj.* Discouraging and depressing; barren; cold; harsh. **bleakness** *n.*, **bleakly** *adv.*

blear•y *adj.* Dull from lack of sleep; unfocused; blurry.

bleat *n.* The cry of a sheep or goat.

bleed *v.* To lose blood, as from an injury; to extort money; to mix or allow dyes to run together; to leak out slowly.

bleed•ing heart *n.* A plant with pink flowers; a person who feels very sympathetic toward the underprivileged.

bleep *n.* A signal with a quick, loud sound.

blem·ish *n.* A flaw or defect.

blend *v.* To mix together smoothly, to obtain a new substance. *n.* A mixture of complementary substances.

blend·er *n.* A kitchen appliance used to blend or liquefy food items; any mechanical device for mixing.

bless *v.* To give one's goodwill to; to honor or praise; to confer prosperity or well-being.

bless·ed *adj.* Holy; enjoying happiness; in a state of favor. **blessedly** *adv.*

bless·ing *n.* A short prayer before a meal; approval or permission; a privilege; evidence of good fortune.

blight *n.* A disease of plants causing complete destruction of crop or species.

blimp *n.* A lighter-than-air large aircraft with a nonrigid gas-filled hull; a zeppelin.

blind *adj.* Not having eyesight; not based on facts; unaware of or incapable of perceiving. *n.* A shelter that conceals hunters.

blind date *n.* A date between two strangers that has been arranged by a third party.

blind·ers *pl. n.* Flaps attached to the bridle of a horse, restricting side vision.

blind·fold *v.* To cover the eyes with a cloth; to block the vision; *n.* a cloth covering for the eyes.

blink *v.* To squint; to open and close the eyes quickly; to take a quick glance; to falter in a mental combat; to weaken.

blink·er *n.* A signaling light that displays a message; a light used to indicate turns.

blintz *n.* A very thin pancake rolled and stuffed with cottage cheese or other fillings.

blip *v.* to remove; erase sounds from a recording. *n.* The brief interruption as the result of blipping.

bliss *n.* The condition of having great happiness or joy; a transcendent state of universal understanding; one's life work or path which gives total satisfaction and happiness. **blissful** *adj.*, **blissfully** *adv.*

blis·ter *n.* The swelling of a thin layer of skin that contains a watery liquid. **blistered** *adj.*

blithe *adj.* Carefree or casual. **blithely** *adv.*, **blitheness** *n.*

blitz *n.* A sudden attack in full force; an intensive and forceful campaign.

bliz·zard *n.* A severe winter storm characterized by cold temperatures, high wind, and blinding snow.

bloat *v.* To swell or puff out. **bloated** *adj.*

blob *n.* A small shapeless mass.

bloc *n.* A united group formed for a common action or purpose.

block *n.* A solid piece of matter; a square or rectangular piece of wood; a platform used at an auction to display goods to be auctioned; the act of obstructing or hindering something. **blockage** *n.*

block *v.* To impede; to prevent from movement or direction; to arrange in blocks.

block·ade *n.* The closure of an area. **blockade** *v.*

blond *adj.* A golden or flaxen color. *n.* A man or boy with yellow hair.

blonde *n.* A woman or girl with yellow hair.

blood *n.* The fluid circulated by the heart throughout the body, carrying oxygen and nutrients to all parts of the body.

blood bank *n.* A place or institution where blood or plasma is processed, typed, and stored for future needs.

blood·hound *n.* A breed of tracking dogs with a very keen sense of smell.

blood·let·ting *n.* The act of bleeding a vein as part of medical therapy.

blood·mo·bile *n.* A portable blood bank that visits different locations, drawing and collecting blood from donors.

blood·shot *adj.* Showing redness or irritation, especially of the eyes.

blood·stream *n.* The tubular circulation of blood in the vascular system of arteries and veins.

blood·suck·er *n.* An animal that sucks blood.

blood ves·sel *n.* Any canal in which

blood circulates, such as a vein, artery, or capillary.

blood•y *adj.* Stained with blood; having the characteristics of blood; violent and destructive to participants, as sports.

bloom *v.* To bear flowers; to flourish; to have a healthy look; to blossom; to mature suddenly from childhood to adulthood. **blooming** *adj.*, **bloomer** *n.*

bloom•ers *pl. n.* Loose trousers that are gathered at the knee or just below; youngsters.

bloop•er *n.* An embarrassing blunder made in public; in baseball, a high pitch lobbed to the batter.

blos•som *n.* A flower or a group of flowers of a plant that bears fruit. *v.* To flourish; to bloom; to grow. **blossomy** *adj.*

blot *n.* A spot or stain. *v.* To dry with an absorbent material.

blotch *n.* A discolored area of skin.

blot•ter *n.* A piece of paper used to blot ink; a book for temporary entries.

blouse *n.* A loosely fitting shirt or top.

blow *v.* To express air or wind; to move or be in motion because of a current of air. *n.* A sudden hit with a hand or fist.

blow•er *n.* A device, mechanical or electric, for moving objects by air; a motor used to vent an area of contaminated air.

blow-dry *v.* To dry one's hair with a hand-held hair dryer.

blow•hole *n.* A hole in the ice that enables aquatic mammals to come up and breathe; the nostril of a whale, located on the top surface of the head.

blow•out *n.* The sudden deflation of a tire occurring while driving.

blow•pipe *n.* A long metal tube used by a glass blower to form shapes made from glass.

blow•torch *n.* A hand-held tool that generates a flame hot enough to melt soft metals.

blow•up *n.* An enlargement; a photograph; an explosion of a violent temper.

blub•ber *n.* The fat removed from whales and other marine mammals. **blubbery** *adj.*

blud•geon *n.* A stick with a loaded end used as a weapon.

blue *n.* A color the same as the color of a clear sky; the hue between violet and green; the color worn by the Union Army during the Civil War. *adj. slang* Sad, melancholy.

blue•ber•ry *n.* A small, edible, seedless berry.

blue•bird *n.* A small North American song bird related to the robin.

blue-col•lar *adj.* Relating to wage earners who wear work clothes to perform their tasks.

blue•gill *n.* A sunfish found in the eastern and central sections of the United States, sought for both eating and sport fishing.

blue•grass *n.* Folk music of the southern United States, played on guitars and banjos.

blue-pen•cil *v.* To correct or edit something before it is printed.

blue•print *n.* A reproduction of technical drawings or plans, using white lines on a blue background; any outline or plan of action.

blue rib•bon *n.* The award given for placing first in a contest.

blues *pl. n.* A style of jazz stemming from African-American post-slavery cultures; a state of depression; the state of being blue.

bluff *v.* To appear differently from one's actual condition; to deceive or mislead; to intimidate by showing more confidence than the facts can support. *n.* A steep and ridged cliff.

blun•der *n.* An error caused by ignorance; an action causing the failure of a project.

blun•der•buss *n.* A short gun with a flared muzzle.

blunt *adj.* Frank and abrupt; without finesse or circumlocution; dull or unsharpened, as an edge.

blur *v.* To smudge or smear; to become hazy. **blurringly** *adv.*, **blur** *n.*

blurt *v.* [with *out*] To speak impulsively.

blush *v.* To turn red in the face from

embarrassment from modesty or humiliation; to feel ashamed. *n.* Make-up used to give color to the cheekbones.

blus·ter *n.* A violent and noisy wind in a storm. *v.* To speak violently but emptily as a defense against reason.

bo·a *n.* A large nonvenomous snake of the Boidea family which coils around prey and crushes it; a feathered accessory that wraps around the neck.

boar *n.* A male pig; wild pig.

board *n.* A flat piece of sawed lumber; a flat area on which games are played; payment for food in a lodging. *v.* To receive meals at a lodging, usually for pay; to enter a ship, train, or plane. **boardlike** *adj.*

board·er *n.* A person who lives in someone's house and is provided food as well as lodging.

board game *n.* A game played by moving pieces on a board.

board·walk *n.* A wooden walkway along a beach.

boast *v.* To brag about one's own accomplishments; to count as one's assets. *n.* A brag or nonhumble statement of one's accomplishments. **boastful** *adj.*, **boastfulness** *n.*

boat *n.* A small open craft, capable of being carried by a larger ship; an open gravy holder or similar container.

boat·er *n.* A straw hat.

bob *v.* To cause to move up and down in a quick, jerky movement; to float in water.

bob·bin *n.* A spool that holds thread in a sewing machine.

bob·by *n.* An English police officer.

bob·by socks *pl. n.* Ankle socks, usually worn by teenaged girls.

bob·sled *n.* Racing sled with steering controls on the front runners. **bobsled** *v.*, **bobsledder** *n.*

bode *v.* To foretell by omen or sign.

bod·ice *n.* The piece of a dress that extends from the shoulder to the waist.

bod·y *n.* The main part of something; the physical part of a person; the corporal element of existence, answering to the laws of physics.

bod·y·guard *n.* A person hired to protect another person.

bog *n.* A poorly drained spongy area.

bo·gey *n.* In golf, one stroke over par for a hole.

bo·gey·man *n.* An imaginary figure used to threaten children.

bog·gle *v.* To pull away from with astonishment.

bo·gus *adj.* Counterfeit; phony; worthless in value.

bo·hea *n.* A black tea from China.

bo·he·mi·an *n.* A person whose lifestyle is artistic or otherwise unconventional.

boil *v.* To raise the temperature of water or other liquid until the gaseous state; to evaporate; reduce in size by boiling.

boil·er *n.* A vessel containing water, heated for steam power.

bois·ter·ous *adj.* Violent from innocent energy; rough and stormy; undisciplined.

bold *adj.* Courageous; showing courage; distinct and clear; visible from a distance.

bold·face *n.* A style of printing type with heavy thick lines.

bole *n.* A tree trunk.

bo·le·ro *n.* A short jacket without sleeves, worn open in the front.

boll *n.* A rounded capsule that contains seeds, as from the cotton plant.

boll wee·vil *n.* A small beetle whose larvae damage cotton bolls.

bo·lo·gna *n.* A seasoned, smoked sausage; baloney.

bo·lo tie *n.* A tie made of cord and fastened with an ornamental clasp.

bol·ster *n.* A long, round pillow. *v.* To provide support.

bolt *n.* A threaded metal pin designed with a head at one end and a removable nut at the other; a thunderbolt; a large roll of fabric or other material. *v.* To run or move suddenly; to flee from punishment.

bomb *n.* An explosive weapon, sometimes projected or dropped through the air, detonating upon impact, releasing destructive material, gas, and smoke.

bom•bard *v.* To attack repeatedly with missiles or bombs. **bombardment** *n.*

bom•bast *n.* Very ornate speech. **bombastic** *adj.*

bomb•er *n.* A military aircraft that carries and drops bombs; a person who makes or detonates explosive weapons.

bo•na•fide *adj.* Performed in good faith; genuine; authentic.

bo•nan•za *n.* A profitable pocket or vein of ore; great prosperity.

bon•bon *n.* Chocolate or fondant candy with a creamy, fruity, or nutty center.

bond *n.* Something that fastens or binds together; a duty or binding agreement; an insurance agreement in which the agency guarantees to pay the employer in the event an employee is accused of causing financial loss. **bonded** *adj.*

bond•age *n.* Slavery; servitude; restraint by physical or mental means.

bonds•man *n.* One who agrees to provide bond for someone else.

bone *n.* The calcified connecting tissue of the skeleton.

bon•fire *n.* An open outdoor fire for cooking and warmth, made from found onsite combustible materials.

bon•go *n.* A pair of small drums played with the hands.

bon•net *n.* A decorative or protective woman's hat with a brim, tying under the chin.

bon•ny *adj.* Attractive or pleasing; pretty.

bon•sai *n.* A small ornamental shrub grown in a shallow pot.

bo•nus *n.* Something given over and above what is expected; extra payment reflecting past overachievement.

boo *interj.* Verbal expression showing disapproval or contempt.

boo•boo *n.* A mistake, blunder, or minor injury.

boo•by prize *n.* A prize given for the worst performance.

book *n.* A group of pages fastened along the left side and bound between a protective cover; literary work written or print-ed. *v.* To reserve or register a room, facility, or performing act.

book•end *n.* A support for holding a row of books upright.

book•ie *n.* A bookmaker; one who handles gambling accounts.

book•ing *n.* A scheduled engagement; a reservation of talent or space in advance.

book•keep•ing *n.* The business of recording the accounts and transactions of a business; the record-keeping aspect of accounting. **bookkeeper** *n.*

book•mak•er *n.* A person who publishes, prints, and binds books; a person who accepts and pays off bets; a bookie.

book•mark *n.* Something inserted in a book to mark one's place; in computers, a feature of browsers to allow easy return to a previous web location.

book•mo•bile *n.* A vehicle equipped as a mobile book-lending service, traveling into communities without libraries.

book•plate *n.* A paper label attached inside a book, giving the owner's name.

book re•port *n.* A written or oral description, criticism, or analysis of a book, given after reading the book.

book•sell•er *n.* A person who specializes in selling books.

book•shelf *n.* An open shelf area used to display and store books.

book•store *n.* A place of business that sells reading material, especially books.

book•worm *n.* Various insect larvae that feed on the paste and binding of books; one who reads insatiably, to the neglect of other activities.

boom *n.* A deep, resonant sound; a long pole extending to the top of a derrick giving support to guide lifted objects; the horizontal spar of a sailing vessel; a sudden prosperity.

boo•mer•ang *n.* A carved, flat missile with aerodynamic properties, thrown so that it returns to the thrower.

boon *n.* Something that is pleasant or beneficial; a blessing; favor.

boon•docks *pl. n.* Back country.

boon·dog·gle *n.* A useless activity; a waste of time.

boor *n.* A person with clumsy manners and little refinement; a rude person. **boorish** *adj.*

boost *v.* To increase; to raise or lift by pushing up from below; to support or raise up by encouragement. *n.* An increase in energy, value, or mood.

boost·er *n.* A promoter or supporter of a cause; a supplementary dose of vaccine.

boot *n.* A protective covering for the foot; any protective sheath or covering; in England, the trunk of a vehicle. *v.* In computers, to load a computer with an operating system or other software.

boo·tee *n.* A soft, knitted sock for a baby.

booth *n.* A small enclosed compartment or area; display area at trade shows for displaying merchandise for sale; an area in a restaurant with a table and benches.

boot·jack *n.* A device shaped like a V, used to pull boots off.

boot·leg *v.* To sell, make, or transport liquor illegally.

booze *n.* An alcoholic drink.

bo·rax *n.* A crystalline compound used in manufacturing detergents and pharmaceuticals.

bor·der *n.* A surrounding decorative or protective margin or edge; a political or geographic boundary.

bor·der·line *n.* A line or mark indicating a border.

bore *v.* To make a hole through or in something using a drill; to make tired; to become repetitious or dull. **boredom** *n.*

bo·re·al *adj.* Located in or of the north.

bor·er *n.* A tool used to bore holes; any larva that penetrates woody stems and surfaces as part of its life cycle.

born *adj.* Brought into life or being; having an innate talent.

bor·ough *n.* A self-governing incorporated town, found in some United States cities; an incorporated British town that sends one or more representatives to Parliament.

bor·row *v.* To receive money with the intentions of returning it; to use as one's own with permission.

borscht *n.* Hot or cold beet soup.

bor·stal *n.* An institution for delinquent boys and girls.

bort *n.* Imperfect diamond fragments used as an abrasive.

bosh *n.* Foolish talk.

bos·om *n.* The female's breasts; the human chest; the heart or center of something. **bosomy** *adj.*

boss *n.* An employer or supervisor for whom one works; one's superior in a hierarchic structure; a projecting block used in architecture. *v.* To command; to supervise. **bossiness** *n.*

bos·sa no·va *n.* A Brazilian dance resembling the samba.

boss·y *adj.* Tending to be domineering.

bo·tan·i·cal *adj.* Relating to plants.

bot·a·ny *n.* The science of plants. **botanist** *n.*

botch *v.* To ruin something by clumsiness; to repair clumsily.

both *adj.* Two in conjunction with one another; one and another; two as a total.

both·er *v.* To pester, harass, or irritate; to be concerned about something. **bothersome** *adj.*

bot·tle *n.* A receptacle, usually made of glass, with a narrow neck and a top that can be capped or corked; formula or milk fed to a baby from such a container.

bot·tle·neck *n.* A narrow, obstructed passage, highway, road, etc.; a hindrance to progress or production.

bot·tom *n.* The lowest or deepest part of anything; the base; underside; the last; the land below a body of water. **bottomed** *v.*

bottom·less *adj.* Extremely deep; seemingly without a bottom. **bottomless·ness** *n.*

bot·tom·most *adj.* Being at the very bottom.

bot·u·lism *n.* Food poisoning, often fatal, caused by bacteria that grow in improperly prepared food.

bouf•fant *adj.* Full; puffed out.

bough *n.* The large branch of a tree.

bouil•lon *n.* A clear broth made from meat.

boul•der *n.* A large round rock.

boul•e•vard *n.* A broad city street lined with trees and separated by lawn or other barrier to opposing traffic.

bounce *v.* To rebound or cause to rebound; to leap or spring suddenly; to be returned by a bank as being worthless or having no value. **bounce** *n.*

bounc•er *n.* A person who removes disorderly people from a public place.

bounc•ing *adj.* Healthy; vigorous; robust; lively and spirited.

bound *n.* A leap or bounce. *v.* To limit; to be tied or restrained; held by an obligation.

bound•a•ry *n.* A limit or border; the edge of an action or right.

bound•en *adj.* Under an obligation or agreement.

bound•er *n.* A vulgar person.

bound•less *adj.* Without limits. **boundlessly** *adv.,* **boundlessness** *n.*

boun•te•ous *adj.* Plentiful or generous; giving freely; beneficent.

boun•ti•ful *adj.* Abundant; plentiful. **bountifully** *adv.*

boun•ty *n.* Generosity; an inducement or reward given for the return of something; a good harvest; the price paid to another to bring a criminal to justice.

bou•quet *n.* A group of cut flowers, held in the hand or arranged in a vessel; the aroma of wine, when first poured.

bour•bon *n.* Whiskey distilled from fermented corn mash.

bour•geoi•sie *coll. n.* The members of the middle class. **bourgeois** *adj.*

bout *n.* A contest or match; the length of time spent in a certain way.

bou•tique *n.* A small retail shop that sells specialized gifts, accessories, and fashionable clothes.

bou•ton•niere *n.* A flower worn in the buttonhole of a man's jacket.

bo•vine *n.* A member of the bovid family, with cloven hooves, four-chamber digestive tracts, and pronounced mammary apertures, such as an ox or cow. **bovine** *adj.*

bow *n.* The front section of a boat or ship; bending of the head or waist to express a greeting or courtesy; a weapon made from a curved stave and strung taut to launch arrows; a rod strung with horsehair, used for playing stringed instruments.

bow *v.* To lower one's upper body in homage or respect; to give in to another's wishes; to bend under a burden.

bow•el *n.* The digestive tract located below the stomach; the intestines.

bow•er *n.* A shelter constructed from tree boughs; an anchor.

bowl *n.* A hemispherical container for food or liquids; a bowl-shaped part, as of a spoon or ladle; a bowl-shaped stadium. *v.* To roll spherical or cylindrical objects; to participate in the game of bowling.

bow•leg•ged *adj.* Characterized by an outward curvature of the leg at the knee.

bowl•er *n.* A person who bowls; a British round-topped, brimmed men's hat.

bow•line *n.* A rope to keep the edge of a square sail taut.

bowl•ing *n.* A game in which a person rolls a ball down a wooden alley in order to knock down a triangular group of nine or ten wooden bowling pins; any lawn game involving rolling balls. **bowler** *n.*

bowl•ing al•ley *n.* A building containing alleys for the game of bowling.

bow•man *n.* An oarsman in the front of a boat.

bow•sprit *n.* A spar that projects forward from the stem of a ship.

box *n.* A small container or chest, usually with a lid; a special area in a theater that holds a small group of people. *v.* To fight with the fists.

box•car *n.* An enclosed railway car used for the transportation of freight, accessed through sliding side doors on both walls.

box•er *n.* A person who boxes

professionally; a German breed of dog with short hair, brownish coat, and a square muzzle.

box·ing *n.* A sport in which two opponents punch each other using padded gloves on their hands, forming fists.

box of·fice *n.* An office where tickets to performances and public events are purchased.

box spring *n.* A cloth-covered frame supporting a mattress.

boy *n.* A male youth or child. **boyhood** *n.*

boy·cott *v.* To abstain from dealing with, buying, or using, as a means of organized protest against practices.

boy·friend *n.* A male companion of a mildly romantic relationship with a young person of the opposite sex.

boy·sen·ber·ry *n.* A trailing fruit-bearing hybrid developed by crossing blackberries and raspberries.

bra *n.* Brassiere.

brace *n.* A device that supports or steadies something; two of a team of work animals. *v.* To support with a brace.

brace·let *n.* An ornamental band for the wrist.

brack·en *n.* A large species of fern with tough stems and finely divided fronts.

brack·et *n.* A support attached to a vertical surface to hold a shelf or other weight; the typographical marks of enclosure. *v.* To enclose in brackets.

brack·ish *adj.* Containing salt; distasteful. **brackishness** *n.*

bract *n.* A leaf-like plant below a flower cluster or flower. **bracteate, bracteal, bracted, bracteolate** *adj.*

brad *n.* A nail that tapers to a small head.

brag *v.* To assert or talk boastfully; to announce one's accomplishments without modesty.

brag·ga·do·ci·o *n.* Cockiness; overconfidence; an arrogant manner; empty bragging.

brag·gart *n.* A person who brags.

braid *v.* To interweave three or more strands of something; to plait. *n.* Fibers or strands that have been braided.

braille *n.* A system of printing for the blind, consisting of six dots, two across and four directly under the first two, with numbers and letters represented by raising certain dots in each group of six.

brain *n.* The large mass of nerve tissue enclosed in the cranium, responsible for the interpretation of sensory impulses, control of the body, and coordination; the center of thought and emotion.

brain·storm *n.* A sudden idea or inspiration. *v.* To think and contribute ideas without censure by reason; to imagine without artificial barriers of practicality.

brain·wash·ing *n.* Intensive indoctrination to radically change a person's convictions. **brainwash** *v.*

braise *v.* To cook by first browning in a small amount of fat, adding a liquid such as water, and then simmering in a covered container.

brake *n.* A device designed to stop or slow the motion of a vehicle or machine; a tool in weaving; a dense covering of shrubbery. **brake** *v.*

brake·man *n.* A train crew member who assists the conductor; the man who operates the brake on a bobsled.

bram·ble *n.* A prickly shrub or plant such as the raspberry or blackberry bush.

bran *n.* The husk of cereal grains separated from the flour.

branch *n.* An extension from the main trunk of a tree; an offshoot or tributary of a river. **branched** *adj.*

brand *n.* A trademark or label that names a product; a mark of disgrace or shame; a piece of charred or burning wood; a mark made by a hot iron to show ownership. **branded** *adj.*

brand name *n.* A company's verbal trademark, protected by law.

brand-new *adj.* Unused and new; fresh; not introduced before.

bran·dy *n.* An alcoholic liquor distilled from fermented fruit juices or wine.

brash *adj.* Hasty, rash, and unthinking;

insolent; impudent.

brass *n.* An alloy of zinc, copper and other metals in lesser amounts.

bras·siere *n.* A woman's undergarment with cups to support the breasts.

brat *n.* An ill-mannered child. **brattiness** *n.*, **bratty** *adj.*

brat·wurst *n.* A fresh pork sausage.

bra·va·do *n.* A false showing of bravery.

brave *adj.* Having or displaying courage; strong in the face of pain; willing to risk harm out of a sense of duty or righteousness. *n.* An honorary term of recognition to a warrior of the Native American tribes.

brav·er·y *n.* The quality of or state of being brave.

bra·vo *interj.* Expressing approval, especially when shouted after a performance or feat.

bra·vu·ra *n.* A musical passage requiring technical skill.

brawl *n.* A noisy argument or fight. **brawl** *v.*, **brawler** *n.*

brawn *n.* Well-developed and solid muscles; sturdy. **brawny** *adj.*

bray *v.* To make a loud cry like a donkey. *n.* A donkey's cry.

braze *v.* To solder using a nonferrous alloy that melts at a lower temperature than that of the metals being joined together.

bra·zen *adj.* Made of brass; shameless or impudent.

bra·zier *n.* A person who works with brass; a metal pan that holds burning charcoal or coals.

breach *n.* Ruptured, broken, or torn condition or area; a break in friendly relations. *v.* To break the law or obligation.

bread *n.* A leavened food made from a flour or meal mixture, and baked; one's livelihood; the reward for labor.

bread·bas·ket *n.* A woven container for carrying bread from market to home; a major grain producing region of the United States.

bread·board *n.* A board used for cutting bread; a board on which electric or elec-

tronic circuit diagrams may be laid out.

breadth *n.* The distance or measurement from side to side; width; thickness in a three-dimensional figure.

break *v.* To separate into parts with violence or suddenness; to collapse or give way; to change suddenly; to temporarily cease discussion or activity.

break *n.* A fissure or division in a solid object; in pool, the first stroke that distributes the balls around the table; a stroke of good luck; a chance from which future successes may grow.

break a leg *v.* To be a theatrical success.

break·down *n.* Failure to function; a mental or nervous collapse.

break·er *n.* A wave that breaks into foam.

break ev·en *v.* To make neither a profit or loss in business.

break·fast *n.* The first meal of the day.

break·through *n.* A sudden advance in knowledge or technique; a thrust that goes farther than anticipated or expected.

break·wa·ter *n.* A barrier that protects a beach from the full force of waves against erosion and damage to moored vessels.

breast *n.* The milk-producing glandular organs on a woman's chest; the mammary glands; the area of the body from the neck to the abdomen.

breast·bone *n.* The sternum.

breast·stroke *n.* A stroke in swimming in which a person lies face down and extends the arms in front of the head, drawing the knees forward and outward, and then sweeping the arms back while kicking outward and backward.

breath *n.* The air inhaled and exhaled in breathing; a very slight whisper, fragrance, or breeze.

breathe *v.* To draw air into and expel from the lungs; to inhale and exhale; to allow air or ventilation to surround a thawing or evaporating substance; to take a short rest.

breath·er *n.* A small opening in an otherwise air-tight enclosure; a pause or rest in an exhaustive activity; one that breathes.

breath·less *adj.* Gasping for breath. **breathlessly** *adv.*, **breathlessness** *n.*

breath·tak·ing *adj.* Astonishing; awesome. **breathtakingly** adv.

breech *n.* The buttocks; the hind end of the body; the part of a gun or firearm located at the rear of the barrel. *pl.* Trousers that fit tightly around the knees.

breed *v.* The genetic strain of domestic animals, developed and maintained by mankind. **breeding** *n.*

breeze *n.* A slight gentle wind; a zephyr; something accomplished with very little effort. **breezy** *adj.*

breeze·way *n.* A roofed connection between two buildings or walls.

breve *n.* The curved mark over a vowel to indicate a short or unstressed syllable.

bre·vi·ar·y *n.* A book that contains prayers and psalms for the canonical hours.

brev·i·ty *n.* A brief duration; conciseness; efficient shortness; briefness.

brew *v.* To make beer from malt and hops by boiling, infusion, and fermentation. **brewer** *n.*

brew·er·y *n.* A building or plant where beer or ale is brewed.

bribe *v.* To influence or induce by giving, illegally or immorally, a token or anything of value for a service. **bribe** *n.*

brib·ery *n.* The practice of giving or receiving a bribe.

bric-a-brac *n.* A collection of small objects displayed on a narrow shelf.

brick *n.* A molded block of baked clay, usually rectangular in shape, used for construction and facing.

brick·bat *n.* A piece of a brick used as a weapon when thrown as a missile.

brick·lay·er *n.* A person who lays bricks as a profession.

bri·dal *adj.* Relating to a bride or a nuptial ceremony.

bri·dal wreath *n.* A flower grown for its small white flowers used in bouquets.

bride *n.* A woman just married or about to be married.

bride·groom *n.* A man just married or about to be married.

brides·maid *n.* A woman who attends a bride at her wedding.

bridge *n.* A structure providing passage over two bodies of land, depressions, obstacles, or other rights of way; a contract-bidding card game for four players.

bridge·head *n.* A military position secured by advance troops in enemy territory, giving protection for the main attack force.

bridge·work *n.* The construction of dental work.

bri·dle *n.* A harness used to restrain or guide a horse. *v.* To restrain or control. **bridler** *n.*

brief *n.* A concise, formal statement of a client's case. *adj.* Short in duration. *v.* To summarize or inform in a short statement. **briefly** *adv.*, **briefness** *n.*

brief·case *n.* A small, flat, flexible case for holding and carrying papers or books.

brief·ing *n.* The act of giving essential information; a meeting at which preliminary information is distributed.

brief·ly *adv.* For a very short span of time.

bri·er *n.* A woody, thorny, or prickly plant.

brig *n.* A prison on a ship; a twin-masted, square-rigged sailing ship.

bri·gade *n.* A military unit organized for a specific purpose.

brig·a·dier *n.* An officer in the British army.

brig·and *n.* A person who lives as a robber; a bandit.

brig·an·tine *n.* A square-rigged two-masted ship.

bright *adj.* Brilliant in color or light; vivid; shining and emitting or reflecting light; happy; cheerful; lovely; intelligent, quick to learn. **brightness** *n.*

bright·en *v.* To make things brighter. **brightener** *n.*

bril·liant *adj.* Very bright and shiny; sparkling; radiant; extremely intelligent.

brim *n.* The edge or rim of a cup; the top

of a cliff or bluff. **brimless** *adj*.

brim·ful *adj*. Completely full.

brim·stone *n*. Sulfur.

brin·dle *adj*. Having dark streaks or flecks on a gray or tawny background.

brine *n*. Water saturated with salt; the water contained in the oceans and seas.

bring *v*. To carry with oneself to a certain place; to cause, act, or move in a special direction.

brink *n*. The upper edge or margin of a very steep slope; the place past which no return is possible.

bri·oche *n*. A roll made from flour, eggs, butter, and yeast.

bri·o·lette *n*. A pear-shaped diamond cut into facets.

bri·quette *n*. A small brick-shaped piece of charcoal.

brisk *adj*. Moving or acting quickly; being sharp in tone or manner; energetic or invigorating. **briskly** *adv*., **briskness** *n*.

bris·ket *n*. The meat from the lower chest or breast of an animal.

bris·tle *n*. Short, stiff, coarse hair. *v*. To react in angry defiance. **bristly** *adj*.

britch·es *pl. n*. Trousers; breeches.

brit·tle *adj*. Very easy to break; fragile.

broach *n*. A tapered and serrated tool used for enlarging and shaping a hole. *v*. In sailing, to fill with water from taking waves broadside.

broad *adj*. Covering a wide area; in proportion measuring from side to side; plain, open, unrefined. **broadly** *adv*.

broad·cast *v*. To transmit a program by radio or television; to make widely known; to scatter or sow seeds. **broadcaster** *n*.

broad·cloth *n*. A textured woolen cloth with a lustrous finish.

broad·en *v*. To become or make broad or broader.

broad·loom *adj*. Woven on a wide loom. *n*. Carpet woven in this manner.

broad·mind·ed *adj*. Tolerant of varied views; liberal; open to the opinions and beliefs of others; not judgmental.

broad·side *n*. The side of a ship that is above the water line; a sheet of paper printed on both sides and then folded.

bro·cade *n*. A silk fabric with raised patterns in silver and gold.

broc·co·li *n*. A green vegetable from the cauliflower family, eaten before the small buds open.

bro·chure *n*. A booklet or pamphlet.

bro·gan *n*. A sturdy oxford shoe.

brogue *n*. A strong regional accent; a heavy shoe with a hobnail sole.

broil *v*. To cook by exposure to direct radiant heat.

broil·er *n*. A device, usually a part of a stove, used for broiling meat; a young chicken.

broke *adj*. Penniless; completely without money. *v*. Past tense of *break*.

bro·ken *adj*. Separated violently into parts; damaged to the point of inoperability; severed or disconnected; difficult to understand, as speech.

bro·ken·heart·ed *adj*. Overcome by despair or grief.

bro·ker *n*. A person who acts as a negotiating agent for contracts, sales, or purchases in return for payment.

bro·ker·age *n*. The establishment of a broker.

bro·mine *n*. A nonmetallic element of a deep red, toxic liquid that gives off a disagreeable odor.

bron·chi·al *adj*. Pertaining to the bronchi or their extensions.

bron·chi·tis *n*. An acute inflammation of the bronchial tubes.

bron·chus *n*. Either of two main branches of the trachea that lead directly to the lungs. **bronchi** *pl*.

bron·co *n*. A wild horse of western North America.

bronze *n*. An alloy of tin, copper, and zinc; moderate olive brown to yellow in color. **bronze** *v*., **bronze** *adj*.

brooch *n*. A large decorative pin.

brood *n*. The young offsprings of an animal; a litter. *v*. To produce by incubation; to hatch; to think about at length; to be in a state of deep gloom or meditation.

brook *n.* A small fresh-water stream.

broom *n.* A long-handled implement used for sweeping.

broth *n.* The liquid in which fish, meat, or vegetables have been cooked; cooking stock.

broth•el *n.* A house of prostitution; whorehouse.

broth•er *n.* A male who shares the same parents as another person; a kindred person by belief or affiliation. **brotherly** *adj.*

broth•er•hood *n.* The state of being brothers; one related to another for a particular purpose; a philanthropic association.

broth•er-in-law *n.* The brother of one's spouse; the husband of one's sister; the husband of one's spouse's sister.

brought *v.* Past tense of *bring*.

brow *n.* The ridge above the eye where the eyebrow grows.

brown *n.* A color between yellow and red; a dark or tanned complexion.

brown•ie *n.* A good-natured elf believed to perform helpful services; a square, chewy piece of chocolate cake.

brown•out *n.* An interruption or severe reduction of community electrical power.

brown•stone *n.* A reddish-brown sandstone used for construction; a building faced with brownstone.

browse *v.* To look over something in a leisurely and casual way; to scan for pertinent information.

bruise *n.* A contusion; an injury that ruptures small blood vessels and discolors the skin without breaking it.

brum•by *n.* An unbroken horse.

brunch *n.* A combination of a late breakfast and an early lunch.

bru•net or **bru•nette** A person with dark brown hair.

brunt *n.* The principal shock, or force.

brush *n.* A device consisting of bristles used for applying paint, scrubbing, or grooming the hair; a very dense growth of bushes. *v.* To touch against lightly.

brush•off *n.* An abrupt dismissal; a disrespectful indifference to a request or communication.

brush up *v.* To refresh one's memory or skills.

brusque *adj.* Blunt or short in manner or speech; harsh. **brusquely** *adv.*, **brusqueness** *n.*

brus•sels sprout *n.* The small head of a green vegetable, resembling the cabbage.

bru•tal *adj.* Very harsh or cruel in treatment; like a brute or animal; violently destructive.

brute *n.* A person characterized by physical power rather than intelligence; one who behaves like an animal. **brutish** *adj.*

brux•ism *n.* The unconscious grinding of the teeth during sleep.

bub•ble *n.* A small body of gas contained inside the adhesive surface strength of a liquid; any small round object, usually hollow. *v.* To produce bubbles.

bub•ble gum *n.* A chewing gum that can be blown into bubbles.

bub•bler *n.* A drinking fountain where water bubbles upward.

bub•bly *adj.* Full of bubbles; high-spirited, cheerful, effervescent of personality. *n.* Champagne.

bu•bo *n.* Inflammatory swelling of the lymphatic glands, especially in the area of the groin or armpits.

bu•bon•ic plague *n.* The contagious and normally fatal disease transmitted by fleas from infected rats, characterized by fever, diarrhea, chills, vomiting, and the appearance of bubos.

buc•ca•neer *n.* A pirate preying on Spanish ships in the West Indies in the 17th century; an unscrupulous adventurer.

buck *n.* The adult male deer; the lowest grade in the military category. *v.* To move violently in a vertical direction; to throw a rider; to oppose the system.

buck•board *n.* An open carriage with four wheels and a seat attached to a flexible board.

buck•et *n.* A vessel used to carry liquids or

solids; a pail.

buck•eye *n.* A tree with flower clusters and glossy brown nuts.

buck•le *v.* To warp, crumple, or bend under pressure; to fasten with a strap. *n.* Metal clasp for fastening a belt.

buck•ram *n.* A coarse, stiff fabric sized with glue and used for interlinings in garments and in book bindings.

buck•shot *n.* A coarse lead shot for shotgun shells.

buck•skin *n.* A soft leather; a light colored horse; riding breeches made from buckskin.

buck•tooth *n.* A large, prominently projecting front tooth. **bucktoothed** *adj.*

bu•col•ic *adj.* Pastoral or natural in tone; peaceful in style or temperament. *n.* A poem.

bud *n.* Something not developed completely; a small structure that contains flowers or leaves that have not developed; early stage of development. **budding** *adj.*

bud•dy *n.* A companion, partner, or friend; a pal; one who shares in an activity.

budge *v.* To give way to; to cause to move slightly; to change position slightly in response to great exertion.

bud•get *n.* The total amount of money allocated for a certain purpose. *v.* To allot funds or resources carefully in advance of expenditure.

buff *n.* A leather made mostly from skins of buffalo, elk, or oxen having the color of light to moderate yellow. *v.* To polish by rubbing with cloth.

buf•fa•lo *n.* A wild ox with heavy forequarters, short horns, and a large muscular hump; a bison.

buff•er *n.* A tool used to polish or shine; in computer science, a part of the memory used to hold information temporarily while data transfers from one place to another. *v.* To lessen, absorb, or protect against the shock of an impact.

buf•fet *n.* A meal placed on a side table so that people may serve themselves; a side table for serving food. *v.* To strike sharply with the hand.

buf•foon *n.* A clown; a stupid person; an uneducated person.

bug *n.* Any small insect or life form; a concealed listening device. *v.* To bother or annoy. **bugged** *adj.*

bug•a•boo *n.* A source of concern or fear.

bug•gy *n.* A small carriage pulled behind a horse; a baby carriage.

bu•gle *n.* A brass wind instrument without keys or valves. *v.* To sound a bugle call. **bugler** *n.*

build *v.* To erect by uniting materials into a composite whole; to fashion or create; to develop or add to; to construct. *n.* The form or structure of a person.

build•er *n.* A person who supervises the construction of a building project.

build•ing *n.* A roofed and walled structure of some size, for permanent use.

bulb *n.* A spherical shape rounded at the bottom, tapering gradually into a point; a rounded underground plant that lies dormant in the winter and blooms in the spring; an incandescent light.

bul•bous *adj.* Resembling a bulb in shape.

bulge *n.* A swelling of the surface caused by pressure from within.

bul•gur *n.* Wheat prepared for human consumption.

bu•lim•i•a *n.* An eating disorder in which a person overeats and then throws up in order to remain thin.

bulk *n.* A large mass; anything that has great size, volume, or units; materials or substances measured by volume rather than number.

bulk•head *n.* The partition that divides a ship into compartments; a retaining wall along a waterfront.

bulk•y *adj.* Having great bulk; out of proportion. **bulkiness** *n.*

bull *n.* The adult male in cattle and other large mammals; one confident that the value of stocks or other marketable commodities will rise in the future.

bull•dog *n.* A short-haired dog with a stocky build and an undershot lower jaw.

bull•doz•er *n.* A tractor-like machine running on metal treads, with a large metal blade in front for moving earth and rocks.

bul•let *n.* A projectile fired from a gun.

bul•le•tin *n.* A broadcast statement of public interest, containing new and important information; a public notice.

bul•le•tin board *n.* A board, often of cork or other soft material, on which messages and temporary notices are posted.

bull•fight *n.* A Spanish or Mexican spectacle in which men known as matadors engage in fighting bulls.

bull•frog *n.* A deep-voiced frog.

bull•head•ed *adj.* Headstrong and stubborn.

bull•horn *n.* A hand-held loudspeaker.

bul•lion *n.* Refined gold or silver in the uncoined state.

bull•ish *adj.* Tending to cause, or hopeful of, rising prices, as in the stock market.

bull•ock *n.* A castrated bull.

bull's eye *n.* The center of a target.

bul•ly *n.* A person who is mean or cruel to weaker people; one who intimidates by oppression or threat of violence.

bul•rush *n.* Tall grass as found in a marsh.

bul•wark *n.* A strong protection or support.

bum *n.* One who begs from others; one who spends time unemployed. *v.* To loaf.

bum•ble•bee *n.* A large hairy bee, solitary in habit and habitat.

bump *v.* To collide with, knock, or strike something; to take advantage of one's rank or seniority to replace someone of lower rank or privilege. *n.* A swelling or lump on a person's body; an area risen up from a relatively flat surface.

bump•er *n.* A device on vehicles that absorbs shock and prevents damage.

bump•kin *n.* An awkward, stupid, or unsophisticated country person.

bump•tious *adj.* Crudely self-assertive and forward; pushy. **bumptiousness** *n.*

bump•y *adj.* Uneven; not smooth; having ups and downs.

bun *n.* Any of a variety of plain or sweet small breads; tightly rolled hair that resembles a bun.

bunch *n.* A cluster or group of like items. *v.* To gather into an informal group.

bun•co *n.* A game of confidence; a swindling scheme.

bun•dle *n.* Anything wrapped or held together. **bundler** *n.*

bun•dle up *v.* To dress warmly, using many layers of clothing.

bung *n.* The cork used to plug the bunghole in a large cask.

bun•ga•low *n.* A small one-story cottage with a pitched roof, usually rural or rustic.

bun•gle *v.* To act awkwardly or clumsily; to damage a project or activity by inexpert or careless handling. **bungler** *n.*

bun•ion *n.* An inflamed, painful swelling of the first joint of the big toe.

bunk *n.* A narrow bed that is built in; one of a tier of berths on a ship.

bun•ker *n.* A tank for storing fuel on a ship; an embankment or a sand trap creating a hazard on a golf course.

bunk•house *n.* A building used as sleeping quarters usually on a ranch.

bun•ny *n.* Child's name for a rabbit.

Bun•sen burn•er *n.* An adjustable gas-burning laboratory burner.

bunt *v.* To tap a pitched ball with a half swing. *n.* The center of a square sail.

bunt•ing *n.* A hooded blanket for a baby; a variety of stout-billed birds.

bu•oy *n.* A floating object to mark a channel or danger; any nautical marker or channel divider.

buoy•an•cy *n.* The tendency of an object or body to remain afloat in liquid or to rise in gas or air.

bur•den *n.* The physical cargo or materials carried by a person or beast; something hard to bear; a duty or responsibility taken on unwillingly but patiently. **burden** *v.*, **burdensome** *adj.*

bur•dock *n.* A coarse plant with purplish flowers.

bu•reau *n.* A low chest for storing clothes;

a branch of the government or a subdivision of a department.

bu•reauc•ra•cy *n.* A body of nonelected officials in a government; the administration of a government through bureaus.

bu•reau•crat *n.* A government official who has great authority in his or her own department. **bureaucratic** *adj.*

bu•rette *n.* A glass tube for measuring quantities of liquid or gas that are discharged or taken in.

burg *n.* A town or city.

bur•gee *n.* A flag used by ships for signals or identification.

bur•geon *v.* To put forth new life, as in leaves and buds.

burg•er *n. slang* A hamburger; ground meat shaped into a patty and served on a bun with condiments and relishes.

bur•gess *n.* A representative of the legislature of colonial Maryland and Virginia.

bur•glar *n.* One who steals personal items from another person's home without detection. **burglarize** *v.*, **burglary** *n.*

bur•gun•dy *n.* A white or red wine produced in Burgundy, an area in southeast France.

burl *n.* A woody, often flat and hard, hemispherical growth on a tree.

bur•lap *n.* A coarse cloth woven from hemp or jute.

bur•lesque *n.* Theatrical entertainment of a low nature, with comedy, mocking imitations, and dance performances.

bur•ley *n.* A tobacco grown in Kentucky.

bur•ly *adj.* Very heavy and strong; stocky.

burn *v.* To be destroyed by fire; to consume fuel and give off heat. *n.* An injury produced by fire, heat, or steam; the firing of a rocket engine in space. **burnable** *adj.*

burn•er *n.* The part of a fuel-burning device where the fire is contained.

bur•nish *v.* To make shiny by rubbing; to polish. **burnishing** *adj.*

bur•noose *n.* A one-piece hooded cloak.

burnt *adj.* Affected by burning; charred or damaged by fire.

bur•ro *n.* A small donkey.

bur•row *n.* A tunnel or dwelling dug in the ground by an animal. *v.* To construct by tunneling through the earth.

bur•sar *n.* The person or official in charge of monies at a college.

bur•sa•ry *n.* The treasury of a college; a grant to a needy student.

bur•si•tis *n.* An inflammation of the small sac between a tendon of the knee, elbow, or shoulder joints.

burst *adj.* To explode or experience a sudden outbreak; to very suddenly become visible or audible. *n.* A sudden explosion or outburst.

bur•y *v.* To hide by covering with earth; to inter a body at a funeral service; to place in an inconspicuous position.

bus *n.* A large passenger vehicle; a small hand truck; a conductor for collecting electric currents. **buses**, **busses** *pl.*

bus•boy *n.* A waiter's assistant; one who removes dirty dishes and resets a table.

bush *n.* A low plant with branches near the ground; a dense tuft or growth; land covered intensely with undergrowth.

bush•el *n.* A unit of dry measurement which equals four pecks or 2,150.42 cubic inches; a basket container that holds a bushel.

bush•fire *n.* A fire burning out of control in the bush.

bush•ing *n.* A cylindrical lining in an opening to limit the size of the opening.

bush•whack *v.* To travel through thick woods by cutting bushes and small trees; to ambush. **bushwhacker** *n.*

bush•y *adj.* Overgrown with a dense growth of bushes; hirsute.

busi•ness *n.* A person's professional dealings or occupation; an industrial or commercial establishment; concerns or activities occupying a period of time.

bus•ing *n.* The practice of transporting children by bus to a school outside their area, to establish racial balance.

busk•er *n.* A juggler, actor, mime, dancer, acrobat, singer, or musician who entertains on a street corner or other public place for handouts.

buss *n.* A light kiss without passion or sexual intent.

bust *n.* A sculpture that resembles the upper part of a human body; the breasts of a woman. *v.* To break or burst; to become short of money.

bust•er *n.* A sturdy child; a person who breaks horses; sudden violent wind coming from the south.

bus•tle *n.* A padding that gives extra bulk to the back of a woman's skirt; hurry, movement, or busyness characterized by vigorous activity. **bustling** *adj.*

bus•y *adj.* Full of activity; engaged in some form of work; occupied with another task; already in use. *v.* To occupy one's self. **busily** *adv.*, **busyness** *n.*

but *conj.* On the contrary to; other than; if not; except for the fact; on the other hand.

bu•tane *n.* A gas produced from petroleum, used as a fuel refrigerant and aerosol propellant.

butch•er *n.* One who slaughters animals and dresses them for food.

bu•te•o *n.* Species of hawk with broad wings and soaring flight.

but•ler *n.* A male servant of a household, in charge of other household employees.

butt *n.* The object of ridicule; the thick large or blunt end of something; a backstop for stopping missiles. *v.* To hit with horns or the head; to be joined at the end.

butte *n.* A small mountain with steep precipitous sides with a smaller summit area than a mesa.

but•ter *n.* A yellow fatty substance churned from milk, used as a spread or cooking oil.

but•ter•fly *n.* A narrow-bodied flying insect with four broad, colorful wings, emerging from the cocoon of the caterpillar; a person occupied with the pursuit of pleasure; a swimming stroke.

but•ter•milk *n.* The liquid that remains after butter has been churned from milk.

but•ter•scotch *n.* A candy made from brown sugar and melted butter.

but•ter•y *n.* A liquor storeroom.

but•tocks *pl. n.* The two round fleshy parts of the rump.

but•ton *n.* A small disk that interlocks with a buttonhole to close a piece of garment; a badge bearing a stamped design or slogan; an immature mushroom. **buttoned** *adj.*

but•ton•hole *n.* The slit through which a button is inserted.

but•ton•hook *n.* A running pattern in football; a hook used to draw buttons thru buttonholes.

but•tress *n.* A support made of either brick or stone and built against or projecting from a building or wall used for the purpose of giving stability; a support or prop.

bu•try•a•ceous *adj.* Having the qualities of butter.

bux•om *adj.* Lively; happy; amply proportioned. **buxomness** *n.*

buy *v.* To purchase in exchange for money; to acquire possession of something. *n.* Anything bought, especially a bargain.

buy•er *v.* A person who buys from a store or an individual; a person employed to make wholesale purchases for a company.

buzz *v.* To make a low vibrating humming sound, as a bee.

buz•zard *n.* A broad-winged vulture from the same family as the hawk.

buzz•er *n.* An electrical signaling device that makes a buzzing sound.

buzz saw *n.* A circular power saw.

by *prep.* Up to and beyond; to go past; not later than; next to; according to; beside or near; according to; in relation to; as a product or creation of.

bye *n.* A position in which a contestant has no opponent after pairs are drawn for a tournament, and, therefore, advances to the next round; something that is aside from the main consideration or course.

bye-bye *interj.* Farewell; goodbye.

by•gone *adj.* Gone by; past; former; departed; out of date.

by·law *n.* A rule or law governing internal affairs of a group or organization.

by·line *n.* A line at the beginning of a newspaper article, news story, or magazine, containing the author's name.

by·pass *n.* A road that goes around an obstructed area; a detour; a secondary route; a freeway that avoids the congestion of the urban business district.

byte *n.* In computer science, a string of binary digits operated on as a unit.

by·way *n.* A secondary field of study; a side road; an unfrequented path.

by·word *n.* A well-known proverb; an object of contempt.

C

C, c The third letter of the English alphabet; the Roman numeral for 100.

ca·bal *n.* A group that conspires against a government or other public institution.

cab·a·ret *n.* A restaurant that provides dancing and live entertainment.

cab·i·net *n.* A unit for displaying and storing dishes and other objects; a selected group of people appointed by the head of state to officially advise and to take charge of government departments.

ca·ble *n.* A heavy rope made from fiber or steel; a bound group of insulated conductors.

ca·ble tel·e·vi·sion *n.* A private television system which picks up signals from stations and transmits them by cable.

ca·boose *n.* The last car of a train, containing the eating and sleeping quarters for the crew.

cache *n.* A safe place to hide and conceal goods.

cack·le *v.* To laugh with the characteristic shrill noise a hen makes after laying an egg; to talk or laugh with a similar sound. **cackler** *n.*

ca·coph·o·ny *n.* A harsh and disagreeable sound. **cacophonous** *adj.*

cac·tus *n.* A leafless plant with a thick, prickly surface, growing primarily in hot and dry regions. **cacti** or **cactuses** *pl.*

ca·dav·er *n.* The body of a person who has died. **cadaverous** *adj.*

cad·die *n.* A person employed by a golfer to assist by carrying clubs and advising the player during the game of golf.

ca·dence *n.* A rhythmic movement or flow; the keeping of time by a marching or musical group.

ca·det *n.* A student in training at a naval or military academy. **cadetship** *n.*

caf·e·te·ri·a *n.* A restaurant where a patron chooses food and then carries it on a tray to the table.

caf·feine *n.* A stimulant found in coffee, tea, and dark colas.

cage *n.* A box-like structure enclosed with bars or grating for the confinement of animals; any enclosure used for confinement. *v.* To capture or restrain in an enclosure.

ca·gey *adj.* Shrewd, wary, or cautious.

ca·jole *v.* To wheedle or coax; to convince by gentle emotional argument.

cake *n.* A sweet, baked dessert food made from flour, eggs, and shortening. *v.* To coat or cover over with a layer. **caked** *adj.*

ca·lam·i·ty *n.* Misfortune or great distress; a disaster. **calamitous** *adj.*, **calamitously** *adv.*

cal·ci·fy *v.* To become or make chalky or stony. **calcification** *n.*

cal·ci·um *n.* The alkaline element found in teeth and bones; the element symbolized by Ca.

cal·cu·late *v.* To figure by a mathematical process, to evaluate; to estimate. **calculable** *adj.*

cal·cu·lat·ed *adj.* Worked out beforehand with careful estimation.

cal·cu·lat·ing *adj.* Shrewdly considering one's self-interest; acting from a thought-out design.

cal·cu·la·tor *n.* A machine with a keyboard for automatic mathematical operation.

cal·cu·lus *n.* The mathematics of integral and differential equations; a stone in the gallbladder or kidneys.

cal•dron *n.* A large boiler or kettle; a cauldron.

cal•en•dar *n.* A system for showing time divisions by years, months, weeks, and days; the twelve months in a year; a printed sheet or book divided into days, weeks, and months.

calf *n.* The young offspring of the domestic cow; the young of large animals as the whale and elephant. **calves** *pl.*

cal•i•ber *n.* The inner diameter of a tube or gun; the quality or worth of something.

cal•i•per *n.* An instrument with two curved, hinged legs, used to measure inner and outer dimensions.

cal•is•then•ics *n.* Exercises that develop muscular tone and promote good physical condition.

call *v.* To speak out to someone; to shout; to name or designate; to telephone.

cal•lig•ra•phy *n.* The art of writing with a pen using different slants and positions.

call•ing *n.* The occupation or profession of a person; one's chosen life work; a natural tendency toward a talent or skill.

cal•lous *adj.* Having calluses; without emotional feelings; hardened or insensitive.

calm *adj.* Absent of motion; having little or no wind, storms, or rough water; even-tempered; judicious.

cal•o•rie *n.* A measurement of the amount of heat or energy produced by food. **caloric** *adj.*

cam *n.* A curved wheel used to produce a reciprocating motion; an off-center portion of a rotating shaft which converts circular to vertical motion.

ca•ma•ra•de•rie *n.* Good will among friends.

cam•ber *n.* A slight curve upward in the middle.

came *v.* Past tense of *come.*

cam•el *n.* A large ruminant mammal used in desert regions as transportation and as a beast of burden, having either one (dromedary) or two (bactrian) humps on its back.

cam•e•o *n.* A gem usually cut with one layer contrasting another, serving as a background; a brief appearance by a famous performer in a single scene on a television show or in a movie.

cam•er•a *n.* An apparatus for taking photographs in a lightproof enclosure with an aperture and shuttered lens through which the image is focused and recorded on photosensitive film.

cam•ou•flage *v.* To disguise by creating the effect of being part of the natural surroundings. *n.* Material or process that disguises.

camp *n.* A temporary lodging or makeshift shelter; a military bivouac; an outdoor-oriented recreational area accommodating groups, especially youth, in organized activities.

cam•paign *n.* An organized operation designed to bring about a particular political, commercial, military, or social goal; a long-range project of the will.

camp•er *n.* A person who camps in makeshift shelters for recreation; a vehicle equipped for casual travel and camping.

camp•fire *n.* An outdoor fire used for cooking and heat while camping, making use of fuel such as twigs and branches.

camp•ground *n.* A specially prepared area for camping; a campsite.

camp•site *n.* The area used for camping.

cam•pus *n.* The buildings and grounds of a college, school, or university.

can *v.* To be able to; to know how to do something; to be physically or mentally able; to have the ability to do something; to preserve fruit or vegetables by sealing in an airtight container; to release from employment suddenly. *n.* An airtight container.

ca•nal *n.* A man-made water channel for irrigating land; a waterway built through land, connecting two bodies of navigable water.

ca•nar•y *n.* A green or yellow songbird popular as a caged pet; a wild finch, brown in winter, turning yellow in spring.

can•cel *v.* To invalidate or annul; to cross out; to neutralize; to abort or stop a procedure or program; in mathematics, to remove a common factor from the numerator and the denominator of a fraction. **cancellation** *n.*

can•cer *n.* A malignant tumor that invades healthy tissue and spreads to other areas; the disease marked by such tumors. **cancerous** *adj.*

can•de•la•bra *n.* A decorative candlestick with several branching arms for candles. **candelabrum** *sing.*

can•did *adj.* Spoken or expressed without regard for subtleties of feelings or reactions; free from bias, malice, or prejudice; honest and sincere.

can•di•date *n.* A person who aspires to or is nominated or qualified for a membership, award, or office; one of a group of possible choices.

can•dor *n.* Straightforwardness; frankness of expression.

can•dy *n.* A confection made from sugar and flavored in a variety of ways. *v.* To preserve, cook, coat, or saturate with syrup or sugar. **candied** *adj.*

cane *n.* A pithy or hollow, flexible, jointed stem of bamboo or rattan split for basketry or wickerwork; a walking stick or other aid to mobility; a crutch for one hand; the stalk of the sugar plant.

ca•nine *adj.* Relating to or resembling a dog; of the dog family.

can•is•ter *n.* A container made of thin metal, used to store dry foods, such as flour, sugar, coffee, and tea.

canned *adj.* Preserved and sealed under pressure; artificial; recorded in advance; *slang* Fired or relieved of employment.

can•ner•y *n.* A company that processes canned meat, vegetables, and other foods.

can•ni•bal *n.* Any animal who survives by eating one of its own kind; a person who survives by eating the flesh of human beings; member of certain primitive tribes whose rituals include the token consumption of human flesh.

can•non *n.* A heavy war weapon made of metal and mounted on wheels or a base for discharging projectiles.

can•non•ball *n.* An iron projectile fired from a cannon.

can•ny *adj.* Thrifty; careful; cautious; shrewd.

ca•noe *n.* A lightweight, slender boat with pointed ends which moves by paddling. **canoe** *v.*, **canoeist** *n.*

can•on *n.* The laws established by a church council; a priest serving in a collegiate church or cathedral. **canonical** *adj.*

can•on•ize *v.* To officially declare a deceased person a saint.

can•o•py *n.* A cloth covering used as ornamental protection over a bed or other structure; the supporting surface of a parachute.

can't *contr.* Contraction of *cannot*.

can•ta•loupe *n.* A sweet-tasting, orange-colored muskmelon.

can•tan•ker•ous *adj.* Bad-tempered and argumentative. **cantankerously** *adv.*

can•teen *n.* A small metal container for carrying water or other drinking liquids; a place where refreshments are sold or served.

can•ter *n.* An easy lope just a little slower than a gallop, but faster than a trot.

can•ti•lev•er *n.* A long structure, such as a beam, supported only at one end.

can•vas *n.* A heavy fabric used in making tents and sails for boats; a piece of such material, or any surface, used for oil paintings.

can•vass *v.* To travel through a region to solicit opinions or votes; to take a poll or survey. **canvasser** *n.*

can•yon *n.* A deep and narrow gorge with steep sides.

cap *n.* A covering for the head, usually brimless and made of a soft material; the top of any container; the final or finishing touch to something; a small explosive charge enclosed in paper and detonated by compression; a small portion; a capsule. **capped** adj.

ca•pa•ble adj. Having the ability to perform in an efficient way; qualified; able. **capability** n., **capably** adv.

ca•pa•cious adj. Roomy; spacious; cavernous.

ca•pac•i•ty n. The ability to contain, receive, or absorb; the aptitude or ability to do something; the maximum production or output.

cap•il•lar•y n. Any of the small vessels that connect the veins and arteries. adj. Having a hair-like bore; very fine or small in size.

cap•i•tal n. The town or city designated as the seat of government for a nation or state; material wealth in the form of money or property used to produce more wealth; funds contributed to a business by the stockholders or owners; net worth of a company or business; an uppercase letter.

cap•i•tal•ism n. The economic system in which the means of distribution and production are privately owned and operated for private profit.

cap•i•tal•ist n. A person who invests in a business. **capitalistic** adj.

ca•pit•u•late v. To surrender under terms of an agreement; to give in to demands.

cap•puc•ci•no n. A hot drink of espresso coffee mixed with hot milk and cinnamon.

cap•size v. To overturn in a boat or ship.

cap•sule n. A small gelatinous case for a dose of oral medicine; a close vehicle housing vital material in a rocket launch; a summary or abstract in a brief form. **capsular** adj.

cap•tain n. The chief leader of a group; the commander or master of a ship; the commissioned naval officer ranking below a commodore or rear admiral.

cap•tion n. A subtitle; a description of an illustration or picture.

cap•tious adj. Deceptive; critical.

cap•ti•vate v. To hold in captivity by attention or emotional influence; to hold the attention, fascinate, or charm a person or group of people.

cap•tive n. A person being held as a prisoner. adj. Held as a captive; captivated.

cap•ture v. To take something or someone by force; to hold after flight. **capturer** n.

car n. An automobile; an enclosed vehicle, as a railroad car.

ca•rafe n. A glass bottle for serving wine or water.

car•a•mel n. A chewy substance primarily composed of sugar, butter, and milk.

car•at n. The unit of weight for gems that equals 200 milligrams.

car•a•van n. A group of people traveling together; a recreational vehicle or trailer for itinerant living.

car•bine n. A short-barreled rifle, light in weight.

car•bo•hy•drate n. A group of compounds, including starches, celluloses, and sugars that contain carbon, hydrogen, and oxygen; one of the essential food groups.

car•bon n. A nonmetallic element that occurs as a powdery noncrystalline solid; the element symbolized by C; the single essential element in carbon-based life forms; the required common substance in organic chemistry.

car•bon•ate v. To add or charge with carbon dioxide gas, as in a beverage.

car•bu•re•tor n. The device in gasoline engines that mixes vapor, fuel, and air for efficient combustion.

car•cass n. The dead body of an animal; something that no longer has life.

car•ci•no•gen•ic adj. Causing or leading to conditions that cause cancer.

car•ci•no•ma n. A malignant tumor; cancer.

card n. A small piece of pasteboard or very stiff paper, used in a wide variety of ways, as a greeting card, a business card, a postcard, and the like; one of a deck of playing cards; a comic person.

card cat•a•log n. An alphabetical catalog of books, composed of individual cards for each book, found in libraries.

car•di•ac *adj.* Relating to the heart.

car•di•gan *n.* A sweater with an opening down the front.

car•di•nal *adj.* Of prime importance; principal; of a number, simple and used for counting.

car•di•ol•o•gy *n.* The study of the heart, its diseases, and treatments. **cardiologist** *n.*

care *n.* A feeling of concern, anxiety, or worry; guardianship or custody; attendance on one's needs or desires, especially of the ill. *v.* To show interest or regard; to concern oneself; to have an emotional reaction toward; [with *for*] to tend or minister to; to have affection for.

ca•reen *v.* To lurch or twist from one side to another while moving rapidly; to turn a boat's hull up, for cleaning or repair.

ca•reer *n.* The profession or occupation a person takes in life; a professional or life-long compensation-earning activity.

care•free *adj.* Free from all cares, worries, and concerns; unworried or unburdened.

care•ful *adj.* Exercising care; cautious; watchful; acting with great attention to detail and subtlety; safe or conscious of preventing damage or injury.

ca•ress *v.* To show affection or admiration by gentle touching or stroking; to pet; to touch in a romantic manner. **caress** *n.*

car•go *n.* Freight; the goods carried on a ship, plane, or other vehicle.

car•nage *n.* A bloody slaughter; war; massacre.

car•nal *adj.* Relating to sensual desires. **carnality** *n.*

car•na•tion *n.* A fragrant perennial flower in a variety of colors, often used as a decoration in a man's lapel.

car•ni•val *n.* A traveling amusement show with side shows, rides such as a ferris wheel, and merry-go-rounds; any kind of a happy celebration.

car•ni•vore *n.* A flesh-eating animal. **carnivorous** *adj.*

ca•rouse *v.* To be rowdy and in a drunken state. **carouser** *n.*

car•ol *n.* A song to celebrate joy or praise, especially Christmas. **caroler** *n.*, **carol** *v.*

ca•rou•sel *n.* A merry-go-round; a child's ride consisting of a menagerie of life-sized carved animals moving around an axis. **carrousel** *var.*

carp *v.* To find unreasonable fault with something or someone; to complain unduly. *n.* A freshwater fish that contains many small bones but can be eaten with caution; a goldfish.

car•pen•ter *n.* A person who builds and repairs wooden structures. **carpentry** *n.*

car•pet *n.* A thick woven or felt floor covering that insulates and protects the floors. **carpeting** *n.*

car•rot *n.* An orange root vegetable.

car•ry *v.* To transport from one place to another; to bear the burden, weight, or responsibility of; to keep or have available for sale; to move a digit to the next decimal place in addition or multiplication; to travel over a long distance, as sound.

cart *n.* A two-wheeled vehicle for moving heavy goods; a small lightweight vehicle that can be moved around by hand.

car•tel *n.* A group of independent companies organized to control prices, production, or distribution

car•ti•lage *n.* A tough, elastic substance of connective tissue attached to the surface of bones near the joints.

car•tog•ra•phy *n.* The art of developing charts and maps. **cartographer** *n.*

car•ton *n.* A container made from cardboard or corrugated material, of various sizes, for transport and storage.

car•toon *n.* A caricature depicting a humorous situation; animated pictures produced by photographing a series of action drawings; a humorous, illustrated story in one or several panels; a comic strip. **cartoonist** *n.*

car•tridge *n.* A case made of metal, pasteboard, or other material, that contains a charge of powder; an inexpensive reel for audio or video tape operation.

cart•wheel *n.* A sideways handspring with the arms over the head and the legs spread like the spokes of a wheel.

carve *v.* To slice meat or poultry; to cut into something; to create by shaping material, as sculpture.

cas•cade *n.* A waterfall that flows over steep rocks.

case *n.* A particular occurrence or instance; an injury or disease; a box or housing to carry things in, as a briefcase; in the law, a suit of action brought against a person.

cash•ew *n.* A tropical American tree that produces an edible nut that can be eaten raw or roasted.

cash•ier *n.* An employee who handles cash as part of the job description; an officer in a bank in charge of receiving or distributing money.

cash•mere *n.* The wool from the Kashmir goat; the yarn from this wool.

cas•ing *n.* A protective covering or container; the framework of a window or door.

ca•si•no *n.* A public establishment open especially for gambling.

cask *n.* A large wooden vessel or barrel; the quantity that a cask will hold.

cas•ket *n.* A coffin; a small chest or box.

cas•sette *n.* A cartridge of magnetic tape used in tape recorders to play and record.

cast *v.* To hurl or throw with force; to direct or turn; to shed; to give a certain part or role; to deposit or give a vote on something; to make or throw, as with a fishing line. *n.* A dressing made from plaster of paris used on a broken bone.

cast•a•way *n.* One who is shipwrecked or discarded.

caste *n.* A social separation based on a profession, hereditary, or financial hierarchy.

cast•er *n.* A small set of swiveling rollers fastened under pieces of furniture and the like.

cas•ti•gate *v.* To punish or criticize severely. **castigation, castigator** *n.*

cast•ing *n.* The act of one who casts; the assignment of roles in a dramatic work.

cas•tle *n.* A fort or fortified dwelling for nobility; any large house or place of refuge; a stronghold.

cast-off *adj.* Discarded; thrown away. *n.* A thing discarded.

cas•trate *v.* To remove the testicles; to remove the ovaries; to spay. **castration** *n.*

ca•su•al *adj.* Informal; occurring by chance; relaxed. **casually** *adv.*, **casual-ness** *n.*

ca•su•al•ty *n.* One who is injured or killed in an accident; a soldier who is killed, wounded, taken prisoner by the enemy, or missing in action.

cat *n.* A small domesticated animal of the feline family, a pet; any animal in the cat family, such as the lion, lynx, or tiger.

cat•a•clysm *n.* A sudden and violent disaster. **cataclysmic, cataclysmal** *adj.*

cat•a•comb *n.* An underground passage with small rooms for coffins.

cat•a•log *n.* A publication containing a list of names, objects, and the like; a book of items for sale; a list of offerings, as in a college.

cat•a•lyst *n.* Any substance that alters or decreases the time of a chemical reaction without altering its own chemical composition.

cat•a•ma•ran *n.* A boat with twin hulls.

cat•a•pult *n.* An ancient military device for throwing arrows or stones; a device for launching aircraft from the deck of a ship.

cat•a•ract *n.* A large waterfall or downpour; a disease of the lens of the eye, causing total or partial blindness.

ca•tas•tro•phe *n.* A terrible and sudden disaster; a cataclysm. **catastrophic** *adj.*

catch *v.* To take; to grasp from flight; to seize or capture; to reach in time; to intercept; to become entangled or fastened.

catch•er *n.* A person who catches a ball, specifically the receiver of a pitched ball.

cat•e•gor•i•cal *adj.* Absolute; certain; related to or included in a category without qualification.

cat•e•go•rize v. To place in categories.

cat•e•go•ry n. A general group to which something belongs; a taxonomical branch of related entries.

ca•ter v. To provide a food service; to bring directly to a location; to attend to diligently; to indulge. **caterer** n.

cat•er•pil•lar n. The very fuzzy, worm-like, brightly-colored spiny larva of a moth or butterfly, often destructive of foliage, and encased in a cocoon during metamorphosis.

ca•the•dral n. A large and important church, containing the seat of a bishop.

CAT scan abbr. Computerized axial tomography; a cross-sectional picture produced by a scanner, used to x-ray the body.

cat•tle pl. n. Farm animals, especially bovines, raised for meat and dairy products.

cau•cus n. A meeting of a political party to make policy decisions and select candidates.

cau•li•flow•er n. A vegetable related to broccoli and cabbage.

caulk v. To seal seams and edges against leakage of water and air.

cause v. To produce a result, consequence, or effect. n. A goal, principle; a reason; motive; a project of the will. **causer** n.

cause•way n. A paved highway through a marsh tract; raised road over water.

cau•ter•ize v. To sear or burn with a hot instrument. **cauterization** n.

cau•tion n. A warning advising careful planning or procedure. **caution** v.

cau•tious adj. Very careful.

cav•al•cade n. A group of horse-drawn carriages or riders, forming a procession.

cav•a•lier n. A very gallant gentleman; a knight.

cav•al•ry n. Army troops trained to fight on horseback or in armored vehicles.

cave n. An underground tomb or chamber with an opening at the ground surface; any underground space.

ca•vern n. A very large underground cave. **cavernous** adj.

cav•i•ar n. The eggs of large fish, eaten as an appetizer.

cav•i•ty n. A decayed place in a tooth; a hollow or hole; any indentation or crevice.

CD abbr. Compact disk.

cease v. To come to an end or put an end to; to stop; to halt.

cease•fire n. An action or agreement to stop fighting, usually the first step in a truce or temporary halt in aggression.

cease•less adj. Endless. **ceaselessly** adv.

ce•dar n. An evergreen tree with fragrant, reddish wood.

ceil•ing n. The overhead covering of a room; the maximum limit to something.

cel•e•brate v. To observe with ceremonies, rejoicing, or festivity; to enjoy the achievement of. **celebration** n.

cel•eb•ri•ty n. A famous, notorious, or well-known person; the condition of being widely recognized.

cel•er•y n. A green vegetable with an edible stalk.

ce•les•tial adj. Heavenly; spiritual; pertaining to astronomy.

cel•i•bate n. A person who remains unmarried because of religious vows; one who is sexually abstinent. **celibacy** n., **celibate** adj.

cell n. A prison; a small room; the smallest unit of any organism capable of independent function, composed of a small mass of cytoplasm, usually enclosing a central nucleus, and surrounded by a membrane or a rigid cell wall; the part of a battery that generates the electricity.

cel•lar n. An underground area, beneath a building, used for storage; a basement room.

cel•lo n. A violoncello; a bass instrument of the violin family, held on the floor and played by bowing or plucking. **cellist** n.

cel•lo•phane n. A transparent paper-like material made from treated cellulose that has been processed in thin, clear strips.

cel•lu•lar adj. Consisting of or pertaining to cells.

cement

ce•ment *n*. A construction material made up of powdered, calcined rock and clay materials which, when added with water, set up as a hard, solid mass.

cem•e•ter•y *n*. A place for burying the dead; a graveyard.

cen•sor *n*. A person who examines documents, films, or printed materials to determine what might be objectionable and remove it before distribution. **censorship** *n*.

cen•sure *n*. An expression of criticism and/or disapproval; a public admonishment by a group to one of its members.

cen•sus *n*. An official count of the population; usually at regular intervals; any survey of opinion or attitude.

cent *n*. One; one hundredth of a dollar; a penny.

cen•ter *n*. The place of equal distance from all sides; the point in a circle equidistant from all points on the circumferential arc of the circle; the heart.

cen•ti•pede *n*. A flat arthropod with numerous (literally, a hundred) body segments and legs.

cen•tral *adj*. In, near, or at the center; of primary importance. **centralize** *v*.

cen•tri•fu•gal *adj*. Moving or directing away from a center location.

cen•tri•pe•tal *adj*. Moving inward or toward the center location.

cen•tu•ry *n*. A period consisting of 100 years.

ce•ram•ic *adj*. Of or relating to a brittle material made by firing a nonmetallic mineral, such as clay.

ce•ram•ics *n*. The art of making a ceramic piece.

ce•re•al *n*. An edible grain eaten as a breakfast food; any grain product or crop.

cer•e•bel•lum *n*. The part of the brain responsible for the coordination of voluntary muscular movements.

cer•e•brum *n*. The brain structure divided into two cerebral hemispheres and occupying most of the cranial cavity.

cer•e•mo•ni•al *adj*. Mark by or relating to

a ceremony. **ceremonially** *adv*.

cer•e•mo•ny *n*. A ritual or formal act performed in a certain manner; a public procedure acknowledging or finalizing an official act.

cer•tain *adj*. Very sure; without any doubt; inevitable; not mentioned but assumed; lacking the possibility of alteration. **certainly** *adv*.

cer•tif•i•cate *n*. A document stating the truth or accuracy of something; a document that certifies fulfillment of duties or requirements, as of a course of study.

cer•ti•fy *v*. To testify in writing that something is true or a fact. **certification** *n*.

ces•sa•tion *n*. The act of stopping or ceasing.

cess•pool *n*. A pit or hole for the collection of drainage from toilets, sinks, and other waste water sources.

chafe *v*. To become sore by rubbing; to irritate.

cha•grin *n*. A feeling of distress caused by disappointment, failure, or humiliation.

chain *n*. A connection of several links; anything that confines or restrains; a combination of linked metal loops, hooks, or other closed forms arranged in a string, giving flexibility without sacrificing strength; any series of events or cause-and-effect occurrences.

chair *n*. A seat with four legs and a back, intended for one person; a seat of office; the person who runs a committee.

chair lift *n*. A chair suspended from cables used to carry people and snow equipment up or down the ski slopes.

chair•per•son *n*. A person of either gender presiding over a committee, board, or other meeting.

chair•wo•man *n*. A female person presiding over a committee, board, or other meeting.

cha•let *n*. A cottage that has a gently sloping and overhanging roof.

chal•ice *n*. A drinking goblet or cup, especially one used in religious rites.

chalk *n*. A soft mineral made from fossil

seashells, used for marking on a surface, such as a slate board. **chalky** *adj*.

chalk•board *n*. A blackboard made from slate, for writing with chalk.

chal•lenge *n*. A demand for a contest; a protest; a difficult endeavor that tests one's abilities. *v*. To call into question; to invite to combat or competition. **challenger** *n*.

cham•ber *n*. A bedroom in a large home; a judge's office; a meeting hall for a legislative body; the compartment of a gun that holds a cartridge about to be fired.

cham•ber•lain *n*. The high-ranking person or official of a royal court; the keeper of the house.

cham•pagne *n*. A white sparkling wine.

cham•pi•on *n*. The holder of first place in a contest; one who defends another person. *v*. To extol or encourage, as a cause.

cham•pi•on•ship *n*. The competition that determines a winner.

chance *n*. The random existence of something happening; a gamble or a risk; a possibility.

chan•cel•lor *n*. The chief director or minister of state in certain countries in Europe.

chanc•y *adj*. Risky; dangerous.

chan•de•lier *n*. A light fixture with many branches for lights suspended from the ceiling.

change *v*. To become or make different; to alter; to mutate; to use to take the place of another; to put on a different wardrobe; to reduce a bill into smaller bills or coins. *n*. Coins; money given back when the payment exceeds the bill. **changeable** *adj*.

chan•nel *n*. The deepest part of a stream, river, or harbor; the course that anything moves through or past; a groove. *pl*. The line of communication, bureaucracy, or instruction.

chant *n*. A melody in which all words are sung on the same note. *v*. To celebrate with a song. **chanter** *n*.

cha•os *n*. Total disorder; the absence of purpose or design; the state of the universe before creation. **chaotic** *adj*.

chap *v*. To dry and split open from the cold and wind; to chafe. *n. slang* A fellow; a man. **chapped** *adj*.

chap•el *n*. A place to worship, usually contained in a church; a small place of meditation or devotion.

chap•er•one *n*. An older person who supervises younger people in social or travel settings.

chap•lain *n*. A member of the clergy who conducts religious services for a group.

chap•ter *n*. One of a major division of a book; a branch of a fraternity, religious order, or society.

char•ac•ter *n*. A quality or trait that distinguishes an individual or group; a person portrayed in a play; a distinctive quality or trait; nobility, integrity, or ethical stability.

cha•rades *pl. n*. A game in which the syllables of words are acted out by players.

char•coal *n*. A carbonaceous material resulting from the imperfect combustion of organic matter, such as wood; material used to draw pictures.

charge *v*. To give responsibility; to ask a price; to accuse; to give power to; to replenish, as a battery; to contain an electrical potential; to record a debt owed; to defer payment for a purchase until receipt of a bill. *n*. Management; custody; supervision; an expense or price; an electrical potential.

char•i•ot *n*. An ancient horse-drawn vehicle used to fight battles; a fine or elaborately decorated horse-drawn vehicle. **charioteer** *n*.

char•i•ty *n*. Money or help given to aid the needy; an organization, fund, or institution whose purpose is to aid those in need; the state of loving generosity.

char•la•tan *n*. One who falsely claims knowledge or a skill not actually in possession.

charm *n*. The ability to delight or please; an inherent power bordering on magic; a small ornament with a special meaning, usually worn on a bracelet or around the neck.

chart *n.* A map, graph, or table that gives information in a form easy to read; a nautical register of depths, distances, aids to navigation, and other details of navigable waters. *v.* To generate, draw, or create a chart; to mark one's anticipated passage on a chart; to plan a voyage or effort.

char·ter *n.* An official document that grants certain privileges and rights; the commission, bylaws, and principles of an organization. *v.* To lease or hire a vehicle, especially a boat or aircraft.

chase *v.* To follow quickly; to pursue; to run after.

chasm *n.* A very deep crack in the earth's surface.

chas·sis *n.* The rectangular framework that supports the body and engine of a motor vehicle or other mechanical assembly.

chaste *adj.* Morally pure; modest; not participating in sexual intercourse.

chas·tise *v.* To severely reprimand; to punish by beating. **chastisement** *n.*

chat *v.* To converse in a friendly manner; to carry on a dialogue without purpose.

chauf·feur *n.* A person hired to drive an automobile for another person.

chau·vin·ism *n.* The unreasonable belief in the superiority of one's own group. **chauvinist** *n.*, **chauvinistic** *adj.*

cheap *adj.* Inexpensive; low in cost; of poor quality.

cheat *v.* To deprive of by deceit; to break the rules; to violate one's own promise.

check *v.* To control or restrain; to examine for correctness or condition; to review for accuracy. *n.* The act of verifying, comparing, or testing; a bill one receives at a restaurant; a written order on one's bank to pay money from funds on deposit; a move in chess which threatens the immediate capture of the king.

check·book *n.* A book containing blank checks for a checking account.

check·er·board *n.* A game board used to play various games, especially checkers; a pattern arranged like a checkerboard.

check·ers *pl. n.* A board game played by two people on a red-and-black checkered board, in which pieces are moved, jumped, and captured; the pieces of the game.

check·mate *n.* The move in chess which places the opponent's king in a position from which escape is impossible.

check·up *n.* A complete physical wellness examination.

ched·dar *n.* A firm, smooth cheese ranging in flavor from mild to sharp.

cheek *n.* The fleshy part of the face just below the eye and above and to the side of the mouth.

cheep *v.* To utter high-pitched sounds. *n.* A young or small bird's sound.

cheer *v.* To give courage to; to instill with courage or hope; to make glad or happy; to shout with encouragement or applause. *n.* Good spirits; happiness.

cheer·ful *adj.* Having or being in good spirits; merry; happy; outwardly positive.

cheer·lead·er *n.* Someone who leads cheers at a sporting event; one who encourages the effort of another.

cheese *n.* A food made from the curd of milk, seasoned and aged.

cheese·cake *n.* A cake made from cream cheese, cottage cheese, eggs, and sugar.

cheese·cloth *n.* A loosely-woven cotton gauze, used in the manufacture of cheese from milk.

chef *n.* A cook who manages a kitchen or supervises a restaurant's cuisine.

chem·i·cal *adj.* Of or related to chemistry; in the nature of molecular and atomic interaction.

chem·ist *n.* A person trained in the science of chemistry; a pharmacist.

chem·is·try *n.* The scientific study of the composition, structure, and properties of substances and their reactions on the molecular level.

cher·ish *v.* To treat with love; to hold dear; to respond with deep emotion and a sense of ownership or belonging.

cher·ry *n.* A fruit tree bearing a small, round, deep, or purplish red fruit with a small, hard stone; the fruit of that tree.

cher•ub *n.* A beautiful young child with angelic features or disposition; a representation of an angel resembling a child with a rosy face and wings.

chess *n.* A game played on a chessboard by two people, each with sixteen pieces of various properties, in which one tries to put the opponent's king in checkmate.

chess•board *n.* A board with sixty-four squares used to play chess or checkers.

chest *n.* The part of the upper body enclosed by the thorax; the ribs; a box for storage, usually having a hinged lid.

chest•nut *n.* A tree bearing edible reddish-brown nuts; a nut from a chestnut tree.

chev•ron *n.* An insignia or emblem consisting of stripes that meet at an angle, indicating rank, length of service, or merit.

chew *v.* To crush or grind with the teeth; to masticate. *n.* The act of chewing.

chick•en *n.* A domestic fowl; the edible meat of a chicken.

chide *v.* To scold or find fault.

chief *n.* The person of highest rank. *adj.* Main, major, most important. **chiefly** *adv.*

chief•tain *n.* The head of a group or tribe.

child *n.* A young person of either sex; an adolescent; a person between infancy and youth. **childish** *adj.*, **children** *pl.*

child a•buse *n.* Sexual or physical maltreatment of a child by a guardian, parent, or other adult.

child•birth *n.* The act of giving birth.

child•hood *n.* The period of being a child.

chil•i *n.* A hot pepper; a sauce made with meat and chili or chili powder; a nonmeat dish of beans, tomatoes, chili powder, onions, and other ingredients.

chill *v.* To be cold, often with shivering; to reduce to a lower temperature. *n.* A feeling of cold. **chilly** *adj.*

chime *n.* A group or set of bells tuned to a scale. *v.* To announce on the hour, by sounding a chime.

chim•ney *n.* A flue for smoke to escape, as from a fireplace.

chim•pan•zee *n.* An anthropoid ape with large ears and dark brown hair, smaller and more intelligent than the gorilla.

chin *n.* The lower part of the face. *v.* To lift oneself up while grasping an overhead bar until the chin is level with the bar.

chink *n.* A narrow crack; a space or hole in a stone or brick wall.

chip *n.* A small piece that has been broken or cut from another source; a disk used as money in gambling; in computers, an integrated circuit engraved on a silicone substrate.

chip•munk *n.* A burrowing striped rodent of the squirrel family.

chis•el *n.* A tool with a sharp edge used to shape and cut metal, wood, or stone.

chit *n.* A voucher indicating the amount owed for food or drink.

chit•chat *n.* Casual conversation or small talk.

chiv•al•ry *n.* The brave and courteous qualities of an ideal knight; any gentlemanly or courteous behavior, especially if protective or attentive of a woman.

chlo•rine *n.* A greenish-yellow compound used to purify water, bleach, and disinfectant.

chlo•ro•phyll *n.* The green pigment found in deciduous vegetation and plant organisms, necessary to photosynthesis but absent in fall foliage.

choc•o•late *n.* A preparation of ground and roasted cacao nuts, usually sweetened; a candy or beverage made from chocolate.

choice *n.* The act of selection; the opportunity, right, or power to choose; freedom of action; the act of selecting among alternatives. **choose** *v.*

choir *n.* An organized group of singers, usually performing religious or celebratory works in a church.

chok•er *n.* A necklace that fits tightly around the neck.

cho•les•ter•ol *n.* A fatty crystalline

substance derived from bile and present in most gallstones, the brain, and blood cells.

choose *v.* To select or pick out; to prefer; to make a choice; to decide among alternatives. **chosen, choosy** *adj.*

chop *v.* To cut by making a sharp downward stroke; to cut into small pieces.

chop•py *adj.* Rough; irregular; jerky.

chop•sticks *pl. n.* Slender sticks of ivory or wood, Chinese in origin, used in pairs of two as eating utensils.

cho•ral *adj.* Pertaining to, written for, or sung by a choir or chorus. **chorally** *adv.*

chore *n.* A daily task; any task that becomes burdensome over time.

cho•re•og•ra•phy *n.* The creation of a dance routine. **choreograph** *v.*, **choreographer** *n.*

chor•tle *v.* To chuckle with glee, especially in triumph or joy.

cho•rus *n.* A group of people who sing together; repeated verses of a song; the singers and dancers in ancient dramas representing the citizens or other collective body.

cho•sen *adj.* Selected or preferred above all; participle of *choose*.

chow•der *n.* A soup dish made with fish or clams, often having a milk base.

chris•ten *v.* To baptize; to give a Christian name at baptism; to use for the first time. **christening** *n.*

chro•mat•ic *adj.* Relating to color.

chro•mo•some *n.* One of several small bodies in the nucleus of a cell, containing genes responsible for the determination and transmission of hereditary characteristics.

chron•ic *adj.* Frequently recurring; continuing for long periods of time; affected by a disease or condition for a long time. **chronically** *adv.*

chron•i•cle *n.* A record of events written in the order in which they occurred; a history, especially of a sovereign, dynasty, or significant period of time.

chub•by *adj.* Plump; rounded; full-faced.

chuck *v.* To tap or pat affectionately under the chin. *n.* A cut of beef extending from the neck to the ribs.

chuck•hole *n.* A hole in the street or the pavement.

chuck•le *v.* To laugh quietly with satisfaction.

chum *n.* A close friend or pal.

chunk *n.* A thick piece of anything; a large quantity of something; a lump.

church *n.* A building for religious worship, especially a Christian ceremony; a congregation of public Christian worship.

churl *n.* A rude or rustic person. **churlish** *adj.*, **churlishness** *n.*

churn *n.* The container in which cream or milk is beaten vigorously to make butter. *v.* To agitate in a churn in order to make butter; to agitate violently.

chute *n.* An inclined passage on or through which water, coal, or other bulk material may travel to a destination by gravity.

ci•der *n.* The juice from apples, fermented or unfermented.

ci•gar *n.* Rolled tobacco leaves used for smoking.

cig•a•rette *n.* A small amount of tobacco rolled in thin paper for smoking, usually sold in packs of twenty.

cinch *n.* The strap for holding a saddle. *v.* To assure or complete something.

cin•der *n.* A piece of something that is partially burned.

cin•e•ma *n.* A motion picture; a motion picture theater; the art or business of making a motion picture.

cin•e•ma•tog•ra•phy *n.* The art of photographing a motion picture. **cinematographer** *n.*

cin•na•mon *n.* The aromatic inner bark of an Asian tree, used as a spice, reddish brown in color.

ci•pher *n.* The symbol for the absence of quantity; a zero; secret writing that has a prearranged key or scheme.

cir•cle *n.* A process that ends at its starting point; a group of people having a common interest or activity; the definition of all points on a plane equidistant from a center point.

cir•cuit *n.* The closed path through which an electric current flows; any prearranged order of passage or distribution; an area of common activity, as theater.

cir•cu•lar *adj.* Moving in a circle or round-like fashion; relating to something in a circle; of a design or direction similar to a circle.

cir•cu•late *v.* To pass from place to place or person to person; to distribute in a wide area; to follow a circuit; to mingle among a group. **circulation** *n.*

cir•cum•fer•ence *n.* The perimeter or boundary of a circle; the arc described by all points equidistant from the center of a circle; the outer boundaries of any area.

cir•cum•scribe *v.* To confine something within drawn boundaries; to surround.

cir•cum•stance *n.* A physical event or series of events; a fact or condition to be considered when making a decision.

cir•cum•stan•tial *adj.* Incidental; not essential; dependent on circumstances; based entirely on physical evidence.

cir•cum•vent *v.* To outwit or gain advantage; to avoid or go around. **circumvention** *n.*

cir•cus *n.* Entertainment traveling from venue to venue, often under temporary facilities, featuring clowns, acrobats, trained animals, and other acts.

cis•tern *n.* A man-made tank or artificial reservoir for holding rain water.

cit•a•del *n.* A fortress commanding a city; a stronghold.

ci•ta•tion *n.* An official summons from a court; a quotation used in literary or legal material; an honor.

cite *v.* To bring forward as proof; to summon to action; to summon to appear in court.

cit•i•zen *n.* A resident of a town or city, especially one entitled to representation or a vote; a native or naturalized person entitled to protection from a government. **citizenship** *n.*

cit•rus *n.* Any of a variety of trees bearing fruit with thick skins, as limes, oranges, lemons, and grapefruits.

cit•y *n.* An urban self-governed permanently located community of residences and businesses, larger than a town but smaller than a metropolis.

civ•ic *adj.* Relating to or of a citizen, city, or citizenship.

civ•il *adj.* Relating to citizens; reasonable and fair in dealings with others.

ci•vil•ian *n.* A person not serving in the military, as a firefighter, or as a policeman.

ci•vil•i•ty *n.* The condition of shared reasonable exchange of freedoms and responsibilities; mutual respect for individuality of choice along with unity of communal values.

civ•i•li•za•tion *n.* A high level of social, cultural, and political development; the human condition after the establishment of laws, history, and generational adhesion.

civ•i•lize *v.* To bring out of a state of savagery into one of education and refinement.

civ•il rights *pl. n.* Rights guaranteed to citizens, specifically the equal rights afforded to all races, creeds, genders, and countries of origin; the rights provided by the 13th and 14th amendments of the United States Constitution.

claim *v.* To ask for one's due; to take into possession as one's own; to hold to be true; to state that something is true.

clair•voy•ance *n.* The ability to visualize in the mind distant objects or objects hidden from the senses. **clairvoyant** *n.* or *adj.*

clam *n.* Any of various marine and fresh-water bivalve mollusks.

clam•ber *v.* To climb by using both the hands and feet.

clam•my *adj.* Damp, cold, and sticky.

clam•or *n.* A loud noise or outcry; a vehement protest or demand. **clamorous** *adj.*, **clamorously** *adv.*

clamp *n.* A device for holding or fastening together, especially temporarily.

clan *n.* A large group of people related to one another by a common ancestor; a community into whose membership one must be related by blood or marriage to enter.

clan•des•tine *adj.* Kept or done in secrecy for a purpose.

clang *v.* To cause or make a loud, ringing, metallic sound.

clan•gor *n.* A loud series of clangs.

clap *v.* To applaud; to strike the hands together with an explosive sound.

clap•board *n.* A narrow board with one end thicker than the other, used to cover the outside of buildings so as to weatherproof the inside.

clap•per *n.* The part of a bell that hits against the side.

clar•i•fy *v.* To become or make clearer; to explain, enlighten, simplify, or restate. **clarification** *n.*

clar•i•net *n.* A woodwind instrument with a single reed.

clar•i•ty *n.* The state or quality of being clear; purity of vision or sound.

clash *v.* To bring or strike together; to collide; to conflict. *n.* A conflict or combat, usually sudden and shortlived.

clasp *n.* A hook to hold parts of objects together; a grasp or grip of the hands. **clasp** *v.*

class *n.* A group or set of units separated from others by specific traits; a group of students who study the same subject in the same room; students who graduate at the same time; quality of behavior; one's inherited social level or position.

clas•sic *adj.* Belonging in a certain category of excellence; having a lasting artistic worth.

clas•si•cal *adj.* Relating to the style of the ancient Roman or Greek classics; standard and authoritative; not new.

clas•si•cism *n.* A belief in the esthetic principles of ancient Rome and Greece. **classicist** *n.*

clas•si•fy *v.* To arrange or assign items, people, and the like into the same class or category; to organize by traits or properties. **classification** *n.*

clat•ter *v.* To make or to cause a rattling sound.

clause *n.* A group of words which are part of a simple compound, or complex sentence, containing a subject and predicate; a section, paragraph, or partition in a document treating a specific element of an agreement or contract.

claus•tro•pho•bi•a *n.* A fear of small or enclosed places.

claw *n.* A sharp, curved nail on the foot of an animal; the pincer of certain crustaceans, such as the crab or lobster.

clay *n.* A fine-grained, pliable earth that hardens when fired, used to make pottery, bricks, and tiles.

clean *adj.* Free from impurities, dirt, or contamination; neat in habits.

cleanse *v.* To make pure or clean.

clear *adj.* Free from precipitation and clouds; able to hear, see, or think easily; free from doubt or confusion; free from a burden, obligation, or guilt. *v.* To free one's name or reputation from accusations; to make clear. **clearly** *adv.*, **clearness**, **clarity** *n.*

clear•ance *n.* The distance that one object clears another by; a permission to proceed.

cleat *n.* A metal projection that provides support, grips, or prevents slipping.

cleav•age *n.* The process, act, or result of splitting; the cleft a woman displays in low-cut clothes.

cleav•er *n.* A knife used by butchers.

clef *n.* A symbol indicating which pitch each line and space represents on a musical staff.

clem•ent *adj.* Merciful; mild.

cler•gy *n.* The group of men and women ordained as religious leaders and servants of God.

cler•i•cal *adj.* Trained to handle office duties; relating to office maintenance, record-keeping, and similar tasks.

clerk *n.* A worker in an office who keeps accounts, records, and correspondence up to date; a person who works in the sales department of a store.

clev•er *adj.* Mentally quick; showing dexterity and skill.

cli•ent *n.* A person who secures the professional services of another; in computers, a program serviced by another program.

cli•en•tele *n.* A collection of patients, customers, or clients.

cliff *n.* A high, steep edge or face of a rock.

cli•mate *n.* The weather conditions of a certain region generalized or averaged over a period of years; the prevailing atmosphere. **climatic** *adj.*

cli•max *n.* The point of greatest intensity and fullest suspense; the culmination; the dramatic structural peak of a work.

climb *v.* To move to a higher or lower location; to advance in rank or status.

clinch *v.* To secure; to fasten; to settle definitely.

cling *v.* To hold fast to; to grasp or stick; to hold on and resist emotional separation.

clin•ic *n.* A medical establishment connected with a hospital; a center that offers instruction or counseling.

clink *v.* To cause a light ringing sound, as of two glasses touching.

clip *v.* To cut off; to curtail; to cut short. *n.* Something that grips, holds, or clasps articles together; a fast pace or cadence.

clip•per *n.* A sailing vessel that travels at a high rate of speed.

clique *n.* A small and exclusive group of people.

cloak *n.* A loose outer garment that conceals or covers.

clock *n.* An instrument that measures time. *v.* To time with a clock, stopwatch, or other timepiece.

clod *n.* A large piece or lump of earth; a stupid, ignorant person.

clog *v.* To choke up. *n.* A shoe with a wooden sole.

clone *n.* An identical reproduction grown from a single cell of the original; an exact duplicate or match.

close *adj.* Near, as in time, space, or relationship; nearly even, as in competition; fitting tightly. *v.* To shut; to seal; to complete. *n.* The end or final action of a story, musical composition, or other action.

closed *adj.* Not open; lidded, protected; not available for business; private, secretive, or uncommunicative.

clo•ser *n.* A sales person who finalizes transactions.

clos•et *n.* A small cabinet, compartment, or room for storage. *v.* To meet with in private.

close•up *n.* A picture taken at close range; a close view or examination of something.

clot *n.* A thick or solid mass, as of blood.

cloth *n.* A knitted, woven, or matted piece of fabric, used to cover a table; the professional clothing of the clergy. **cloths** *pl.*

clothe *v.* To provide clothes; to cover with clothes; to wrap.

cloud *n.* A visible body of water or ice particles floating in the atmosphere; something that obscures.

clout *n.* A heavy blow with the hand.

clo•ver *n.* A plant with a dense flower and trifoliate leaves, frequented by bees.

clo•ver•leaf *n.* A junction of highways that cross each other at different levels and are connected by curving ramps; the leaf of a clover.

clown *n.* A professional comedian who entertains by jokes, tricks, and jest; a circus comedian who dresses in outlandish costumes and heavy makeup. **clownish** *adj.*

cloy *v.* To make one sick or disgusted with too much sweetness.

club *n.* A heavy wooden stick, used as a weapon; a group of people who have organized themselves with or for a common purpose.

clump *n.* A very thick cluster or group; a dull, heavy sound. *v.* To plant or place in a clump.

clum•sy *adj.* Lacking coordination, grace, or dexterity; not tactful or skillful.

clus•ter *n.* A bunch; a bouquet; a group or gathering, especially spontaneous.

clutch *v.* To seize or attempt to seize and

hold tightly. *n.* A tight grasp; a device for connecting and disconnecting the engine and the drive shaft in the automobile or other mechanism.

clut•ter *n.* A confused mass of disorder; a mess; any unorganized collection of miscellaneous items.

coach *n.* A closed carriage; a bus or large passenger vehicle; a trainer or director of athletics, drama, or other skill.

co•ag•u•late *v.* To clot. **coagulation** *n.*

coal *n.* A mineral composed of fossilized organic matter, mainly carbon, widely used as a natural fuel; an ember or burning carbon substance in a fireplace or stove.

co•a•lesce *v.* To come together or to grow as one.

co•a•li•tion *n.* A temporary alliance.

coarse *adj.* Lacking in refinement; of inferior or low quality; having large particles.

coast *v.* To move without propelling oneself; to use the force of gravity alone; to slide or glide along. *n.* The land bordering the sea.

coat *n.* An outer garment with sleeves, worn over other clothing; a layer that covers a surface. **coat** *v.*, **coating** *n.*

coax *v.* To persuade by tact, gentleness, or flattery.

cob *n.* A male swan; a corncob; a thickset horse with short legs.

cob•ble *v.* To make or repair shoes; to make or put together roughly.

CO•BOL *n.* In computer science, a simple computer programming language.

co•bra *n.* A venomous snake from Asia or Africa whose neck, when excited, dilates into a broad hood.

cob•web *n.* The fine thread from a spider spun into a web and used to catch prey.

co•caine *n.* An alkaloid used as an anesthetic and narcotic.

cock *n.* The adult male in the domestic fowl family; the rooster; the hammer of a firearm and the readiness for firing. *v.* To raise in preparation for hitting; to ready a firearm for firing.

cock•pit *n.* The compartment of an airplane containing the pilot, crew, and operating controls and instruments.

cock•roach *n.* A flat-bodied, fast running, chiefly nocturnal, hard-shelled insect.

co•coa *n.* The powder from the roasted husked seed kernels of the cacao plant.

co•coon *n.* The protective fiber or silk pupal case spun by insect larvae.

cod *n.* A large fish of the North Atlantic, important as food.

cod•dle *v.* To cook just below the boiling point; to simmer; to baby or treat carefully; to indulge.

code *n.* A system of set rules; a set of secret words, numbers, or letters used as a means of communication; in computers, the method of representing information or data by using a set sequence of characters, symbols, or words.

co•dex *n.* An ancient manuscript of the classics or Scriptures; a book form in which pages face each other bound at one end.

co•ed•u•ca•tion *n.* An educational system for both men and women at the same institution. **coeducational** *adj.*

co•erce *v.* To restrain or dominate with force; to compel by law, authority, fear, or force.

co•e•val *adj.* Of the same time period.

co•ex•ist *v.* To exist at the same time or together; to live peaceably with others in spite of differences.

cof•fee *n.* A beverage prepared from ground beans of the coffee tree.

cof•fer *n.* A strongbox or chest made for valuables; one's saving place.

cof•fin *n.* A box in which a corpse is buried.

cog *n.* A tooth or one of a series of teeth on the rim of a wheel in a machine or a mechanical device.

co•gent *adj.* Compelling; forceful; convincing.

cog•i•tate *v.* To think carefully about or to ponder. **cogitation** *n.*

co•gnac *n.* A fine brandy made in France.

cog•nate *adj.* From a common ancestor;

identical or similar in nature; related.

cog•ni•zance *n.* Perception of fact; awareness; recognition; observation.

cog•no•men n. A person's surname; nickname.

co•hab•it *v.* To live together as husband and wife. **cohabitation** *n.*

co•here *v.* To stick or hold together.

co•hort *n.* One of a group of people united in one effort; an accomplice; a colleague in an enterprise or project.

coif *n.* A close-fitting hat worn under a nun's veil; a hairstyle.

coil *n.* A series of connecting rings; part of an electrical system delivering power to a mechanism. *v.* To wind in spirals; to retract into a striking position.

coin *n.* A flat, rounded piece of metal used as money. *v.* To invent or make a new phrase or word.

co•in•cide *v.* To happen at the same time; to agree exactly; to be congruent in all temporal respects.

co•in•ci•dence *n.* Two events happening at the same time by accident but appearing to have some connection.

coke *n.* A solid, carbonaceous fuel made by heating soft coal until some of its gases have been removed; cocaine.

cold *adj.* Having a low temperature; feeling uncomfortable; without sufficient warmth; lacking in affection or desire; frigid; without preparation or rehearsal. *n.* An infection of the upper respiratory tract resulting in coughing, sneezing, and other symptoms.

cold-blood•ed *adj.* Done without feeling; having a body temperature that varies according to the temperature of the surroundings.

cold boot *n.* In computers, the startup of operations performed when power is turned on for the first time each day.

cold cuts *pl. n.* A selection of freshly sliced cold meats.

col•ic *n.* A sharp pain in the abdomen caused by muscular cramps or spasms, occurring most often in very young babies.

col•lide *v.* To come together with a direct impact; to clash; to come into conflict.

col•i•se•um *n.* A large amphitheater used for sporting games.

col•lab•o•rate *v.* To cooperate or work with another person. **collaboration**, **collaborator** *n.*

col•lapse *v.* To fall; to give way; to fold and assume a smaller size; to lose all or part of the air in a lung.

col•lar *n.* The upper part of a garment that encircles the neck, often folded over.

col•late *v.* To compare in a critical fashion; to assemble in correct sequence or order.

col•lat•er•al *adj.* Serving to support; guaranteed by stocks, property, bonds, etc. *n.* Assets held to guarantee a loan or other financial transaction.

col•league *n.* Someone who works in the same profession or official body; a partner of equal rank; a cohort.

col•lect *v.* To gather or assemble; to gather donations or payments. **collectible**, **collection** *n.*

col•lege *n.* An institution of higher education which grants a bachelor's degree; one division of a university.

col•lo•cate *v.* To compare facts and arrange in correct order.

co•lon *n.* A punctuation mark (:) used to introduce an example or series; the section of the large intestine that extends from the cecum to the rectum.

colo•nel *n.* An officer in the armed forces who ranks above a lieutenant colonel and below a brigadier general.

col•o•ny *n.* A group of emigrants living in a new land away from, but under the control of, the parent country; a group of insects, as ants.

col•or *n.* The aspect of things apart from the shape, size, and solidity; a hue or tint caused by the different degrees of light reflected or emitted by them.

col•or•a•tion *n.* The arrangement of different colors or shades.

col•or-blind *adj.* Unable to distinguish colors, either totally or partially.

co•los•sal *adj.* Very large or gigantic in degree or size.

co•los•sus *n.* Something that is very large, as a huge state, thing, or person.

colt *n.* A very young male horse.

col•umn *n.* A decorative or supporting pillar used in construction; a vertical division of typed or printed lines on paper; a regular news or magazine feature, usually by one person.

col•um•nist *n.* A person who writes a newspaper or magazine column.

co•ma *n.* A deep sleep or unconsciousness caused by an illness or injury.

co•ma•tose *adj.* Unconscious.

comb *n.* A toothed instrument made from a material such as plastic used for smoothing and arranging hair or other fibers; the fleshy crest on the head of a fowl. *v.* To search diligently by careful examination.

com•bat *v.* To fight against; to oppose; to contend. *n.* A struggle; a fight or contest especially with armed conflict, as a battle.

com•bi•na•tion *n.* The process of combining or the state of being combined; a series of numbers or letters needed to open certain locks.

com•bine *v.* To unite; to merge. *n.* A farm machine that harvests by cutting, threshing, and cleaning the grain.

com•bus•ti•ble *adj.* Having the capability of burning.

com•bus•tion *n.* A chemical change occurring rapidly and producing heat and light; a burning.

come *v.* To arrive; to approach; to reach a certain position, state, or result; to appear; to come into view.

com•e•dy *n.* A humorous, entertaining performance with a happy ending; a real-life comical situation. **comedian** *n.*

co•mes•ti•ble *n.* Something that is fit to eat.

com•et *n.* A celestial body that moves in an orbit around the sun, consisting of a solid head surrounded by a bright cloud with a long, vaporous conical section called a tail, but actually a stream of particles driven away from the sun.

com•fort *v.* To console in time of grief or fear; to make someone feel better; to help.

com•fort•a•ble *adj.* In a state of comfort; financially secure. **comfortably** *adv.*

com•fort•er *n.* A heavy blanket or quilt; someone who comforts.

com•ic *adj.* Characteristic of comedy; lighthearted or laughable; not serious. *n.* A comedian.

com•ma *n.* The punctuation mark used to indicate separation of ideas or a series in a sentence, or to clarify meaning for the reader.

com•mand *v.* To rule; to give orders; to dominate; to act in charge of a force. *n.* In computers, the instruction that specifies an operation to be performed.

com•mand•ing *adj.* Dominating by size or position.

com•mem•o•rate *v.* To honor the memory of; to create a memorial to. **commemoration** *n.*

com•mence *v.* To begin; to start.

com•mence•ment *n.* A graduation ceremony; the beginning of a project or activity.

com•mend *v.* To give praise; to applaud. **commendable** *adj.*, **commendation** *n.*

com•men•su•rate *adj.* Equal in duration, extent, or size.

com•ment *n.* A statement of criticism, analysis, or observation. **comment** *v.*

com•merce *n.* The exchanging of products or materials; buying and selling.

com•mer•cial *adj.* Of or relating to a product; supported by advertising; business-like in nature. *n.* An advertisement on radio or television.

com•mis•er•ate *v.* To display or feel sympathy for someone.

com•mis•sion *n.* The moneys paid to a person for service in the area of sales; the act of entrusting to another; the command or authorization to act as specified.

com•mit•tee *n.* A group of persons appointed or elected to perform a particular task or function.

com•mode *n.* A movable washstand with storage underneath; a toilet; a low chest of drawers or bureau.

com•mo•di•ous *adj.* Roomy; spacious.

com•mo•dore *n.* A naval officer ranking above a captain and below a rear admiral; the senior captain of a naval squadron or merchant fleet.

com•mon *adj.* Having to do with, belonging to, or used by an entire community or public; usual; ordinary; of the expected variety; vulgar; unrefined.

com•mon de•nom•i•na•tor *n.* A number that can be evenly divided by all the denominators of a set of fractions.

com•mon frac•tion *n.* A fraction with whole numbers in the denominator and numerator.

com•mon law *n.* The unwritten system of law that is based on judicial decisions, customs, and usages.

com•mon•wealth *n.* The common good of the whole group of people; the general population of a political unit.

com•mu•ni•ca•ble *adj.* Capable of being transmitted, as with a disease.

com•mu•ni•cate *v.* To make known; to cause others to partake or share something; to talk or commune with.

com•mu•ni•ca•tion *n.* The act of transmitting ideas through writing or speech; the means to transmit messages between person or places. *pl.* The profession, specialty, or commercial field of communicating.

com•mun•ion *n.* The mutual sharing of feelings and thoughts; a religious fellowship among members of a church.

com•mu•nism *n.* A system of government in which goods and production are commonly owned.

com•mu•ni•ty *n.* A group of people living in the same area and under the same government; a class or group having common interests and likes.

com•mute *v.* To travel a long distance to one's job each day; to exchange or to sub-stitute; to alter a prison sentence from one kind to another.

com•mut•er *n.* One who travels a long distance on a regular basis.

com•pact *adj.* Packed together or solidly united; firmly and closely united.

com•pac•tor *n.* A device for compressing trash into a small mass for disposal.

com•pan•ion *n.* An associate; a close friend or fellow traveller; a partner in life activities; a person employed to accompany or assist another. **companionship** *n.*

com•pan•ion•a•ble *adj.* Friendly; sociable.

com•pa•ny *n.* The gathering of persons for a social purpose; a number of persons associated for a common purpose, as in business; a business or corporation created and maintained for profit of its owners.

com•pa•ra•ble *adj.* Capable of comparison; worthy of comparison; similar. **comparability** *n.*, **comparative** *adj.*

com•pare *v.* To speak of or represent as similar or equal to; to note the similarities or likenesses of.

com•par•i•son *n.* Likeness; similarity; the evaluation or measurement of two entities to detect similarity; the grammatical modification of an adjective to indicate degree or relationship between two quantities or qualities.

com•part•ment *n.* One of the sections into which an enclosed area is divided.

com•pass *n.* An instrument used to determine geographic direction by magnetic attraction or other means; a device shaped like a V used for drawing circles.

com•pas•sion *n.* Deep, sincere, and long-standing sympathy for someone suffering or distressed in some way; an empathetic relationship.

com•pat•i•ble *adj.* Able to function, exist, or live together harmoniously. **compatibility** *n.*

com•pel *v.* To urge or force action.

com•pen•sate *v.* To make up for; to make amends; to pay; to neutralize or counterbalance. **compensation** *n.*,

compensatory *adj.*

com•pete *v.* To vie or contend with others; to engage in a contest or competition.

com•pe•tent *adj.* Having sufficient ability; capable; possessing the necessary skills.

com•pe•ti•tion *n.* The act of rivalry or competing; a trial of skill or ability; a contest among teams or individuals.

com•pet•i•tor *n.* One who competes against another; a company vying for the same business.

com•pile *v.* To put together material gathered from a number of sources; in computer science, to convert a logical language into machine language. **compilation** *n.*, **compiler** *n.*

com•plain•ant *n.* A person filing a formal charge.

com•plaint *n.* An expression of pain, dissatisfaction, or resentment; a cause or reason for complaining; a legal registered grievance to be settled by a court of law.

com•plai•sance *n.* The willingness to please, to oblige. **complaisant** *adj.*

com•ple•ment *n.* Something that perfects, completes, or adds to; a harmonious addition. **complementary** *adj.*

com•plete *adj.* Having all the necessary parts; whole; concluded. *v.* To finish; to make whole; to come to the conclusion of. **completion** *n.*

com•plex *adj.* Consisting of various intricate parts; not simple; containing more than one clause.

com•plex•ion *n.* The natural color and texture of the skin. **complexioned** *adj.*

com•pli•ance *n.* The act of agreeing passively to a request, rule, or demand; the tendency to yield to others; obedience to regulation. **compliant** *adj.*

com•pli•cate *v.* To make or become involved or complex; to introduce a variation.

com•plic•i•ty *n.* An involvement or association with a crime.

com•pli•ment *n.* An expression of praise or admiration; a statement of satisfaction or approval. **complimentary** *adj.*

com•ply *v.* To agree, to consent to, or obey a command or wish.

com•po•nent *n.* A constituent part; one of a series of assembled units performing a task.

com•port *v.* To behave or conduct oneself in a certain way.

com•pose *v.* To make up from elements or parts; to produce or create a song; to arrange, as to typeset. **composer** *n.*

com•posed *adj.* Calm; in control of one's emotion or reaction; centered or balanced.

com•pos•ite *adj.* Made up from separate elements or parts; combined or compounded.

com•po•si•tion *n.* The act of putting together artistic, musical, or literary work; a short essay written for school.

com•post *n.* A fertilizing mixture of decomposed vegetable matter.

com•po•sure *n.* Tranquillity; calm self-possession.

com•pound *n.* The combination of two or more parts, elements, or ingredients; in grammar, a new word composed of two or more words joined with a hyphen or written as a solid word; in chemistry, a definite substance that results from combining specific radicals or elements in certain or fixed proportions. *v.* To combine; to increase.

com•pre•hend *v.* To perceive, to grasp mentally, or to understand fully; to comprise; to include. **comprehension** *n.*, **comprehensible** *adj.*

com•pre•hen•sive *adj.* Large in content or scope; covering all aspects.

com•press *v.* To press together into a smaller space; to condense. *n.* A soft pad, sometimes medicated, for applying cold, heat, moisture, or pressure to a part of the body. **compression** *n.*

com•pres•sor *n.* Something that compresses; a machine used for compressing air to utilize its expansion.

com•prise *v.* To consist of; to be made up of.

com•pro•mise *n.* The process of settling

or the settlement of differences between opposing sides, with each side making concessions.

comp·trol·ler *n.* A person appointed to examine and verify accounts.

com·pul·sion *n.* The act or state of being compelled; an irresistible urge or impulse to act, especially irrationally. **compulsive** *adj.*

com·pute *v.* To ascertain or determine by the use of mathematics; to determine something by the use of a computer.

com·put·er *n.* A person who computes; a high-speed electronic machine for performing logical calculations, processes, storage, and retrieval of programmed information.

com·put·er lan·guage *n.* The various codes and information used to give data and instructions to computers.

com·rade *n.* An associate, friend, or companion who shares one's interest or occupation. **comradeship** *n.*

con·cave *adj.* Hollowed and curved inward.

con·ceal *v.* To keep from disclosure, sight, or knowledge; to hide.

con·cede *v.* To grant or yield to a right or privilege; to acknowledge as true. **concession** *n.*

con·ceive *v.* To become pregnant; to create a mental image. **conceivable** *adj.*

con·cen·trate *v.* To give intense thought to; to draw to a common point; to intensify by removing certain elements; to become compact.

con·cen·tra·tion *n.* The state of being concentrated or the act of concentrating; the process or act of giving complete attention to a problem or task; total absorption in a mental or physical activity.

con·cept *n.* A generalized idea formed from particular instances; an abstraction; an opinion. **conceptual** *adj.*

con·cep·tion *n.* The union of sperm and egg; a mental thought or plan.

con·cern *n.* Something to consider; sincere interest; something that affects one's business or affairs; an important element in one's attention. *v.* To be interested in; to be involved with. **concerned** *adj.*

con·cert *n.* A musical performance for a group of people; agreement in purpose, action, or feeling.

con·cer·to *n.* A musical composition, usually in three parts, featuring one or more solo instruments along with an orchestra.

con·ces·sion *n.* The act of conceding; something that has been conceded; a tract of land that is granted by a government for a particular use.

conch *n.* A tropical marine mollusk having a large spiral shell and edible flesh.

con·cil·i·ate *v.* To win over or to gain a friendship. **conciliation, conciliator** *n.*, **conciliatory** *adj.*

con·cise *adj.* Short and to the point; brief.

con·clave *n.* A private or secret meeting; the private meeting of the Roman Catholic cardinals to elect a new pope.

con·clude *v.* To close or bring to an end; to bring about an agreement; to arrive at a decision; to resolve. **conclusion** *n.*

con·clu·sive *adj.* Putting an end to any questions or doubt.

con·coct *v.* To make by combining ingredients; to devise or plan. **concoction** *n.*

con·com·i·tant *adj.* Accompanying; adjoining or connected.

con·cord *n.* Accord; harmony; friendly and peaceful relationships.

con·cor·dance *n.* A condition of concord or agreement; the alphabetical index of major words used by an author, listed in the order of use in a book.

con·crete *adj.* Pertaining to a specific instance or thing; naming a specific class of things; real and measurable; actual; not abstract. *n.* A construction material made from sand, gravel, and cement.

con·cu·bine *n.* A woman living with a man without marriage, but with a financial arrangement. **concubinage** *n.*

con·cur *v.* To agree or express approval; to cooperate; to happen at the same time; to coincide. **concurrence** *n.*

con•cur•rent *adj.* Referring to an event that happens at the same time as another; acting together.

con•cus•sion *n.* A sudden and violent jolt; a violent injury to an organ, especially the brain. **concussive** *adj.*

con•demn *v.* To find to be wrong; to show the guilt; to announce judgment upon; to officially declare unfit for use; to rule as damned.

con•dense *v.* To make more concentrated or compact; to change something from a liquid state to a solid state or from a gaseous to a liquid state; to abstract, summarize, or edit for essentials.

con•di•ment *n.* A relish, spice, or sauce used to season food.

con•di•tion *n.* The mode or state of existence of a thing or person; a circumstance found to be necessary to the occurrence of another; a provision in a contract or will that leaves room for modification or changes at a future date; a medical determination of wellness or illness.

con•di•tion *v.* To train or manipulate in preparation for strenuous activity; to soften to a more malleable state, as leather.

con•di•tion•al *adj.* Tentative; depending on a condition; implying or expressing a condition. **conditionally** adv.

con•di•tioned *adj.* Prepared for a certain process or action by past experience.

con•di•tion•er *n.* An application that improves the usability of a substance.

con•do•min•i•um *n.* A joint ownership; an apartment in which all units are owned separately; a building in which the units are owned by each tenant. **condo** *abbr.*

con•done *n.* To overlook; to forgive; to disregard.

con•du•cive *adj.* Contributing toward or promoting; helpful. **conduce** *v.*

con•duct *v.* To lead and direct a performance of a band or orchestra; to guide or show the way; to lead; to transmit heat, electricity, or sound. *n.* Behavior.

con•duc•tor *n.* A person who conducts a musical ensemble; one who is in charge of a railroad or streetcar; in physics, any substance that conducts light, electricity, heat, or sound.

con•duit *n.* A pipe used to pass electric wires or cable through a solid object; a channel or pipe that water passes through.

cone *n.* A solid body tapered evenly to a point from a base that is circular; a cone-shaped wafer used for holding ice cream.

con•fec•tion•er•y *n.* Candy and sweets as a whole; a store that sells candy and sweets. **confection** *n.*

con•fed•er•a•cy *n.* The union of eleven southern states that seceded from the United States during the Civil War of 1861-1865 and established the Confederate State of America; any such political or social organization.

con•fed•er•ate *n.* An ally or friend; a person who supports the Confederacy.

con•fer *v.* To consult with another; to hold a conference; to give or grant a title, honor, or other recognition.

con•fer•ence *n.* A formal meeting for discussion; a league of churches, schools, or athletic teams.

con•fess *v.* To disclose or admit to a crime, fault, sin, or guilt; to tell a priest or God of one's sins. **confession** *n.*

con•fes•sion•al *n.* The small enclosure where a priest hears confessions.

con•fet•ti *pl. n.* Small pieces of paper thrown during a happy occasion.

con•fide *v.* To entrust a secret to another. **confidante** *n.*

con•fi•dence *n.* A feeling of self-assurance; trust in the success of an endeavor; a feeling of trust in a person; reliance.

con•fi•den•tial *adj.* Held as a secret; having another's entrusted confidence. **confidentiality** *n.*, **confidentially** *adv.*

con•fig•u•ra•tion *n.* An arrangement of parts or things; the arrangement of elements.

con•fine *v.* To keep within a certain boundary or limit. **confines** *pl.*, **confinement** *n.*

con•firm *v.* To establish or support the

truth of something; to make stronger; to ratify and bind by a formal approval.

con•fir•ma•tion *n*. The act of confirming to show proof; a religious rite that admits a person to full membership in a church.

con•fis•cate *v*. To seize for public use; to officially seize. **confiscation** *n*.

con•flict *n*. A battle; clash; a disagreement of ideas, or interests.

con•form *v*. To be similar in form or character; to adhere to prevailing customs or modes.

con•for•ma•tion *n*. The manner in which something is shaped, structured, or arranged.

con•found *v*. To amaze, confuse, or perplex; to confuse one thing for another.

con•front *v*. To put or stand face to face with defiance; to physically, mentally, or verbally address opposition or impediment directly.

con•fuse *v*. To mislead or bewilder; to jumble or mix up. **confusion** *n*.

con•fute *v*. To prove to be invalid or false. **confutation** *n*.

con•geal *v*. To jell; to solidify; to change from a liquid to a solid form.

con•gen•i•al *adj*. Having similar character habits or tastes; sociable; friendly. **congeniality** *n*.

con•gen•i•tal *adj*. Existing from the time of birth, but not from heredity.

con•gest *v*. To enlarge with an excessive accumulation of blood; to clog. **congestion** *n*., **congestive** *adj*.

con•glom•er•ate *n*. A business consisting of many different companies; gravel that is embedded in cement material.

con•grat•u•late *v*. To acknowledge an achievement with praise; to join others in praise or acknowledgment.

con•grat•u•la•tions *pl. n*. The expression of or the act of congratulating.

con•gre•gate *v*. To assemble together in a crowd.

con•gre•ga•tion *n*. A group of people meeting together, especially for worship.

con•gru•ent *adj*. Agreeing to conform; in

mathematics, having exactly the same size and shape.

con•ic or **con•i•cal** *adj*. Related to and shaped like a cone.

con•jec•ture *n*. A guess or conclusion based on incomplete evidence. **conjecture** *v*.

con•ju•gal *adj*. Pertaining to the relationship or marriage of husband and wife.

con•ju•gate *adj*. To change the form of a verb; to join in pairs.

con•jure *v*. To bring into the mind; to appeal or call on solemnly; to practice magic.

con•nect *v*. To join; to unite; to associate, as to relate.

con•nec•tion *n*. An association of one person or thing to another; a link, or bond.

con•nec•tive *adj*. Capable of connecting; tending to connect. *n*. Something that connects as a word.

con•nive *v*. To ignore a known wrong, therefore implying sanction; to conspire; to cooperate in secret.

con•nois•seur *n*. A person whose expertise in an area of art or taste demonstrates clear judgment; an expert or appreciator of the subtleties of an area; a collector of refinement.

con•no•ta•tion *n*. The associative meaning of a word in addition to the literal meaning. **connotative** *adj*.

con•note *v*. To imply along with the literal meaning.

con•quer *v*. To subdue; to win; to overcome by physical or mental force; to replace a government by physical usurpation of power.

con•science *n*. The ability to recognize right and wrong regarding one's own behavior; the internal sense of self-assessment.

con•sci•en•tious *adj*. Honest; scrupulous; careful; self-disciplined in care or honesty.

con•scious *adj*. Aware of one's own existence and environment; aware of facts or objects; in a state of mental alertness; not comatose.

conscript

con·script *n.* One who is drafted or forced to enroll for a service or a job.

con·se·crate *v.* To declare something to be holy; to dedicate to sacred uses. **consecration** *n.*

con·sec·u·tive *adj.* Following in uninterrupted succession. **consecutively** *adv.*

con·sen·sus *n.* A general agreement; a collective opinion.

con·sent *v.* To agree; to allow; to give approval.

con·se·quence *n.* The natural result from a preceding condition or action; the effect.

con·se·quent *adj.* Following as a natural result or effect. **consequently** adv.

con·se·quen·tial *adj.* Having or showing self-importance. **consequentially** *adv.*

con·serv·a·tive *adj.* Opposed to change; desiring the preservation of the existing order of things; moderate; cautious; wanting to conserve. **conservatively** *adv.*

con·ser·va·to·ry *n.* A school of dramatic art or music; a greenhouse.

con·serve *v.* To save something from decay, loss, or depletion; to maintain; to preserve fruits with sugar; to use a perishable or depletable commodity with thrift and care. *n.* A mixture of several fruits cooked together with sugar and sometimes raisins or nuts.

con·si·der *v.* To think about with some care; to examine mentally; to believe or hold as an opinion; to deliberate.

con·sid·er·a·ble *adj.* Large or substantial in amount or extent; important; worthy of consideration.

con·sid·er·a·tion *n.* The taking into account of circumstance before forming an opinion; care and thought; a kind or thoughtful treatment or feeling.

con·sid·er·ing *prep.* In regard to; taking into account.

con·sign *v.* To commit to the care of another; to deliver or forward, as merchandise; to put aside, as for specific use. **consignee, consignment** *n.*

con·sist *v.* To be made up of.

con·sis·ten·cy n. Agreement or compatibility among ideas, events, or successive acts; the degree of texture, viscosity, or density. **consistent** *adj.*

con·sole *v.* To give comfort to someone. **consolation** *n.*

con·sol·i·date *v.* To combine in one or to form a union of; to form a compact mass. **consolidation, consolidator** *n.*

con·so·nant *n.* A sound produced by complete or partial blockage of the air from the mouth, as the sound of b,f,k,s,t; the letter of the alphabet that represents such a sound. *adj.* In agreement; in harmony.

con·sort *n.* A spouse; companion or partner. *v.* to unite or keep in company.

con·sor·ti·um *n.* An association with banks or corporations that require vast resources.

con·spic·u·ous *adj.* Noticeable. **conspicuously** *adv.*

con·spir·a·cy *n.* A plan or act of two or more persons to do an evil or secret act.

con·spire *v.* To plan a wrongful act in secret; to work or act together. **conspirator** *n.*

con·stant *adj.* Faithful; unchanging; steady in action, purpose, and affection; permanently present. *n.* A quantity whose presence or value remains the same throughout an activity. **constancy** *n.*

con·ster·na·tion *n.* Sudden confusion or amazement.

con·stit·u·en·cy *n.* A group of voters represented by an elected legislator.

con·stit·u·ent *adj.* Having the power to elect a representative. *n.* A necessary element or part.

con·sti·tu·tion *n.* The fundamental laws that govern a nation; structure or composition; health of state or wellness.

con·strain *v.* To restrain by physical or moral means. **constrained** *adj.*, **constraint** *n.*

con·struct *n.* To create, make, or build.

con·struc·tion *n.* The act of constructing or building something; the product of building with materials; an organized and ordered arrangement of ideas or arguments.

con•struc•tive *adj.* Useful; helpful; building, advancing, or improving; resulting in a positive conclusion; not destructive.

con•strue *v.* To interpret; to translate; to guess at the connotations of; to analyze grammatical structure.

con•sul *n.* An official residing in a foreign country and representing the government's political and commercial interests and citizens.

con•sul•ate *n.* The official premises occupied by a consul.

con•sult *v.* To seek advice or information from; to compare views; to use as reference. **consultant, consultation** *n.*

con•sume *v.* To ingest; to eat or drink; to destroy completely; to absorb.

con•sum•er *n.* A person who buys services or goods.

con•sump•tion *n.* Fulfillment; the act of consuming; the quantity consumed; tuberculosis.

con•tact *n.* The place, spot, or junction where two or more surfaces or objects touch; the connection between two electric conductors. *pl.* Contact lenses; connections in a network of influential persons or offices.

con•tact lens *n.* A thin lens of plastic or glass with an optical prescription, worn directly on the cornea of the eye.

con•ta•gion *n.* The transmitting of a disease by contact. **contagious** *adj.*

con•tain *v.* To include or enclose; to restrain or hold back.

con•tain•er *v.* Something that holds or carries, as a box or can.

con•tam•i•nate *v.* To pollute or make inferior by adding undesirable elements; to taint; to infect; to make dirty or to soil. **contamination** *n.*

con•tem•plate *v.* To look over; to ponder; to consider thoughtfully. **contemplation** *n.*, **contemplative** *adj.*

con•tem•po•ra•ne•ous *adj.* Occurring or living at the same time; contemporary.

con•tempt *n.* The act of viewing something as mean, vile, or worthless scorn; legally, the willful disrespect or disregard of authority. **contemptible** *adj.*

con•temp•tu•ous *adj.* Feeling or showing contempt. **contemptuously** *adv.*

con•tend *v.* To dispute; to fight; to debate; to argue. **contender** *n.*

con•tent *adj.* Satisfied; calm and happy; in agreement with prevailing conditions.

con•ten•tion *n.* Competition; rivalry; controversy; argument. **contentious** *adj.*

con•tents *pl. n.* Something contained within; the subject matter of a book or document; the proportion of a specified part.

con•test *n.* A competition; strife; conflict; any activity in which participants can earn or win a prize. *v.* To challenge. **contestant** *n.*

con•text *n.* A sentence, phrase, or passage so closely connected to a word or words that it affects their meaning; the environment in which an event occurs.

con•ti•nent *n.* One of the seven large land masses of the earth: Africa, Asia, Australia, Europe, North America, South America, and Antarctica.

con•ti•nen•tal *adj.* Of or characteristic of a continent.

con•tin•ue *v.* To maintain without interruption a course or condition; to resume; to postpone or adjourn.

con•ti•nu•i•ty *n.* The quality of being continuous; the element of filmmaking calling for logical sequencing of events after editing.

con•tin•u•ous *adj.* Uninterrupted. **continuously** *adv.*

con•tort *v.* To severely twist out of shape.

con•tor•tion•ist *n.* An acrobat who exhibits unnatural body positions.

con•tour *n.* The outline of a body, figure, or mass.

con•tra•band *n.* Illegal or prohibited traffic; smuggled goods.

con•tra•cep•tion *n.* The voluntary

prevention of impregnation. **contraceptive** *adj.*, *n.*

con•tract *v.* To pull in; to become smaller.

con•tract *n.* A formal agreement among two or more parties to perform the duties as stated.

con•trac•tion *n.* The act of contracting; a shortening of a word by omitting a letter or letters and replacing them with an apostrophe (').

con•tra•dict *v.* To say against; to express the opposite side or idea; to be inconsistent.

con•trap•tion *n.* A gadget.

con•trar•y *adj.* Unfavorable; incompatible with another.

con•trast *v.* To note the differences between two or more people or things.

con•tra•vene *v.* To be contrary; to violate; to oppose; to go against.

con•trib•ute *v.* To give something to someone; to submit for publication; to offer without pay or compensation. **contribution** *n.*

con•trite *adj.* Grieving for sin or shortcoming. **contrition** *n.*

con•trol *v.* To have the authority or ability to regulate, direct, or dominate a situation; to enclose inside rules or parameters; to regulate, steer, or limit.

con•tro•ver•sy *n.* A dispute, especially of ideas or ideologies, in which both sides are polarized; a debate; a quarrel. **controversial** *adj.*

co•nun•drum *n.* A riddle with an answer that involves a pun; a question or problem with only a surmise for an answer.

con•va•lesce *v.* To grow strong after a long illness. **convalescence** *n.*, **convalescent** *adj.*

con•vec•tion *n.* The transfer of heat by the movement of air, gas, or heated liquid between areas of unequal density.

con•vene *v.* To meet or assemble formally; to gather for a purpose. **convener** *n.* **con•ven•ience** *n.* The quality of being suitable; something easy to use or made simple to operate.

con•vent *n.* A local house or community of a religious order, especially for nuns.

con•ven•tion *n.* A formal meeting; a regulatory meeting among people, states, or nations on matters that affect all of them.

con•ven•tion•al *adj.* Commonplace, ordinary; expected or assumed from experience.

con•verge *v.* To come to a common point; to move toward intersection in time or space. **convergence** *n.*, **convergent** *adj.*

con•ver•sa•tion *n.* An informal talk, generally void of argument.

con•ver•sion *n.* The act of changing from one state to another; changing to adopt new opinions or beliefs; a formal acceptance of a different religion.

con•vert•i•ble *n.* A car with a top that folds back or can be removed completely.

con•vex *adj.* Curved outward like the outer surface of a ball.

con•vey *v.* To transport; to pass information on to someone else; to conduct.

con•vey•ance *n.* The action of conveying; the legal transfer of property or the document effecting it; a means of transportation.

con•vict *v.* To prove someone guilty; to find for the prosecution in a criminal trial. *n.* A prisoner.

con•vic•tion *n.* The act of being convicted; a strong belief.

con•vince *v.* To cause to believe without doubt; to change another's opinion or point of view.

con•vo•ca•tion *n.* A formal or ceremonial assembly or meeting, especially with speeches. **convoke** *v.*

con•voy *n.* A group of cars, trucks, etc., traveling together. *v.* To escort or guide.

con•vulse *v.* To move or shake violently; to contract, as muscles. **convulsive** *adj.*, **convulsion** *n.*

cook *v.* To apply heat to food before eating; to prepare food for a meal. *n.* A person who prepares food.

cook•book *n.* A book containing directions for preparing and cooking food; a book of recipes.

cook•ie *n.* A sweet, flat cake; a biscuit; in computers, a customized web site feature sent to a browser.

cool *adj.* Without warmth; indifferent or unenthusiastic; neither cold nor lukewarm.

coop *n.* A cage or enclosed area to contain animals, as chickens.

co•op•er•ate *v.* To work together toward a common cause. **cooperation** *n.*

co•or•di•nate *v.* To organize and orchestrate a series of acts toward harmonious completion; to plan a wardrobe or outfit so that it goes well together. *n.* Any of a set of numbers which establishes position on a graph, map, etc. **coordinator**, **coordination** *n.*

cope *v.* To strive; to struggle or contend with something.

cop•i•er *n.* A machine that makes copies of original material.

co•pi•lot *n.* The assistant pilot on an aircraft.

co•pi•ous *n.* Large in quantity; abundant. **copiously** *adv.*

cop•per *n.* A metallic element that is a good conductor of electricity and heat, reddish-brown in color.

cop•y *v.* To reproduce an original; to make a duplicate of; to emulate or imitate. *n.* A single printed text.

cop•y•right *n.* The statutory right to sell, publish, or distribute a literary or artistic work.

cor•al *n.* The stony skeleton of a small sea creature, forming large islands under and just above the surface of tropical seas, often used for jewelry.

cord *n.* A string or twine; an insulated wire used to supply electricity to another source; a measurement for firewood that equals 128 cubic feet; a raised rib of fabric, as corduroy.

cor•dial *adj.* Formal, but warm-hearted and sincere. *n.* A liqueur.

cor•don *n.* A circle of men or ships positioned to guard or enclose an area; an ornamental ribbon or braid worn as an insignia of honor.

core *n.* The innermost or central part of something; the inedible center of a fruit that contains the seeds.

cork *n.* The elastic bark of the oak tree used for bottle stoppers and craft projects.

cork•screw *n.* A pointed metal spiral attached to a handle used for removing corks from bottles.

corn *n.* An American-cultivated cereal plant bearing seeds on a large ear or cob; any grain crop; the seed of this plant.

cor•ne•a *n.* The transparent membrane of the eyeball. **corneal** *adj.*

cor•ner *n.* The point formed when two surfaces or lines meet and form an angle; the location where two streets meet. *v.* To enclose in a corner; to hold; to gain control of.

cor•ner•stone *n.* A stone that forms part of the corner of a building's foundation.

corn•meal *n.* Meal made from corn.

corn•row *v.* To braid the hair in rows very close to the head.

cor•nu•co•pi•a *n.* A curved goat's horn overflowing with flowers, fruit, and corn to signify prosperity.

corn•y *adj.* Trite or mawkishly old-fashioned.

co•rol•la *n.* The petals of a flower.

cor•ol•lar•y *n.* Something that naturally or incidentally follows or accompanies.

cor•o•nar•y *adj.* Of or relating to the two arteries that supply blood to the heart muscles.

cor•po•ral *n.* A noncommissioned officer who ranks above a private first class but below a sergeant. *adj.* Relating to the body.

cor•po•rate *adj.* Combined into one joint body; relating to a corporation.

cor•po•ra•tion *n.* A group of merchants united in a trade guild; any group or persons that act as one; an organization limiting its responsibilities to its own assets and not those of the members.

cor·po·re·al *adj.* Of a physical nature.

corpse *n.* A dead body.

cor·pu·lence *n.* The excessive accumulation of body fat; obesity. **corpulent** *adj.*

cor·pus·cle *n.* A minute particle or living cell, especially as one in the blood.

cor·ral *n.* An enclosure for containing animals.

cor·rect *v.* To make free from fault or mistakes; to change toward rightness; to adjust toward a true course. **correction**, **correctness** *n.*, **correctly** *adv.*

cor·rel·a·tive *adj.* Having a mutual relation.

cor·re·spond *v.* To communicate by letter or written words; to be harmonious, equal or similar.

cor·ri·dor *n.* A long hallway.

cor·rob·o·rate *v.* To support a position or statement with evidence. **corroboration** *n.*

cor·rode *v.* To eat away through chemical action. **corrodible** *adj.*, **corrosion** *n.*, **corrosive** *adj.* or *n.*

cor·rupt *adj.* Dishonest; evil. *v.* To become or make corrupt. **corrupter** *n.*

cor·sage *n.* A small bouquet of flowers worn on a woman's shoulder or wrist.

cor·set *n.* An undergarment tightened with laces and reinforced with stays, worn to give shape and support to a woman's body.

cos·met·ic *n.* A preparation designed to beautify, especially the face.

cos·me·tol·o·gy *n.* The study of cosmetics and their use. **cosmetologist** *n.*

cos·mo·naut *n.* A Soviet astronaut.

co·sign *v.* To sign a document jointly.

cos·mog·o·ny *n.* The creation of the universe.

cos·mo·pol·i·tan *adj.* At home anywhere in the world.

cos·mos *n.* An orderly and harmoniously systematic universe.

cos·set *v.* To pamper; pet.

cost *n.* The amount paid or charged for a purchase.

cost·ly *adj.* Expensive; taking a large expenditure of energy or effort; damaging in its results.

cos·tume *n.* A suit, dress, or set of clothes characteristic of a particular season or occasion; clothes worn by a person playing a part or dressing up in disguise.

cot *n.* A small, often collapsible bed.

cot·tage *n.* A small house; a rural dwelling.

cot·ton *n.* A plant or shrub cultivated for the fiber surrounding its seeds; a fabric created by the weaving of cotton fibers; yarn spun from cotton fibers.

cot·ton can·dy *n.* Spun sugar, served on a paper cone.

couch *n.* A piece of furniture, such as a sofa or bed on which one may sit or recline for rest or sleep. *v.* To phrase in a certain manner; to lie in ambush.

cough *v.* To suddenly expel air from the lungs with an explosive noise. *n.* The harsh sound from clearing one's throat or lungs.

could *v.* Past tense of *can.*

coun·cil *n.* A group of people assembled for consultation or discussion; an official legislative or advisory body.

coun·sel *n.* Advice given through consultation; a lawyer engaged in the management or trial of a court case.

coun·sel·or *n.* One who gives advice; a lawyer.

count *v.* To name or number so as to find the total number of units involved; to name numbers in order; to take account of in a tally or reckoning; to rely or depend on; to have significance.

count·down *n.* An audible counting in descending order to mark the time remaining before an event.

coun·te·nance *n.* The face as an indication of mood or character; bearing or expression that would suggest approval or sanction.

coun·ter *n.* A level surface over which transactions are conducted, on which food is served, or on which articles are displayed. *v.* To move or act in a contrary, or opposing direction or wrong way; to balance with an opposing action.

coun•ter•act *v.* To oppose and, by contrary action, make ineffective.

coun•ter•at•tack *n.* An attack made in response to an enemy attack.

coun•ter•bal•ance *n.* A force or influence that balances another; a weight that balances another.

coun•ter•feit *v.* To closely imitate or copy with the intent to deceive; to forge. *adj.* Marked by false pretense. *n.* Something counterfeit.

coun•ter•mand *v.* To reverse or revoke a command by issuing a contrary order.

coun•ter•point *n.* In music, the combining of melodies into a harmonic relationship while retaining the linear character.

coun•ter•pro•duc•tive *adj.* Tending to hinder rather than aid in the attainment of a goal.

coun•ter•sign *v.* To give a signature confirming the authenticity of a document already signed by another. *n.* A sign or signal given in response to another.

coun•ter•weight *n.* An equivalent weight, used as a counterbalance.

count•ess *n.* The wife or widow of an earl or count; a woman who, in her own right, holds the rank of earl or count.

count•less *adj.* Too many or too numerous to be counted.

coun•tri•fied *adj.* Of or relating to country life; rural; unsophisticated.

coun•try *n.* A given area or region; the land of one's birth, residence, or citizenship; a state, nation, or its territory.

coun•try mu•sic *n.* Music derived from the folk style of the southern United States, or from the culture of the pioneer, cowboy, and adventurer.

coun•ty *n.* A territorial division for local government within a state.

coup *n.* A brilliant, sudden move that joins two things together.

cou•ple *v.* To join two together; to pair. *n.* A pair.

cou•plet *n.* Two rhyming lines of poetry in succession, with the same number of syllables and stresses.

cou•pon *n.* A statement of interest due, to be removed from a bearer bond and presented for payment when it is payable; a form surrendered to obtain a product, service, or discount.

cour•age *n.* Mental or moral strength to face danger with fear; bravery over an extended period.

cou•ri•er *n.* A messenger; a person who carries contraband for another.

course *n.* The act of moving in a path from one point to another; the path over which something moves; a period of time; a series or sequence; a series of studies.

court *n.* The residence of a sovereign or similar dignitary; an assembly for the transaction of judicial business; a place where trials are conducted; an area marked off for game playing.

cour•te•ous *adj.* Marked by respect for and consideration of others; graciously thoughtful and considerate; cognizant of and following the practices of unspoken social etiquette. **courtesy** *n.*

cour•te•san *n.* A prostitute who associates with or caters to high-ranking or wealthy men.

court•house *n.* A building for holding courts of law.

court•i•er *n.* One in attendance at a royal court.

court•yard *n.* An open space enclosed by walls.

cous•in *n.* A child of one's uncle or aunt; any person whose parent was a sibling to one's own parent; a member of a culturally similar race or nationality; a relative.

cove *n.* A small inlet or bay, generally sheltered; a deep recess or small valley in the side of a mountain.

cov•e•nant *n.* A formal, binding agreement; a promise or pledge.

cov•er *v.* To place something on or over; to lie over; to spread over; to guard from attack; to hide or conceal; to act as a stand-in during another's absence. *n.* Any object used to protect or cover.

cov•et *v.* To wish for enviously; to crave possession of that which belongs to someone else.

cow *n.* The mature female of cattle or of any bovine; the female of any species when the adult male is referred to as a bull.

cow•ard *n.* One who shows great fear or timidity. **cowardice** *n.*

cox•comb *n.* A conceited foolish person.

coy *adj.* Quiet or shy, or pretending to be so.

coz•en *v.* To swindle, cheat, deceive, win over, or induce by coaxing or trickery. **cozener** *n.*

co•zy *adj.* Comfortable and warm; snug.

crab•by *adj.* Uncivil, ill-tempered and cross.

crack *v.* To make a loud explosive sound; to break, snap, or split apart; to break open without completely separating; to lose control under pressure (often used with *up*). *n.* A fissure or opening in a long, deep shape; a sharp, witty remark; a weakness caused by decay or age.

crack•le *v.* To make sharp, sudden, repeated noises; to develop a network of fine cracks.

cra•dle *n.* A small bed for infants, usually on rockers or rollers; a framework of support, such as that for a telephone receiver.

craft *n.* A special skill or ability; a trade that requires dexterity or artistic skill; an aircraft, boat, or ship.

crag *n.* A steep jagged rock or cliff. **crag•gy** *adj.*

cram *v.* To pack tightly or stuff; to thrust in a forceful manner; to eat in a greedy fashion; to prepare hastily for an exam.

cramp *n.* A painful involuntary contraction of a muscle; sharp abdominal pain.

cran•ber•ry *n.* A North American shrub which grows in damp soil and bears edible, tart red berries.

crane *n.* A large bird with long legs and a long neck; a machine used for lifting or moving heavy objects. *v.* To strain or stretch the neck.

crank *n.* An arm bent at right angles to a shaft and turned to transmit motion; an eccentric person; a bad-tempered person; a grouch. *v.* To operate or start by crank. **cranky** *adj.*

cran•ny *n.* A small break or crevice; an obscure nook or corner.

craps *v.* A gambling game played with two dice.

crash *v.* To break violently or noisily; to damage in landing, usually a vehicle; to collapse suddenly, usually a business; to cause to make a loud noise. *n.* A collision; in computers, the unplanned termination of a computer operation or program; the failure of a computer to respond.

crass *adj.* Insensitive and unrefined.

crate *n.* A container, usually made of wooden slats, for protection during shipping or storage.

cra•ter *n.* A bowl-shaped depression at the mouth of a volcano; a depression formed by a meteorite; a hole made by an explosion.

cra•vat *n.* A necktie.

crave *v.* To desire intensely. **craving** *n.*

cra•ven *adj.* Completely lacking courage.

crawl *v.* To move slowly by dragging the body along the ground in a prone position; to move on hands and knees.

cray•on *n.* A stick of white or colored wax, covered with paper and ending in a point, used for writing or drawing.

craze *v.* To make insane or as if insane; to become insane; to develop a fine mesh of narrow cracks. *n.* Something that lasts for a short period of time; a fad.

cra•zy *adj.* Insane; impractical; unusually fond; without sense.

creak *n.* A squeaking or grating noise.

cream *n.* The yellowish, fatty part of milk, containing a great amount of butterfat; something having the consistency of cream; the best part; a pale yellow-white color. **creaminess** *n.*, **creamy** *adj.*

crease *n.* A line or mark made by folding

and pressing a pliable substance; a slim space between two guarded areas.

cre•ate *v.* To bring something into existence; to give rise to; to make.

cre•a•tion *n.* The act of creating; something created; the universe.

cre•a•tive *adj.* Marked by the ability to create; inventive; imaginative; artistic. **creativity** *n.*

cre•a•tor *n.* One who creates or has created. *cap.* The Creator; God.

crea•ture *n.* Something created; a living being; a member of the animal kingdom.

cred•i•ble *adj.* Offering reasonable grounds for belief. **credibility, credence** *n.*

cred•it *n.* An amount at a person's disposal in a bank; one's ability to borrow or to buy in advance of payment; recognition by name for a contribution.

cred•u•lous *adj.* Gullible; ready to believe on slight or uncertain evidence.

creed *n.* A belief; a saying or maxim from which one builds one's behavior; a brief authoritative statement of religious belief.

creek *n.* A narrow stream or brook, navigable only by small craft.

creel *n.* A wicker basket for holding fish.

creep *v.* To advance at a slow pace; to go timidly or cautiously; to move on one's knees; to crawl.

cre•mate *v.* To reduce to ashes by burning.

cres•cent *n.* The shape of the moon in its first and fourth quarters, defined with a convex and a concave edge; a curved portion of a sphere.

crest *n.* A tuft or comb on the head of a bird or animal; the top line of a mountain or hill; a helmet or crown.

cre•vasse *n.* A deep crack or crevice.

crev•ice *n.* A narrow crack; a long space between hard surfaces.

crew *n.* A group of people who work together in the operation or completion of a project; the whole company belonging to an aircraft or ship.

crib *n.* A small bed with high sides for an infant; a feeding bin for animals.

crick•et *n.* A leaping orthopteran insect, the male of the species producing a high pitched chirping sound by rubbing the front wings together; a game played with a bat and ball by two teams of eleven players each.

cri•er *n.* One who calls out public notices.

crime *n.* The commission of an act forbidden by law.

crimp *v.* To cause to become bent or crinkled; to pinch in or together.

cringe *v.* To shrink or recoil in fear.

crin•kle *v.* To wrinkle. **crinkly** *adj.*

crip•ple *n.* One who is lame or partially disabled; something flawed or imperfect. *adj.* Being a cripple. *v.* To deprive one of the use of a limb or limbs.

cri•sis *n.* An unstable or uncertain time or state of affairs, the outcome of which will have a major impact; the turning point for better or worse in a disease or fever. **crises** *pl.*

crisp *adj.* Easily broken; brittle; brisk or cold; sharp; clear. *v.* To make or become crisp.

cri•te•ri•on *n.* A standard by which something can be judged. **criteria** *pl.*

crit•ic *n.* A person who is critical; a person who examines a subject and expresses an opinion as to its value; a person who judges or evaluates art or artistic creations, as a theatre critic.

crit•i•cal *adj.* Very important, as a decision; serious, or at the point of most tension.

crit•i•cism *n.* The act of close analysis and examination; discussion of the details of a work or product; severe or negative observation.

crit•i•cize *v.* To be a critic; to find fault with; to judge critically; to blame.

croak *n.* A hoarse, raspy cry such as that made by a frog. *v.* To utter a croak.

crock *n.* An earthenware pot or jar used for cooking or storing food.

croc•o•dile *n.* Any of various large, thick-skinned, long-bodied reptiles of tropical and subtropical regions.

crone *n.* A witch-like, withered old

woman.

crook *n.* A bent or hooked implement; a bend or curve; a person given to dishonest acts. *v.* To bend or curve.

croon *v.* To sing in a gentle, low voice; to make a continued moaning sound.

crop *n.* A plant which is grown and harvested for use or for sale.

cro•quet *n.* An outdoor game played by driving wooden balls through hoops by means of long-handled mallets.

cross *n.* A structure consisting of an upright post and a crossbar; a method of execution used especially by the Romans; a symbol of the Christian religion. *v.* To go over; to intersect; in biology, to interbreed a plant or an animal with one of a different kind. *adj.* Discourteous, or short of patience.

cross•bow *n.* A weapon consisting chiefly of a bow mounted crosswise near the end of a wooden stock.

crotch *n.* The angle formed by the junction of two parts, such as legs or branches.

crouch *v.* To bend at the knees and lower the body close to the ground.

croup *n.* A spasmodic laryngitis, especially of children, marked by a loud, harsh cough and difficulty in breathing. **croupy** *adj.*

crou•pi•er *n.* One who collects and pays bets at a gambling table.

crou•ton *n.* A small piece of toasted or fried bread.

crow *n.* A large, black bird.

crowd *n.* A large group of people gathered together. *v.* To assemble in large numbers; to press close; to fill so that elements are touching or pressed together.

crown *n.* A circular ornament or head covering made of precious metal and jewels, worn as the headdress of a sovereign; the highest point; top-most part of the skull.

cru•cial *adj.* Extremely important; critical.

cru•ci•ble *n.* A vessel used for melting materials at high temperatures; a hard test of someone.

cru•ci•fy *v.* To put to death by nailing to a cross; to treat cruelly; to torment.

crude *adj.* Unrefined; lacking refinement or tact; haphazardly made. *n.* Unrefined petroleum; crude oil. **crudity** *n.*

cruel *adj.* Inflicting suffering; causing pain; intentionally destructive without regard to feelings. **cruelty** *n.*

cruise *v.* To drive or sail about for pleasure; to move about the streets at leisure; to travel at a speed that provides maximum efficiency. *n.* A trip, usually by boat, taken for pleasure at a leisurely pace.

crumb *n.* A small fragment of material, particularly bread or other baked material.

crum•ble *v.* To break into small pieces; to flake off; to lose structural integrity.

crunch *v.* To chew with a crackling noise; to run, walk, or move with a crushing noise; to summarize or condense toward a conclusion or final amount.

crush *v.* To squeeze or force by pressure so as to damage or injure; to reduce to particles by pounding or grinding; to put down or suppress.

crust *n.* The hardened exterior or surface of bread; a hard or brittle surface layer; the outer layer of the earth; the shell of a pie, normally made of pastry. *v.* To cover or become covered with crust; to cake over.

crutch *n.* A support usually designed to fit in the armpit and to be used as an aid in walking; any support or prop.

crux *n.* An essential or vital moment; a main or central feature.

cry *v.* To shed tears; to call out loudly; to utter a characteristic call or sound; to proclaim publicly.

crypt *n.* An underground chamber or vault primarily used to bury the dead.

cryp•tic *adj.* Intended to be obscure; serving to conceal.

cryp•tog•ra•phy *n.* The writing and deciphering of messages in secret code. **cryptographer** *n.*

crys•tal *n.* Quartz that is transparent or nearly transparent; a body formed by the solidification of a chemical element; a clear, high-quality glass. **crystalline** *adj.*

crys•tal ball *n.* A glass globe for

foretelling the future.

crys•tal•ize *v.* To cause to form crystals or assume crystalline form; to cause to take a definite form; to coat with crystals, especially sugar crystals.

cub *n.* The young of the lion, wolf, or bear; an awkward child or youth.

cub•by•hole *n.* A small enclosed area.

cube *n.* A regular solid with six equal squares, having all its angles right angles; a number expressed in the third power; a number multiplied by the square of itself.

cube root *n.* A number whose cube is a given number.

cu•bic *adj.* Having the shape of a cube; having three dimensions; having the volume of a cube with the edges of a specified unit.

cu•bi•cle *n.* A small partitioned area.

cub•ism *n.* An art style that portrays the subject matter with geometric forms. **cubist** *n.*

cu•bit *n.* An ancient unit of measurement that equals approximately eighteen to twenty inches.

cu•cum•ber *n.* A fruit with a green rind and white, seedy flesh.

cud *n.* Food forced up into the mouth of a ruminating animal from the first stomach and chewed again.

cud•dle *v.* To caress fondly and hold close; to snuggle; to hug. **cuddly** *adj.*

cue *n.* A signal given to a technician or operator calling for a specific response; a line or action on stage signalling an actor to perform.

cuff *n.* The lower part of a sleeve; the turned-up part of the pant legs. *v.* To strike someone lightly.

cui•sine *n.* A style of cooking and preparing food; the food prepared.

cu•li•nar•y *adj.* Relating to cooking.

cull *v.* To select the best from a group.

cul•mi•nate *v.* To reach or rise to the highest point. **culmination** *n.*

cul•pa•ble *adj.* Meriting blame. **culpability** *n.*

cul•prit *n.* A person guilty of a crime.

cult *n.* A group or system of religious worship.

cul•ti•vate *v.* To improve land for planting by fertilizing and plowing; to improve by study; to nourish or improve, as in friendship; to encourage.

cul•ture *n.* The act of developing intellectual ability with education; the cumulative habits, beliefs, and shared experiences of a social, political, or hereditary group; a form of civilization, particularly the beliefs, arts, and customs; in biology, the growth of living material in a prepared nutrient media.

cul•vert *n.* A drain that runs under a road or railroad.

cum•ber•some *adj.* Clumsy; unwieldy.

cum•mer•bund *n.* A wide sash worn by men in formal attire.

cun•ning *adj.* Crafty; sly; carefully and cleverly planned or thought out.

cup *n.* A small, open container with a handle, used for drinking; a measure of capacity that equals 1/2 pint, 8 ounces, or 16 tablespoons.

cu•po•la *n.* A rounded roof; a small vaulted structure that usually rises above a roof.

cur *n.* A mongrel; a dog of mixed breeds.

cu•ra•tor *n.* A person in charge of a museum.

curb *n.* Something that restrains or controls; the raised border along the edge of a street. *v.* To restrain or restrict.

curd *n.* The coagulated portion of milk used for making cheese.

cure *n.* Recovery from a sickness; a medical treatment; the process of preserving food with the use of salt, smoke, or aging.

cu•ret•tage *n.* Surgical cleaning and scraping.

cur•few *n.* An order for people to clear the streets at a certain hour; the hour at which an adolescent has been told to be home.

cu•ri•o *n.* An unusual or rare object.

cu•ri•ous *adj.* Questioning; inquisitive; eager for information; strangely inconsistent in fact or sense.

curl *v.* To twist into curves; to shape like a

coil; to play the sport of curling. *n.* A ringlet of hair.

cur•mudg•eon *n.* An ill-tempered person.

cur•ren•cy *n.* Money in circulation.

cur•rent *adj.* Belonging or occurring in the present time; in use or valid now; most recent. *n.* Water or air with a steady flow in a definite direction; the flow of electrical power.

cur•ric•u•lum n. The courses offered in a school. **curricula** *pl.*

cur•ry *v.* To groom a horse with a brush. *n.* A pungent spice used in cooking.

curse *n.* A prayer or wish for harm to come to someone or something.

cur•sive *n.* A flowing writing in which the letters are joined together.

cur•sor *n.* In computers, the flashing square, underline, or other indicator on the screen that shows where the next character will be deleted or inserted.

curt *adj.* Abrupt; rude.

cur•tail *v.* To shorten. **curtailment** *n.*

cur•tain *n.* A piece of material that covers a window and can be either drawn to the sides or raised; the drape in front of a proscenium stage concealing the set.

curt•sy *n.* A respectful gesture made by bending the knees and lowering the body. *v.* To make such a gesture.

cush•ion *n.* A pillow with a soft filling. *v.* To absorb the shock or effect.

cus•pi•dor *n.* A spittoon.

cuss *v.* To use profanity.

cus•tard *n.* A baked mixture of milk, eggs, sugar, and flavoring.

cus•to•di•an *n.* One who has the custody or care of something or someone; one who maintains, cleans, replenishes, and repairs a building; a caretaker; a janitor.

cus•to•dy *n.* The act of guarding; the care and protection of a minor; any ownership or possession.

cus•tom *n.* An accepted practice of a community or people; the usual manner of doing something; habitual way.

cus•to•mer *n.* One who purchases from a buyer; a person with whom a merchant or business person must deal, usually on a regular basis.

cut *v.* To penetrate with a sharp edge, as with a knife; to omit or leave out; to separate from a larger group; to reap or harvest crops in the fields. *n.* A laceration that penetrates the skin; any reduction or separation; a share of the profits.

cute *adj.* Attractive in a delightful way; pretty; mildly pleasing.

cut•lass *n.* A thick, short, curved sword.

cut•ler•y *n.* Cutting instruments used at the dinner table and to prepare food for cooking.

cut•let *n.* A thin piece of meat for broiling or frying, usually lamb or veal.

cut•off *n.* A short cut; the act of cutting something off.

cut•throat *n.* A murderer; a thug.

cy•ber•space *n.* Theoretical and metaphorical universe of interconnected computers.

cy•cle *n.* A recurring time in which an event occurs repeatedly; a bicycle or motorcycle.

cy•clist *n.* A person who rides a cycle.

cyl•in•der *n.* A long, round body that is either hollow or solid; a barrel or tube shape; a geometric design whose top and bottom are circles. **cylindrical** *adj.*

cyn•ic *n.* One who believes that all people have selfish motives; a skeptic of humanistic tendencies or principles. **cynical** *adj.*, **cynicism** *n.*

cy•tol•o•gy *n.* The scientific study of cell formation, function, and structure.

czar *n.* One of the former emperors or kings of Russia; any powerful and influential leader of an enterprise or group, especially one wielding autocratic rule.

deadline

D

D, d The fourth letter of the English alphabet; the Roman numeral for 500.

dab v. To touch quickly with light, short strokes.

dab·ble v. To play in a liquid with the hands. **dabbler** n.

daf·fo·dil n. A bulb plant with solitary yellow flowers.

daft adj. Crazy; foolish.

dag·ger n. A short pointed hand weapon.

dai·ly adj. Happening every day. n. A newspaper published every day.

dain·ty adj. Delicately beautiful.

dai·qui·ri n. A cocktail made with rum and lime juice.

dair·y n. A place where milk is made and bottled for sale.

dai·sy n. Flowers with yellow disks and white rays.

dale n. A small valley.

dal·ly v. To waste time; to dawdle.

dam n. A barrier across a river that makes a lake or gives power; an animal mother.

dam·age n. An injury to person or property.

damn v. To express anger; to swear or curse at.

damp adj. Between dry and wet.

dam·sel n. A maiden; a young unmarried woman.

dance v. To move the body to music.

dan·de·li·on n. A common yellow wildflower found on lawns.

dan·druff n. Scaly dry skin on the scalp and in the hair.

dan·dy n. A fashionable man who dresses well. adj. Excellent, very fine.

dan·ger n. Something unsafe, causing injury or loss. **dangerous** adj.

dan·gle v. To hang loosely and swing to and fro.

dank adj. Uncomfortably damp; wet and cold.

dap·per adj. Stylishly dressed.

dap·pled adj. Spotted in color.

dare v. To be brave or bold; to challenge a person to show courage.

dark adj. Dim; having little or no light. **darken** v.

dark·en v. To become or make dark or darker. **darkish** adj., **darkly** adv.

dar·ling n. A favorite person; someone very dear.

darn v. To mend a hole with stitches in cloth.

dart n. A small pointed arrow either shot or thrown.

dash v. To move quickly; to rush; to break.

da·ta pl. n. The numbers or facts of a study or survey.

da·ta bank n. The place where a computer stores information.

date n. The day, month, and year; a social appointment.

date·line n. The line or phrase at the beginning of a periodical giving the date and place of publication; the 180th meridian on a map or globe where a day begins.

da·tum n. A single piece of information.

daub v. To coat or smear with something gooey.

daugh·ter n. The female child of a man or woman.

daugh·ter-in-law n. One's son's wife.

daunt v. To intimidate or discourage.

daw·dle v. To waste; to take more time than is needed.

dawn n. The beginning of a new day; a sunrise.

day n. The time between dawn and nightfall; one rotation of the earth upon its axis; twenty-four hours.

day·care n. A service giving daytime safekeeping for children.

daze v. To stun with a heavy blow or shock.

dea·con n. The clergyman who ranks immediately below a priest. **deaconess** n.

dead adj. Without life; not living.

dead·end n. A street having no outlet; the end of a path.

dead·line n. A time limit for something to

101

be done.

dead·ly *adj.* Very dangerous; likely to cause death.

deaf *adj.* Totally or partially unable to hear.

deal *v.* To pass out playing cards; to be in business.

deal·er·ship *n.* A franchise to sell a certain item in a specified area, as a car dealership.

dean *n.* The academic head of a college or university.

dear *adj.* Loved; greatly cherished.

death *n.* The end of life; the stopping of all vital functions.

death·less *adj.* Immortal; not subject to death.

death·ly *adj.* Fatal; causing death.

de·ba·cle *n.* A sudden downfall, failure, or collapse.

de·base *v.* To lower in character or value; demean.

de·bate *v.* To discuss or argue opposite points reasonably.

de·bil·i·tate *v.* To make feeble or weak.

deb·it *n.* A debt or item recorded in an account. *v.* To enter a debt in a ledger.

de·brief *v.* To interrogate or question in order to obtain information.

de·bris *n.* Waste; garbage on the ground or in water.

debt *n.* The money or promise someone owes to someone else.

de·bug *v.* To find and remove a concealed electronic listening device; in computer science, to remove errors in a computer program.

de·but *n.* A first public appearance of someone or something.

deb·u·tante *n.* A young woman making her debut into society.

dec·ade *n.* A period of ten years.

de·ca·dence *n.* A process of decay or deterioration; a period or condition of decline, as in morals. **decadent** *adj.*

de·caf·fein·at·ed *adj.* Having the caffeine removed.

dec·a·gon *n.* A polygon with ten sides and ten angles.

dec·a·gram *n.* A measure of weight equal to 10 grams.

de·cal *n.* A design or picture transferred onto a surface.

de·camp *v.* To break camp; to leave or depart suddenly.

de·cant *v.* To pour off liquid without disturbing the sediments; to pour from one container to another. **decantation** *n.*

de·cant·er *n.* A decorative stoppered bottle for serving wine or other liquids.

de·cap·i·tate *v.* To cut off the head; to behead.

de·cath·lon *n.* An athletic event with ten different track and field events in all of which each contestant participates.

de·cay *v.* To rot; to fall apart slowly.

de·ceased *adj.* Dead; not living.

de·ceit *n.* Deception; the quality of being deceptive; falseness. **deceitful** *adj.*

de·ceive *v.* To mislead or trick by falsehood.

de·cel·er·ate *v.* To decrease in velocity. **deceleration** *n.*

de·cent *adj.* Satisfactory; kind; generous.

de·cen·tral·ize *v.* To divide the administrative functions of a central authority among several local authorities; to reorganize into smaller and more dispersed parts. **decentralization** *n.*

de·cep·tive *adj.* Having the tendency or power to deceive.

de·ci·bel *n.* A measurement of sound.

de·cide *v.* To settle; to make up one's mind.

de·cid·u·ous *adj.* Shedding leaves in the fall.

dec·i·mal *n.* A proper fraction based on the number 10 and indicated by the use of a decimal point.

dec·i·mal point *n.* A period placed to the left of a decimal fraction.

dec·i·mate *v.* To destroy or kill a large proportion of something; to select by lot and kill one out of every ten. **decimation** *n.*

de·ci·pher *v.* To decode; to figure out.

de·ci·sion *n.* The act of deciding; a

judgment or conclusion reached by deciding; in boxing, a victory decided when there has not been a knockout.

de•ci•sive *adj.* Ending uncertainty or dispute; conclusive; characterized by firmness; unquestionable; unmistakable. **decisively** *adv.*

deck *n.* A set of playing cards; the outside floor of a boat.

de•claim *v.* To speak or deliver loudly and rhetorically; to give a formal speech; to attack verbally. **declamation** *n.*, **declamatory** *adj.*

de•clare *v.* To make known or clear; to state officially. **declaration** *n.*

de•clas•si•fy *v.* To remove the security classification of a document.

de•cline *v.* To reject or refuse something politely.

de•code *v.* To turn a coded message into plain language.

de•com•pose *v.* To decay; to separate into constituent parts.

de•com•press *v.* To relieve of pressure; to bring a person back to normal air pressure, as divers or caisson workers. **decompression** *n.*

de•con•ges•tant *n.* An agent that relieves congestion.

de•cor *n.* The decoration of a room, office, or home.

dec•o•rate *v.* To make fancy or pleasing; to add beautiful things.

dec•o•ra•tion *n.* The art of decorating; something that makes a place more pleasing; an emblem, badge, or medal.

dec•o•ra•tive *adj.* Suitable for decoration; ornamental. **decoratively** *adv.*

de•co•rum *n.* Proper behavior; good or fitting conduct. **decorous** *n.*

de•coy *n.* A make-believe animal used to lure real animals; anything misleading or distracting.

de•crease *v.* To grow less or smaller.

de•cree *n.* An authoritative and formal order or decision; a judicial judgment.

de•crep•it *adj.* Broken down or worn out by old age or excessive use. **decrepitude** *n.*

de•crim•i•nal•ize *v.* To remove the criminal classification of; to no longer prohibit.

de•cry *v.* To disparage or condemn openly; to denounce.

ded•i•cate *v.* To set apart for special use or purpose; to promise to do something. **dedication** *n.*

de•duce *v.* To derive a conclusion by reasoning. **deductive** *adj.*

de•duct *v.* To subtract or take away from. **deductible** *adj.*

de•duc•tion *n.* The act of deducing or subtracting; an amount that is or may be deducted; the process or act of deducting.

deed *n.* Something done; a task or act; proof of ownership of property.

deem *v.* To judge or consider.

deep *adj.* Going far below a surface; low in voice or sound.

deep•freeze *n.* A food freezer for storing frozen foods.

deer *n.* A hoofed mammal with antlers, living in the forests and farmlands. **deer** *pl.*

de•face *v.* To spoil or mar the appearance or surface of something.

de•fame *v.* To slander or libel. **defamation** *n.*

de•fault *v.* To neglect to fulfill an obligation or requirement, as to pay money due or to appear in court; to forfeit by default.

de•feat *v.* To win a victory; to beat someone in a contest.

de•fect *n.* The lack of something desirable or necessary for completeness or perfection; a fault or imperfection. **defection, defector** *n.*

de•fec•tive *adj.* Having a defect; imperfect.

de•fend *v.* To protect against attack; to explain a choice. **defense** *n.*

de•fend•ant *n.* The person charged with a crime

de•fense *n.* The action of defending.

de•fer *v.* To delay or postpone. **deferment** *n.*

de•fi•ance *n.* The instance or act of

defying; a challenge. **defiant** *adj.*

de·fi·cient *adj.* Lacking in a necessary element.

def·i·cit *n.* Deficiency in amount.

de·flate *v.* To cause to collapse by removing gas or air; to remove self-esteem or conceit.

de·flect *v.* To turn aside; to swerve from a course.

de·form *v.* To distort the form of; to be distorted; to mar the beauty or excellence of; to spoil the natural form of.

de·fraud *v.* To cheat; to swindle.

de·fray *v.* To provide for or to make payment on something.

de·frost *v.* To thaw out; to remove ice or frost.

deft *adj.* Skillful and neat in one's actions. **deftly** *adv.*, **deftness** *n.*

de·funct *adj.* Dead; deceased.

de·fuse *v.* To remove the detonator or fuse from; to remove or make less dangerous, tense or hostile.

de·fy *v.* To resist boldly and openly; to challenge someone; to dare.

de·gen·er·ate *v.* To decline in quality, value, or desirability; to deteriorate; to become worse. *adj.* Morally depraved or sexually deviant. **degenerate, degeneracy** *n.*

de·grade *v.* To reduce in rank, status, or grade; to demote; to reduce in quality or intensity. **degraded** *adj.*, **degradation** *n.*

de·gree *n.* A unit of cold or heat on a thermometer; a stage or step toward a goal; an academic title for passing all the courses of a special study.

de·hu·man·ize *v.* To deprive of human qualities, especially to make mechanical and routine.

de·hy·drate *v.* To cause to lose moisture or water. **dehydration** *n.*

de·i·fy *v.* To glorify or idealize; to raise in high regard; to worship as a god. **deification** *n.*

deign *v.* To think it barely worthy of one's dignity; to condescend.

de·ism *n.* A belief in the existence of God but a denial of the validity of revelation. **deist** *n.*

de·ject *v.* To lower the spirits; to dishearten. **dejection** *n.*

de·lay *v.* To put off until a later time; to make something late.

de·lec·ta·ble *adj.* Giving great pleasure; delightful; savory; delicious.

de·lec·ta·tion *n.* Enjoyment or pleasure.

del·e·gate *n.* A person with power to act as a representative for another; a deputy or agent; a person appointed or elected to represent a territory in the House of Representatives. *v.* To entrust and commit to another.

del·e·ga·tion *n.* The act of delegating or the state of being delegated; a person or group of people appointed to represent others.

de·lete *v.* To cancel; to take out. **deletion** *n.*

del·e·te·ri·ous *adj.* Causing moral or physical injury; harmful.

de·lib·er·ate *adj.* Done on purpose; thought out and careful.

del·i·ca·cy *n.* A special tasty or dainty food.

del·i·cate *adj.* Pleasing in color, taste, or aroma; made finely and carefully; fragile.

del·i·ca·tes·sen *n.* A store that sells cooked meats, preserved cheeses, pickles, and other delicacies.

de·li·cious *adj.* Extremely pleasant to the taste. *n.* A variety of red, sweet apples.

de·light *n.* A great joy or pleasure. *v.* To give or take great pleasure. **delightful** *adj.*

de·lin·e·ate *v.* To represent by a drawing; to draw or trace the outline of something; to sketch; to represent in gestures or words. **delineation** *n.*

de·lin·quent *adj.* Neglecting to do what is required by obligation or law; falling behind in a payment. *n.* A juvenile who is out of control, as violating the law. **delinquency** *n.*

de·lir·i·um *n.* A temporary or sporadic

mental disturbance associated with fever, shock, or intoxication and marked by excitement, incoherence, and hallucination; uncontrolled excitement and emotion.

de•liv•er *v.* To take to another place; to hand over; to assist in the birth of an offspring. **delivery** *n.*

dell *n.* A small secluded valley.

de•lude *v.* To mislead the mind or judgment; to deceive; to cause to be deceived.

del•uge *n.* A great flood. *v.* To flood with water; to cover over.

de•lu•sion *n.* A false, fixed belief held in spite of contrary evidence. **delusional** *adj.*

de•luxe *adj.* The best quality; filled with luxury.

de•mand *v.* To ask for in a firm tone; to claim as due.

de•mar•cate *v.* To set boundaries or limits; to separate or limit. **demarcation** *n.*

de•mean *v.* To behave or conduct oneself in a particular manner; to degrade; to humble oneself or another.

de•mean•or *n.* A person's conduct toward others; a person's general behavior.

de•men•tia *n.* An irreversible deterioration of intellectual faculties. **demented** *adj.*

de•mer•it *n.* A fault; a mark against the school record for bad conduct.

de•mise *n.* Death; in law, a transfer of an estate by lease or will.

de•moc•ra•cy *n.* A form of government by the people or through their elected representatives; rule by the majority. **democrat** *n.*

de•mog•ra•phy *n.* Study of the characteristics of human population, such as growth, size, and vital statistics. **demographic** *adj.*

de•mol•ish *v.* To tear down; to raze; to completely do away with; to end. **demolition** *n.*

de•mon *n.* An evil spirit; a devil. **demonic** *adj.*

de•mon•stra•ble *adj.* Obvious or apparent. **demonstrably** *adv.*

dem•on•strate *v.* To show how something works; to prove by reasoning or evidence.

de•mon•stra•tive *adj.* Serving to point out or demonstrate; able to prove beyond any doubt; conclusive and convincing.

de•mor•al•ize *v.* To undermine the morale or confidence of someone; to degrade; to corrupt.

de•mote *v.* To reduce in rank, grade, or position. **demotion** *n.*

de•mur *v.* To take issue; to object.

de•mure *adj.* Reserved and modest; coy.

den *n.* A wild animal's shelter; a small study room in a home.

de•ni•al *n.* A refusal to grant a request; the act of saying accusations are not true.

den•i•grate *v.* To slander; to defame.

den•im *n.* A strong woven cotton used for blue jeans.

de•nom•i•na•tor *n.* The bottom half of a fraction, showing the number of equal parts into which the unit is divided.

de•no•ta•tion *n.* The meaning of, or the object or objects designated by a word; an indication, as a sign.

de•note *v.* To make known; to point out; to indicate; to signify; to designate; to mean, to represent by a symbol.

de•noue•ment *n.* The final solution of a novel, play, or plot.

de•nounce *v.* To attack or condemn openly and vehemently; to accuse formally; to announce the ending of something in a formal way.

dense *adj.* Compact; thick.

den•si•ty *n.* The state or quality of being dense or close in parts; the quantity or amount of something per unit measure, area, volume, or length.

dent *n.* A small hollow fault on a surface, caused by bumping or pressing.

den•tal *adj.* Having to do with the teeth.

den•tist *n.* A person who inspects, cleans, and repairs teeth. **dentistry** *n.*

den•ture *n.* A set of artificial teeth either partial or full; a dental plate.

de•nun•ci•a•tion *n.* Open disapproval of

a person or action; an accusation; warning or threat.

de•ny *v.* To declare as untrue; to withhold; to refuse to grant.

de•o•dor•ant *n.* A product designed to prevent, mask, or destroy unpleasant odors.

de•ox•y•ri•bo•nu•cle•ic ac•id *n.* A main message-carrying ingredient of genes, known as DNA.

de•part *v.* To leave; to go away; to start on a trip.

de•part•ment *n.* The division or part of a company, college, or store.

de•part•ment store *n.* A large retail store selling many types of merchandise.

de•par•ture *n.* The act of taking leave or going away; a divergence; a deviation; the act of starting out on a new course of action or going on a trip.

de•pend *v.* To rely on; to trust with responsibilities.

de•pend•a•ble *adj.* Trustworthy; able to be depended upon.

de•pend•ent *n.* A person who depends on another person for financial support.

de•pict *v.* To represent in a sculpture or a picture; to describe or represent in words. **depiction** *n.*

dep•i•late *v.* To remove hair from. **depilation, depilator, depilatory** *n.*

de•plete *v.* To exhaust, empty, or use up a supply of something. **depletion** *n.*

de•plor•a•ble *adj.* Grievous; lamentable; very bad; wretched.

de•plore *v.* To have, show, or feel great disapproval of something.

de•ploy *v.* To spread out; to place or position according to plans.

de•port *v.* To banish or expel someone from a country.

de•port•ment *n.* The way one behaves or acts.

de•pos•it *v.* To put, place, or set something down; to put money in a bank. *n.* A layer or formation of natural substance in the ground.

de•pot *n.* A railroad or bus station.

de•prave *v.* To render bad or worse; in morals, to corrupt or pervert. **depravity** *n.*

dep•re•cate *v.* To express regret for or disapproval of; to belittle.

de•pre•ci•a•tion *n.* A loss in efficiency or value resulting from age or usage; the decline in the purchasing value of money. **depreciate** *v.*

de•pressed *adj.* Dejected; sad; low in spirits.

de•pres•sion *n.* The state of being or the act of depressing; a dent or hollow in a surface.

de•prive *v.* To take something away from; to keep from using acquiring, or enjoying.

depth *n.* The state of being deep; the measurement of distance downward; seriousness or complexity.

dep•u•ty *n.* A person authorized to act for another, especially a police officer helping a sheriff.

de•rail *v.* To run off the rails; to cause a train to run off the rails.

der•by *n.* An annual horse race open to all; an old-fashioned stiff hat with a round crown.

de•reg•u•late *v.* To decontrol or remove from regulation or control. **deregulation** *n.*

der•e•lict *adj.* Neglectful of obligations; remiss; abandoned or deserted, as a ship at sea. *n.* A vagrant; a social outcast.

der•e•lic•tion *n.* Voluntary neglect, as of responsibility; the fact or state of being abandoned.

de•ride *v.* To ridicule; to treat with scornful mirth. **derision** *n.*

der•i•va•tion *n.* The act of or process of deriving; the process used to form new words by the addition of affixes to roots, stems, or words.

de•rive *v.* To receive or obtain from a source; to produce a compound from other substances by chemical reaction. **derivative** *adj.*

de•rog•a•tor•y *adj.* Having the effect of belittling; lessening.

des•cant *v.* To play or sing a varied melody.

de•scend *v.* To move from a higher to a lower level; to go down. **descent** *n.*

de•scen•dant *adj.* Proceeding downward; descending from an ancestor. *n.* One who descends from another individual; an offspring.

de•scent *n.* A slope; lowering or decline, as in level or status.

de•scribe *v.* To tell how something looks or feels; to explain in written or spoken words. **descriptive** *adj.*

de•scrip•tion *n.* The technique or act of describing; an account or statement that describes.

des•e•crate *v.* To violate something sacred, turning it into something common or profane. **desecration** *n.*

de•seg•re•gate *v.* To remove or eliminate racial segregation. **desegregation** *n.*

de•sen•si•tize *v.* To make less sensitive; to eliminate the sensitivity of an individual, tissue, or organ, as to an allergen.

de•sert *v.* To abandon or leave; to be absent without leave (AWOL) in the armed forces.

des•ert *n.* A dry, barren region of land without adequate water supply.

de•served *adj.* Merited; earned. **deserving** *adj.*

de•sign *v.* To invent or create in the mind; to draw and sketch an idea or outline.

des•ig•nate *v.* To assign a name or title to; to point out; to specify; to appoint or select, as to an office. **designation** *n.*

de•sir•a•ble *adj.* Pleasing, attractive, or valuable.

de•sire *v.* To long for; to wish; to crave; to request.

de•sist *v.* To stop doing something; to cease from an action.

desk *n.* A table with drawers and a top for writing.

des•o•late *adj.* Made unfit for habitation; useless; forlorn; forsaken. **desolation** *n.*

de•spair *v.* To lose or give up hope. *n.* A sense of hopelessness.

des•per•a•do *n.* A dangerous, desperate, or violent criminal.

des•per•ate *adj.* Rash, violent, reckless, and without care, as from despair; intense; overpowering.

des•per•a•tion *n.* The state of being desperate.

des•pi•ca•ble *adj.* Deserving scorn or contempt.

de•spise *v.* To regard with contempt; to regard as worthless.

de•spite *prep.* Nevertheless; in spite of; even though.

de•spon•den•cy *n.* A dejection of spirits from loss of courage or hope. **despondent** *adj.*

des•sert *n.* A serving of sweet foods at the end of a meal.

des•ti•na•tion *n.* The point or place where someone or something is going; the purpose or end for which something is created or intended.

des•ti•ny *n.* The fate or final outcome of an act or person; a course of events whose end is already determined.

des•ti•tute *adj.* Utterly impoverished; not having; extremely poor. **destitution** *n.*

de•stroy *v.* To ruin; to tear down; to demolish. **destruction** *n.*, **destructive** *adj.*

de•tach *v.* To unfasten, disconnect, or separate; to extricate oneself; to withdraw.

de•tached *adj.* Separate; apart.

de•tach•ment *n.* The process of separating.

de•tail *n.* A small part or item looked at separately and carefully.

de•tect *v.* To find out or perceive ; to expose or uncover, as a crime. **detection** *n.*

de•tec•tive *n.* A person who investigates crimes and discovers evidence.

de•ten•tion *n.* A punishment by holding or stopping; a time of temporary custody while the court decides guilt or innocence.

de•ter *v.* To prevent or discourage someone from acting by arousing fear, uncertainty, intimidation, or other strong emotion.

de·ter·gent *n.* A cleansing agent which is chemically different from soap.

de·te·ri·o·rate *v.* To worsen; to depreciate. **deterioration** *n.*

de·ter·mine *v.* To settle or decide by the facts; to figure out.

de·ter·mined *adj.* Showing or having a fixed purpose; firm and resolute.

de·test *v.* To dislike strongly. **detestable** *adj.*

det·o·nate *v.* To explode suddenly and violently. **detonation** *n.*

det·o·na·tor *n.* The device, such as a fuse or percussion cap, used to detonate an explosive.

de·tour *n.* A road used temporarily instead of a main road; a sidetrack from the goal.

de·tract *v.* To take away from; to diminish; to divert. **detractor** *n.*

det·ri·ment *n.* Damage; injury; loss; something which causes damage, injury, or loss. **detrimental** *adj.*

deuce *n.* Two; a playing card with two spots; in tennis, an even score.

dev·as·tate *v.* To destroy; to ruin; to overwhelm; to overpower. **devastation** *n.*

de·vel·op *v.* To bring out or expand; to make fancier; to turn exposed film into pictures.

de·vice *n.* Something made and used for a special purpose; a gadget.

dev·il *n.* The spirit of evil, the ruler of Hell; Satan.

dev·il's ad·vo·cate *n.* One who argues a side of a debate just for the sake of argument.

de·vi·ous *adj.* Leading away from the straight, regular, or direct course; rambling; straying from the proper way.

de·vise *v.* To form in the mind; to contrive; to plan; to invent; in law, to transmit or give by will.

de·void *adj.* Empty; utterly lacking; without.

de·vote *v.* To apply time completely to some activity; to concentrate time or ener-

gy. **devoted** *adj.*

de·vo·tion *n.* A strong attachment or affection to a person or cause; zeal.

de·vour *v.* To destroy or waste; to eat up greedily; to engulf.

de·vout *adj.* Extremely and earnestly religious; showing sincerity; displaying piety or reverence. **devoutly** *adv.*, **devoutness** *n.*

dew *n.* Early morning moisture from the atmosphere in minute drops on cool surfaces.

dex·ter·i·ty *n.* Proficiency or skill in using the hands or body; cleverness.

dex·ter·ous *adj.* Skillful or adroit in the use of the hands, body, or mind.

di·a·bol·i·cal *adj.* Wicked; proceeding from the evil; satanic or infernal.

di·a·crit·ic *n.* A mark near or through a phonetic character or combination of characters, to indicate a special phonetic value or to distinguish words otherwise graphically identical.

di·a·dem *n.* A crown or headband worn to symbolize or indicate royalty or honor.

di·ag·no·sis *n.* An analysis and examination to identify a disease; the result of diagnosis. **diagnose** *v.*, **diagnostic** *adj.*, **diagnostician** *n.*

di·ag·o·nal *adj.* Joining two opposite corners of a polygon *n.* A diagonal or slanting plane or line.

di·a·gram *n.* A sketch or drawing that outlines a plan or process. **diagrammatic**, **diagrammatical** *adj.*

di·al *n.* Any circular plate or face with measuring marks; the face of a clock, watch, or sundial; a control for selecting a radio or television station. *v.* To make a phone call with a dial telephone.

di·a·lec·tic *n.* The act or practice of argument or exposition in which the conflict between contradictory facts or ideas is resolved.

di·a·logue *n.* A conversation among several persons; a passage of talking in a literary work; the lines said in a play.

di·am·e·ter *n.* A straight line passing

through the center of a circle or sphere and stopping at the circumference.

dia•mond *n.* A very hard colorless or white crystalline of carbon used as a gem; something in the shape of a diamond.

dia•mond•back *n.* A large venomous U.S. rattlesnake.

di•a•per *n.* A folded piece of absorbent material placed between a baby's legs and fastened at the waist.

di•aph•a•nous *adj.* Of such fine texture as to be transparent or translucent; delicate.

di•a•phragm *n.* The muscular wall which separates the abdominal and thoracic cavities; a contraceptive device usually made of a rubber or rubberlike material and shaped like a cap to cover the uterine cervix.

di•a•ry *n.* A daily record; a journal or day-book, especially one containing one's personal experiences.

di•a•tribe *n.* A bitter, often malicious criticism or denunciation.

dice *pl. n.* Two or more small cubes of wood, bone, or ivory marked with dots.

dic•tate *v.* To read or speak aloud for another to record or transcribe; to give commands, terms, rules, or other orders with authority. *n.* A directive or guiding principle. **dictation** *n.*

dic•ta•tor *n.* A person having absolute authority and supreme governmental powers; one who dictates. **dictatorship** *n.*, **dictatorial** *adj.*

dic•tion *n.* The selection and arrangement of words in speaking and writing; the manner of uttering speech sounds.

dic•tion•ar•y *n.* A reference book containing alphabetically arranged words together with their definitions and usages.

did *v.* Past tense of *do.*

di•dac•tic *adj.* Inclined to teach or moralize excessively. **didacticism** *n.*

die *v.* To expire; to stop living; to cease to exist; to stop working.

die•sel *n.* A diesel engine or a vehicle driven by a diesel engine.

di•et *n.* The selection of food and drink one eats regularly.

dif•fer *v.* To disagree; to be different from.

dif•fer•ence *n.* The amount by which a number is less or greater than another.

dif•fer•ent *adj.* Not the same; separate; other; out of the ordinary.

dif•fi•cult *adj.* Hard to do; hard to please.

dif•fi•cul•ty *n.* A hardship or obstruction; something not easy.

dig *v.* To make a hole in the ground; to break up or remove earth with a shovel; to investigate.

di•gest *v.* To change ingested food into usable form, to mentally assimilate; to endure; to tolerate patiently; to decompose or soften with moisture or heat.

di•ges•tion *n.* The chemical and muscular action of transforming food into an assimilable state.

dig•it *n.* A toe or finger; the Arabic numerals 0 through 9.

dig•i•tal *adj.* Pertaining to or like the fingers or digits; expressed in digits, especially for computer use.

dig•ni•fied *adj.* Showing dignity; noble.

dig•ni•ty *n.* The quality or state of being excellent, poised, or reserved; nobility.

di•gress *v.* To turn away or aside from the main subject in a discourse; to wander. **digression** *n.*

dike *n.* An embankment of earth to hold and control flood waters; a levee.

di•lap•i•dat•ed *adj.* In a state of decay or disrepair, especially of stone structures.

di•late *v.* To become or make enlarged; to expand. **dilation, dilator** *n.*

di•lem•ma *n.* A predicament requiring a choice between equally undesirable alternatives.

dil•et•tante *n.* One who has an amateurish and superficial interest in something.

dil•i•gent *adj.* Showing painstaking effort and application in whatever is undertaken; industrious. **diligence** *n.*

di•lute *v.* To weaken, thin, or reduce the concentration of by adding a liquid. **dilution** *n.*

dim *adj.* Dull; lacking sharp perception;

faint; poorly lit.

dime *n.* A U.S. coin worth one tenth of a dollar.

di•men•sion *n.* A measurement, as length, thickness, or breadth.

di•min•ish *v.* To become or make smaller or less; to reduce in power, rank, or authority; to decrease; to taper. **diminution** *n.*

di•min•ished *adj.* Reduced; lessened.

di•min•u•tive *adj.* Very small; tiny.

dim•mer *n.* A device used to soften or turn down the intensity of an electric light.

dim•ple *n.* A slight depression in the surface of the skin.

din *n.* A loud, confused, harsh noise.

dine *v.* To eat, especially dinner.

din•ner *n.* The chief meal of the day.

di•no•saur *n.* Any extinct reptile from prehistoric times, some of which were the largest animals in existence.

dip *v.* To put down into a liquid for a moment.

di•plo•ma *n.* A document issued by a college, school, or university testifying that a student has earned a degree or completed a course of study.

dip•per *n.* A long-handled cup container for ladling liquids.

dire *adj.* Dreadful or terrible in consequence.

di•rect *v.* To command or order; to supervise or instruct the performance of a job. **director** *n.*

di•rec•tion *n.* An instruction, order or command; the path or line along which something points.

di•rec•tor *n.* A person who manages or directs; one of a group of persons who supervises the affairs of an institute, corporation or business.

di•rec•to•ry *n.* A book listing data, alphabetically or classified, containing the names and addresses of a specific group, persons, organizations, inhabitants, or businesses.

dirt *n.* Soil or earth; broken ore or rock; washed-down earth.

dirt•y *adj.* Not clean; grimy; indecent; obscene.

dis•a•ble *v.* To make powerless; to stop from working.

dis•ad•van•tage *n.* An unfavorable condition; a handicap.

dis•a•gree *v.* To vary in opinion; to differ; to argue.

dis•a•gree•a•ble *adj.* Offensive or unpleasant.

dis•ap•pear *v.* To vanish; to drop from sight.

dis•ap•point *v.* To fail to satisfy; to let down.

dis•ap•prove *v.* To refuse to approve; to reject; to condemn *n.* **disapproval** *n.*

dis•arm *v.* To make harmless; to deprive or take away the weapons or any means of attack or defense. **disarmament** *n.*

dis•ar•ray *n.* A state of confusion or disorder; an upset or turmoil.

dis•as•ter *n.* A catastrophe or great ruin.

dis•a•vow *v.* To disclaim or deny any responsibility for or knowledge of. **disavowal** *n.*

dis•band *v.* To disperse; to break up.

dis•bar *v.* In law, to be expelled officially from the legal profession.

dis•burse *v.* To pay out or distribute according to budgetary guidelines. **disbursement**, **disbursal** *n.*

disc or **disk** *n.* A phonograph record

dis•card *v.* To remove a playing card from one's hand; to throw out. *n.* The act of discarding; something which is cast aside or rejected.

dis•cern *v.* To detect visually; to detect with senses other than that of vision; to comprehend mentally; to perceive as separate and distinct. **discernment** *n.*

dis•charge *v.* To relieve of a charge, duty, load, or burden; to release as from confinement, custody, care, or duty; to dismiss from employment; to send forth; to shoot or fire a weapon; to get rid of; to release from service or duty; to fulfill an obligation, duty, or debt. *n.* The act of discharging or the condition of being discharged.

dis•ci•ple *n.* One who accepts and assists in spreading the doctrines of another; one of Christ's followers.

dis•ci•pline *n.* Training which corrects, molds, or perfects the mental facilities or moral character; behavior which results from such training; obedience to authority or rules; punishment meant to correct poor behavior. *v.* To train or develop by teaching and by control; to bring order to; to penalize.

dis•claim *v.* To disavow any claim to or association with. **disclaimer** *n.*

dis•close *v.* To make known; to bring into view. **disclosure** *n.*

dis•con•cert *v.* To upset; to discompose; to perturb.

dis•con•nect *v.* To sever or break the connection of or between. **disconnected** *adj.*

dis•con•so•late *adj.* Without consolation; dejected; cheerless; sorrowful.

dis•con•tent *n.* Lack of contentment; dissatisfaction.

dis•con•tin•ue *v.* To come or bring to an end; to break the continuity of; to interrupt; to stop trying, taking, or using.

dis•cord *n.* Lacking accord or harmony; a harsh combination of musical sounds. **discordant** *adj.*

dis•co•theque *n.* A nightclub where music is provided for dancing. **disco** *abbrev.*

dis•count *n.* A special price lower than the normal one; a deduction or bargain.

dis•cour•age *v.* To take enthusiasm away; to advise against.

dis•course *n.* A conversation; a formal and lengthy discussion of a subject. *v.* To write or converse extensively.

dis•cov•er *v.* To make known or visible; to find for the first time.

dis•creet *adj.* Tactful; careful of appearances; modest.

dis•crep•an•cy *n.* A difference in facts; an instance of being discrepant.

dis•crete *adj.* Separate; made up of distinct parts.

dis•cre•tion *n.* The quality or act of being discreet; the ability to make responsible choices; power to decide; the result of separating or distinguishing. **discretionary** *adj.*

dis•crim•i•nate . To distinguish or differentiate between someone or something on the basis of race, sex, class, or religion. **discrimination** *n.*

dis•cur•sive *adj.* Covering a wide field of subjects in a quick manner; rambling from subject to subject.

dis•cus *n.* A heavy disk made of wood, rubber, or metal, hurled for distance in athletic competitions.

dis•cuss *v.* To hold a conversation; to talk; to exchange ideas about. **discussion** *n.*

dis•ease *n.* An illness; a sickness, often spread from one person to another; a group of symptoms with its own name.

dis•fa•vor *n.* Disapproval; the state of being disliked.

dis•fig•ure *v.* To mar, deface, or deform the appearance of something or someone.

dis•grace *n.* Loss of grace, favor, or respect. *v.* To bring shame to; to humiliate.

dis•guise *v.* To change appearance to hide; to conceal the actual existence or character of. *n.* Clothes or make-up that hides the identity.

dis•gust *v.* To cause ill feeling or even sickness; to repel from ugliness.

dish *n.* A vessel for serving food; one part of a multi-course meal; any flat curved object shaped like a plate.

dis•hon•est *adj.* Lacking honesty; coming from falseness.

dis•hon•or *n.* The deprivation of honor; disgrace; the state of one who has lost honor; a cause of disgrace; failure to pay a financial obligation.

dish•wash•er *n.* A person or a machine for washing dishes.

dis•in•te•grate *v.* To break or reduce into separate elements, parts, or small particles; to destroy the unity or integrity of; to

111

disk

explode; to undergo a change in structure, as an atomic nucleus.

disk *n.* A thin, flat, circular object; a round, flat plate coated with a magnetic substance for storing data.

disk op•er•at•ing sys•tem *n.* In computer science, the software that controls the disk drives and disk accessing; abbreviated as DOS.

dis•like *v.* To regard with disapproval; to feel badly toward.

dis•lo•cate *v.* To put out of place or proper position.

dis•lodge *v.* To remove or drive out from a dwelling or position; to force out of a settled position.

dis•loy•al *adj.* Not loyal; untrue to obligations or duty.

dis•mal *adj.* Gloomy; depressing; low in merit.

dis•miss *v.* To allow to leave; to take off the list; to remove from position.

dis•o•bey *v.* To refuse or fail to follow commands; to be disobedient.

dis•or•der *n.* Lack of good order; messiness; chaos; an ailment.

dis•pa•rate *adj.* Altogether dissimilar; unequal.

dis•pense *v.* To give out; to distribute; to administer; to let go or exempt. **dispenser** *n.*

dis•perse *v.* To break up or scatter in various directions; to spread or distribute from a common source; to distribute. **dispersal** *n.*

dis•play *v.* To show or put on exhibit; to give a demonstration of; to show off. *n.* The part of a computer or other device that shows data visually on a screen.

dis•pose *v.* To put in place; to finally settle or come to terms. dispose of *v.* To get rid of; to attend to or settle; to transfer or part with, as by selling.

dis•pute *v.* To debate or argue; to question the validity of. *n.* A verbal controversy; a quarrel.

dis•rupt *v.* To throw into disorder or confusion; upset; to cause to break down.

disruption *n.*

dis•sat•is•fy *v.* To fail to satisfy; to disappoint.

dis•sect *v.* To cut into pieces for examination; to expose; to analyze in detail. **dissection** *n.*

dis•sem•ble *v.* To conceal or hide the actual nature of; to put on a false appearance; to conceal facts.

dis•sem•i•nate *v.* To scatter or spread, as if by sowing, over a wide area. dissemination, disseminator n.

dis•sen•sion *n.* Difference of opinion; discord; strife.

dis•sent *v.* To differ in opinion or thought. *n.* Difference of opinion; refusal to go along with an established church.

dis•ser•ta•tion *n.* A formal written discourse or treaties, especially one submitted for a doctorate.

dis•si•dent *adj.* Strong and open difference with an opinion or group. **dissident, dissidence** *n.*

dis•si•pate *v.* To disperse or drive away; to squander or waste; to separate into parts and scatter or vanish; to become dispersed; to lose irreversibly. **dissipation** *n.*

dis•so•lute *adj.* Loose in morals; lacking moral restraint.

dis•so•lu•tion *n.* The act or process of changing from a solid to a fluid form; the separation of body and soul; death.

dis•solve *v.* To pass into solution; to absorb solid particles into a liquid; to lose structure.

dis•tance *n.* Separation in time or space; the measure between two points; a large amount of space between. **distant** *adj.*

dis•taste *v.* To feel aversion to; to have an offensive taste; dislike.

dis•tem•per *n.* Bad humor or temper; a highly contagious viral disease of dogs.

dis•tend *v.* To expand from internal pressure.

dis•till *v.* To condense by boiling or other means; to give off in drops. **distillery** *n.*

dis•tinct *adj.* Separate from all others;

clearly seen; different.

dis·tin·guish *v.* To recognize as being different; to make important the differences between two things.

dis·tin·guished *adj.* Set apart; honored; worthy of praise.

dis·tort *v.* To twist or bend out of shape; to warp the true meaning of.

dis·tract *v.* To draw or divert one's attention away from something; to cause one to feel conflicting emotions. **distraction** *n.*

dis·tress *v.* To cause suffering of mind or body; to upset or make tense. *n.* Pain or suffering; severe physical or mental strain.

dis·trib·ute *v.* To divide among many; to deliver or give out to many.

dis·trict *n.* A section of a territory; a distinctive area.

dis·turb *v.* To destroy the balance or rest; to unsettle; to bother.

ditch *n.* A trench in the earth; an excavation for pipes or lines. *v.* To discard.

dit·to *n.* An exact copy; the same as stated before.

dive *v.* To plunge into water headfirst; to plunge downward at a sharp angle. **diver** *n.*

di·verse *adj.* Unlike in characteristics; having various forms or qualities. **diverse-ness, diversity** *n.*

di·ver·si·fy *v.* To give variety to something; to engage in varied operations; to distribute over a wide range of types or classes.

di·ver·sion *n.* The act of diverting from a course, activity or use; something that diverts or amuses.

di·vert *v.* To turn from a set course; to give pleasure by distracting the attention from something burdensome or oppressive.

di·vest *v.* To undress or strip, especially of clothing or equipment; to deprive or dispossess of property, authority, or title.

di·vide *v.* To separate into halves or portions and give out in shares; to cause to be apart; to do mathematical division on a number.

di·vine *adj.* Of or pertaining to God.

di·vi·sion *n.* Separation; something which divides, separates, or marks off; the act, process, or instance of separating or keeping apart.

di·vi·sor *n.* The number by which a dividend is to be divided.

di·vorce *n.* The legal breaking up of a marriage; the complete separation of things.

diz·zy *adj.* Whirling until balance is lost; confused; giddy.

do *v.* To bring to pass; to bring about; to perform or execute; to put forth; to exert; to bring to an end.

do·cent *n.* A teacher at a college or university; a guide or lecturer in a museum.

do·cile *adj.* Easily led, taught, or managed.

dock *n.* A pier or parking place for ships or boats; a loading area for trucks or trains.

dock·yard *n.* A shipyard; a place where ships are repaired or built.

doc·tor *n.* A person who practices medicine, such as a physician, surgeon, dentist, or veterinarian; a person holding the highest degree offered by a university.

doc·trine *n.* A body of principles; a statement of beliefs.

doc·u·ment *n.* An official paper or written record.

dodge *v.* To avoid by moving suddenly; to shift suddenly.

do·do *n.* An extinct flightless bird.

doe *n.* A mature female deer, hare, or kangaroo.

dog *n.* A domesticated member of the wolf family; a canine.

dog·ma *n.* A rigidly held doctrine proclaimed to be true by a religious group; a principle or idea considered to be the absolute truth.

dog·mat·ic *adj.* Marked by an authoritative assertion of unproved or unprovable principles.

dog pad·dle *n.* A beginner's swimming stroke.

dole *n.* The distribution of food, money, or clothing to the needy; a grant of government funds to the unemployed; something portioned out and distributed bit by bit.

doll *n.* A child's toy having a human form.

dol•lar *n.* A unit of money in the U.S. and elsewhere; one hundred cents.

dol•ly *n.* A child's word for a doll

dol•phin *n.* Any of various intelligent marine animals with the snout in the shape of a beak.

do•main *n.* A territory under one government; a field of activity or interest; in computers, the host destination of a uniform resource location (URL).

dome *n.* A roof resembling a hemisphere.

do•mes•tic *adj.* Relating to the home, household, or family life.

dom•i•nant *adj.* Having the most control or influence; strongest.

dom•i•nate *v.* To rule or control; to stand above.

dom•i•no *n.* A small rectangular block of wood or plastic with the face marked with dots. **dominoes** *pl.* A game containing 28 of such pieces.

done *adj.* Completely finished or through; cooked adequately.

don•key *n.* The domesticated beast of burden.

do•nor *n.* One who gives or contributes.

doo•dle *v.* To scribble, design, or sketch aimlessly.

doom *n.* To condemn to a severe penalty or death.

door *n.* A swinging or sliding panel, by which an entry is closed and opened; a means of entrance or exit.

dor•mant *adj.* Asleep; a state of inactivity or rest.

DOS *abbr.* Disk operating system.

dose *n.* The measured amount of a substance.

dot *n.* A small round spot; a period used in punctuation.

dou•ble *adj.* Twice as much; composed of two like parts; designed for two.

doubt *v.* To be uncertain about something; to distrust.

dough *n.* A soft mixture of flour, liquids, and other ingredients baked to make bread, pastry, and other foods.

dough•nut or **do•nut** *n.* A small cake with a hole in the middle, made of rich, light, deep-fried dough.

dour *adj.* Stern and forbidding; morose; ill-tempered.

douse *v.* To plunge into liquid; to throw water on; to drench; to extinguish.

dove *n.* Any of numerous pigeons; a gentle, innocent person.

dow•a•ger *n.* A widow holding a title or property from her dead husband; a dignified, elderly woman.

dow•el *n.* A round wooden pin which fits tightly into a hole to fasten together the two pieces.

down *adv.* Toward a lower position or condition; the direction that is opposite of up.

dowse *v.* To search for with a divining rod to find underground water or minerals. **dowser** *n.*

doz•en *n.* Twelve of a kind; a set of twelve things.

drab *adj.* Light, dull brown or olive brown color; commonplace or dull.

draft *n.* A current of air; a sketch or plan of something to be made.

drag *v.* To pull along or haul by force; to move with painful or undue slowness; to bring by force.

drag•on *n.* A mythical, giant, serpentlike, winged, fire-breathing monster.

drain *v.* To draw off liquid gradually; to use up; to exhaust.

drake *n.* A male duck.

dra•ma *n.* An imitation of an action without narrator, acted on the stage or composed in a story.

drank *v.* Past tense of *drink*.

drape *v.* To cover or adorn with something; to arrange or hang in loose folds. *n.* A heavy cloth curtain for windows.

dras•tic *adj.* Acting extremely harsh or severe.

draw *v.* To move toward a direction; to lead; to sketch.

draw•bridge *n.* A bridge that can be raised or lowered to allow ships and boats to pass.

draw•er *n.* One that draws pictures; a sliding box or receptacle in furniture.

draw•ing *n.* The art of representing something or someone by means of lines.

dread *v.* To fear greatly; to imagine with alarm or worry. **dreadful** *adj.*

dream *n.* Thoughts, images, or emotions occurring during sleep; something that is strongly desired; something that fully satisfies a desire.

drea•ry *adj.* Bleak and gloomy; dull.

drench *v.* To wet thoroughly.

dress *n.* An outer garment for women and girls. *v.* To put clothes on.

drew *v.* Past tense of *draw*.

drib•ble *v.* To drip; to slobber or drool; to bounce a ball repeatedly.

drift *v.* To be carried along by currents of air or water; to move aimlessly; to float. *n.* A hill or dune of blown snow or sand.

drill *n.* A tool used in boring holes; the act of training soldiers in marching and the use of weapons. *v.* To make a hole by boring with a hard sharp point.

drink *v.* To take liquid into the mouth and swallow.

drip *v.* To fall in drops. *n.* Liquid which falls in drops; the sound made by falling drops.

drive *v.* To push, or press onward; to operate a vehicle; to supply a moving force.

drive-in *n.* A place of business where customers stay in their vehicles to be served.

driz•zle *n.* A fine, quiet, gentle rain.

drom•e•dar•y *n.* A one-humped camel.

drool *v.* To dribble from the mouth.

droop *v.* To hang or bend downward; to lose stiffness.

drop *n.* A tiny, pear-shaped or rounded mass of liquid; a small quantity of a substance; the smallest unit of liquid measure. *v.* To fall or let go of an object in air.

drove *n.* A herd being driven in a body; a crowd. *v.* Past tense of *drive*.

drown *v.* To kill or die by suffocating in a liquid; to cause not to be heard by making a loud noise.

drows•y *adj.* Sleepy.

drudge *n.* A person who does tiresome or menial tasks. **drudgery** *n.*

drug *n.* A substance used to treat a disease or illness; a narcotic.

drum *n.* A musical instrument made of a hollow frame with a cover stretched across one or both ends, played by beating or pounding.

drunk *adj.* Intoxicated with alcohol.

drunk•ard *adj.* A person who is intoxicated by liquor.

dry *adj.* Free from moisture or liquid; having little or no rain.

dry•ad *n.* A wood nymph.

du•al *adj.* Made up or composed of two parts; having a double purpose.

du•bi•ous *adj.* Causing doubt; unsettled in judgment; reluctant to agree; question as to quality or validity; verging on impropriety.

duck *n.* Any of various swimming birds with short necks and legs. *v.* To lower the head and body quickly; to plunge quickly under water.

duct *n.* A bodily tube or canal, especially one carrying a secretion; a tubular passage through which something flows.

due *adj.* Owed; payable; owed or owing as a right.

du•et *n.* A musical piece for two performers or musical instruments.

dull *adj.* Not sharp; stupid; lacking in intelligence or understanding; boring or not exciting.

dumb *adj.* Unable to speak; temporarily speechless.

dum•my *n.* A human shaped imitation or copy, used as a substitute.

dump•ling *n.* A small mass of dough cooked in soup or stew; sweetened dough wrapped around fruit and baked.

dunce *n.* A slow-witted person; a person not prepared for lessons.

dune *n.* A ridge or hill of sand blown or drifted by the wind.

dun•ga•rees *pl. n.* Trousers made of sturdy, coarse, cotton fabric.

dun•geon *n.* A dark, confining, underground prison chamber.

dunk *v.* To dip a piece of food into liquid before eating; to submerge someone in a playful fashion.

du•o *n.* An instrument duet; two people in close association.

du•plex *n.* An apartment with rooms on two adjoining floors.

du•pli•cate *adj.* Identical with another; existing in or consisting of two corresponding parts; a copy.

du•ra•ble *adj.* Able to continue for a prolonged period of time without damage; physically strong; able to last.

du•ress *n.* Constraint by fear or force; in law, coercion illegally applied; forced restraint.

dur•ing *prep.* While; throughout the time of; within the time of.

dusk *n.* The earliest part of the evening, just before darkness.

dust *n.* Fine, dry particles of matter. *v.* To remove fine particles from a surface with a cloth.

du•ty *n.* Something a person must or ought to do; an obligation.

dwarf *n.* A human, plant, or animal of a much smaller than normal size.

dwell *v.* To live, as an inhabitant.

dwell•ing *n.* A house or building where one lives.

dy•na•mite *n.* An explosive composed of nitroglycerin and other materials, usually packaged in stick form. *v.* To blow up with dynamite.

dy•nam•ics *n.* The part of physics which deals with force, energy, and motion and the relationship between them.

dys•lex•i•a *n.* An impairment in one's ability to read. **dyslexic** *adj.*

E

E, e The fifth letter of the English alphabet; in music, the third tone in the natural scale of C.

each *adj.* Every one of two or more considered separately. *adv.* Apiece.

ea•ger *adj.* Enthusiastic or anxious; having a great desire or wanting something.

ea•gle *n.* A large bird of prey having a powerful bill, broad strong wings, and soaring flight.

ear *n.* The hearing organ in vertebrates, located on either side of the head; the ability to hear keenly.

earl *n.* A British title for a nobleman ranking above a viscount and below a marquis. **earldom** *n.*

ear•ly *adj.* Occurring near the beginning of a period of time; before the usual or expected time; occurring in the near future.

ear•ly bird *n.* An early riser; a person who arrives early.

earn *v.* To receive payment in return for work done or services rendered; to gain as a result of one's efforts.

ear•nest *adj.* Serious; sincere; without trickery or guile;

earn•ings *pl. n.* Something earned, such as a salary.

earth *n.* The third planet from the sun and the planet on which there is life; the outer layer of the world; ground; soil; dirt.

ease *n.* A state of being comfortable; relaxation; freedom from pain, discomfort, or care.

ea•sel *n.* A frame used by artists to support a canvas or picture.

east *n.* The direction opposite of west; the direction in which the sun rises.

eas•y *adj.* Done with little difficulty; free from worry or pain; simple.

eas•y•go•ing *adj.* Taking life easy; without worry, concern, or haste.

eat *v.* To chew and swallow food; to take a meal.

eaves *pl. n.* The overhanging edge of a roof.

ebb *n.* The return of the tide towards the sea; a time of decline. *v.* To recede, as the tide does; to fall or flow back; to weaken.

ebb tide *n.* The tide while at ebb; a period

of decline.

eb•o•ny *n.* The dark, hard, colored wood from the center of the ebony tree of Asia and Africa. *adj.* Resembling ebony; black.

e•bul•lient *adj.* Filled with enthusiasm. **ebullience** *n.*, **ebulliently** *adv.*

ec•cen•tric *adj.* Differing from an established pattern or accepted norm; deviating from a perfect circle; not located at the geometrical center. *n.* An odd or erratic person; a disk or wheel with its axis not situated in the center. **eccentrically** *adv.*, **eccentricity** *n.*

ec•cle•si•as•ti•cal *n.* A clergyman; a person officially serving a church. *adj.* Of or relating to a church.

ech•e•lon *n.* A formation, as of military aircraft or naval vessels, resembling a series of steps where each rank is positioned slightly to the right or left of the preceding one; a level of command or authority; a hierarchy.

ech•o *n.* Repetition of a sound by reflecting sound waves from a surface; the sound produced by reflection; a repetition. *v.* To repeat or be repeated by; to imitate. **echoes** *pl.*

ec•lec•tic *adj.* Having components from many different sources or styles.

e•clipse *n.* A total or partial blocking of one celestial body by another. *v.* To fall into obscurity or decline; to cause an eclipse of.

e•clip•tic *n.* The circle formed by the intersection of the plane of the earth's orbit and the celestial sphere.

ec•o•cide *n.* The deliberate destruction of the natural environment, caused by pollutants.

e•col•o•gy *n.* The branch of science concerned with how organisms relate to their environments. **ecologist** *n.*

ec•o•nom•i•cal *adj.* Not wasteful; frugal; operating with little waste.

ec•o•nom•ics *n.* The science relating to the development, production, and management of material wealth, and which treats production, distribution, and consumption of commodities.

e•con•o•mize *v.* To manage thriftily; to use sparingly.

e•con•o•my *n.* Careful management of money, materials, and resources; a reduction in expenses.

ec•ru *n.* A light yellowish brown, as the color of unbleached linen.

ec•sta•sy *n.* The state of intense joy or delight. **ecstatic** *adj.*, **ecstatically** *adv.*

ec•ze•ma *n.* A noncontagious inflammatory skin condition, marked by itching and scaly patches. **eczematous** *adj.*

ed•dy *n.* A current, as of water, running against the direction of the main current, especially in a circular motion.

edge *n.* The thin, sharp, cutting side of a blade; keenness; sharpness.

ed•i•ble *adj.* Safe or fit to eat.

e•dict *n.* A public decree; an order or command officially proclaimed.

ed•i•fy *v.* To benefit and enlighten, morally or spiritually. **edification** *n.*

ed•it *v.* To prepare and correct for publication; to put together for an edition; to delete or change. **editor** *n.*

e•di•tion *n.* The form in which a book is published; the total number of copies printed at one time.

ed•i•to•ri•al *n.* An article in a newspaper or magazine which expresses the opinion of a publisher or editor.

ed•u•cate *v.* To supply with training or schooling; to supervise the mental or moral growth of. **educator** *n.*

e•duce *v.* To call forth or bring out; to develop from given facts.

eel *n.* A snake-like marine or freshwater fish without scales or pelvic fins.

ee•rie or **ee•ry** *adj.* Suggesting the unexplainable or strange; spooky. **eerily** *adv.*, **eeriness** *n.*

ef•face *v.* To remove or rub out; to make unnoticeable

ef•fect *n.* Something produced by a cause; the power to produce a desired result.

ef•fec•tive *adj.* Producing an expected

effeminate

effect or proper result.

ef·fem·i·nate *adj.* Having a more woman-like quality or trait than a man. **effeminacy** *n.*, **effeminately** *adv.*

ef·fete *adj.* Exhausted of effectiveness or force; worn-out; decadent.

ef·fi·ca·cious *adj.* Producing an intended effect. **efficaciously** *adv.*

ef·fi·cient *adj.* Adequate in performance with a minimum of waste or effort.

ef·fi·gy *n.* A life-size sculpture or painting representing a crude image or dummy, especially of a disliked person.

ef·flu·ence *n.* An act of flowing out; something that flows out or forth. **effluent** *adj.*, *n.*

ef·fort *n.* Voluntary exertion of physical or mental energy; a normally earnest attempt or achievement.

ef·ful·gent *adj.* Shining brilliantly; radiant. **effulgence** *n.*

ef·fu·sion *n.* An instance of pouring forth; an unrestrained outpouring of feeling. **effuse** *v.*, **effusive** *adj.*, **effusively** *adv.*

egg *n.* The hard-shelled reproductive cell of female animals, especially one produced by a chicken, used as food.

egg·head *n.* An intellectual; highbrow.

egg·nog *n.* A drink of beaten eggs, sugar, and milk, often mixed with alcohol.

egg·roll *n.* A thin egg-dough fried casing filled with minced vegetables and sometimes meat or seafood.

e·go *n.* The self-thinking, feeling, and acting distinct from the external world; the consciousness of self.

e·go·cen·tric *adj.* Self-centered; thinking, observing, and regarding oneself as the object of all experiences.

e·go·ma·ni·a *n.* Self-obsession. **egomaniac** *n.*, **egomaniacal** *adj.*

e·gre·gious *adj.* Outstandingly or remarkably bad; flagrant.

e·gress *n.* The act of coming out; emergence; a means of departing; exit.

e·gret *n.* Any of several species of white wading birds having long plumes.

eight *n.* The cardinal number which follows seven.

ei·ther *pron.* One or the other. *adj.* One or the other of two. *adv.* Likewise; also. *conj.* Used before the first of two or more alternatives linked by or.

e·ject *v.* To throw out; to expel.

e·lab·o·rate *adj.* Planned or carried out with great detail; very complex; intricate. *v.* To give more detail.

e·lapse *v.* To slip or glide away; to pass in time.

e·las·tic *adj.* Flexible; capable of easy adjustment. **elasticity** *n.*

e·late *v.* To fill with joy; to become exuberant; to make proud of.

el·bow *n.* The outer joint of the arm between the upper arm and forearm; a sharp turn, as in a river or road, which resembles an elbow.

el·bow·room *n.* Ample room to move about; enough space for comfort.

eld·er *adj.* Older. *n.* One who is older than others; a person of great influence; an official of the church; a shrub bearing reddish fruit.

e·lect *v.* To choose or select by vote, as for an office; to make a choice.

e·lec·tric *adj.* Relating to electricity.

e·lec·tri·cian *n.* A person who installs or maintains electric equipment.

e·lec·tric·i·ty *n.* An interchange of charged particles on the atomic level; a force that causes bodies to attract or repel each other, responsible for a natural phenomena as lightning; electric current as a power source; emotional excitement.

e·lec·tro·car·di·o·gram *n.* The record produced by an electrocardiograph machine.

e·lec·tro·cute *v.* To kill or execute by the use of electric current.

e·lec·trode *n.* A conductor by which an electric current enters or leaves.

e·lec·tro·dy·nam·ics *n.* The study of the interactions of moving electric charges. **electrodynamic** *adj.*

e·lec·trol·y·sis *n.* A chemical decomposition by an electric current; destruction of tumors or hair roots by an electric current.

e•lec•tro•mag•net *n.* A magnet consisting of a soft iron core magnetized by electric current passing through a wire which is coiled around the core.

e•lec•tron *n.* A subatomic particle with a negative electric charge found outside of an atom's nucleus.

e•lec•tro•stat•ic *adj.* Pertaining to static electric charges.

el•e•gance *n.* Refinement in appearance, movement, or manners.

el•e•gy *n.* A poem expressing sorrow for one who is dead.

el•e•ment *n.* A basic part of a construction; a substance not separable into less complex substances by chemical means. *pl.* The conditions of the weather; natural forces.

el•e•men•ta•ry *adj.* Fundamental, essential; referring to elementary school.

el•e•phant *n.* A large mammal with thick grey hide, a long flexible trunk, and curved tusks.

el•e•vate *v.* To lift up or raise; to promote to a higher rank.

e•lev•en *n.* A cardinal number with a sum equal to ten plus one.

elf *n.* An imaginary being with magical powers, often mischievous; a small, mischievous child. **elves** *pl.*, **elfish** *adj.*

e•lic•it *v.* To bring or draw out; to evoke.

e•lide *v.* To omit, especially to slur over in pronunciation, as a vowel, consonant, or syllable. **elision** *n.*

e•lim•i•nate *v.* To get rid of, remove; to omit.

e•lite *n.* The most skilled members of a group; a small, powerful group.

e•lix•ir *n.* A sweetened aromatic liquid of alcohol and water, used as a vehicle for medicine; a medicine regarded as a cure-all.

elk *n.* The largest deer of Europe and Asia.

ell *n.* An extension of a building at right angles to the main structure.

el•lipse *n.* A closed curve, somewhat oval in shape, with two focal points. **elliptic,**

elliptical *adj.*

elm *n.* Any of various valuable timber and shade trees with arching branches.

el•o•cu•tion *n.* The art of effective public speaking. **elocutionary** *adj.*, **elocutionist** *n.*

e•lope *v.* To run away, especially in order to get married, usually without parental permission. **elopement** *n.*

el•o•quent *adj.* Having the power to speak fluently and persuasively; vividly expressive.

else *adj.* Different; other; more; additional. *adv.* In addition; besides.

else•where *adv.* To or in another place.

e•lu•ci•date *v.* To make clear, clarify; to explain. **elucidator**, **elucidation** *n.*

e•lude *v.* To evade or avoid; to escape understanding.

e•ma•ci•ate *v.* To become or cause to become extremely thin from the loss of appetite. **emaciation** *n.*

e-mail or **e•mail** *n.* In computers, electronic messages sent to specific network addresses.

em•a•nate *v.* To come or give forth, as from a source. **emanation** *n.*

e•man•ci•pate *v.* To liberate; to set free from bondage.

e•mas•cu•late *v.* To castrate; to deprive of masculine vigor.

em•balm *v.* To treat with preservatives in order to protect from decay.

em•bank•ment *n.* A support or defense made of a bank of earth or stone.

em•bar•go *n.* A prohibition or restraint on trade, as a government order forbidding the entry or departure of merchant vessels.

em•bark *v.* To board a ship; to set out on a venture.

em•bar•rass *v.* To cause to feel self-conscious; to make one feel confusion or inadequacy.

em•bas•sy *n.* The headquarters of an ambassador; the center of representation of a government on foreign soil.

em•bat•tle *v.* To prepare or arrange for battle.

em•bed v. To fix or enclose tightly in a surrounding mass.

em•bel•lish v. To adorn or make beautiful with ornamentation; to decorate; to add to the details of.

em•ber n. A small piece of glowing coal or wood, as in a dying fire. pl. The smoldering ashes or remains of a fire.

em•bez•zle v. To take money or other items fraudulently and secretly.

em•bit•ter v. To make bitter; to create feelings of hostility.

em•blem n. A symbol of something; a distinctive design.

em•bo•dy v. To give a bodily form to; to personify. **embodiment** n.

em•bold•en v. To encourage; to make bold.

em•boss v. To shape or decorate in relief; to represent in relief.

em•bou•chure n. In music, the part of a wind instrument applied to the lips to produce a musical tone.

em•brace v. To clasp or hold in the arms; to hug; to surround.

em•broi•der v. To decorate with ornamental needlework; to add fictitious details to.

em•broil v. To involve in contention or violent actions; to throw into confusion.

em•bry•o n. An organism in its early developmental stage, before it has a distinctive form. **embryonic** adj.

e•mend v. To correct or remove faults; to edit or repair. **emendation** n.

em•er•ald n. A bright-green, transparent gemstone variety of beryl.

e•merge v. To rise into view; to come into existence.

e•mer•gen•cy n. A sudden and unexpected situation requiring prompt action.

e•mer•i•tus adj. Retired from active duty but retaining the honorary title held immediately before retirement. **emeritus** n.

em•er•y n. A grainy, mineral substance having impure corundum, used for polishing and grinding.

e•met•ic n. A medicine used to induce vomiting.

em•i•grate v. To move from one country or region to settle elsewhere. **emigrant** n.

em•i•nent adj. High in esteem, rank, or office.

em•i•nent do•main n. The claim of a government's right to take or control property for public use.

em•is•sar•y n. A person sent out on a mission; an ambassador.

e•mit v. To send forth; to throw or give out.

e•mol•lient n. A substance for the soothing and softening of the skin.

e•mol•u•ment n. Profit; compensation, as a salary or perquisite.

e•mote v. To show emotion, as in acting; to express one's feelings.

e•mot•i•con n. In computers, a combination of keyboard symbols representing caricatures of human emotions such as happiness, skepticism, and surprise.

e•mo•tion n. A strong surge of feeling; any of the feelings of fear, sorrow, joy, hate, or love.

em•pa•thy n. Identification with and understanding the feelings of another person. **empathetic**, **empathic** adj.

em•per•or n. The ruler of an empire made of many countries.

em•pha•sis n. Special attention, significance or importance attached to anything.

em•phat•ic adj. Expressed or spoken with emphasis. **emphatically** adv.

em•pire n. Several territories or nations governed by a single supreme authority, the emperor.

em•pir•i•cal adj. Depending on or gained from observation or experiment rather than from theory and science. **empirically** adv.

em•ploy v. To engage the service or use of; to hire; to use.

em•ploy•ee or **em•ploy•e** n. A person who works for another in return for salary or wages.

em•po•ri•um *n.* A large store carrying general merchandise; a department store.

em•pow•er *v.* To authorize; to give power to; to license.

em•press *n.* A woman who rules an empire; an emperor's wife or widow.

emp•ty *adj.* Containing nothing; vacant; lacking substance. **emptiness** *n.*

e•mu *n.* A swift-running flightless Australian bird related to the ostrich.

em•u•late *v.* To strive to equal by imitating; to admire and follow as a role model.

e•mul•sion *n.* A suspended mixture of small droplets, one within the other; a light-sensitive coating on photographic paper, film, or plates. **emulsive** *adj.*

en•a•ble *v.* To give the power or ability to; to supply with adequate power, knowledge, or opportunity.

en•act *v.* To make into law; to carry out a plan.

e•nam•el *n.* A decorative or protective coating on a surface, as of pottery; a paint that dries to a hard, glossy surface; the hard outermost covering of a tooth.

en•am•or *v.* To inflame with love; to charm.

en•camp *v.* To form or stay in a camp; to settle into temporary shelter. **encampment** *n.*

en•cap•su•late *v.* To enclose or encase in a capsule. **encapsulation** *n.*

en•chain *v.* To put in chains; to enslave.

en•chant *v.* To put under a spell; to bewitch; to charm; to delight greatly.

en•cir•cle *v.* To form a circle around; to move around.

en•clave *n.* A country surrounded by a foreign country; a cultural group living within a larger group.

en•close *v.* To surround on all sides; to put in the same envelope or package with something else. **enclosure** *n.*

en•com•pass *v.* To surround; to form a circle; to enclose.

en•core *n.* An audience's demand for a repeat performance; a performance in response to an encore. *v.* To call for an encore.

en•coun•ter *n.* A meeting or conflict. *v.* To come upon unexpectedly; to confront in a hostile situation.

en•cour•age *v.* To inspire with courage or hope. **encouragingly** *adv.*

en•croach *v.* To intrude upon the rights or possessions of another; to step over onto another's property

en•crust *v.* To cover with a crust; to crust. **encrustation** *n.*

en•cryp•tion *n.* In computers, the process of encoding electronic information for privacy and security during transfer.

en•cum•ber *v.* To hinder or burden with difficulties or obligations. **encumbrance** *n.*

en•cy•clo•pe•di•a *n.* A comprehensive work with articles covering a broad range of subjects. **encyclopedic** *adj.*

end *n.* A part lying at a boundary; the terminal point.

en•dan•ger *v.* To expose or put into danger or imperil.

en•dan•gered *adj.* Threatened with extinction; in danger.

en•dear *v.* To make beloved or dear. **endearment** *n.*

en•deav•or *n.* A valiant try; a sincere attempt to attain or do something.

en•dem•ic *adj.* Peculiar to a particular area or people.

en•do•cri•nol•o•gy *n.* The area of science or study of the endocrine glands and various secretions. **endocrinologist** *n.*

en•dor•phin *n.* Hormones with tranquilizing and pain-killing capabilities, secreted by the brain.

en•dorse *v.* To support or recommend; to sign the back of a check.

en•dow *v.* To supply with a permanent income or income-producing property; to bestow upon. **endowment** *n.*

en•dure *v.* To undergo; to put up with; to bear.

end•wise *adv.* On end; lengthwise.

en•e•my *n.* One who seeks to inflict injury

on another; a foe; a hostile force or power.

en•er•gy *n.* Power for working or acting; vigor; strength; vitality.

en•er•vate *v.* To deprive of vitality or strength; to weaken. **enervation** *n.*

en•fee•ble *v.* To weaken; to make feeble.

en•fold *v.* To enclose; to wrap in layers; to embrace.

en•force *v.* To carry out the rules; to demand obedience.

en•fran•chise *v.* To grant with civil rights, as the right to vote; to give a franchise to. **enfranchisement** *n.*

en•gage *v.* To employ or hire; to hook together parts of a machine; to pledge oneself to marry.

en•gen•der *v.* To give rise to; to exist; to cause.

en•gine *n.* A machine that converts energy into mechanical motion; a mechanical instrument; a locomotive.

en•gorge *v.* To swallow greedily. Pathol. To fill an artery with blood. **engorgement** *n.*

en•grave *v.* To carve or etch into a surface, such as stone, metal, or wood for printing; to print from plates made by such a process.

en•grav•ing *n.* The act or technique of one that engraves; the impression printed from an engraved plate.

en•gross *v.* To occupy the complete attention of; to copy or write in a large, clear hand.

en•gulf *v.* To enclose completely; to submerge; to swallow up.

en•hance *v.* To make greater; to raise to a higher degree.

e•nig•ma *n.* Something that baffles; anything puzzling; a riddle.

en•join *v.* To command to do something; to prohibit, especially by legal action.

en•joy *v.* To feel joy or find pleasure in something.

en•large *v.* To make larger; to speak or write in greater detail.

en•light•en *v.* To give broadening or revealing knowledge; to give spiritual guidance or light to.

en•list *v.* To secure the help or active aid of; to sign up for the armed forces.

en•liv•en *v.* To make livelier or more or vigorous.

en•mesh *v.* To catch in a net; to entangle.

en•mi•ty *n.* Deep hatred; hostility.

en•no•ble *v.* To make noble or honorable in quality or nature; to confer the rank of nobility.

en•nui *n.* Boredom; weariness; a sense of meaninglessness and futility.

e•nor•mi•ty *n.* Excessive wickedness; an outrageous offense or crime.

e•nor•mous *adj.* Very great in size or degree; huge. **enormously** *adv.*, **enormousness** *n.*

e•nough *adj.* Adequate to satisfy demands or needs. *adv.* To a satisfactory degree.

en•rage *v.* To put or throw into a rage; to make very angry.

en•rap•ture *v.* To enter into a state of rapture; to delight.

en•rich *v.* To make rich or richer; to make more productive.

en•roll or **en•rol** *v.* To sign up for; to enter one's name on a roll or register.

en•sconce *v.* To settle securely; to shelter.

en•sem•ble *n.* A group of parts in harmony; a coordinated outfit of clothing; a group performing music together.

en•shrine *v.* To place in a shrine; to hold sacred.

en•sign *n.* An identifying flag or banner; as one displayed on a ship or aircraft.

en•slave *v.* To make a slave of; to put in bondage.

en•snare *v.* To catch; to trap in a snare.

en•sue *v.* To follow as a consequence; to occur afterwards.

en•sure *v.* To make certain of; to guarantee.

en•tail *v.* To have as a necessary accompaniment or result; to restrict the inheritance of property to a certain line of heirs. **entailment** *n.*

en•tan•gle *v.* To tangle; to make more complex.

en·ter *v.* To go or come into; to penetrate; to begin.

en·ter·prise *n.* A large or risky undertaking; a business organization; boldness and energy in practical affairs.

en·ter·tain *v.* To receive as a guest; to amuse; to consider as a possibility. **entertainer**, **entertainment** *n.*

en·thrall *v.* To fascinate; to captivate.

en·throne *v.* To place on a throne; to crown as leader.

en·thu·si·asm *n.* Intense feeling for a cause; eagerness.

en·tice *v.* To attract by arousing desire; to coax or convince.

en·tire *adj.* Having no part left out; whole; complete.

en·ti·tle *v.* To give a name to; to furnish with a right.

en·ti·tle·ment *n.* The right by birth and equality; one's automatic consideration and due.

en·ti·ty *n.* The fact of real existence; something that exists alone.

en·tomb *v.* To place in a tomb. **entombment** *n.*

en·to·mol·o·gy *n.* The study of insects.

en·trails *pl. n.* Internal organs of man or animals.

en·trance *n.* The act of entering; the means or place of entry; the first appearance of an actor in a play.

en·trance *v.* To fascinate; to put in a trance. **entrancing** *adj.*

en·trap *v.* To catch in a trap. **entrapment** *n.*

en·treat *v.* To make an earnest request; to beg for favor or permission.

en·trench *v.* To dig a trench, as for defense; to fix or sit firmly. **entrenchment** *n.*

en·tre·pre·neur *n.* A person who launches or manages a business venture. **entrepreneurial** *adj.*

en·trust *v.* To transfer to another for care; to share with.

en·try *n.* An opening or place for entering; an item entered in a book list.

en·twine *v.* To twine about or together.

e·nu·mer·ate *v.* To count off one by one; to number

e·nun·ci·ate *v.* To pronounce with clarity; to announce; proclaim.

en·ve·lope *n.* Something that covers or encloses; a paper case, especially for a letter, having a flap for sealing.

en·vi·a·ble *adj.* Highly desirable; able to be envied.

en·vi·ron·ment *n.* Surroundings; the combination of external conditions affecting the development and existence of an individual group or organism.

en·vi·ron·men·tal·ist *n.* A person who seeks to preserve the natural environment.

en·vi·rons *pl. n.* A surrounding region; a place; outskirts, especially of a city.

en·vis·age *v.* To have or form a mental image of.

en·voy *n.* A messenger or agent; an ambassador.

en·vy *n.* A feeling of discontent or resentment for someone else's possessions or advantages.

en·zyme *n.* Proteins produced by living organisms that function as biochemical catalysts in animals and plants.

e·on *n.* An indefinite but very long period of time.

e·phem·er·al *adj.* Lasting a very short time. **ephemera** *n.*

ep·ic *n.* A long narrative poem or story celebrating the adventures and achievements of a hero.

ep·i·cen·ter *n.* The part of the earth's surface directly above the focus of an earthquake.

ep·i·cure *n.* One having refined tastes, especially in food and wine.

ep·i·dem·ic *adj.* Breaking out suddenly and affecting many individuals at the same time. *n.* A fast-moving contagious disease.

ep·i·der·mis *n.* The outer, nonvascular layer of the skin. **epidermal** *adj.*

ep·i·gram *n.* A clever, brief, pointed

remark or observation; a terse, witty poem or saying. **epigrammatic** *adj*.

ep·i·graph *n*. An inscription on a tomb, monument, etc.; a motto or quotation placed at the beginning of a literary work.

ep·i·lep·sy *n*. A nervous disorder marked by attacks of unconsciousness with or without convulsions. **epileptic** *n*. or *adj*.

ep·i·logue *n*. A short speech given by an actor to the audience at the end of a play; an appended chapter placed at the end of a novel or book.

e·piph·a·ny *n*. The Christian festival held on January 6th, celebrating the manifestation of Christ to the Gentiles as represented by the Magi; also known as the Twelfth Day.

e·pis·co·pal *adj*. Pertaining to or governed by bishops.

ep·i·sode *n*. A section of a novel or drama complete in itself; an occurrence; an incident.

ep·och *n*. A point in time marking the beginning of a new era.

ep·ox·y *n*. A durable, corrosion-resistant resin used especially in surface glues and coatings.

eq·ua·ble *adj*. Not changing or varying; free from extremes; evenly proportioned; uniform; not easily upset. **equability** *n*.

e·qual *adj*. Of the same measurement, quantity, or value as another; having the same privileges or rights.

e·qual·ize *v*. To become or make equal or uniform. **equalization, equalizer** *n*.

e·qua·nim·i·ty *n*. Composure.

e·quate *v*. To consider or make equal.

e·qua·tion *n*. The act or process of being equal; a mathematical statement expressing the equality of two quantities.

e·qua·tor *n*. The great imaginary circle around the earth. **equatorial** *adj*.

e·ques·tri·an *n*. A person who rides or performs on a horse. **equestrienne** *n*.

e·qui·an·gu·lar *adj*. Having all angles equal.

e·qui·dis·tant *adj*. Having equal distances.

e·qui·lat·er·al *adj*. Having all sides equal.

e·qui·lib·ri·um *n*. The state of balance between two opposing forces or influences.

e·quine *adj*. Pertaining to or like a horse.

e·qui·nox *n*. Either of the two times a year when the sun crosses the celestial equator and the days and nights are equal in time. **equinoctial** *adj*.

e·quip *v*. To furnish or fit with whatever is needed for any undertaking or purpose.

e·quip·ment *n*. The materials used for a special purpose; gear; tools.

eq·ui·ta·ble *adj*. Being impartial in treatment or judgment.

eq·ui·ty Fairness or impartiality; the value of property beyond a mortgage or liability.

e·quiv·a·lent *adj*. Being equal or virtually equal, as in effect or meaning. **equivalence, equivalency, equivalent** *n*.

e·quiv·o·cal *adj*. Ambiguous; questionable.

e·quiv·o·cate *v*. To use intentionally evasive or vague language. **equivocation, equivocator** *n*.

er·a *n*. An extended period of time or point in the past used as the basis of a chronology.

e·rad·i·cate *v*. To destroy utterly; to remove by the roots. **eradicator, eradication** *n*.

e·rase *v*. To remove something written; to wipe out. **erasure** *n*.

e·rect *adj*. In a vertical position; standing up straight. *v*. To construct; build.

er·e·mite *n*. A hermit.

er·mine *n*. A weasel whose fur changes from brown to white depending on the season.

e·rode *v*. To wear away gradually by constant friction; to corrode; to eat away. **erosion** *n*.

e·rog·e·nous *adj*. Responsive to sexual stimulation.

e·ro·sion *n*. The state or process of being eroded.

e·rot·ic *adj*. Pertaining to or promoting sexual desire. **eroticism** *n*.

e•rot•i•ca *n.* Act or literature with an erotic quality.

err *v.* To make a mistake; to sin.

er•rand *n.* A short trip to carry a message or to perform a specific task, usually for someone else.

er•rant *adj.* Wandering or traveling about in search of adventure; straying from what is proper or customary.

er•rat•ic *adj.* Lacking a fixed course; irregular; inconsistent.

er•ro•ne•ous *adj.* Containing an error.

er•ror *n.* Something said, believed, or done incorrectly; a mistake; the state of being wrong or mistaken.

erst•while *adj.* Former.

er•u•dite *adj.* Scholarly; possessed of great learning. **erudition** *n.*

e•rupt *v.* To burst forth violently and suddenly; to explode with steam or lava, as a volcano or geyser.

es•ca•late *v.* To intensify, increase, or raise in energy.

es•ca•la•tor *n.* A moving stairway with steps attached to an endless belt.

es•ca•pade *n.* An adventure, especially a dangerous or illegal one.

es•cape *v.* To break free from capture or restraint; to enjoy temporary freedom from unpleasant realities.

es•cap•ism *n.* An escape from unpleasant realities through daydreams or other mental diversions.

es•chew *v.* To shun or avoid. **eschewal** *n.*

es•cort *n.* A person or persons accompanying another to give protection or guidance.

es•crow *n.* In law, a written deed, contract, or money placed in the custody of a third party until specified conditions are met.

es•cutch•eon *n.* A shield-shaped surface with an emblem bearing a coat of arms; a protective plate, as for a keyhole.

e•soph•a•gus *n.* The muscular, membranous tube through which food passes on the way from the mouth to the stomach.

es•o•ter•ic *adj.* Confidential; kept secret; understood or meant for only a particular and often very small group.

es•pi•o•nage *n.* The act or practice of spying to obtain secret intelligence information.

es•pou•sal *n.* Support or adoption, as of a cause; a wedding.

es•pouse *v.* To make something one's own; to take as a spouse; to marry; to give in marriage.

es•pres•so *n.* A strong coffee brewed by steam pressure from darkly roasted beans.

es•prit *n.* Spirit; wit; mental liveliness.

es•py *v.* To catch a quick view or sight of.

es•quire *n.* The title of courtesy or respect; sometimes written as Esq. behind a man's last name.

es•say *n.* A short composition on a single topic, expressing the author's viewpoint on a subject; an effort or attempt.

es•sence *n.* The real nature; the central true element.

es•sen•tial *adj.* Necessary; indispensable; containing of, or being an essence.

es•tab•lish *v.* To make permanent, stable, or secure; to install; to prove.

es•tab•lish•ment *n.* A place of business or residence; those who occupy positions of influence and status in a society.

es•tate *n.* An unusually large or extensive piece of land containing a large house.

es•teem *v.* To regard with respect. *n.* High regard; admiration.

es•thet•ic *adj.* Variation of aesthetic.

es•ti•ma•ble *adj.* Worthy of respect or admiration.

es•ti•mate *v.* To form or give an approximate opinion or calculation. *n.* A preliminary opinion or statement of the approximate cost for certain work.

es•trange *v.* To arouse hatred or indifference where there has been love and caring; to disassociate or remove oneself. estrangement *n.*

es•tu•ar•y *n.* The wide mouth of a river where the current meets the sea and is influenced by tides.

etch *v.* To engrave or cut into the surface

etching

by the action of acid; to sketch or outline by scratching lines with a pointed instrument.

etch·ing *n.* The process of engraving in which lines are scratched with a sharp instrument on a plate covered with wax or other coating after which the exposed parts are subjected to the corrosive action of an acid; a picture or impression made from an etched plate.

e·ter·nal *adj.* Existing without beginning or end; unending; meant to last indefinitely.

e·ter·ni·ty *n.* Existence without beginning or end; forever; the immeasurable extent of time; the endless time after a person dies.

e·the·re·al *adj.* Very airy and light; highly refined; delicate; heavenly. **ethereally** *adv.*

eth·ics *pl. n.* The system of moral values; the principle of right or good conduct. **ethical** *adj.*

eth·nic *adj.* Relating to or of a national, cultural, or racial group. **ethnicity** *n.*

eth·nog·ra·phy *n.* The branch of anthropology dealing with the classification and description of primitive human cultures.

eth·nol·o·gy *n.* The branch of anthropology concerned with the study of ethnic and racial groups, their cultures, origins, and distribution.

e·ti·ol·o·gy *n.* The science and study of causes or origins; the theory of the cause of a particular disease.

et·i·quette *n.* The prescribed rules, forms and practices for behavior in polite society; manners.

eu·ca·lyp·tus *n.* A large, native Australian tree with very aromatic leaves that yield an oil used medicinally.

eu·chre *n.* A card game for two to four players played with 32 cards in which the winning side must take three of five tricks.

eu·gen·ics *n.* The science of improving the physical and mental qualities of human beings through genetics. **eugenic**

adj., **eugenicist** *n.*

eu·lo·gize *v.* To write or deliver a eulogy for.

eu·lo·gy *n.* A speech that honors a person or thing, usually delivered at a funeral; high praise.

eu·nuch *n.* A castrated man.

eu·phe·mism *n.* A substitution for a word or expression that is thought to be too strong, blunt, or painful for another person. **euphemistic** *adj.*, **euphemistically** *adv.*

eu·pho·ny *n.* The agreeable sound of spoken words. **euphonious** *adj.*

eu·re·ka *inter.* An expression of triumph, discovery, understanding, or achievement.

eu·tha·na·sia *n.* The act or practice of putting to death painlessly a person suffering from an incurable disease; mercy killing.

eu·then·ics *n.* The study of improving the physical and mental qualities of human beings by controlling the environmental factors.

e·vac·u·ate *v.* To leave a threatened area or building.

e·vade *v.* To baffle; to elude; to get away from by using cleverness or tricks.

e·val·u·ate *v.* To examine carefully; to determine the value of; to appraise.

ev·a·nes·cent *adj.* Vanishing or passing quickly; fleeting. **evanescence** *n.*

e·van·gel·i·cal *adj.* Relating to the Christian gospel, especially the four Gospels of the New Testament; maintaining the doctrine that the Bible is the only rule of faith. **evangelicalism** *n.*, **evangelically** *adv.*

e·van·gel·ism *n.* The zealous preaching and spreading of the gospel.

e·vap·o·rate *v.* To convert into vapor; to remove the liquid or moisture from fruit, milk, or other products.

e·va·sion *n.* The act or means of evading.

e·va·sive *adj.* Being intentionally vague; equivocal.

eve *n.* The evening before a special day or holiday; the period immediately preceding some event; evening.

e•ven *adj.* Having a flat, smooth, and level surface; having no irregularities; smooth; equal in strength or number.

e•ven•hand•ed *adj.* Fair; impartial.

eve•ning *n* The time between sunset and bedtime.

eve•ning star *n.* The brightest planet visible in the west just after sunset, especially Venus.

e•vent *n.* A significant occurrence; something that takes place; a scheduled activity.

e•ven•tide *n.* Evening.

e•ven•tu•al *adj.* Happening or expected to happen in due course of time. **eventually** *adv.*

e•ven•tu•al•i•ty *n.* A likely or possible occurrence; the conceivable outcome.

e•ven•tu•ate *v.* To result ultimately; to come out eventually.

ev•er *adv.* At any time; on any occasion; by any possible chance or conceivable way.

ev•er•green *n.* A tree that has green foliage throughout the year.

ev•er•last•ing *adj.* Lasting or existing forever; eternal.

e•vert *v.* To turn inside out or outward.

eve•ry *adj.* Without exceptions; the utmost; all possible.

eve•ry•bo•dy *pron.* Every person.

eve•ry•day *adj.* Happening every day; daily; suitable for ordinary days.

eve•ry•one *pron.* Everybody; every person.

eve•ry•place *adv.* Everywhere.

eve•ry•thing *pron.* All things; whatever exists; whatever is needed, relevant, or important.

eve•ry•where *adv.* In, at, or to every place; in all places.

e•vict *v.* To put out or expel a tenant by legal process.

ev•i•dence *n.* Signs or facts on which a conclusion can be based.

ev•i•dent *adj.* Easily understood or seen; obvious.

e•vil *adj.* Morally bad or wrong; causing injury or any other undesirable result.

e•voke *v.* To call or summon forth; to draw forth or produce a reaction; to summon up the spirits by or as by incantations. **evocation** *n.*

ev•o•lu•tion *n.* The gradual process of development or change; a theory that all forms of life originated by descent from earlier forms.

e•volve *v.* To develop or change gradually; to emerge gradually as a result of a series of actions; to develop by evolutionary processes; to develop or work out. **evolvement** *n.*

ewe *n.* A female sheep.

ex•ac•er•bate *v.* To make more severe or worse; to aggravate. **exacerbation** *n.*

ex•act *adj.* Perfectly complete and clear in every detail; accurate in every detail with something taken as a model; similar. *v.* To force unjustly for the payment of something; to insist upon as strict right or obligation.

ex•act•ing *adj.* Making severe demands; rigorous; involving constant attention, hard work, and precision.

ex•act•i•tude *n.* The quality of being exact.

ex•act•ly *adv.* Precisely; entirely accurately.

ex•ag•ger•ate *v.* To represent something as being greater than it really is; to make greater in intensity or size than would be normal or expected.

ex•alt *v.* To raise in character, honor, rank, etc.; to praise or glorify; to increase the intensity of. **exalted** *adj.*, **exaltation** *n.*

ex•am *n.* An examination; a test of skill or knowledge; the act of examining or the state of being examined; medical testing and scrutiny.

ex•am•ine *v.* To observe or inspect; to test by questions or exercises, as to fitness or qualification. **examination** *n.*

ex•am•ple *n.* A representative as a sample; one worthy of imitation; a problem or exercise in arithmetic to show a rule or practice.

ex•as•per•ate *v.* To make frustrated or

angry; to irritate. **exasperatingly** *adv.*, **exasperation** *n.*

ex•ca•vate *v.* To dig a hole or cavity; to dig, scoop, or hollow out.

ex•ceed *v.* To surpass in quality or quantity; to go beyond the limit.

ex•ceed•ing•ly *adv.* Greater than; to an extraordinary degree or extreme.

ex•cel *v.* To surpass or to do better than others.

ex•cel•lence *n.* The state or quality of being superior or outstanding; the highest grade; a superior trait or quality. **excellent** *adj.*

ex•cel•si•or *n.* Long, firm wood shavings used in packing to protect delicate materials. *adj.* Upward; higher.

ex•cept *prep.* With the omission or exclusion of; aside from; not including.

ex•cep•tion *n.* Something excluded from; an example not conforming to the general class.

ex•cep•tion•a•ble *adj.* Open to objection or exception.

ex•cep•tion•al *adj.* Being an exception to the rule; well above average; outstanding.

ex•cerpt *n.* A passage from a book, speech, or other work.

ex•cess *n.* The condition of going beyond what is necessary, usual, or proper; overindulgence, as in drink or food. **excessive** *adj.*

ex•change *v.* To give in return for something else; to trade; to return as unsatisfactory and get a replacement; to barter.

ex•cise *n.* The indirect or internal tax on the production, consumption, or sale of a commodity, such as liquor or tobacco, that is produced, sold, and used or transported within a country.

ex•cit•a•ble *adj.* To be easily excited.

ex•cite *v.* To stir up strong feeling, action, or emotion.

ex•claim *v.* To cry out abruptly; to utter suddenly, as from emotion.

ex•cla•ma•tion *n.* An abrupt or sudden forceful utterance.

ex•cla•ma•tion point *n.* A punctuation mark used after an interjection or exclamation.

ex•clude *v.* To keep out; to omit from consideration.

ex•clu•sive *adj.* Intended for the sole use and purpose of a single individual or group. **exclusivity**, **exclusiveness** *n.*

ex•com•mu•ni•cate *v.* To deprive the right of church membership; to remove from membership or communality **excommunication** *n.*

ex•co•ri•ate *v.* To tear the skin or wear off; to censure harshly. **excoriation** *n.*

ex•cre•ment *n.* Bodily waste, especially feces. **excremental** *adj.*

ex•crete *v.* To throw off or eliminate waste matter by normal discharge from the body. **excretion** *n.*, **excretory** *adj.*

ex•cru•ci•at•ing *adj.* Intensely painful; agonizing.

ex•cul•pate *v.* To free from wrongdoing; to prove innocent of guilt. **exculpation** *n.*, **exculpatory** *adj.*

ex•cur•sion *n.* A short trip, usually made for pleasure; a trip available at a special reduced fare.

ex•cuse *v.* To ask forgiveness or pardon for oneself; to grant pardon or forgiveness. *n.* A reason or explanation.

ex•e•crate *v.* To detest; to feel or express detestation for; to abhor. **execration** *n.*

ex•e•cute *v.* To carry out; to put into effect; to validate.

ex•e•cu•tion *n.* The act of executing a job or task; a putting to death as a result of a legal decision, as the death penalty.

ex•ec•u•tion•er *n.* A person who puts others to death; a person who carries out a legal execution.

ex•ec•u•tive *n.* A manager or administrator in an organization; the branch of the government responsible for activating or putting laws into effect.

ex•ec•u•tor *n.* The person appointed to carry out the reading and execution of a will.

ex•e•ge•sis *n.* An interpretation or explanation of a text. **exegetical** *adj.*

ex•em•plar *n.* Something that serves as a worthy model or imitation; a typical example.

ex•em•pla•ry *adj.* Serving as a model; worthy of imitation; commendable as an example.

ex•em•pli•fy *v.* To show by giving examples; to be an example of. **exemplification** *n.*

ex•empt *adj.* Free from an obligation or duty to which others are subject.

ex•er•cise *n.* A drill or repeated activity to gain skill, such as practice on the piano.

ex•ert *v.* To put into action; to put oneself through a strenuous effort.

ex•hale *v.* To breathe out; the opposite of inhale; to breathe forth or give off, as air, vapor, or aroma.

ex•haust *v.* To make extremely tired; to drain oneself of resources or strength. *n.* The escape or discharge of waste gases from a machine or factory. **exhaustible** *adj.*, **exhaustion** *n.*

ex•haus•tive *adj.* Tending to exhaust or having the ability to exhaust; thorough, without exception or deletion; done in a way that eliminates all other effort. **exhaustively** *adv.*

ex•hib•it *v.* To display, as to put up for public view; to bring documents or evidence into a court of law. *n.* An exhibition or display of objects.

ex•hi•bi•tion•ism *n.* The practice of deliberately drawing undue attention to oneself. **exhibitionist** *n.*

ex•hil•a•rate *v.* To elate, make cheerful, or refresh. **exhilaration** *n.*

ex•hort *v.* To urge by earnest appeal or argument; to advise or recommend strongly. **exhortation** *n.*

ex•hume *v.* To dig up and remove from a grave; to disinter. **exhumation** *n.*

ex•i•gen•cy *n.* A pressing need or necessity. **exigence** *n.*, **exigent** *adj.*

ex•ile *n.* The separation by necessity or choice from one's native country or home; banishment; one who has left or been driven from his or her country.

ex•ist *v.* To have actual being or reality; to live.

ex•is•tence *n.* The state of existing, living, or occurring; the manner of existing.

ex•is•ten•tial•ism *n.* A philosophy that stressed the active role of the will rather than of reason in facing problems posed by a hostile universe. **existentialist** *n.*

ex•it *n.* A way or passage out; the act of going away or out; the departure from a stage.

ex•o•dus *n.* A going forth; a departure of large numbers of people, as that of Moses and the Israelites as described in Exodus, the second book of the Old Testament.

ex•on•er•ate *v.* To free or clear one from accusation or blame; to relieve or free from responsibility. **exoneration** *n.*

ex•or•bi•tant *adj.* Beyond usual and proper limits, as in price or demand.

ex•or•cise *v.* To cast out or expel an evil spirit by prayers or incantations; to free from an evil spirit. **exorcism**, **exorcist** *n.*

ex•ot•ic *adj.* Belonging by nature or origin to another part of the world; foreign; strangely different and fascinating.

ex•pand *v.* To increase the scope, range, volume, or size; to open up or spread out. **expansion** *n.*

ex•panse *n.* A wide, open space.

ex•pan•sion *n.* The act of or state of being expanded; the amount of increase in range, size, or volume.

ex•pan•sive *adj.* Capable of expanding or inclined to expand; characterized by expansion; broad and extensive; open and generous; outgoing. **expansively** *adv.*, **expansiveness** *n.*

ex•pa•ti•ate *v.* To leave one's country and reside in another; to send into exile; to banish. *n.* One who leaves a homeland to live elsewhere while maintaining citizenship. **expatriate**, **expatriation** *n.*

ex•pect *v.* To look forward to something as probable or certain; to look for as proper, right, or necessary.

ex·pec·tan·cy *n.* The action or state of expecting; expectation; an object or amount of expectation.

ex·pec·tant *adj.* Expecting; pregnant; anticipatory. **expectantly** *adv.*

ex·pec·ta·tion *n.* The state or act of expecting; something that is expected and looked forward to.

ex·pec·to·rate *v.* To spit. **expectoration** *n.*

ex·pe·di·ent *adj.* Promoting narrow or selfish interests; pertaining to or prompted by interest rather than by what is right. **expediently** *adv.*, **expedience** *n.*

ex·pe·dite *v.* To speed up the progress or process of something; to do with quick efficiency. **expediter** *n.*

ex·pe·di·tion *n.* A journey of some length for a definite purpose.

ex·pe·di·tious *adj.* Quick; speedy; capable of expediting.

ex·pel *v.* To drive or force out, as to dismiss from a school. **expulsion** *n.*

ex·pend *v.* To consume; to pay out or use up.

ex·pend·a·ble *adj.* Available for spending; capable of being sacrificed or done without. **expendability** *n.*

ex·pen·di·ture *n.* An amount spent; the act or process of expending.

ex·pense *n.* The outlay or cost; the amount of money required to buy or do something.

ex·pen·sive *adj.* Costing a lot of money; high-priced.

ex·pe·ri·ence *n.* The actual participation in something; the direct contact with; the knowledge or skill acquired from actual participation. **experienced** *adj.*

ex·per·i·ment *n.* The act or test performed to demonstrate or illustrate a truth. **experimentation** *n.*

ex·pert *n.* A person having great knowledge, experience, or skill in a certain field. *adj.* Skilled as the result of training or experience.

ex·per·tise *n.* A specialized knowledge, ability, or skill in a particular area.

ex·pi·ate *v.* To atone for; to make amends for. **expiation**, **expiator** *n.*, **expiatory** *adj.*

ex·pi·ra·tion *n.* The emission of breath; the act of breathing out; the time when something is no longer allowed or alive.

ex·pire *v.* To come to an end; to breathe out, as from the mouth; to exhale.

ex·plain *v.* To make understandable; to clarify; to give reasons for.

ex·ple·tive *n.* An exclamation, often profane.

ex·pli·ca·ble *adj.* Capable of explanation.

ex·pli·cate *v.* To clear up the meaning of; to interpret or analyze; to translate from metaphor or symbolism to common language. **explication** *n.*

ex·plic·it *adj.* Plainly expressed; specific; unreserved in expression; straightforward. **explicitly** *adv.*, **explicitness** *n.*

ex·plode *v.* To burst or blow up violently with a loud noise; to increase rapidly without control.

ex·ploit *n.* A notable or difficult deed or act. *v.* To use to the best advantage of; to make use of in a selfish or unethical way.

ex·plore *v.* To examine and investigate in a systematic way; to travel through unfamiliar territory. **exploration** *n.*, **exploratory** *adj.*

ex·plo·sion *n.* A sudden, violent release of energy; the sudden, violent outbreak of personal feelings. **explosive** *adj.*

ex·po·nent *n.* A person who represents or speaks for a cause or group; in mathematics, a number or symbol that indicates the number of times an expression is used as a factor. **exponential** *adj.*, **exponentially** *adv.*

ex·port *v.* To carry or send merchandise or raw materials to other countries for resale or trade. *n.* A commodity exported.

ex·pose *v.* To lay open, as to criticism or ridicule; to lay bare and uncovered.

ex·po·si·tion *n.* A statement of intent or meaning; a detailed presentation of subject matter; a commentary or interpretation; a large public exhibition.

ex•po•sure *n.* The act or state of being exposed; an indication of which way something faces; the act of exposing a sensitive plate or film; the time required for the film or plate to be exposed.

ex•pound *v.* To give a detailed statement of something; to explain the meaning at length.

ex•press *v.* To formulate in words; to verbalize; to state; to communicate through some medium other than words or signs; to release outward without regard to effect.

ex•pres•sion *n.* Communication of opinion, thought, or feeling; the outward indication of a condition, feeling, or quality; a particular phrase or word from a certain region of the country.

ex•pres•sion•ism *n.* An early twentieth century movement in the fine arts that emphasizes subjective expression of the artist's inner experiences rather than realistic representation.

ex•pres•sive *adj.* Of or characterized by expression; serving to indicate or express; full of expression. **expressively** *adv.*, **expressiveness** *n.*

ex•press•ly *adv.* Plainly; in direct terms.

ex•pro•pri•ate *v.* To transfer or take property from the owner for public use; to deprive a person or property or ownership. **expropriation** *n.*

ex•pul•sion *n.* The act of expelling or the state of being expelled.

ex•punge *v.* To delete or remove; to erase.

ex•pur•gate *v.* To remove obscene or objectionable material from a play, book, etc., before it is available to the public.

ex•qui•site *adj.* Delicately or intricately beautiful in design or craftsmanship; highly sensitive.

ex•tant *adj.* Still in existence; not lost or destroyed; surviving.

ex•tem•po•ra•ne•ous *adj.* Acting or performing with little or no advance preparation; spoken with regard to content, but not memorized or read word for word; designed for a sudden and singular occasion.

ex•tem•po•rize *v.* To make, do, or perform with little or no advance preparation; to improvise to meet circumstances.

ex•tend *v.* To stretch or open to full length; to make longer, broader, or wider.

ex•tend•ed *adj.* Pulled or extended out; stretched out.

ex•ten•sion *n.* The act or state of being extended; something protruding past its normal point.

ex•ten•sive *adj.* Widespread; far-reaching; having a wide range; broad in scope.

ex•tent *n.* The degree, dimension, or limit to which anything is extended; the area over which something extends; the size.

ex•ten•u•ate *v.* To minimize the seriousness of something as a crime or fault. **extenuating** *adj.*

ex•te•ri•or *adj.* Pertaining to or of the outside; the external layer.

ex•ter•mi•nate *v.* To annihilate; to destroy completely; to cause to cease to exist.

ex•tern or **ex•terne** *n.* A person associated with but not officially residing in a hospital or an institution.

ex•ter•nal *adj.* For or on the outside; acting from the outside.

ex•tinct *adj.* Inactive; no longer existing; extinguished.

ex•tin•guish *v.* To put an end to; to put out, as a fire; to make extinct.

ex•tol *v.* To praise highly; to compliment by a listing of accomplishments or qualities.

ex•tort *v.* To obtain money from a person by threat, oppression, or abuse of authority. **extortion**, **extortionist** *n.*

ex•tra *adj.* Over and above what is normal, required, or expected.

ex•tract *v.* To pull or draw out by force; to obtain in spite of resistance; to obtain from a substance as by pressure or distillation.

ex•trac•tion *n.* The process or act of extracting; a person's origin or ancestry.

ex•tra•cur•ric•u•lar *adj.* Pertaining to

activities not directly a part of the curriculum of a school or college.

ex•tra•dite *v.* To obtain or surrender by extradition. **extraditable** *adj.*

ex•tra•di•tion *n.* The legal surrender of an alleged criminal to the jurisdiction of another country, government, or state for trial.

ex•tra•mar•i•tal *adj.* Adulterous.

ex•tra•ne•ous *adj.* Coming from without; foreign; not vital or essential. **extraneously** *adv.*

ex•tra•or•di•nar•y *adj.* Outstanding; unusual; beyond what is usual or common; remarkable.

ex•trap•o•late *v.* To infer the possibility beyond the strict evidence of a series of events, facts, or observations; in mathematics, to infer the unknown information by projecting or extending known information. **extrapolation** *n.*

ex•tra•sen•so•ry *adj.* Beyond the range of normal sensory perception; pertaining to sensitivities beyond the five measurable senses.

ex•tra•ter•res•tri•al *adj.* Occurring, or originating outside the earth or its atmosphere.

ex•trav•a•gant *adj.* Overly lavish in expenditure; wasteful; exceeding reasonable limits; immoderate; unrestrained.

ex•trav•a•gan•za *n.* A lavish, spectacular, showy entertainment.

ex•treme *adj.* Greatly exceeding; going far beyond the bounds of moderation; exceeding what is considered moderate, usual, or reasonable.

ex•trem•ist *n.* A person who advocates or resorts to extreme measures or holds extreme views.

ex•trem•i•ty *n.* The utmost or farthest point; the greatest degree of distress or peril; an extreme measure; an appendage or limb of a body; a hand or foot.

ex•tri•cate *v.* To free from hindrance, entanglement, or difficulties; to disengage. **extrication** *n.*

ex•trin•sic *adj.* Not inherent; outside the nature of something; from the outside; external. extrinsically *adv.*

ex•tro•vert *n.* A person who is more interested in people and things outside himself than in his own private feelings and thoughts. **extroversion** *n.*

ex•trude *v.* To push or thrust out; to shape by forcing through dies under pressure; to project or protrude. **extrusion** *n.*

ex•u•ber•ant *adj.* Full of high spirits, vitality, vigor, and joy.

eye *n.* An organ of sight consisting of the cornea, iris, pupil, retina, and lens; a look; gaze; the ability to judge, perceive, or discriminate.

eye•ball *n.* The ball of the eye, enclosed by the socket and eyelids and connected at the rear to the optic nerve.

eye•brow *n.* The short hairs covering the bony ridge over the eye.

eye•glass *n.* A corrective lens used to assist vision. *pl.* A pair of corrective lenses set in a frame.

eye•lash *n.* The stiff, curved hairs growing from the edge of the eyelids.

eye•lin•er *n.* Makeup used to highlight the outline of the eyes.

eye•piece *n.* The lens or combination of lenses of an optical instrument closest to the eye.

eye•sight *n.* The faculty or power of sight; the range of vision.

eye•strain *n.* Fatigue or discomfort of the eyes, caused by excessive or improper use and marked by symptoms such as pain and headache.

eye•wit•ness *n.* A person who has seen something and can testify to it firsthand.

F

F, f The sixth letter of the English alphabet; in music, the fourth tone in the scale of C major; a failing grade.

fab•ri•cate *v.* To make or manufacture; to build; to construct by combining or assembling parts; to make up in order to deceive; to invent, as a lie or story. **fabrication, fabricator** *n.*

fa•ble *n.* A brief, fictitious story embodying a moral and using persons, animals, or inanimate objects as characters. **fabulist, fabler** *n.*, **fabled** *adj.*

fab•ric *n.* A cloth produced by knitting, weaving, or spinning fibers.

fab•u•lous *adj.* Past the limits of belief; incredible. **fabulously** *adv.*

face *n.* The front surface of the head from ear to ear and from forehead to chin; the principal, front, finished, or working surface of anything. *v.* To confront with awareness.

fac•et *n.* One of the flat, polished surfaces cut upon a gemstone; the small, smooth surface on a bone or tooth; a phase, aspect, or side of a person or subject. **faceted, facetted** *adj.*

fa•ce•tious *adj.* Given to or marked by playful jocularity; humorous.

fa•cial *adj.* Near, of, or for the face; a massage or other cosmetic treatment for the face.

fac•ile *adj.* Requiring little effort; easily achieved or performed; arrived at without due care, effort, or examination; superficial. **facilely** *adv.*, **facileness** *n.*

fa•cil•i•tate *v.* To make easier or less difficult. **facilitator** *n.*

fa•cil•i•ty *n.* Ease in performance, moving, or doing something; something that makes an operation or action easier.

fac•ing *n.* The lining or covering sewn to a garment.

fac•sim•i•le *n.* An exact copy, as of a document; the method of transmitting drawings, messages, or such by an electronic method. **fax** *abbrev.*

fact *n.* Something that actually occurred or exists; something that has real and demonstrable existence; actuality.

fac•tion *n.* A group or party within a government that is often self-seeking and usually in opposition to a larger group; discord.

fac•tious *adj.* Given to dissension; creating friction; divisive. **factiously** *adv.*

fac•ti•tious *adj.* Produced artificially; lacking authenticity or genuineness. **factitiously** *adv.*, **factitiousness** *n.*

fac•tor *n.* One of the elements or causes that contribute to produce the result; in mathematics, one of two or more quantities that when multiplied together give or yield a given product

fac•to•ry *n.* An establishment where goods are manufactured; an industrial plant.

fac•tu•al *adj.* Containing or consisting of facts, literal and exact. **factually** *adv.*

fac•ul•ty *n.* A natural ability or power; the complete teaching staff of a school or any other educational institution.

fad *n.* A temporary fashion adopted with wide enthusiasm.

fade *v.* To lose brightness, brilliance, or loudness gradually; to vanish slowly; to disappear gradually.

Fahr•en•heit *adj.* Of or relating to the temperature scale in which the freezing point of water is 32 degrees and the boiling point of water is 212 degrees under normal atmospheric pressure.

fail *v.* To be totally ineffective, unsuccessful; to go bankrupt; to receive an academic grade below the acceptable standards.

fail•ing *n.* A minor fault; a defect.

fail•ure *n.* The fact or state of failing; a breaking down in health, action, strength, or efficiency; in school, a failing grade.

faint *adj.* Having a little strength or vigor; feeble; lacking brightness or clarity; dim. *n.* A sudden, temporary loss of consciousness; a swoon. **faintly** *adv.*, **faintness** *n.*

faint•heart•ed *adj.* Lacking courage or conviction; cowardly; timid.

fair *adj.* Visually light in coloring; pleasing to the eye; beautiful; impartial; not stormy; without precipitation.

fair•way *n.* The part of a golf course between the tees and putting greens; the usual course through a harbor or channel.

fair•weath•er *adj.* Friendly only during good times.

fair•y *n.* A tiny imaginary being, capable of working good or ill.

fair•y•land *n.* Any delightful, enchanting place; the land of the fairies.

fair•y tale *n.* An incredible or fictitious tale of fanciful creatures; a tale about fairies.

faith *n.* A belief in the value, truth, or trustworthiness of someone or something; belief and trust in God; a system of religious beliefs.

faith•ful *adj.* True and trustworthy in the performance of duty, promises or obligations.

faith•less *adj.* Not being true to one's obligations or duties; lacking a religious faith; unworthy of belief or trust.

fake *adj.* Having a false or misleading appearance; not genuine.

fall *v.* To drop down from a higher place or position due to the removal of support or loss of hold or attachment; to collapse; to become less in rank or importance. *n.* The act of falling; a moral lapse or loss of innocence; autumn.

fal•la•cy *n.* A deception; an error in logic.

fall•back *n.* A place or position to which one can retreat.

fall guy *n.* A person left to receive the blame or penalties; scapegoat.

fal•li•ble *adj.* Capable of making an error; liable to be deceived or misled; apt to be erroneous. **fallibility** *n.*

fall•ing-out *n.* A fight, disagreement, or quarrel.

fall-off *n.* A decrease in something.

fal•lo•pi•an tube *n.* One of a pair of long, slender ducts serving as a passage for the ovum from the ovary to the uterus.

fal•low *n.* Ground that has been plowed but left unseeded during the growing season. **fallowness** *n.*

fal•low *adj.* Light yellowish-brown in color.

false *adj.* Contrary to truth or fact; incorrect. **falsity** *n.*

false•hood *n.* The act of lying; an intentional untruth.

fal•set•to *n.* An artificially high singing voice, usually male.

fal•si•fy *v.* To give an untruthful account of; to misrepresent

fal•ter *v.* To be uncertain or hesitant in action or voice; to waver.

fame *n.* Public esteem; a good reputation.

fa•mil•iar *adj.* Being well acquainted with; common; having good and complete knowledge of something. **familiarity** *n.*

fa•mil•iar•ize *v.* To make oneself or someone familiar with something.

fam•i•ly *n.* Parents and their children; a group of people connected by blood or marriage and sharing common ancestry.

fam•i•ly name *n.* A last name shared by family members.

fam•i•ly tree *n.* A genealogical diagram showing family descent.

fam•ine *n.* A widespread scarcity of food; severe hunger; starvation.

fam•ish *v.* To starve or cause to starve. **famished** *adj.*

fa•mous *adj.* Well known; renowned.

fan *n.* A device for putting air into motion, especially a flat, lightweight, collapsible, wedge-like shape; a machine that rotates thin, rigid vanes; an enthusiastic devotee of a sport, celebrity, or diversion.

fa•nat•ic *n.* One moved by a frenzy of enthusiasm or zeal. **fanatically** *adv.*, **fanaticism** *n.*

fan•ci•er *n.* A person having a special enthusiasm for or interest in something.

fan•ci•ful *adj.* Existing or produced only in the fancy; indulging in fancies.

fan•cy *n.* Imagination of a fantastic or whimsical nature; a notion or idea not based on evidence or fact; a whim or caprice.

fan•dan•go *n.* A Spanish or Spanish-American dance in triple time; the music for this dance.

fan•fare *n.* A short, loud trumpet flourish; a spectacular public display.

fang *n.* A long, pointed tooth or tusk an animal uses to seize or tear at its prey; a snake's hollow tooth.

fan•jet *n.* An aircraft with turbojet engines.

fan•ta•sia *n.* A composition structured according to the composer's fancy and not observing any strict musical form.

fan•ta•size *v.* To create mental fantasies; to imagine or indulge in fantasies. **fantasy** *n.*

fan•tas•tic *adj.* Existing only in fantasy; unreal; wildly fanciful or exaggerated; impulsive or capricious; coming from the imagination or fancy; superb.

fan•ta•sy *n.* A creative imagination; a creation of the fancy; an unreal or odd mental image.

FAQ *abbr.* Frequently asked questions; in computers, a list of informational answers to queries from network browsers to specific web sites.

far *adv.* From, to, or at a considerable distance; very remote in time, quality, or degree.

far•a•way *adj.* Very distant; remote; absent-minded; dreamy.

fare *v.* To be in a specific state; to turn out. *v.* A fee paid for hired transportation; food or a variety of foods.

fare•well *n.* Good-bye; a departure. *adj.* Closing; parting.

far-fetched *adj.* Neither natural nor obvious; highly improbable.

far-flung *adj.* Widely distributed over a great distance.

fa•ri•na *n.* A fine meat obtained chiefly from nuts, cereals, potatoes, or Indian corn, used as a breakfast food or in puddings.

farm *n.* Land cultivated for agricultural production or to breed and raise domestic animals.

farm•house *n.* The homestead on a farm.

farm•land *n.* Land that is suitable for agricultural production.

farm•stead *n.* A farm, including its land and all of the buildings.

farm•yard *n.* The area surrounded by farm buildings and enclosed for confining stock.

far-off *adj.* Distant; remote.

far-out *adj.* Very unconventional; at the edges of accepted or expected behavior.

far-reach•ing *adj.* Having a wide range, effect, or influence.

far•row *n.* A litter of pigs.

far-see•ing *adj.* Having foresight; prudent; wise; having the ability to see distant objects clearly.

far-sight•ed *adj.* Able to see things at a distance more clearly than things nearby; wise.

far•ther *adv.* To or at a more distant point.

far•thing *n.* Something of little worth; a former British coin worth 1/4 of a penny.

fas•ci•nate *v.* To attract irresistibly, as by beauty or other qualities.

fas•cism *n.* A one-party system of government marked by a centralized dictatorship, social and economic controls, and strong nationalism.

fash•ion *n.* The mode or manner of dress, living, and style that prevails in society; good form or style; current style.

fast *adj.* Swift; rapid; performed quickly; constant; steadfast. *v.* To give up food, especially for a religious reason.

fast•en *v.* To join something else; to connect; to securely fix.

fas•tid•i•ous *adj.* Exceedingly delicate or refined; hard to please in matters of taste. **fastidiousness** *n.*

fat *adj.* Having superfluous flesh or fat; obese; plump; containing much fat or oil. *n.* Any of a large class of yellowish to white, greasy liquids or solid substances widely distributed in animal and plant tissues.

fat•al *adj.* Causing death; deadly; bringing ruin or disaster; destructive; decisively important; fateful.

fa•tal•ism *n.* The belief that events or things are predetermined by fate and cannot be altered. **fatalist** *n.*, **fatalistic** *adj.*

fa•tal•i•ty *n.* A death caused by a disaster or accident.

fate *n.* The force or power held to predetermine events; fortune; inevitability.

fate•ful *adj.* Determining destiny; governed by fate; bringing death or disaster. **fatefully** *adv.*

fa•ther *n.* The male parent; any male forefather; ancestor; a male who establishes or founds something; a priest.

fa•ther-in-law *n.* The father of one's spouse.

fath•om•less *adj.* Too deep to measure; too difficult to understand.

fa•tigue *n.* The condition of extreme tiredness or weariness from prolonged physical or mental exertion.

fat•ten *v.* To make or become fat; to increase the amount of something. **fatted** *adj.*

fat•ty *adj.* Greasy; oily; having an excess of fat.

fau•cet *n.* A fixture with an adjustable valve to draw liquids from a pipe or cask.

fault *n.* An impairment or defect; a weakness; a minor offense or mistake; a break in the earth's crust allowing adjoining surfaces to shift in a direction parallel to the crack.

faun *n.* A woodland deity represented in Roman mythology as part goat and part man.

fau•na *n.* Animals living within a given area or environment. **faunal** *adj.*

fa•vor *n.* A helpful or considerate act; the attitude of friendliness or approval. *v.* To benefit; to give advantage; to prefer or like one more than another.

fa•vor•a•ble *adj.* Beneficial; advantageous; building up hope or confidence.

fa•vor•ite *n.* Anything regarded with special favor or preferred above all others.

fa•vor•it•ism *n.* Preferential treatment; a display of often unjust partiality.

fawn *n.* A young deer less than a year old; a light yellowish-brown color.

faze *v.* To worry; to disconcert. **fazed**, **fazing** *v.*

fe•al•ty *n.* The obligation of allegiance owed to a feudal lord by his vassal or tenant; faithfulness; loyalty.

fear *n.* The agitated feeling caused by the anticipation or the realization of danger; an uneasy feeling that something may happen contrary to one's hopes. **fearfulness** *n.*, **fearful** *adj.*, **fearfully** *adv.*

fear•less *adj.* Without fear; brave; courageous.

fear•some *adj.* Causing fear; timid.

fea•si•ble *adj.* Able to be put into effect or accomplished; practical. **feasibility** *n.*, **feasibly** *adv.*

feast *n.* A delicious meal; a banquet.

feat *n.* A notable act or difficult physical achievement.

feath•er *n.* One of the light, hollow-shafted structures that form the covering of birds.

fea•ture *n.* The appearance or shape of the face; the main presentation at a movie theater; a special article in a magazine or newspaper.

fed *v.* Past tense of *feed*.

fed•er•al *adj.* Relating to an agreement between two or more states or groups retaining certain controlling powers while being united under a central authority.

fe•do•ra *n.* A soft hat with a low crown creased lengthwise and a brim that can be turned up or down.

fee *n.* A fixed charge or payment for something; a charge for professional services.

fee•ble *adj.* Very weak; lacking in strength; ineffective.

feed *v.* To supply with food; to provide as food; to consume food; to keep supplied.

feed•back *n.* The return to the input of a portion of the output of a machine; the return of data for corrections or control.

feel *v.* To examine, explore, or perceive through the sense of touch; to perceive as a physical sensation; to believe.

feet *n.* The plural of *foot*.

feign *v.* To make a false show of; to dream up a false story and tell it as the truth; to fabricate; to imitate to deceive; to pretend. **feigned** *adj.*

feint *n.* Deceptive or misleading movement intended to draw defensive action away from the real target.

fe·lic·i·tous *adj.* Most appropriate; well chosen; pertinent or effective in manner or style; possessing qualities of balance and beauty beyond the ability to describe. **felicitously** *adv.*

fe·lic·i·ty *n.* Happiness; bliss; a natural and suitable juxtaposition of conditions.

fe·line *adj.* Of or relating to cats, including wild and domestic cats.

fell *v.* Past tense of *fall*; to strike or cause to fall down, as a tree.

fel·low *n.* A boy or man; an associate, comrade; one of a pair.

fel·low·ship *n.* A friendly relationship; the condition or fact of having common interests, ideals, or experiences.

fel·on *n.* A person who has committed a felony.

fel·o·ny *n., pl.* **-ies** A serious crime, such as rape, murder, or burglary, punishable by a severe sentence. **felon** *n.*, **felonious** *adj.*

felt *v.* Past tense of *feel*. *n.* An unwoven fabric made from pressed animal fibers, as wool or fur.

fe·male *n.* The sex that produces ova or bears young; a plant with a pistil but no stamen, capable of being fertilized and producing fruit. *adj.* Of or relating to the sex that produces ova or bears young.

fem·i·nine *adj.* Pertaining to or of the female gender; female.

fem·i·nism *n.* The movement of advocating the granting of the same social, political, and economic rights to women as the ones granted to men. **feminist** *n.*, **feministic** *adj.*

fe·mur *n.* The bone extending from the pelvis to the knee.

fen *n.* A low, marshy land; a bog.

fence *n.* A structure made from rails, stakes, or strung wire functioning as a boundary or barrier.

fenc·ing *n.* The sport of using a foil or saber; the material used to make fences; fences collectively.

fend *v.* To ward off or to keep off; to offer resistance.

fend·er *n.* The protective device over the wheel of a car or other vehicle; a metal guard set in front of an open fireplace; the projection on the front of a locomotive or streetcar, designed to push obstructions from the tracks, also known as cow-catcher.

fen·nel *n.* A tall herb from the parsley family which produces an edible stalk and aromatic seeds used as a flavoring.

fe·ral *adj.* Not tame nor domesticated; returned to a wild state; in an untamed state; wolf-like.

fer-de-lance *n.* A large, venomous snake of tropical America, with gray and brown markings.

fer·ment *n.* Any substance or agent producing fermentation, as yeast, mold, or enzyme; excitement; unrest; agitation.

fer·men·ta·tion *n.* The decomposition of complex organic compounds into simpler substances; the conversion of glucose into ethyl alcohol through the action of zymase; great agitation; commotion.

fern *n.* Any of a number of flowerless, seedless plants, having fronds with divided leaflets and reproducing by spores.

fe·ro·cious *adj.* Extremely savage, fierce, or bloodthirsty. **ferocity** *n.*

fer·ry *n.* A boat or other craft used to transport people and vehicles across a body of water; a ferryboat.

fer·tile *adj.* Having the ability to reproduce; rich in material required to maintain plant growth. **fertility**, **fertileness** *n.*

fer·til·ize *v.* To make fertile; to cause to be productive or fruitful.

fer·til·iz·er *n.* A material that fertilizes and enriches soil, such as nitrates or manure.

fer·vent *adj.* Passionate; ardent; very hot.

fer·vid *adj.* Fervent to an extreme degree; impassioned; very hot; burning. **fervidly** *adv.*

fer·vor *n.* Great emotional warmth or intensity.

fes·tal *adj.* Pertaining to or typical of a festival, holiday, or feast.

fes•ter *v.* To develop or generate pus; to be a constant source of irritation or resentment.

fete *n.* A festival or feast; a very elaborate outdoor celebration.

fet•id *adj.* Having a foul odor; stinking. **fetidly** *adv.*, **fetidness** *n.*

fet•ish *n.* An object regarded as having magical powers; something that one is devoted to excessively or irrationally; a nonsexual object that arouses or gratifies sexual desires. **fetishistic** *adj.*, **fetishist** *n.*

fes•ti•val *n.* A particular holiday or celebration or a regularly occurring occasion.

fes•tive *adj.* Relating to or suitable for a feast or other celebration. **festively** *adv.*, **festiveness**, **festivities** *n.*

fetch *v.* To go after and return with; to draw forth.

fe•tus *n.* The individual unborn organism carried within the womb from the time major features appear. **fetal** *adj.*

feud *n.* A bitter quarrel between two families, usually lasting a long period of time.

feu•dal•ism *n.* The political, social, and economic system of the Medieval period offering labor in exchange for protection from marauding hordes. **feudalist** *n.*, **feudalistic** *adj.*

fe•ver *n.* Abnormally high body temperature and rapid pulse; a craze; a heightened emotion or activity.

few *adj.* Small in number; not many; several. *n.* A select or limited group.

fey *adj.* Seemingly spellbound; having clairvoyance; acting as if under a spell.

fez *n.* A red felt, black-tasseled hat worn by Egyptian men.

fi•an•ce *n.* A man to whom a woman is engaged to be married.

fi•an•cee *n.* A woman to whom a man is engaged to be married.

fi•as•co *n.* A complete or total failure.

fi•at *n.* A positive and authoritative order or decree.

fib *n.* A trivial lie. **fib** *v.*, **fibber** *n.*

fi•ber *n.* A fine, long, continuous piece of natural or synthetic material made from a filament of asbestos, spun glass, textile, or fabric; internal strength; character. **fibrous** *adj.*

fib•ril•la•tion *n.* The rapid and uncoordinated contraction of the muscle fibers of the heart.

fick•le *adj.* Inconstant in purpose or feeling; changeable.

fic•tion *n.* Something created or imaginary; a literary work produced by the imagination and not based on fact. **fictional** *adj.*

fic•ti•tious *adj.* Nonexistent; not genuine; false; not real.

fid•dle *n.* A violin. *v.* To play the violin; to fidget or make nervous or restless movements.

fi•del•i•ty *n.* Faithfulness or loyalty to obligations, vows, or duties; a sound system's ability to deliver pure rich sound without distortion.

fidg•et To move nervously or restlessly.

field *n.* A piece of land with few or no trees; a cultivated piece of land devoted to the growing of crops; an area in which a natural resource such as oil is found; an airport; the complete extent of knowledge in a given area; in sports, the playing area.

fierce *adj.* Savage, violent, or frightening.

fier•y *adj.* Containing or composed of fire; brightly glowing; blazing; hot and inflamed.

fife *n.* A small, shrill-toned instrument similar to a flute.

fif•teen *n.* The cardinal number equal to 14 + 1. **fifteenth** *adj.*

fifth *adj.* The ordinal of five; one of five equal parts.

fif•ty *n.* The cardinal number equal to 5 x 10. **fiftieth** *adj.*

fif•ty-fif•ty *adj.* Divided into two equal portions or parts; shared evenly.

fig *n.* A tree or shrub bearing a sweet, pear-shaped, edible fruit.

fight *v.* To struggle against in combat; to quarrel; to argue; to make one's way by struggling.

fight•er *n.* A person who fights; a fast,

highly maneuverable airplane used in combat.

fig•ure *n.* A symbol or character that represents a number; anything other than a letter; the visible form of something; the human form or body. *v.* To represent; to depict; to compute.

fig•ure eight *n.* A skating maneuver shaped like an 8; anything shaped like the number 8.

fig•u•rine *n.* A small sculptured or molded figure; a statuette.

fil•a•ment *n.* A very thin, finely spun fiber, wire, or thread; the fine wire enclosed in an electric lamp bulb which is heated electrically to incandescence.

filch *v.* To steal by secretive removal of small amounts. **filcher** *n.*

file *n.* A device for storing papers in proper order; a collection of papers so arranged; a hard, steel instrument with ridged cutting surfaces, used to smooth or polish. *v.* To march as a soldier; to make an application as for a job.

fil•i•bus•ter *n.* An attempt to prolong, prevent, or hinder legislative action by using delaying tactics such as long speeches. **filibuster** *v.*

fil•i•gree *n.* Delicate, lace-like ornamental work made of silver or gold intertwined wire.

fi•lings *pl. n.* Particles removed by a file.

fill *v.* To put into or hold as much of something as can be contained; to supply fully.

fill•er *n.* Something added to increase weight or bulk or to take up space; a material used to fill cracks, pores, or holes.

fill•ing *n.* That which fills something, especially the substance put into a prepared cavity in a tooth.

fill•ing sta•tion *n.* A retail business where vehicles are serviced with gasoline, oil, water, and air for tires.

fil•lip *n.* A snap of the finger that has been pressed down by the thumb and then suddenly released; something that arouses or excites.

film *n.* A thin covering, layer, or membrane; a photosensitive strip or sheet of flexible cellulose material used to make photographic negatives or transparencies; an entertainment on film; a movie.

fil•ter *n.* A cloth, paper, or charcoal device that separates matter from liquid. *v.* To strain or use a filter. **filterability** *n.*

filth *n.* Anything dirty or foul; something considered offensive.

filth•y *adj.* Highly unpleasant; morally foul; obscene.

fil•trate *v.* To pass or cause to pass through something. *n.* Anything which has passed through the filter. **filtration** *n.*

fin *n.* A thin membranous extension of the body of a fish or other aquatic animal, used for swimming and balancing.

fi•na•gle *v.* To get something by trickery or deceit.

fi•nal *adj.* Coming to the end; last or terminal. **finality** *n.*, **finally** *adv.*

fi•na•le *n.* The last part, as the final scene in a play or the last part of a musical composition.

fi•nal•ist *n.* A contestant taking part in the final round of a contest.

fi•nal•ize *v.* To put into final and complete form.

fi•nals *pl. n.* Something decisively final, as the last of a series of athletic contests; the final academic examination.

fi•nance *n.* The science of monetary affairs. *pl.* Monetary resources; funds. *v.* To supply the capital or funds for something; to sell or provide on a credit basis. **financial** *adj.*, **financially** *adv.*

finch *n.* A small bird, as a grosbeak, canary, or goldfinch, having a short stout bill.

find *v.* To discover unexpectedly; to achieve, attain, or ascertain; to determine; to recover or regain. **finding** *n.*

find•er *n.* A person who finds; the device on a camera that indicates what will be in the picture.

find•ing *n.* Something found or discovered. *pl.* Conclusions or statistics that are the result of a study, examination, or investigation.

fine

fine *adj.* Superior in skill or quality; very enjoyable and pleasant; light and delicate in workmanship, texture, or structure.

fine arts *pl. n.* The arts of painting, sculpture, architecture, literature, music, dance, and drama.

fin•er•y *n.* Elaborate jewels and clothes.

fi•nesse *n.* A highly refined skill; the skillful handling of a situation; graceful or subtle handling.

fin•ger *n.* One of the digits of the hand, usually excluding the thumb.

fin•ger•ing *n.* In music, the technique of using the fingers in order to play a musical instrument; the marking that indicates which fingers are to be used.

fin•ger•nail *n.* The transparent covering on the dorsal surface of each fingertip.

fin•ger•print *n.* An inked impression of the pattern formed by the ridges of the skin on the tips of each finger and thumb.

fin•ger•tip *n.* The extreme end of a finger.

fin•i•al *n.* The ornamental projection or terminating part, as on a lamp shade or chair back.

fin•ick•y *adj.* Hard to please; choosy.

fin•ish *v.* To bring to or reach an end; to conclude; to give a glossy polish. *n.* The surface texture or gloss of a flat structure.

fi•nite *adj.* Having bounds or limits; of or relating to a number which can be determined, counted, or measured.

fir *n.* An evergreen tree with flat needles and erect cones.

fire *n.* The chemical reaction of burning, which releases heat and light; combustion; rapid oxidation. *v.* To bake in a kiln; to discharge a firearm or explosive; to let a person go from a job; to dismiss.

fire a•larm *n.* A safety device to signal the outbreak of a fire.

fire•arm *n.* A small weapon used for firing a missile.

fire•ball *n.* A very bright meteor; a hot, incandescent sphere of air and vaporized debris; a remarkably energetic person or thing.

fire•box *n.* A box that contains a fire alarm; the compartment in which the fuel of a locomotive or furnace is burned.

fire•brand *n.* A piece of glowing or burning wood; one who stirs up or agitates conflict or trouble.

fire•break *n.* A strip of land that is cleared to prevent a fire from spreading.

fire•brick *n.* A highly heat-resistant brick, used to line furnaces and fireplaces.

fire•bug *n.* One who enjoys setting fire to buildings or homes; a pyromaniac.

fire•crack•er *n.* A small paper cylinder charged with an explosive to make noise.

fire en•gine *n.* A large motor vehicle equipped to carry firefighters and their equipment to a fire.

fire es•cape *n.* A structure, often metal, used as an emergency exit from a building.

fire ex•tin•guish•er *n.* A portable apparatus for fire extinguishing chemicals, ejected through a short nozzle and hose.

fire fight•er *n.* A person who fights fires.

fire•fly *n.* A beetle that flies at night, having an abdominal organ that gives off a flashing light.

fire•place *n.* An open recess in which a fire is built, especially the base of a chimney that opens into a room.

fire•plug *n.* A hydrant for supplying water in the event of a fire.

fire•pow•er *n.* The capacity to deliver fire or missiles, as from a weapon, military unit, or ship.

fire•proof *adj.* Resistant to fires.

fire•wall *n.* In computers, a security system using software to prevent unauthorized entry to files or information.

fire•works *pl. n.* Explosives used to generate colored lights, smoke, and noise for entertainment or celebrations.

firm *adj.* Relatively solid, compact, or unyielding to pressure or touch; strong and sure. *n.* A partnership of two or more persons for conducting a business.

fir•ma•ment *n.* The expanse of the heavens; the sky.

first *adj.* Preceding all others in the order of numbering; taking place or acting prior to all others; earliest.

first aid *n.* The emergency care given to a person before full treatment and medical care can be obtained.

first·hand *adj.* Coming directly from the original source.

first per·son *n.* A category for verbs or pronouns indicating the speaker or writer of a sentence in which they are used.

fis·cal *adj.* Relating to or of the finances or treasury of a nation or a branch of government; financial.

fish *n.* A cold-blooded, vertebrated aquatic animal with fins, gills, and usually scales. *v.* To try to catch fish.

fish·er·man *n.* Any person who fishes commercially or for sport and relaxation; a commercial fishing boat; an angler.

fis·sion *n.* The process or act of splitting into parts; the exploding of the nucleus of an atom and the release of large quantities of energy. **fissionable** *adj.*

fis·sure *n.* A narrow opening, crack, or cleft in a rock.

fist *n.* The hand closed lightly with the fingers bent into the palm.

fis·tu·la *n.* A duct or other passage formed by the imperfect closing of a wound or abscess and leading either to the body surface or to another hollow organ.

fit *v.* To be the proper size and shape; to come together well; to be in good physical condition. *adj.* Adapted or adequate for a particular circumstance or purpose.

fit·ful *adj.* Characterized by irregular actions; capricious; restless. fitfully adv.

fit·ting *adj.* Suitable or proper. *n.* The act of trying on clothes for alteration; a piece of equipment or an appliance used in an adjustment.

five *n.* The cardinal number equal to 4 + 1; any symbol of this number, as 5; anything with five units, parts, or members.

fix *v.* To make stationary, firm, or stable; to direct or hold steadily; to repair; to prepare, as a meal. *n.* A position of embarrassment or difficulty; the position of a ship under way.

fix·a·tion *n.* The act or state of being fixed; a strong, often unhealthy preoccupation. **fixate** *v.*

fix·ture *n.* Anything installed as a part of structure or building.

fizz *n.* A hissing or bubbling sound; effervescence; tiny gas bubbles.

flab *n.* Excessive, loose, and flaccid body tissue. **flabby** *adj.*, **flabbiness** *n.*

flab·ber·gast *v.* To astound; to amaze. **flabbergasted** *adj.*

flac·cid *adj.* Lacking resilience or firmness. **flaccidity** *n.*, **flaccidly** *adv.*

flag *n.* A piece of cloth, usually oblong, bearing colors and designs to designate a nation, state, city, or organization.

flag·on *n.* A vessel or container with a handle, spout, and hinged lid, used for holding wines or liquors.

fla·grant *adj.* Obvious; glaring; disgraceful; notorious; outrageous. **flagrancy** *n.*, **flagrantly** *adv.*

flair *n.* An aptitude or talent for something; a dashing style.

flake *n.* A small, flat, thin piece split or peeled off from a surface.

flam·boy·ant *adj.* Extravagantly ornate; showy; florid; brilliant and rich in color.

flame *n.* A mass of burning vapor or gas rising from a fire, often having a bright color and forming a tongue-shaped area of light.

fla·min·go *n.* A large, long-necked, tropical wading bird, having very long legs, and pink or red plumage.

flam·ma·ble *adj.* Capable of catching fire and burning rapidly.

flange *n.* A projecting rim or collar used to strengthen or guide a wheel or other object, keeping it on a fixed track.

flank *n.* The fleshy part between the ribs and the hip on either side of the body of an animal or human being; the lateral part of something; the right or left side of a military bastion or formation. *v.* To stand or place oneself at the side of something.

flan·nel *n.* A woven fabric made of wool or a wool, cotton or synthetic blend.

flan•nel•ette *n.* Cotton flannel.

flan•nels *pl. n.* Trousers made of flannel.

flap•per *n.* A young woman of the 1920s whose dress and behavior were considered unconventional; a young bird unable to fly.

flare *v.* To blaze up with a bright light; to break out suddenly or violently; to open or spread outward. *n.* An incendiary device for signalling for help.

flash *v.* To burst forth suddenly into a brilliant fire or light; to occur or appear briefly or suddenly. *n.* A short and important news break or transmission. **flashed**, **flashing** *v.*

flash card *n.* A card printed with numbers or words and displayed as a learning drill.

flash•y *adj.* Showing brilliance for a moment; tastelessly showy; gaudy.

flask *n.* A small laboratory container of glass.

flat *adj.* Extending horizontally with no curvature or tilt; stretched out level; below the correct pitch.

flat•ten *v.* To make flat; to knock down.

flat•ter *v.* To praise without sincerity; to gratify the vanity of. **flattery** *n.*

flat•u•lent *adj.* Marked by or affected with gases generated in the intestine or stomach. **flatulence** *n.*

flat•ware *n.* Tableware that is fairly flat and designed usually of a single piece, as plates; table utensils, as knives, forks, and spoons.

flaunt *v.* To display showily; to show off, especially talent or privilege.

flau•tist *n.* A flutist; a person who plays the flute.

fla•vor *n.* A distinctive taste of something; a distinctive, characteristic quality.

fla•vor•ing *n.* A substance, as an extract, used to increase the flavor.

flaw *n.* A defect or blemish, often hidden, that may cause failure under stress; a weakness in character.

flaw•less *adj.* Without flaws or defects.

flax *n.* A plant with blue flowers, with seeds that yield oil, and slender stems from which a fine textile fiber is derived.

flea *n.* A small, wingless, blood-sucking, parasitic jumping insect.

flea mar•ket *n.* A place where antiques and used items are bought and sold.

fleck *n.* A tiny spot or streak.

fledg•ling or **fledge•ling** *n.* A young bird with newly acquired feathers; a beginner.

flee *v.* To run away from; to move swiftly away.

fleece *n.* A coat of wool covering a sheep. *v.* To shear the fleece from; to swindle; to cover with fleece.

fleet *n.* A number of warships operating together under the same command; a number of vehicles, as taxicabs or fishing boats, operated under one command. *adj.* Moving rapidly or nimbly.

flesh *n.* Soft tissue on the body of a human or animal, especially skeletal muscle.

flex *v.* To bend the arm repeatedly; to contract a muscle. **flexed** *adj.*

flex•i•ble *adj.* Capable of being bent or flexed; pliable.

flick *n.* A light, quick snapping movement or the sound accompanying it. *v.* To strike or hit with a quick, light stroke; to cause to move with a quick movement.

flick•er *v.* To burn or shine unsteadily, as a candle. *n.* A North American woodpecker having a brownish back and a spotted breast.

fli•er or **fly•er** *n.* An aviator; a daring or risky venture; a printed handbill.

flight *n.* The act or manner of flying; a scheduled airline trip; a group of stairs leading from one floor to another; an instance of fleeing.

flight at•ten•dant *n.* A person employed to assist passengers on an aircraft; a steward or stewardess.

flight•y *adj.* Inclined to act in a fickle fashion; marked by irresponsible behavior, impulse, or whim; easily excited, skittish. **flightiness** *n.*

flim•sy *adj.* Lacking in physical strength or substance; thin and weak.

flinch *v.* To wince or pull back, as from pain; to draw away.

fling *v.* To throw or toss violently.

flint *n.* A hard quartz that produces a spark when struck by steel.

flip *v.* To turn or throw over suddenly with a jerk.

flip-flop *n.* The sound or motion of something flapping loosely; a backward somersault; a sudden reversal of direction or point of view.

flip•pant *adj.* Marked by or showing disrespect, impudence, or the lack of seriousness. **flippancy** *n.*

flip•per *n.* A broad flat limb, as of a seal, adapted for swimming; a paddle-like rubber shoe used by swimmers.

flip side *n.* The reverse or opposite side.

flirt *v.* To make teasing romantic or sexual overtures; to act so as to attract attention.

flit *v.* To move rapidly or abruptly.

float *n.* Something that floats on the surface of or in a liquid; a device used to buoy the baited end of a fishing line.

flock *n.* A group of animals of all the same kind, especially birds or sheep, living, feeding, or kept together.

floe *n.* A large, flat mass of floating ice or a detached part of such a mass.

flog *v.* To beat hard with a whip or stick.

flood *n.* An overflow of water onto land that is normally dry; an overwhelming quantity.

flood•gate *n.* A valve for controlling the flow or depth of a large body of water.

flood•light *n.* An electric lamp that gives off a broad and intensely bright light.

floor *n.* The level base of a room; the lower inside surface of a structure; a ground surface. *v.* To overwhelm, to knock out.

flop *v.* To fall down clumsily; to move about in a clumsy way.

flop•py disk *n.* In computer science, a flexible plastic disk coated with magnetic material, used to record and store data.

flo•ra *n.* Plants growing in a specific region or season.

flo•ral *adj.* Of or pertaining to flowers.

flo•res•cence *n.* A state or process of blossoming.

flor•id *adj.* Flushed with a rosy color or redness.

flo•rist *n.* One who grows or sells real or artificial flowers.

floss *n.* A loosely-twisted embroidery thread; a soft, silky fiber, such as the tassel on corn; dental floss. *v.* To clean between the teeth with dental floss.

flo•ta•tion *n.* The act or state of floating.

flo•til•la *n.* A fleet of small vessels; a group resembling a small fleet.

flot•sam *n.* Any goods remaining afloat after a ship has sunk.

flounce *n.* A gathered piece of material attached to the upper edge of another surface, as on a curtain. *v.* To move with exaggerated tosses of the body.

floun•der *v.* To struggle clumsily, as to gain footing; to act or speak in a confused way. *n.* Any of various edible marine flatfish.

flour *n.* A soft, fine, powder-like substance obtained by grinding the meal of grain, especially wheat.

flour•ish *v.* To thrive; to fare well; to prosper and succeed.

flow *v.* To move freely, as a fluid; to circulate, as blood; to proceed or move steadily and easily; to rise.

flow chart *n.* A chart or diagram showing the sequence and progress of a series of operations on a specific project.

flow•er *n.* A cluster of petals, bright in color, near or at the tip of a seed-bearing plant.

flu *n.* Influenza.

fluc•tu•ate *v.* To shift irregularly; to change; to undulate. **fluctuation** *n.*

flue *n.* A conduit or passage through which air, gas, steam, or smoke can pass.

flu•ent *adj.* Having an understanding of a language use; flowing smoothly and naturally. **fluency** *n.*, **fluently** *adv.*

fluff *n.* A ball, tuft, or light cluster of loosely gathered fibers of cotton or wool.

flu•id *n.* A substance, as water or gas, capable of flowing. *adj.* Changing readily, as a liquid.

fluke

fluke *n.* A flatfish, especially a flounder; a flattened, parasitic trematode worm; the triangular head of an anchor at the end of either of its arms; a barb or point on an arrow; an unexpected piece of good luck.

flunk *v.* To fail in, as an examination or course.

fluo·res·cence *n.* Emission of electromagnetic radiation, especially of visible light, resulting from and occurring during the absorption of radiation from another source; the radiation emitted. **fluorescent** *adj.*

flur·ry *n.* A sudden gust of wind; a brief, light fall of snow or rain.

flush *v.* To flow or rush out suddenly and abundantly; to become red in the face; to blush; to glow with a reddish color; to wash out with a brief, rapid gush of water.

flute *n.* A high-pitched musical woodwind instrument with finger holes and keys.

flut·ist *n.* A flute player; a flautist.

flut·ter *v.* To flap or wave rapidly and irregularly; to fly as with a light, rapid beating of the wings.

flux *n.* A flowing or discharge; a constant flow or movement; a state of constant fluctuation or change; a substance that promotes the fusing of metals and prevents oxide formation.

fly *v.* To move through the air on wings or wing-like parts; to travel by air; to float or cause to float in the air. *n.* Any of numerous winged insects, including the housefly and the tsetse; a fishing lure that resembles an insect.

foal *n.* The young animal, as a horse, especially one under a year old. *v.* To give birth to a foal.

foam *n.* A mass of bubbles produced on the surface of a liquid by agitation; a froth; a firm, spongy material used especially for insulation and upholstery.

fo·cus *n.* A point at which rays converge or from which they appear to diverge; a center of activity or interest. *v.* To produce a sharp, clear image of; to adjust a lens in order to produce a clean image; to direct; to come together at a point of focus. **focuses, foci** *pl.,* **focal** *adj.,* **focally** *adv.*

fod·der *n.* A coarse feed for livestock.

foe *n.* An enemy in war; an opponent or adversary.

fog *n.* A vapor mass of condensed water which lies close to the ground; a state of mental confusion or bewilderment. *v.* To obscure or cover with.

fo·gey *n.* A person with old-fashioned attitudes and ideas.

fog·horn *n.* A horn sounded in fog.

foi·ble *n.* A minor flaw, weakness, or failing.

foil *v.* To prevent from being successful; to thwart. *n.* A very thin, flexible sheet of metal; a fencing sword.

foist *v.* To pass off something as valuable or genuine.

fold *v.* To double or lay one part over another; to bring from an opened to a closed position; to put together and intertwine; to envelop or wrap.

fo·li·age *n.* The leaves of growing plants and trees.

fo·li·o *n.* A large sheet of paper folded once in a middle.

folk *n.* An ethnic group of people forming a nation or tribe.

fol·li·cle *n.* A small anatomical cavity or sac.

fol·low *v.* To proceed or come after; to pursue; to follow the course of; to obey.

fol·ly *n.* Lack of good judgment; an instance of foolishness.

fo·ment *v.* To rouse; to incite; to treat therapeutically with moist heat. **fomentation** *n.*

fond *adj.* Affectionate; liking; cherished with great affection.

fon·dle *v.* To stroke, handle, or caress affectionately.

font *n.* A source of nourishment; a holy water receptacle in a church; printing type of the same size and face.

food *n.* A substance to be eaten, used to sustain life and growth in the body of an organism; nourishment.

fool *n.* One lacking good sense or judgment. *v.* To trick or mislead someone.

foot *n.* The lower extremity of the vertebrate leg upon which one stands; a unit of measurement equal to 12 inches. **feet** *pl.*

foot·ball *n.* A team game whose object is to get the ball over a goal line or between goalposts by running, passing or kicking; the oval ball used in the game of football.

foot·fall *n.* A footstep; the sound of a footstep.

foot·hill *n.* A low hill near the foot of a mountain or a higher hill.

foot·ing *n.* Secure and stable position for placement of the feet; a foundation.

foot·note *n.* A note of reference or comment below the text on a printed page; a commentary.

foot·print *n.* The outline or impression of the foot on a surface.

for *prep.* Used to indicate the extent of something; used to indicate the number or amount of; considering the usual characteristics of; on behalf of someone; to be in favor of. *conj.* Because; in as much as; with the purpose of.

for·age *n.* Food for cattle or other domestic animals. *v.* To make a raid so as to find supplies; to plunder or rummage through.

for·ay *n.* A raid to plunder.

for·bade *v.* Past tense of *forbid*.

for·bear *v.* To refrain from; to cease from. **forbearance** *n.*

for·bid *v.* To command someone not to do something; to prohibit by law; to prevent.

for·bid·ding *adj.* Very difficult; disagreeable.

force *n.* Energy or power; strength; a group organized for a certain purpose. *v.* To compel or make happen by force.

for·ceps *n.* A pair of tongs used for manipulating, grasping or extracting, especially in surgery. **forceps** *pl.*

forc·i·ble *adj.* Accomplished or achieved by force; marked by force.

ford *n.* A shallow place in a body of water that can be crossed without a boat. *v.* To wade across a body of water.

fore *adj.* or *adv.* Situated in, at, or toward the front; forward. *n.* The front of something. *interj.* A cry used by a golfer to warn others that a ball is about to land in their direction.

fore-and-aft *adj.* Lying or going lengthwise on a ship; from stem to stern.

fore·arm *v.* To prepare in advance, as for a battle. *n.* The part of the arm between the elbow and the wrist.

fore·bear *n.* An ancestor.

fore·bode *v.* To give an indication or warning in advance; to have a premonition of something evil. **foreboding** n.

fore·cast *v.* To predict, as weather; to calculate in advance.

fore·close *v.* To recall a mortgage in default and take legal possession of the mortgaged property; to exclude; to shut out. foreclosure n.

fore·fa·ther *n.* An ancestor.

fore·fin·ger *n.* The finger next to the thumb.

fore·go *v.* To go before; to precede in time.

fore·gone *adj.* Already finished or gone; established in advance.

fore·ground *n.* The part of a picture represented as nearest to the viewer.

fore·head *n.* The part of the face from the eyebrows to the hair.

for·eign *adj.* Situated outside one's native country; belonging to a country or region other than one's own.

for·eign·er *n.* A person from a different place or country; an alien.

fore·knowl·edge *n.* Prior knowledge of something; knowledge beforehand.

fore·lock *n.* A lock of hair growing from the front of the scalp and hanging over the forehead.

fore·man *n.* A person of either gender who oversees a group of people; the spokesperson for a jury. **forewoman** *n.*

fore·most *adj.* First in rank, position, time, or order.

fore·noon *n.* The period between sunrise and noon.

fo•ren•sic *adj.* Of, relating to, or used in courts of justice or formal debate.

fo•ren•sic med•i•cine *n.* A science dealing with the application of medicine in legal problems.

fore•run•ner *n.* One sent before to give notice of the approach of others; a harbinger.

fore•see *v.* To know or see beforehand.

fore•shad•ow *v.* To represent or warn of beforehand.

fore•short•en *v.* In drawing, to shorten parts of an object in order to give the illusion of depth.

fore•sight *n.* The act or capacity of foreseeing; the act of looking forward; concern for the future; prudence. **foresighted** *adj.*, **foresightedness** *n.*

for•est *n.* A large tract of land covered with trees.

fore•taste *n.* A sample or indication beforehand.

fore•tell *v.* To tell about in advance; to predict.

fore•thought *n.* Prior thought or planning; a plan for the future.

for•ev•er *adv.* For eternity; without end.

fore•ward *n.* An introductory statement before the text of a book.

fore•warn *v.* To warn in advance. **fore•warned** *adj.*

for•feit *n.* Something taken away as punishment; a penalty; something placed in escrow and redeemed on payment of a fine.

forge *n.* A furnace where metals are heated and wrought; a smithy. *v.* To form by heating and hammering; to give shape to; to imitate falsely.

for•get *v.* To lose the memory of; to fail to remember.

for•give *v.* To pardon; to cease to feel resentment against.

for•go *v.* To give up or refrain from; to do without.

fork *n.* A tool consisting of a handle at one end of which are two or more prongs; a division of something into two or more parts that continue, as a river or road. **forked** *adj.*

forked *adj.* Shaped like or having a fork.

fork lift *n.* A self-propelled industrial vehicle with a pronged platform for hoisting and transporting heavy objects.

for•lorn *adj.* Abandoned or left in distress; hopeless.

form *n.* The shape or contour of something; a body of a living being; the basic nature of or particular state of something; a document with blank spaces to fill out with information.

for•mal *adj.* Of or pertaining to the outward aspect of something; based on accepted conventions.

for•mal•de•hyde *n.* A colorless, gaseous chemical used chiefly as a preservative and disinfectant in synthesizing other compounds.

for•mat *n.* A general style of a publication; the general form or layout of a publication. *v.* In computers, to produce data in a specified form.

for•ma•tion *n.* The act or state of being formed; the manner in which something is formed.

for•ma•tive *adj.* Forming or having the power to form; of or pertaining to formation, growth, or development.

for•mer *adj.* Previous; preceding in place.

for•mer•ly *adv.* Previously.

form-fit•ting *adj.* Following closely to the contours of the body.

for•mi•da•ble *adj.* Extremely difficult; exciting fear by reason of size or strength. **formidably** *adv.*

form let•ter *n.* A standardized format of an impersonal letter sent to a large number of people.

for•mu•la *n.* A prescribed method of words or rules for use in a certain ceremony or procedure; a nutritious food for an infant in liquid form; a combination used to express an algebraic or symbolic form; a symbolic representation of the composition of a chemical compound. **formulas, formulae** *pl.*, **formulaic** *adj.*

for•mu•late *v.* To state or express as a formula. **formulation, formulator** *n.*

for•ni•ca•tion *n.* Voluntary sexual intercourse between two unmarried people. **fornicate** *v.,* **fornicator** *n.*

for•sake *v.* To abandon or renounce; to give up.

for•sooth *adv.* In truth; certainly.

for•swear *v.* To renounce emphatically or upon oath; to forsake; to swear falsely; to perjure oneself.

fort *n.* A fortified structure for defense against invasion.

forte *n.* An activity one does with excellence; a person's strong point.

forth *adv.* Out into plain sight; forward in order, place, or time.

forth•com•ing *adj.* Ready or about to appear or occur; readily available.

forth•right *adj.* Straightforward; direct; frank.

forth•with *adv.* At once; promptly; immediately.

for•ti•fy *v.* To make more secure; to provide physical strength or courage to; to strengthen.

for•ti•tude *n.* Strength of mind in adversity, pain, or peril.

fort•night *n.* A period of two weeks.

for•tress *n.* A fort; a fortified place.

for•tu•i•tous *adj.* Occurring by chance; accidental and unplanned. **fortuitously** *adv.*

for•tu•nate *adj.* Brought about by good fortune; having good fortune.

for•tune *n.* A force that determines events and issues favorably and unfavorably; success that results from luck; wealth.

for•tune-tell•er *n.* A person who claims to predict the future.

fo•rum *n.* A public marketplace in an ancient Roman city; any place or opportunity for group discussion or expression.

for•ward *adv.* At, near, or toward a place or time in advance; overstepping the usual bounds.

fos•sil *n.* The remains of an animal or plant of a past geologic age preserved in the rocks of the earth's surface.

fos•ter *v.* To give parental care to; to nurture; to encourage.

foul *adj.* Revolting to the senses; spoiled or rotten; unfavorable. *v.* To physically contact or entangle; to become foul or dirty.

found *v.* To establish; to set up; to establish the basis or lay the foundation of.

foun•da•tion *n.* The basis on which anything is founded; an institution supported by an endowment.

foun•dry *n.* A place where metal is cast.

fount *n.* A fountain; an abundant source.

foun•tain *n.* A natural spring coming from the earth; an artificially created spray of water.

foun•tain pen *n.* A pen having a reservoir of ink that automatically feeds the writing point.

four *n.* The cardinal number that equals 3 + 1; anything consisting of four units.

four•score *adj.* Being four times twenty; eighty.

fowl *n.* A bird used as food or hunted as game.

fox *n.* A wild mammal having a pointed snout, upright ears, and a long bushy tail.

foy•er *n.* The public lobby of a hotel, theater, etc.; an entrance hall.

fra•cas *n.* A noisy quarrel or disturbance; fight or dispute.

frac•tion *n.* A small part; in mathematics, an indicated quantity less than a whole number that is expressed as a decimal.

frac•ture *n.* The act of breaking; the state of being broken; something broken or cracked, as a bone.

frag•ile *adj.* Easily damaged or broken; frail; tenuous; flimsy.

frag•ment *n.* A part detached or broken; part unfinished or incomplete. *v.* To break into fragments.

fra•grant *adj.* Having an agreeable, especially sweet odor. **fragrance** *n.*

frail *adj.* Delicate; weak; easily damaged.

frame *v.* To put into a frame, as a picture; to build; to design.

fran•chise *n.* A privilege or right granted

to a person or group by a government.

fran•gi•ble *adj*. Breakable. **frangibility** *n*.

frank *adj*. Sincere and straightforward; open and honest.

frank•furt•er *n*. A smoked sausage.

frank•in•cense *n*. An aromatic gum resin obtained from African and Asian trees used as incense and in medicine.

fran•tic *adj*. Emotionally out of control with worry or fear. **frantically** *adv*.

fra•ter•nal *adj*. Relating to brothers; of a fraternity.

frat•er•nize *v*. To associate with others in a friendly way; to mingle intimately with the enemy, often in violation of military law.

frat•ri•cide *n*. The killing of one's brother or sister; one who has killed his brother or sister. **fratricidal** *adj*.

fraud *n*. A deliberate and willful deception for unlawful gain. **fraudulent** *adj*.

fraught *adj*. Full of or accompanied by something specified.

fray *n*. A brawl, or fight; a heated argument or dispute. *v*. To wear out by rubbing; to irritate one's nerves.

fraz•zle *v*. To wear out; to completely fatigue. **frazzled** *adj*.

freak *n*. A capricious event; a whimsical quality or disposition.

freck•le *n*. One of the small brownish spots on the skin, usually due to pigmentation, and increased by the sun.

free *adj*. Not imprisoned; not under obligation; able to choose. *v*. To give freedom to; to unlock or disentangle; to give away.

free•dom *n*. The condition or state of being free; political independence.

free-lanc•er *n*. One whose services are offered without long-term commitments to any one employer. **free-lance** *v*.

free trade *n*. Unrestricted international exchange between nations or states.

free•way *n*. A highway with more than two lanes; a superhighway.

free will *n*. The ability to choose freely; the belief that a human being's choices can be made freely, without external constraint.

freeze *v*. To become ice or a similar solid through loss of heat; to preserve by cooling at an extremely low temperature.

freeze-dry *v*. To preserve by drying in a frozen state under a high vacuum.

freez•er *n*. An insulated cabinet for freezing and storing perishable foods.

freight *n*. A service of transporting commodities by air, land or water; the price paid for such transportation; a train that transports goods only.

freight•er *n*. A ship used for transporting cargo.

fren•zy *n*. A state of extreme excitement or agitation; temporary insanity.

fre•quent *adj*. Happening often or time after time. *v*. To go to a place repeatedly.

fres•co *n*. A painting on moist plaster with water-based paint.

fresh *adj*. Newly made, gathered, or obtained; not spoiled, musty, or stale; new.

fresh•man *n*. A student in the first year of studies in a high school, university, or college; a beginner.

fret *v*. To be anxious or irritated; a ridge of metal fixed across the finger-board of a stringed instrument, as a guitar.

fri•a•ble *adj*. Easily crumbled or pulverized brittle. **friability, friableness** *n*.

fri•ar *n*. A member of a religious order, usually reclusive.

fric•as•see *n*. A dish of meat or poultry stewed in gravy.

fric•tion *n*. The rubbing of one surface or object against another.

friend *n*. Someone personally well known and liked; a supporter of a cause or group.

frieze *n*. A decorative horizontal band along the upper part of a wall in a room.

frig•ate *n*. An early square-rigged sailing warship; a U.S. warship smaller than a cruiser but larger than a destroyer.

fright *n*. Sudden violent alarm or fear; a feeling of alarm.

fright•en *v*. To fill with fear; to force by arousing fear.

frig•id *adj*. Very cold; lacking warmth of

feeling or emotional warmth.

frill *n.* A decorative ruffled or gathered border.

fringe *n.* An edging that consists of hanging threads, cords, or loops.

frip•per•y *n.* Showy and often cheap ornamentation; a pretentious display.

frisk *v.* To skip or leap about playfully; to search for a concealed weapon by running the hands over the clothing quickly.

friv•o•lous *adj.* Trivial; insignificant; lacking importance.

frizz *v.* To form into small, tight curls. **frizzy** *adj.*

fro *adv.* Away from; back, as running to and fro.

frock *n.* A smock or loose-fitting robe; a robe worn by monks; a pretty dress.

frog *n.* Any of various small, smooth-skinned, web-footed, largely aquatic, tailless, leaping amphibians.

frol•ic *n.* Merriness; a playful, carefree occasion.

from *prep.* Starting at a particular time or place; used to indicate a specific place.

frond *n.* A large leaf, as of a tropical fern, usually divided into smaller leaflets.

front *n.* The forward surface of an object or body; the area or position located before or ahead.

fron•tier *n.* A part of an international border or the area adjacent to it; an unexplored area of knowledge or thought.

fron•tis•piece *n.* An illustration preceding the title page of a book or periodical.

frost *n.* A feathery covering of minute ice crystals on a cold surface; the act or process of freezing.

frost•bite *n.* The local destruction of bodily tissue due to exposure to freezing temperatures, often resulting in gangrene.

frost•ing *n.* Icing; a mixture of egg whites, sugar, and butter.

froth *n.* A mass of bubbles on or in a liquid, resulting from agitation or fermentation; a salivary foam.

fro•ward *adj.* Obstinate. **frowardness** *n.*

frown *v.* To contract the brow as in displeasure or concentration.

fro•zen *adj.* Covered with or made into ice; extremely cold, as a climate; immobilized or made rigid, as by fear.

fru•gal *adj.* Economical; thrifty.

fruit *n.* The ripened, mature, seed-bearing part of a flowering plant, especially the edible, fleshy kind, as an apple or plum.

frump•y *adj.* Unfashionable; dowdy. **frump, frumpiness** *n.*

frus•trate *v.* To thwart; to prevent; to keep from attaining a goal or fulfilling a desire.

fry *v.* To cook in hot fat or oil, especially over direct heat. *n.* A dish of any fried food.

fudge *n.* A soft, cooked candy containing sugar, butter, and a flavoring, as chocolate. *v.* To falsify or fit together in a clumsy way; to evade.

fuel *n.* A combustible matter consumed to generate energy, especially a material such as wood, coal, or oil burned to generate heat.

fu•gi•tive *adj.* Fleeing or having fled, as from arrest or pursuit. *n.* One who has fled from a place.

ful•crum *n.* The point on which a lever turns. **fulcrums, fulcra** *pl.*

ful•fill or **ful•fil** *v.* To convert into actuality; to complete; to carry out; to satisfy. **fulfillment** *n.*

ful•mi•nate *v.* To condemn severely; to explode. **fulmination, fulminator** *n.*, **fulminated** *adj.*

fum•ble *v.* To handle idly; to blunder; to mishandle.

fumes *pl. n.* An irritating smoke, gas, or vapor.

fu•mi•gate *v.* To spray or apply airborne insecticides to exterminate vermin or insects.

func•tion *n.* The purpose of a thing or process; the reason something is used or made; a specific occupation, duty, or role; an official ceremony.

fund *n.* A source of supply; a sum of money reserved for a specific purpose.

fun•da•men•tal *adj.* Basic or essential; of

major significance; most important.

fu•ner•al *n.* The service performed in conjunction with the burial or cremation of a dead person; an interment.

fun•gus *n.* Any of numerous spore-bearing plants which have no chlorophyll, such as yeasts, molds, mildews, and mushrooms. **fungous, fungal** *adj.*

funk *n.* Cowardly fright or panic; fear; a state of depression.

fun•nel *n.* A cone-shaped utensil having a tube for channeling a substance into a container.

fur•bish *v.* To make bright, as by rubbing; to polish; to renovate.

fu•ri•ous *adj.* Extremely angry; marked by rage or activity.

furl *v.* To roll up and secure to something, as a pole or mast; to curl or fold.

fur•long *n.* A distance equal to approximately 201 meters or 230 yards.

fur•lough *n.* Permission granted to be absent from duty, especially to members of the armed forces.

fur•nace *n.* A large enclosure designed to produce intense heat.

fur•nish *v.* To outfit or equip, as with fittings or furniture.

fur•ni•ture *n.* Movable articles, such as chairs and tables, used in a home, office, or other interior.

fu•ror *n.* Violent anger; rage; great excitement; commotion.

fur•row *n.* A long, narrow trench in the ground, made by a plow or other tool.

fur•tive *adj.* Done in secret; surreptitious; obtained underhandedly; stolen.

fu•ry *n.* Uncontrolled anger; turbulence; in mythology, an angry or spiteful woman.

fu•sil•lage *n.* The central section of an airplane, containing the wings and tail assembly.

fus•tian *n.* A sturdy, stout cotton cloth. *adj.* Pompous, pretentious language; bombastic.

fu•tile *adj.* Ineffectual; of no avail.

fuzz *n.* A mass of fine, loose particles, fibers, or hairs.

G

G, g The seventh letter of the English alphabet; in music, the fifth tone in the scale of C major.

gad *v.* To wander about restlessly with little or no purpose.

gadg•et *n.* A small device or tool used in performing odd tasks.

gag *n.* An obstacle to or any restraint of free speech; a practical joke or hoax.

gag•gle *n.* A flock of geese; a group; a cluster.

gai•e•ty *n.* The state of being happy; cheerfulness; fun.

gai•ly *adv.* In a cheerful manner.

gain *v.* To acquire possession of something; to succeed in winning a victory; to develop an increase of; to put on weight.

gain•ful *adj.* Producing profits; lucrative. **gainfully** *adv.*

gain•say *v.* To deny; to contradict; dispute. **gainsayer** *n.*

gait *n.* A way or manner of moving on foot; one of the foot movements in which a horse steps or runs.

ga•la *n.* A festive celebration.

gal•ax•y *n.* Any of the very large systems of stars, nebulae, or other celestial bodies that constitute the universe; a brilliant, distinguished group or assembly.

gale *n.* A very powerful wind.

gall *n.* The bitter fluid secreted by the liver; bile; bitterness of feeling; animosity; impudence; something that irritates. *v.* To injure the skin by friction; to chafe.

gal•lant *adj.* Dashing in appearance or dress; chivalrously attentive to women; courteous.

gal•lant•ry *n.* Nobility and bravery; a gallant act.

gal•ler•y *n.* A long, narrow passageway; a place for showing artwork.

gal•ley *n.* A long medieval ship propelled by sails and oars.

garland

gal·lon *n.* A liquid measurement used in the U.S., equal to 4 quarts.

gal·lop *n.* A horse's gait faster than a canter and characterized by regular leaps during which all four feet are off the ground at once.

gal·lows *n.* A framework of two or more upright beams and a crossbeam, used for execution by hanging.

gall·stone *n.* A small, hard concretion of cholesterol crystals that sometimes form in the gall bladder or bile passages.

ga·lore *adj.* In great numbers; abundant.

ga·loshes *pl. n.* Waterproof overshoes worn in bad weather.

gal·va·nism *n.* Electricity produced by chemical action; a therapeutic application of continuous electric current from voltaic cells.

gal·va·nize *v.* To stimulate or shock muscular action by an electric current; to protect iron or steel with rust resistant zinc; to infuse with energy. **galvanization**, **galvanizer** *n.*

gam·bit *n.* In chess, an opening in which a piece is sacrificed for a favorable position; a carefully planned maneuver.

gam·ble *v.* To take a chance on an uncertain outcome as a contest or a weekly lottery number. *n.* Any risky venture.

game *n.* A contest governed by specific rules; a way of entertaining oneself; amusement; animals or birds hunted for sport or food.

game·keep·er *n.* A person in charge of protecting and maintaining wildlife on a private preserve.

gam·ma ray *n.* Electromagnetic radiation that has energy greater than several hundred thousand electron volts.

gam·ut *n.* The whole range or extent of anything.

gam·y *adj.* Having the strong flavor of game, especially when slightly tainted; scandalous.

gan·der *n.* A male goose; a quick glance; a look or peek.

gang *n.* A group of persons organized to work or socialize regularly; a group of adolescent hoodlums or criminals.

gan·gling *adj.* Tall and thin; lanky.

gan·gli·on *n.* A collection of nerve cells located outside the spinal cord or brain.

gang·plank *n.* A temporary board or ramp used to board or leave a ship.

gan·grene *n.* The death and decay of tissue in the body caused by a failure in the circulation of the blood supply. **gangrenous** *adj.*

gang·ster *n.* A member of a criminal gang.

gan·try *n.* A bridge-like framework support, especially a movable vertical structure with platforms, used in assembling or servicing rockets before they are launched.

gap *n.* An opening or wide crack, as in a wall; a cleft; a deep notch or ravine in a mountain ridge, offering passage.

gape *v.* To open the mouth wide, as in yawning; to stare in amazement with the mouth wide open.

gar *n.* A fish having a spearlike snout and elongated body covered with bony plates; a garfish.

ga·rage *n.* A building or structure to store or repair motor vehicles.

gar·bage *n.* Food wastes, consisting of unwanted or unusable pieces of meat, vegetables, and other food products; trash.

gar·ble *v.* To mix up or confuse; to change or distort the meaning of.

gar·den *n.* A place for growing flowers, vegetables, or fruit; a piece of ground commonly used as a public resort. *v.* To work in or make into a garden.

gar·gan·tu·an *adj.* Of enormous size; immense.

gar·gle *v.* To force air from the lungs through a liquid held in the back of the mouth and throat.

gar·goyle *n.* A waterspout made or carved to represent a grotesque animal or human figure, projecting from a gutter to throw rain away from the side of a building.

gar·ish *adj.* Too showy and bright; gaudy.

gar·land *n.* A wreath, chain, or rope of

flowers or leaves.

gar•lic *n.* A plant related to the onion with a compound bulb which contains a strong odor and flavor, used as a seasoning. **garishly** *adv.*, **garishness** *n.*

gar•ment *n.* An article of clothing.

gar•ner *v.* To gather and store; to accumulate.

gar•net *n.* A dark-red silicate mineral used as a gemstone or abrasive.

gar•nish *v.* To add something to, as to decorate or embellish; to add decorative or flavorful touches to food or drink. **garnish** *n.*

gar•ret *n.* A room in an attic with a steep roof.

gar•ri•son *n.* The military force that is permanently placed in a fort or town; a military post.

gar•ru•lous *adj.* Given to continual talkativeness; chatty. **garrulity**, **garrulousness** *n.*

gas *n.* A form of matter capable of expanding to fill a container and taking on the shape of the container; a combustible mixture used as fuel; gasoline.

gash *n.* A long, deep cut.

gas•ket *n.* A rubber seal, disk, or ring used between matched machine parts or around pipe joints to prevent the escape of fluid or gas.

gas mask *n.* A protective respirator for the face, containing a chemical air filter to protect against poisonous gases.

gas•o•line *n.* A colorless, highly flammable mixture of liquid hydrocarbons made from crude petroleum and used as a fuel.

gasp *v.* To inhale suddenly and sharply, as from fear or surprise; to make labored or violent attempts to breathe.

gas•tric *adj.* Of or pertaining to the stomach.

gate *n.* A movable opening in a wall or fence, commonly swinging on hinges, that closes or opens.

gath•er *v.* To bring or come together into one place or group; to harvest or pick; to accumulate slowly.

gauche *adj.* Socially awkward; clumsy; boorish.

gaud•y *adj.* Too highly decorated to be in good taste.

gauge *n.* A standard measurement, dimension, or capacity; an instrument used for measuring, testing, or registering. *v.* To measure or estimate.

gaunt *adj.* Thin and bony; haggard.

gauze *n.* A loosely woven, transparent material used for surgical bandages; any thin, open-mesh material, a mist.

gav•el *n.* A mallet used by a presiding officer to call for order or attention.

gawk *v.* To gape; to stare stupidly.

gay *adj.* Merry; happy and carefree.

gaze *v.* To look intently at something in admiration or wonder; to stare.

ga•zelle *n.* A small antelope, having curved horns and large eyes.

ga•zette *n.* A newspaper; an official publication.

gear *n.* A toothed wheel which interacts with another toothed part to transmit motion; equipment for a special task.

gel•a•tin *n.* An almost tasteless, odorless, dried protein derived from boiled animal tissues, used in making foods, drugs, and photographic film.

geld *v.* To castrate or spay, especially a horse.

geld•ing *n.* A gelded animal.

gel•id *adj.* Very cold; frigid. **gelidity** *n.*

gem *n.* A cut and polished precious or semiprecious stone.

gen•der *n.* Any of two or more categories for pronouns, as feminine, masculine, and neuter; the quality of being of the male or female sex.

gene *n.* A functional unit on a chromosome, responsible for the transmission of hereditary characteristics.

ge•ne•al•o•gy *n.* A record, table, or account showing the descent of a family, group, or person from an ancestor; the study of ancestry. **genealogical** *adj.*, **genealogist** *n.*

gen•er•al *adj.* Including or affecting the

whole or every member of a group or class; common to or typical of most.

gen•er•al•i•ty *n.* The state or quality of being general; an inadequate, inexact or vague statement or idea.

gen•er•al•i•za•tion *n.* Something arrived at by generalizing, such as a broad, overall statement or conclusion.

gen•er•al•ize *v.* To draw a general conclusion from particular facts, experiences, or observations.

gen•er•al store *n.* A retail store selling a large variety of merchandise but not subdivided into departments.

gen•er•ate *v.* To cause to be; to produce; to bring into existence, especially by a chemical or physical process. **generative** *adj.*

gen•er•a•tion *n.* A group of individuals born at about the same time; the average time interval between the birth of parents and that of their offspring. **generational** *adj.*

gen•er•a•tor *n.* A machine that changes mechanical energy into electrical energy.

ge•ner•ic *adj.* Relating to or indicating an entire class or group; general; pertaining to a genus or class of related things; of or relating to a class of; product, or merchandise that does not bear a trademark or trade name. **generically** *adv.*

gen•er•ous *adj.* Sharing freely; abundant. **generosity** *n.*, **generously** *adv.*

ge•net•ic *adj.* Of or pertaining to the origin or development of something; of or relating to genetics.

ge•net•ic code *n.* The biochemical basis of heredity that specifies the amino acid sequence in the synthesis of proteins and on which heredity is based.

gen•ial *adj.* Cheerful, kind, pleasant and good-humored in disposition or manner. **geniality** *n.*, **genially** *adv.*

gen•ius *n.* Exceptional intellectual ability or creative power; a strong, natural talent.

gen•o•cide *n.* The systematic extermination of a political, racial, or cultural group. **genocidal** *adj.*

gen•til•i•ty *n.* The quality of being genteel; the members of the upper class; well-born or well-bred persons collectively.

gen•tle *adj.* Not harsh, severe, rough, or loud; easily handled or managed; docile; not sudden or steep.

gen•tle•man *n.* A man of noble birth and social position; a courteous or polite man.

gen•tle•wo•man *n.* A woman of noble birth and social position; a well-bred or polite woman.

gen•try *n.* People of good family or high social standing; the aristocracy; in England, the social class that is considered the upper ranks of the middle class.

gen•u•flect *v.* To bend down on one knee, as in worship. **genuflection** *n.*

gen•u•ine *adj.* Real; authentic; not counterfeit; sincere. **genuinely** *adv.*, **genuineness** *n.*

ge•nus *n.* A group or category of plants and animals usually including several species.

ge•o•cen•tric *adj.* Of or relating to the earth's center; formulated on the assumption that the earth is the center of the universe.

ge•og•ra•phy *n.* The science of the earth's natural climate, resources, and population. **geographer** *n.*

ge•ol•o•gy *n.* The science of the history, origin, and structure of the earth. **geologist** *n.*

ge•om•e•try *n.* The branch of mathematics that deals with the measurement, properties, and relationship of lines, angles, points, surfaces and solids.

ge•ra•ni•um *n.* A plant having rounded leaves and clusters of pink, red, or white flowers.

ger•bil *n.* An animal of the rodent family having long hind legs and a long tail.

ger•i•at•rics *n.* The medical study that deals with the structural changes, diseases, physiology, and hygiene of old age.

germ *n.* A small cell or organic structure from which a new organism may develop; a microorganism which causes disease.

ger·mane *adj*. Relevant to what is being considered or discussed.

ger·mi·nate *v*. To begin to grow, develop, or sprout. **germination** *n*.

ges·ta·tion *n*. The carrying of a developing offspring in the uterus; pregnancy. **gestate** *v*.

ges·tic·u·late *v*. To make expressive or emphatic gestures, as in speaking.

ger·und *n. gram*. A verb form used as a noun.

ges·ture *n*. A bodily motion, especially with the hands in speaking, to emphasize some idea or emotion.

get *v*. To come into possession of, as by receiving, winning, earning, or buying.

gey·ser *n*. A natural hot spring that intermittently ejects hot water and steam.

ghast·ly *adj*. Horrible; terrifying; very unpleasant or bad; ghost-like in appearance; deathly pale.

ghet·to *n*. A run-down section of a city in which a minority group lives because of poverty or social pressure.

ghost *n*. The spirit of a dead person believed to appear to or haunt living persons; a spirit; a ghostwriter.

ghoul *n*. A person who robs graves; in Moslem legend, an evil spirit which plunders graves and feeds on corpses. **ghoulish** *adj*.

gi·ant *n*. A legendary man-like being of supernatural size and strength; one of great power, importance, or size.

gib·ber·ish *n*. Meaningless speech.

gib·bon *n*. A slender, long-armed ape.

gibe *v*. To ridicule or make taunting remarks.

gid·dy *adj*. Affected by a reeling or whirling sensation; dizzy; frivolous and silly.

GIF *abbr*. Graphic Interchange Format; in computers, a system for compressing visual material otherwise too large for easy electronic transfer.

gift *n*. Something given from one person to another; a natural aptitude; a talent.

gift·ed *adj*. The state of having a special talent or ability.

gi·gan·tic *adj*. Of tremendous or extraordinary size; huge.

gig·gle *v*. To laugh in high-pitched, repeated, short sounds.

gill *n*. The organ, as of fishes and various other aquatic invertebrates, used for taking oxygen from water.

gilt *adj*. Covered with or of the color of gold. *n*. A thin layer of gold or a gold-colored substance applied to a surface.

gim·mick *n*. A tricky feature obscured or misrepresented; a tricky device, especially when used dishonestly or secretly.

gin *n*. An aromatic, clear, alcoholic liquor distilled from grain and flavored with juniper berries; a machine used to separate seeds from cotton fibers.

gin·ger *n*. A tropical Asian plant that has a pungent aromatic root, used in medicine and cooking.

gin·ger·bread *n*. A dark, ginger and molasses flavored cake or cookie.

gin·ger·snap *n*. A brittle, molasses and ginger cookie.

gin·seng *n*. An herb native to China and North America with an aromatic root believed to have medicinal properties.

gi·raffe *n*. The tallest mammal, having an extremely long neck and very long legs.

gird *v*. To surround, encircle, or attach with or as if with a belt.

gird·er *n*. A strong, horizontal beam, as of steel or wood, which is the main support in a building.

gir·dle *n*. A cord or belt worn around the waist; a supporting undergarment worn by women to give support and to shape.

girl *n*. A female child or infant; a very young, unmarried woman.

girl·friend *n*. A female friend; a regular female companion of a boy or man.

girth *n*. The circumference or distance around something; a strap that encircles an animal's body to secure something on its back, as a saddle.

gis·mo *n*. A part or device whose name is

unknown or forgotten; a gadget.

gist *n.* The central or main substance, as of an argument or question.

give *v.* To make a present of; to bestow; to accord or yield to another; to put into the possession of another.

give·a·way *n.* Something given free as a premium; something that betrays, generally unintentionally.

giv·en *adj.* Bestowed; presented; specified or assumed.

gi·ven name *n.* The name bestowed or given at birth or baptism.

gla·cial *adj.* Relating to glaciers; extremely cold.

gla·cier *n.* A large mass of compacted snow that moves slowly until it either breaks off to form icebergs or melts when it reaches warmer climates.

glad *adj.* Displaying or experiencing; a state of being happy; being willing to help.

glad·den *v.* To make glad.

glade *n.* A clearing in a forest or woods.

glad·i·a·tor *n.* An ancient Roman slave, captive, or paid freeman who entertained the public by fighting to the death; one who engages in an intense struggle or controversy.

glad·some *adj.* Giving cheer; showing joy. **gladsomely** *adv.*, **gladsomeness** n.

glam·or·ize *v.* To make glamorous; to portray or treat in a romantic way.

glam·our *n.* Alluring fascination or charm. **glamourous** *adj.*

glance *v.* To take a brief or quick look at something; to give a light, brief touch; to brush against.

gland *n.* Any of various body organs which excrete or secrete substances. **glandular** *adj.*

glare *v.* To stare fiercely or angrily; to shine intensely; to dazzle. *n.* An uncomfortably harsh or bright light.

glass *n.* A hard, amorphous, brittle, usually transparent material which hardens from the molten state; a mirror, tumbler, windowpane, lens, or other material made of glass.

glass blow·ing *n.* The art or process of shaping objects from molten glass by blowing air into them.

glass·es *pl. n.* A pair of eyeglasses used as an aid to vision; glassware.

glaze *n.* A thin, smooth coating as on ceramics. *v.* To become covered with a thin glassy coating of ice; to coat or cover with a glaze; to fit with glass.

gleam *n.* A momentary ray or beam of light. *v.* To shine or emit light softly; to appear briefly.

glean *v.* To collect or gather facts by patient effort; to collect part by part; to pick bits of a crop left in a reaper. **glean·er** *n.*, **gleanings** *pl. n.*

glee *n.* Joy; merriment. **gleeful** *adj.*

glee club *n.* A singing group organized to sing short pieces of choral music.

glen *n.* A small, secluded valley.

glib *adj.* Spoken easily and fluently; superficial. **glibly** *adv.*, **glibness** *n.*

glide *v.* To pass or move smoothly with little or no effort; to fly without motor power.

glid·er *n.* One that glides; a swing gliding in a metal frame; an aircraft without an engine, constructed to soar on air currents.

glim·mer *n.* A faint suggestion; an indication; a dim unsteady light.

glimpse *n.* A momentary look; a brief view.

glis·ten *v.* To shine softly as reflected by light.

glitch *n.* A minor mishap or malfunction.

glit·ter *n.* A brilliant sparkle; small bits of light-reflecting material used for decoration. *v.* To sparkle with brilliance. **glittery** *adj.*

gloat *v.* To express, feel, or observe with malicious pleasure or self-satisfaction.

glob·al *adj.* Spherical; involving the whole world. **globalize** *v.*

globe *n.* A spherical object; anything perfectly rounded; the earth.

globe-trot·ter *n.* One who travels all over the world.

gloom *n.* Partial or total darkness;

depression of the mind or spirits.

glo•ri•fy *v.* To worship and give glory to; to give high praise. **glorification** *n.*

glo•ri•ous *adj.* Magnificent; resplendent; full of glory.

glo•ry *n.* Distinguished praise or honor; exalted reputation; adoration and praise offered in worship.

gloss *n.* The sheen or luster of a polished surface; a deceptively or superficially attractive appearance.

glos•sa•ry *n.* A list of terms and their meanings.

gloss•y *adj.* Having a bright sheen; lustrous; superficially attractive.

glove *n.* A covering for the hand with a separate section for each finger; an oversized protective covering for the hand.

glow *v.* To give off heat or light, especially without a flame; to have a bright, warm, ruddy color.

glow•er *v.* To look sullenly or angrily at; to glare. **glower** *n.*, **gloweringly** *adv.*

glow•worm *n.* A luminous larva or grub-like female of an insect which displays phosphorescent light; the firefly.

glue *n.* Any of various adhesives used to stick and hold items together.

glum *adj.* Moody and silent.

glut *v.* To feed or supply beyond capacity; to provide with a supply that exceeds demand.

glut•ton *n.* Someone who eats immoderately. **gluttony** *n.*

gnarl *n.* A hard, protruding knot on a tree. **gnarled** *adj.*

gnash *v.* To grind or strike the teeth together, as in a rage or pain.

gnat *n.* A small, winged insect, specially one that bites or stings.

gnaw *v.* To chew or eat with persistence.

gnome *n.* In folklore, a dwarf-like creature who lives underground and guards precious metals and treasures.

gnu *n.* South African antelope with an ox-like head, curved horns, a long tail, and a mane.

go *v.* To proceed or pass along; to leave; to move away from; to follow a certain course of action; to function.

goal *n.* A purpose; the terminal point of a race or journey.

goal•keep•er *n.* The player responsible for defending the goal in hockey, soccer, and other games.

goat *n.* A horned, cud-chewing mammal related to the sheep.

goat•ee *n.* A short, pointed beard on a man's chin.

goat•skin *n.* The skin of a goat, often used for leather.

gob•ble *v.* To eat and swallow food greedily; to take greedily.

gob•bler *n.* A male turkey.

gob•let *n.* A drinking glass, typically with a base and stem.

gob•lin *n.* In folklore, an ugly, grotesque creature said to be mischievous and evil.

god *n.* A male deity; a male considered to be extremely important or valuable.

god•child *n.* A child for whom an adult serves as sponsor at baptism and other rites.

god•dess *n.* A female deity; a female considered to be extremely important or valuable.

god•fa•ther *n.* A man who sponsors a child at his or her baptism or other such ceremony.

god•moth•er *n.* A woman who sponsors a child at his or her baptism or other such ceremony.

god•par•ent *n.* A godfather or godmother.

god•send *n.* Something received unexpectedly and needed or wanted.

god•son *n.* A male godchild.

go-get•ter *n.* An enterprising, aggressive person.

gog•gles *pl. n.* Spectacles or eyeglasses to protect the eyes against dust, wind, sparks, and other debris.

go•ing *n.* The act of moving, leaving, or departing; the condition of roads or ground that affects walking, riding, and other movement.

gold *n.* A soft, yellow, metallic element

highly ductile and resistant to oxidation; used especially in coins and jewelry.

gold•en *adj.* Made of or containing gold; bright yellow in color; rich; lustrous; marked by prosperity.

gold•en an•ni•ver•sa•ry *n.* The fiftieth anniversary.

gold•en rule *n.* The principle of treating others as one wants to be treated.

gold•fish *n.* A reddish or brass-colored freshwater fish, cultivated as an aquarium fish; a carp.

gold mine *n.* A mine which produces gold ore; any source of great riches or profit.

golf *n.* A game played outdoors with a hard ball and various clubs, on a grassy course with nine or eighteen holes.

gon•do•la *n.* A long, narrow, flat-bottomed boat propelled by a single oar and used on the canals of Venice.

gone *adj.* Past; bygone; dead; beyond hope; participle of *go*.

gon•or•rhe•a *n.* A contagious venereal infection transmitted chiefly by sexual intercourse. **gonorrheal** *adj.*

good *adj.* Having desirable or favorable qualities or characteristics; morally excellent; virtuous; well-behaved.

good-by or **good-bye** *interj.* Used to express farewell. *n.* A farewell; a parting word; an expression of farewell.

good-heart•ed *adj.* Having a kind and generous disposition. **good-hearted-ness** *n.*

good-hu•mored *adj.* Having a cheerful temper or mood; amiable.

good-look•ing *adj.* Handsome; having a pleasing appearance.

good-na•tured *adj.* Having an easygoing and pleasant disposition.

good•ness *n.* The state or quality of being good.

good•will *n.* A desire for the well-being of others; the pleasant feeling or relationship between a business and its customers.

goose *n.* A large water bird related to swans and ducks. **geese** *pl.*

go•pher *n.* A burrowing North American rodent with large cheek pouches.

gore *v.* To stab or pierce. *n.* Blood that has been shed; a triangular or tapering piece of cloth as in a sail or skirt.

gorge *n.* A deep, narrow ravine; deep or violent disgust.

gor•geous *adj.* Beautiful; dazzling; extremely attractive.

go•ril•la *n.* A large African jungle ape, having a massive, stocky body, long arms, and tusk-like canine teeth.

go•ry *adj.* Covered or stained with blood; marked by much bloodshed or violence.

gos•ling *n.* A young goose.

gos•pel or **Gos•pel** *n.* The teachings of Christ and the apostles; any information accepted as unquestionably true; any of the first four books of the New Testament.

gos•pel mus•ic *n.* American religious music based on simple folk melodies blended with rhythmic and melodic elements of spirituals and jazz.

gos•sa•mer *n.* The fine film or strands of a spider's web floating in the air; anything sheer, delicate, light, or flimsy. **gossamer** *adj.*

gos•sip *n.* Idle, often malicious talk; a person who spreads sensational or intimate facts.

gouge *n.* A chisel with a scoop-shaped blade used for woodcarving; a groove or hole made with or as if with a gouge. *v.* To make a hole or groove with a gouge; to cheat, as to charge exorbitant prices. **gouger** *n.*

gou•lash *n.* A stew made from beef or veal and vegetables seasoned chiefly with paprika.

gourd *n.* A vine fruit related to the pumpkin, squash, and cucumber and bearing inedible fruit with a hard rind.

gour•met *n.* Someone who appreciates and understands fine food and drink.

gout *n.* A disease caused by a defect in metabolism and characterized by painful inflammation of the joints. **gouty** *adj.*

gov•ern *v.* To guide, rule, or control by right or authority; to control or guide the action of something. **governable** *adj.*, **governance** *n.*

gov•ern•ess *n.* A woman employed in a private household to train and instruct children.

gov•ern•ment *n.* The authoritative administration of public policy and affairs of a nation, state, or city; the system or policy by which a political unit is governed.

gov•er•nor *n.* Someone who governs, as the elected chief executive of any state in the United States.

gown *n.* A woman's dress, especially for a formal affair; any long, loose-fitting garment; a robe worn by certain officials.

grab *v.* To snatch or take suddenly; to take possession of by force.

grace *n.* Seemingly effortless beauty and charm of movement, proportion, or form; a charming quality or characteristic.

gra•cious *adj.* Marked by having or showing kindness and courtesy; full of compassion; merciful.

gra•da•tion *n.* A gradual and orderly arrangement or progression according to quality; size, rank, or other value; the act of grading. **gradational** *adj.*

grade *n.* A step or degree in a process or series; a group or category; a level of progress in school, usually constituting a year's work.

grade school *n.* Elementary school, which will usually teach from kindergarten to grade six or eight.

gra•di•ent *n.* A slope or degree of inclination; a rate of change in variable factors, as temperature or pressure.

grad•u•al *adj.* Moving or changing slowly by degrees; not steep or abrupt. **gradually** *adv.*

grad•u•ate *v.* To receive or be granted an academic diploma or degree upon completion of a course of study. **graduation** *n.*

graf•fi•to *n.* An inscription or drawing made on a public wall, subway train, rock, or any other surface. **graffiti** *pl.*

graft *v.* To insert a shoot from a plant into another living plant so that the two will grow together as a single plant; to transplant a piece of tissue or an organ. *n.* Living tissue or skin used to replace damaged or destroyed tissue or skin; the act of acquiring or getting personal profit or advantage by dishonest or unfair means through one's public position.

gra•ham *n.* Whole wheat flour.

grain *n.* A small, hard seed or kernel of cereal, wheat, or oats; the seeds or fruits of such plants as a group; a very small amount; the direction of growth in a fibrous substance such as wood.

grain•y *adj.* Having a granular texture; resembling the grain of wood. **graini-ness** *n.*

gram *n.* A metric unit of mass and weight equal to 1/1000 kilogram and nearly equal to one cubic centimeter of water at its maximum density.

gram•mar *n.* The study and description of the classes of words, their relations to each other, and their arrangement into sentences.

gram•mar school *n.* An elementary school.

gran•a•ry *n.* A building for storing threshed grain; an area or region where grain grows in abundance.

grand *adj.* To be large in size, extent, or scope; magnificent; of high rank or great importance.

grand•child *n.* The child of one's son or daughter.

grand•dad *n.* The father of one's mother or father.

grand•daugh•ter *n.* The daughter of one's son or daughter.

gran•deur *n.* The quality or condition of being grand; splendor.

grand•fa•ther *n.* The father of one's father or mother; an ancestor.

grand•fa•ther clock *n.* A pendulum clock enclosed in a tall narrow cabinet.

gran•di•ose *adj.* Impressive and grand; pretentiously pompous; bombastic.

grand•moth•er *n.* The mother of one's father or mother; a female ancestor.

grand•par•ent *n.* A parent of one's mother or father.

grand pi•an•o *n.* A piano with the strings arranged horizontally in a curved, wooden case.

grand•son *n.* A son of one's son or daughter.

grand•stand *n.* A raised stand of seats, usually roofed, for spectators at a racetrack or sports event.

gran•ite *n.* A hard, coarse-grained igneous rock composed chiefly of quartz and mica, used for building material and in sculpture.

gra•no•la *n.* Rolled oats mixed with dried fruit and seeds and eaten as a snack.

grant *v.* To allow; to consent to; to admit something as being the truth. *n.* An award of money for a study or experiment.

gran•u•lar *adj.* The state of being composed or seeming to be composed or containing grains or granules. **granularity** *n.*

gran•u•late *v.* To make or form into granules or crystals; to become or cause to become rough and grainy. **granulation** *n.*

gran•ule *n.* A very small grain or particle.

grape *n.* Any of numerous woody vines bearing clusters of smooth-skinned, juicy, edible berries.

grape•fruit *n.* A tropical, large, round citrus fruit with a pale yellow rind and tart, juicy pulp.

grape•vine *n.* A climbing vine that produces grapes; a secret or informal means of transmitting information or rumor from person to person.

graph *n.* A visual diagram representing the relationship between sets of things.

graph•ic or **graph•i•cal** *adj.* Describing in full detail; of or pertaining to drawings or blueprints, as in architecture.

graph•ite *n.* A soft black form of carbon having a metallic luster and slippery texture, used in lead pencils, lubricants, paints, and coatings.

grap•ple *n.* An instrument with iron claws used to fasten an enemy ship alongside for boarding. *v.* To struggle or contend with; to fasten, seize or drag as with a grapple. **grappler** *n.*

grasp *v.* To seize and grip firmly; to comprehend; to understand.

grasp•ing *adj.* Urgently desiring material possessions; greedy.

grass *n.* Any of numerous plants having narrow leaves and jointed stems; the ground on which grass is growing.

grass•hop•per *n.* Any of several jumping insects with long powerful hind legs.

grate *v.* To reduce, shred or pulverize by rubbing against a rough or sharp surface; to make or cause to make a harsh sound. *n.* A framework or bars placed over a window or other opening; an iron frame to hold burning fuel in a fireplace or furnace.

grate•ful *adj.* Thankful or appreciative for benefits or kindnesses; expressing gratitude.

grat•i•fy *v.* To give pleasure or satisfaction to; to fulfill the desires of; to indulge. **gratification** *n.*

grat•ing *n.* A grate.

grat•i•tude *n.* Appreciation and gratefulness; thankfulness.

gra•tu•i•tous *adj.* Given or obtained without payment; unjustified; unwarranted. **gratuitousness** *n.*

gra•tu•i•ty *n.* A gift, as money, given in return for a service rendered; a tip.

grave *n.* A burial place for a dead body, usually an excavation in the earth. *adj.* Very serious or important in nature; filled with danger; critical.

grav•el *n.* Loose rock fragments often with sand.

grave•stone *n.* A stone that marks a grave; a tombstone.

grave•yard *n.* An area set aside as a burial place; a cemetery.

grav•i•tate *v.* To be drawn as if by an irresistible force; to sink or settle to a lower level.

grav·i·ta·tion *n.* The force or attraction any two bodies exert towards each other. **gravitational** *adj.*

grav·i·ty *n.* The gravitational force manifested by the tendency of material bodies to fall toward the center of the earth.

gra·vy *n.* The juices exuded by cooking meat; a sauce made by seasoning and thickening these juices.

gray or **grey** *adj.* A neutral color between black and white; gloomy; dismal; characteristic of old age.

graze *v.* To feed upon growing grasses or herbage; to put livestock to feed on grass or pasturage; to brush against lightly in passing.

grease *n.* Melted or soft animal fat; any thick fatty or oily substance; lubrication.

great *adj.* Very large in size or volume; prolonged in duration or extent; more than ordinary.

greed *n.* Selfish desire for more than one needs or deserves.

greed·y *adj.* Excessively eager to acquire or gain something.

green *adj.* Of the color between yellow and blue in the spectrum; not fully matured or developed; lacking in skill or experience.

green·house *n.* An enclosed structure equipped with heat and moisture designed for the cultivation of plants.

greet *v.* To address someone in a friendly way; to welcome.

greet·ing *n.* A word of salutation.

gre·gar·i·ous *adj.* Habitually associating with others as in groups, flocks, or herds; enjoying the company of others; sociable. **gregariousness** *n.*

grem·lin *n.* A mischievous elf said to cause mechanical trouble in airplanes and other machinery.

grew *v.* Past tense of *grow.*

grey·hound *n.* One of a breed of slender, swift-running dogs with long legs.

grid *n.* An arrangement of regularly spaced bars; the system of intersecting parallel lines that divide maps, charts, and aerial photographs, used as a reference for locating points.

grid·dle *n.* A flat pan used for cooking.

grid·i·ron *n.* A metal framework used for broiling meat, fish, and other foods; a football field.

grief *n.* Deep sadness or mental distress caused by a loss or bereavement.

griev·ance *n.* A real or imagined wrong regarded as cause for complaint or resentment; a complaint of unfair treatment.

grieve *v.* To cause or feel grief or sorrow. **grievous** *adj.*

griev·ous *adj.* Causing grief, sorrow, anguish, or pain; causing physical suffering. **grievously** *adv.*

grill *n.* A cooking utensil made from parallel metal bars; a grating with open metalwork used as a decorative screen or room divider.

grim *adj.* Stern or forbidding in appearance or character.

grim·ace *n.* A facial expression of pain, disgust, or disapproval. **grimace** *v.*

grime *n.* Dirt, especially soot clinging to or coating a surface. **griminess** *n.*, **grimy** *adj.*

grin *v.* To smile broadly.

grind *v.* To reduce to fine particles; to sharpen, polish, or shape by friction.

grip *n.* A firm hold; a grasp; the ability to seize or maintain a hold; a suitcase. *v.* To grasp and keep a firm hold on.

gripe *v.* To anger; to annoy; to complain.

gris·ly *adj.* Ghastly; gruesome.

grist *n.* Grain that is to be ground; a batch of such grain.

gris·tle *n.* Cartilage of meat. **gristly** *adj.*

grist·mill *n.* A mill for grinding grain.

grit *n.* Small, rough granules, as of sand or stone; having great courage and fortitude. *v.* To clamp the teeth together. **gritty** *adj.*

grits *pl. n.* Coarsely ground hominy; coarse meal; eaten primarily in the southern states of the U.S.

griz·zle *v.* To become or cause to become gray.

groan *v.* To utter a deep, prolonged sound

of pain or disapproval.

gro•cer *n.* A storekeeper who deals in foodstuffs and various household supplies. **grocery** *n.*

gro•cer•ies *pl. n.* The merchandise sold in a grocery.

grog *n.* Any alcoholic liquor, especially rum, mixed with water.

grog•gy *adj.* Dazed, weak, or not fully conscious.

groin *n.* Anat. The crease or fold where the thigh meets the abdomen. Archit. The curved edge of a building formed by two intersecting vaults.

groom *n.* A male person hired to tend horses; a stableman; a bridegroom. *v.* To make neat in appearance.

groove *n.* A long, narrow channel or indentation; a fixed, settled habit or routine; a rut. **groove** *v.*

groo•vy *adj. slang* A state or condition of being wonderful; delightful.

grope *v.* The act of feeling about, as in the dark; to look for uncertainly or blindly.

gross *adj.* Relating to the total amount received; excessively large or fat; lacking refinement or delicacy; coarse; vulgar. *n.* An amount that equals 12 dozen or 144 items.

gro•tesque *adj.* Distorted or incongruous in appearance or style; bizarre; outlandish.

grot•to *n.* A cave or cave-like structure; a natural place of meditation or prayer.

grouch *n.* A habitually irritable or complaining person.

ground *n.* The surface of the earth; soil, sand, and other natural material at or near the earth's surface.

ground *v.* Past tense of *grind*; to prohibit flight; to run a boat onto the bottom.

ground•less *adj.* Without foundation or basis.

grounds *n.* The land that surrounds a building; the basis for an argument, action or belief; the sediment at the bottom of a liquid, such as coffee or tea.

group *n.* A collection or assemblage of people, objects, or things having some-

thing in common.

grouse *n.* Any of a family of game birds characterized by mottled, brownish, plumage and rounded bodies. *v.* To complain; to grumble.

grout *n.* A material used to fill cracks in masonry or spaces between tiles.

grove *n.* A small group of trees, lacking undergrowth.

grow *v.* To increase in size, develop, and reach maturity; to expand; to increase.

growl *v.* To utter a deep, guttural, threatening sound.

grown•up *n.* A mature adult.

growth *n.* The act or process of growing; a gradual increase in size or amount.

grub *v.* To dig up by the roots; to lead a dreary existence; to drudge. *n.* The thick, worm-like larva of certain insects, as of the June beetle.

grub•by *adj.* Sloppy; unkempt. **grubbily** *adv.,* **grubbiness** *n.*

grudge *n.* A feeling of ill will, rancor, or deep resentment. *v.* To be displeased, resentful, or envious of the possessions or good fortune of another.

gru•el *n.* A thin liquid made by boiling meal in water or milk.

gru•el•ing or **gru•el•ling** *adj.* Extremely tiring; exhausting.

grue•some *adj.* Causing horror or fright.

gruff *adj.* Surly or ill-tempered; deep-voiced; rough.

grum•ble *v.* To complain in low, throaty sounds; to growl.

grump•y *adj.* Irritable and moody; sour of temperament.

grun•gy *adj.* Dirty, run-down, or inferior in condition or appearance.

grunt *n.* The deep, guttural sound of a hog.

guar•an•tee *v.* To promise or assure the durability or quality of a product.

guar•an•ty *n.* A pledge or promise to be responsible for the debt, duty, or contract of another person in case of default; something that guarantees.

guard *v.* To watch over or shield from danger or harm; to keep watch.

guard·i·an *n.* One legally assigned responsibility for the care of the person and property of an infant, minor or other person.

guard·rail *n.* The protective rail, as on a highway or any area that poses danger.

gu·ber·na·to·ri·al *adj.* Of or pertaining to a governor.

guer·ril·la *n.* A member of an irregular military force capable of great speed and mobility, often operating behind enemy lines.

guess *v.* To make a judgment or form an opinion on uncertain or incomplete knowledge; to suppose; to believe.

guest *n.* A person who is the recipient of hospitality from another; a customer who pays for lodging.

guf·faw *n.* A loud burst of laughter.

guid·ance *n.* The act, process, or result of guiding.

guide *n.* One who leads or directs another, as in a course of action; a person employed to conduct others on trips through museums and sightseeing tours.

guide·book *n.* A handbook containing directions and other information for tourists and visitors.

guide·line *n.* Any suggestion, statement, or outline of policy or procedure.

guild *n.* An association of persons of the same trade or occupation.

guil·lo·tine *n.* An instrument of capital punishment in France during the French Revolution, used for beheading condemned prisoners.

guilt *n.* The condition or fact of having committed a crime or wrongdoing.

guilt·less *adj.* A state or condition of being without guilt; innocent.

guilt·y *adj.* Deserving of blame for an offense that has been committed; convicted of some offense.

gui·tar *n.* A musical instrument with six strings, played by plucking or strumming.

gulf *n.* A large area of ocean or sea partially enclosed by land; a wide, impassable difference.

gull *n.* A long-winged, web-footed sea bird, usually white and gray, with a hooked upper mandible.

gul·let *n.* The passage from the mouth to the stomach; esophagus; the throat; the pharynx.

gul·li·ble *adj.* Easily cheated or fooled. **gullibility** *n.*

gul·ly *n.* A ditch or channel cut in the earth by running water.

gulp *v.* To swallow rapidly or in large amounts; to gasp or choke.

gum *n.* A sticky, viscous substance exuded from various trees and plants, soluble in water and hardening on exposure to air; chewing gum.

gum·drop *n.* A small, round, firm piece of jelly-like, sugar-coated candy.

gump·tion *n.* Boldness; initiative; enterprise.

gun *n.* A weapon made of metal from which a projectile is thrown by the force of an explosion; a portable firearm.

gun·pow·der *n.* An explosive powder used in blasting, fireworks, and guns.

gun·shot *n.* A shot fired from a gun.

gun·smith *n.* A person who makes or repairs guns.

gup·py *n.* A small, tropical freshwater fish, popular in home aquariums.

gur·gle *v.* To flow in a broken, uneven current, making low bubbling sounds; to make a soft moist sound. **gurgle** *n.*

gu·ru *n.* A spiritual teacher of Hinduism.

gush *v.* To flow forth in volume and with sudden force; to be overly sentimental or enthusiastic. **gush** *n.*, **gushy** *adj.*

gush·er *n.* An oil well with a plentiful natural flow of oil; a person who gushes.

gust *n.* A sudden, violent rush of wind or air; a sudden outburst, as of emotion.

gut *n.* The alimentary canal or part of it.

gut·ter *n.* A channel or ditch at the side of a street for carrying off water; a trough for carrying off rain water from the roof.

gut·tur·al *adj.* Pertaining to the throat; having a harsh, muffled, or grating quality. guttural *n.*

guz•zle *v.* To drink greedily or to excess. **guzzler** *n.*

gym *n.* A gymnasium.

gym•na•si•um *n.* A room or building equipped for indoor sports.

gym•nas•tics *pl. n.* Physical exercises requiring strength and flexibility, especially those performed with special apparatus in a gymnasium.

gy•ne•col•o•gy *n.* The branch of medicine dealing with the female reproductive organs, female diseases, and female organs. **gynecological** *adj.*.

gy•rate *v.* To rotate or revolve around a fixed point or axis; to move or turn in a spiral motion.

H

H, h The eighth letter of the English alphabet.

hab•it *n.* Involuntary pattern of behavior acquired by frequent repetition; manner of conducting oneself; an addiction.

hab•it•able *adj.* Suitable for habitation.

hab•i•tat *n.* The region in which an animal or plant lives or grows; the place of residence of a person or group.

hab•i•ta•tion *n.* A place of residence.

hab•it-form•ing *adj.* Producing physiological addiction.

ha•bit•u•al *adj.* Practicing by or acting according to habit; resorted to on a regular basis; regular. **habitually** *adv.*

ha•ci•en•da *n.* A large estate or ranch in Spanish-speaking countries.

hack *v.* To cut with repeated irregular blows; to enter a computer memory without permission. *n.* A tool used for hacking; a rough, dry cough; a taxi driver.

hack•er *n.* In computers, an electronics expert capable of improvising creative solutions; especially, intruders who use such expertise to enter unauthorized files.

hack•le *n.* One of the long, slender, often narrow glossy feathers on the neck of a rooster; the hairs on the back of the neck, especially of a dog, that rise in anger or fear.

hack•ney *n.* A horse of medium size for ordinary driving or riding; a carriage or coach available for hire. *v.* To make common or frequent use of.

hack•neyed *adj.* Trite; commonplace.

hack•saw *n.* A saw in a narrow frame for cutting metal.

had•dock *n.* A food fish that is usually smaller than the related cod and is found on both sides of the Atlantic.

hadn't *contr.* Had not.

haft *n.* A handle of a weapon or tool.

hag *n.* A woman who will not be wooed; a witch. **haggish** *adj.*

hag•gard *adj.* Worn-out, exhausted; gaunt, as from hunger or fatigue. **haggardly** *adv.*, **haggardness** *n.*

hag•gle *v.* To argue or bargain on price or terms.

hai•ku *n.* An unrhymed Japanese verse form with three short lines of five, seven, and five syllables.

hail *n.* Precipitation of small, hard lumps of ice and snow; a hailstone; an exclamation, greeting, acclamation. *v.* To call loudly in greeting or welcome; to shout with enthusiasm.

hail•stone *n.* A type of hard pellet made of frozen snow and ice.

hair *n.* One of the pigmented filaments that grow from the skin of most mammals; a covering of such structures, as on the human head and on the skin; a slender margin. **hairy** *adj.*

hair•brush *n.* An instrument used for grooming the hair.

hair•cloth *n.* A wiry, stiff fabric of horsehair.

hair•split•ting *n.* The process of making petty distinctions. **hairsplitter** *n.*

hair•spring *n.* A fine, coiled spring that regulates and controls the movement of the balance wheel in a clock or watch.

hair trig•ger *n.* A gun trigger set to react to the slightest pressure. *adj.* Reacting immediately to the slightest provocation.

hake *n.* A marine food fish related to the cod.

hale *adj.* Healthy and robust; free from defect.

half *n.* One of two equal divisible parts; part of a thing approximately equal to the remainder; one of a pair.

half•back *n.* In football, either of two players who, along with the fullback and quarterback, make up the backfield.

hal•i•but *n.* Any of the edible flat fishes of the North Atlantic or Pacific waters.

hal•ite *n.* Large crystal or masses of salt.

hal•i•to•sis *n.* A condition or state of having bad breath.

hall•mark *n.* An official mark placed on gold and silver products to attest to their purity.

hal•low *v.* To sanctify; to make holy; to honor.

hal•lu•ci•na•tion *n.* An illusion of seeing something nonexistent; a delusion. **hallucinate** *v.*

ha•lo *n.* A ring of colored light surrounding the head; an aura.

hal•o•gen *n.* Any of the group of nonmetallic elements including flourine, chlorine, bromine, iodine, and astatine.

hal•ter *n.* A rope or strap for leading or tying an animal; a woman's upper garment tied behind the neck and across the back.

halve *v.* To divide into two equal parts; to lessen by half.

hal•yard *n.* A rope for hoisting or lowering a sail or flag.

ham *n.* The meat of a hog's thigh; the back of the knee or thigh; an amateur or showy actor or performer.

ham•let *n.* A small rural village or town.

ham•mer *n.* A hand tool with a heavy head used to drive or strike forcefully, especially nails.

ham•mer•lock *n.* A hold in wrestling where the opponent's arm is twisted upward behind his back.

ham•mer•toe *n.* A toe that is bent downward and malformed.

ham•mock *n.* A hanging bed or couch of fabric or heavy netting, suspended from supports at each end.

ham•per *v.* To interfere with movement or progress of. *n.* A ventilated, covered, receptacle used to store dirty laundry.

ham•ster *n.* Any of various rodents with large cheek pouches and a short tail.

ham•string *n.* Either of two tendons located at the back of the human knee; the large tendon at the back of the hock of four-footed animals.

hand *n.* The part of the arm below the wrist, consisting of the palm, four fingers, and a thumb; a set of cards dealt to a player in a card game.

hand•ball *n.* A court game in which the players bat a small rubber ball against the wall with their hands.

hand•bill *n.* A hand-distributed advertisement.

hand•book *n.* A small guide or reference book giving information or instructions.

hand•cuff *v.* To put handcuffs on; to make ineffective. *pl.* A pair of circular metal shackles chained together that can be fastened around the wrists.

hand•gun *n.* A gun that can be held and fired with one hand.

hand•i•cap *n.* Any disadvantage that makes achievement unusually difficult; a contest in which odds are equalized; an obstacle. *v.* To give a handicap to.

hand•i•craft or **hand•craft** *n.* Skill and expertise in working with the hands; an occupation requiring manual dexterity.

hand•ker•chief *n.* A small piece of cloth used for wiping the face or nose; a kerchief or scarf.

han•dle *v.* To touch, pick up, or hold with the hands; to represent.

hand•made *adj.* Made by hand or by a hand process.

hand•maid•en *n.* A female maid or personal servant.

hand•out *n.* Free food, clothing, or cash given to the needy; a folder distributed free of charge; a flyer.

hand•pick *v.* To select with care; to choose

personally or after careful screening.

hand•set *n.* A telephone receiver and transmitter combined in a single unit.

hand•shake *n.* The act of clasping hands by two people, as in greeting, agreement, or parting.

hand•some *adj.* Very good-looking or attractive.

hand•spring *n.* An acrobatic feat in which the body flips entirely backward or forward, while the feet pass quickly in an arc over the head.

hand•stand *n.* The feat of supporting the body on the hands with feet balanced in the air.

hand•writ•ing *n.* Writing performed with the hand, especially cursive, the type of writing of a person.

hand•y *adj.* Easy to use or reach; helpful or useful. **handily** *adv.*

hand•y•man *n.* A person who does odd jobs and repairs.

hang *v.* To be attached from above and unsupported from below; to fasten or be suspended so as to swing freely.

hang•ar *n.* A building for housing aircraft.

hang•er *n.* A device from which something may be hung or on which something hangs.

hang gli•der *n.* A device shaped like a kite from which a person hangs suspended in a harness while gliding through the air.

hang•man *n.* One hired to execute people by hanging.

hang•nail *n.* The small piece of skin that hangs loose from the side or root of a fingernail.

hang•o•ver *n.* Something remaining from what has passed; the effects of excessive alcohol intake.

hang-up *n.* A psychological or emotional problem; an obstacle.

hank *n.* A loop, coil, or piece of hair, thread, or yarn.

han•ker *v.* To have a yearning or craving for something.

hap•haz•ard *adj.* Occurring by accident; happening by chance or at random; hit-or-miss.

hap•less *adj.* Unfortunate; unlucky. **haplessly** *adv.*

hap•pen *v.* To occur or come to pass; to take place; to discover by chance; to turn up or appear by chance.

hap•pen•ing *n.* A spontaneous event or performance, with high contingency, accident, or improvisation, and low probability of repetition; an important event.

hap•pen•stance *n.* An event occurring by chance.

hap•py *adj.* Enjoying contentment and well-being; glad, joyous, satisfied or pleased. **happily** *adv.*, **happiness** *n.*

hap•py-go-luck•y *adj.* Carefree and unconcerned.

ha•ra-ki•ri *n.* A Japanese suicide ritual committed by ripping open the abdomen with a knife.

ha•rangue *n.* A long, extravagant, speech; a lecture.

ha•rass *v.* To disturb or annoy constantly; to torment persistently. **harassment**, **harasser** *n.*

har•bin•ger *n.* A person or event that initiates or pioneers a major change; something that foreshadows what is to come; a messenger.

har•bor *n.* A place of refuge or shelter; a bay or cove; an anchorage for ships. *v.* To provide shelter.

hard *adj.* Difficult to perform, endure, or comprehend; solid in texture or substance; resistant to cutting or penetration.

hard-boiled *adj.* Boiled or cooked in the shell to a hard or solid state.

hard co•py *n.* In computer science, the printed information from a computer.

hard-core *adj.* Extremely graphic in presentation; obstinately resistant to change.

hard disk *n.* In computer science, magnetic storage consisting of a rigid disk of aluminum coated with a magnetic recording substance, contained within a removable cartridge or mounted in the hard disk of a microcomputer.

harden

hard•en *v.* To make or become hard or harder; to make or become physically or mentally tough.

hard hat *n.* A protective head covering made of rigid material, worn by construction workers.

hard•head•ed *adj.* Having a stubborn character; obstinate.

hard•heart•ed *adj.* Heartless; unfeeling.

hard•ly *adj.* Very little; almost certainly not. *adv.* Forcefully; painfully; barely.

hard-nosed *adj.* Stubborn; hard-headed; unyielding.

hard pal•ate *n.* The bony forward part of the palate that forms the roof of the mouth.

hard•pan *n.* A layer of very hard clay-like matter or subsoil which roots cannot penetrate.

hard rock *n.* Rock music featuring amplified sound and modulations.

hard sell *n.* A sales method involving aggressive, high-pressure selling and closing techniques.

hard•ship *n.* A painful, difficult condition.

hard•tack *n.* A hard, cracker-like biscuit made from flour and water.

hard•top *n.* A car with a permanent top designed to resemble a convertible.

hard•ware *n.* Manufactured machine parts, such as tools and utensils; the mechanical components of a computer installation.

hard•wood *n.* The wood of an angiospermous tree as opposed to that of a coniferous tree; a tree that yields hardwood.

har•dy *adj.* Bold and robust; able to survive very unfavorable conditions as extreme cold; daring. **-iness** *n.*, **-ily** *adv.*

hare *n.* Various mammals related to the rabbits but having longer ears and legs.

hare-brained *adj.* Foolish or silly.

hare•lip *n.* A congenital deformity in which the upper lip is split.

har•em *n.* The women living in a Muslim residence; the living quarters of a harem.

hark *v.* To listen closely.

har•le•quin *n.* A jester; a clown. *adj.* Patterned with vividly colored diamond shapes.

harm *n.* Emotional or physical damage or injury. *v.* To cause damage or injury to. **harmful** *adj.* **harmless** *adj.*

har•mon•ic *adj.* Relating to musical harmony; in harmony; concordant. **harmonically** *adv.*

har•mon•i•ca *n.* A small, rectangular musical instrument having a series of tuned metal reeds that vibrate with the player's breath.

har•mo•ni•ous *adj.* Pleasing to the ear; characterized by agreement and accord; having components agreeably combined.

har•mo•ny *n.* Complete agreement, as of feeling or opinion; an agreeable combination of components; pleasing sounds; a combination of musical tones into chords.

har•ness *n.* The working gear of a horse or other draft animal.

harp *n.* A musical instrument having a triangular upright frame with strings plucked with the fingers. **harpist** *n.*

har•poon *n.* A barbed spear used in hunting whales and fish.

harp•si•chord *n.* A piano-like instrument whose strings are plucked by using quills or leather points.

har•py *n.* A vicious woman; a predatory person. **harpies** *pl.*

har•ri•dan *n.* A mean, hateful old woman.

har•ri•er *n.* A slender, narrow-winged hawk that preys on small animals; a hunting dog; a cross-country runner.

har•row *n.* A tool with sharp teeth for breaking up and smoothing soil.

har•ry *v.* To harass.

harsh *adj.* Disagreeable; extremely severe.

hart *n.* A fully grown male deer after it has passed its fifth year.

har•vest *n.* The process or act of gathering a crop; the season or time for gathering crops. *v.* To reap; to obtain as if by gathering. **harvester** *n.*

hash *n.* A fried or baked mixture of chopped meat and potatoes. *v.* To chop up into small pieces.

hash•ish *n.* The leaves and flowering tops of the hemp plant, chewed, drunk, or smoked for their intoxicating and narcotic effect.

hasp *n.* A clasp or hinged fastener that passes over a staple and is secured by a pin, bolt, or padlock.

has•sle *n.* A type of quarrel or argument. **hassle** *v.*

has•sock *n.* A firm upholstered cushion used as a footstool.

haste *n.* Speed; swiftness of motion or action; excessive eagerness to act.

has•ten *v.* To act or move with speed.

hast•y *adj.* Rapid; swift; made or done with excessive speed.

hat *n.* A covering for the head with a crown and brim.

hat•box *n.* A container or box used for storing or carrying hats.

hatch *n.* A small opening or door, as in a ship's deck. *v.* To bring forth, as young from an egg; to devise.

hatch•back *n.* An automobile with a sloped roof in the back that opens upward.

hatch•way *n.* An opening covered by a hatch in a ship's deck.

hatch•et *n.* A small ax with a short handle.

hate *v.* To feel hostility or animosity toward; to dislike intensely.

ha•tred *n.* A deep-seated animosity.

haugh•ty *adj.* Arrogantly proud; disdainful. **haughtiness** *n.*

haul *v.* To pull or draw with force; to move or transport, as in a truck or cart. *n.* The distance over which someone travels or something is transported; an amount collected at one time.

haul•age *n.* The process or act of hauling; a charge for hauling.

haunch *n.* The hip; the buttock and upper thigh of an animal; the loin and leg of a four-footed animal.

haunt *v.* To appear to or visit as a ghost or spirit; to linger in the mind. **haunting** *adj.*

hau•teur *n.* A disdainful arrogance.

have *n.* To hold or own, as a possession or as property; to possess.

hav•oc *n.* Mass confusion; widespread destruction; devastation.

haw *n.* A hesitating sound made by a speaker who is groping for words. *v.* To hesitate in speaking; to falter in speaking.

hawk *n.* Any of several predatory birds, with a short, hooked bill and strong claws for seizing small prey; one who advocates a war-like foreign policy.

haw•ser *n.* A heavy cable or rope for towing or securing a ship.

haw•thorn *n.* A thorny shrub or tree bearing white or pink flowers and red fruit.

hay *n.* Alfalfa or grass that has been cut and dried for animal food.

hay fe•ver *n.* An acute allergy to certain airborne pollens, marked by severe irritation of the upper respiratory tract and the eyes.

hay•fork *n.* A hand tool used to move hay.

hay•loft *n.* An upper loft in a barn or stable used to store hay.

hay•stack *n.* A pile of hay stored outdoors.

hay•wire *adj., Slang* Broken; emotionally out of control; crazy.

haz•ard *n.* A risk; chance; an accident; a danger or source of danger.

haze *n.* A fog-like suspension of dust, smoke, and vapor in the air; a confused or vague state of mind. *v.* To harass as part of an initiation ceremony.

ha•zel *n.* A small tree or shrub bearing edible brown nuts with smooth shells; a light brown or yellowish brown.

ha•zel•nut *n.* The edible nut of the hazel.

haz•y *adj.* Lacking clarity; vague; seen through a haze.

head *n.* The upper part of a human or animal body, containing the brain, the principal nerve centers, the eyes, ears, nose and mouth.

head•ache *n.* A pain or ache in the head.

head•band *n.* A band of cloth worn around the head.

head•board *n.* A frame or panel that stands at the head of a bed.

head cold *n.* A common cold or viral

infection that centers primarily in the nasal passages.

head·first *adv.* With the head in a forward position; headlong.

head·hunt·ing *n.* A tribal custom of decapitating slain enemies and preserving the heads as trophies.

head·ing *n.* A title or caption that acts as a front or upper part of anything; the direction or course of a ship or aircraft.

head·land *n.* A high ridge or cliff projecting into the water.

head·line *n.* A title, caption, or summarizing words of a newspaper story or article printed in large type. *v.* To serve as the star performer. **headliner** *n.*

head·lock *n.* A wrestling hold in which the head of a wrestler is locked under the arm of his opponent.

head·long *adv.* Headfirst; not having deliberation.

head·mas·ter *n.* A school principal of a private school.

head·mis·tress *n.* A female school principal of a private school.

head·piece *n.* A helmet, cap or other covering for the head; a headset.

head·quar·ters *pl. n.* The official location from which a leader directs a complex activity; the home offices of a corporation.

head·set *n.* A pair of headphones.

head·stall *n.* The part of a bridle that goes over a horse's head.

head·stand *n.* The act of balancing the body's weight on the top of the head, with the aid of the arms.

head start *n.* An early or advance start; an advantage.

head·stone *n.* A memorial stone marker at the head of a grave, indicating a name, date of birth and date of death.

head·strong *adj.* Not easily restrained; obstinate.

head·wait·er *n.* The waiter in charge of a restaurant or dining room staff.

head·wat·er *n.* The source of a river or stream.

head·way *n.* Motion in a forward direction; progress toward a goal; clearance beneath an arch or ceiling.

head wind *n.* A wind blowing in the direction opposite the course of a ship or aircraft.

head·y *adj.* Tending to intoxicate; affecting the senses.

heal *v.* To restore to good health; to mend. **healable** *adj.*

health *n.* The overall sound condition or function of a living organism at a particular time; freedom from disease or defect. **healthful** *adj.*, **healthfully** *adv.*, **healthfulness** *n.*

health·y *adj.* In a state of or having good health; characteristic of a sound condition.

heap *n.* A haphazard assortment of things; a large number or quantity; a pile. *v.* To throw or pile into a heap.

hear *v.* To perceive by the ear; to listen with careful attention; to be informed of; to listen to officially or formally.

hear·ing *n.* One of the five senses; the range by which sound can be heard; an opportunity to be heard.

hear·ing aid *n.* An electronic device used to amplify the hearing of partially deaf persons.

heark·en *v.* To listen carefully.

hear·say *n.* Information heard from another; common talk; rumor.

hearse *n.* A vehicle for conveying a dead body to the place of burial.

heart *n.* The hollow, primary muscular organ of vertebrates which circulates blood throughout the body; the emotional center, such as in love, hate, consideration, or compassion; the most essential part of something.

heart·ache *n.* Emotional grief; sorrow.

heart at·tack *n.* An acute malfunction or interrupted heart function.

heart·beat *n.* A pulsation of the heart, consisting of one contraction and one relaxation.

heart·break *n.* Great sorrow; deep grief. **heartbreaking** *adj.*

heart·burn *n.* A sensation of burning in

the stomach and esophagus, usually caused by excess acid in the stomach.

heart•en *v.* To give courage to; to strengthen the heart.

heart•felt *adj.* Deeply felt; sincere.

hearth *n.* The floor of a fireplace, furnace; the stone that forms the front of a fireplace.

heart•land *n.* A strategically important central region, or one regarded as vital to a nation's character.

heart•less *adj.* Having no sympathy; lacking compassion. **heartlessness** *n.*, **heartlessly** *adv.*

heart-rend•ing *adj.* Causing great distress, suffering emotional anguish.

heart•sick *adj.* Profoundly dejected.

heart•throb *n.* One pulsation of the heart; tender emotion; a loved one.

heart-to-heart *adj.* Sincere; frank.

heart-warm•ing *adj.* A feeling of warm sympathy.

heart•wood *n.* The older, no longer active central wood of a tree.

heart•y *adj.* Marked by exuberant warmth; full of vigor; nourishing; substantial.

heat *n.* A quality of being hot or warm; a degree of warmth; depth of feeling.

heat ex•haus•tion *n.* A reaction to intense heat, a mild form of heat stroke.

heath *n.* An open tract of uncultivated wasteland covered with low-growing shrubs and plants.

hea•then *n.* A person or nation that does not recognize the God of Christianity, Judaism, or Islam.

heath•er *n.* A shrub that grows in dense masses and has small evergreen leaves and small pinkish flowers.

heat light•ning *n.* Flashes of electric light, without thunder, seen near the horizon.

heat stroke *n.* A state of collapse or exhaustion, accompanied by fever and marked by clammy skin, caused by excessive heat.

heave *v.* To raise or lift, especially forcibly; to hurl or throw.

heav•en *n.* The sky; the region above and around the earth; the abode of God, the angels, and the blessed souls of the dead; a state or place of blissful happiness.

heav•y *adj.* Of great weight; very thick or dense; forceful; powerful; rough and violent, as stormy weather.

heav•y-du•ty *adj.* Designed for hard use; sturdy and durable.

heav•y-hand•ed *adj.* Clumsy; not tactful; oppressive.

heav•y-heart•ed *adj.* Melancholy; depressed; sad.

heav•y-set *adj.* Having a stocky build.

heav•y-weight *n.* A person of above average weight; a competitor in the heaviest class; a boxer weighing more than 175 pounds.

heck•le *v.* To badger or annoy.

hec•tic *adj.* Intensely active, rushed, or excited; confusingly complex.

hedge *n.* A boundary or fence formed of shrubs or low-growing trees.

hedge•hog *n.* A small nocturnal mammal with dense spines on the back for defense.

hedge•hop *v.* To fly an aircraft close to the ground, as in spraying crops.

hedge•row *n.* A dense row of bushes, shrubs, or trees forming a hedge.

he•don•ism *n.* The doctrine devoted to the pursuit of pleasure; the philosophy that pleasure is the principal good in life.

heed *v.* To pay attention; to take notice of something.

heel *n.* The rounded back part of the human foot under and behind the ankle; the part of a shoe supporting or covering the heel; a lower or bottom part; the crusty ends of a loaf of bread.

heft *n.* Weight; bulk. *v.* To gauge or estimate the weight of by lifting; to lift up.

heft•y *adj.* Bulky; heavy; sizable.

he•gem•o•ny *n.* Dominance or leadership, as of one country over another.

heif•er *n.* A young cow that has not yet produced a calf.

height *n.* The quality of being high; the highest or most advanced point; the distance from the base of something.

height·en *v.* To increase or become high in quality or degree.

Heim·lich ma·neu·ver *n.* An emergency maneuver used to dislodge food from a choking person's throat; the closed fist is placed below the rib cage and pressed inward to force air from the lungs upward.

hei·nous *adj.* Extremely wicked; hateful or shockingly wicked.

heir *n.* A person who inherits another's property or title.

heir ap·par·ent *n.* An heir who is legally assured of his right to inherit if he survives his ancestor.

heir·ess *n.* A female heir, especially to a large fortune.

heir·loom *n.* A family possession handed down from generation to generation.

heist *v.* To take from; to steal. *n.* A robbery.

hel·i·cal *adj.* Of or pertaining to the shape of a helix.

hel·i·con *n.* A large, circular tuba that encircles the player's shoulder.

hel·i·cop·ter *n.* An aircraft propelled by rotors which can take off vertically.

hel·i·port *n.* A designed area where helicopters land and take off.

hel·i·um *n.* An extremely light, nonflammable, odorless, gaseous element, symbolized by He.

hell or **Hell** *n.* The abode of the dead souls condemned to eternal punishment; a place of evil, torment, or destruction.

hell hole *n.* A place of extreme wretchedness or horror.

helm *n.* A wheel or steering apparatus for a ship.

hel·met *n.* A protective covering for the head made of metal, leather, or plastic.

helms·man *n.* One who guides a ship.

help *v.* To assist or aid. *n.* Assistance; relief; one who assists; one hired to help.

help·ing *n.* A single serving of food.

help·less *adj.* Without help; powerless; lacking strength.

help·mate *n.* A helper, partner or companion.

hel·ter-skel·ter *adv.* In a confused or hurried manner; in an aimless way. *adj.* Rushed and confused. *n.* Great confusion; a tumult.

helve *n.* A handle on a tool such as an axe or hatchet.

hem *n.* A finished edge of fabric folded under and stitched.

he·ma·tol·o·gy *n.* The branch of biological science that deals with blood and blood-generating organs.

hem·i·sphere *n.* A half sphere divided by a plane passing through its center; either symmetrical half of an approximately spherical shape; the northern or southern half of the earth.

hem·lock *n.* An evergreen tree of North America and eastern Asia, having flat needles and small cones; the wood of a hemlock; any of several poisonous herbaceous plants, having compound leaves and small whitish flowers; a poison obtained from the hemlock plant.

he·mo·glo·bin *n.* The respiratory pigment in the red blood cells of vertebrates containing iron and carrying oxygen to body tissues.

he·mo·phil·i·a *n.* An inherited blood disease characterized by severe, protracted, sometimes spontaneous bleeding. **hemophiliac** n.

hem·or·rhage *n.* Bleeding, especially excessive bleeding. **hemorrhage** *v.*

hem·or·rhoid *n.* A painful mass of dilated veins in swollen anal tissue.

he·mo·stat *n.* An agent that stops bleeding; a clamp-like instrument for preventing or reducing bleeding.

hemp *n.* An Asian herb whose tough fiber is used in the manufacture of rope.

hen *n.* A mature female bird, especially an adult female domestic fowl.

hench·man *n.* A loyal and faithful follower; one who supports a political figure chiefly for personal gain; a confederate in an unsavory enterprise.

hen·na *n.* An Asian and North African

ornamental tree bearing fragrant white or reddish flowers; a brownish-red dye derived from henna leaves and used as a cosmetic dye; a strong reddish brown.

hen•peck *v.* To domineer over one's husband by persistent nagging.

he•pat•ic *adj.* Of or like the liver.

hep•a•ti•tis *n.* Inflammation of the liver causing jaundice.

her•ald *n.* A person who announces important news; an official whose duty is to announce royal proclamations.

her•ald•ry *n.* The art or science of tracing genealogies and devising and granting coats of arms.

herb *n.* A soft-stemmed plant without woody tissue that usually withers and dies each year; an often pleasant-smelling plant. **herbal** *adj.*

her•ba•ceous *adj.* Like, or consisting of herbs; green and leaf-like.

herb•age *n.* Grass or vegetation used especially for grazing; the succulent edible parts of plants.

herb•al•ist *n.* One who gathers, grows, and deals in herbs.

her•bar•i•um *n.* A collection of dried plant specimens that are scientifically arranged for study; a place housing a herbarium.

her•bi•cide *n.* A chemical agent used to kill weeds.

her•bi•vore *adj.* Feeding chiefly on plant life or vegetables. **herbivore** *n.*

her•cu•le•an *adj.* Of unusual size, force, or difficulty; having great strength.

herd *n.* A number of cattle or other animals of the same kind, kept or staying together as a group.

here•af•ter *adv.* From now on; at some future time. *n.* Existence after death.

here•by *adv.* By means or by virtue of this.

he•red•i•tar•y *adj.* Passing or transmitted from an ancestor to a legal heir; transmitted or transmissible by genetic inheritance.

he•red•i•ty *n.* The genetic transmission of physical traits from parents to offspring.

here•in *adv.* In or into this place.

here•of *adv.* Relating to or in regard to this.

her•e•sy *n.* A belief in conflict with orthodox religious beliefs; any belief contrary to set doctrine.

her•e•tic *n.* A person holding opinions different from orthodox beliefs, especially religious beliefs.

here•to *adv.* To this matter, proposition, or thing.

here•to•fore *adv.* Up to the present time; previously.

here•un•to *adv.* Hereto; to this.

here•up•on *adv.* Immediately following or resulting from this.

here•with *adv.* Together or along with this; hereby.

her•i•tage *n.* Property inherited; something handed down from past generations.

her•maph•ro•dite *n.* A person having both male and female reproductive organs. **hermaphroditic** *adj.*

her•met•ic *adj.* Tightly sealed against air and liquids; made impervious to outside influences. **hermetically** *adv.*

her•mit *n.* A person who lives in seclusion, often for religious reasons.

her•mit•age *n.* The dwelling place or retreat of a hermit; a secluded hideaway.

her•ni•a *n.* The protrusion of a bodily organ, as the intestine, through an abnormally weakened wall that usually surrounds it; a rupture. **hernial** *adj.*

he•ro *n.* A figure in mythology and legend renowned for exceptional courage and fortitude. **heroes** *pl.*

he•ro•ic coup•let *n.* A verse consisting of two rhyming lines of iambic pentameter.

her•o•in *n.* A highly addictive narcotic derivative of morphine.

her•o•ine *n.* A woman of heroic character; the principal female character in a story or play.

her•o•ism *n.* Heroic behavior.

her•on *n.* A wading bird with a long slender bill and long legs and neck.

her•pes *n.* A viral infection, characterized

by small blisters on the skin or mucous membranes.

her·pe·tol·o·gy *n.* The scientific study and treatment of reptiles and amphibians.

her·ring *n.* A valuable food fish of the North Atlantic, the young of which are prepared as sardines, the adults are pickled, salted, or smoked.

her·ring·bone *n.* A pattern utilizing rows of short slanted parallel lines with connected rows slanting in the opposite direction.

hertz *n.* A unit of frequency equaling one cycle per second.

hes·i·tant *adj.* Given to hesitating; lacking decisiveness. **hesitancy** *n.*

hes·i·tate *v.* To pause or to be slow before acting, speaking, or deciding; to be uncertain.

het·er·o·sex·u·al *adj.* Of or having sexual desire to the opposite sex; involving different sexes.

hew *v.* To make or shape with an axe; to adhere strictly; to conform.

hex *n.* One held to bring bad luck; a jinx. *v.* To put under an evil spell; to bewitch.

hex·a·gon *n.* A polygon having six sides and six angles.

hex·am·e·ter *n.* A line of verse containing six metrical feet.

hey·day *n.* A time of great power, prosperity or popularity; a peak.

hi·ber·nate *v.* To pass the winter in an inactive, dormant, sleep-like state. **hibernation** *n.*

hi·a·tus *n.* A slight gap, break, or lapse in time from which something is missing; a break.

hi·ba·chi *n.* A deep, portable charcoal grill used for cooking food.

hic·cup or **hic·cough** *n.* An involuntary contraction of the diaphragm that occurs on inhalation and spasmodically closes the glottis, producing a short, sharp sound.

hick·o·ry *n.* A North American tree with a smooth or shaggy bark, hard edible nuts, and heavy, tough wood.

hide *v.* To put, or keep out of sight; to keep secret; to obscure from sight. *n.* The skin of an animal.

hid·e·ous *adj.* Physically repulsive; extremely ugly.

hi·er·ar·chy *n.* An authoritative body or group of things or persons arranged in successive order; a ranked series of persons or things.

hi·er·o·glyph·ic *n.* A pictorial symbol representing an idea, object, or sound.

hi-fi *n.* High fidelity; electronic equipment, such as a phonograph, radio, or recording equipment capable of reproducing high-fidelity sound.

high *adj.* Extending upward; located at a distance above the ground; more than normal in degree or amount.

high·born *adj.* Of noble birth or ancestry.

high·boy *n.* A tall chest of drawers often in two sections with the lower one mounted on four legs.

high·bred *adj.* Highborn; descending from superior breeding stock.

high·brow *n.* One who claims superior knowledge or culture.

high fash·ion *n.* The newest in fashion, style, or design.

high·fi·del·i·ty *n.* The reproduction of sound with minimal distortion, as on records or tapes.

high-flown *adj.* Pretentious in language or style.

high fre·quen·cy *n.* A radio frequency in the band from three to thirty megacycles.

high-hand·ed *adj.* Overbearing and arbitrary.

high-hat *adj.* Supercilious; patronizing; snobbish; fashionable.

high jump *n.* A jump for height in athletics.

high·land *n.* Land elevated as a plateau; a hilly or mountainous region.

high·light *n.* A significant event or detail of special importance. *v.* To give emphasis to; to provide with highlights.

high-pres·sure *adj.*, Informal Using insistent persuasive methods or tactics. *v.* To try to persuade by using high-pressure techniques.

high-rise *n.* An extremely tall residential building; a skyscraper.

high•road *n.* A main road; a direct or honorable method or course.

high school *n.* A secondary school of grades nine through twelve or grades ten through twelve.

high seas *pl. n.* The open waters of an ocean or sea beyond the territorial jurisdiction of any one nation.

high-stick•ing *n.* In hockey, an offense in which a player holds the stick above the shoulders of other players or himself.

high-strung *adj.* A state of being very nervous and excitable.

high tech•nol•o•gy *n.* The technology that involves highly advanced or specialized systems or devices. **high tech** *abbrev.*

high tide *n.* The highest level reached by the incoming tide each day.

high•way *n.* A main or principal road or thoroughfare of some length connecting towns and cities.

high•way•man *n.* Formerly, a robber who waylaid travelers on highways.

hi•jack *v.* To seize illegally or steal while in transit; to commandeer a vehicle, especially an airplane in flight. **hijacker** *n.*

hike *v.* To walk for a lengthy amount of time, usually through rugged terrain or woods.

hi•lar•i•ous *adj.* Boisterously happy or cheerful. **hilarity** *n.*

hill *n.* A rounded, elevation of the earth's surface, smaller than a mountain; a pile or heap.

hill•bil•ly *n.* A person living or coming from an isolated rural region, as from the mountains or a backwoods area, especially of the southern U.S.

hill•ock *n.* A small or low hill or mound.

hill•side *n.* The side or slope of a hill.

hill•top *n.* The summit or top of a hill.

hilt *n.* The handle of a dagger or sword.

him *pron.* The objective case of the pronoun *he.*

him•self *pron.* That identical male one; a form of the third person, singular masculine pronoun.

hind *adj.* Located at or toward the rear part; posterior.

hin•der *v.* To interfere with the process or action of.

hind•most *adj.* Farthest to the rear or back.

hind•quar•ter *n.* The back or hind part of a side of meat. **hindquarters** *pl.* The rump.

hin•drance *n.* The act of hindering or state of being hindered.

hind•sight *n.* Comprehension or understanding of an event after it has happened.

hinge *n.* A jointed device which allows a part, as a door or gate, to swing or turn on another frame.

hint *n.* An indirect indication or suggestion. *v.* To make something known by a hint.

hip *n.* The part of the human body that projects outward below the waist and thigh; the hip joint.

hip *n.* The bright, red seed case of a rose; a rosehip.

hip•pie *n.* A young person who adopts unconventional dress and behavior, questioning the middle class life its values.

hip•po•pot•a•mus *n.* A large, aquatic mammal, native to Africa, having short legs, a massive, thick-skinned hairless body, and a broad wide-mouthed muzzle.

hire *v.* To obtain the service of another for pay. **hirer** *n.*

his *adj.* The possessive case of the pronoun *he.*

hiss *n.* A sound resembling a prolonged, sibilant sound, as that of *sss.* *v.* To remit such a sound as an expression of disapproval. **hisser** *n.*

his•ta•mine *n.* A white, crystalline substance that occurs in plant and animal tissue, found to reduce blood pressure and to have a contracting action on the uterus and believed to cause allergic reactions.

his•to•ri•an *n.* A person who specializes in

the writing or study of history.

his·tor·ic *adj.* Significant or famous in history; historical.

hi·stor·i·cal *adj.* Relating to or taking place in history; serving as a source of knowledge of the past; historic. **historically** *adv.*, **historicalness**, **historicity** *n.*

his·to·ry *n.* Past events, especially those involving human affairs; an account or record of past events written in chronological order.

his·tri·on·ics *pl. n.* Theatrical acts; feigned emotional display.

hit *v.* To give a blow to; to strike with force; to come forcibly in contact with; to collide with.

hitch *v.* To fasten or tie temporarily with a hoot or knot. *n.* A device for attaching a trailer to a vehicle; a delay or difficulty.

hitch·hike *v.* To travel by signaling and obtaining rides from a passing driver. **hitchhiker** *n.*

hive *n.* A natural or man-made structure serving as a habitation for honeybees; a beehive.

hoard *n.* The accumulation of something stored away for safekeeping or future use. *v.* To amass and hide or store valuables, money. **hoarder** *n.*

hoarse *adj.* Having a husky, gruff, or croaking voice.

hoar·y *adj.* Ancient; aged; frosty; gray or white with age.

hoax *n.* A trick or deception. *v.* To deceive by a hoax. **hoaxer** *n.*

hob·ble *v.* To limp or walk with a limp; to progress irregularly or clumsily; to fetter a horse or other animal.

hob·by *n.* An activity or interest undertaken for pleasure during one's leisure time.

ho·bo *n.* A vagrant who travels aimlessly about; a vagabond; a tramp. **hoboes**, **hobos** *pl.*

hock *n.* The joint of the hind leg of a horse, ox, or other animal which corresponds to the ankle in man.

hock·ey *n.* A game played on ice between two teams of skaters whose object is to drive a puck into the opponent's goal using curved wooden sticks.

ho·cus-po·cus *n.* Any deception or trickery, as misleading gestures; nonsense words or phrases used in conjuring or sleight of hand.

hodge·podge *n.* A jumbled mixture or collection.

hoe *n.* A tool with a long handle and flat blade used for weeding, cultivating, and loosening the soil.

hog *n.* A pig, especially one weighing more than 120 pounds and raised for the market.

hoist *v.* To haul or raise up. *n.* A machine used for raising large objects.

hold *v.* To take and keep as in one's hand; to grasp; to possess; to put or keep in a particular place, position, or relationship.

hold·ing *n.* Property, such as land, money, or stocks.

hold·up *n.* A robbery at gun point; a delay.

hole *n.* A cavity or opening in a solid mass or body.

hol·i·day *n.* A day set aside by law to commemorate a special person or event; a day free from work; any day of rest.

ho·li·ness *n.* The state of being holy.

hol·ler *v.* To shout loudly; to yell.

hol·low *adj.* Having a cavity or space within; concaved or sunken; not genuine; empty; meaningless.

hol·ly *n.* A tree or shrub with glossy spiny leaves and bright-red berries.

hol·ly·hock *n.* A tall, cultivated plant of the mallow family, widely cultivated for its tall spikes of large, variously colored flowers.

hol·mi·um *n.* A metallic element of the rare-earth group, symbolized by Ho.

hol·o·caust *n.* A widespread or total destruction, especially by fire.

hol·o·graph *n.* A handwritten document, as a letter or will, signed by the person who wrote it.

hol·ster *n.* A leather case designed to hold a pistol or gun.

ho•ly *adj.* Regarded with or characterized by divine power; sacred.

hom•age *n.* Great respect or honor, especially when expressed publicly.

home *n.* The place where one resides; a place of origin; one's birthplace or residence during the formative years.

home•com•ing *n.* A return to one's home; a yearly celebration during which graduates return to their old schools.

home•sick *adj.* Longing or yearning for home and family. **homesickness** *n.*

home•work *n.* Work done at home, especially school assignments.

home•y or **hom•y** *adj.* Suggesting the coziness, intimacy, and comforts of home.

hom•i•cide *n.* The killing of one person by another; a person killed by another.

hom•ing pi•geon *n.* A pigeon trained to find its way home from great distances.

ho•mog•e•nize *v.* To process with milk by breaking up fat globules and dispersing them uniformly.

hom•o•nym *n.* A word that has the same sound and often the same spelling as another, but a different meaning and origin.

hom•o•phone *n.* One of two or more words that have the same sound but different spelling, origin, and meaning.

hon•cho *n.* The main person in charge; the boss; the manager.

hon•est *adj.* Truthful; not lying, cheating, or stealing; having or giving full worth or value. **honestly** *adv.*, **honesty** *n.*

hon•ey *n.* A sweet, sticky substance made by bees from the nectar gathered from flowers; sweetness; dear; darling.

hon•ey•bee *n.* Any of various bees living in colonies and producing honey.

hon•ey•comb *n.* A structure of hexagonal cells made by bees for the storage of honey, pollen, or their eggs.

hon•ey•moon *n.* A trip taken by a newly married couple.

honk *n.* The harsh, loud sound made by a goose; the sound made by an automobile horn.

hon•or *n.* High regard or respect; personal integrity; reputation.

hon•or•a•ble *adj.* Worthy of honor.

hon•or•ar•y *adj.* Relating to an office or title bestowed as an honor, without the customary powers, duties, or salaries.

hood *n.* A covering for the head and neck, often attached to a garment; the metal hinged cover of an automobile engine.

hood•lum *n.* A young, tough, wild, or destructive fellow.

hoof *n.* The horny covering of the foot in various mammals, as horses, cattle, and oxen. **hooves** *pl.*, **hoofed** *adj.*

hook *n.* A curved or bent piece of metal used to catch, drag, suspend, or fasten something.

hoop *n.* A circular band of metal or wood used to hold staves of a cask or barrel together; in basketball, the basket.

hoot *n.* The loud sound or cry of an owl.

hop *n.* A perennial herb with lobed leaves and green flowers, used in brewing beer; an informal dance; a quick trip on a plane. *v.* To move with light springing motions.

hope *v.* To want or wish for something with a feeling of confident expectation.

hope•ful *adj.* Manifesting or full of hope. *n.* A young person who shows signs of succeeding.

hope•less *adj.* Totally without hope; despairing; having no grounds for hope.

ho•ri•zon *n.* The line along which the earth and sky seem to meet.

hor•i•zon•tal *adj.* Parallel to the horizon.

horn *n.* A hard, bone-like, permanent projection on the heads of certain hoofed animals, as cattle, sheep, or deer; the two antlers of a deer which are shed annually.

hor•net *n.* Any of various wasps capable of inflicting a severe sting.

hor•o•scope *n.* A chart or diagram of the relative positions of the planets and signs of the zodiac at a certain time.

hor•ri•ble *adj.* Shocking; inducing or producing horror.

hor•rid *adj.* Horrible; terrible; frightening.

hor•ri•fy *v.* To cause a feeling of horror; to

dismay or shock.

hor•ror *n.* The painful, strong emotion caused by extreme dread, fear, or repugnance.

horse *n.* A large, strong, hoofed quadruped mammal with a long mane and tail, used for riding and for pulling heavy objects.

horse•man *n.* A person who rides horseback; an equestrian; one who breeds or raises horses. **horsemanship** *n.*

horse•pow•er *n.* A unit of power equal to 746 watts and nearly equivalent to the gravitational unit of 550 foot-pounds per second.

horse•shoe *n.* A protective U-shaped shoe for a horse, consisting of a narrow plate of iron shaped to fit the rim of a horse's hoof. *pl.* A game pitching horseshoes at a post target.

hose *n.* A sock; a stocking; a flexible tube for carrying fluids or gases under pressure. *v.* To wash; to water; to squirt with a hose.

ho•sier•y *n.* Stockings or socks.

hos•pice *n.* A lodging for travelers or the needy; a home taking care of terminally ill patients.

hos•pi•ta•ble *adj.* Treating guests with warmth and generosity; receptive.

hos•pi•tal *n.* An institution where the injured or sick receive medical, surgical, and emergency care.

hos•pi•tal•i•ty *n.* Hospitable treatment, disposition, or reception.

hos•pi•tal•ize *v.* To place or admit in a hospital as a patient for care or treatment.

host *n.* One who receives or entertains guests; one who provides a room or building for an event or function.

hos•tage *n.* A person held as security that promises will be kept or terms met by a third party.

host•ess *n.* A woman who entertains socially; a woman who greets patrons at a restaurant and escorts them to their tables.

hos•tile *adj.* Of or relating to an enemy; antagonistic. **hostility** *n.*

hot *adj.* Having heat that exceeds normal body temperature; electrically charged.

ho•tel *n.* A business that provides lodging, meals, entertainment, and other services.

hot•head•ed *adj.* Having a fiery temper.

hot•house *n.* A heated greenhouse.

hound *n.* Any of several kinds of long-eared dogs with deep voices which follow their prey by scent.

hour *n.* A measure of time equal to 60 minutes; one 24th of the day; the time of day or night.

hour•ly *adj.* Something that happens or is done every hour.

house *n.* A building that serves as living quarters for one or more families; home; a shelter or refuge.

how *adv.* In what manner or way; to what effect; in what condition or state.

how•ev•er *adv.* In whatever way. *conj.* Nevertheless.

howl *v.* To utter a loud, sustained, plaintive sound, as a wolf.

hub *n.* The center of a wheel; the center of activity.

hub•cap *n.* The removable metal cap that covers the end of an axle, as on the wheel of a motor vehicle.

hud•dle *n.* To crowd together; in football, a brief meeting of teammates to prepare for the next play.

hue *n.* A gradation of color running from red through yellow, green and blue to violet; a particular color; a shade.

huff *n.* A fit of resentment or of ill temper. *v.* To exhale or breathe heavily, as from extreme exertion.

hug *v.* To embrace; to hold fast; to keep, cling, or stay close to.

huge *adj.* Of great quantity, size, or extent.

hu•la *n.* A Hawaiian dance characterized by beautiful rhythmic movement of the hips and gestures with the hands.

hulk *n.* A heavy, bulky ship; the body of an old ship no longer fit for service.

hulk•ing *adj.* Unwieldy or awkward.

hull *n.* The outer cover of a fruit or seed; the framework of a boat.

hum *v.* To make a continuous low-pitched

sound; to be busily active; to sing with the lips closed.

hu•man *adj.* Of, relating to, or typical of man; having or manifesting human form or attributes.

hu•mane *adj.* To be marked by compassion, sympathy, or consideration for other people or animals. **humanely** *adv.*, **humaneness** *n.*

hu•man•i•tar•i•an *n.* A person who is concerned for human welfare, especially through philanthropy. **humanitarian** *adj.*, **humanitarianism** *n.*

hu•man•i•ty *n.* The quality or state of being human; humankind.

hum•ble *adj.* Marked by meekness or modesty; unpretentious; lowly. *v.* To make humble. **humility** *n.*

hu•mid *adj.* Containing or characterized by a large amount of moisture; damp.

hu•mid•i•ty *n.* A moderate amount of wetness in the air; dampness.

hu•mil•i•ate *v.* To reduce one's dignity or pride to a lower position; to shame.

hum•ming•bird *n.* A very small bird with narrow wings, a slender bill, and a very long tongue.

hu•mor *n.* Something with the ability to be comical or amusing.

hump *n.* The rounded lump or protuberance, as on the back of a camel.

hunch *n.* A strong, intuitive feeling about a future event or result.

hun•dred *n.* The cardinal number equal to 10 x 10. **hundred** *adj.*

hun•ger *n.* A strong need or desire for food. **hungrily** *adv.*, **hungry** *adj.*

hunt *v.* To search or look for food; to pursue with the intent of capture; to look in an attempt to find.

hur•dle *n.* A portable barrier used to jump over in a race; an obstacle one must overcome. *v.* To leap over.

hurl *v.* To throw with great force.

hur•rah *interj.* Used to express approval, pleasure, or exultation.

hur•ri•cane *n.* A tropical cyclone with winds exceeding 74 miles per hour, usually accompanied by rain, thunder, and lightning.

hur•ry *v.* To move or cause to move with haste. **hurriedly** *adv.*

hurt *v.* To experience or inflict with physical pain; to cause physical or emotional harm to; to damage. **hurtful** *adj.*

hus•band *n.* A man who is married.

hush *v.* To make or become quiet; to calm; to keep secret.

husk *n.* The dry or membranous outer cover of certain vegetables, fruits, and seeds.

husk•y *adj.* Having a dry cough or grating sound; burly or robust.

husk•y *n.* A heavy-coated working dog of the arctic region.

hus•tle *v.* To urge or move hurriedly along; to work busily and quickly.

hut *n.* An often small and temporary dwelling made of simple construction; a shack.

hy•drant *n.* A pipe with a valve and spout which supplies water from a main source.

hy•drau•lic *adj.* Operated, moved, or effected by the means of water, hardening or setting under water.

hy•drau•lics *pl. n.* The scientific study that deals with practical applications of liquids in motion.

hy•dro•gen *n.* A colorless, normally odorless, highly flammable gas that is the simplest and lightest of the elements.

hy•dro•gen bomb *n.* An extremely destructive bomb with an explosive power obtained from the rapid release of atomic energy.

hy•e•na *n.* Any of several strong carnivorous scavenger mammals of Africa and Asia, with coarse hair and powerful jaws.

hy•giene *n.* The science of the establishment and maintenance of good health and the prevention of disease. **hygienic** *adj.*, **-ically** *adv.*

hy•per•link *n.* In computers, a specialized text allowing one network site to contact another; a web page feature allowing such transfer.

hy·per·text *n.* In computers, a selectable part of a text, usually highlighted, allowing immediate linking to related areas of inquiry.

hy·phen *n.* A punctuation mark used to show connection between two or more words. **hyphenate** *v.*, **hyphenation** *n.*

hyp·no·sis *n.* A state that resembles sleep but is brought on or induced by another person whose subconscious suggestions are accepted by the subject.

hyp·not·ic *adj.* Inducing sleep. *n.* An agent, such as a drug, which induces sleep

I

I, i The ninth letter of the English alphabet; the Roman numeral for one.

I *pron.* The person speaking or writing. *n.* The self; the ego.

i·amb *n.* A metrical foot consisting of a short or unstressed syllable followed by an accented syllable. **iambic** *adj.* or *n.*

i·bex *n.* An Old World mountain goat with long curved horns.

ibid *abbr.* Ibidem, in the same place.

i·bi·dem *adv.* Used in footnotes to indicate a part of literary work that was just mentioned.

ice *n.* Solidly frozen water; a dessert of flavored and sweetened crushed ice.

ice age *n.* A time of widespread glaciation.

ice ax *n.* A pick and adze that has a spiked handle, used for mountain climbing.

ice bag *n.* A small, flexible, waterproof bag designed to hold ice, used on parts of the body.

ice·berg *n.* A thick mass of floating ice separated from a glacier.

ice·blink *n.* A luminous appearance under a cloud or near the horizon, caused by the reflection of light on distant formations of ice.

ice·boat *n.* A vehicle with runners and usually a sail, used for sailing over ice; an icebreaker. **iceboater** *n.*

ice·boat·ing *n.* A sport of sailing in ice-boats. **iceboater** *n.*

ice·bound *adj.* Obstructed or covered by ice so as to be inaccessible or immovable.

ice·box *n.* A structure designed for holding ice in which food and other perishables are stored.

ice·break·er *n.* A sturdy vessel for breaking a path through icebound waters; a pier or dock apron for deflecting floating ice from the base of a pier or bridge.

ice cap *n.* An extreme perennial covering of ice and snow that covers a large area.

ice cream *n.* A smooth mixture of milk, cream, flavoring, sweeteners, and other ingredients, beaten and frozen.

ice-cream cone *n.* A crisp and edible cone for the purpose of holding ice cream.

ice·fall *n.* A waterfall which is frozen.

ice field *n.* Pieces of glaciers that have joined and frozen together causing a sheet of ice so large that one cannot see its end.

ice floe *n.* A mass of sea ice that floats free upon the water.

ice·house *n.* A building for the purpose of storing ice.

ice·land moss *n.* A kind of lichen of the arctic areas which can be used for food.

ice·land pop·py *n.* A type of perennial poppy having small pastel flowers.

ice·man *n.* A man who is able to travel upon the ice with ease; one who delivers and sells ice.

ice milk *n.* A food similar to ice cream but made from skim milk.

ice nee·dle *n.* A slender ice particle which floats in the air in cold weather.

ice pack *n.* A large mass of floating, compacted ice; a folded bag filled with ice and applied to sore parts of the body.

ice pick *n.* A pointed tool used for breaking ice into small pieces.

ice plant *n.* An herb of the Old World that is related to the carpetweed.

ice point *n.* A temperature of zero degrees centigrade.

ice skate *n.* A shoe or boot with a runner fixed to it for skating on ice.

ice storm *n.* A storm with frozen rain.

ice wa•ter *n.* Water cooled by ice.

ich•nol•o•gy *n.* The study of fossil footprints of animals. **ichnological** *adj.*

ich•thy•ol•o•gy *n.* The zoological study of fishes.

i•ci•cle *n.* A hanging spike of ice formed by dripping water that freezes.

i•ci•ness *n.* The state of being very cold or icy.

ic•ing *n.* A sweet preparation for coating cakes and cookies.

i•con or **i•kon** *n.* A sacred Christian pictorial representation of Jesus Christ, the Virgin Mary, or other sacred figures.

i•con•o•clasm *n.* The attitude or practice of an iconoclast.

i•con•o•clast *n.* One who opposes the use of sacred images; one who attacks traditional or cherished beliefs. **iconoclastic** *adj.*

i•co•nog•ra•phy *n.* A pictorial material illustrating a subject; a published work dealing with iconography.

i•con•o•scope *n.* A camera tube containing an electron gun and a mosaic screen which produces a charge proportional to the light intensity of the image on the screen.

i•cy *adj.* Covered with or consisting of ice; extremely cold; freezing; characterized by coldness.

i•de•a *n.* Something existing in the mind; conception or thought; an opinion; a plan of action.

i•de•al *n.* A concept or imagined state of perfection; highly desirable; perfect; an ultimate objective; an honorable principle or motive. *adj.* Conforming to absolute excellence.

i•de•al•ism *n.* The practice or tendency of seeing things in ideal form; pursuit of an ideal; a philosophical system believing that reality consists of ideas or perceptions.

i•de•al•ist *n.* A person who practices or advocates idealism in writing.

i•de•al•is•tic *adj.* To be pertaining to idealism or idealists.

i•de•al•i•ty *n.* The state of being ideal.

i•de•al•ize *v.* To regard or represent as ideal. **idealization** *n.*

i•de•al•ly *adv.* In respect to an ideal; theoretically.

i•de•al point *n.* The point added to a space to eliminate special cases.

i•de•ate *v.* To make an idea of something.

i•de•a•tion *n.* The act of forming ideas.

i•de•a•tion•al *adj.* Pertaining to ideation; referring to ideas of objects not immediately present to the senses.

i•dem•po•tent *adj.* Pertaining to a mathematical quantity that is not zero.

i•den•ti•cal *adj.* Being the same; exactly equal or much alike; designating a twin or twins developed from the same ovum. **identically** *adv.,* **-ness** *n.*

i•den•ti•fi•a•ble *adj.* Having the capability of being identified or recognized.

i•den•ti•fy *v.* To recognize the identity of; to establish as the same or similar; to equate; to associate oneself closely with an individual or group. **identifiable** *adj.,* **identification** *n.*

i•den•ti•ty *n.* The condition or state of being a specific person or thing and recognizable as such.

id•e•o•gram or **id•e•o•graph** *n.* A pictorial symbol used in a writing system to represent an idea or thing, as Chinese characters; a graphic symbol, as $ or %.

id•e•og•ra•phy *n.* A representation of some ideas by use of graphic symbols.

id•e•o•log•i•cal *adj.* Concerned with ideas.

id•e•o•logue *n.* A person who adheres to a particular ideology.

i•de•ol•o•gy *n.* A body of ideas that influence a person, group, culture, or political party.

id•i•o•cy *n.* A condition of an idiot.

id•i•o•graph•ic *adj.* Pertaining to the concrete or unique.

id•i•om *n.* A form of expression having a meaning not readily understood from the meaning of its component words; the dialect of people or a region; a kind of language or vocabulary.

id•i•o•path•ic *adj.* To be peculiar to an individual. **idiopathically** *adv.*

id•i•o•syn•cra•sy *n.* A peculiarity, as of behavior. **idiosyncratic** *adj.*

id•i•ot *n.* A mentally deficient person; an extremely foolish or stupid person.

id•i•ot•ic *adj.* Showing of complete lack of thought or common sense by someone. **idiotically** *adv.*

id•i•ot sa•vant *n.* A person who is mentally defective but exhibits exceptional skill in a specific area, such as mathematics or music.

i•dle *adj.* Doing nothing; inactive; moving lazily; unemployed or inactive.

id•ler wheel *n.* A kind of wheel or roller used to transfer motion to something.

i•dol *n.* A symbol or representation of a god or deity that is worshiped; a person or thing adored.

i•dol•a•try *n.* An immoderate attachment to something. **idolatrous** *adj.*

i•dol•ize *v.* To admire with excessive admiration or devotion; to worship as an idol.

i•dyll or **i•dyl** *n.* A poem or prose piece about country life; a scene, event, or condition of rural simplicity; a romantic interlude.

if *conj.* On the condition that; allowing that; supposing or granting that.

ig•loo *n.* A dome-shaped Eskimo dwelling or hut often made of blocks of snow.

ig•ne•ous *adj.* Relating to fire; formed by solidification from a molten magma.

ig•nes•cent *adj.* To be capable of giving off sparks.

ig•nite *v.* To start or set a fire; to render luminous by heat.

ig•ni•tion *n.* An act or action of igniting; a process or means for igniting the fuel mixture in an engine.

ig•no•ble *adj.* Dishonorable in character or purpose, not of noble rank; mean, worthless; of a low family or birth right.

ig•no•min•i•ous *adj.* Marked by or characterized by shame or disgrace; dishonorable. **ignominiously** *adv.*

ig•no•min•y *n.* A disgraceful conduct or action; dishonor, shame.

ig•no•ra•mus *n.* A totally ignorant person.

ig•no•rant *adj.* Lacking education or knowledge; not aware; lacking comprehension. **ignorance** *n.*

ig•nore *v.* To pay no attention to; to reject; to disregard; refuse to consider, recognize or notice.

i•gua•na *n.* A large, dark-colored tropical American lizard.

i•guan•o•don *n.* A member of the genus of the gigantic herbivorous dinosaurs.

il•e•um *n.* The lower part of the small intestine between the jejunum and the large intestine.

il•i•um *n.* The largest bone of the pelvis.

ilk *n.* Sort; kind.

ill *adj.* Not healthy; sick; destructive in effect; harmful.

I'll *contr.* I will; I shall.

il•la•tive *n.* A phrase which introduces an inference. **illatively** *adv.*

ill-bred *adj.* Ill-mannered; impolite; rude.

il•le•gal *adj.* Contrary to law or official rules.

il•leg•i•ble *adj.* Not readable; not legible.

il•le•git•i•mate *adj.* Against the law; unlawful; born out of wedlock. **illegitimacy** *n.*, **illegitimately** *adv.*

ill-fat•ed *adj.* Destined for misfortune; doomed; unlucky; that which causes or marks the beginnings of misfortune.

ill-fa•vored *adj.* Unattractive; objectionable; offensive; unpleasant.

ill-got•ten *adj.* Obtained in an illegal or dishonest way.

ill-hu•mored *adj.* Irritable; cross.

il•lic•it *adj.* Not permitted by custom or law; unlawful. **illicitly** *adv.*

il•lim•it•a•ble *adj.* To be incapable of being bounded or limited in any way. **illimitably** *adv.*, **illimitability** *n.*

il•lit•er•ate *adj.* Unable to read and write; uneducated; having or showing a lack of knowledge of fundamentals on a particular subject.

ill·man·nered *adj.* Lacking or showing a lack of good manners; rude.

ill·na·tured *adj.* Disagreeable or unpleasant disposition.

ill·ness *n.* Sickness; a state of being in poor health; the unhealthy condition of one's body or mind.

il·log·i·cal *adj.* Contrary to the principles of logic; not logical.

ill·tem·pered *adj.* Having or showing a cross temper or disposition.

il·lu·mi·nate *v.* To give light; to make clear; to provide with understanding; to decorate with pictures or designs.

il·lu·sion *n.* A misleading perception of reality; an overly optimistic idea or belief; misconception; the act of deceiving.

il·lu·sion·ar·y *adj.* To be factual; a matter-of-fact.

il·lus·trate *v.* To explain or clarify, especially by the use of examples; to clarify by serving as an example; to provide a publication with explanatory features. **illustrator** *n.*

il·lus·tra·tion *n.* The act of illustrating; an example or comparison used to illustrate.

il·lus·tri·ous *adj.* Greatly celebrated; renowned; brilliantly outstanding because of actions or achievements.

il·lu·vi·um *n.* The material that is leached from one soil horizon to another soil horizon.

ill will *n.* Unfriendly or hostile feelings; malice.

ill·wish·er *n.* A person who wishes ill or harm to another.

I'm *contr.* I am.

im·age *n.* A representation of the form and features of someone or something; an optically formed representation of an object made by a mirror or lens; a mental picture of something imaginary.

im·age·ry *n.* Mental pictures; existing only in the imagination.

im·ag·in·a·ble *adj.* Capable of being imagined. **imaginably** *adv.*

im·ag·i·nar·y *adj.* Existing only in the imagination.

im·ag·i·na·tion *n.* The power of forming mental images of unreal or absent objects; such power used creatively; resourcefulness.

im·ag·ine *v.* To form a mental picture or idea of; to suppose; to guess.

im·ag·ism *n.* The movement in poetry in the 20th century where expression of ideas and emotions are through precise images. **imagistically** *adj.*, **imagist** *n.*

im·bal·ance *n.* A lack of functional balance; defective coordination.

im·be·cile *n.* A mentally deficient person who requires supervision in the daily routine of caring for himself. **imbecilic** *adj.*

im·bibe *v.* To drink; to take into the mind and retain; to absorb light, heat, gas, or moisture. **imbiber** *n.*

im·bri·cate *adj.* With edges overlapping in a regular arrangement, as roof tiles or fish scales. **imbricately** *adv.*

im·brue *v.* To drench something.

im·i·tate *v.* To copy the actions or appearance of another; to adopt the style of; to duplicate; to appear like. **imitator** *n.*

im·i·ta·tion *n.* An act of imitating; something copied from an original.

im·i·ta·tive *adj.* To be marked by imitation.

im·mac·u·late *adj.* Free from sin, stain, or fault; impeccably clean.

im·ma·te·ri·al *adj.* Lacking material body or form; of no importance or relevance.

im·ma·ture *adj.* Not fully grown; undeveloped; suggesting a lack of maturity.

im·meas·ur·a·ble *adj.* Not capable of being measured.

im·me·di·a·cy *n.* The quality of being immediate; directness; something of urgent importance.

im·me·di·ate *adj.* Acting or happening without an intervening object, agent, or cause; directly perceived; occurring at once.

im·me·di·ate·ly *adv.* In direct relationship or connection.

im·me·mo·ri·al *adj.* Beyond the limits of memory, tradition, or records.

im·me·mo·ri·al·ly *adv.*

im·mense *adj.* Exceptionally large. **immensely** *adv.*, **immenseness** *n.*

im·men·si·ty *n.* The state of something being immense or very large in size.

im·merse *v.* To put into a liquid; to baptize by submerging in water; to engross; to absorb.

im·mersed *adj.* To be growing completely underwater such as a plant.

im·mers·i·ble *adj.* Having the capability of being totally underwater without damaging any working parts.

im·mer·sion *n.* The act or state of being totally immersed.

im·mi·grant *n.* One who leaves his country to settle in another and who takes up permanent residence in the new country.

im·mi·grate *v.* To leave one country and settle in another; to bring in as immigrants. **immigration** *n.*, **immigrational** *adj.*

im·mi·nent *adj.* About to happen or take place. **imminentness, imminence** *n.*, **imminently** *adv.*

im·mit·i·ga·ble *adj.* To not be capable of being mitigated. **immitigably** *adv.*

im·mo·bile *adj.* Not moving or incapable of motion. **immobility** *n.*

im·mo·bi·lize *v.* To render motionless, preventing movement. **immobilization, immobilizer** *n.*

im·mod·er·ate *adj.* Exceeding normal bounds.

im·mod·est *adj.* Lacking modesty; indecent; boastful.

im·mo·late *v.* To kill, as a sacrifice; to destroy completely. **immolator** *n.*

im·mor·al *adj.* Not moral; conflict with moral principles.

im·mo·ral·i·ty *n.* Lack of morality; an immoral act or practice.

im·mor·tal *adj.* Exempt from death; lasting forever, as in fame. *n.* A person of lasting fame.

im·mor·tal·ize *v.* To make something immortal.

im·mov·a·ble *adj.* Not capable of moving or being moved.

im·mune *adj.* Not affected or responsive; resistant, or protected as to a disease.

im·mu·ni·ty *n.* The state at which something is immune.

im·mu·nize *v.* To make immune.

im·mu·no·ge·net·ics *n.* A branch of immunology concerned with heredity, disease, and the immune system and its components.

im·mu·nol·o·gy *n.* The study of immunity to diseases.

imp *n.* A mischievous child.

im·pact *n.* A collision; the impetus or force produced by a collision; an initial, usually strong effect. *v.* To pack firmly together; to strike or affect forcefully.

im·pac·ted *adj.* Wedged together at the broken ends, as an impacted bone; wedged inside the gum in such a way that normal eruption is prevented, as an impacted tooth.

im·pair *v.* To diminish in strength, value, quantity, or quality.

im·pa·la *n.* A large African antelope, the male of which has slender curved horns.

im·pale *v.* To pierce with a sharp stake or point; to kill by piercing in this fashion. **impalement** *n.*

im·pal·pa·ble *adj.* Not perceptible to touch; not easily distinguished. **impalpability** *n.*, **impalpably** *adv.*

im·part *v.* To grant; to bestow; to convey; to make known; to communicate.

im·par·tial *adj.* Not partial; unbiased.

im·pass·a·ble *adj.* Impossible to travel over or across.

im·passe *n.* A road or passage having no exit; a difficult situation with no apparent way out; a deadlock.

im·pas·sioned *adj.* To be filled with passion.

im·pas·sive *adj.* Unemotional; showing no emotion; expressionless.

im·pa·tience *n.* The quality of being impatient.

im·pa·tient *adj.* Unwilling to wait or tolerate delay; expressing or caused by irritation at having to wait; restlessly eager; intolerant. **impatiently** *adv.*

im•peach *v.* To charge with misconduct in public office before a proper court of justice; to make an accusation against. **impeachable** *adj.*, **impeachment** *n.*

im•pec•ca•ble *adj.* Having no flaws; perfect; not capable of sin.

im•pe•cu•ni•ous *adj.* Having no money. **impecuniousness**, **impecuniosity** *n.*

im•ped•ance *n.* A measure of the total opposition to the flow of an electric current, especially in an alternating current circuit.

im•pede *v.* To obstruct or slow down the progress of.

im•ped•i•ment *n.* One that stands in the way; something that impedes, especially an organic speech defect.

im•pel *v.* To spur to action; to provoke; to drive forward; to propel.

im•pend *v.* To hover threateningly; to be about to happen. .

im•pen•dent *adj.* To be near at hand.

im•pen•e•tra•bil•i•ty *n.* The inability of two parts of anything to occupy the same space at exactly the same time.

im•pen•e•tra•ble *adj.* Not capable of being penetrated; not capable of being seen through or understood; unfathomable.

im•per•a•tive *adj.* Expressing a command or request; empowered to command or control; compulsory.

im•per•cep•ti•ble *adj.* Not perceptible by the mind or senses; extremely small.

im•per•fect *adj.* Not perfect; of or being a verb tense which shows an uncompleted or continuous action or condition.

im•per•fec•tion *n.* The quality or condition or being imperfect; a defect.

im•pe•ri•al *adj.* Of or relating to an empire or emperor; designating a nation or government having dependent colonies; majestic; regal.

im•pe•ri•al•ism *n.* The national policy or practice of acquiring foreign territories or establishing dominance over other nations.

im•per•il *v.* To put in peril; endanger.

im•pe•ri•ous *adj.* Commanding; domineering; urgent.

im•per•ish•a•ble *adj.* Not perishable; permanently enduring.

im•pe•ri•um *n.* An absolute dominion; the right to employ the force of the state.

im•per•ma•nent *adj.* Not permanent; temporary.

im•per•me•a•ble *adj.* Not permeable; incapable of penetration. *adv.*

im•per•mis•si•ble *adj.* Not allowed.

im•per•son•al *adj.* Having no personal reference or connection; showing no emotion or personality.

im•per•son•ate *v.* To assume the character or manner of.

im•per•ti•nent *adj.* Overly bold or disrespectful; not pertinent; irrelevant.

im•per•vi•ous *adj.* Incapable of being penetrated or affected. **imperviously** *adv.*, **imperviousness** *n.*

im•pe•ti•go *n.* A contagious skin disease marked by pustules.

im•pet•u•ous *adj.* Marked by sudden action or emotion; impulsive.

im•pe•tus *n.* A driving force; an incitement; a stimulus; momentum.

im•pi•ous *adj.* Not pious; irreverent; disrespectful.

imp•ish *adj.* Mischievous. **impishness** *n.*

im•pla•ca•ble *adj.* Not capable of being placated or appeased. **implacability** *n.*, **implacably** *adv.*

im•pli•ca•tion *n.* The act of implicating or state of being implicated; the act of implying.

im•plode *v.* To collapse or burst violently inward.

im•plant *v.* To set in firmly; to fix in the mind; to insert surgically.

im•plau•si•ble *adj.* Difficult to believe; unlikely.

im•ple•ment *n.* A utensil or tool. *v.* To put into effect; to carry out; to furnish with implements. **implementation** *n.*

implicate

im•pli•cate v. To involve, especially in illegal activity; to imply. implication n.

im•plic•it adj. Contained in the nature of someone or something but not readily apparent; understood but not directly expressed; complete; absolute.

im•plore v. To appeal urgently to.

im•ply v. To infer by logical necessity; to express indirectly; to suggest.

im•po•lite adj. Rude; without courtesy.

im•pon•der•a•ble adj. Incapable of being weighed or evaluated precisely.

im•port v. To bring in goods from a foreign country for trade or sale; to mean; to signify; to be significant. n. Something imported; meaning; significance.

im•por•tant adj. Likely to determine or influence events; significant; having fame or authority.

im•pose v. To enact or apply as compulsory; to obtrude or force oneself or a burden on another; to take unfair advantage.

im•pos•ing adj. Awesome; impressive. imposingly adv.

im•po•si•tion n. The act of imposing upon someone or something; an excessive or uncalled for burden.

im•pos•si•ble adj. Not capable of existing or happening; unlikely to take place or be done; unacceptable; difficult to tolerate or deal with. impossibility n., impossibly adv.

im•pos•tor or im•pos•ter n. One who assumes a false identity or title.

im•pos•ture n. Deception by the assumption of a false identity.

im•po•tent adj. Without strength or vigor; having no power; ineffectual.

im•pound v. To confine in or as if in a pound; to seize and keep in legal custody; to hold water, as in a reservoir.

im•pov•er•ish v. To make poor; to deprive or be deprived of natural richness or fertility. impoverishment n.

im•pov•er•ish•ed adj. To be poor.

im•prac•ti•ca•ble adj. Incapable of being done or put into practice.

im•prac•ti•cal adj. Unwise to put into effect; unable to deal with practical or financial matters efficiently.

im•pre•cate v. To utter curses or to invoke evil upon someone or something.

im•preg•nate v. To make pregnant; to fertilize; as an ovum; to fill throughout; to saturate.

im•press v. To apply or produce with pressure; to stamp or mark with or as if with pressure; to fix firmly in the mind; to affect strongly and usually favorably.

im•pres•sion n. A mark or design made on a surface by pressure; an effect or feeling retained in the mind as a result of experience; an indistinct notion or recollection; a satiric or humorous imitation; the copies of a publication printed at one time.

im•pres•sion•a•ble adj. Easily influenced. impressionably adv.

im•pres•sion•ism n. A style of late nineteenth century painting in which the immediate appearance of scenes is depicted with unmixed primary colors applied in small strokes to simulate reflected light. impressionist n., impressionistic adj.

im•pres•sive adj. Making a strong impression; striking.

im•press•ment n. An act of seizing something for public use.

im•pres•sure n. A type of mark made by the application of pressure.

im•pri•ma•tur n. Official permission to print or publish; authorization.

im•print v. To make or impress a mark or design on a surface; to make or stamp a mark on; to fix firmly in the mind. n. A mark or design made by imprinting; a lasting influence or effect; a publisher's name, often with the date and place of publication, printed at the bottom of a title page.

im•print•ing n. A type of behavior pattern which is established early in the life of a member of a social species.

im•pris•on v. To put in prison.

im•prob•a•ble adj. Not likely to occur or be true.

im•promp•tu *adj.* Devised or performed without prior planning or preparation.

im•prop•er *adj.* Unsuitable; indecorous; incorrect.

im•pro•pri•e•ty *n.* The quality or state of being improper; an improper act or remark.

im•prove *v.* To make or become better; to increase something's productivity or value.

im•prove•ment *n.* The act or process of improving or the condition of being improved; a change that improves.

im•pro•vise *v.* To make up, compose, or perform without preparation; to make from available materials.

im•pru•dent *adj.* Not prudent; unwise.

im•pu•dent *adj.* Marked by rude boldness or disrespect.

im•puis•sance *n.* A weakness.

im•pulse *n.* A driving force or the motion produced by it; a sudden spontaneous urge; a motivating force; a general tendency.

im•pulse buy•ing *n.* The buying of items and merchandise on an impulse.

im•pul•sive *adj.* Acting on impulse rather than thought; resulting from impulse; uncalculated.

im•pure *adj.* Not pure; unclean; unchaste or obscene; mixed with another substance; adulterated; deriving from more than one source or style.

in•a•bil•i•ty *n.* A lack of sufficient power or capacity.

in•ac•ces•si•ble *adj.* Not accessible.

in•ac•cu•ra•cy *n.* The state of being inaccurate.

in•ac•tion *n.* The lack of activity or lack of action.

in•ac•ti•vate *v.* To make something or someone inactive.

in•ac•tive *adj.* Not active or inclined to be active; out of current use or service.

in•ad•e•quate *adj.* Not adequate.

in•ad•ver•tent *adj.* Unintentional; accidental; inattentive. **inadvertently** *adv.*

in•ad•vis•a•ble *adj.* Being not advisable.

in•al•i•en•a•ble *adj.* Not capable of being given up or transferred.

in•al•ter•a•ble *adj.* Being not alterable. **inalterability** *n.*

in•an•i•mate *adj.* Not having the qualities of life; not animated.

in•ap•pro•pri•ate *adj.* Being not appropriate; out of place in a setting; out of proportion.

in•ar•tic•u•late *adj.* Not uttering or forming intelligible words or syllables; unable to speak; speechless; unable to speak clearly or effectively; unexpressed.

in•as•much as *conj.* Because of the fact that; since.

in•at•ten•tive *adj.* Not paying attention.

in•au•gu•ral *adj.* Of or for an inauguration.

in•au•gu•rate *v.* To put into office with a formal ceremony; to begin officially. **inaugurator, inauguration** *n.*

in be•tween *adv.* or *prep.* Between.

in•board *adj.* Within a ship's hull; close to or near the fuselage of an aircraft.

in•born *adj.* Possessed at birth; natural; hereditary.

in•bound *adj.* Incoming.

in•bounds *adj.* Pertaining to putting the ball into play by throwing or passing it onto a court such as with the game of basketball.

in•breed *v.* To produce by repeatedly breeding closely related individuals.

in•breed•ing *n.* The act of interbreeding of individuals which are closely related to preserve desirable characteristics of the stock or thing being breed.

in•cal•cu•la•ble *adj.* Not calculable; indeterminate; unpredictable; very large.

in•can•des•cent *adj.* Giving off visible light when heated; shining brightly; ardently intense. **incandescence** *n.*

in•can•ta•tion *n.* A recitation of magic charms or spells; a magic formula for chanting or reciting.

in•ca•pa•ble *adj.* Lacking the ability for doing or performing.

in•ca•pac•i•tate *v.* To render incapable; to disable; in law, to disqualify.

185

incapacitation *n.*, **incapacitated** *adj.*

in·ca·pac·i·ty *n.* Inadequate ability or strength; a defect; in law, a disqualification.

in·car·cer·ate *v.* To place in jail.

in·car·nate *v.* To give actual form to.

in·car·na·tion *n.* The act of incarnating or state of being incarnated; one regarded as personifying a given abstract quality or idea; the embodiment.

in·cen·di·ar·y *adj.* Causing or capable of causing fires; of or relating to arson; tending to inflame; inflammatory.

in·cense *v.* To make angry. *n.* A substance, as gum or wood, burned to produce a pleasant smell; the smoke or odor produced.

in·cen·tive *n.* Something inciting one to action or effort; a stimulus.

in·cep·tion *n.* A beginning; an origin. **inceptive** *adj.*

in·cer·ti·tude *n.* Uncertainty; lack of confidence; instability.

in·ces·sant *adj.* Occurring without interruption; continuous. **incessantly** *adv.*

in·cest *n.* Sexual intercourse between persons so closely related that they are forbidden by law to marry. **incestuous** *adj.*, **incestuously** *adv.*

inch *n.* A unit of measurement equal to one twelfth of a foot. *v.* To move slowly.

in·ci·dence *n.* The extent or rate of occurrence.

in·ci·dent *n.* An event; an event that disrupts normal procedure or causes a crisis.

in·ci·den·tal *adj.* Occurring or likely to occur at the same time or as a result; minor; subordinate. *n.* A minor attendant occurrence or condition.

in·cin·er·ate *v.* To burn up.

in·cin·er·a·tor *n.* One that incinerates; a furnace for burning waste.

in·cip·i·ent *adj.* Just beginning to appear or occur.

in·cise *v.* To make or cut into with a sharp tool; to carve into a surface; to engrave.

in·ci·sion *n.* The act of incising; a cut or notch, especially a surgical cut.

in·ci·sive *adj.* Having or suggesting sharp intellect; penetrating; cogent and effective; telling. **incisively** *adv.*, **incisiveness** *n.*

in·ci·sor *n.* A cutting tool at the front of the mouth.

in·cite *v.* To provoke to action. **incitement** *n.*

in·cli·na·tion *n.* An attitude; a disposition; a tendency to act or think in a certain way; a preference; a bow or tilt; a slope.

in·cline *v.* To deviate or cause to deviate from the horizontal or vertical; to slant; to dispose or be disposed; to bow or nod. *n.* An inclined surface.

in·clude *v.* To have as a part or member; to contain; to put into a group or total. **inclusion** *n.*

in·cog·ni·to *adv.* or *adj.* With one's identity hidden.

in·co·her·ent *adj.* Lacking order; connection, or harmony; unable to think or speak clearly or consecutively.

in·come *n.* Money or its equivalent received in return for work or as profit from investments.

in·com·ing *adj.* Coming in or soon to come in.

in·com·mu·ni·ca·do *adv.* or *adj.* Without being able to communicate with others.

in·com·pa·ra·ble *adj.* Incapable of being compared; without rival.

in·com·pat·i·ble *adj.* Not suited for combination or association; inconsistent.

in·com·pe·tent *adj.* Not competent; not capable of performance. **incompetence**, **incompetency** *n.*

in·com·plete *adj.* Not complete; lacking completeness.

in·com·pre·hen·si·ble *adj.* Being unable to understand; opaque to reason.

in·con·ceiv·a·ble *adj.* Impossible to understand.

in·con·clu·sive *adj.* Having no definite result.

in·con·gru·ous *adj.* Not corresponding; disagreeing; made up of diverse or discordant elements; unsuited to the surrounding or setting. **incongruity** n.

in·con·se·quen·tial adj. Without importance; petty. **inconsequentially** adv.

in·con·sid·er·a·ble adj. Unimportant; trivial. **inconsiderably** adv.

in·con·sid·er·ate adj. Not considerate; thoughtless.

in·con·sis·tent adj. Lacking firmness, harmony, or compatibility; incoherent in thought or actions.

in·con·sol·a·ble adj. Not capable of being consoled.

in·con·spic·u·ous adj. Not readily seen or noticed.

in·con·stant adj. Likely to change; unpredictable; faithless; fickle. **inconstancy** n., **inconstantly** adv.

in·con·sum·a·ble adj. Unfit to be consumed.

in·con·ti·nent adj. Not restrained; uncontrolled; unable to contain or restrain something specified; incapable of controlling the excretory functions. **incontinence** n.

in·con·tro·vert·i·ble adj. Unquestionable; indisputable.

in·con·ven·ience n. The quality or state of being inconvenient; something inconvenient. v. To cause inconvenience to; to bother.

in·con·ven·ient adj. Not convenient; awkward or out of the way.

in·cor·po·rate v. To combine into a unified whole; to unite; to form or cause to form a legal corporation; to give a physical form to; to embody.

in·cor·po·re·al adj. Without material form or substance. **incorporeally** adv.

in·cor·ri·gi·ble adj. Incapable of being reformed or corrected. **incorrigibility**, **incorrigible** n.

in·cor·rupt·i·ble adj. Not capable of being corrupted morally; not subject to decay.

in·crease v. To make or become greater or larger; to have offspring; to reproduce. n. The act of increasing; the amount or rate of increasing.

in·cred·i·ble adj. Too unlikely to be believed; unbelievable; astonishing.

in·cred·u·lous adj. Skeptical; disbelieving; expressive of disbelief. **incredulity** n., **incredulously** adv.

in·cre·ment n. An increase; something gained or added, especially one of a series of regular additions.

in·crim·i·nate v. To involve in or charge with a wrongful act, as a crime. **incrimination** n.

in·cu·bate v. To warm and hatch eggs, as by bodily heat or artificial means; to maintain a bacterial culture in favorable conditions for growth.

in·cu·ba·tor n. A cabinet in which a desired temperature can be maintained, used for bacterial culture; an enclosure for maintaining a premature infant in a controlled environment; a temperature controlled enclosure for hatching eggs.

in·cu·bus n. An evil spirit believed to seize or harm sleeping persons; a nightmare; a nightmarish burden.

in·cul·cate v. To impress on the mind by frequent repetition or instruction. **in·cur·able** adj. Unable to be cured.

in·cum·bent adj. Lying or resting on something else; imposed as an obligation; obligatory; currently in office. n. A person currently in office. **incumbency** n.

in·debt·ed adj. Obligated to another, as for money or a favor; beholden. **indebtedness** n.

in·de·cent adj. Morally offensive or contrary to good taste. **indecency** n., **indecently** adv.

in·de·ci·pher·a·ble adj. Not capable of being deciphered or interpreted.

in·de·ci·sion n. Inability to make up one's mind; irresolution.

in·de·ci·sive adj. Without a clear-cut result; marked by indecision. **indecisively** adv., **indecisiveness** n.

in·deed adv. Most certainly; without doubt; in reality; in fact. interj. Used to express surprise; irony; or disbelief.

in·de·fen·si·ble *adj.* Incapable of being justified; not able to protect against a physical fight.

in·def·i·nite *adj.* Not decided or specified; vague; unclear; lacking fixed limits. **indefinitely** *adv.*

in·del·i·ble *adj.* Not able to be erased or washed away; permanent.

in·del·i·cate *adj.* Lacking sensitivity; tactless. **indelicacy** *n.*, **indelicately** *adv.*

in·dem·ni·ty *n.* Security against hurt, loss, or damage; a legal exemption from liability for damages; compensation for hurt, loss, or damage.

in·dent *v.* To set in from the margin; to notch the edge of; to serrate; to make a dent or depression in; to impress; to stamp. *n.* An indentation.

in·den·ta·tion *n.* The act of indenting or the state of being indented; an angular cut in an edge; a recess in a surface.

in·den·ture *n.* A legal deed or contract; a contract obligating one party to work for another for a specified period of time. *v.* To bind into the service of another.

in·de·pend·ence *n.* The quality or state of being independent.

in·de·pend·ent *adj.* Politically self-governing; free from the control of others; not committed to a political party or faction; not relying on others; especially for financial support; providing or having enough income to enable one to live without working. *n.* One who is independent, especially a candidate or voter not committed to a political party.

in-depth *adj.* Thorough; detailed.

in·de·scrib·a·ble *adj.* Surpassing description; incapable of being described.

in·de·struc·ti·ble *adj.* Unable to be destroyed.

in·de·ter·mi·nate *adj.* Not determined; not able to be determined; unclear or vague.

in·dex *n.* A list for aiding reference, especially an alphabetized listing in a printed work which gives the pages on which various names, places, and subjects are mentioned. *v.* To provide with or enter in an index; to indicate; to adjust through. **indexer** *n.*, **indexes, indices** *pl.*

in·dex·a·tion *n.* The linkage of economic factors, as wages or prices, to a cost-of-living index so they rise and fall within the rate of inflation.

in·dex fin·ger *n.* The finger next to the thumb.

In·di·an sum·mer *n.* A period of mild weather in late autumn.

in·di·cate *v.* To point out; to show; to serve as a sign or symptom; to signify; to suggest the advisability of; to call for. **indication, indicator** *n.*

in·dic·a·tive *adj.* Serving to indicate; of or being a verb mood used to express actions and conditions that are objective facts. *n.* The indicative mood; a verb in the indicative mood.

in·di·ca·tor *n.* A pressure gauge; a dial that registers pressures, etc.

in·dif·fer·ent *adj.* Having no marked feeling or preference; impartial; neither good nor bad. **indifference** *n.*

in·dict *v.* To accuse of an offense; to charge; to make a formal accusation against a party or an individual by the findings of a grand jury.

in·di·ges·tion *n.* Difficulty or discomfort in digesting food.

in·dig·nant *adj.* Marked by or filled with indignation. **indignantly** *adv.*

in·dig·na·tion *n.* Anger aroused by injustice, unworthiness, or unfairness.

in·dig·ni·ty *n.* Humiliating treatment; something that offends one's pride.

in·di·go *n.* A blue dye obtained from a plant or produced synthetically; a dark blue.

in·di·rect *adj.* Not taking a direct course; not straight to the point.

in·dis·creet *adj.* Lacking discretion. **indiscreetly** *adv.*, **indiscretion** *n.*

in·dis·pen·sa·ble *adj.* Necessary; essential. **indispensability, indispensable** *n.*, **indispensably** *adv.*

in·dis·tin·guish·a·ble *adj.* Unable to

determine in shape or structure; not clearly recognizable; lacking identity.

in•di•vid•u•al *adj.* Of, for, or relating to a single human being. **individually** *adv.*

in•di•vis•i•ble *adj.* Not able to be divided.

in•doc•tri•nate *v.* To instruct in a doctrine or belief; to train to accept a system or thought uncritically.

in•do•lent *adj.* Disinclined to exert oneself; lazy.

in•dom•i•ta•ble *adj.* Incapable of being subdued or defeated.

in•duce *v.* To move by persuasion or influence; to cause to occur; to infer by inductive reasoning.

in•dulge *v.* To give in to the desires of, especially to excess; to yield to; to allow oneself a special pleasure.

in•dus•tri•al *adj.* Of, relating to, or used in industry.

in•dus•tri•ous *adj.* Working steadily and hard; diligent.

in•dus•try *n.* The commercial production and sale of goods and services; a branch of manufacture and trade; industrial management; diligence.

in•e•bri•ate *v.* To make drunk; to intoxicate. **inebriated** *adj.*, **inebriant**, **inebriation** *n.*

in•ef•fa•ble *adj.* Beyond expression; indescribable; unsayable.

in•ef•fi•cient *adj.* Wasteful of time, energy, or materials.

in•ept *adj.* Awkward or incompetent; not suitable.

in•e•qual•i•ty *n.* The condition or an instance of being unequal; social or economic disparity; lack of regularity.

in•ert *adj.* Not able to move or act; slow to move or act; sluggish; displaying no chemical activity.

in•er•tia *n.* The tendency of a body to remain at rest or to stay in motion unless acted upon by an external force; resistance to motion or change. **inertial** *adj.*, **inertially** *adv.*

in•ev•i•ta•ble *adj.* Not able to be avoided.

in•ex•pe•ri•ence *n.* Lack of experience.

in•ex•pli•ca•ble *adj.* Not capable of being explained. **inexplicably** *adv.*

in•fal•li•ble *adj.* Not capable of making mistakes; not capable of failing; never wrong. **infallibility** *n.*, **infallibly** *adv.*

in•fa•mous *adj.* Having a very bad reputation; shocking or disgraceful. **infamously** *adv.*

in•fa•my *n.* Evil notoriety or reputation; the state of being infamous; a disgraceful, publicly known act.

in•fan•cy *n.* The condition or time of being an infant; an early stage of existence; in law, minority.

in•fant *n.* A child in the first period of life; a very young child; in law, a minor.

in•fan•ti•cide *n.* The killing of an infant.

in•fan•tile *adj.* Of or relating to infants or infancy; immature; childish.

in•fat•u•ate *v.* To arouse an extravagant or foolish love in. **infatuated** *adj.*, **infatuation** *n.*

in•fect *v.* To contaminate with disease-causing microorganisms; to transmit a disease to; to affect as if by contagion.

in•fec•tion *n.* Invasion of a bodily part by disease-causing microorganisms; the condition resulting from such an invasion; an infectious disease.

in•fe•lic•i•tous *adj.* Not happy; unfortunate; not apt, as in expression.

in•fer *v.* To conclude by reasoning; to deduce; to have as a logical consequence; to lead to as a result or conclusion. **inference** *n.*

in•fe•ri•or *adj.* Located under or below; low or lower in order, rank, or quality. **inferiority** *n.*

in•fer•nal *adj.* Of, like, or relating to hell; damnable; abominable.

in•fer•no *n.* A place or condition suggestive of hell.

in•fest *v.* To spread in or over so as to be harmful or offensive. **infestation** *n.*

in•fi•del *n.* One who has no religion; an unbeliever in a religion, especially Christianity.

in•field *n.* In baseball, the part of a playing

field within the base lines.

in•fil•trate *v.* To pass or cause to pass into something through pores or small openings; to pass through or enter gradually or stealthily.

in•fi•nite *adj.* Without boundaries; limitless; immeasurably great or large; in mathematics, greater in value than any specified number, however large. **infinity** *n.*

in•fin•i•tes•i•mal *adj.* Immeasurably small.

in•fin•i•ty *n.* The quality or state of being infinite; unbounded space, time, or amount; an indefinitely large number.

in•firm *adj.* Physically weak, especially from age; feeble; not sound or valid.

in•fir•ma•ry *n.* An institution for the care of the sick or disabled.

in•flame *v.* To set on fire; to arouse to strong or excessive feeling; to intensify; to produce, affect or be affected by inflammation.

in•flam•ma•ble *adj.* Tending to catch fire easily; easily excited.

in•flam•ma•tion *n.* Localized redness, swelling, heat, and pain in response to an injury or infection.

in•flate *v.* To fill and expand with a gas; to increase unsoundly; to puff up; to raise prices abnormally. **inflatable** *adj.*

in•fla•tion *n.* The act or process of inflating; a period during which there is an increase in the monetary supply, causing a continuous rise in the price of goods.

in•flect *v.* To turn; to veer; to vary the tone or pitch of the voice, especially in speaking; to change the form of a word to indicate number, tense, or person. **inflective** *adj.*, **inflection** *n.*

in•flex•i•ble *adj.* Not flexible; rigid; not subject to change; unalterable. **inflexibility** *n.*, **inflexibly** *adv.*

in•flict *v.* To cause to be suffered; to impose.

in•flu•ence *n.* The power to produce effects, especially indirectly or through an intermediary; the condition of being affected; one exercising indirect power to sway or affect. *v.* To exert influence over; to modify. **influential** *adj.*

in•flu•en•za *n.* An acute, infectious viral disease marked by respiratory inflammation, fever, muscular pain, and often intestinal discomfort; the flu.

in•flux *n.* A stream of people or things coming in.

in•form•ant *n.* One who discloses or furnishes information which should remain secret.

in•for•ma•tive *adj.* Providing information; instructive.

in•fra•struc•ture *n.* An underlying base or foundation; the basic facilities needed for the functioning of a system.

in•fringe *v.* To break a law; to violate; to encroach; to trespass. **infringement** *n.*

in•fu•ri•ate *v.* To make very angry or furious; to enrage.

in•fuse *v.* To introduce, instill or inculcate, as principles; to obtain a liquid extract by soaking a substance in water.

in•gen•ious *adj.* Showing great ingenuity; to have inventive ability; clever. **ingeniously** *adv.*, **ingeniousness, ingenuity** *n.*

in•gen•u•ous *adj.* Frank and straightforward; lacking sophistication; innocent and guileless.

in•got *n.* A mass of cast metal shaped in a bar or block.

in•grain *v.* To impress firmly on the mind or nature. *n.* Fiber or yarn that is dyed before being spun or woven.

in•gre•di•ent *n.* An element that enters into the composition of a mixture; a part of anything.

in•grown *adj.* Growing into the flesh; growing abnormally within or into.

in•hab•it *v.* To reside in; to occupy as a home.

in•hab•i•tant *n.* A person who resides permanently.

in•hale *v.* To breathe or draw into the lungs, as air or tobacco smoke; the opposite of exhale. **inhalation** *n.*

in•hal•er *n.* One that inhales; a respirator.

in•her•ent *adj.* Forming an essential element or quality of something.

in•her•it *v.* To receive something, as property, money, or other valuables, by legal succession or will. In biology, to receive traits or qualities from one's ancestors or parents.

in•her•i•tance *n.* The act of inheriting; that which is inherited or to be inherited by legal transmission to a heir.

in•hu•mane *adj.* Lacking compassion or pity; cruel. **inhumanely** *adv.*

in•hu•man•i•ty *n.* The lack of compassion or pity; an inhumane or cruel act.

in•i•tial *adj.* Of or pertaining to the beginning. *n.* The first letter of a name or word. *v.* To mark or sign with initials. **initially** *adv.*

in•i•ti•ate *v.* To begin or start; to admit someone to membership in an organization, fraternity, or group; to instruct in fundamentals. **initiator** *n.*, **initiatory** *adj.*

in•i•ti•a•tive *n.* The ability to originate or follow through with a plan of action.

in•ject *v.* To force a drug or fluid into the body through a blood vessel or the skin with a hypodermic syringe; to throw in or introduce a comment abruptly.

in•jure *v.* To cause physical harm, damage, or pain.

in•ju•ry *n.* Damage or harm inflicted or suffered.

in•jus•tice *n.* The violation of another person's rights; an unjust act; a wrong.

ink *n.* Any of variously colored liquids or paste, used for writing, drawing, and printing. **inky** *adj.*

ink•ling *n.* A slight suggestion or hint; a vague idea or notion.

ink•well *n.* A small container or reservoir for holding ink.

in•laid *adj.* Ornamental with wood, ivory, or other materials embedded flush with the surface.

in•land *adj.* Pertaining to or located in the interior of a country.

in•law *n.* A relative by marriage.

in•lay *v.* To set or embed something, as gold or ivory, into the surface of a decorative design.

in•let *n.* A bay or stream that leads into land; a passage between nearby islands.

in•mate *n.* A person who dwells in a building with another; one confined in a prison, asylum, or hospital.

inn *n.* A place of lodging where a traveler may obtain meals and/or lodging.

in•nate *adj.* Inborn and not acquired; having as an essential part; inherent.

in•ner *adj.* Situated or occurring farther inside; relating to or of the mind or spirit.

in•ner ear *n.* The part of the ear which includes the semicircular canals, vestibule, and cochlea.

inn•keep•er *n.* The proprietor or manager of an inn.

in•no•cent *adj.* Free from sin, evil, or moral wrong; pure; legally free from blame or guilt; not maliciously intended; lacking in experience or knowledge; naive. **innocence** *n.*

in•noc•u•ous *adj.* Having no harmful qualities or ill effect; harmless.

in•nu•mer•a•ble *adj.* Too numerous or too much to be counted; countless.

in•oc•u•late *v.* To introduce a mild form of a disease or virus to a person or animal in order to produce immunity.

in•op•er•a•ble *adj.* Unworkable; incapable of being treated or improved by surgery.

in•op•er•a•tive *adj.* Not working; not functioning.

in•op•por•tune *adj.* Inappropriate; untimely; unsuitable.

in•or•di•nate *adj.* Exceeding proper or normal limits; not regulated; unrestrained. **inordinately** *adv.*

in•or•gan•ic *adj.* Not having or involving living organisms, their remains, or products.

in•put *n.* The amount of energy delivered to a machine; in computer science, information that is put into a data processing system.

in•quire *v.* To ask a question; to make an

investigation.

in•quir•y *n*. The act of seeking or inquiring; a request or question for information; a very close examination; an investigation or examination of facts or evidence.

in•quis•i•tive *adj*. Curious; probing; questioning.

in•sane *adj*. Afflicted with a serious mental disorder impairing a person's ability to function; the characteristic of a person who is not sane. **insanity** *n*.

in•san•i•tar•y *adj*. Not sanitary; not hygienic and dangerous to one's health.

in•scribe *v*. To write, mark, or engrave on a surface; to enter a name in a register or on a formal list; to write a short note on a card.

in•sect *n*. Any of a numerous cosmopolitan class of small to minute winged invertebrate animals with three pairs of legs, a segmented body, and usually two pairs of wings.

in•se•cure *adj*. Troubled by anxiety and apprehension; threatened; not securely guarded; unsafe; liable to break, fail, or collapse. **insecurely** *adv*., **insecurity** *n*.

in•sem•i•nate *v*. To introduce semen into the uterus of; to make pregnant; to sow seed.

in•sep•a•ra•ble *adj*. Incapable of being separated or parted.

in•sert *v*. To put in place; to set. *n*. In printing, something inserted or to be inserted. **insertion** *n*.

in•side *n*. The part, surface, or space that lies within.

in•sides *n*. The internal parts or organs.

in•sid•i•ous *adj*. Cunning or deceitful; treacherous; seductive; attractive but harmful.

in•sight *n*. Perception into the true or hidden nature of things. **insightful** *adj*., **insightfully** *adv*.

in•sig•ni•a *n*. A badge or emblem used to mark membership, honor, or office.

in•sin•cere *adj*. Not sincere; hypocritical. **insincerely** *adv*., **insincerity** *n*.

in•sin•u•ate *v*. To suggest something by giving a hint; to introduce by using ingenious and sly means. **insinuating** *adv*., **insinuation** *n*.

in•sip•id *adj*. Lacking of flavor; tasteless; flat; dull; lacking interest.

in•sist *v*. To demand firmly; to dwell on something repeatedly for emphasis. **insistent** *adj*., **insistently** *adv*.

in•sol•vent *adj*. In law, unable to meet debts; bankrupt.

in•som•ni•a *n*. The chronic inability to sleep. **insomniac** *n*.

in•spect *v*. To examine or look at very carefully for flaws; to examine or review officially. **inspection**, **inspector** *n*.

in•spi•ra•tion *n*. The stimulation within the mind of some idea, feeling, or impulse which leads to creative action; a divine or holy presence which inspires; the act of inhaling air.

in•spire *v*. To exert or guide by a divine influence; to arouse and create high emotion; to exalt; to inhale; breathe in.

in•stall or **in•stal** *v*. To put in position for service; to place into an office or position; to settle. **installation**, **installer** *n*.

in•stall•ment or **in•stal•ment** *n*. One of several payments due in specified amounts at specified intervals.

in•stance *n*. An illustrative case or example; a step in proceedings.

in•stant *n*. A very short time; a moment; a certain or specific point in time. *adj*. Instantaneously; immediate; urgent.

in•stan•ta•ne•ous *adj*. Happening with no delay; instantly; completed in a moment. **instantaneously** *adv*.

in•stant•ly *adv*. Immediately; at once.

in•stead *adv*. In lieu of that just mentioned.

in•stinct *n*. The complex and normal tendency or response of a given species to act in ways essential to its existence, development, and survival. **instinctive**, **instinctual** *adj*.

in•sti•tute *v*. To establish or set up; to find; to initiate; to set in operation; to start. *n.* An organization set up to promote or further a cause; an institution for educating.

in•sti•tu•tion *n.* The principle custom that forms part of a society or civilization; an organization which performs a particular job or function, such as research, charity, or education; a place of confinement such as a prison or mental hospital.

in•struct *v.* To impart skill or knowledge; to teach; to give orders or direction. **instructive** *adj.*

in•struc•tion *n.* The act of teaching or instructing; important knowledge; a lesson; an order or direction.

in•struc•tor *n.* One who instructs; a teacher; a low-rank college teacher, not having tenure.

in•stru•ment *n.* A mechanical tool or implement; a device used to produce music; a person who is controlled by another; a dupe; in law, a formal legal document, deed, or contract.

in•stru•men•tal *adj.* Acting or serving as a means; pertaining to, composed for, or performed on a musical instrument.

in•sub•or•di•nate *adj.* Not obedient; not obeying orders.

in•suf•fi•cient *adj.* Not enough.

in•su•late *v.* To isolate; to wrap or surround with nonconducting material in order to prevent the passage of heat, electricity, or sound into or out of; to protect with wrapping or insulation.

in•sult *v.* To speak or to treat with insolence or contempt; to abuse verbally. *n.* An act or remark that offends someone. **insulting** *adj.*, **insultingly** *adv.*

in•sur•ance *n.* Protection against risk, loss, or ruin; the coverage an insurer guarantees to pay in the event of death, loss, or medical bills; a contract guaranteeing such protection on future specified losses in return for annual payments; any safeguard against risk or harm. **insurability** *n.*, **insurable** *adj.*

in•sure *v.* To guarantee against loss of life, property, or other types of losses; to make

certain; to ensure; to buy or issue insurance. **insurability** *n.*

in•sured *n.* A person protected by an insurance policy.

in•sur•er *n.* The person or company which insures someone against loss or damage.

in•sur•mount•a•ble *adj.* Incapable of being overcome. **insurmountably** *adv.*

in•sur•rec•tion *n.* An open revolt against an established government.

in•tact *adj.* Remaining whole and not damaged in any way. **intactness** *n.*

in•take *n.* The act of taking in or absorbing; the amount or quantity taken in.

in•tan•gi•ble *adj.* Incapable of being touched; vague or indefinite to the mind. **intangibility**, **intangibleness** *n.*, **intangibly** *adv.*

in•te•ger *n.* Any of the numbers 1, 2, 3, etc., including all the positive whole numbers and all the negative numbers and zero; a whole entity.

in•te•gral *adj.* Being an essential and indispensable part of a whole; made up, from, or formed of parts that constitute a unity.

in•te•grate *v.* To make into a whole by joining parts together; to unify; to be open to people of all races or ethnic groups. **integration** *n.*

in•teg•ri•ty *n.* Uprightness of character; honesty; the condition, quality, or state of being complete or undivided.

in•tel•lect *n.* The power of the mind to understand and to accept knowledge; the state of having a strong or brilliant mind; a person of notable intellect.

in•tel•lec•tu•al *adj.* Pertaining to, possessing, or showing intellect; inclined to rational or creative thought. *n.* A person who pursues and enjoys matters of the intellect and of refined taste.

in•tel•li•gence *n.* The capacity to perceive and comprehend meaning; information; news; the gathering of secret information, as by military or police authorities.

in•tel•li•gent *adj.* Having or showing intelligence.

in·tel·li·gi·ble *adj.* Having the capabilities of being understood; understanding.

in·tend *v.* To have a plan or purpose in mind; to design for a particular use.

in·tense *adj.* Extreme in strength, effect, or degree; expressing strong emotion, concentration, or strain; profound. **intensely** *adv.*, **intenseness** *n.*

in·ten·si·fy *v.* To become or make more intense or acute. **intensification** *n.*

in·ten·si·ty *n.* The quality of being intense or acute; a great effect, concentration, or force.

in·ten·sive *adj.* Forceful and concentrated; marked by a full and complete application of all resources. **intensively** *adv.*

in·ten·sive care *n.* The hospital care provided for a gravely ill patient in specially designed rooms with monitoring devices and life-support systems.

in·tent *n.* A purpose, goal, aim, or design. **intently** *adv.*, **intentness**, **intention** *n.*

in·ten·tion·al *adj.* To be deliberately intended or done. **intentionality** *n.*, **intentionally** *adv.*

in·ter·act *v.* To act on each other or with each other. **interactive** *adj.*

in·ter·cede *v.* To argue or plead on another's behalf.

in·ter·cept *v.* To interrupt the course of; to seize or stop. **interception** *n.*

in·ter·change *v.* To put each in the place of another; to give and receive in return. *n.* The intersection of a highway which allows traffic to enter or turn off without obstructing other traffic.

in·ter·change·a·ble *adj.* To be capable of being interchanged with something.

in·ter·de·pen·dence *n.* A mutual dependence. **interdependency** *n.*

in·ter·de·pen·dent *adj.* To be mutually dependent.

in·ter·dict *v.* To forbid or prohibit by official decree.

in·ter·dis·ci·plin·ar·y *adj.* To be involving or containing two or more artistic, academic, or scientific disciplines.

in·ter·est *n.* Curiosity or concern about something; that which is to one's benefit; legal or financial right, claim or share, as in a business; a charge for a loan of money, usually a percent of the amount borrowed.

in·ter·est·ed *adj.* Having or displaying curiosity; having a right to share in something. **interestedly** *adv.*

in·ter·est group *n.* A group of people who have a common identifying interest.

in·ter·est·ing *adj.* Stimulating interest, attention, or curiosity.

in·ter·face *n.* A surface forming a common boundary between adjacent areas; in computer science, the software or hardware connecting one device or system to another. **interface** *v.*

in·ter·fere *v.* To come between; to get in the way; to be an obstacle or obstruction. **interferer** *n.*

in·ter·fer·ence *n.* The process of interfering in something.

in·ter·ga·lac·tic *adj.* To be occurring between galaxies.

in·ter·grade *v.* To come together or to merge gradually one with another.

in·ter·im *n.* A time between events or periods. *adj.* Temporary.

in·te·ri·or *adj.* Of, or contained in the inside; inner; away from coast or border; inland; private; not exposed to view.

in·te·ri·or de·sign *n.* The practice of supervising and planning the design for a home in order to make it look better through the use of architectural interiors and the furnishings.

in·ter·jec·tion *n.* A word used to express excitement or emotion, as an exclamation; a casual insertion into a conversation.

in·ter·li·brar·y *adj.* To be taking place between two or more libraries.

in·ter·lock *v.* To join closely.

in·ter·lope *v.* To intrude or interfere in the rights of others. **interloper** *n.*

in·ter·lude *n.* A period of time that occurs in and divides some longer process; light entertainment between the acts of a show, play, or other more serious entertainment.

in·ter·me·di·ar·y *n.* A mediator. *adj.*

Coming between; intermediate.

in·ter·mi·na·ble *adj.* Seeming to have no end; without cessation.

in·ter·mis·sion *n.* A temporary interval of time between events or activities; the pause in the middle of a performance.

in·ter·mit·tent *adj.* Ceasing from time to time; coming at intervals.

in·tern *n.* A medical school graduate undergoing supervised practical training in a hospital.

in·ter·nal *adj.* Of or pertaining to the inside; pertaining to the domestic affairs of a country; intended to be consumed by the body from the inside. **internally** *adv.,* **internality** *n.*

in·ter·nal-com·bus·tion en·gine *n.* An engine in which fuel is burned inside the engine.

in·ter·na·tion·al *adj.* Relating to more than one nation; global in scope.

in·ter·na·tion·al·ism *n.* The policy of cooperation among nations where politics and economics are concerned. **internationalist** *n.,* **internationalize** *v.*

in·ter·net *n.* In computers, any interconnecting series of electronic networks. The Internet: a widely used networking interface, connecting several very large information servers.

in·ter·per·son·al *adj.* To be relating or to pertaining to relations between people.

in·ter·plan·e·tar·y *adj.* To be happening or operating between the planets.

in·ter·pret *v.* To convey the meaning of something by explaining or restating; to present the meaning of something, as in a picture; to take words spoken or written in one language and put them into another language. **interpretation** *n.*

in·ter·pret·er *n.* A person who will interpret things, such as languages, for others.

in·ter·ra·cial *adj.* Between, among, or affecting different races.

in·ter·re·lat·ed *adj.* Having a mutual relation with someone or something. **interrelatedly** *adv.,* **interrelatedness** *n.*

in·ter·ro·gate *v.* To question formally. **interrogation, interrogator** *n.*

in·ter·rog·a·tive *adj.* Asking or having the nature of a question. *n.* A word used to ask a question.

in·ter·rupt *v.* To break the continuity of something; to intervene abruptly while someone else is speaking or performing.

in·ter·sect *v.* To divide by cutting through or across; to form an intersection; to cross.

in·ter·sec·tion *n.* A place of crossing; a place where streets or roads cross; in mathematics, the point common to two or more geometric elements.

in·ter·state *adj.* Between, involving, or among two or more states.

in·ter·twine *v.* To unite by twisting together. **intertwinement** *n.*

in·ter·ur·ban *adj.* Between or among connecting urban areas.

in·ter·val *n.* The time coming between two points or objects; a period of time between events or moments.

in·ter·vene *v.* To interfere or take a decisive role so as to modify or settle something; to interfere with force in a conflict. **intervention** *n.*

in·ter·view *n.* A conversation conducted by a reporter to elicit information; a conversation led by an employer who is trying to decide whether to hire someone. **interview** *v.,* **interviewer** *n.*

in·ter·weave *v.* To weave things together; to intertwine.

in·tes·tine *n.* The section of the alimentary canal from the stomach to the rectum.

in·ti·mate *adj.* Characterized by close friendship or association. **intimacy** *n.*

in·tim·i·date *v.* To make timid or fearful; to frighten; to discourage or suppress by threats or by violence. **intimidation, intimidator** *n.*

in·to *prep.* Inside of; to a form or condition of; to a time in the midst of.

in·tol·er·a·ble *adj.* Unbearable.

in·tol·er·ant *adj.* Not able to endure; not tolerant of the rights or beliefs of others. **intolerance** *n.*

intone

in•tone v. To utter or recite in a monotone; to chant.

in•tra•ca•cy n. The state of something being intricate.

in•tra•ga•lac•tic adj. Occurring within a single galaxy.

in•tra•mu•ral adj. Taking place within a school, college, or institution; the competition which is limited to a school community. **intramurally** adv.

in•tran•si•gent adj. Refusing to moderate a position; uncompromising. **intransigency**, **intransigent** n.

in•tra•state adj. To be occurring or happening within a state.

in•tra•ve•nous adj. To be occurring within a vein. **intravenously** adv.

in•trep•id adj. Courageous; unshaken by fever; bold. **intrepidly** adv., **intrepidity**, **intrepidness** n.

in•tri•cate adj. Having many perplexingly entangled parts or elements; complex; difficult to understand. **intricately** adv.

in•trigue v. To arouse the curiosity or interest; to fascinate; to plot; to conspire; to engage in intrigues. n. A secret or illicit love affair; a secret plot or plan.

in•trigu•ing adj. Engaging the interest of something or of someone to a marked degree.

in•trin•sic adj. Belonging to the true or fundamental nature of a thing; inherent.

in•tro•duce v. To present a person face to face to another; to make acquainted; to bring into use or practice for the first time; to bring to the attention of. **introductory** adj.

in•tro•duc•tion n. A passage of a book that will introduce the story or the content of a book; something which introduces.

in•tro•ject v. To incorporate ideas in someone's personality unconsciously.

in•tro•vert n. A person who directs his interest to himself and not to friends or social activities. **introversion** n., **introverted** adj.

in•trude v. To thrust or push oneself in; to come in without being asked or wanted. **intruder** n.

in•tru•sion n. The act of intruding; an invasion of another's space or attention. **intrusive** adj., **intrusiveness** n.

in•tu•i•tion n. The direct knowledge or awareness of something without conscious attention or reasoning; knowledge that is acquired in this way. **intuitive** adj., **intuitively** adv.

in•un•date v. To overwhelm with abundance or excess, as with work. **inundation** n., **inundatory** adj.

in•vade v. To enter by force with the intent to conquer or to pillage; to penetrate and to overrun harmfully; to violate; to encroach upon. **invader** n.

in•va•lid n. A chronically sick, bedridden, or disabled person.

in•val•id adj. Disabled by injury or disease; not valid; unsound. **invalidity** n., **invalidly** adv.

in•val•i•date v. To nullify; to make invalid. **invalidation**, **invalidator** n.

in•val•u•a•ble adj. Priceless; of great value; to be of great help or use.

in•var•i•a•ble adj. Constant and not changing. **invariably** adv.

in•va•sion n. The act of invading; an entrance made with the intent of overrunning or occupying.

in•vent v. To desire or create by original effort or design. **inventor** n.

in•ven•tion n. The act or process of inventing; a new process, method, or device conceived from study and testing.

in•ven•to•ry n. A list of items with descriptions and quantities of each; the process of making such a list.

in•ver•te•brate adj. Lacking a backbone or spinal column. **invertebrate** n.

in•vest v. To use money for the purchase of stocks or property in order to obtain profit or interest; to place in office formally; to install; to make an investment. **investor** n.

in•ves•ti•gate v. To search or inquire into; to examine carefully. **investigation**, **investigator** n.

in•vest•ment n. The act of investing

money or capital to gain interest or income; property acquired and kept for future benefit.

in•vig•o•rate *v.* To give strength or vitality to.

in•vis•i•ble *adj.* Not capable of being seen; not visible; not open to view; hidden. **invisibility** *n.*, **invisibly** *adv.*

in•vi•ta•tion *n.* The act of inviting; the means or words that request someone's presence or participation.

in•vite *v.* To request the presence or participation of; to make a formal or polite request for; to provoke; to entice; to issue an invitation.

in•vit•ing *adj.* Tempting; attractive. **invitingly** *adv.*

in•vo•ca•tion *n.* An appeal to a deity or other agent for inspiration, witness, or help; a prayer which is used at the opening of a ceremony or a service.

in•voice *n.* An itemized list of merchandise shipped or services rendered, including prices, shipping instructions, and other costs; a bill.

in•vol•un•tar•y *adj.* Not done by choice or willingly.

in•volve *v.* To include as a part; to make a participant of; to absorb; to engross. **involvement** *n.*

in•volved *adj.* To be complex in an extreme manner.

in•vul•ner•a•ble *adj.* To be immune to attack; impregnable; not able to be physically injured or wounded. **invulnerability** *n.*, **invulnerably** *adv.*

in•ward *adj.* To be situated toward the inside, the center, or the interior; of or existing in the mind or thoughts. **inwardness** *n.*, **inwardly** *adv.*

i•o•dine *n.* A grayish-black, corrosive, poisonous element, symbolized by I; a solution made up of iodine, alcohol, and sodium iodide or potassium iodide which is used as an antiseptic.

i•rate *adj.* To be raging; to be angry. **irately** *adv.*, **irateness** *n.*

ir•i•des•cent *adj.* Displaying the colors of the rainbow in shifting hues and patterns.

i•ris *n.* The pigmented part of the eye which regulates the size of the pupil by contracting and expanding around it; in botany, a plant with narrow sword-shaped leaves and large, handsome flowers, as the gladiolus and crocus.

irk *v.* To annoy or to weary someone.

irk•some *adj.* Tending to irk someone or something. **irksomeness** *n.*

i•ron *n.* A type of heavy malleable ductile magnetic metallic element that is silver-white and will rust easily in moist air.

i•ron•ic *adj.* To be marked by or characterized by irony.

i•ron•ing *n.* The process or action of pressing or smoothing with a heated iron; clothes that have been ironed or are to be ironed.

i•ro•ny *n.* A literary device for conveying meaning by saying the direct opposite of what is really meant.

ir•ra•tion•al *adj.* Unable to reason; contrary to reason; absurd; in mathematics, a number which is not expressible as an integer or a quotient of integers. **irrationality** *n.*

ir•reg•u•lar *adj.* Not according to the general rule or practice; not straight, uniform, or orderly; uneven. *n.* One who is irregular. **irregularity** *n.*, **irregularly** *adv.*

ir•rel•e•vant *adj.* Not pertinent or related to the subject matter.

ir•re•place•a•ble *adj.* Unable to be replaced; precious; unique.

ir•re•sist•i•ble *adj.* Completely fascinating; impossible to resist.

ir•re•spon•si•ble *adj.* Lacking in responsibility; not accountable. **irresponsibility** *n.*, **irresponsibly** *adv.*

ir•re•vers•i•ble *adj.* Impossible to reverse.

ir•ri•gate *v.* To water land or crops artificially, as by means of ditches or sprinklers; to refresh with water. **irrigation** *n.*

ir•ri•ta•ble *adj.* Easily annoyed; ill-tempered.

ir•ri•tate *v.* To annoy or bother; to

provoke; to be sore, chafed, or inflamed. **irritator, irritation** *n*.

is *v*. Third person, singular, present tense of the verb *to be*.

is•land *n*. A piece of land smaller than a continent, completely surrounded by water.

is•n't *contr*. Is not.

i•so•bu•tyl•ene *n*. A type of gaseous butylene used for the purpose of making gasoline compounds.

i•so•gen•ic *adj*. To be characterized by having identical genes.

i•so•gon•ic *adj*. To be growing so that sizes of parts remain equivalent.

i•so•late *v*. To set apart from the others; to put by itself; to place or be placed in quarantine. **isolation, isolator** *n*.

i•so•la•tion•ism *n*. A national policy of avoiding political or economic alliances or relations with other countries. **isolationist** *n*.

i•so•mer *n*. A compound having the same kinds and numbers of atoms as another compound but differing in chemical or physical properties due to the linkage or arrangement of the atoms.

i•sos•ce•les tri•an•gle *n*. A triangle which has two equal sides.

i•so•tope *n*. Any of two or more species of atoms of a chemical element which contain in their nuclei, the same number of protons but different numbers of neutrons. **isotopically** *adv*.

i•so•trop•ic *adj*. Having the same value in all directions.

is•sue *n*. The act of giving out; something that is given out or published; a matter of importance to solve. *v*. To come forth; to flow out; to emerge; to distribute or give out, as supplies. **issuable** *adj.*, **issuer** *n*.

it *pron*. Used as a substitute for a specific noun or name when referring to places, things, or animals of unspecified sex; used to refer to the general state of something.

i•tal•ic *adj*. A style of printing type in which the letters slant to the right.

i•tal•i•cize *v*. To print in italics. **italiciza-**

tion *n*.

itch *n*. A skin irritation which causes a desire to scratch; a contagious skin disease accompanied by a desire to scratch; a restless desire or craving. **itch** *v*., **itchiness** *n*., **itchy** *adj*.

i•tem *n*. A separately-noted unit or article included in a category or series; a short article, as in a magazine or newspaper.

i•tem•ize *v*. To specify by item; to list. **itemizer, itemization** *n*.

it•er•ate *v*. To state or do again; to repeat. **iteration** *n*.

i•tin•er•ant *adj*. Traveling from place to place; wandering. **itinerant** *n*.

its *adj*. The possessive case of the pronoun *it*.

it's *contr*. It is; it has.

i•vo•ry *n*. A hard, smooth, yellowish-white material which forms the tusks of elephants, walruses, and other animals; any substance similar to ivory. *pl*. The keys on a piano; teeth.

i•vy *n*. A climbing plant having glossy evergreen leaves.

iz•zard *n*. The letter Z.

J

J, j The tenth letter of the English alphabet.

jab *v*. To poke or thrust sharply with short blows; a rapid punch.

jab•ber *v*. To speak quickly or without making sense.

jack *n*. The playing card that ranks just below a queen and bears a representation of a knave; any of various tools or devises used for raising heavy objects.

jack•al *n*. An African or Asian dog-like, carnivorous mammal.

jack•ass *n*. A male donkey or ass; a stupid person or one who acts in a stupid fashion.

jack•et *n*. A short coat worn by men and women; a protective cover for a book.

jack•ham•mer *n*. A tool operated by air pressure, used to break pavement and to drill rock.

jack•knife *n.* A large pocketknife; a dive executed by doubling the body forward with the knees unbent and the hands touching the ankles and then straightening before entering the water.

jack-of-all-trades *n.* A person who is able to do many types of work.

jack-o-lan•tern n. A lantern made from a hollowed out pumpkin which has been carved to resemble a face.

jack•pot *n.* Any post, prize, or pool in which the amount won is cumulative.

jack rab•bit *n.* A large American hare with long back legs and long ears.

jacks *n.* A game played with a set of six-pronged metal pieces and a small ball.

jade *n.* A hard, translucent, green gemstone; an old, worn-out unmanageable horse.

jag•ged *adj.* Having jags or sharp notches; serrated. **jaggedness** *n.*

jag•uar *n.* A large, spotted feline mammal of tropical America with a tawny coat and black spots.

jai a•lai *n.* A game similar to handball in which players catch and throw a ball with long, curved, wicker baskets strapped to their arms.

jail *n.* A place of confinement for incarceration.

jail•bird *n.* A prisoner or ex-prisoner.

jail•er *n.* The officer in charge of a jail and its prisoners.

ja•lop•y *n.* *slang* An old, rundown automobile.

jam *v.* To force or wedge into a tight position; to apply the brakes of a car suddenly; to be locked in a position; to block; to crush.

jam *n.* A preserve or whole fruit boiled with sugar.

jam•bo•ree *n.* A large, festive gathering.

jan•i•tor *n.* A person who cleans and cares for a building.

jar *n.* A deep, cylindrical vessel with a wide mouth; a harsh sound. *v.* To strike against or bump into; to affect one's feelings unpleasantly.

jar•gon *n.* The technical or specialized vocabulary used among members of a particular profession. **jargonistic** *adj.*

jas•mine *n.* A shrub with fragrant yellow or white flowers.

jas•per *n.* An opaque red, brown, or yellow variety of quartz, having a high polish.

jaun•dice *n.* A diseased condition of the liver due to the presence of bile pigments in the blood and characterized by yellowish staining of the eyes, skin, and body fluids.

jaunt *n.* A short journey for pleasure.

jaun•ty *adj.* Having a buoyantly carefree and self-confident air or manner about oneself. **jauntily** *adv.*, **jauntiness** *n.*

jav•e•lin *n.* A light spear thrown as a weapon; a long spear with a wooden shaft, used in competition of distance throwing.

jaw *n.* Either of two bony structures forming the framework of the mouth and holding the teeth.

jay *n.* Any of various corvine birds of brilliant coloring, as the blue jay.

jay•walk *v.* To cross a street carelessly, violating traffic regulations. **jaywalker** *n.*

jazz *n.* A kind of music which has a strong rhythmic structure with frequent syncopation and often involving ensemble and solo improvisation.

jeal•ous *adj.* Suspicious or fearful of being replaced by a rival; resentful or bitter in rivalry; demanding exclusive love. **jealousness, jealousy** *n.*

jean *n.* A strong, twilled cotton cloth. *pl.* Pants made of denim.

jeep *n.* A trademark for a small, military, and civilian vehicle with four-wheel drive.

jeer *v.* To speak or shout derisively.

jel•ly *n.* Any food preparation made with pectin or gelatin and having a somewhat elastic consistency; a food made of boiled and sweetened fruit juice and used as a filter or spread.

jel•ly•bean *n.* A small candy having a hard colored coating over a gelatinous center.

jel•ly•fish *n.* Any of a number of free-swimming marine animals of jellylike substance, often having bell or umbrella-shaped bodies with trailing tentacles.

jeop•ard•ize *v.* To put in jeopardy; to expose to loss or danger.

jeop•ard•y *n.* Exposure to loss or danger.

jerk *v.* To give a sharp twist or pull to. *n.* A sudden movement, as a tug or twist; an involuntary contraction of a muscle resulting from a reflex action.

jer•kin *n.* A close-fitting jacket, usually sleeveless.

jer•sey *n.* A soft ribbed fabric of wool, cotton, or other material; a knitted sweater, jacket, or shirt; fawn-colored, small dairy cattle which yield milk rich in butter fat.

jest *n.* An action or remark intended to provoke laughter; a joke; a playful mood. **jester** *n.*

jet *n.* A sudden spurt or gush of liquid or gas emitted through a narrow opening; a jet airplane; a hard, black mineral which takes a high polish and is used in jewelry; a deep glossy black.

jet lag *n.* Mental and physical fatigue resulting from rapid air travel.

jet stream *n.* A high-velocity wind near the troposphere, generally moving from west to east, often at speeds over 250 mph.

jet•ti•son *v.* To throw cargo overboard; to discard a useless or hampering item.

jet•ty *n.* A wall made of piling rocks, or other materials which extends into a body of water to protect a harbor or influence the current; a pier.

jew•el *n.* A precious stone used for personal adornment; a person or thing of very rare excellence or value. *v.* To furnish with jewels. **jewelry** *n.*

jew•el•er or **jew•el•ler** *n.* A person who makes or deals in jewelry.

jif•fy *n.* A very short time; in a hurry.

jig *n.* Any of a variety of fast, lively dances; the music for such a dance; a device used to hold and guide a tool.

jig•ger *n.* A small measure holding 1 1/2 oz used for measuring liquor.

jig•gle *v.* To move or jerk lightly up and down. *n.* A jerky, unsteady movement.

jig•saw *n.* A saw having a slim blade set vertically, used for cutting curved and irregular lines.

jig•saw puz•zle *n.* A puzzle consisting of many irregularly shaped pieces which fit together and form a picture.

jilt *v.* To discard a romantic interest.

jim•my *n.* A short crowbar, often used by a burglar. *v.* To force open or break into with a jimmy.

jin•gle *v.* To make a light clinking or ringing sound. *n.* A short, catchy song or poem, as one used for advertising.

jinx *n.* A person or thing thought to bring bad luck; a period of bad luck.

jit•ney *n.* A vehicle carrying passengers for a fee; a taxi running a regular route and carrying several fares at a time.

jit•ter•bug *n.* A lively dance or one who performs this dance.

jit•ters *n.* Nervousness; uneasiness caused by external forces.

jive *n.* Jazz or swing music and musicians.

job *n.* Anything that is done; work that is done for a set fee; the project worked on; a position of employment.

job•ber *n.* One who buys goods in bulk from the manufacturer and sells them to retailers; a person who works by the job; a pieceworker.

job•name *n.* In computers, a code assigned to a specific job instruction in a computer program, for the operator's use.

jock•ey *n.* A person who rides a horse as a professional in a race; one who works with a specific object or device.

joc•u•lar *adj.* Marked by joking; playful.

joc•und *adj.* Cheerful; merry; suggestive of high spirits and lively mirthfulness.

jog *n.* A slight movement or a slight shake; the slow steady trot of a horse, especially when exercising or participating in a sport; a projecting or retreating part in a surface or line. *v.* To shift direction abruptly; to exercise by running at a slow but steady pace.

join *v.* To bring or put together so as to

form a unit; to become a member of an organization; to participate.

join·er *n.* A person whose occupation is to build articles by joining pieces of wood; a cabinetmaker; a carpenter.

joint *n.* The place where two or more things or parts are joined; a point where bones are connected.

join·ture *n.* A settlement of property arranged by a husband which is to be used for the support of his wife after his death.

joist *n.* Any of a number of small parallel beams set from wall to wall to support a floor.

joke *n.* Something said or done to cause laughter, such as a brief story with a punch line; something not taken seriously. *v.* To tell or play jokes.

jok·er *n.* A person who jokes; a playing card, used in certain card games as a wild card; an unsuspected or unapparent fact which nullifies a seeming advantage.

jol·ly *adj.* Full of good humor; merry.

jolt *v.* To knock or shake about. *n.* A sudden bump or jar, as from a blow.

jon·quil *n.* A widely grown species of narcissus related to the daffodil, having fragrant white or yellow flowers and long narrow leaves.

joss stick *n.* A stick of incense burnt by the Chinese.

jos·tle *v.* To make one's way through a crowd by pushing or shoving. **jostler** *n.*

jot *v.* To make a brief note of something. *n.* A tiny bit.

jour·nal *n.* A diary or personal daily record of observations and experiences; in bookkeeping, a book in which daily financial transactions are recorded.

jour·nal·ism *n.* The occupation, collection, writing, editing, and publishing of newspapers and other periodicals. **journalist** *n.*, **journalistic** *adj.*

jour·ney *n.* A trip from one place to another over a long distance; the distance that is traveled. *v.* To make a trip; to travel a long distance.

jour·ney·man *n.* A worker who has served an apprenticeship in a skilled trade.

joust *n.* A formal combat between two knights on horseback as a part of a medieval tournament.

jo·vi·al *adj.* Good-natured; good-humored; jolly. **joviality** *n.*

jowl *n.* The fleshy part of the lower jaw; the cheek. **jowly** *adj.*

joy *n.* A strong feeling of great happiness; delight; a state or source of contentment or satisfaction; anything which makes one delighted or happy. **joyfully** *adv.*, **joyfulness** *n.*

joy·ous *adj.* Joyful; causing or feeling joy. **joyously** *adv.*, **joyousness** *n.*

ju·bi·lant *adj.* Exultantly joyful or triumphant; expressing joy. **jubilation** *n.*, **jubilantly** *adv.*

ju·bi·lee *n.* A special anniversary of an event; any time of rejoicing.

judge *n.* A public officer who passes judgment in a court. *v.* To decide authoritatively after deliberation.

judg·ment *n.* The ability to make a wise decision or to form an opinion; the act of judging. In law, the sentence or determination of a court. **judgmental** *adj.*

ju·di·ca·ture *n.* The function of administration of justice, law, courts, or judges as a whole.

ju·di·cial *adj.* Pertaining to the administering of justice, to courts of law, or to judges; enforced or decreed by a court of law. **judicially** *adv.*

ju·di·ci·ar·y *adj.* Of or pertaining to judges, courts, or judgments. *n.* The department of the government which administers the law; a system of courts of law.

ju·di·cious *adj.* Having, showing, or exercising good sound judgment. **judiciously** *adv.*, **judiciousness** *n.*

ju·do *n.* A system or form of self-defense, developed from jujitsu in Japan in 1882, which emphasizes principles of balance and leverage.

jug *n.* A small pitcher or similar vessel for holding liquids.

jug•gle *v.* To keep several objects continuously moving from the hand into the air. **juggler** *n.*

jug•u•lar *adj.* Of or pertaining to the region of the throat or the jugular vein.

juice *n.* The liquid part of a vegetable, fruit, or animal.

juic•er *n.* A device for extracting juice from fruit.

juic•y *adj.* Full of; abounding with juice; full of interest; richly rewarding, especially financially. **juiciness** *n.*

juke box *n.* A large, automatic, coin-operated record player.

jum•ble *v.* To mix in a confused mass; to throw together without order; to confuse or mix something up in the mind.

jump *v.* To spring from the ground, floor, or other surface into the air by using a muscular effort of the legs and feet; to move in astonishment; to leap over; to increase greatly, as prices.

jump•er *n.* One who or that which jumps; a sleeveless dress, usually worn over a blouse.

jump•ing jack *n.* A toy puppet whose joined limbs are moved by strings; an exercise performed by jumping to a position with legs spread wide and hands touching overhead and then back to a standing position with arms down at the sides.

jump-start *v.* To start an automobile by connecting a jumper cable from its battery to one of another automobile and turning the engine over.

jump•y *adj.* Nervous; jittery.

junc•tion *n.* The place where lines or routes meet, as roads or railways; the process of joining or the act of joining.

jun•gle *n.* A densely covered land with tropical vegetation, usually inhabited by wild animals.

jun•ior *adj.* Younger in years or rank; used to distinguish a son from a father of the same first name; the younger of two. *n.* The third year of high school or college.

ju•ni•per *n.* An evergreen shrub or tree of Europe and America with dark blue berries, prickly foliage, and fragrant wood.

junk *n.* Discarded material, as glass, scrap iron, paper, or rags; a flat-bottomed Chinese ship with battened sails; rubbish.

jun•ket *n.* A party, banquet, or trip; a trip taken by a public official with all expenses paid for by public funds; a custard-like dessert of flavored milk set with rennet. **junket** *v.*, **junketeer** *n.*

junk food *n.* Food containing very little nutritional value in proportion to the number of calories.

ju•ris•dic•tion *n.* The lawful right or power to interpret and apply the law; the territory within which power is exercised. **jurisdictional** *adj.*

ju•ror *n.* A person who serves on a jury.

ju•ry *n.* A group of persons summoned to serve on a judicial tribunal to give a verdict according to evidence presented.

just *adj.* Fair and impartial in acting or judging; morally right; merited; deserved; based on sound reason. *adv.* To the exact point; precisely; exactly right. **justly** *adv.*, **justness** *n.*

jus•tice *n.* The principle of moral or ideal rightness; conformity to the law; the abstract principle by which right and wrong are defined; a judge.

jus•ti•fy *v.* To be just, right, or valid; to declare guiltless; to adjust or space lines to the proper length.

jut *v.* To extend beyond the main portion; to project.

ju•ve•nile *adj.* Young, youthful; not yet an adult. *n.* A young person; an actor who plays youthful roles; a child's book.

ju•ve•nile court *n.* A court which deals only with cases involving dependent, neglected, and delinquent children.

ju•ve•nile de•lin•quent *n.* A person who is guilty of violations of the law, but is too young to be punished as an adult criminal; a young person whose behavior is out of control.

K

K, k The eleventh letter of the English alphabet; symbol for *kilo*, one thousand; in computers, a unit of capacity equal to 1024 bytes.

ka·bob *n.* Cubed meat and vegetables placed on a skewer.

ka·bu·ki *n.* A traditional Japanese drama in which dances and songs are performed in a stylized fashion.

kale *n.* A green cabbage having crinkled leaves which do not form a tight head.

ka·lie·do·scope *n.* A tubular instrument rotated to make successive symmetrical designs by using mirrors reflecting the changing patterns made by pieces of loose colored glass.

ka·mi·ka·ze *n.* A Japanese pilot in World War II trained to make a suicidal crash; an aircraft loaded with explosives used in a suicide attack.

kan·ga·roo *n.* Any of various herbivorous marsupials of Australia, with short forelegs and large hind limbs, capable of jumping, and a large tail.

kar·at *n.* A unit of measure for the fineness of gold; a measure of weight for precious gems.

ka·ra·te *n.* The Japanese art of self-defense.

kar·ma *n.* The over-all effect of one's behavior, held in Hinduism and Buddhism to determine one's destiny in a future existence. **karmic** *adj.*

ka·ty·did *n.* Any of various green insects related to grasshoppers and crickets.

kay·ak *n.* A watertight Eskimo boat with a light frame and covered with sealskin.

kay·o *n.* To knock out (K.O.) an opponent, in boxing.

ka·zoo *n.* A toy musical instrument with a paper membrane which vibrates when a player hums into the tube.

kedge *n.* A small anchor. *v.* Pull a ship by the rope of an anchor.

keel *n.* The central main stem of a ship or aircraft which runs lengthwise along the center line from bow to stern.

keel·boat *n.* A boat used on rivers; shallow boat used for freight.

keen *adj.* Having a sharp edge or point; acutely painful or harsh; intellectually acute; strong; intense.

keep *v.* To have and hold; to not let go; to maintain, as business records; to know a secret and not divulge it; to protect and defend.

keep·er *n.* One who keeps, guards, or maintains something; a person who respects or observes a requirement.

keep·ing *n.* Charge or possession; conformity or harmony; maintenance or support.

keep·sake *n.* A memento or souvenir; a token or remembrance of friendship.

kef *n.* A tranquil and dreamy state; a narcotic.

keg *n.* A small barrel usually having the capacity of five to ten gallons; the unit of measure for nails which equals 100 pounds.

kelp *n.* Any of a variety of large brown seaweed.

Kel·vin *adj.* Designating or relating to the temperature scale having a zero point of approximately −273 degrees C.

ken·nel *n.* A shelter for or a place where dogs or cats are bred, boarded, or trained.

ke·no *n.* A game of chance resembling bingo; a lottery game.

ker·a·tin *n.* A fibrous protein that forms the basic substance of nails, hair, horns, and hoofs. **keratinous** *adj.*

ker·chief *n.* A piece of cloth usually worn around the neck or on the head; scarf. **kerchiefed** *adj.*

ker·nel *n.* A grain or seed, as of corn, enclosed in a hard husk; the inner substance of a nut; the central, most important part; a device for holding something in place, as a latch, or clasp.

ker·o·sene or **ker·o·sine** *n.* An oil distilled from petroleum or coal.

kes·trel *n.* A small falcon, with gray and

brown plumage.

ketch *n*. A small two-masted sailing vessel with the foremast larger than the aftmast, and both forward of the helm.

ketch•up *n*. A thick, smooth sauce made from tomatoes; catsup.

ket•tle *n*. A large metal pot for stewing or boiling.

ket•tle•drum *n*. A musical instrument with a parchment head tuned by adjusting the tension.

key *n*. An object used to open a lock; button or lever used on a keyboard of a typewriter or piano; the crucial or main element. **keyed** *adj*.

key•board *n*. A bank of keys, as on a piano, typewriter, or computer terminal.

key•hole *n*. Lock; area that a key is inserted into.

key•note *n*. The first and harmonically fundamental tone of a scale; main principle or theme.

key•punch *n*. A machine operated from a keyboard that uses punched holes in tapes or cards for data processing systems. **keypunch** *n*., **keypuncher** *v*.

key•stone *n*. The wedge-shaped stone at the center of an arch that locks its parts together; an essential part.

key•stroke *n*. A stroke of a key.

kha•ki *n*. A yellowish brown or olive-drab color; a sturdy cloth, khaki in color. *pl*. Trousers or a uniform of khaki cloth.

khan *n*. An Asiatic title of respect; a medieval Turkish, Mongolian or Tartar ruler. **khanate** *n*.

kick *v*. To strike something with force by the foot.

kick•back *n*. A secret payment to a person who can influence a source of income; repercussion; a strong reaction.

kick•off *n*. The play that begins a game of soccer or football.

kick•stand *n*. The swiveling bar for holding a two-wheeled vehicle upright.

kid *n*. A young goat; leather made from the skin of a young goat. *slang* A child; youngster. *v*. To mock or tease playfully,

to deceive for fun; to fool.

kid•nap *v*. To seize and hold a person unlawfully, often for ransom. **kidnapper** *n*.

kid•ney *n*. Either of two organs situated in the abdominal cavity of vertebrates whose function is to keep proper water balance in the body and to excrete wastes in the form of urine.

kid•ney bean *n*. A bean whose edible seeds are in the shape of a kidney.

kill *v*. To put to death; nullify; cancel; to slaughter for food; to deprive of life.

kill•er whale *n*. A black and white carnivorous whale, found in the colder waters of the seas.

kil•lick *n*. An anchor for a boat, sometimes consisting of a stone secured by wood.

kill•ing *n*. The act of a person who kills; a slaying.

kill•joy *n*. One who spoils the enjoyment of others.

kiln *n*. An oven or furnace for hardening or drying a substance, especially one for firing ceramics or pottery.

ki•lo *n*. A kilogram.

kil•o•bit *n*. In computer science, one thousand binary digits.

kil•o•cal•o•rie *n*. One thousand gram calories.

ki•lo•cy•cle *n*. A unit equal to one thousand cycles; one thousand cycles per second.

kil•o•gram *n*. A measurement of weight in the metric system equal to slightly more than one third of a pound.

kil•o•li•ter *n*. Metric measurement equal to one thousand liters.

kil•o•me•ter *n*. Metric measurement equal to one thousand meters.

kil•o•ton *n*. One thousand tons; an explosive power equal to that of one thousand tons of TNT.

kil•o•volt *n*. One thousand volts.

kil•o•watt *n*. A unit of power equal to one thousand watts.

kil•o•watt hour *n*. A unit of electric power consumption of one thousand watts throughout one hour.

kilt *n.* A knee-length wool skirt with deep pleats, usually of tartan, worn especially by men in the Scottish Highlands.

kil·ter *n.* Good condition; proper or working order.

ki·mo·no *n.* A loose Japanese robe with a wide sash; a loose robe worn chiefly by women.

kin *n.* One's relatives by blood; relatives collectively.

kind *n.* A characteristic; a variety.

kind *adj.* Of a friendly, or good-natured disposition; coming from a good-natured readiness to please others. **kindness** *n.*

kin·der·gar·ten *n.* A school or class for young children from the ages of four to six. **kindergartner** *n.*

kind·heart·ed *adj.* Having much generosity and kindness.

kin·dle *v.* To ignite; to catch fire; to stir up; to excite, as feelings.

kind·less *adj.* Mean, cruel, unkind, unfriendly.

kin·dling *n.* Easily ignited material such as sticks and wood chips, used to start a fire.

kind·ly *adv.* Pleasantly, in a natural way; with a good disposition, or character; benevolently. **kindliness** *n.*

kind·ness *n.* An act of good will; state or quality of being kind.

kin·dred *n.* A person's relatives by blood. *adj.* Having a like nature; similar.

kin·e·mat·ics *n.* The branch of dynamics that deals with motion considered apart from force and mass. **kinematic, kinematical** *adj.*, **kinematically** *adv.*

kin·e·scope *n.* A cathode-ray tube in a television set which translates received electrical into a visible picture on a screen; a film of a television on broadcast.

ki·ne·sics *n.* To study the relationship between communication and body language. **kinesic** *adj.*

ki·ne·si·ol·o·gy *n.* Science that investigates organic and anatomy processes in reference to human motion.

ki·net·ic *adj.* Relating to, or produced by, motion.

king *n.* One who rules over a country; a male monarch; a playing card with a picture of a king; the main piece in the games of chess and checkers.

king·bolt *n.* A vertical bolt connecting the body of a vehicle with the front axle.

king crab *n.* A large crab-like crustacean common in the coastal waters of Japan, Alaska, and Siberia.

king·craft *n.* The art of ruling as a king; the profession and techniques used by a king.

king·dom *n.* The area or the country ruled by a king or queen.

king·fish *n.* A large fish used for food.

king·fish·er *n.* A bright colored bird having a long stout bill and short tail, which feeds on fish and insects.

king·let *n.* A very small bird; a king of little importance.

king·ly *adj.* Pertaining to or belonging to a king or kings; monarchical; splendid.

king·pin *n.* The foremost pin of a set arranged in order for playing bowling or tenpins; the most important or essential person.

king post *n.* A post located between the tie beam and the apex of a roof truss.

kink *n.* A tight twist or knot-like curl; a sharp painful muscle cramp. **kinky** *adj.*

kin·ka·jou *n.* A tropical American mammal having large eyes, brown fur and a long prehensile tail.

kink·y *adj.* Tightly curled; sexually uninhibited.

ki·osk *n.* A small building used as a refreshment booth or newsstand.

kip·per *n.* A salted and smoked herring or salmon. *v.* To cure by salting, smoking, or drying.

kir·tle *n.* A woman's long skirt or petticoat; a man's tunic or coat.

kis·met *n.* Fate; appointed lot.

kiss *v.* To touch two lips together in greeting between two people. **kissable** *adj.*

kit *n.* A collection of tools, supplies, or items for a special purpose.

kitch•en *n.* A room in a house or building used to prepare and cook food.

kitch•en•ette *n.* A small area that functions as a kitchen.

kitch•en•ware *n.* Dishes, pots, pans, and other utensils used in a kitchen.

kite *n.* A light-weight framework of wood and paper designed to fly in a steady breeze at the end of a string.

kith or **kin** *n.* Acquaintances or family.

kit•ten *n.* A young cat.

kit•ty *n.* A small collection or accumulation of objects or money; a young cat or kitten.

ki•va *n.* A Pueblo Indian chamber, used in ceremonies, often underground.

ki•wi *n.* A flightless bird, of New Zealand, having vestigial wings and a long, slender bill; a vine, native to Asia, which yields a fuzzy-skinned, edible fruit.

klep•to•ma•ni•a *n.* Obsessive desire to steal or impulse to steal, especially without economic motive.

klutz *n.* A clumsy person. **klutzy** *adj.*

knack *n.* A natural talent; aptitude.

knack•wurst or **knock•wurst** *n.* A thick or short, heavily seasoned sausage.

knap•sack *n.* A supply or equipment bag, as of canvas or nylon, worn strapped across the shoulders.

knave *n.* A tricky or dishonest person.

knead *v.* To work dough into a uniform mass by folding over; to shape by or as if by kneading.

knee *n.* The hinged joint in the leg connecting the calf with the thigh.

knee•cap *n.* Patella; bone covering the joint of the knee.

knee-deep *adj.* So deep that it reaches one's knees.

kneel *v.* To go down upon one's knees. **kneeler** *n.*

knell *v.* To sound a bell, especially when rung for a funeral; to toll. *n.* An act or instance of knelling; a signal of disaster.

knick•knack *n.* A trinket; trifling article.

knife *n.* An instrument used to cut an item.

knife edge *n.* A very sharp edge; the edge of a knife.

knife switch *n.* A switch used to close a circuit.

knight *n.* A medieval soldier serving a monarch; a chess piece bearing the shape of a horse's head. **knighthood** *n.*, **knightly** *adj.*

knit *v.* To form by intertwining thread or yarn, by interlocking loops of a single yarn by means of needles; to fasten securely; to draw together.

knit•ting nee•dle *n.* A long, slender, pointed rod for knitting.

knob *n.* A rounded protuberance; a lump; a rounded mountain; a rounded handle. **knobbed** *adj.*, **knobby** *adj.*

knock *v.* To hit or strike with a hard blow; to criticize; to collide.

knock•er *n.* A metal ring for knocking on a door.

knock•knee *n.* A condition in which one or both knees turn inward and knock or rub together while walking. **knock-kneed** *adj.*

knoll *n.* A small round hill; a mound.

knot *n.* An interwinding of string or rope; a fastening made by typing together lengths of material, as string; a unifying bond, especially of marriage; a hard node on a tree from which a branch grows; a nautical unit of speed, also called a nautical mile, which equals approximately 1.15 statute miles per hour.

knot•hole *n.* A hole in lumber left by the falling out of a knot.

knout *n.* A whip or scourge for flogging criminals. **knout** *v.*

know *v.* To perceive directly as fact or truth; to believe to be true; to be certain of; to be familiar with or have experience.

know•how *n.* Craft or expertise in something.

know•ing *adj.* Astute, knowledgeable; possessing secret knowledge. **knowingly** *adv.*

know•ledge *n.* Facts, information; the state of knowing. **knowledgeable** *adj.*

knuck•le *n.* The hinge or joint of the finger where it joins the hand or fist.

knuck•le•bone *n.* The bone of the finger which forms the knuckle.

knuck•le•head *n.* A person who is not very smart; affectionate term for an ignorant person.

ko•a•la *n.* An Australian marsupial with large hairy ears and gray fur, which feeds on eucalyptus leaves.

kohl *n.* Dark powder used as cosmetics to darken under the eyes.

kohl•ra•bi *n.* A variety of cabbage having a thick stem and eaten as a vegetable.

L

L, l The twelfth letter of the English alphabet; the Roman numeral for fifty.

la•bel *n.* Something that identifies or describes. *v.* To attach a label to.

lab•y•rinth *n.* A system of winding, intricate passages; a maze.

lac *n.* The resinous secretion left on certain trees by the lac insect and used in making paints and varnishes.

lace *n.* A delicate open-work fabric of silk, cotton, or linen made by hand or on a machine. *v.* To fasten or tie together; to interlace or intertwine. **lacy** *adj.*

lac•er•ate *v.* To open with a jagged tear; to wound the flesh by tearing. **laceration** *n.*

lack *n.* The deficiency or complete absence of something. *v.* To have little of something or to be completely without.

lack•lus•ter *adj.* Lacking sheen; dull.

lac•quer *n.* A transparent varnish which is dissolved in a volatile solution and dries to give surfaces a glossy finish.

la•crosse *n.* A game of American Indian origin played with a ball and long-handled rackets, by two teams of ten men each, to advance the ball into the opponents' goal.

lac•tate *v.* To secrete or to milk. **lactation** *n.*

lad *n.* A boy or young man.

lad•der *n.* An implement used for climbing up or down in order to reach another place or area.

lad•en *adj.* Heavily burdened; oppressed; weighed down; loaded.

lad•ing *n.* Cargo; freight.

la•dle *n.* A cup-shaped vessel with a deep bowl and a long handle, used for dipping or conveying liquids.

la•dy *n.* A woman showing refinement, cultivation, and often high social position; an address or term of reference for any woman.

la•dy•bug or **la•dy•bird** *n.* Any of a family of brightly colored beetles, black with red spots which feed mainly on aphids and other insects.

la•dy•like *adj.* Having the characteristics of a lady; delicate; gentle.

lag *v.* To stray or fall behind; to move slowly; to weaken gradually.

la•goon *n.* A body of shallow water separated from the ocean by a coral reef or sandbars.

laid *v.* Past tense of *lay.*

lain *v.* Past tense of *lie.*

lais•sez-faire *n.* A policy stating that a government should exercise very little control in trade and industrial affairs; noninterference.

la•i•ty *n.* Laymen, as distinguished from clergy.

lake *n.* A large inland body of either salt or fresh water.

La•maze meth•od *n.* A method of childbirth in which the mother is prepared psychologically and physically to give birth without the use of drugs.

lamb *n.* A young sheep; the meat of a lamb used as food; a gentle person.

lame *adj.* Disabled or crippled, especially in the legs or feet so as to impair free movement.

la•me *n.* A brocaded fabric woven with gold or silver thread, sometimes mixed with other fiber.

la•ment *v.* To express sorrow; to mourn. *n.* An expression of regret or sorrow.

lam•i•nate *v.* To form or press into thin

sheets; to form layers by the action of pressure and heat. **lamination** *n.*, **laminated** *adj.*

lamp *n.* A device for generating heat or light.

lam•poon *n.* A satirical, humorous, attack in verse or prose, especially one that ridicules a group, person, or institution.

lance *n.* A spear-like implement used as a weapon by mounted knights or soldiers.

land *n.* The solid, exposed surface of the earth as distinguished from the waters. *v.* To arrive at a destination from water.

lan•dau *n.* A four-wheeled vehicle with a closed carriage and a back seat with a collapsible top.

land•er *n.* A space vehicle for landing on a celestial body.

land•fill *n.* A system of trash and garbage disposal in which the waste is buried in low-lying land to build up the ground surface; a section built up by landfill.

land grant *n.* A grant of land made by a government, especially for railroads, roads, or agricultural colleges.

land•ing *n.* The act of coming, going, or placing ashore from any kind of vessel or craft; the act of descending and settling on the ground in an airplane.

land•locked *adj.* Almost or completely surrounded by land.

land•lord *n.* A person who owns property and rents or leases to another.

land•mark *n.* A fixed object that serves as a boundary marker.

land•scape *n.* A view or vista of natural scenery as seen from a single point. *v.* To decorate outside with flowers, shrubbery, and lawns.

lane *n.* A small or narrow path between walls, fences, or hedges.

lan•guage *n.* The words, sounds, pronunciation and method of combining words used and understood by people.

lan•guid *adj.* Lacking in energy; drooping; weak. **languidness** *n.*

lan•guish *v.* To become weak; to be or live in a state of depression. **languisher** *n.*,

languishment *n.*

lank *adj.* Slender; lean.

lan•o•lin *n.* Wool grease obtained from sheep's wool and refined for use in ointments and cosmetics.

lan•tern *n.* A portable light having transparent or translucent sides.

la•pel *n.* The front part of a garment, especially a coat, that is turned back, usually a continuation of the collar.

lap•in *n.* Rabbit fur that is sheared and dyed.

lap•is laz•u•li *n.* A semi-precious stone that is azure blue in color.

lapse *n.* A temporary deviation or fall to a less desirable state.

lar•ce•ny *n.* The unlawful taking of another person's property.

lard *n.* The soft, white, solid or semi-solid fat obtained after rendering the fatty tissue of the hog.

lar•der *n.* A place, such as a pantry or room, where food is stored.

large *adj.* Greater than usual or average in amount or size.

lar•gess or **lar•gesse** *n.* Liberal or excessive giving to an inferior; generosity.

lar•go *adv.* In a very slow, broad, and solemn manner. **largo** *adj.*

lar•i•at *n.* A long, light rope with a running noose at one end to catch livestock.

lark *n.* A bird having a melodious ability to sing; a merry or carefree adventure.

lar•va *n.* The immature, wingless, often worm-like form of a newly hatched insect; the early form of an animal that differs greatly from the adult, such as the tadpole. **larval** *adj.*, **larvae** *pl.*

lar•yn•gi•tis *n.* Inflammation of the larynx.

lar•ynx *n.* The upper portion of the trachea which contains the vocal cords.

la•ser *n.* A device which utilizes the natural oscillations of molecules or atoms between energy levels for generating coherent electromagnetic radiation in the visible, ultraviolet, or infrared parts of the spectrum.

lash *v.* To strike or move violently or suddenly; to attack verbally; to whip. *n.* An eyelash.

lass *n.* A young girl or woman.

las•si•tude *n.* A condition of weariness; fatigue.

las•so *n.* A long rope or long leather thong with a running noose used to catch horses and cattle.

last *adj.* Following all the rest; of or relating to the final stages, as of life; worst; lowest in rank. *adv.* After all others in sequence or chronology. *v.* To continue; to endure.

latch *n.* A device used to secure a gate or door, consisting of a bar that usually fits into a notch.

latch•et *n.* A narrow leather strap or thong used to fasten a shoe or sandal.

latch•key *n.* A key for opening an outside door.

latch•key child *n.* A child whose parent or parents work during the day and who carries a key to the front door because he or she returns home from school to an empty house.

late *adj.* Coming, staying, happening after the proper or usual time; having recently died.

lat•er•al *adj.* Relating to or of the side. *n.* In football, an underhand pass thrown sideways or away from the line of scrimmage. **laterally** *adv.*

la•tex *n.* The milky, white fluid produced by certain plants, such as the rubber tree; a water emulsion of synthetic rubber or plastic globules used in paints and adhesives.

lath *n.* A thin, narrow strip of wood nailed to joists, rafters, or studding and used as a supporting structure for plaster.

lathe *n.* A machine for holding material while it is spun and shaped by a tool.

lath•er *n.* A foam formed by detergent or soap and water.

lat•i•tude *n.* The angular distance of the earth's surface north or south of the equator, measured in degrees along a meridian;

freedom to act and to choose.

lat•ter *adj.* Being the second of two persons or two things.

lat•tice *n.* A structure made of strips of wood, metal, or other materials, interlaced or crossed, framing regularly spaced openings.

laugh *v.* To express amusement, satisfaction, or joy with a smile and inarticulate sounds. **laughable** *adj.*, **laughter** *n.*

launch *v.* To push or move a vessel into the water for the first time; to set a rocket or missile into flight. *n.* A large boat carried by a ship.

laun•der *v.* To wash clothes or other materials in soap and water.

laun•dro•mat *n.* A place to wash and dry clothes in coin operated machines.

laun•dry *n.* A business where laundering is done professionally; clothes or other articles to be or that have been laundered.

lau•re•ate *n.* A person honored for accomplishment; a recipient of laurels.

la•va *n.* Molten rock which erupts or flows from an active volcano; the rock formed after lava has cooled and hardened.

lav•a•to•ry *n.* A room with permanently installed washing and toilet facilities.

lav•en•der *n.* An aromatic plant having spikes of pale violet flowers; light purple in color. **lavender** *adj.*

lav•ish *adj.* Generous and extravagant in giving or spending.

law *n.* A rule of conduct or action, recognized by custom or decreed by formal enactment, considered binding on the members of a nation, community, or group; a system or body of such rules.

lawn *n.* A stretch of ground covered with grass mowed regularly.

law•suit *n.* A case or proceeding brought before a court of law for settlement.

law•yer *n.* A person trained in the legal profession who acts for and advises clients or pleads in court.

lax *adj.* Lacking disciplinary control; lacking rigidity or firmness.

lax•a•tive *n.* A medicine taken to

stimulate evacuation of the bowels. **laxa-tive** *adj.*

lay *v.* To cause to lie; to place on a surface; past tense of *lie*.

lay•er *n.* A single thickness, coating, or covering that lies over or under another. **layered** *adj.*

lay•ette *n.* The clothing, bedding, and equipment for a newborn child.

lay•man *n.* A person not belonging to a particular profession or specialty; one who is not a member of the clergy.

lay•off *n.* A temporary dismissal of employees.

la•zy *adj.* Unwilling to work; moving slowly; sluggish. **lazily** *adv.*

la•zy•bones *n.* A lazy person.

leach *v.* To cause a liquid to pass through a fiber; to remove or wash out by filtering. **leachable** *adj.*

lead *v.* To go ahead so as to show the way; to control the affairs or action of.

leaf *n.* A flat outgrowth from a plant structure or tree, usually green in color and functioning as the principal area of photosynthesis; a page in a book. **leafy** *adj.*

leaf•let *n.* A part or a segment of a compound leaf; a small printed handbill or circular, often folded.

league *n.* An association of persons, organizations, or states for common interest; an association of athletic competition.

leak *n.* An opening, as a flaw or small crack, permitting an escape or entrance of light or fluid. **leakage** *n.*

lean *v.* To rest or incline the weight of the body for support; to rest or incline anything against a large object or wall; to rely or depend on; to have a tendency or preference for. *adj.* Having little or no fat; thin. **leanly** *adv.*, **leanness** *n.*

lean•ing *n.* An inclination; a predisposition.

leap *v.* To rise or project oneself by a sudden thrust from the ground with a spring of the legs; to spring; to jump.

leap•frog *n.* A game in which two players leap over each other by placing one's hands on the back of another who is bending over and leaping over in a straddling position.

leap year *n.* A year containing 366 days, occurring every fourth year, with the extra day added to make 29 days in February.

learn•ing *n.* The process of acquiring knowledge, understanding, or mastery of a study or experience. **learner** *n.*, **learnable** *adj.*, **learn** *v.*

lease *n.* A contract for the temporary use or occupation of property or premises in exchange for payment of rent.

leash *n.* A strong cord or rope for restraining a dog or other animal.

leath•er *n.* An animal skin or hide with the hair removed, prepared for use by tanning.

leave *v.* To go or depart from; to permit to remain behind or in a specified place or condition; to forsake; to abandon; to bequeath, as in a will.

leav•en *n.* An agent of fermentation, as yeast, used to cause batters and doughs to rise; any pervasive influence that produces a significant change.

lech•er•y *n.* Unrestrained indulgence in sexual activity. **lecher** *n.*, **lecherous** *adj.*

lec•tern *n.* A stand or tall desk, usually with a slanted top, on which a speaker or instructor may place books or papers.

lec•ture *n.* A speech on a specific subject, delivered to an audience for information or instruction. *v.* To give a speech or lecture; to criticize or reprimand.

led *v.* Past tense of *lead*.

ledge *n.* A narrow, shelf-like projection forming a shelf.

ledg•er *n.* A book in which sums of money received and paid out are recorded.

leech *n.* Any of various carnivorous or bloodsucking worms; a person who clings or preys on others.

leek *n.* A culinary herb of the lily family, related to the onion, with a slender, edible bulb.

leer *n.* A sly look or sideways glance expressing desire or malicious intent.

left *adj.* Pertaining to or being on the side of the body that faces north when the subject is facing east.

leg *n.* A limb or appendage serving as a means of support and movement in animals and man.

leg•a•cy *n.* Personal property, money, and other valuables bequeathed by will; anything handed down from an ancestor, predecessor, or earlier era.

le•gal *adj.* Of, pertaining to, or concerned with the law or lawyers; something based on or authorized by law.

le•ga•to *adv.* Smooth and flowing with successive notes connected. **legato** *adj.*

leg•end *n.* An unverifiable story handed down from the past; a body of such stories, as those connected with a culture or people. **legendary** *adj.*

leg•i•ble *adj.* Capable of being read or deciphered. **legibility** *n.*, **legibly** *adv.*

le•gion *n.* In ancient Rome, an army unit that comprised between 4,200 and 6,000 men; any of various honorary or military organizations, usually national in character.

leg•is•la•tion *n.* The act or procedures of passing laws; lawmaking; an enacted law. **legislate** *v.*, **legislative** *adj.*

leg•is•la•ture *n.* A body of persons officially constituted and empowered to make and change laws.

leg•ume *n.* A plant of the pea or bean family, that bears pods which split when mature; the seeds or pod of a legume used as food. **leguminous** *adj.*

lei•sure *n.* A time of freedom from work or duty.

lem•on *n.* An oval citrus fruit grown on a tree, having juicy, acid pulp and a yellow rind that yields an essential oil used as a flavoring and as a perfuming agent.

lem•on•ade *n.* A drink made from water, lemon juice, and sugar.

lend *v.* To allow the temporary use or possession of something with the understanding that it is to be returned; to offer oneself as to a specific purpose. **lender** *n.*

length *n.* The linear extent of something from end to end, usually the longest dimension of a thing as distinguished from its thickness and width. **lengthy** *adj.*, **lengthen** *v.*

le•ni•ent *adj.* Gentle, forgiving, and mild; merciful; undemanding; tolerant. **leniency, lenience** *n.*

len•i•tive *adj.* Having the ability to ease pain or discomfort. **lenitive** *n.*

lens *n.* In optics, the curved piece of glass or other transparent substance used to refract light rays so that they converge or diverge to form an image; the transparent structure in the eye, situated behind the iris, which serves to focus an image on the retina.

lent *v.* Past tense of *lend.*

len•til *n.* A leguminous plant, having broad pods and containing edible seeds.

leo•pard *n.* A large member of the cat family of Africa and Asia, having a tawny coat with dark brown or black spots grouped in rounded clusters, also called a panther.

le•o•tard *n.* A close-fitting garment worn by dancers and acrobats.

lep•er *n.* One who suffers from leprosy.

lep•re•chaun *n.* A mischief-making elf of Irish folklore, supposed to own hidden treasure.

lep•ro•sy *n.* A chronic communicable disease characterized by nodular skin lesions and the progressive destruction of tissue.

les•bi•an *n.* A homosexual woman. **lesbian** *adj.*

le•sion *n.* An injury; a wound; any well-defined bodily area where the tissue has changed in a way that is characteristic of a disease.

less *adj.* Smaller; of smaller or lower importance or degree. *prep.* With the subtraction of; minus.

les•son *n.* An instance from which something is to be or has been learned; an assignment to be learned or studied.

let *v.* To give permission; to allow.

let•down *n.* A decrease or slackening, as in

energy or effort.

le·thal *adj.* Pertaining to or being able to cause death.

leth·ar·gy *n.* A state of excessive drowsiness or abnormally deep sleep; laziness.

let's *contr.* Let us.

let·ter *n.* A standard character or sign used in writing or printing to represent an alphabetical unit or speech sound; a written or printed means of communication sent to another person.

let·ter·head *n.* Stationery printed with a name and address, usually of a company or business establishment.

let·tuce *n.* A plant having crisp, edible leaves used specially in salads.

le·vee *n.* An embankment along the shore of a body of water, especially a river, built to prevent overflowing.

lev·el *n.* A relative position, rank, or height on a scale; a standard position from which other heights and depths are measured. *adj.* Balanced in height; even. *v.* To make or become flat or level.

lev·er *n.* A handle that projects and is used to operate or adjust a mechanism.

lev·er·age *n.* The use of a lever; the mechanical advantage gained by using a lever; power to act effectively.

lev·i·tate *v.* To rise and float in the air in apparent defiance of gravity.

lev·i·ty *n.* Lack of seriousness; frivolity; lightness; humor.

lev·y *v.* To impose and collect by authority or force, as a fine or tax; to draft for military service; to prepare for, begin, or wage war. **levy** *n.*

lewd *adj.* Preoccupied with sex; lustful. **lewdly** *adv.*, **lewdness** *n.*

lex·i·cog·ra·phy *n.* The practice or profession of compiling dictionaries. **lexicographer** *n.*, **lexicographical** *adj.*

lex·i·con *n.* A dictionary; a vocabulary or list of words that relate to a certain subject, occupation, or activity. **lexical** *adj.*

li·a·bil·i·ty *n.* The condition or state of being liable; that which is owed to another. **liable** *adj.*

li·a·ble *adj.* Legally or rightly responsible.

li·ai·son *n.* A communication, as between different parts of an armed force or departments of a government; a close connection or relationship; an illicit love affair.

li·ar *n.* A person who tells falsehoods.

li·bel *n.* A written statement in published form that damages a person's character or reputation. **libel** *v.*, **libelous** *adj.*

lib·er·al *adj.* Characterized by generosity or lavishness in giving; abundant; ample. **liberalism**, **liberality** *n.*, **liberally** *adv.*

lib·er·al arts *pl. n.* Academic courses that include literature, philosophy, history, languages, etc., which provide general cultural information.

lib·er·ate *v.* To set free, as from bondage, oppression, or foreign control. **liberation** *n.*

lib·er·ty *n.* The state of being free from oppression, tyranny, confinement, or slavery; freedom.

li·bi·do *n.* One's sexual desire or impulse; the psychic energy drive that is behind all human activities. **libidinous** *adj.*

li·brar·i·an *n.* A person in charge of a library; one who specializes in library work.

li·brar·y *n.* A collection of books, pamphlets, magazines, and reference books kept for reading, reference, or borrowing; a commercial establishment, usually in connection with a city or school, which rents books.

lice *n.* Plural of *louse.*

li·cense *n.* An official document that gives permission to engage in a specified activity or to perform a specified act. **license** *v.*, **licenser** *n.*

li·cen·ti·ate *n.* A person licensed to practice a specified profession.

li·cen·tious *adj.* Lacking in moral restraint; immoral. **licentiously** *adv.*, **licentiousness** *n.*

li·chen *n.* Any of various flowerless plants consisting of fungi, commonly growing in flat patches on trees and rocks.

lick *v.* To pass the tongue over or along the surface of.

lic·o·rice *n.* A perennial herb of Europe, the dried root of which is used to flavor medicines and candy.

lid *n.* A hinged or removable cover for a container; an eyelid. **lidded**, **lidless** *adj.*

lie *v.* To be in or take a horizontal recumbent position; to recline. *n.* A false or untrue statement.

liege *n.* A feudal lord or sovereign.

lien *n.* The legal right to claim, hold, or sell the property of another to satisfy a debt or obligation.

lieu *n.* Place; stead.

lieu·ten·ant *n.* A commissioned officer in the U.S. Army, Air Force, or Marine Corps who ranks below a captain.

life *n.* The form of existence that distinguishes living organisms from dead organisms or inanimate matter in the ability to carry on metabolism, respond to stimuli, reproduce, and grow.

life·guard *n.* An expert swimmer employed to protect people in and around water.

life pre·serv·er *n.* A buoyant device, as one in the shape of a ring or jacket, used to keep a person afloat in water.

life raft *n.* A raft made of wood or an inflatable material used by people who have been forced into the water.

life·time *n.* The period between one's birth and death.

life·work *n.* The main work of a person's lifetime.

lift *v.* To raise from a lower to a higher position; to elevate; to take from. *n.* The act or process of lifting; force or power available for lifting; an elevation of spirits; a device or machine designed to pick up, raise, or carry something.

lig·a·ment *n.* A tough band of tissue joining bones or holding a body organ in place. **ligamentous** *adj.*

li·gate *v.* To tie with a ligature.

lig·a·ture *n.* Something, as a cord, that is used to bind.

light *n.* Electromagnetic radiation that can be seen by the naked eye; brightness; a source of light; spiritual illumination; enlightenment. *adj.* Having light; bright; of less force, quantity, intensity, or weight than normal.

light·er *n.* A device used to light a pipe, cigar or cigarette; a barge used to load and unload a cargo ship.

light·ning *n.* The flash of light produced by a high-tension natural electric discharge into the atmosphere. *adj.* Moving with or as if with the suddenness of lightning.

light·ning rod *n.* A grounded metal rod positioned high on a building to protect it from lightning.

light-year or **light year** *n.* A measure equal to the distance light travels in one year, approximately 5,878 trillion miles.

like·ness *n.* Resemblance; a copy.

light show *n.* A display of colored lights in kaleidoscopic patterns, often accompanied by film, slides, or music.

light·weight *n.* A person who weighs very little; a boxer or wrestler weighing between 127 and 135 pounds.

lig·ne·ous *adj.* Of or resembling wood; woody.

like·wise *adv.* In a similar way.

li·lac *n.* A shrub widely grown for its large, fragrant purplish or white flower cluster; a pale purple.

lilt *n.* A light song; a rhythmical way of speaking.

lil·y *n.* Any of various plants bearing trumpet-shaped flowers, associated with Easter.

li·ma bean *n.* Any of several varieties of tropical American plants having flat pods with light green edible seeds.

limb *n.* A large bough of a tree; an animal's appendage used for movement or grasping; an arm or leg.

lim·ber *adj.* Bending easily; pliable; moving easily; agile. *v.* To make or become limber.

lim·bo *n.* The abode of souls kept from

lime

entering Heaven; a place or conditions of oblivion or neglect; a state awaiting decision or resolution of a dynamic event.

lime *n.* A tropical citrus tree with evergreen leaves, fragrant white flowers, and edible green fruit; calcium oxide.

lime•light *n.* A focus of public attention; the center of attention.

lim•er•ick *n.* A humorous verse of five lines.

lime•stone *n.* A form of sedimentary rock composed mainly of calcium carbonate, used in building and in making lime and cement.

lim•it *n.* A boundary; a maximum or a minimum number or amount; a restriction on frequency or amount. *v.* To restrict; to establish boundaries. **limitation** *n.*

lim•ou•sine *n.* A luxurious large vehicle; a small bus used to carry passengers to airports and hotels.

limp *v.* To walk lamely.

lin•den *n.* Any of various shade trees having heart-shaped leaves.

lin•e•age *n.* A direct line of descent from an ancestor.

lin•e•ar *adj.* Of, pertaining to, or resembling a line; long and narrow.

lin•en *n.* Thread, yarn, or fabric made of flax; household articles, such as sheets and pillow cases, made of linen or a similar fabric.

lin•er *n.* A ship belonging to a ship line or an aircraft belonging to an airline; one that lines or serves as a lining.

lin•ger *v.* To be slow in parting or reluctant to leave; to be slow in acting; to procrastinate. **lingeringly** *adv.*

lin•ge•rie *n.* Women's undergarments.

lin•go *n.* Language that is local, unfamiliar, or highly idiomatic; a specialized vocabulary; jargon.

lin•guist *n.* One who is fluent in more than one language; a person specialized in linguistics.

lin•i•ment *n.* A liquid or semi-liquid medicine applied to the skin.

lin•ing *n.* A material which is used to cover an inside surface.

link *n.* One of the rings forming a chain; something in the form of a link; a tie or bond. *v.* To connect by or as if by a link or links. **linkage** *n.*

li•no•le•um *n.* A floor covering consisting of a surface of hardened linseed oil and a filler, as wood or powdered cork, on a canvas or burlap backing.

lin•seed *n.* The seed of flax, used in paints and varnishes.

lin•tel *n.* A horizontal beam across the top of a door which supports the weight of the structure above it.

li•on *n.* A large carnivorous mammal of the cat family, found in Africa and India, having a short, tawny coat and a long, heavy mane in the male. **lioness** *n.*

li•on•ize *v.* To treat someone as a celebrity.

lip serv•ice *n.* An expression of acquiescence that is not acted upon.

liq•ue•fy or **liq•ui•fy** *v.* To make liquid.

li•queur *n.* A sweet alcoholic beverage; a cordial.

liq•uid *adj.* Being in the physical state between gas and solid at room temperature. *n.* A substance that takes on the form of the vessel containing it; a beverage or drink.

liq•ui•date *v.* To settle a debt by payment or other settlement; to close a business by settling accounts and dividing up assets; to get rid of, especially to kill.

liq•uor *n.* A distilled alcoholic beverage; a liquid substance, as a watery solution of a drug.

lisp *n.* A speech defect or mannerism marked by lisping. *v.* To mispronounce the s and z sounds; usually as th. **lisper** *n.*

list *n.* A series of numbers or words; a tilt to one side. **list** *v.*

list•less *adj.* Lacking energy.

list•serv *n.* In computers, a mailing list capable of sending information to sites linked by common interests.

lit•a•ny *n.* A prayer in which phrases recited by a leader are alternated with answers from a congregation; any list, especially recited.

lit·er·al *adj.* Conforming to the exact meaning of a word; concerned primarily with facts; without embellishment or exaggeration. **literally** *adv.*

lit·er·ar·y *adj.* Pertaining to literature; appropriate to or used in literature; of or relating to the knowledge of literature.

lit·er·a·ture *n.* Printed material; written words of lasting excellence.

lithe *adj.* Bending easily; supple. **lithely** *adv.*, **litheness** *n.*

lit·i·gate *v.* To conduct a legal contest by judicial process.

lit·mus *n.* A blue powder obtained from lichens which turns red in acid solutions and blue in alkaline solutions, used as an acid-base indicator.

lit·to·ral *adj.* Relating to or existing on a shore. *n.* A shore.

lit·ter *n.* A stretcher used to carry a sick or injured person; material used as bedding for animals; the offspring at one birth of a multiparous animal; an accumulation of waste material. **litter** *v.*, **litterer** *n.*

lit·tle *adj.* Small

lit·ur·gy *n.* A prescribed rite or body of rites for public worship.

live·ly *adj.* Vigorous, active. **liveliness** *n.*

liv·er *n.* The large, vascular, glandular organ of vertebrates which secretes bile.

live·stock *n.* Farm animals raised for human use.

liv·id *adj.* Discolored from a bruise; very angry.

liz·ard *n.* One of various reptiles, usually with an elongated scaly body, four legs, and a tapering tail.

lla·ma *n.* A South American ruminant, related to the camel family and raised for its soft wool.

load *n.* A mass or weight that is lifted or supported; anything as cargo, put in a ship, aircraft, or vehicle for conveyance; something that is a heavy responsibility; a burden.

loaf *n.* A food, especially bread, shaped into a mass. *v.* To spend time in idleness. **loafer** *n.*

loan *n.* Money lent with interest to be repaid; something borrowed for temporary use. *v.* To lend.

loathe *v.* To dislike intensely. **loathing** *n.*, **loathsome** *adj.*

lob *v.* To hit or throw in a high arc.

lob·by *n.* An entranceway, as in a hotel or theatre; a group of private persons trying to influence legislators. **lobbyist** *n.*

lobe *n.* A curved or rounded projection or division, as the fleshy lower part of the ear.

lo·bot·o·my *n.* Surgical severance of nerve fibers by incision into the brain.

lob·ster *n.* Any of several large, edible marine crustaceans with five pairs of legs, the first pair being large and claw-like.

lo·cal *adj.* Pertaining to, being in, or serving a particular area or place. **locally** *adv.*

lo·cale *n.* A locality where a particular event takes place; the setting or scene.

lo·cal·i·ty *n.* A specific neighborhood, place, or district.

lo·cate *v.* To determine the place, position, or boundaries of; to look for and find. **location** *n.*

lock *n.* A device used to secure or fasten; a part of a waterway closed off with gates to allow the raising or lowering of boats by changing the level of the water; a strand or curl of hair. **lock** *v.*

lock·et *n.* A small, ornamental case for a keepsake, often a picture, worn as a pendant on a necklace.

lock·jaw *n.* Tetanus; a form of tetanus in which a spasm of the jaw muscles locks the jaws closed.

lock·smith *n.* A person who makes or repairs locks.

lo·co·mo·tive *n.* A self-propelled vehicle, generally steam, electric, or diesel-powered, used for moving railroad cars.

lo·cust *n.* Any of numerous grasshoppers which often travel in swarms and damage vegetation; any of various hardwood leguminous trees, such as carob, black locust, or honey locust.

lode•star *n.* A star; the North Star, used as a reference point.

lodge *n.* A house, such as a cabin, used as a temporary or seasonal dwelling or shelter; an inn. **lodger** *n.*

loft *n.* One of the upper, generally unpartitioned floors of an industrial or commercial building, such as a warehouse; an attic; a gallery in a church or hall.

loge *n.* A small compartment, especially a box in a theatre.

log•ic *n.* The science of dealing with the principles of reasoning, especially of the method and validity of deductive reasoning. **logical** *adj.*, **logically** *adv.*

lo•gis•tics *pl. n.* The logical apparatus of an operation or undertaking; the methods of procuring, maintaining, and replacing material and personnel, as in a military operation.

loi•ter *v.* To stay for no apparent reason; to dawdle or delay.

lone *adj.* Single; isolated; sole.

lone•ly *adj.* Being without companions; dejected from being alone. **loneliness** *n.*

lon•er *n.* A person who avoids the company of others.

lone•some *adj.* Dejected because of the lack of companionship.

long•bow *n.* A wooden bow, approximately five to six feet in length.

lon•gev•i•ty *n.* Long life; long duration; seniority.

lon•gi•tude *n.* The angular distance east and west of the prime meridian at Greenwich, England, measured in degrees. **longitudinal** *adj.*

look *v.* To examine with the eyes; to see; to glance, gaze, or stare at. *n.* The act of looking; the physical appearance of something or someone; a glance.

look•out *n.* A person positioned to keep watch or look for something or someone.

loom *v.* To come into view as a image; to seem to be threatening. *n.* A machine used for interweaving thread or yarn to produce cloth.

loop *n.* A circular length of line folded over and joined at the ends; a loop-shaped pattern, figure, or path. *v.* To form into a loop; to join, fasten, or encircle with a loop.

loose *adj.* Not tightly fastened; not confined or fitting; free.

loot *n.* Goods; usually of significant value, taken in time of war; goods that have been stolen. *v.* To plunder; to steal. **looter** *n.*

lop *v.* To remove branches from; to trim.

lope *v.* To run with a steady gait. **lope** *n.*

lop•sid•ed *adj.* Larger or heavier on one side than on the other; tilting to one side.

lo•qua•cious *adj.* Overly talkative. **loquaciously** *adv.*, **loquacity** *n.*

lore *n.* Traditional fact; knowledge gained through education or experience.

lose *v.* To mislay; to fail to keep; to be beaten in a competition.

loss *n.* The suffering or damage caused by losing; someone or something that is lost.

lost *adj.* Unable to find one's way; out of a familiar place.

lot *n.* Fate; fortune; a parcel of land having boundaries; a plot.

lo•tion *n.* A liquid medicine for external use on the hands and body.

lot•ter•y *n.* A contest in which winners are selected by a random drawing among paying participants.

lo•tus *n.* An aquatic plant having fragrant pinkish flowers and large leaves; any of several plants similar or related to the lotus.

loud *adj.* Marked by intense sound and high volume. **loudly** *adv.*, **loudness** *n.*

lounge *v.* To move or act in a lazy, relaxed manner. *n.* A room, as in a hotel or theatre, where people may wait; a couch.

lous•y *adj.* Lice-infested; mean; poor; inferior; abundantly supplied. **lousily** *adv.*

lout *n.* An awkward, stupid person. **loutish** *adj.*

love *n.* Intense affection for another arising out of kinship or personal ties; a strong feeling of attraction resulting from sexual desire; enthusiasm or fondness.

love•ly *adj.* Beautiful. **loveliness** *n.*

lov•er *n.* A person who loves another; a sexual partner; one who greatly enjoys an activity or thing, as a lover of music.

love seat *n.* A small couch which seats two.

love•sick *adj.* Languishing with love; expressing a lover's yearning.

low *adj.* Not high; being below or under normal height, rank, or level; depressed.

low•er•class *n.* The group in society that ranks below the middle class in social and economic status.

low•land *n.* Land that is low and level in relation to the surrounding countryside.

low•ly *adj.* Low in position or rank.

lox *n.* Smoked salmon.

loy•al *adj.* Faithful in allegiance to one's country and government; faithful to a person, cause, ideal, or custom. **loyalty** *n.*

loz•enge *n.* Small medicated candy, normally having the shape of a lozenge.

lu•au *n.* A traditional Hawaiian feast.

lu•cid *adj.* Easily understood; mentally clear; rational; shining. **lucidity** *n.*

luck *n.* Good fortune; the force or power which controls odds and which brings good fortune or bad fortune. **lucky** *adj.*, **luckily** *adv.*

lu•cra•tive *adj.* Producing profits or great wealth. **lucratively** *adv.*

lu•cre *n.* Money; profit.

lu•cu•brate *v.* To study or work laboriously.

lu•di•crous *adj.* Amusing or laughable through obvious absurdity; ridiculous.

lug•gage *n.* Suitcases or other traveler's baggage.

luke•warm *adj.* Mildly warm; tepid; unenthusiastic; average.

lull *v.* To cause to rest or sleep; to cause to have a false sense of security. *n.* A temporary period of quiet or rest.

lul•la•by *n.* A song to lull a child to sleep.

lum•bar *adj.* Part of the back and sides between the lowest ribs and the pelvis.

lum•ber *n.* Timber, sawed or split into boards.

lum•ber•jack *n.* One who cuts and pre-

pares timber for the sawmill.

lum•ber•yard *n.* A place where lumber and other building materials are sold.

lu•mi•nous *adj.* Emitting or reflecting light; bathed in steady light; illuminated.

lump *n.* A projection; a protuberance; a swelling, as from a bruise or infection. *v.* To group things together.

lu•na•cy *n.* Insanity.

lu•nar *adj.* Of, relating to, caused by the moon.

lu•nar e•clipse *n.* An eclipse where the moon passes partially or wholly through the umbra of the earth's shadow.

lu•na•tic *n.* A crazy person.

lunch•eon *n.* A lunch.

lunch•eon•ette *n.* A modest restaurant at which light meals are served.

lung *n.* One of the two spongy organs that constitute the basic respiratory organ of air-breathing vertebrates.

lunge *n.* A sudden forward movement.

lure *n.* A decoy; something appealing; an artificial bait to catch fish. *v.* To attract or entice with the prospect of reward or pleasure.

lurk *v.* To lie in concealment.

lus•cious *adj.* Very pleasant to smell or taste; appealing to the senses.

lush *adj.* Producing luxuriant growth or vegetation. **lushly** *adv.*, **lushness** *n.*

lust *n.* Intense sexual desire; an intense longing; a craving.

lus•ter or **lus•tre** *n.* A glow of reflected light; sheen; brilliance or radiance; brightness. **lusterless** *adj.*

lute *n.* A medieval musical stringed instrument with a fretted finger board, a pear-shaped body, and usually a bent neck.

lux•u•ri•ant *adj.* Growing or producing abundantly; lush; plentiful.

M

M, m The thirteenth letter of the English alphabet; the Roman numeral for 1,000.

ma·ca·bre *adj.* Suggesting death and decay.

mac·a·ro·ni *n.* Dried pasta made into short tubes and prepared as food.

mac·a·roon *n.* A small cookie made of sugar, egg whites, coconut, and ground almonds.

ma·caw *n.* Any of various tropical American parrots with long tails, brilliant plumage, and harsh voices.

mace *n.* An aromatic spice made by grinding the cover of the nutmeg.

ma·chet·e *n.* A large, heavy knife with a broad blade, used as a weapon.

ma·chine *n.* A device or system built to use energy to do work; a political organization. *v.* To produce precision tools.

ma·chine lan·guage *n.* In computers, the system of numbers or instructions for coding input data.

ma·chin·er·y *n.* A collection of machines as a whole; the mechanism or operating parts of a machine.

ma·chin·ist *n.* One skilled in the operation or repair of machines.

ma·chis·mo *n.* An exaggerated sense of masculinity.

ma·cho *adj.* Exhibiting machismo.

mack·er·el *n.* A fish with dark, wavy bars on the back and a silvery belly, found in the Atlantic Ocean.

mac·ra·me *n.* The craft or hobby of tying knots into a pattern.

mac·ro·scop·ic *adj.* Large enough to be seen by the naked eye.

mad *adj.* Angry; afflicted with a mental disorder; insane.

mad·am *n.* A title used to address a married woman; used without a name as a courtesy title when addressing a woman.

mad·cap *adj.* Impulsive, rash or reckless.

mad·den *v.* To craze; to enrage; to make mad; to become mad.

made *v.* Past tense of *make*.

mad·ri·gal *n.* An unaccompanied song, usually for four to six voices, developed during the early Renaissance.

mael·strom *n.* Any irresistible or dangerous force.

maes·tro *n.* A person mastering any art, but especially a famous conductor of music.

mag·a·zine *n.* A publication with a paper cover containing articles, stories, illustrations and advertising; the part of a gun which holds ammunition.

ma·gen·ta *n.* A purplish red color.

mag·got *n.* The legless larva of any of various insects, as the housefly, often found in decaying matter.

mag·ic *n.* The art which seemingly controls foresight of natural events and forces by means of supernatural agencies.

mag·is·trate *n.* A civil officer with the power to enforce the law.

mag·nan·i·mous *adj.* Generous in forgiving insults or injuries. **magnanimity**, **magnanimousness** *n.*

mag·nate *n.* A person notable or powerful, especially in business.

mag·ne·sia *n.* A light, white powder used in medicine as an antacid and laxative.

mag·ne·si·um *n.* A light, silvery metallic element which burns with a very hot, bright flame and is used in lightweight alloys, symbolized by Mg.

mag·net *n.* A body having the property of attracting iron and other magnetic material. **magnetism** *n.*

mag·net·ic *adj.* Pertaining to magnetism or a magnet; capable of being attracted by a magnet; having the power or ability to attract. **magnetically** *adv.*

mag·net·ic field *n.* The area in the neighborhood of a magnet or of an electric current, marked by the existence of a detectable magnetic force in every part of the region.

mag·net·ize *v.* To have magnetic properties; to attract by personal charm.

mag·nif·i·cent *adj.* Having an extraordinarily imposing appearance; beautiful; outstanding; exceptionally pleasing.

mag·ni·fy *v.* To increase in size; to cause to seem more important or greater; to glorify or praise someone or something.

magnification, magnifier *n*.

mag·nil·o·quent *adj*. Speaking or spoken in a lofty and extravagant manner.

mag·ni·tude *n*. Greatness or importance in size or extent; the relative brightness of a star expressed on a numerical scale, ranging from one for the brightest to six for those just visible.

mag·no·lia *n*. An ornamental flowering tree or shrub with large, fragrant flowers of white, pink, purple, or yellow.

mag·num *n*. A wine bottle holding about two quarts or approximately 2/5 gallon.

mag·num o·pus *n*. A great work of art; literary or artistic masterpiece; the greatest single work of an artist, writer, or other creative person.

mag·pie *n*. Any of a variety of large, noisy birds found the world over having long tapering tails and black and white plumage.

ma·hat·ma *n*. In some Asian religions, a person venerated for great knowledge; a title of respect.

ma·hog·a·ny *n*. Any of various tropical trees having hard, reddish-brown wood, much used for cabinet work and furniture.

maid *n*. A young unmarried woman or girl; a female servant. **maiden** *n*.

mail *n*. Letter, printed matter, or parcel handled by the postal system.

mail or·der *n*. Goods which are ordered and sent by mail.

maim *v*. To disable or to deprive of the use of a bodily part; to impair.

main *adj*. Being the most important part of something. *n*. A large pipe used to carry water, oil, or gas. **mainly** *adv*.

main·land *n*. The land part of a country as distinguished from an island.

main·tain *v*. To carry on or to keep in existence; to preserve in a desirable condition. **maintenance** *n*.

maize *n*. Corn.

maj·es·ty *n*. Stateliness; exalted dignity. **majestic** *adj*.

ma·jor *adj*. Greater in importance, quantity, number, or rank; serious; a subject or field of academic study.

ma·jor·i·ty *n*. The greater number of something; more than half; the age at which a person is considered to be an adult, usually 21 years old.

make *v*. To cause something to happen; to create; to provide, as time; to manufacture a line of goods. *n*. A brand name.

mal·a·droit *adj*. Lacking skill; awkward; clumsy. **maladroitness** *n*.

mal·a·dy *n*. A chronic disease or sickness.

mal·aise *n*. The vague discomfort sometimes indicating the beginning of an illness.

mal·a·prop·ism *n*. A foolish misuse of a word.

mal·ap·ro·pos *adj*. Not appropriate. **malapropos** *adv*.

ma·lar·i·a *n*. The infectious disease introduced into the blood by the bite of the infected female anophelene mosquito, and characterized by cycles of fever, chills, and profuse swelling. **malarial** *adj*.

ma·lar·key *n*. Foolish or insincere talk; nonsense.

mal·con·tent *adj*. Unhappy with existing conditions or affairs. **malcontent** *n*.

mal de mer *n*. Seasickness.

male *adj*. Of or belonging to the sex that has organs to produce spermatozoa.

mal·e·dic·tion *n*. A curse; execration. **maledictory** *adj*.

mal·e·fac·tor *n*. A person who commits a crime or an unlawful act; a criminal. **malefaction** *n*.

mal·e·vo·lent *adj*. Full of spite or ill will for another; malicious. **malevolently** *adv*., **malevolence** *n*.

mal·func·tion *n*. Failure to function correctly.

mal·ice *n*. The direct intention or desire to harm others.

ma·lign *v*. To speak slander or evil of.

ma·lig·nant *adj*. Of or relating to tumors and abnormal or rapid growth; opposed to benign; causing death or great harm. **malignancy** *n*., **malignantly** *adv*.

mall *n*. A walk or other shaded public

promenade; a street with shops, restaurants, and businesses, closed to vehicles.

mal·lard *n.* A wild duck having brownish plumage, the male of which has a green head and neck.

mal·le·a·ble *adj.* Able to be bent, shaped, or hammered without breaking; capable of being molded, altered, or influenced. **malleability** *n.*

mal·let *n.* A hammer with a head made of wood or rubber and a short handle; a tool for striking an object without marring it.

mal·nour·ished *adj.* Undernourished.

mal·nu·tri·tion *n.* Insufficient nutrition.

mal·prac·tice *n.* Improper treatment of a patient by his doctor during surgery or treatment which results in damage or injury; failure to perform a professional duty in a proper or correct fashion, resulting in injury, loss, or other problems.

malt *n.* Grain, usually barley, used chiefly in brewing and distilling; an alcoholic beverage.

ma·ma *n.* Mother.

mam·ba *n.* A venomous snake found in the tropics and in southern Africa.

mam·bo *n.* A dance resembling the rumba of Latin America.

mam·mal *n.* Any member of a class whose females secrete milk for nourishing their young, including man. **mammalian** *adj.*

mam·ma·ry gland *n.* The milk-producing organ of the female mammal, consisting of small cavity clusters with ducts ending in a nipple.

mam·moth *n.* An extinct, early form of elephant whose tusks curved upwards and whose body was covered with long hair; *adj.* anything of great or huge size.

man *n.* An adult or fully-grown male; the human race; any human being, regardless of sex [not current].

man·a·cle *n.* A device for restraining the hands; handcuffs. **manacle** *v.*

man·age *v.* To direct or control the affairs or use of; to organize. **manageability** *n.*, **manageable** *adj.*

man·ag·er *n.* One in charge of managing an enterprise or business.

man·da·to·ry *adj.* Required by; having the nature of, or relating to a mandate; obligatory.

man·di·ble *n.* The lower jaw bone; either part of the beak of a bird. **mandibular** *adj.*

man·do·lin *n.* A musical instrument having a pear-shaped body and a fretted neck.

man·drake *n.* A poisonous plant having purplish flowers and a branched root formerly used as a narcotic.

man·drel or **man·dril** *n.* A spindle or shaft on which material is held for working on a lathe.

mane *n.* The long hair growing on the neck of some animals, as the lion, and horse.

ma·neu·ver *n.* A planned strategic movement or shift, as of warships, or troops; any planned, skillful, or calculated move. **maneuver** *v.*, **maneuverability** *n.*, **maneuverable** *adj.*

man·ga·nese *n.* A hard, brittle, gray-white metallic element which forms an important component of steel alloys, symbolized by Mn.

mange *n.* A contagious skin disease of dogs and other domestic animals caused by parasitic mites and marked by itching and hair loss. **mangy** *adj.*

man·ger *n.* A trough or box which holds livestock feed.

man·gle *v.* To disfigure or mutilate by bruising, battering, or crushing; to spoil.

man·go *n.* A tropical evergreen tree that produces a fruit having a slight acidic taste.

man·grove *n.* A tropical evergreen tree or shrub having aerial roots which form dense thickets along tidal shores.

man·han·dle *v.* To handle very roughly.

man·hole *n.* A circular covered opening usually in a street, through which one may enter a sewer, drain, or conduit.

ma·ni·a *n.* An extraordinary enthusiasm or craving for something; intense excitement and physical overactivity, often a symptom of manic-depressive psychosis.

ma•ni•ac *n.* A violently insane person. **maniac, maniacal** *adj.*

man•ic-de•pres•sive *adj.* Of a mental disorder characterized by alternating periods of manic excitation and depression. **manic-depressive** *n.*

man•i•cot•ti *n.* Pasta shaped like a tube, filled with meat or ricotta cheese and served with hot tomato sauce.

man•i•cure *n.* The cosmetic care of the hands and fingernails. **manicurist** *n.*

man•i•fest *adj.* Clearly apparent; obvious. *v.* To display, reveal, or show. *n.* A list of cargo or passengers. **manifestly** *adv.*

man•i•fes•ta•tion *n.* The act or state of being manifest.

man•i•fes•to *n.* A public or formal expectation of principles or intentions, usually of a political nature. **manifestos** or **manifestoes** *pl.*

man•i•fold *adj.* Having many and varied parts, forms, or types; having an assortment of features; a pipe with several or many openings, as for the escaping of exhaust gas.

ma•nip•u•late *v.* To handle or manage; to control shrewdly and deviously for one's own profit. **manipulation, manipulator** *n.*, **manipulative** *adj.*

man•kind *n.* The human race.

manned *adj.* Operated by a human being.

man•ne•quin *n.* A life-sized model of a human figure, used to fit or display clothes; a woman who models clothes.

man•ner *n.* The way in which something happens or is done; an action or style of speech; one's social conduct and etiquette. **mannered** *adj.*

man•ner•ism *n.* A person's distinctive behavioral trait or traits.

man•ner•ly *adj.* Well-behaved; polite.

man•nish *adj.* Resembling a man; masculine. **mannishness** *n.*

man•or *n.* A landed estate; the house or hall of an estate. **manorial** *adj.*

man•sion *n.* A very large, impressive house.

man•slaugh•ter *n.* The unlawful killing without malice of a person by another.

man•tel also **man•tle** *n.* A shelf over a fireplace; the ornamental brick or stone around a fireplace.

man•til•la *n.* A light scarf worn over the head and shoulders by women in Latin America and Spain.

man•tis *n.* A tropical insect with a long body, large eyes, and swiveling head, which stands with its forelegs folded as if in prayer.

man•tle *n.* A loose-fitting coat which is usually sleeveless; something that covers or conceals; a device consisting of a sheath of threads, used in gas lamps to give off brilliant illumination when heated by a flame.

man•u•al *adj.* Used or operated by the hands. *n.* A small reference book which gives instructions on how to operate or work something. **manually** *adv.*

man•u•fac•ture *v.* To make a product; to invent or produce something. **manufacturer** *n.*

ma•nure *n.* The fertilizer used to fertilize land, obtained from animal dung.

man•u•script *n.* A typed or written material copy of an article, book, or document, which is being prepared for publication.

man•y *adj.* Amounting to a large or indefinite number or amount.

map *n.* A plane surface representation of a region. *v.* To plan anything in detail. **mapmaker** *n.*, **mapper** *n.*

ma•ple *n.* A tall tree having lobed leaves and a fruit of two joined samaras; the wood of this tree, amber in color when finished, used for furniture and flooring.

mar *v.* To scratch or deface; to blemish; to ruin; to spoil.

mar•a•thon *n.* A foot race of slightly more than 26 miles, usually run on the streets of a city; any contest of endurance.

mar•ble *n.* A limestone which is partly crystallized and irregular in color. *pl.* A game played with balls of glass.

march *v.* To walk with measured, regular

steps in a solemn or dignified manner; a musical composition for marching.

mare *n.* The female of the horse and other equine animals.

mar•ga•rine *n.* A butter substitute made from vegetable oils and milk.

mar•gin *n.* The edge or border around the body of written or printed text.

ma•ri•a•chi *n.* A Mexican band; the music performed by a musician playing in a mariachi.

mar•i•gold *n.* Any of a variety of plants having golden yellow flowers.

mar•i•jua•na *n.* Hemp; the dried flower tops and leaves of this plant, capable of producing disorienting or hallucinogenic effects when smoked in cigarettes or ingested.

ma•ri•na *n.* A docking area for boats, furnishing moorings and supplies for small boats.

mar•i•nade *n.* A brine made from vinegar or wine and oil with various herbs and spices for soaking meat, fowl, or fish before cooking.

mar•i•nate *v.* To soak meat in a marinade.

ma•rine *adj.* Of, pertaining to, existing in, or formed by the sea. *n.* A soldier trained for service on land and at sea.

mar•i•tal *adj.* Pertaining to marriage.

mar•i•time *adj.* Located and situated on or near the sea; pertaining to the sea and its navigation and commerce.

mark *n.* A visible impression, trace, dent, or stain; an identifying seal, inscription, or label.

mar•ket *n.* The trade and commerce in a certain service or commodity; a public place for purchasing and selling merchandise; the possible consumers of a particular product. *v.* To sell. **marketability** *n.,* **marketable** *adj.*

mar•ket•place *n.* A place, such as a public square, where ideas, opinions, and works are traded and tested.

mar•ma•lade *n.* A preserve made from the pulp and rinds of fruits.

ma•roon *v.* To put ashore and abandon on a desolate shore. *n.* A dull purplish red.

mar•quis *n.* The title of a nobleman ranking below a duke.

mar•qui•sette *n.* A fabric of cotton, silk, nylon, or a combination of these, used in curtains, clothing, and mosquito nets.

mar•riage *n.* The state of being married; wedlock; the act of marrying or the ceremony entered into by a man and woman so as to live together as husband and wife.

mar•row *n.* The soft, vascular tissue which fills bone cavities; the main part or essence of anything.

mar•ry *v.* To take or join as husband and wife; to unite closely.

marsh *n.* An area of low, wet land; a swamp. **marshy** *adj.*

mar•shal *n.* A military officer of high rank in foreign countries; the person in the U.S. in charge of a police or fire department. *v.* To bring troops together to prepare for a battle.

marsh•mal•low *n.* A soft, white confection made of sugar, corn syrup, starch, and gelatin and coated with powdered sugar.

mar•su•pi•al *n.* An animal, such as a kangaroo, koala, or opossum, which has no placenta, but which in the female has an abdominal pouch with teats to feed and carry the offspring.

mart *n.* A trading market; a center.

mar•tial *adj.* Of, pertaining to, or concerned with war or the military life.

mar•tial arts *pl. n.* Oriental arts of self-defense, such as karate or judo, which are practiced as sports.

mar•tial law *n.* Temporary rule by military forces over the citizens in an area where civil law and order no longer exist.

mar•tin *n.* A bird of the swallow family with a tail that is less forked than that of the common swallow.

mar•ti•ni *n.* A cocktail of gin and dry vermouth, served with an olive or lemon peel.

mar•tyr *n.* A person who would rather die than renounce his religious principles; one making great sacrifices to advance a cause, belief, or principle. **martyr** *v.,*

martyrdom *n.*

mar•vel *n.* Anything causing surprise, wonder, or astonishment.

mar•vel•ous or **mar•vel•lous** *adj.* Causing astonishment and wonder; wondrous; excellent; very good, admirable.

mar•zi•pan *n.* A confection of grated almonds, sugar, and egg whites.

mas•car•a *n.* A cosmetic preparation used for coloring or darkening the eyelashes.

mas•cot *n.* A person, animal, or object thought to bring good luck.

mas•cu•line *adj.* Of or pertaining to the male sex; male; the masculine gender. **masculinity** *n.*

mash *n.* A soft, pulpy mass or mixture used to distill alcohol or spirits. *v.* To crush into a soft, pulpy mass.

mask *n.* A covering used to conceal the face in order to disguise or protect. *v.* To hide or conceal.

mas•o•chism *n.* A condition in which sexual gratification is marked by pleasure from being subjected to physical pain or abuse. **masochist** *n.*

ma•son *n.* A person working with brick or stone.

ma•son•ic *adj.* Pertaining to or like Freemasonry or Freemasons.

masque *n.* An elaborately staged dramatic performance, popular during the 16th and 17th centuries in England; a masquerade.

mas•quer•ade *n.* A costume party in which the guests are masked and dressed in fancy costumes. *v.* To disguise oneself.

mass *n.* A body of matter that does not have definite shape but is relatively large in size; physical volume; the measure of a body's resistance to acceleration.

mas•sa•cre *n.* The indiscriminate and savage killing of human beings in large numbers.

mas•sage *n.* The manual or mechanical manipulation of the skin to improve circulation and to relax muscles.

mas•sive *adj.* Of great intensity, degree, or size.

mast *n.* The upright pole or spar which supports the sails and rigging of a sail boat.

mas•tec•to•my *n.* The surgical removal of a breast.

mas•ter *n.* A person with control or authority over others; one who is exceptionally gifted or skilled in an art, science, or craft; the title given for respect or in address. *v.* To learn a skill, craft, or job; to overcome defeat.

mas•ter•piece *n.* Something having notable excellence; an unusually brilliant achievement considered the greatest achievement of its creator.

mas•ti•cate *v.* To chew. **mastication** *n.*

mas•to•don *n.* A large extinct mammal which resembles an elephant.

mat *n.* A flat piece of material made of fiber, rubber, rushes, or other material and used to cover floors.

mat•a•dor *n.* A bullfighter who kills the bull after completing various maneuvers with a cape.

match *n.* Anything that is similar or identical to another; a short, thin piece of wood, or cardboard with a specially treated tip which ignites as a result of friction. *v.* To equal; to oppose successfully.

mate *n.* A spouse; something matched, joined, or paired with another; in chess, a move which puts the opponent's king in jeopardy. **mate** *v.*

ma•te•ri•al *n.* The substance from which anything is or may be composed or constructed of; anything used in creating, working up, or developing something.

ma•te•ri•al•ism *n.* The doctrine that physical matter is the only reality and that everything, including thought, feeling, will, and mind is explainable in terms of matter; a preference for material objects as opposed to spiritual or intellectual pursuits. materialist *n.*, **materialistic** *adj.*, **materialistically** *adv.*

ma•te•ri•al•ize *v.* To give actual, physical form to something; to assume material or visible appearance; to take form or shape.

ma•te•ri•el *n.* The equipment and supplies of a military force, including guns and ammunition.

ma•ter•nal *adj.* Relating to a mother or motherhood; inherited from one's mother.

ma•ter•ni•ty *n.* The state of being a mother; the qualities of a mother; the department in a hospital for the prenatal and postnatal care of babies and their mothers.

math *n.* Mathematics.

math•e•mat•ics *n.* The study of form, arrangement, quantity, and magnitude of numbers and operational symbols. **mathematical** *adj.*, **mathematician** *n.*

mat•i•nee *n.* An afternoon performance of a play, concert, or movie.

ma•tri•arch *n.* A woman ruler of a family, tribe, or clan. **matriarchy** *n.*

mat•ri•cide *n.* The killing of one's own mother; one who kills one's mother. **matricidal** *adj.*

ma•tric•u•late *v.* To enroll or to be admitted into a college or university. **matriculation** *n.*

mat•ri•mo•ny *n.* The condition of being married; the act, sacrament, or ceremony of marriage. **matrimonial** *adj.*

ma•trix *n.* Something within which something develops, originates, or takes shape; a mold or die. **matrices, matrixes** *pl.*

ma•tron *n.* A married woman or widow of dignity and social position; the woman supervisor in a prison.

mat•ter *n.* Something that makes up the substance of anything; that which is material and physical, occupies space, and is perceived by the senses; something that is sent by mail; something written or printed.

mat•tress *n.* A large cloth case filled with soft material and used on or as a bed.

ma•ture *adj.* Completely developed; at full growth; something, as a bond at a bank, that is due and payable. **maturely** *adv.*, **maturity** *n.*

mat•zo *n.* A large, flat piece of unleavened bread eaten during Passover.

maud•lin *adj.* Overly sentimental; tearfully and overwhelmingly emotional.

maul *n.* A heavy hammer or mallet used to drive wedges, piles, and other materials. *v.* To handle roughly; to abuse.

maun•der *v.* To wander or talk in an incoherent manner.

mau•so•le•um *n.* A large and stately tomb.

mauve *n.* A purplish rose shade; a moderately reddish to gray purple.

mav•er•ick *n.* An unbranded or orphaned calf or colt; a person who is unorthodox in his ideas or attitudes.

maw *n.* The jaws, mouth, or gullet of a hungry or ferocious animal; the stomach.

mawk•ish *adj.* Disgustingly sentimental; sickening or insipid. **mawkishly** *adv.*, **mawkishness** *n.*

max•il•la *n.* The upper jaw or jawbone. **maxillary** *adj.*

max•im *n.* A brief statement of truth, general principle, or rule of conduct.

max•i•mize *v.* To increase as greatly as possible; to intensify to the maximum.

max•i•mum *n.* The greatest possible number, measure, degree, or quantity. **maximum** *adj.*

may *v.* To be permitted or allowed; used to express a wish, purpose, desire, contingency, or result.

may•be *adv.* Perhaps; possibly.

may•on•naise *n.* A dressing for salads, made by beating raw egg yolk, oil, lemon juice, or vinegar and seasonings.

may•or *n.* The chief magistrate of a town, borough, municipality, or city. **mayoral** *adj.*, **mayoralty, mayorship** *n.*

may•pole *n.* A decorated pole hung with streamers around which May Day dancing takes place.

maze *n.* A complicated, intricate network of passages or pathways; a labyrinth; a state of uncertainty or bewilderment.

me *pron.* The objective case of the pronoun I.

mead•ow *n.* A tract of grassland used for grazing or growing hay.

mea•ger or **mea•gre** *adj.* Thin; lean;

deficient in quantity, vigor, or fertility.

meal *n.* The edible seeds of coarsely ground grain; any powdery material; the food served or eaten at one sitting at certain times during the day; the time or occasion of taking such food.

mean *v.* To have in mind as a purpose or intent; to have a specified importance or significance. *adj.* Poor or inferior in appearance or quality. *n.* The medium point.

me·an·der *v.* To wander about without a certain course or a fixed direction.

mean·ing *n.* That which is meant or intended; the aim, end, or purpose; the significance; an interpretation. **meaningful, meaningfulness** *adj.*

mean·while *adv.* At the same time.

mea·sles *n.* A contagious viral disease usually occurring in children, characterized by the eruption of red spots.

mea·sly *adj. Slang* Very small; meager.

meas·ure *n.* The range, dimension, extent, or capacity of anything; in music, the group of beats marked off by regularly recurring primary accents; the notes and rests between two successive bars on a musical staff. *v.* To determine the range, dimension, extent, volume, or capacity of anything. **measurable** *adj.*, **measurably** *adv.*, **measurement** *n.*

meat *n.* The flesh of an animal which is used as food; the core or essential part of something.

me·chan·ic *n.* A person skilled in the making, operation, or repair of machines.

me·chan·i·cal *adj.* Involving or having to do with the construction, operation, or design of tools or machines; produced or operated by a machine.

me·chan·ics *pl. n.* The scientific study and analysis of the action of forces and motion on material bodies.

mech·a·nism *n.* The arrangement or parts of a machine; the technique or process by which something works.

mech·a·nize *v.* To make mechanical; to equip with tanks, trucks, mechanical and other equipment, as in the military.

mechanization *n.*

med·al *n.* A small piece of metal with a commemorative image or inscription presented as an award.

me·dal·lion *n.* A large circular or oval medal used as a decorative element.

med·dle *v.* To interfere or participate in another person's business or affairs. **meddler** *n.*, **meddlesome** *adj.*

med·i·a *pl. n.* The instruments of news communication, as radio, television, and newspapers.

me·di·al *adj.* Pertaining to or situated in the middle; ordinary.

me·di·an *n.* Something that is halfway between two different parts. *adj.* Relating to or constituting the median or a set of numbers.

me·di·an strip *n.* The strip which divides highway traffic lanes going in opposite directions.

me·di·ate *v.* To help settle or reconcile opposing sides in a dispute. **mediation, mediator** *n.*

med·ic *n.* A physician or intern; a medical student; in the armed forces, a corpsman or enlisted person trained to give first aid.

med·i·cal *adj.* Relating to the study or practice of medicine. **medically** *adv.*

med·i·cine *n.* Any agent or substance used in the treatment of disease or in the relief of pain; the science of diagnosing and treating disease; the profession of medicine.

me·di·e·val or **mediae·val** *adj.* Like or characteristic of the Middle Ages.

me·di·o·cre *adj.* Common; fair; undistinguished.

med·i·tate *v.* To be in continuous, contemplative thought; to think about doing something. **meditative** *adj.*, **meditation** *n.*

me·di·um *n.* Something which occupies a middle position between two extremes; the means of communicating information or ideas through publishing, radio, or television.

med·ley *n.* A mixture or confused mass or

come into conjunction or contact with someone or something; to cope or deal with; to handle; to fulfill an obligation of need.

meet·ing *n.* An assembly or gathering of persons; a coming together.

meg·a·byte *n.* Literally, a million bytes. In computers, a measurement of computer and storage disk capacity, or size of a file.

mel·an·cho·li·a *n.* A mental disorder of great depression of spirits and excessive brooding without apparent cause. **melancholic** *adj.*

mel·an·chol·y *adj.* Excessively gloomy or sad.

mel·low *adj.* Sweet and soft; rich and full-flavored; rich and soft in quality, as in sounds or colors.

me·lo·di·ous *adj.* Characterized by a melody; tuneful; pleasant to hear. **melodiously** *adv.*

mel·o·dra·ma *n.* A dramatic presentation which is marked by suspense and romantic sentiment and contains clearly defined forces of good and evil in opposition; sensational and highly emotional language or behavior. **melodramatic** *adj.*

mel·o·dy *n.* An agreeable succession of pleasing sounds. **melodic** *adj.*, **melodically** *adv.*

mel·on *n.* The large fruit of any of various plants of the gourd family, as the watermelon.

mem·oir *n.* Personal records or reminiscences; an autobiography.

mem·o·ra·ble *adj.* Worth remembering or noting. **memorably** *adv.*

me·mo·ri·al *n.* Something that serves to keep in remembrance, as a person or event. *adj.* Perpetuating remembrance. **memorialize** *v.*

mem·o·rize *v.* To commit something to memory. **memorization** *n.*

mem·o·ry *n.* The mental function or capacity of recalling or recognizing something that has been previously learned or experienced.

men *pl.* The plural of *man.*

men·ace *n.* Something or someone who threatens; an annoying person. **menacingly** *adv.*

mend *v.* To fix; to repair; to correct.

men·da·cious *adj.* Prone to lying; deceitful; untrue; false. **mendacity** *n.*

me·ni·al *adj.* Relating to a household servant or household chores requiring little responsibility or skill.

men·o·pause *n.* The time of final menstruation, occurring normally between the ages of 45 and 50. **menopausal** *adj.*

men·stru·a·tion *n.* The process, act, or periodical flow of bloody fluid from the uterus, also called period.

men•u *n.* A list of food or dishes available at a restaurant; in computer science, a list of options displayed on the screen.

me•ow *n.* The cry of a cat.

mer•can•tile *adj.* Of or relating to merchants, trading, or commerce.

mer•ce•nar•y *n.* A person who is concerned only with making money and obtaining material gain; a person paid to serve as a soldier in a foreign country. **mercenary** *adj.*

mer•chan•dise *n.* Commodities or goods that are bought and sold.

mer•chant *n.* A person who operates a retail business for profit.

mer•cu•ry *n.* A silvery, metallic, liquid element used in thermometers and barometers, symbolized by Hg.

mer•cy *n.* Compassionate and kind treatment. **merciful, merciless** *adj.*, **mercilessly** *adv.*

mere *adj.* Absolute; no more than what is stated. **merest** *adj.*, **merely** *adv.*

merge *v.* To unite or bring together as one; in computers, to combine two or more files into one.

mer•ger *n.* The act of combining two or more corporations into one.

me•ringue *n.* A mixture of stiffly beaten egg whites and sugar, used as a topping for cakes and pies or baked into crisp shells.

mer•it *n.* A characteristic act or trait which is worthy of praise. *v.* To earn; to be worthy of.

mer•maid *n.* An imaginary sea creature having the upper body of a woman and the tail of a fish. **merman** *n.*

mer•ry *adj.* Delightful; gay; entertaining; festive; happy; joyous. **merrily** *adv.*, **merriness** *n.*

me•sa *n.* A flat-topped hill or small plateau with steep sides.

mesh *n.* Open spaces in a thread, wire, or cord net; something that entraps or snares; the fitting or coming together of gear teeth for transmitting power. *v.* To coincide; to fit well.

mes•mer•ize *v.* To hypnotize or put into a trance.

mess *n.* A disorderly or confused heap; a jumble; a dish or portion of soft or liquid food; a meal eaten by a group of persons, usually in the military.

mes•sage *n.* Any information, command, or news transmitted from one person to another.

mes•sen•ger *n.* A person who carries a message or does an errand for another person or company.

mess•y *adj.* Untidy; upset; dirty; lacking neatness. **messily** *adv.*, **messiness** *n.*

me•tab•o•lism *n.* The chemical and physical changes in living cells which involve the maintenance of life. **metabolic** *adj.*, **metabolize** *v.*

met•al *n.* One of a category of opaque, fusible, ductile, and typically lustrous elements. **metallic** *adj.*, **metallically** *adv.*

met•al•lur•gy *n.* The technology and science which studies methods or extracting metals from their ores and of preparing them for use. **metallurgical** *adj.*, **metallurgist** *n.*

met•a•mor•pho•sis *n.* The transformation and change in the structure and habits of an animal during normal growth, as the metamorphosis of a tadpole into a frog. **metamorphose** *v.*

met•a•phor *n.* A figure of speech in which the context demands that a word or phrase not be taken literally, as the sun is smiling; a comparison which doesn't use *like* or *as*.

me•te•or *n.* A moving particle in the solar system which appears as a trail or streak in the sky as it comes into contact with the atmosphere of the earth.

me•te•or•ic *adj.* Of or relating to a meteor or meteors; resembling a meteor in speed, brilliance, or brevity.

me•te•or•ite *n.* A stony or metallic mass of a meteor which reaches the earth after partially burning in the atmosphere.

me•te•or•ol•o•gy *n.* The science concerned with the study of weather, weather conditions and weather forecasting. **meteorologic** *adj.*, **meteorologically**

adv., **meteorologist** *n.*

me•ter *n.* The arrangement of words, syl-lables, or stanzas in verse or poetry; a measure equaling 39.37 inches.

meth•ane *n.* A colorless, odorless flam-mable gas used as a fuel; a product of the decomposition of organic matter.

meth•a•nol *n.* A colorless, odorless flam-mable alcohol that is used as an antifreeze, as a fuel, and as a raw material in chemi-cal synthesis.

meth•od *n.* A manner, a process, or the regular way of doing something; the orderly arrangement, development, or classification.

me•tic•u•lous *adj.* Very precise; careful; concerned with small details. **meticu-lously** *adv.*, **meticulousness** *n.*

met•ric *adj.* Of or relating to the metric system. **metrical** *adj.*, **metrication** *n.*

met•ric sys•tem *n.* A decimal system of weights and measures based on the meter as a unit of length and the kilogram as a unit of mass, originated in France around 1790.

met•ro *n.* A subway system for transporta-tion.

met•ro•nome *n.* An instrument designed to mark time by means of a series of clicks at exact intervals.

me•trop•o•lis *n.* A large or capital city of a state, region, or country. **metropolitan** *adj.*

mew *n.* A hideaway; a secret place.

mez•za•nine *n.* A low story between two main stories of a building; the lowest bal-cony in a theatre.

mice *pl.* The plural of *mouse.*

mi•cro•phone *n.* An instrument which converts acoustical waves into electrical signals and feeds them into a recorder, amplifier or broadcasting transmitter. **microphonic** *adj.*

mi•cro•proc•es•sor *n.* In computers, a semiconductor processing unit which is contained on an integrated circuit chip.

mi•cro•scope *n.* An optical instrument consisting of a lens or combination of lenses, used to produce magnified images of very small objects.

mi•cro•scop•ic *adj.* Too small to be seen by the eye alone.

mi•cro•wave *n.* A very short electromag-netic wave.

mid•air *n.* A point in the air just above the ground surface.

mid•day *n.* Noon; the middle of the day.

mid•dle *adj.* Being equally distant from extremes or limits; central. *n.* Anything which occupies a middle position; the waist.

mid•dle age *n.* The period of life from about 40 to 60 years.

mid•dle ear *n.* A small membrane-lined cavity between the tympanic membrane and the inner ear through which sound waves are carried.

mid•night *n.* 12 o'clock a.m.; the middle of the night.

midst *n.* The central or middle part or position; a person positioned among oth-ers in a group.

might *n.* Force, power, or physical strength. *v.* Past tense of *may*; used to indicate a present condition contrary to fact.

might•y *adj.* Showing or having great power.

mi•graine *n.* A condition of severe, recur-ring headaches often accompanied by nausea.

mi•grant *n.* A person who moves from one place to another to find work in the fields.

mi•grate *v.* To move from one place to another or from one climate to another. **migration** *n.*

mild *adj.* Gentle in manner, behavior, or disposition; not severe or extreme. **mild-ly** *adv.*, **mildness** *n.*

mil•dew *n.* A fungal growth which is usu-ally white in color. **mildew** *v.*, **mildewy** *adj.*

mile *n.* A unit of measurement equaling 5,280 feet.

mile•age *n.* The distance traveled or meas-ured in miles; an allowance given for traveling expenses at a set rate per mile; the average distance of miles a vehicle will travel on a gallon of gas.

mile·stone *n.* A stone marker serving as a mile-post; an important point in development or progress.

mil·i·tant *adj.* Engaged in warfare or combat; aggressive. **militancy** *n.*

mil·i·ta·rize *v.* To train or equip for war.

mil·i·tar·y *adj.* Of or related to arms, war, or soldiers. *n.* A nation's armed forces. **militarily** *adv.'*

mi·li·tia *n.* A military service or armed forces called upon in case of an emergency.

milk *n.* A whitish fluid produced by the mammary glands of all mature female mammals as a source of food for their young. *v.* To draw milk from the breast or udder. **milkiness** *n.*, **milky** *adj.*

mill *n.* A building housing machinery for grinding grain into meal or flour; any of various machines which grind, crush, or press; a unit of money which equals 1/1000 of a U.S. dollar. *v.* To grind.

mill·er *n.* A person who operates, works, or owns a grain mill; a moth whose wings are covered with a powdery substance.

mil·li·ner *n.* Someone who designs, sells, or makes women's hats.

mil·lion *n.* A large number equal to 1,000 x 1,000. **million** *adj.*, **millionth** *n.* or *adj.*

mil·lion·aire *n.* A person whose wealth is estimated at $1,000,000 or more.

mime *v.* To act a part or performance without using words. *n.* An actor who portrays a part, emotion, or situation using only gestures and body language.

mim·ic *v.* To imitate another person's behavior or speech.

mince *v.* To cut or chop something into small pieces.

mind *n.* The element of a human being which controls perception, thought, feeling, memory, and imagination. *v.* To obey; to take care of; to bring; to remem-

ber; to object to.

mine *n.* A pit or underground excavation from which metals or coal can be uncovered and removed. **miner** *n.*

mine *pron.* The one that belongs to me.

min·er·al *n.* A solid inorganic substance, such as silver, diamond, or quartz, which is taken from the earth. **mineral** *adj.*

min·gle *v.* To mix or come together.

min·i·a·ture *n.* A copy or model of something that has been greatly reduced in size.

min·i·com·put·er *n.* In computers, a computer designed on a very small scale.

min·i·mum *n.*, *pl.* **-ums** or **-uma** The least, smallest, or lowest amount, degree, number, or position.

min·is·ter *n.* The pastor of a Protestant church; a high officer of state who is in charge of a governmental division.

mink *n.* A semiaquatic animal of the weasel family whose thick, lustrous fur is used for making fur coats.

min·now *n.* A small, fresh-water fish used as bait.

mi·nor *adj.* Not of legal age; lesser in degree, size, or importance.

mi·nor·i·ty *n.* The smaller in number of two groups constituting a whole; a part of the population that differs, as in race, sex, or religion.

min·strel *n.* A medieval traveling musician or poet.

mint *n.* A place where coins are made by a government; any of a variety of aromatic plants used for flavoring; candy flavored by such a plant.

min·u·et *n.* A slow, stately dance.

mi·nus *prep.* Reduced by subtraction.

min·ute *n.* The unit of time which equals 60 seconds.

mi·nute *adj.* Extremely small in size.

mir·a·cle *n.* A supernatural event or happening regarded as an act of God.

mi·rage *n.* An optical illusion in which nonexistent bodies of water with reflections of objects are seen.

mire *n.* Soil or heavy mud.

mir•ror *n.* A surface of glass which reflects light, forming the image of an object.

mirth *n.* Merriment or joyousness expressed by laughter.

mis•ad•ven•ture *n.* An unlucky mishap; a misfortune.

mis•an•thrope *n.* Someone who hates mankind.

mis•ap•pre•hend *n.* To understand something incorrectly; to misunderstand. **misapprehension** *n.*

mis•ap•pro•pri•ate *v.* To embezzle money; to use wrongly for one's own benefit. **misappropriation** *n.*

mis•car•riage *n.* The premature birth of a fetus from the uterus.

mis•cel•la•ne•ous *adj.* Consisting of a mixed variety of parts, elements, or characteristics.

mis•chance *n.* Bad luck or mishap.

mis•chief *n.* Behavior which causes harm, damage, or annoyance.

mis•chie•vous *adj.* Tending to behave in a playfully annoying way.

mis•con•duct *n.* Improper conduct or behavior; bad management.

mis•deed *n.* A wrong or improper act; an evil deed.

mis•de•mean•or *n.* A crime less serious than a felony.

mis•er *n.* A person who hoards money; a person who lives a meager life in order to hoard his money.

mis•er•a•ble *adj.* Very uncomfortable or unhappy; causing misery. **miserableness** *n.* **miserably** *adv.*

mis•er•y *n.* A state of great unhappiness, distress, or pain.

mis•fire *v.* To fail to explode, ignite, or fire. **misfire** *n.*

mis•fit *n.* A person who is not adjusted to his environment; anything which does not fit correctly.

mis•for•tune *n.* Bad luck or fortune.

mis•giv•ing *n.* A feeling of doubt

mis•hap *n.* An unfortunate accident; bad luck.

mis•lead *v.* To lead in a wrong direction; to deliberately deceive. **misleading** *adj.*

mis•no•mer *n.* A wrong or inappropriate name.

mi•sog•a•my *n.* Hatred of marriage.

mi•sog•y•ny *n.* Hatred of women.

mis•place *v.* To mislay; to put in a wrong place.

mis•pro•nounce *v.* To pronounce a word incorrectly.

mis•read *v.* To read or interpret incorrectly.

mis•rep•re•sent *v.* To represent wrongly, misleadingly, or falsely. **misrepresentation** *n.*

miss *v.* To fail to hit, reach, or make contact with something; to omit; to feel the absence or loss of.

mis•sile *n.* An object that is thrown or shot at a target.

mis•sion *n.* An instance or the act of sending; an assignment to be carried out.

mis•sion•ar•y *n.* A person sent to do religious or charitable work, usually in a foreign country.

mis•spell *v.* To spell a word incorrectly. **misspelling** *n.*

mis•take *n.* A wrong statement, action, or decision. **mistaken, mistakable** *adj.*, **mistakably** *adv.*, **mistake** *v.*

mis•treat *v.* To treat badly or wrongly. **mistreatment** *n.*

mite *n.* A very small insect; a small amount of money.

mi•ter *n.* A joint made by cutting two pieces at an angle and then fitting them together.

mit•i•gate *v.* To make or become less severe or painful.

mi•to•sis *n.* A process of cell division in which chromatin divides into chromosomes.

mitt *n.* In baseball, a glove worn to protect the hand while catching; short for mitten.

mix *v.* To blend or combine into one; to come or bring together. **mixable** *adj.*

mix•ture *n.* The state of being mixed; the process or act of mixing; a combination of two or more substances.

mix•up *n.* An instance or state of confusion.

moan *n.* A very low, dull sound indicative of pain or grief.

moat *n.* A deep, wide trench surrounding a castle, usually filled with water.

mob *n.* A large, unruly crowd. *v.* To overcrowd.

mo•bi•lize *v.* To put into motion; to make ready. **mobilization** *n.*

moc•ca•sin *n.* A shoe or slipper made of a soft leather.

mo•cha *n.* An Arabian coffee of superior quality; a flavoring with coffee, often used with chocolate.

mock *v.* To treat with contempt or scorn; to imitate a mannerism or sound closely; to mimic. *adv.* In an insincere manner. *n.* An imitation; a copy. **mockingly** *adv.*

mock•er•y *n.* Insulting or contemptuous action or speech; a subject of laughter or sport; a false appearance.

mode *n.* A way or method of doing something; a particular manner or form; the value or score that occurs most frequently in a set of data.

mod•el *n.* A small representation of an object; a pattern that something will be based on; a design or type; one serving as an example; one who poses for an artist or photographer. **model** *v.*, **modeler** *n.*

mo•dem *n.* In computers, a digital-to-analog converter for converting telephone lines into conveyers of digitized information.

mod•er•ate *adj.* Not excessive; tending toward the mean or average extent or quality; opposed to extreme political views. **moderate** *v.*, **moderation** *n.*

mod•er•a•tor *n.* A person who moderates; a person who presides over a discussion or meeting but takes no sides.

mod•ern *adj.* Typical of the recent past or the present; advanced or up-to-date. **modernity** *n.*, **modernly** *adv.*

mod•ern•ism *n.* A thought, action, or belief characteristic of modern times. **modernistic** *adj.*

mod•est *adj.* Placing a moderate estimate on one's abilities or worth; retiring or reserved; limited in size or amount. **modesty** *n.*

mod•i•cum *n.* A small amount.

mod•i•fy *v.* To alter; to make different in character or form; to change to less extreme; to moderate. **modification** *n.*

mod•u•late *v.* To soften; to temper; to vary the intensity of; to change from one key to another; to vary the tone or intensity of. **modulation, modulator** *n.*, **modulative, modulatory** *adj.*

mod•ule *n.* One of a series of standardized components in a system.

moi•e•ty *n.* A half; any portion; part or share.

moil *v.* To work hard; to drudge. **moil** *n.*

moist *adj.* Slightly wet; damp; saturated with moisture or liquid.

mois•ten *v.* To make or become moist or slightly wet.

mois•ture *n.* Liquid diffused or condensed in a relatively small quantity; dampness. **moisturize** *v.*, **moisturizer** *n.*

mo•lar *n.* A grinding tooth which has a broad surface for grinding food, located in the back of the mouth.

mo•las•ses *n.* A thick, dark syrup produced when sugar is refined.

mold *n.* A superficial, often woolly growth produced on damp or decaying organic matter or on living organisms; a fungus that produces such a growth; crumbling, soft, friable earth suited to plant growth; distinctive nature or character; the frame on or around which an object is constructed; a cavity in which an object is shaped; general shape; form. **moldable** *adj.*

mo•lec•u•lar *adj.* Of, relating to, or caused by molecules.

mol•e•cule *n.* The simplest structural unit into which a substance can be divided and still retain its identity.

mole•hill *n.* A small ridge of earth thrown up by a mole.

mo•lest *v.* To bother or persecute; to accost sexually. **molestation, molester** *n.*

mol·li·fy *v*. To make less angry; to soften; to make less intense or severe. **mollifes-tation** *n*.

mol·lusk or **mol·lusc** *n*. Any of various largely marine invertebrates, including the edible shellfish.

mol·ly·cod·dle *v*. To spoil by pampering; to coddle.

molt *v*. To cast off or shed an external covering, as horns, feathers, or skin, which is periodically replaced by new growth. **molt** *n*.

mol·ten *adj*. Transformed to liquid form by heat.

mo·men·tar·y *adj*. Lasting just a moment; occurring presently or at every moment.

mo·men·tous *adj*. Of great importance or consequence; significant. **momen-tously** *adv*., **momentousness** *n*.

mo·men·tum *n*. A property of a moving body which determines the length of time required to bring it to rest when under the action of a constant force.

mon·arch *n*. A person who reigns over a kingdom or empire; a large orange and black butterfly.

mon·ar·chy *n*. Government by a monarch; sovereign control; a government or nation ruled by a monarch.

mon·ey *n*. Anything which has or is assigned value and is used as a medium of exchange.

mon·goose *n*. A chiefly African or Asian mammal which has the ability to kill venomous snakes. **mongooses** *pl*.

mon·grel *n*. An animal or plant, especially a dog, produced by interbreeding.

mo·ni·tion *n*. A caution or warning, as for an impending danger.

mon·i·tor *n*. A student assigned to assist a teacher; a receiver used to view the picture being picked up by a television camera; the image being generated by a computer.

monk *n*. A man who is a member of a religious order and lives in a monastery.

mon·key *n*. A member of the older primates, excluding man, having a long-tail; a small species as distinguished from the larger apes.

mo·nog·a·my *n*. Marriage or sexual relationship with only one person at a time. **monogamist** *n*., **monogamous** *adj*.

mon·o·logue *n*. A speech by one person which precludes conversation; a series of jokes and stories delivered by a comedian. monologist n.

mo·nop·o·ly *n*. Exclusive ownership or control, as of a service or commodity, by a single group, person, or company; a group, person, or company having a monopoly; exclusive possession; a service or commodity controlled by a single group.

mon·o·tone *n*. The utterance of sounds, syllables, or words in a single tone.

mo·not·o·nous *adj*. Spoken in a monotone; lacking in variety. **monotonous-ly** *adv*., **monotony** *n*.

mon·soon *n*. A periodic wind, especially in the Indian Ocean and southern Asia; the season of the monsoon.

mon·ster *n*. An animal or plant having an abnormal form or structure; an animal, plant, or object having a frightening or deformed shape; one unusually large for its kind. **-ity**, **-ousness** *n*., **-ous** *adj*., **-ously** *adv*.

mon·tage *n*. A composite picture made by combining several separate pictures or parts of several pictures; a rapid succession of images in a motion picture, designed to illustrate an association of ideas.

month *n*. One of the twelve divisions of a calendar year.

month·ly *adj*. Occurring, done, or payable each month. *n*. A publication issued once a month. **monthly** *adv*.

mon·u·ment *n*. An object, such as a statue, built as a memorial to a person or an event; a burial vault; an area set aside for public use because of its aesthetic, historical, or ecological significance.

mon·u·men·tal *adj*. Serving as or similar to a monument; massive; extremely important. **monumentally** *adv*.

mood *n*. A conscious yet temporary state

of mind or emotion; the prevailing spirit; a verb form or set of verb forms inflected to show the understanding of the person speaking regarding the condition expressed.

mood•y *adj.* Subject to moods, especially depression; gloomy.

moon *n.* The earth's only natural satellite; a natural satellite which revolves around a planet.

moon•beam *n.* A ray of moonlight.

moon•light *n.* The light of the moon. *v.* To hold a second job in addition to a regular one. **moonlighter** *n.*

mope *v.* To be uncaring or dejected; to move in a leisurely manner. **moper** *n.*

mor•al *adj.* Of or pertaining to conduct or character from the point of right and wrong; teaching a conception of right behavior. *n.* The lesson to be learned from a story, event, or teaching. *pl.* Standards of right and wrong. **morally** *adv.*

mo•rale *n.* An individual's state of mind with respect to the tasks he or she is expected to perform.

mo•ral•i•ty *n.* The quality of being morally right; moral behavior.

mor•bid *adj.* Of, pertaining to, or affected by disease; suggesting an unhealthy mental state of being; gruesome.

more *adj.* Greater number, size, or degree; additional. *n.* An additional or greater number, degree, or amount. *adv.* To a greater extent or degree; in addition. *pron.* Additional things or persons.

more•o•ver *adv.* Furthermore; besides.

mo•res *pl. n.* The moral customs and traditional customs of a social group.

morgue *n.* A place in which dead bodies are kept until claimed or identified; the reference file at a newspaper or magazine office.

mor•i•bund *adj.* Approaching extinction; at the point of death. **moribundity** *n.*

morn•ing *n.* The early part of the day; the time from midnight to noon.

mor•sel *n.* A small piece or quantity of

food; a tasty dish.

mor•tal *adj.* Having caused or about to cause death; fatal; subject to death; very tedious or prolonged; unrelentingly hostile; of, relating to, or connected with death. *n.* A human being. **mortally** *adv.*

mor•tal•i•ty *n.* The state or condition of being mortal; the death rate; deaths.

mor•tar *n.* A strong vessel in which materials can be crushed or ground with a pestle; a muzzle-loading cannon for firing shells at short ranges and at high angles; a mixed building material, as cement with sand and water, which hardens and is used with masonry or plaster.

mort•gage *n.* A temporary conveyance of property to a creditor as security for the repayment of a debt; a contract or deed defining the terms of a mortgage. *v.* To pledge or transfer by means of a mortgage.

mor•ti•cian *n.* An undertaker.

mor•ti•fy *v.* To destroy the strength or functioning of; to subdue or deaden through pain or self-denial; to subject to severe humiliation; to become gangrenous. **mortification** *n.*

mor•tu•ar•y *n.* A place in which dead bodies are temporarily held until burial or cremation.

mo•sa•ic *n.* A decorative inlaid design of small pieces, as of colored glass or tile, in cement. **mosaic** *adj.*

mos•qui•to *n.* Any of various winged insects of which the females suck the blood of animals or humans.

moss *n.* Delicate, small green plants which often form a dense, mat-like growth. **mossiness** *n.*, **mossy** *adj.*

most *adj.* The majority of. *n.* The greatest amount. *pron.* The largest part or number. *adv.* In or to the highest degree.

most•ly *adv.* For the most part.

mo•tel *n.* A temporary, roadside dwelling for motorists with rooms opening directly onto a parking area.

moth *n.* A usually nocturnal insect of the order Lepidoptera, having antennae that are often feathered, duller in color and literary work.

mo·tile *adj.* Exhibiting or capable of movement.

mo·tion *n.* The act or process of changing position; a purposeful movement of the body or a bodily part; a formal proposal or suggestion that action be taken. **motion** *v.*, **motionless** *adj.*

mo·tion pic·ture *n.* A sequence of filmed pictures that gives the illusion of continuous movement, when projected on a screen.

mo·ti·vate *v.* Causing to act.

mo·tive *n.* Something, as a need or desire, which causes a person to act; a musical motif.

mo·tor *n.* Any of various devices which develop energy or impart motion.

mo·tor·cy·cle *n.* A two-wheeled automotive vehicle. **motorcycle** *v.*, **motorcyclist** *n.*

mot·to *n.* A sentence, phrase, or word expressing purpose, character, or conduct; an appropriate phrase inscribed on something.

mound *n.* A small hill of earth, sand, gravel or debris; a burial place of primitive cultures.

mount *v.* To rise or ascend; to get up on; climb upon; to increase in amount or extent; to organize and equip; to launch and carry out. *n.* A horse or other animal used for riding; a support to which some-

which food is taken in.

move *v.* To set in motion; to change one's place or location; to make a recommendation in a formal manner. **movable, moveable** *adj.*, **moveably** *adv.*

move·ment *n.* The act of moving; a part of a musical composition; a political or ethical organization for change.

mov·er *n.* One that moves; a person employed to help in moving the contents of a home or business.

mov·ie *n.* A motion picture.

mow *v.* To cut down, as with a machine. *n.* The part of the barn where hay or grain is stored. **mower** *n.*

much *adj.* In great amount, quantity, degree, or extent. *adv.* To a great extent.

mud *n.* A mixture of water and earth. **muddily** *adv.*, **muddiness** *n.*, **muddy** *adj.*

mud·dle *v.* To make muddy; to mix up or confuse; to make a mess of; to think or act in a confused way.

muf·fin *n.* A soft, cap-shaped bread that is cooked in a muffin pan.

muf·fle *v.* To wrap up so as to conceal or protect; to deaden the sound of; to suppress.

muf·fler *n.* A scarf worn around the neck; a device which deadens noise, especially as part of the exhaust system of an vehicle.

mug *n.* A large drinking cup; a person's face; a photograph of someone's face. *v.*

mulch *n.* A loose protective covering, as of sawdust, compost, or wood chips spread on the ground to prevent moisture evaporation, to protect roots from freezing, and to retard the growth of weeds.

mule *n.* A hybrid animal that is the offspring of a female horse and a male ass.

mull *v.* To mix or grind thoroughly; to ponder; to think about.

mul·ti·na·tion·al *adj.* Involving or relating to several countries.

mul·ti·ple *adj.* Relating to or consisting of more than one individual, part, or element. *n.* A number into which another number can be divided with no remainders.

mul·ti·ple-choice *adj.* Offering several answers from which the correct one is to be chosen.

mul·ti·pli·ca·tion *n.* The mathematical operation by which a number indicates how many times another number is to be added to itself.

mul·ti·ply *v.* To increase in amount or number; to combine by multiplication.

mum·ble *v.* To speak or utter in a low, confused manner. **mumbler** *n.*

mum·my *n.* A body embalmed or treated for burial in the manner of the ancient Egyptians. **mummies** *pl.*

mur·der *n.* The crime of unlawfully killing a person.

mur·der·ous *adj.* Intending or having the purpose or capability of murder. **murderously** *adv.*

murk *n.* Darkness; gloom. **murkily** *adv.*, **murkiness** *n.*, **murky** *adv.*

mur·mur *n.* A low, indistinct, and often continuous sound; a gentle or soft utterance. **murmur** *v.*

mus·cle *n.* Bodily tissue which consists of long cells that contract when stimulated. **muscular** *adj.*

mush *n.* A thick porridge of cornmeal boiled in water or milk; soft matter. **mushiness** *n.*, **mushy** *adj.*

mush·room *n.* A fungus having an umbrella-shaped cap on a stalk. *v.* To grow or multiply quickly.

mu·sic *n.* Organized tones in sequences and combinations which make up a continuous composition. **musical** *adj.*

mu·si·cian *n.* A composer or performer of music. **musicology** *n.*

musk *n.* A substance with a strong, powerful odor which is secreted by the male musk deer. **muskiness** *n.*, **musky** *adj.*

mus·ket *n.* A heavy, large-caliber shoulder gun with a long barrel. **musketeer** *n.*

musk·mel·on *n.* A sweet melon having a rough rind and juicy, edible flesh.

must *v.* To be forced to; to have to; to be obligated to do something; to be necessary to do something. *n.* A requirement; absolute; something indispensable.

mus·tache or **mous·tache** *n.* The hair growing on the human upper lip.

mus·tard *n.* A condiment or medicinal preparation made from the seeds of the mustard plant.

must·n't *contr.* Must not.

mus·ty *adj.* Moldy or stale in odor or taste.

mute *adj.* Unable to speak. *n.* A person who cannot speak.

mut·ter *v.* To speak or utter in a low voice; to grumble; to complain.

mu·tu·al *adj.* Having the same relationship; received and directed in equal amounts. **mutuality** *n.*

muz·zle *n.* The projecting mouth of certain animals; the open end or mouth of an implement such as the barrel of a gun.

my *adj.* Relating to or of myself or one. *interj.* An expression of surprise, dismay, or pleasure.

myr·i·ad *adj.* Having extremely large, indefinite aspects or elements.

my·self *pron.* The one identical with me; used reflexively; my normal, healthy state or condition.

mys·te·ri·ous *adj.* Relating to or being a mystery; impossible or difficult to comprehend. **mystery** *n.*

mys·tic *adj.* Relating to mystics, mysticism, or mysteries. *n.* A person practicing or believing in mysticism. **mystical** *adj.*, mystically *adv*.

mys·ti·fy *v*. To perplex, to bewilder. **mys-tification** *n*., **mystifyingly** *adv*.

myth *n*. A traditional story dealing with supernatural ancestors; a person or thing having only an unverifiable or imaginary existence. **mythical, mythic** *adj*., **mythically** *adv*.

my·thol·o·gy *n*. A body of myths dealing with gods and heroes. **mythological** *adj*., **mythologist** *n*.

N

N, n The fourteenth letter of the English alphabet.

nab *v*. To seize; to arrest.

na·cho *n*. A tortilla, often small and triangular in shape, topped with cheese or chili sauce and baked.

nag *v*. To bother by scolding or constant complaining. *n*. A worthless horse.

nai·ad *n*. A nymph presiding over and living in springs, brooks, and fountains.

nail *n*. A thin pointed piece of metal for hammering into wood and other materials to hold pieces together.

nail·brush *n*. A small brush with trim bristles used to clean the hands and nails.

nail file *n*. A small instrument with a rough surface, used to shape the fingernails.

na·ive *adj*. Simple and trusting; not sophisticated. **naiveness, naivete** *n*.

na·ked *adj*. Without clothes on the body; nude. **nakedness** *n*.

name *n*. A title or word by which something or someone is known. *v*. To give a name. **nameable** *adj*.

name·less *adj*. Having no name; anonymous. **namelessly** *adv*.

name·plate *n*. A plaque or plate bearing one's name.

name·sake *n*. A person named after someone with the same name.

nan·ny *n*. A child's nurse; one who cares for small children.

nap *n*. A short rest or sleep, often during the day. *v*. The surface of a piece of leather or fabric.

na·palm *n*. A mixture of aluminum soaps used in jelling gasoline for use in bombs or by flame throwers.

nape *n*. The back of the neck.

nap·kin *n*. A cloth or soft paper, used at the table for wiping the lips and fingers.

na·po·le·on *n*. A pastry of several flaky layers filled with custard cream.

nar·cis·sus *n*. A widely grown type of bulbous plant which includes the jonquil, narcissus, and daffodil.

nar·co·sis *n*. A deep drug induced state of stupor or unconsciousness.

nar·cot·ic *n*. A drug which dulls the senses, relieves pain, and induces a deep sleep; if abused, it can become habit-forming and cause convulsions or comas.

nar·rate *v*. To tell a story or give a description in detail. **narration** *n*., **narrator** *v*.

nar·row *adj*. Slender or small in width; of less than standard width. **narrowly** *adj*.

nar·row-mind·ed *adj*. Lacking sympathy or tolerance. **narrow-mindedness** *n*.

na·sal *adj*. Of or pertaining to the nose.

nas·ty *adj*. Dirty, filthy, or indecent; unpleasant. **nastily** *adv*., **nastiness** *n*.

na·tal *adj*. Pertaining to or associated with birth.

na·tion *n*. A group of people made up of one or more nationalities under one government.

na·tion·al·ism *n*. Devotion to or concern for one's nation.

na·tion·al·i·ty *n*. The fact or condition of belonging to a nation.

na·tion·al·ize *v*. To place a nation's resources and industries under the control of the state.

na·tive *n*. A person born in a country or place.

na·tiv·i·ty *n*. Birth, circumstances, or conditions.

nat·ty *adj*. Tidy and trimly neat. **nattily** *adj*.

nat·u·ral *adj*. Produced or existing by

nature; a note that is not sharp or flat. **naturalness** *n.*, **naturally** *adv.*

na•ture *n.* The universe and its phenomena; one's own character or temperament.

naught *n.* Nothing; the number 0; zero.

naugh•ty *adj.* Unruly; ill-behaved.

nau•se•a *n.* An upset stomach with a feeling that one needs to vomit. **nauseous** *adj.*, **nauseate** *v.*, **nauseatingly** *adv.*

nau•ti•cal *adj.* Pertaining to ships or seamanship.

na•val *adj.* Of or relating to ships.

na•vel *n.* A small mark on the abdomen where the umbilical cord was attached.

nav•i•ga•ble *adj.* Sufficiently deep and wide enough to allow ships to pass. **navigability** *n.*, **navigably** *adv.*

nav•i•gate *v.* To plan the course of a ship or aircraft; to steer a course. **navigator** *n.*, **navigational** *adj.*

na•vy *n.* One of a nation's organizations for defense; a nation's fleet of ships; a very dark blue.

neap tide *n.* A tide in the minimum range which occurs during the first and third quarter of the moon.

near *adv.* At, to, or within a short time or distance. **nearness** *n.*

near•by *adj.* or *adv.* Close by; near at hand; adjacent.

near•sight•ed *adj.* Able to see clearly at short distances only. **nearsightedness** *n.*

neat *adj.* Tidy and clean; free from disorder and dirt. **neatly** *adv.*, **neatness** *n.*

neat•en *v.* To make neat; to set in order.

nec•es•sar•y *adj.* Unavoidable; required; essential; needed. **necessarily** *adv.*

ne•ces•si•ty *n.* The condition of being necessary; the condition making a particular course of action necessary.

neck *n.* The part of the body which connects the head and trunk; a narrow part or projection, as of land; a stringed instrument, or bottle.

neck•tie *n.* A narrow strip of material worn around the neck and tied.

nec•tar *n.* A sweet fluid in various flowers,

gathered by bees to help make honey. **nectarous** *adj.*

need *n.* The lack of something desirable, useful, or necessary.

need•ful *adj.* Necessary.

nee•dle *n.* A slender, pointed steel implement which contains an eye through which thread is passed. *v.* To tease. **needlelike** *adj.*

need•less *adj.* Unnecessary; not needed. **needless** *adv.*, **needlessness** *n.*

need•n't *contr.* Need not.

neg•a•tive *adj.* Expressing denial or disapproval; not positive. *n.* In photography, a negative photo. **negativity** *n.*

ne•glect *v.* To ignore; to pay no attention to; to fail to perform. **neglectful** *adj.*

neg•li•gent *adj.* To neglect what needs to be done.

ne•go•ti•ate *v.* To confer with another person to reach an agreement. **negotiation, negotiator** *n.*

neigh•bor *n.* One who lives near another. **neighboring** *adj.*, **neighbor** *v.*

neigh•bor•hood *n.* A section or small region that possesses a specific quality.

neigh•bor•ly *adj.* Characteristic of good neighbors; friendly. **neighborliness** *n.*

nei•ther *adj.* Not one or the other. *pron.* Not the one or the other.

ne•on *n.* An inert gaseous element used in lighting fixtures, symbolized by *Ne*; the light from such fixtures.

ne•o•na•tol•o•gy *n.* The medical study of the first 60 days of a baby's life.

neph•ew *n.* The son of one's sister, brother, sister-in-law, or brother-in-law.

nerve *n.* The bundles of fibers which convey sensation and originate motion through the body.

nerve•less *adj.* Lacking courage or strength. **nervelessness** *n.*

nerv•ous *adj.* Affecting the nerves or the nervous system; agitated; worried. **nervously** *adv.*, **nervousness** *n.*

nerv•ous sys•tem *n.* The body system that coordinates, regulates, and controls the various internal functions and

ness in the exchange of electronic information.

net·work n. A system of interlacing tracks, channels, or lines; an interconnected system.

neu·ral adj. Relating to a nerve or the nervous system. **neurally** adv.

neu·ral·gia n. Pain that occurs along the course of a nerve.

neu·ro·sis n. Any one of various functional disorders of the mind or emotions having no physical cause.

neu·ter adj. Neither feminine nor masculine.

neu·tral adj. Not supporting either side of a debate, quarrel, or party; a color which does not contain a decided hue; in chemistry, neither alkaline nor acid. **neutrality** n.

neu·tral·ize v. To make or declare neutral.

nev·er adv. Not over; absolutely not.

nev·er·the·less adv. Nonetheless; however; in spite of this.

new adj. Not used before; unaccustomed; unfamiliar. **newness** n.

news pl. n. Current information and happenings.

news·cast n. A television or radio news broadcast.

news·group n. In computers, a group of users with a similar interest communicating and sharing information.

news·pa·per n. A weekly or daily publication which contains recent information.

news·print n. An inexpensive machine-

U.S. coin worth five cents.

nick·el·o·de·on n. A movie theatre which charged five cents for admission; a coin-operated juke box.

nick·name n. The familiar form of a proper name, expressed in a shortened form.

nic·o·tine or **nic·o·tin** n. A poisonous alkaloid found in tobacco and used in insecticides and medicine.

niece n. The daughter of one's sister, brother, sister-in-law, or brother-in-law.

nigh adv. Near in relationship, time, or space.

night n. The time between dusk and dawn or the hours of darkness.

night·cap n. An alcoholic drink usually taken before retiring for the night.

night·in·gale n. A songbird with brownish plumage, noted for the sweet, nocturnal song of the male.

night·mare n. A frightening and horrible dream.

nim·ble adj. Marked by a quick, light movement; quick-witted. **nimbleness** n., **nimbly** adv.

nine n. The cardinal number that is equal to 8 + 1.

nip v. To pinch, bite, or grab something. n. To pinch, bite, or grab; a sharp, stinging feeling caused by cold temperatures. **nipper** n.

nip·ple n. The small projection of a mammary gland through which milk passes; an artificial teat usually made from a type of element which is essential to life.

no *adv.* Used to express rejection, disagreement, or denial; not so; not at all.

no•ble *adj.* Morally good; superior in character or nature. *n.* A person of rank or noble birth. **noblemen, nobleness** *n.,* **nobly** *adv.*

no•bod•y *pron.* Not anybody; no person.

noc•tur•nal *adj.* Pertaining to or occurring during the night.

nod *n.* A quick downward motion of the head as one falls off to sleep; a downward motion of the head indicating acceptance or approval.

node *n.* A swollen or thickened enlargement.

no•el *n.* A Christmas carol.

noise *n.* A sound which is disagreeable or loud; in computers, unwanted data in an electronic signal. **noisy** *adj.,* **noisily** *adv.*

no•mad *n.* A member of a group of people who wander from place to place. **nomadic** *adj.,* **nomadism** *n.*

no•men•cla•ture *n.* The set of names used to describe the elements of art, science, and other fields.

nom•i•nal *adj.* Of or relating to something that is in name or form only.

nom•i•nate *v.* To select a candidate for an elective office. **-tion, -tor** *n.*

non•cha•lant *adj.* Giving an effect of casual unconcern. **nonchalance** *n.,* **nonchalantly** *adv.*

non•con•form•ist *n.* A person who does not feel compelled to follow or accept community traditions.

none *pron.* Not any; not one.

non•sense *n.* Something that seems senseless or foolish. **nonsensical** *adj.*

non seq•ui•tur *n.* An inference that does not follow as the logical result of what has preceded it.

noo•dle *n.* A flat strip of dried dough made with eggs and flour.

nook *n.* A corner, recess, or secluded place.

noon *n.* The middle of the day; 12:00 o'clock.

noose *n.* A loop of rope secured by a slip-knot, allowing it to decrease in size as the rope is pulled.

nor *conj.* Not either; not.

norm *n.* A rule, model, or pattern typical for a particular group.

nor•mal *adj.* Ordinary, average, usual; having average intelligence. **normalcy, normality** *n.,* **normally** *adv.*

north *n.* The direction to a person's left while facing east.

nose *n.* The facial feature containing the nostrils; the sense of smell.

nose•dive *n.* A sudden plunge as made by an aircraft.

nos•tal•gia *n.* A yearning to return to the past. **nostalgic** *adj.*

nos•tril *n.* The external openings of the nose.

nos•y or **nos•ey** *adj.* Prying; inquisitive.

not *adv.* In no manner; used to express refusal or denial.

no•ta•ble *adj.* Remarkable, distinguished. **notably** *adv.*

no•ta•rize *v.* To acknowledge and certify as a notary public.

no•ta•ry pub•lic *n.* A person who is legally authorized as a public officer to witness and certify documents.

no•ta•tion *n.* A process or system of figures or symbols used in specialized fields to represent quantities, numbers, or values. **notational** *adj.*

notch *n.* A v-shaped indentation or cut.

note *n.* A record or message in short form; a musical tone or written character. **note** *v.*

not•ed *adj.* Famous; well-known.

noth•ing *n.* Not anything; no part or portion.

no•tice *n.* An announcement; a notification. **noticeable** *adj.,* **noticeably** *adv.*

no•ti•fy *v.* To give notice of; to announce. **notifier, notification** *n.*

no•tion *n.* An opinion; a general concept; an idea.

no•to•ri•ous *adj.* Having a widely known and usually bad reputation.

not•with•stand•ing *prep.* In spite of.

adv. Nevertheless; anyway. *conj.* Although.

noun *n.* A word which names a person, place, or thing.

nour·ish *v.* To furnish with the nutriment and other substances needed for growth and life; to support. **nourishing** *adj.*, **nourishment** *n.*

nou·veau riche *n.* A person who has recently become rich.

no·va *n.* A star that flares up and fades away after a few years or months.

nov·el *n.* An inventive narrative dealing with human experiences; a book. **novel·ist** *n.*

nov·el·ty *n.* Something unusual or new.

nov·ice *n.* A person who is new and unfamiliar with an activity or business.

now *adv.* At the present time; immediately.

no·where *adv.* Not in or at any place.

nox·ious *adj.* Harmful; obnoxious; corrupt.

noz·zle *n.* A projecting spout or vent.

nu·ance *n.* A slight variation.

nub *n.* A knob; a small piece or lump.

nu·cle·ar *adj.* Pertaining to and resembling a nucleus; relating to atomic energy.

nu·cle·us *n.* A central element around which other elements are grouped. **nuclei** *pl.*

nude *adj.* Unclothed; naked. **nudity, nudist** *n.*

nudge *v.* To poke or push gently.

nug·get *n.* A lump, as of precious metal.

nui·sance *n.* A source of annoyance.

null *adj.* Invalid; having no value or consequence. **nullification, nullity** *n.*

nul·li·fy *v.* To counteract.

numb *adj.* Lacking physical sensation. **numb** *v.*, **numbness** *n.*

num·ber *n.* A word or symbol which is used in counting or which indicates how many or which one in a series.

num·ber·less *adj.* Too many to be counted.

nu·mer·al *n.* A symbol, figure, letter, word, or a group of these which represents a number.

nu·mer·a·tor *n.* The term in mathematics indicating how many parts are to be taken; the number in a fraction which appears above the line.

nun *n.* A woman who has joined a religious group and has taken vows to give up worldly goods and never to marry.

nup·tial *adj.* Of or pertaining to a wedding.

nup·tials *pl. n.* A wedding.

nurse *n.* A person who is specially trained to care for disabled or sick persons. *v.* To feed a baby from a mother's breast.

nurs·er·y *n.* A room reserved for the special use of infants or small children; a business or place where trees, shrubs, and flowers are raised.

nur·ture *n.* The upbringing, care, or training of a child. **nurture** *v.*, **nurturer** *n.*

O, o The fifteenth letter of the English alphabet.

oaf *n.* A stupid or clumsy person. **oafish** *adj.*, **oafishly** *adv.*

oar *n.* A long pole, flat at one end, used in rowing a boat.

oars·man *n.* A person who rows in a racing crew.

o·a·sis *n.* A fertile section in the desert which contains water. **oases** *pl.*

oat *n.* A cultivated cereal grass whose grain or seed is used as food.

oath *n.* A solemn promise in the name of God or on a Bible that a person will speak only the truth.

oat·meal *n.* A cooked cereal made from rolled oats.

ob·du·rate *adj.* Stubborn; hard-hearted; not giving in.

o·be·di·ent *adj.* Obeying or willing to do what one is told. **obedience** *n.*

o·bese *adj.* Very fat. **obesity** *n.*

o·bey *v.* To carry out instructions; to be guided or controlled; to follow directions.

o·bit·u·ar·y *n.* A published announcement

that a person has died, often containing a short biography. **obituary** *adj.*

ob•ject *v.* To voice disapproval; to protest. *n.* Something visible which can be touched; a word in a sentence which explains who or what is acted upon.

ob•jec•tion *n.* A feeling of opposition or disagreement; the reason for a disagreement.

ob•jec•tive *adj.* Pertaining to or dealing with material objects rather than mental concepts. *n.* Something that one works toward, a goal; a purpose. **objectivity** *n.*

ob•la•tion *n.* A religious offering or the act of sacrifice; that which is offered.

ob•li•ga•tion *n.* A promise or feeling of duty; something one must do because one's conscience or the law demands it; a debt which must be repaid.

o•blige *v.* To constrain; to put in one's debt by a service or favor; to do a favor. **obliger** *n.*, **obligingly** *adv.*

ob•li•gee *n.* The person to whom another is obligated.

o•blique *adj.* Inclined; not level or straight up and down; slanting; indirect. **obliqueness**, **obliquity** *n.*

o•blit•er•ate *v.* To blot out or eliminate completely; to wipe out.

ob•liv•i•on *n.* The condition of being utterly forgotten; the act of forgetting.

ob•liv•i•ous *adj.* Not aware or conscious of what is happening; unmindful. **obliviously** *adv.*

ob•long *adj.* Rectangular; longer in one direction than the other; normally, the horizontal dimension; the greater in length. **oblong** *n.*

ob•lo•quy *n.* Abusive language; a strongly condemnatory utterance.

ob•nox•ious *adj.* Very unpleasant; repugnant. **obnoxiousness** *n.*

o•boe *n.* A double-reed, tube-shaped woodwind instrument. **oboist** *n.*

ob•scene *adj.* Indecent; disgusting. **obscenity** *n.*

ob•scure *adj.* Remote; not clear; faint. *v.* To make dim; to conceal by covering.

obscurity, obscureness *n.*

ob•ser•vant *adj.* Paying strict attention to something.

ob•ser•va•tion *n.* The act of observing something; that which is observed; a judgment or opinion. **observational** *adj.*, *adv.*

ob•ser•va•to•ry *n.* A building or station furnished with instruments for studying the natural phenomenon; a high tower affording a panoramic view.

ob•serve *v.* To pay attention; to watch. **observable**, **observably** *adv.*, **observer** *n.*

ob•sess *v.* To preoccupy the mind with an idea or emotion; to be abnormally preoccupied. **obsession** *n.*

ob•so•lete *adj.* No longer in use; out-of-date. **obsolescence** *n.*, **obsolescent** *adj.*

ob•sta•cle *n.* An obstruction; anything which opposes or stands in the way.

ob•stet•rics *pl. n.* The branch of medicine which deals with pregnancy and childbirth. **obstetric** *adj.*

ob•sti•nate *adj.* Stubbornly set to an opinion or course of action; difficult to control or manage; hardheaded. **obstinacy** *n.*, **obstinately** *adv.*

ob•struct *v.* To block, hinder or impede. **obstructor**, **obstruction** *n.*

ob•tain *v.* To acquire or gain possession of. **obtainable** *adj.*, **obtainer** *n.*

ob•tuse *adj.* Lacking acuteness of feeling; insensitive; obscure; not distinct or clear to the senses, as pain or sound; rounded or blunt at the end, as a petal or leaf.

ob•vert *v.* To turn in order to present a different view or surface.

ob•vi•ate *v.* To counter or prevent by effective measures; to provide for.

ob•vi•ous *adj.* Easily seen, discovered, or understood. **obviously** *adv.*

oc•ca•sion *n.* The time an event occurs; the event itself; a celebration.

oc•ca•sion•al *adj.* Appearing or occurring irregularly or now and then; intended, made, or suitable for a certain occasion;

rom a position or place; no longer
d or on. *adj.* Canceled. *prep.*
om.

v. To make angry; to arouse
ent; to break a law. **offender** *n.*

n. A violation of a duty, rule, or a
v; the act of causing displeasure;
f assaulting or attacking.

To present for acceptance or rejec-
present as an act of worship; to
ailable; to present in order to sat-
quirement.

n. The act of one who offers; a
tion, as money, given to the sup-
church.

adv. or *adj.* Without preparation
:dition.

A place where business or pro-
duties are conducted; an impor-
duty, or position.

n. A person who holds a title,
or office; a policeman.

adj. Something derived from
authority. *n.* One who holds a
or office; a person who referees a
ch as football, basketball, or soc-
cialism *n.*, **officially** *adv.*

te *v.* To carry out the duties and
s of a position or office.

g n. The descendants of a person,
animal.

v. Frequently; many times.

Used to express surprise, fear, or

ny of various substances, usually
nich can be burned or easily melt-
ricant. *v.* To lubricate.

n. A cloth treated with oil which
e becomes waterproof.

a. An area rich in petroleum; an

area which has been made ready for oil production.

oil slick *n.* A layer of oil floating on water.

oint•ment *n.* An oily substance used on the skin as an aid to healing or to soften the skin.

old *adj.* Having lived or existed for a long time; of a certain age. *n.* Former times.

old•en *adj.* Of or relating to times long past; ancient.

old-fash•ioned *adj.* Pertaining to or characteristic of former times or old customs; not modern or up-to-date.

o•li•gar•chy *n.* A government controlled by a small group for corrupt and selfish purposes; the group exercising such control.

ol•ive *n.* A small oval fruit from an evergreen tree with leathery leaves and yellow flowers, valuable as a source of oil.

om•buds•man *n.* A government official appointed to report and receive grievances against the government; any negotiator between two unequal layers of organization.

o•men *n.* A phenomenon thought of as a sign of something to come, whether good or bad.

om•i•nous *adj.* Foreshadowed by an omen or by a presentiment of evil; threatening.

o•mit *v.* To neglect; to leave out; to overlook.

om•ni•bus *n.* A public vehicle designed to carry a large number of people; a bus. *adj.* Covering a complete collection of objects or cases.

om•nip•o•tent *adj.* Having unlimited or infinite power or authority.

on *prep.* Positioned upon; indicating proximity; indicating direction toward; with respect to. *adv.* In a position of covering; forward.

once *adv.* A single time; at any one time. *conj.* As soon as.

one *adj.* Single; undivided. *n.* A single person; a unit; the first cardinal number (1).

one•self *pron.* One's own self.

on•line or **on-line** *adj.* or *adv.* In computers, connected with a network of other users and therefore capable of contact and exchange of electronic information.

on•ly *adj.* Sole; for one purpose alone. *adv.* Without anyone or anything else. *conj.* Except; but.

on•o•mat•o•poe•ia *n.* The use of a word, as buzz or hiss, which vocally imitates the sound it denotes.

on•shore *adj.* Moving or coming near or onto the shore.

on•to *prep.* To a position or place; aware of.

on•ward *adv.* Moving forward in time or space. **onwards** *adj.*

ooze *n.* A soft deposit of slimy mud on the bottom of a body of water; muddy or marshy ground; a bog. *v.* To flow or leak slowly; to disappear little by little.

o•paque *adj.* Not transparent; dull; obscure. **opacity**, **opaqueness** *n.*

o•pen *adj.* Having no barrier; not covered, sealed, locked, or fastened. *n.* A contest for both amateurs and professionals. *v.* To begin. **openness** *n.*, **openly** *adv.*

op•er•a *n.* A drama having music as a dominant factor, an orchestral accompaniment, acting, and scenery.

op•er•ate *v.* To function, act, or work effectively; to perform an operation, as surgery. **operative** *adj.*

op•er•a•tion *n.* The system or method of operating; a series of acts to effect a certain purpose; a process; a procedure performed on the human body with surgical instruments to restore health.

o•pin•ion *n.* A judgment held with confidence; a conclusion held without positive knowledge.

o•pi•um *n.* A bitter, highly addictive drug; a narcotic.

op•po•nent *n.* An adversary; one who opposes another.

op•por•tu•ni•ty *n.* A favorable position; a chance for advancement.

op•pose *v.* To be in direct contention with; to resist; to be against. **opposable** *adj.*, **opposition** *n.*

op•po•site *adj.* Situated or placed on

opposing sides. **oppositeness** *n.*

op•press *v.* To worry or trouble the mind; to weigh down; to burden as if to enslave. **oppression, oppressor** *n.*

op•tic *adj.* Pertaining or referring to sight or the eye.

op•ti•mism *n.* A doctrine which emphasizes that everything is for the best.

op•ti•mum *n.* The degree or condition producing the most favorable result. *adj.* Conducive to the best result.

op•tion *n.* The act of choosing or the power of choice; a choice. **optionally** *adv.*

op•u•lence *n.* Wealth in abundance; affluence; visible excess, especially indicative of rich taste.

or *conj.* A word used to connect the second of two choices or possibilities, indicating uncertainty.

or•a•cle *n.* A seat of worship where ancient Romans and Greeks consulted the gods for answers; a person of unquestioned wisdom.

o•ral *adj.* Spoken or uttered through the mouth; taken or administered through the mouth. **orally** *adv.*

or•ange *n.* A citrus fruit round and orange in color. *adj.* Yellowish red.

or•bit *n.* The path of a celestial body or a man-made object. *v.* To revolve or move in an orbit; to circle. **orbital** *adj.*

or•chard *n.* Land devoted to the growing of fruit trees.

or•ches•tra *n.* A group of musicians performing together on various instruments. **orchestral** *adj.*

or•dain *v.* To appoint as a minister, priest, or rabbi by a special ceremony; to decree.

or•deal *n.* A painful or severe test of character or endurance.

or•der *n.* A condition where there is a logical arrangement or disposition of things; sequence or succession; method; an instruction for a person to follow; a request for certain objects. *v.* To command; to demand.

or•di•nar•y *adj.* Normal; having no exceptional quality; common; average; plain.

ore *n.* A natural underground substance, as a mineral or rock, from which valuable matter is extracted.

or•gan *n.* A musical instrument of pipes, reeds, and keyboards which produces sound by means of compressed air; a part of an animal, human, or plant that performs a definite function, as the heart or kidney.

or•gan•ic *adj.* Pertaining to the organs of an animal or plant; of or relating to the process of growing plants with natural fertilizers with no chemical additives. **organically** *adv.*

or•gan•i•za•tion *n.* The state of being organized or the act of organizing; a group of people united for a particular purpose. **organizational** *adj.*, **organize** *v.*

or•i•gin *n.* The cause or beginning of something; the source; a beginning place.

o•rig•i•nal *adj.* Belonging to the first or beginning. *n.* A new idea produced by one's own imagination; the first of a kind. **originality** *n.*, **originally** *adv.*

or•na•ment *n.* A decoration. *v.* To adorn or beautify. **ornamental** *adj.*, **ornamentally** *adv.*, **ornamentation** *n.*

or•nate *adj.* Excessively ornamental; elaborate; showy, as a style of writing.

or•phan *n.* A child whose parents are deceased. **orphan** *v.*, **orphanage** *n.*

oth•er *adj.* Additional; alternate; different from what is implied or specified. *pron.* A different person or thing.

oth•er•wise *adv.* Under different conditions or circumstances.

ouch *interj.* An exclamation to express sudden pain.

ought *v.* Used to show or express a moral duty or obligation; to be advisable or correct.

ounce *n.* A unit of weight which equals 1/16 of a pound.

our *adj.* Of or relating to us; ourselves. *pron.* The possessive case of the pronoun *we.*

oust *v.* To eject; to remove with force.

out *adv.* Away from the center or inside.

adj. Away. *n.* A means of escape. *prep.* Through; forward from.

out•cast *n.* A person who is excluded; a homeless person.

out•come *n.* A consequence or result.

out•dat•ed *adj.* Old-fashioned; obsolete.

out•do *v.* To excel in achievement.

out•fit *n.* The equipment or tools required for a specialized purpose; the clothes a person is dressed in. *v.* To supply.

out•law *n.* A person who habitually defies or breaks the law; a criminal. *v.* To ban; prohibit; to deprive of legal protection.

out•let *n.* An exit.

out•line *n.* A rough draft showing the main features of something. **outline** *v.*

out•look *n.* A person's point of view; an area offering a view of something.

out•num•ber *v.* To go over or exceed in number.

out•post *n.* Troops stationed at a distance away from the main group as a guard against attack; a frontier or outlying settlement.

out•put *n.* Production or yield during a given time.

out•rage *n.* An extremely violent act of violence or cruelty; the violent emotion such an act engenders. **outrageous** *adj.*, **outrage** *v.*

out•side *n.* The area beyond the boundary lines or surface; extreme.

out•spo•ken *adj.* Spoken without reserve; candid. **outspokenly** *adv.*

out•stand•ing *adj.* Excellent; prominent; unsettled, as a bill owed; projecting.

out•ward *adj.* Pertaining to the outside or exterior; superficial. **outwards** *adv.*

out•wit *v.* To trick, baffle, or outsmart.

o•val *adj.* Having the shape of an egg; an ellipse.

o•va•ry *n.* One of the pair of female reproductive glands.

ov•en *n.* An enclosed chamber used for baking, drying, or heating.

o•ver *prep.* Above; across; upon. *adv.* Covering completely; thoroughly; again; repetition. *adj.* Higher; upper. *prefix* Excessive, beyond normal boundaries.

o•ver•act *v.* To act in an exaggerated way.

o•ver•all *adj.* Including or covering everything; from one side or end to another; generally. *pl.* Pants with a bib and shoulder straps.

o•ver•board *adv.* Over the side of a boat or ship into the water.

o•ver•cast *adj.* Gloomy; obscured; clouds covering more than nine tenths of the sky.

o•ver•coat *n.* A coat worn over a suit for extra warmth.

o•ver•come *v.* To prevail; to conquer or defeat. **overcomer** *n.*

o•ver•do *v.* To do anything excessively.

o•ver•dose *v.* To take an excessive dose of medication, especially narcotics.

o•ver•due *adj.* Past the time of return or payment.

o•ver•haul *v.* To make all needed repairs; to catch up with; to overtake.

o•ver•look *v.* To disregard or fail to notice something purposely; to ignore.

o•ver•rule *v.* To put aside by virtue of higher authority.

o•ver•seas *adv.* Abroad; across the seas. **overseas** *adj.*

o•ver•size or **o•ver•sized** *adj.* Larger than the average size of something.

o•void *adj.* Having the shape of an egg.

o•vu•late *n.* To discharge or produce eggs from an ovary.

o•vum *n.* The female reproductive cell.

owe *v.* To be in debt for a certain amount; to have a moral obligation.

owl *n.* A predatory nocturnal bird, having large eyes, a short hooked bill, and long powerful claws. **owlish** *adj.*

own *adj.* Belonging to oneself. *v.* To possess; to confess; to admit. **owner** *n.*

ox *n.* A bovine animal used domestically in much the same way as a horse; an adult castrated bull. **oxen** *pl.*

ox•ide *n.* A compound of oxygen and another element.

ox•y•gen *n.* A colorless, odorless, tasteless gaseous element essential to life, symbolized by O.

pace *n.* A person's step or length of a step; stride; the gait of a horse in which the legs on the same side are moved at the same time. **pace** *v.*, **pacer** *n.*

pace•mak•er *n.* The person who sets the pace for another in a race; a surgically implanted electronic instrument used to stabilize or stimulate the heartbeat.

pac•er *n.* One that sets a particular speed.

pac•i•fy *v.* To quiet or soothe anger or distress; to calm. **pacification** *n.*

pack *n.* A bundle; a group of things tied or wrapped up; a full set of associated or like things, such as a pack of cards; a group of wolves or wild dogs that hunt together. *v.* To put things together in a trunk, box, or suitcase; to put away for storage.

pack•age *n.* Something tied up, wrapped or bound together.

pack an•i•mal *n.* An animal used to carry heavy packs.

pact *n.* An agreement between nations,

pail *n.* A cylindrical container usually having a handle; a bucket.

pain *n.* The unpleasant feeling resulting from injury or disease; any distress or suffering of the mind; sorrow. *v.* To cause or experience pain. **painful**, **painless** *adj.*

paint *n.* A mixture of colors or pigments spread on a surface as protection or as a decorative coating. *v.* To apply paint to a surface; to express oneself creatively on canvas. **painter**, **painting** *n.*

pair *n.* Two things similar and used together; something made of two parts used together; two persons or animals which live or work together.

pa•ja•mas *pl. n.* A garment for sleeping, consisting of a jacket and pants.

pal•ace *n.* The residence of a sovereign, as of a king; a mansion. **palatial** *adj.*

pal•at•a•ble *adj.* Pleasant to the taste; agreeable to one's feelings or mind.

pale *n.* The pointed stake of a fence; a

sparkle. **pallidly** *adv.*, **pallidness** *n.*

pal·lor *n.* Lacking color; paleness.

palm *n.* The inner area of the hand between the fingers and the wrist; any of a large group of tropical evergreen trees, having an unbranched trunk with a top or crown of fan-like leaves. *v.* To hide something small in or about the hand.

pal·sy *n.* Paralysis; the loss of ability to control one's movements.

pam·per *v.* To treat with extreme care.

pam·phlet *n.* A brief publication.

pan·a·ce·a *n.* A remedy for all diseases, difficulties, or ills; a cure-all.

pan·cake *n.* A thin, flat cake made from batter and fried on a griddle, served with butter, syrup, and other toppings.

pan·cre·as *n.* A large, irregularly shaped gland situated behind the stomach which releases digestive enzymes and produces insulin. **pancreatic** *adj.*

pan·da *n.* A large bear-like animal of China and Tibet with black and white fur and rings around the eyes; a raccoon-like animal of the south-eastern Himalayas with a ringed tail and reddish fur.

pan·de·mo·ni·um *n.* A place marked with disorder and wild confusion; disorder; confusion.

pan·el *n.* A flat, rectangular piece of material, often wood, which forms a part of a surface; a group of people selected to participate in a discussion group or to serve on a jury. **panelist** *n.*, **panel** *v.*

pan·ic *n.* A sudden unreasonable fear which overpowers. *v.* To cause or to experience panic. **panicky** *adj.*

pan·o·rama *n.* An unlimited or complete view in all directions of what is visible.

pant *v.* To breathe in rapid or short gasps; to yearn. *n.* A short breath.

pan·the·ism *n.* The belief that the laws and forces of nature are all manifestations of God. **pantheist** *n.*, **pantheistic** *adj.*

pan·ther *n.* A black leopard in its unspotted form. **pantheress** *n.*

pan·to·mime *n.* Communication done solely by means of facial and body gestures. *v.* To express or act in pantomime.

pan·try *n.*, *pl.* **-ies** A closet or room for the storage of food, dishes, and other kitchen items.

pants *pl. n.* Trousers; underpants.

pap *n.* A soft food for invalids or babies.

pa·per *n.* A substance made of pulp from wood and rags, formed into sheets for printing, wrapping and writing.

par·a·ble *n.* A short, fictitious story which illustrates a moral lesson.

par·a·chute *n.* A folding umbrella-shaped apparatus of light fabric used to make a safe landing after a free fall from an airplane. **parachute** *v.*, **parachutist** *n.*

pa·rade *n.* An organized public procession; a march. **parader** *n.*

par·a·dise *n.* A state or place of beauty, bliss or delight; heaven.

par·a·dox *n.* A statement which seems opposed to common sense or contradicts itself, but is perhaps true. **paradoxical** *adj.*, **paradoxically** *adv.*

par·a·gon *n.* A pattern or model of excellence or perfection.

par·a·graph *n.* A section of a composition dealing with a single idea, containing one or more sentences with the first line usually indented.

par·a·keet *n.* A small parrot with a long, wedge-shaped tail.

par·al·lel *adj.* Moving in the same direction but separated by a distance, as railroad tracks. *n.* A parallel curve, line, or surface; a comparison; one of the imaginary lines which circle the earth paralleling the equator and mark the latitude. **parallel** *v.*, **parallelism** *n.*

par·al·lel·o·gram *n.* A four-sided figure having parallel, opposite, equal sides.

pa·ral·y·sis *n.* Complete or partial loss of the ability to feel any sensation or to move. **paralytic** *adj.*

par·a·lyze *v.* To cause to be inoperative or powerless.

par·a·med·ic *n.* A person trained to give emergency medical treatment until a doctor is available.

par•a•mount *adj.* Superior to all others in rank, importance, and power.

par•a•noi•a *n.* Mental insanity marked by systematic delusions of persecution or grandeur.

par•a•pher•na•lia *n.* Personal effects or belongings; the apparatus or articles used in some activities; equipment.

par•a•phrase *v.* To put something written or spoken into different words while retaining the same meaning.

par•a•site *n.* An organism which lives, grows, feeds, and takes shelter in or on another organism; a person depending entirely on another without providing something in return.

par•a•sol *n.* A small umbrella used as protection from the sun.

par•cel *n.* A wrapped package; a bundle; a portion or plat of land. **parcel** *v.*

parch *v.* To become very dry from intense heat; to become dry from thirst or the lack of water. **parched** *adj.*

parch•ment *n.* Goatskin or sheepskin prepared with a pumice stone and used as a material for writing or drawing.

par•don *v.* To forgive someone for an offense; in law, to allow a convicted person freedom from the penalties of an office or crime. **pardonable** *adj.*, **pardonably** *adv.*, **pardon** *n.*

pare *v.* To cut away or remove the outer surface gradually.

par•ent *n.* A mother or father; a forefather; an ancestor; a source; a cause. **parentage**, **parenthood** *n.*, **parental** *adj.*

pa•ren•the•sis *n.* One of a pair of curved lines ( ) used to enclose a qualifying or explanatory remark. **parentheses** *pl.*

park *n.* A tract of land used for recreation. *v.* To leave something temporarily in a parking garage or lot, as a car. **parker** *n.*

par•ka *n.* A jacket with an attached hood.

par•lia•ment *n.* The assembly which constitutes the lawmaking body of various countries, as the United Kingdom.

par•lor *n.* A room for entertaining visitors or guests; a business offering a personal service, such as beauty parlor, ice cream parlor, or funeral parlor.

par•o•dy *n.* A composition, song, or poem which mimics another in a ridiculous way.

pa•role *n.* The conditional release of a prisoner before his sentence expires. **parole** *v.*

par•rot *n.* A brightly colored, semitropical bird with a strong, hooked bill. *v.* To imitate or repeat.

par•ry *v.* To avoid something; to turn aside. **parry** *n.*

parse *v.* To identify the parts of speech in a sentence and to indicate their relationship to each other.

par•son *n.* A pastor or clergyman.

par•son•age *n.* The home provided by a church for its parson.

part *n.* A segment, portion, or division of a whole; a component for a machine; the role of a character, as in a play; the line which forms where the hair is parted by combing or brushing. *v.* To leave or go away from; to be separated into pieces; to give up control or possession.

par•tial *adj.* Incomplete; inclined to favor one side more than the other. **partiality** *n.*, **partially** *adv.*

par•tic•i•pate *v.* To join in or share; to take part. **participant, participation, participator** *n.*, **participatory** *adj.*

par•ti•cle *n.* A very small piece of solid matter; a group of words, such as articles, prepositions, and conjunctions which convey very little meaning but help to connect, specify, or limit the meanings of other words.

par•tic•u•lar *adj.* Having to do with a specific person, group, thing, or category; noteworthy; precise. **particularly** *adv.*

par•ti•tion *n.* A separation or division. *v.* To divide.

part•ner *n.* One who shares something with another.

part•ner•ship *n.* Two or more persons who run a business together and share in the profits and losses.

par•tridge *n.* A plump or stout-bodied

game bird.

par•ty *n.* A group of persons who gather for pleasure or entertainment; a group of persons associated together for a common purpose; a group which unites to promote or maintain a policy or a cause.

pass *v.* To proceed; to move; to transfer; to go away or come to an end; to get through a course, trial or test; to approve; to vote for; to give as an opinion or judgment; to hit or throw a ball to another player. *n.* A ticket or note that allows a person to come and go freely.

pas•sage *n.* The act of going, proceeding, or passing; a small portion or part of a whole book or speech; something, as a path or channel, through, over or along which something else may pass.

pas•sen•ger *n.* One who travels in a vehicle, car, plane, boat, or other conveyance.

pas•sion *n.* A powerful feeling; sexual desire; an outburst of strong feeling; violence or anger. **passionless, passionate** *adj.*

pas•sive *adj.* Not working, acting, or operating; inactive; acted upon, influenced, or affected by something external; designating the form of a verb which indicates the subject is receiving the action. **passively** *adv.*, **passivity, passiveness** *n.*

pass•port *n.* An official permission issued to a person allowing travel out of the country and return; a document of identification.

pass•word *n.* A secret word allowing a person to prove authorization to pass or enter.

past *adj.* Having to do with or existing at a former time. *n.* Before the present time; a person's history or background. *adv.* To go by. *prep.* After; beyond in time; beyond the power, reach, or influence.

paste *n.* A mixture usually made from water and flour, used to stick things together; dough used in making pastry; a brilliant glass used in imitating precious stones. **paste** *v.*

pas•tel *n.* A crayon made of ground pigments; a drawing made with crayons of this kind. *adj.* Pale and light in color or shade.

pas•teur•i•za•tion *n.* The process of killing disease-producing microorganisms by heating the liquid to a high temperature for a period of time.

pas•time *n.* A means of spending spare time in a pleasant way; a diversion.

pas•tor *n.* A Christian clergy member in charge of a church or congregation.

pas•tor•al *adj.* Referring to the duties of a pastor; pertaining to life in the country; rural or rustic. *n.* A poem dealing with country life.

pas•try *n.* Food made with dough or having a crust made of dough, as pies, tarts, or other desserts.

pas•ture *n.* An area for grazing of domestic animals.

pat *v.* To tap lightly with something flat. *n.* A soft, caressing stroke.

patch *n.* A piece of fabric used to repair a weakened or torn area in a garment; a piece of cloth with an insignia which represents an accomplishment. *v.* To repair or put together hastily. **patchy** *adj.*

pat•ent *n.* A governmental protection assuring an inventor the exclusive right of manufacturing, using, exploiting, and selling an invention. *adj.* Evident; obvious. **patentee, patency** *n.* **patently** *adv.*

pa•ter•nal *adj.* Relating to or characteristic of a father; inherited from a father. **paternally** *adv.*, **paternalism** *n.*

path *n.* A track or course; a route; a course of action or life.

pa•thet•ic *adj.* Arousing pity, tenderness, or sympathy. **pathetically** *adv.*

pa•thol•o•gy *n.* The science that deals with facts about diseases, their nature and causes. **pathologic, pathological** *adj.*, **pathologist** *n.*

pa•thos *n.* A quality in a person that evokes sadness or pity.

pa•tience *n.* The quality, state, or fact of being patient; the ability to be patient.

pa•tient *adj.* Demonstrating

thing; a regular customer. **patroness** n.

pat•tern n. Anything designed or shaped to serve as a guide in making something else; a sample. v. To make according to a pattern.

pause v. To linger, hesitate, or stop for a time.

pave v. To surface with gravel, concrete, asphalt, or other material.

pave•ment n. A paved surface.

paw n. The foot of an animal. v. To handle clumsily or rudely.

pawn n. Something given as security for a loan; a hostage; a chessman of little value.

pay v. To give a person what is due for a debt, purchase, or work completed; to compensate; to suffer the consequences.

pay•ment n. The act of paying.

pay•roll n. The amount of money to be paid to a list of employees.

pea n. A round edible seed contained in a pod and grown on a vine.

peace n. A state of physical or mental tranquillity; calm; serenity; the absence of war; the state of harmony between people.

peach n. A round, sweet, juicy fruit having a thin, downy skin, a pulpy yellow flesh, and a hard, rough single seed.

pea•cock n. A male bird with brilliant blue or green plumage and a long iridescent tail that fans out to approximately six feet.

peb•ble n. A small, smooth stone.

pe•can n. A large tree of the central and southern United States with an edible oval, thin-shelled nut.

peck v. To strike with the beak; to eat taking only small bites. n. A measure which equals one fourth of a bushel.

pe•cu•liar adj. Odd; strange. **peculiarity** n., **peculiarly** adv.

ped•al n. A lever usually operated by the foot.

ped•dle v. To travel around in an attempt to sell merchandise.

ped•es•tal n. A support or base for a statue.

pe•des•tri•an n. A person traveling by foot.

pe•di•at•rics n. The branch of medicine dealing with the care of children and infants. **pediatric** adj., **pediatrician** n.

ped•i•gree n. A line of ancestors, especially of an animal of pure breed.

ped•i•ment n. A broad, triangular architectural or decorative part above a door.

pe•dom•e•ter n. An instrument which indicates the number of miles one has walked.

peek v. To look shyly or quickly from a place of hiding; to glance. **peek** n.

peel n. The natural rind or skin of a fruit. v. To pull or strip the skin or bark off; to remove in thin layers.

peep *v.* To utter a very small and weak sound, as of a young bird.

peer *v.* To look searchingly; to come partially into one's view. *n.* An equal; a member of the British nobility, as a duke or earl.

pee•vish *adv.* Irritable in mood; cross. **peevishly** *adv.*, **peevishness** *n.*

peg *n.* A small pin, usually of wood or metal; a projecting pin on which something may be hung. *slang* An artificial leg, often made of wood.

pel•i•can *n.* A large, web-footed bird with a large pouch under the lower bill for the temporary storage of fish.

pel•let *n.* A small round ball made from paper or wax; a small bullet or shot.

pelt *n.* The skin of an animal with the fur.

pen *n.* An instrument used for writing.

pe•nal *adj.* Of or pertaining to punishment or penalties.

pen•al•ty *n.* The legal punishment for an offense or crime; something forfeited when a person fails to meet a commitment; in sports, a punishment or handicap imposed for breaking a rule.

pen•ance *n.* A voluntary act to show sorrow or repentance for sin.

pen•cil *n.* A writing or drawing implement made from graphite. *v.* To make, write, or draw with a pencil.

pen•du•lum *n.* A suspended object free to swing back and forth.

pen•e•trate *v.* To force a way through or into; to pierce; to enter; to pass through something. **penetrable, penetrating** *adj.*, **penetration** *n.*

pen•guin *n.* A web-footed, flightless, marine bird of the southern hemisphere.

pen•i•cil•lin *n.* A powerful antibiotic derived from mold and used to treat certain types of bacterial infections.

pen•in•su•la *n.* A piece of land projecting into water from a larger land mass. **peninsular** *adj.*

pe•nis *n.* The male sex organ; the male organ through which urine leaves the body.

pen•i•tent *adj.* Having a feeling of guilt or remorse for one's sins or misdeeds; sorry. **penitence** *n.*, **penitential** *adj.*

pen•ny *n.* A U.S. coin worth one hundredth of a dollar.

pen•sion *n.* The amount of money a person receives regularly after retirement. **pensioner** *n.*

pen•sive *adj.* Involved in serious, quiet reflection; causing melancholy thought. **pensively** *adv.*, **pensiveness** *n.*

pen•ta•gon *n.* Any object or building having five sides and five interior angles.

peo•ple *n.* Human beings; a body of persons living in the same country, under the same government, and speaking the same language; one's relatives or family.

pep•per *n.* A strong, aromatic condiment. *v.* To pelt or sprinkle.

per•ceive *v.* To become aware of by the senses; to understand; to feel or observe.

per•cent•age *n.* The rate per hundred; a part or proportion in relation to a whole.

per•cep•tive *n.* Discerning; capable of close observation; having the ability to perceive. **perception** *n.*

perch *n.* A place on which birds rest or alight; any place for standing or sitting; a small, edible freshwater fish.

per•cip•i•ent *adj.* Having the power of perception. **percipience, percipiency** *n.*

per•co•late *v.* To pass or cause to pass through a porous substance; to filter. **percolation, percolator** *n.*

per•cus•sion *n.* The sharp striking together of one body against another; the striking of a cap in a firearm; an instrument which makes music when it is struck, as a drum or cymbal.

per•en•ni•al *adj.* Lasting from year to year; perpetual. *n.* A plant which lives through the winter and blooms again in the spring. **perennially** *adv.*

per•fect *adj.* Having no defect or fault; flawless; accurate; absolute. *v.* To make perfect. **perfectness, perfection** *n.*

per·form *v.* To execute or carry out an action; to act or function in a certain way; to act; to give a performance or exhibition. **performer, performance** *n.*

per·fume *n.* A fragrant substance which emits a pleasant scent; one distilled from flowers. **perfume** *v.*

per·haps *adv.* Possibly; maybe; not sure.

per·il *n.* A source of danger; exposure to the chance of injury; danger. **perilous** *adj.*, **perilously** *adv.*

pe·ri·od *n.* An interval of time marked by certain conditions; an interval of time regarded as a phase in development; the punctuation mark which indicates the end of a sentence or an abbreviation.

per·ish *v.* To ruin or spoil; to suffer an untimely or violent death.

per·ma·nent *adj.* Continuing in the same state; lasting indefinitely; enduring. *n.* A hair wave which gives long-lasting curls or body to the hair. **permanence, permanency** *n.*, **permanently** *adv.*

per·me·ate *v.* To spread through; to pervade; to pass through the pores. **permeation** *n.*, **permeable** *adj.*

per·mis·sion *n.* The act of permitting something; consent.

per·mit *v.* To consent to; to allow. *n.* An official document giving permission.

per·ni·cious *adj.* Very harmful; malicious. **perniciousness** *n.*

per·ox·ide *n.* Oxide containing the highest proportion of oxygen for a given series; a chemical used with other ingredients to bleach the hair.

per·pen·dic·u·lar *adj.* Being at right angles to the plane of the horizon; in math, meeting a plane or given line at right angles.

per·pe·trate *v.* To perform; to commit; to be guilty. **perpetrator** *n.*

per·pet·u·al *adj.* Lasting or continuing forever or an unlimited time.

per·plex *v.* To confuse or be confused; to make complicated. **perplexing** *adj.*, **perplexedly** *adv.*, **perplexity** *n.*

per·se·cute *v.* To harass or annoy persistently; to oppress because of one's religion, beliefs, or race. **persecution, persecutor** *n.*, **persecutive** *adj.*

per·se·vere *v.* To persist in any purpose or idea; to strive in spite of difficulties. **perseverance** *n.*, **perseveringly** *adv.*

per·sist *v.* To continue firmly despite obstacles; to endure. **persistence** *n.*, **persistent** *adj.*, **persistently** *adv.*

per·son *n.* A human being; an individual; the personality of a human being.

per·son·al *adj.* Belonging to a person or persons; of the body or person; relating to oneself; done by oneself.

per·son·i·fy *v.* To think of or represent as having human qualities or life; to be a symbol of. **personifier, personification** *n.*

per·son·nel *n.* The body of people working for a business or service; human resources.

per·spec·tive *n.* A painting or drawing technique in which objects seem to have depth and distance.

per·spi·ra·tion *n.* The salty fluid excreted from the body by the sweat glands.

per·spire *v.* To give off perspiration.

per·suade *v.* To cause to convince or believe by means of reasoning or argument. **persuasion** *n.*, **persuasive** *adj.*

per·tain *v.* To relate to; to refer to; to belong as a function, adjunct, or quality; to be appropriate or fitting.

per·ti·na·cious *adj.* Adhering firmly to an opinion, belief, or purpose; stubbornly persistent. **pertinaciously** *adv.*, **pertinacity** *n.*

per·ti·nent *adj.* Relating to the matter being discussed.

per·turb *v.* To disturb, make anxious, or make uneasy; to cause confusion. **perturbation** *n.*

per·vade *v.* To spread through every part of something; to permeate. **pervasive** *adj.*

per·ver·sion *n.* The act of being led away from the accepted course; a deviant form of sexual behavior; a distorted variation.

per•vert *v.* To lead away from the proper cause; to use in an improper way. *n.* A person practicing or characterized by sexual perversion. **perverted, pervertible** *adj.*

pes•si•mism *n.* The tendency to take a gloomy view of affairs or situations and to anticipate the worst.

pest *n.* A person or thing which is a nuisance; an annoying person or thing; a destructive insect, plant, or animal.

pes•ter *v.* To harass with persistent annoyance; to bother.

pes•ti•cide *n.* A chemical substance used to destroy rodents, insects, and pests. **pesticidal** *adj.*

pet *n.* An animal, bird, or fish one keeps for companionship; any favorite or treasured thing. *adj.* Treated or tamed as a pet. *v.* To stroke or caress gently.

pet•al *n.* One of the leaf-like parts of a flower.

pe•tite *adj.* Small in size; little. **petiteness** *n.*

pe•ti•tion *n.* A solemn request or prayer; a written request addressed to a group or person in authority. **petitioner** *n.*

pet•ri•fy *v.* To convert into a stony mass; to make fixed or immobilize, as in the face of danger or surprise. **petrification** *n.*, **petrifactive, petrified** *adj.*

pe•tro•le•um *n.* An oily, thick liquid which develops naturally below the ground surface, used in products such as gasoline, fuel oil, and kerosene.

pet•ty *adj.* To have little importance or value; insignificant; trivial; having a low position or rank; minor; small-minded. **pettiness** *n.*

pet•ty cash *n.* Cash held on hand for minor bills or expenditures.

pew•ter *n.* An alloy of tin with copper, silver-gray in color and used for tableware and kitchen utensils.

phal•lus *n.* A representation of the penis, often as a symbol of generative power. **phallic** *adj.*

phan•tasm *n.* The creation of an imaginary image; a fantasy; a phantom. **phantasmal, phantasmic** *adj.*

phan•tom *n.* Something which exists but has no physical reality; a ghost. **phantom** *adj.*

phar•ma•cy *n.* A place of business which specializes in preparing, identifying, and disbursing drugs; a drugstore.

phase *n.* Any decisive stage in development or growth.

pheas•ant *n.* A long-tailed game bird noted for the plumage of the male.

phe•nom•e•non *n.* Something that can be observed or perceived; a rare occurrence; an outstanding person with remarkable power, ability, or talent. **phenomena** *pl.*

phi•los•o•phy *n.* The logical study of the nature and source of human knowledge or human values; the set of values, opinions, and ideas of a group or individual.

pho•bi•a *n.* A compulsive fear of a specified situation or object.

phone *n.* A telephone. *v.* To call or communicate by telephone.

phon•ic *adj.* Pertaining to sounds in speech; using the same symbol for each sound. **phonetics** *n.*

pho•ny *adj.* Counterfeit; fraudulent; not real or genuine.

phos•phate *n.* A salt or phosphoric acid which contains mostly phosphorus and oxygen.

phos•pho•rus *n.* A highly flammable, poisonous, nonmetallic element used in safety matches, symbolized by P.

pho•to *n.* A photograph.

pho•to•cop•y *v.* To reproduce printed material using a photographic process. **photocopier, photocopy** *n.*

pho•to•graph *n.* A picture or image recorded by a camera and reproduced on photosensitive paper. **photography** *n.*

pho•to•syn•the•sis *n.* The chemical process by which plants use light to change carbon dioxide and water into carbohydrates, releasing oxygen as a by-product.

phrase *n.* A brief or concise expression which does not contain both a predicate and a subject.

phys•i•cal *adj.* Relating to the human body apart from the mind or emotions; pertaining to material rather than imaginary subjects. *n.* A medical exam to determine a person's physical condition. **physically** *adv.*

phy•si•cian *n.* A person licensed to practice medicine.

phys•ics *n.* The scientific study which deals with energy, matter, motion, and related areas of science.

phys•i•ol•o•gy *n.* The scientific study of living animals, plants, and their activities and functions; the vital functions and processes of an organism. **physiological, physiologic** *adj.*, **physiologist** *n.*

pi•an•o *n.* A musical instrument with a manual keyboard and felt-covered hammers which produce musical tones when struck upon steel wires.

pic•co•lo *n.* A small flute with a brilliant sound pitched an octave above the flute.

pick *v.* To select or choose from a number or group; to remove the outer area of something with the fingers or a pointed instrument; to remove by tearing away little by little; to open a lock without using a key; to harass or tease someone or something; to pluck a musical instrument. *n.* A pointed metal tool sharpened at both ends, used to break up hard surfaces; a small flat piece of plastic or of bone, used to pluck or strum the strings of an instrument, as a guitar or banjo.

pick•et *n.* A pointed stake driven into the ground as support for a fence; a person positioned outside of a place of employment during a strike.

pick•le *n.* A cucumber preserved in a solution of brine or vinegar.

pic•nic *n.* An outdoor social gathering where food is provided usually by the people attending. **picnicker** *n.*

pic•ture *n.* A visual representation on a surface, printed, drawn or photographed; the mental image or impression of an event or situation.

piece *n.* An element, unit, or part of a whole; a musical or literary work.

pier *n.* A structure extending into the water, used to secure, protect, and provide access to vessels.

pierce *v.* To penetrate or make a hole in something; to force into or through. **piercing** *adj.*

pi•e•ty *n.* Devoutness toward God.

pig *n.* A cloven-hoofed mammal with short legs, bristly hair, and a snout for rooting; the edible meat of a pig; pork.

pi•geon *n.* A bird with short legs, a sturdy body, and a small head.

pig•ment *n.* A material used as coloring matter, suitable for making paint.

pile *n.* A quantity of anything thrown in a heap; a massive or very large building or a group of buildings.

pil•grim *n.* A person who travels to a sacred place; a wanderer.

pill *n.* A small tablet containing medicine taken by mouth; someone or something disagreeable but that must be dealt with.

pil•lar *n.* A freestanding column which serves as a support.

pil•low *n.* A cloth case filled with feathers or other soft material, used to cushion the head during sleep.

pi•lot *n.* A person licensed to operate an aircraft; someone trained and licensed to guide ships in and out of port. *v.* To act or serve as a pilot.

pin *n.* A small, stiff piece of wire with a blunt head and a sharp point, used to fasten something, usually temporarily.

pinch *v.* To squeeze between a finger and thumb causing pain or discomfort; to be miserly. *n.* The small amount that can be held between the thumb and forefinger.

pine *n.* Any of various cone-bearing evergreen trees; the wood of such a tree.

pine•ap•ple *n.* A tropical American plant with spiny, curved leaves bearing a large edible fruit.

pink *n.* Any of various plants related to the

carnation, having fragrant flowers; a light or pale hue of crimson; the highest or best possible degree.

pin•na•cle *n.* The highest peak; a sharp point; a pointed summit.

pi•noch•le *n.* A card game for two, three, or four people, played with a double deck of 48 cards.

pint *n.* A liquid or dry measurement equal to half of a quart or two cups.

pi•o•neer *n.* One of the first settlers of a new region or country; the first developer or investigator in a new field of enterprise, research, or other endeavor.

pi•ous *adj.* Reverently religious; devout. **piously** *adv.,* **piousness, piety** *n.*

pipe *n.* A hollow cylinder for conveying fluids; a small bowl with a hollow stem for smoking tobacco.

pipe-line *n.* A pipe used to transfer gas or oil over long distances; a smoking container; a means for conveying information.

pi•rate *n.* A robber of the high seas; someone who uses or reproduces someone else's work without authorization. **piracy** *n.*

pis•ta•chi•o *n.* A small tree of western Asia; the edible fruit from this tree.

pis•til *n.* The seed-producing female reproductive organ of a flower.

pis•tol *n.* A small hand-held firearm.

pis•ton *n.* A solid cylinder fitted into a larger cylinder, moving back and forth under liquid pressure.

pit *n.* An artificial or manmade hole in the ground; a slight indentation in the skin, as a scar from the chicken pox; an area for refueling or repair at a car race; the stone in the middle of some fruit, as peaches.

pitch *n.* A thick, sticky, dark substance which is the residue of the distillation of petroleum or coal tar; the degree of slope of an incline; the property of a musical tone which makes it high or low. *v.* To cover with pitch; to throw; to throw out; to slope.

pitch•er *n.* The person who throws the ball to the batter; a container for holding and pouring liquids.

pitch•fork *n.* A large fork with a wide prong span, used as a garden or farm tool.

pit•y *n.* A feeling of compassion or sorrow for another's misfortune. **pitiful** *adj.,* **pitifully** *adv.*

piv•ot *n.* A thing or person upon which development, direction, or effect depends. *v.* To turn.

piz•za *n.* An Italian food consisting of a doughy crust covered with tomato sauce, cheese, and toppings and then baked.

place *n.* A region; an area; a building or location used for a special purpose; the position of something in a series or sequence. *v.* To put in a particular order or place.

pla•cen•ta *n.* The vascular, membranous structure which supplies a fetus with nourishment before its birth.

place•ment *n.* The act of being placed; a business or service which finds positions of employment for applicants.

plague *n.* Anything troublesome; a highly contagious and often fatal epidemic disease, as the bubonic plague.

plaid *n.* A rectangular wool cloth or garment, usually worn by men and women, having a crisscross or checkered design.

plain *adj.* Level; flat; clear; open, as in view; not rich or luxurious; not highly gifted or cultivated. **plainly** *adv.,* **plainness** *n.*

plain•tiff *n.* A person who brings suit.

plan *n.* A scheme or method for achieving something; a drawing to show proportion and relationship to parts. *v.* To have in mind as an intention or purpose.

plane *n.* A tool for smoothing or leveling a wood surface; a surface on which any two points can be joined with a straight line; an airplane.

plan•et *n.* A celestial body illuminated by light from the star around which it revolves.

plan•e•tar•i•um *n.* A projection device for exhibiting celestial bodies as they exist at any time and for any place on earth.

plank *n.* A broad piece of wood; one of the issues or principles of a political platform.

plant *n.* A living organism belonging to the vegetable kingdom, having cellulose cell walls. *v.* To place a living organism in the ground for growing; to place so as to deceive or to spy.

plaque *n.* A flat piece, made from metal, porcelain, ivory, or other materials, engraved for mounting; the bacteria deposit that builds up on the teeth.

plas•ma *n.* The clear fluid part of blood, used for transfusions.

plas•tic *adj.* Pliable; capable of being molded. *n.* A synthetic material molded and then hardened into objects.

plate *n.* A flat flexible, thin piece of material, as metal; a shallow, flat vessel made from glass, crockery, plastic, or other material from which food is eaten.

pla•teau *n.* An extensive level expanse of elevated land; a period of stability.

plat•form *n.* Any elevated surface used by speakers, or by other performers or for display purposes; a formal declaration of principles or policy of a political party.

plat•i•num *n.* A silver-white, metallic element which is corrosive-resistant, used in jewelry; symbolized by Pt.

plat•ter *n.* A large, oblong, shallow dish for serving food.

plau•si•ble *adj.* Seeming to be probable; appearing to be trustworthy or believable.

play *v.* To amuse or entertain oneself, as in recreation; to take part in a game; to perform in a dramatic role; to perform with a musical instrument; in fishing, to allow a hooked fish to tire itself out; to pretend to do something. *n.* A dramatic presentation.

play•ful *adj.* Lightly humorous; full of high spirits.

play•ground *n.* The area set aside for children's recreation.

pla•za *n.* An open-air marketplace or square; a shopping mall.

plea *n.* An urgent request; a legal allegation made by either party in a lawsuit.

plead *v.* To argue for one or against something in court; to ask earnestly.

pleas•ant *adj.* Giving or promoting the feeling of pleasure; very agreeable. **pleasantly** *adv.*, **pleasantness** *n.*

please *v.* To make happy; to give pleasure; to be the will or wish of; to prefer.

pleas•ur•a•ble *adj.* Pleasant; gratifying.

pleas•ure *n.* A feeling of satisfaction or enjoyment; one's preference or wish.

pleat *n.* A fold in a cloth made by doubling the cloth back and fastening it down.

pledge *n.* A solemn promise; a deposit of something as security for a loan; a promise to join a fraternity; a person who is pledged to join a fraternity. *v.* To promise or vow.

plen•ti•ful *adj.* Having great abundance. **plentifully** *adv.*, **plentifulness** *n.*

plen•ty *n.* An ample amount; prosperity or abundance.

pli•a•ble *adj.* Flexible; easily controlled or persuaded. **pliability**, **pliableness** *n.* **pliably** *adv.*

pli•ers *pl. n.* A pincers-like implement used for holding, bending, or cutting.

plight *n.* A distressing circumstance, situation, or condition.

plod *n.* To walk in a heavy, slow way.

plot *n.* A small piece of ground usually used for a special purpose; the main story line in a piece of fiction; a plan; an intrigue; a conspiracy. *v.* To represent something by using a map or chart; to scheme secretly. **plotter** *n.*

plow *n.* An implement for breaking up or turning over the soil. *v.* To dig out. *slang* To hit with force.

pluck *v.* To remove by pulling out or off; to pull and release the strings on a musical instrument.

plug *n.* Anything used to stop or close a hole or drain; a two-pronged device attached to a cord and used in a jack or socket to make an electrical connection.

plum *n.* A small tree bearing an edible fruit with a smooth skin and a single hard seed; the fruit from such a tree.

plum•age *n.* The feathers of a bird.

plumb *n.* A lead weight tied to the end of

a string, used to test the exact perpendicular line of something.

plumb•er *n.* A person who repairs or installs plumbing in a home or business.

plumb•ing *n.* The profession or trade of a plumber; the connecting of pipes and fixtures used to carry water and waste.

plume *n.* A feather used as an ornament.

plun•der *v.* To deprive of goods or property in a violent way. **plunderer** *n.*

plunge *v.* To thrust or cast something, as into water; to submerge; to descend sharply or steeply.

plu•ral *adj.* Consisting of or containing more than one. **plural** *n.*

ply *v.* To mold, bend, or shape. *n.* A layer of thickness; the twisted strands of thread, yarn, or rope.

pneu•mo•nia *n.* An inflammation caused by bacteria, virus of the lungs, or irritation.

poach *v.* To cook in a liquid just at the boiling point; to trespass on another's property with the intent of taking fish or wild game. **poacher** *n.*

pock•et *n.* A small pouch within a garment, having an open top and used for carrying items. *v.* To put in or deposit in a pocket.

pod *n.* A seed vessel, as of a bean or pea. A separate and detachable compartment in a spacecraft.

po•di•a•try *n.* Professional care and treatment of the feet.

po•di•um *n.* A small raised platform for an orchestra conductor or a speaker.

po•em *n.* A composition in verse with language selected for its beauty and sound.

po•et *n.* A person who writes poetry.

po•et•ry *n.* The art of writing stories, poems, and thoughts into verse.

point *n.* The sharp or tapered end of something; a mark of punctuation, as a period; a geometric object which does not have property or dimensions other than location; a degree, condition, or stage; a particular or definite spot in time. *v.* To aim; to indicate direction by using the finger.

poise *v.* To bring into or hold one's balance. *n.* Equilibrium; self-confidence; the ability to stay calm in all social situations.

poi•son *n.* A substance which kills, injures, or destroys. **poisoner** *n.*, **poisonous** *adj.*

poke *v.* To push or prod at something with a finger or other implement.

po•lar *adj.* Having to do with the poles of a magnet or sphere; relating to the geographical poles of the earth.

po•lar•ize *v.* To cause something to vibrate in an exact pattern; to break up into opposite groups. **polarization** *n.*

pole *n.* A long, slender rod; either of the two ends of the axis of a sphere, as the earth; the two points called the North and South Poles, where the axis of the earth's rotation meets the surface.

po•lice *n.* A division or department organized to maintain order; the members of such a department; a law enforcement officer. *v.* To patrol; to enforce the law and maintain order. **policeman, policewoman** *n.*

pol•i•cy *n.* Any plan or principle which guides decision making.

pol•ish *v.* To make lustrous and smooth by rubbing; to become refined or elegant.

po•lite *adj.* Refined, mannerly, and courteous.

po•lit•i•cal *adj.* Pertaining to government; involved in politics.

poll *n.* The recording of votes in an election; a public survey taken on a given topic. **poll** *v.*

pol•len *n.* The yellow dust-like powder which contains the male reproductive cells of a flowering plant.

pol•lute *v.* To contaminate; to make unclear or impure; to dirty. **pollution** *n.*

po•lo *n.* A game played on horseback in which players try to drive a wooden ball through the opposing team's goal using long-handled mallets. **poloist** *n.*

po•lo•ni•um *n.* A radioactive metallic element symbolized by Po.

pol•ter•geist *n.* A mischievous ghost or spirit which makes much noise.

pol•y•es•ter *n.* A strong lightweight synthetic resin used in fibers.

pol•y•graph *n.* A machine designed to record different signals given off by the body, as respiration, blood pressure, or heartbeats, and which may be used to detect physiological changes in a person who may be lying.

pom•pa•dour *n.* A hairstyle which is puffed over the forehead.

pomp•ous *adj.* Displaying a showing or appearance of dignity or importance.

pond *n.* A body of still water, smaller in size than a lake.

pon•der *v.* To weigh or think about very carefully; to meditate.

pon•der•ous *adj.* Massive; having great weight.

po•ny *n.* A small horse.

pool *n.* A small body of water; the collective stake in gambling games.

poor *adj.* Lacking possessions and money; not satisfactory; broke; needy; destitute.

pop *v.* To cause something to burst; to make a sharp, explosive sound. *n.* Soda; a carbonated sweet drink.

pop•corn *n.* A type of corn which explodes when heated, forming white puffs.

pope *n.* The head of the Roman Catholic Church.

pop•lar *n.* A rapidly growing tree having a light, soft wood.

pop•u•lar *adj.* Approved of; widely liked; suited to the means of the people.

pop•u•la•tion *n.* The total number of people in a given area, country, or city.

por•ce•lain *n.* A hard, translucent ceramic which has been fired and glazed.

porch *n.* A covered structure forming the entrance to a house.

por•cu•pine *n.* A clumsy rodent covered with long sharp quills.

pore *v.* To ponder or meditate on something. *n.* A minute opening, as in the skin.

pork *n.* The edible flesh of swine. *informal* Favors given by a government for political reasons and not public necessity.

por•nog•ra•phy *n.* Pictures, films, or writings that deliberately arouse sexual excitement.

por•poise *n.* An aquatic mammal with a blunt, rounded snout.

port *n.* A city or town with a harbor for loading and unloading cargo from ships; the left side of a ship; a dark-red, sweet, fortified wine; in computers, the hardware connection by which elements of a computer system are physically linked to enable electronic transfer among devices.

port•a•ble *adj.* Capable of being moved easily.

por•ter *n.* A person hired to carry baggage.

port•fo•li•o *n.* A carrying case for holding papers, drawings, and other flat items.

port•hole *n.* A small opening in the side of a ship providing light and ventilation.

por•tion *n.* A section or part of a whole; a share. *v.* To allot; to assign.

por•tray *v.* To represent by drawing, writing, or acting.

pose *v.* To place or assume a position, as for a picture.

po•si•tion *n.* The manner in which something is placed; an attitude; a viewpoint; a job. *v.* To place in proper order.

pos•i•tive *adj.* Containing, expressing, or characterized by affirmation; very confident; absolutely certain; not negative. **positively** *adv.*, **positiveness** *n.*

pos•se *n.* A deputized group or squad.

pos•ses•sion *n.* The fact or act of possessing property; the state of being possessed, as by an evil spirit.

pos•ses•sive *adj.* Having a strong desire to possess; not wanting to share. *n.* The noun or pronoun case which indicates ownership.

pos•si•ble *adj.* Capable of being true, happening, or being accomplished. **possibility** *n.*, **possibly** *adv.*

post *n.* An upright piece of wood or metal support; a position of employment. *v.* To put up information in a public place.

post•age *n*. The charge or fee for mailing something.

pos•te•ri•or *adj*. Located in the back. *n*. The buttocks.

post•mor•tem *n*. The examination of a body after death; an autopsy.

post•pone *v*. To put off; to defer to a later time. **postponement, postponer** *n*.

pos•ture *n*. The position of the body.

pot *n*. A rounded, deep container used for cooking and other domestic purposes.

po•tas•si•um *n*. A silvery white, highly reactive metallic element symbolized by K.

po•ta•to *n*. A thick, edible, underground tuber plant native to America.

po•tent *adj*. Having great strength or physical powers; having a great influence on the mind or morals; sexually competent.

po•ten•tial *adj*. Possible, but not yet actual; having the capacity to be developed; the energy of an electric charge that depends on its position in an electric field. **potentiality** *n*., **potentially** *adv*.

pot•pour•ri *n*. A mixture of sweet-smelling dried flower petals and spices, kept in an airtight jar.

pot•ter•y *n*. Objects molded from clay and fired by intense heat.

pouch *n*. A small bag or other container for holding or carrying money, tobacco, and other small articles; the sac-like structure in which some animals carry their young.

poul•try *n*. Domestic fowl as ducks and hens, raised for eggs or meat.

pound *n*. A measure of weight equal to sixteen ounces; a public enclosure where stray animals are fed and housed. *v*. To strike repeatedly or with force; to throb or beat violently or rapidly.

pov•er•ty *n*. The condition or state of being poor and needing money.

pow•der *n*. A dry substance which has been finely ground or pulverized; dust; an explosive, such as gunpowder. *v*. To dust or cover.

pow•er•ful *adj*. Possessing energy or great force; having authority.

prac•ti•cal *adj*. Serving an actual use or purpose; inclined to act instead of thinking or talking about something; useful.

prac•tice *n*. A custom or habit of doing something. *v*. To work at a profession; to apply; to put into effect; to rehearse.

prai•rie *n*. A wide area of level or rolling land with grass and weeds but no trees.

praise *v*. To express approval; to glorify.

prank *n*. A mischievous, playful action or trick. **prankster** *n*.

prawn *n*. An edible shrimp-like crustacean found in both salt and fresh water.

pray *v*. To address prayers to God; to ask or request.

pray•er *n*. A devout request; the act of praying; a formal or set group of words used in praying.

preach *v*. To advocate; to proclaim; to deliver a sermon. **preacher, preachment** *n*., **preachy** *adj*.

pre•am•ble *n*. An introduction to something, as a law, which states the purpose and reasons for the matter which follows.

pre•cau•tion *n*. A measure of caution taken in advance to guard against harm.

pre•cede *v*. To be or go before in time, position, or rank. **precedence** *n*.

prec•e•dent *n*. An instance which may serve as a rule or example in the future.

pre•cept *n*. A rule, order, or commandment meant to guide one's conduct.

pre•cinct *n*. An electoral district of a county, township, city, or town; an enclosure with definite boundaries.

pre•cious *adj*. Having great worth or value; beloved; cherished.

pre•cip•i•ta•tion *n*. Condensed water vapor which falls as snow, rain, sleet, or hail; the act of causing crystals to separate and fall to the bottom of a liquid.

pre•cise *adj*. Exact; definite; strictly following rules; very strict.

pre•ci•sion *n*. Exactness; the quality of being precise; accuracy.

pre•clude *v*. To shut out; to come before

so as to prevent; to make impossible.

pre·co·cious *adj.* Showing and developing skills and abilities very early in life.

pre·con·ceive *v.* To form a notion or conception before knowing all the facts. **preconception** *n.*

pre·da·cious *adj.* Living by preying on other animals.

pred·a·tor *n.* A person who steals from others; an animal that survives by killing and eating other animals.

pre·des·ti·na·tion *n.* Destiny; fate; the act by which God has predestined all events.

pred·i·ca·ble *adj.* Capable of being predicated; dependent on; necessary for continuation.

pred·i·cate *n.* The word or words which say something about the subject of a clause or sentence; the part of a sentence which contains the verb. *v.* To establish.

pre·dict *v.* To tell beforehand; to foretell; to forecast. **predictability, prediction** *n.*, **predictable** *adj.*

pref·ace *n.* The introduction at the beginning of a book or speech.

pre·fer *v.* To select as being the favorite; to promote; to present.

pref·er·ence *n.* A choice; a special liking for something. **preferential** *adj.*

pre·fix *v.* To put at the beginning; to put before.

preg·nant *adj.* Carrying an unborn fetus; significant. **pregnancy** *n.*

prej·u·dice *n.* A biased opinion based on emotion rather than reason; bias against a group, race, or creed.

pre·lim·i·nar·y *adj.* Leading up to the main action. **preliminaries** *n. pl.*

prel·ude *n.* An introductory action; the movement at the beginning of a piece of music.

pre·ma·ture *adj.* Occurring or born before the natural time. **prematurely** *adv.*

pre·med·i·tate *v.* To plan in advance or beforehand.

pre·mier *adj.* First in rank or importance. *n.* The chief executive of a government.

premiership *n.*

pre·mi·um *n.* An object offered free as an inducement to buy; the fee or amount payable for insurance; an additional amount charged above the nominal value.

pre·na·tal *adj.* Existing prior to birth.

prep·a·ra·tion *n.* The process of preparing for something.

pre·pare *v.* To make ready or qualified; to equip. **preparedly** *adv.*

pre·oc·cu·py *v.* To engage the mind or attention completely. **preoccupied** *adj.*

prep·o·si·tion *n.* A word placed in front of a noun or pronoun to show a connection with or to something or someone.

pre·pos·ter·ous *adj.* Absurd; ridiculous; beyond all reason.

pre·rog·a·tive *n.* The unquestionable right belonging to a person.

pres·age *n.* An omen or indication of something to come; a premonition. **presage**

pre·school *adj.* Of or for children usually between the ages of two and five. **preschooler** *n.*

pre·scribe *v.* To impose as a guide; to recommend; to authorize or order medicines.

pre·scrip·tion *n.* A physician's written order for medicine.

pres·ence *n.* The state of being present; the immediate area surrounding a person or thing; poise.

pres·ent *adj.* Now going on; not past or future; denoting a tense or verb form which expresses a current state or action. *v.* To bring into the acquaintance of another; to introduce; to make a gift of. *n.* A gift.

pres·en·ta·tion *n.* A formal introduction of one person to another; to present something as an exhibition, show, or product.

pre·serv·a·tive *adj.* Keeping something from decay or injury. **preservation** *n.*, **preservable** *adj.*

pre·serve *v.* To keep or save from destruction or injury; to prepare fruits or vegetables to prevent spoilage or decay. *n. pl.* Fruit preserved with sugar.

pre•side *v.* To have a position of authority or control; to run or control a meeting.

pres•i•dent *n.* The chief executive officer of a government, corporation, or association. **presidency** *n.*

press *v.* To act upon or exert steady pressure or force; to squeeze out or extract by pressure; to smooth by heat and pressure; to iron clothes. *n.* A machine used to produce printed material.

pres•sure *n.* The act of or state of being pressed; a constraining moral force; any burden, force, painful feeling, or influence; a depressing feeling or influence; the depressing effect of something.

pres•tige *n.* Importance based on past reputation and achievements.

pre•sume *v.* To take for granted; to take upon oneself without permission; to proceed overconfidently. **presumably** *adv.*

pre•sump•tion *n.* Arrogant conduct or speech; something that can be logically assumed true until disproved.

pre•tend *v.* To make believe; to act in a false way. **pretender** *n.*

pre•tense *n.* A deceptive and false action or appearance; a false purpose.

pre•ten•tion *n.* The assumption or claim of worth, excellence, rank, or privilege. **pretentious** *adj.*

pre•text *n.* A motive assumed in order to conceal the true purpose.

pret•ty *adj.* Pleasant; attractive; characterized by gracefulness; pleasing to look at; *informal* Sitting pretty; in a favorable position; good circumstances. **prettier**, **prettiest** *adj.*

pre•vail *v.* To succeed; to win control over something; to predominate. **prevailer** *n.*, **prevailing** *adj.*

pre•vent *v.* To keep something from happening; to keep from doing something.

pre•ven•tive or **pre•ven•ta•tive** *adj.* Protecting or serving to ward off harm, disease, or other problems. **preventive** *n.*

pre•view *n.* An advance showing or viewing to invited guests.

pre•vi•ous *adj.* Existing or occurring earlier. **previously** *adv.*

price *n.* The set amount of money expected or given for the sale of something.

prick *n.* A small hole made by a sharp point. *v.* To pierce something lightly.

pride *n.* A sense of personal dignity; a feeling of pleasure because of something achieved, done, or owned.

priest *n.* A clergyman in the Catholic church who serves as mediator between God and His worshippers.

pri•ma•ry *adj.* First in origin, time, series, or sequence; basic; fundamental.

prime *adj.* First in importance, time, or rank. *n.* A period of full vigor, success, or beauty. *v.* To make ready by putting something on before the final coat.

prim•i•tive *adj.* Of or pertaining to the beginning or earliest time; resembling the style or manners of an earlier time.

primp *v.* To dress or arrange with superfluous attention to detail.

prince *n.* The son of a king; a king.

prin•cess *n.* The daughter of a king.

prin•ci•pal *adj.* Chief; most important. *n.* The principal administrator; the headmaster or chief official of a school; a sum of money invested or owed separate from the interest.

prin•ci•ple *n.* The fundamental law or truth upon which others are based; a moral standard.

print *n.* An impression or mark made with ink; the design or picture transferred from an engraved plate or other impression. *v.* To stamp designs; to publish something.

print•er *n.* A person whose occupation is printing.

print•out *n.* The output of a computer, printed on paper; hard copy.

pri•or *adj.* Previous in order or time.

pri•or•i•ty *n.* Something which takes precedence; something which must be done or taken care of first.

prism *n.* A solid figure with triangular ends and rectangular sides, used to disperse light into a spectrum.

pris·on *n.* A place of confinement where people are kept while waiting for a trial or while serving time for breaking the law; jail. **prisoner** *n.*

pri·vate *adj.* Secluded or removed from the public view; secret; intimate; owned or controlled by a group or person rather than by the public or government. *n.* An enlisted person holding the lowest rank in military service.

priv·i·lege *n.* A special right or benefit granted to a person. **privileged** *adj.*

prize *n.* An award or something given to the winner of a contest; something exceptional or outstanding.

pro *n.* An argument in favor of something.

prob·a·bil·i·ty *n.* The state or quality of being probable; a mathematical statement or prediction of the odds of something happening or not happening.

prob·a·ble *adj.* Likely to become a reality, but not certain or proved.

pro·ba·tion *n.* A period used to test the qualifications and character of a new employee; the early release of lawbreakers who must be under supervision.

probe *n.* An instrument used for investigating an unknown environment; a careful investigation or examination. *v.* To examine by insertion or careful investigation.

prob·lem *n.* A perplexing situation or question; a question presented for consideration or solution. **problematic** *adj.*

pro·ce·dure *n.* A certain pattern or way of doing something; the normal methods or forms to be followed.

pro·ceed *v.* To carry on or continue an action or process.

proc·ess *n.* The course, steps, or methods toward a desired result. *v.* To compile, compute, or assemble data.

pro·ces·sion *n.* A group which moves along in a formal manner; a parade.

pro·ces·sion·al *n.* A hymn sung during a procession; the opening of a church service. **processional** *adj.*

pro·ces·sor *n.* In computer science, the central unit of a computer which processes data; any device used in the refinement of a manufactured product; a person who processes or facilitates bureaucratic operations.

pro·claim *v.* To announce publicly in a ceremony.

proc·la·ma·tion *n.* An official public declaration or announcement.

pro·cras·ti·nate *v.* To put off, defer, or postpone to a later time. **procrastination, procrastinator** *n.*

proc·tor *n.* A person in a university or college whose job it is to see that order is maintained during exams. **proctorial** *adj.*

pro·cure *v.* To acquire; to accomplish; to provide for another's use.

prod *v.* To arouse mentally; to poke with a pointed instrument. *n.* A pointed implement used to prod or poke.

pro·duce *v.* To bear or bring forth by a natural process; to manufacture; to make; to present or bring into view.

prod·uct *n.* Something produced, manufactured, or obtained; the answer obtained by multiplying.

pro·duc·tion *n.* The process or act of producing; something produced, as a play.

pro·fess *v.* To admit or declare openly; to make an open vow.

pro·fes·sor *n.* A faculty member of the highest rank in a college or university; a highly skilled teacher.

pro·fi·cient *adj.* Highly skilled in a field of knowledge. **proficiency** *n.*

pro·file *n.* The outline of a person's face or figure as seen from the side; a short biographical sketch.

prof·it *n.* The financial return after all expenses have been accounted for. *v.* To gain an advantage or a financial reward. **profitable** *adj.*

pro·found *adj.* Deeply held or felt; intellectually penetrating.

pro·fuse *adj.* Extravagant; giving forth lavishly; overflowing. **profusely** *adv.*, **profuseness** *n.*

prog•e•ny *n.* One's offspring, children, or descendants.

prog•no•sis *n.* A prediction of the outcome and course a disease may take; an assessment of future possibility or consequence.

pro•gram *n.* Any prearranged plan or course; a show or performance; a sequence of commands which tell a computer how to perform a task or sequence of tasks. **program** *v.*

prog•ress *n.* Forward motion or advancement to a higher goal; an advance; steady improvement.

pro•hib•it *v.* To forbid legally; to prevent.

pro•ject *n.* A plan or course of action; a proposal; a large job. *v.* To give an estimation on something.

pro•jec•tile *n.* Anything hurled forward through the air.

pro•jec•tion *n.* The act or state of being projected; estimation of future values or features; the state or part that sticks out; an image of light and shadow cast on a surface for viewing. **projector** *n.*

pro•lif•er•ate *v.* To grow or produce with great speed, as cells in tissue formation; to multiply and scatter; to become ubiquitous.

pro•logue *n.* An introductory statement at the beginning of a poem, song, or play.

pro•long *v.* To extend or lengthen in time.

prom•e•nade *n.* An unhurried walk for exercise or amusement; a public place for such a walk, as the deck of a ship.

prom•i•nent *adj.* Jutting out; widely known; held in high esteem.

pro•mis•cu•ous *adj.* Lacking selectivity or discrimination, especially in sexual relationships.

prom•ise *n.* An assurance given that one will or will not do something; a pledge. **promise** *v.*

prompt *adj.* Arriving on time; punctual; immediate. *v.* To suggest or inspire.

prone *adj.* Lying flat; face down.

pro•noun *n.* A word used in the place of a noun or noun phrase.

pro•nounce *v.* To deliver officially; to articulate the sounds.

proof *n.* The establishment of a fact by evidence; the act of showing that something is true; a trial impression from the negative of a photograph. *v.* To proofread.

prop *n.* A support to keep something upright. *v.* To sustain.

prop•a•gate *v.* To reproduce or multiply by natural causes; to pass on qualities or traits. **propagation** *n.*

prop•er *adj.* Appropriate; especially adapted or suited; conforming to social convention; correct.

prop•er•ty *n.* Any object of value owned or lawfully acquired; a piece of land.

proph•e•cy *n.* A prediction made under divine influence.

proph•et *n.* One who delivers divine messages; one who foretells the future. **prophetess** *n.*

pro•pi•ti•ate *v.* To win the goodwill of; to stop from being angry; to appease or reconcile those in power. **propitiation** *n.*

pro•po•nent *n.* One who supports or advocates a cause or proposal.

pro•por•tion *n.* The relation of one thing to another in size, degree, or amount. *v.* To adjust or arrange with balance and harmony.

pro•pose *v.* To present or put forward for consideration or action; to suggest someone for an office or position; to make an offer; to offer marriage. **proposal** *n.*

prop•o•si•tion *n.* A scheme or plan offered for consideration; a subject or idea to be proved or discussed. *v.* To make a sexual suggestion.

pro•pri•e•ty *n.* The quality or state of being proper in accordance with recognized principles or usage.

pro•pul•sion *n.* The act or process of propelling. **propulsive** *adj.*

pro•rate *v.* To distribute or divide proportionately. **proration** *n.*

pro•scribe *v.* To banish; to outlaw; to prohibit.

prose *n.* Ordinary language, speech, or

the male bladder.

pros•ti•tute *n.* One who sells one's body for the purpose of sexual intercourse.

pros•trate *adj.* Lying with the face down to the ground. *v.* To overcome; to adopt a submissive posture.

pro•tect *v.* To guard or shield from attack or injury; to shield. **protective** *adj.*, **protectively** *adv.*

pro•tein *n.* Any of a very large group of highly complex nitrogenous compounds occurring in living matter and composed of amino acids essential for tissue repair and growth.

pro•test *v.* To make a strong formal objection; to object to. *n.* The act of protesting. **protester** *n.*

pro•to•col *n.* In computers, an electronically defined set of transmission and communication rules, by which various software devices can be interchanged.

pro•ton *n.* A unit of positive charge found in the nucleus of an atom, equal in magnitude to an electron.

pro•tract *v.* To extend in space; to protrude; to lengthen or prolong. **protracted** *adj.*

pro•trude *v.* To project; to thrust outward. **protrusion** *n.*

proud *adj.* Showing or having a feeling that one is better than the others; having a feeling of satisfaction; having proper self-respect or proper self-esteem.

prove *v.* To show with valid evidence that something is true. **provable** *adj.*

prov•erb *n.* An old saying which illustrates very carefully.

prune *n.* The dried fruit of a plum. *v.* To cut off that which is not wanted or not necessary.

psalm *n.* A sacred hymn, taken from the Book of Psalms in the Old Testament.

pso•ri•a•sis *n.* A non-contagious, chronic, inflammatory skin disease characterized by reddish patches and white scales.

psych *v.* To prepare oneself emotionally or mentally; to outwit or out-guess.

psy•chi•a•try *n.* The branch of medicine that deals with the diagnosis and treatment of mental disorders.

psy•chic *adj.* Having the quality of supernatural forces which cannot be explained by natural or physical laws. *n.* A person who communicates with the spirit world.

psy•chol•o•gy *n.* The science of emotions, behavior, and the mind. **psychological** *adj.*, **psychologist** *n.*

psy•cho•path *n.* A person suffering from a mental disorder characterized by aggressive antisocial behavior. **psychopathic** *adj.*

pu•ber•ty *n.* The stage of development in which sexual reproduction can first occur; the process of the body which culminates in sexual maturity.

pub•lic *adj.* Pertaining to or affecting the people or community; for everyone's use; widely or well known.

pub•li•ca•tion *n.* The business of publishing; any pamphlet, book, or magazine.

pub•lic•i•ty *n.* The state of being known to the public; common knowledge.

public. **publisher** *n.*

puck *n.* A hard rubber disk used in playing ice hockey.

pud•dle *n.* A small pool of water or other liquid.

puff *n.* A brief discharge of air or smoke. *v.* To breathe in short heavy breaths.

pull *v.* To apply force; to cause motion toward or in the same direction of; to remove from a fixed place; to stretch.

pulp *n.* The soft juicy part of a fruit; a soft moist mass; inexpensive paper.

pul•pit *n.* The elevated platform lectern used in a church, from which a service is conducted and sermons delivered.

pul•sate *v.* To beat rhythmically, with a steady, measurable pace. **pulsation, pulsator** *n.*

pulse *n.* The rhythmical beating of the arteries caused by the action of the heart. **pulse** *v.*

pul•ver•ize *v.* To be reduced to dust or powder by crushing.

pump *n.* A mechanical device for moving a gas or liquid. *v.* To raise with a pump; to obtain information through persistent questioning.

pump•kin *n.* A large, edible yellow-orange fruit having a thick rind and many seeds.

punch *n.* A tool used for perforating or piercing; a blow with the fist; a drink made of an alcoholic beverage and a fruit juice or other non-alcoholic beverage. *v.* To use a punch on something; to hit sharply with the hand or fist.

punc•tu•al *adj.* Prompt; arriving on time.

pun•ish *v.* To subject a person to confinement or impose a penalty for a crime.

pun•ish•ment *n.* A penalty imposed for breaking the law or a rule.

punt *n.* A narrow, long, flat-bottomed boat; in football, a kick of a football dropped from the hands. *v.* To kick a football; to go boating.

pup *n.* A puppy, young dog, or the young of other animals.

pu•pil *n.* A person who attends school and receives instruction by a teacher.

pup•pet *n.* A small figure of an animal or person manipulated by hand or by strings. **puppeteer, puppetry** *n.*

pur•chase *v.* To receive by paying money as an exchange. **purchaser** *n.*

pure *adj.* Free from anything that damages, weakens, or contaminates; innocent; clean.

purge *v.* To make clean; to free from guilt or sin; to rid of anything undesirable, as unwanted persons; to cause or induce emptying of the bowels. **purge** *n.*

pu•ri•fy *v.* To make clean or pure. **purification, purifier** *n.*

pu•ri•ty *n.* The quality of being pure; freedom from guilt or sin.

pur•ple *n.* A color between red and violet. **purplish** *adj.*

pur•port *v.* To give the appearance of intending; to imply, usually with the intent to deceive.

pur•pose *n.* A desired goal; an intention. **purposeful, purposeless** *adj.*, **purposely** *adv.*

purr *n.* The low, murmuring sound characteristic of a cat.

purse *n.* A small pouch or bag for money; a handbag; a pocketbook; the sum of money offered as a prize.

pur•sue *v.* To seek to achieve; to follow in an attempt to capture. **pursuer** *n.*

pur•suit *n.* The act of pursuing an occupation.

push *v.* To move forward by exerting force; to force oneself through a crowd; to sell illegally.

put *v.* To cause to be in a location; to bring into a specific relation or state; to bring forward for debate or consideration.

pu•ta•tive *adj.* Commonly supposed; arguable; supportable but not proven.

pu•tre•fy *v.* To cause to decay; to decay. **putrefaction** *n.*, **putrefied, putrid** *adj.*

putt *n.* In golf, a light stroke made on a putting green to get the ball into the hole.

puz•zle *v.* To bewilder; to confuse. *n.* A toy, board game, or word game which tests one's patience and skills.

qual·i·fy v. To prove something able.

qual·i·ty n. A distinguishing character which makes something such as it is; a high degree of excellence.

qualm n. A sudden feeling of sickness; sensation of uneasiness or doubt.

quan·da·ry n. A state of perplexity.

quan·ti·ty n. Number; amount; bulk; weight; a portion; as a large amount.

quar·an·tine n. A period of enforced isolation for a period of time used to prevent

metal by thrusting into water; to drink to satisfy a thirst.

quer·u·lous adj. Complaining or fretting; expressing complaints.

que·ry n. An inquiry; a question. v. To question.

quest n. A search; pursuit; an expedition to find something.

ques·tion n. An expression of inquiry which requires an answer; a problem; an unresolved matter; the act of inquiring.

ques·tion mark n. A mark of punctuation

arrangement; in computers, a sequence of stored programs or data on hold for processing.

quib·ble *v.* To raise a trivial objection. **quibble**, **quibbler** *n.*

quick *adj.* Moving swiftly; occurring in a short time; responding, thinking, or understanding something rapidly and easily. **quickly** *adv.*, **quickness** *n.*

quick·sand *n.* A bog of very fine, wet sand of considerable depth, that engulfs and sucks down objects, people, or animals.

quid *n.* A small portion of tobacco; a cow's cud.

qui·es·cent *adj.* Being in a state of quiet repose.

qui·et *adj.* Silent; making very little sound; still; tranquil; calm. *v.* To become or make quiet. *n.* The state of being quiet.

qui·nine *n.* A very bitter, colorless, crystalline powder used in the treatment of malaria.

quin·tes·sence *n.* The most essential and purest form of anything.

quin·tet *n.* A musical composition written for five people; any group of five.

quin·til·lion *n.* A thousand quadrillions, one followed by eighteen zeros.

quin·tu·ple *adj.* Increased five times; multiplied by five; consisting of five parts.

quip *n.* A sarcastic remark. **quipster** *n.*

quire *n.* Twenty-five sheets of paper removed from a complete ream of paper; a set of all the sheets of paper necessary to form a book.

quirk *n.* A sudden, sharp bend or twist; a personal mannerism.

quis·ling *n.* A person who is a traitor, working against his own country from within.

quit *v.* To cease; to give up; to depart; to abandon; to resign from a job or position.

quite *adv.* To the fullest degree; really; actually; to a great extent.

quiz *v.* To question, as with an informal oral or written examination. **quiz** *n.*

quiz·zi·cal *adj.* Being odd; teasing; questioning.

quon·dam *adj.* Former.

quo·rum *n.* The number of members needed in order to validate a meeting.

quo·ta *n.* An allotment or proportional share.

quote *v.* To repeat exactly what someone else has previously stated.

quo·tid·i·an *adj.* Occurring or recurring daily; everyday; pedestrian.

quo·tient *n.* In math, the amount or number which results when one number is divided by another.

R

R, r The eighteenth letter of the English alphabet.

rab·bet *n.* A recess or groove along the edge of a piece of wood cut to fit another piece to form a joint. **rabbeted** *adj.*

rab·bi *n.* An ordained leader and teacher of a Jewish congregation.

rab·bit *n.* A burrowing mammal related to but smaller than the hare.

rab·ble *n.* A disorderly crowd.

rab·id *adj.* Affected with rabies; mad; furious, rabidly adv. **rabidness** *n.*

ra·bies *n.* An infectious viral disease of the central nervous system, often fatal, transmitted by the bite of an infected animal.

rac·coon *n.* A nocturnal mammal with a black, mask-like face and a black-and-white ringed, bushy tail.

race *n.* The zoological division of the human population having common origin and other physical traits, such as hair, form and pigmentation; a contest judged by speed; any contest, such as a race for an elective office. **raced**, **racer** *n.*

ra·cial *adj.* A characteristic of a race of people.

rac·ism *n.* A thought or belief that one race is better than another race.

rack *n.* An open framework or stand for displaying or holding something; an instrument of torture used to stretch the body; a triangular frame used to arrange the balls on a pool table.

rack•et•eer *n.* One who engages in ads which are illegal.

rac•on•teur *n.* One who is skilled in the act of telling stories.

ra•dar *n.* A system which uses radio signals to detect the presence or speed of an object.

ra•di•al *adj.* Pertaining to or resembling a ray or radius; developing from a center axis.

ra•di•ant *adj.* Emitting rays of heat or light; beaming with kindness or love; projecting a strong quality.

ra•di•ate *v.* To move out in rays, such as heat moving through the air.

ra•di•a•tion *n.* An act of radiating.

ra•di•a•tor *n.* Something which radiates; a cooling device on automobiles and other vehicles; a heating device that uses hot water or radiant energy.

rad•i•cal *adj.* Making extreme changes in views, conditions, or habits; carrying theories to their fullest application.

ra•di•o *n.* The technique of communicating by radio waves; the business of broadcasting programmed material to the public via radio waves.

ra•di•o•ac•tive *adj.* Exhibiting radioactivity.

ra•di•o•ac•tiv•i•ty *n.* A spontaneous emission of electromagnetic radiation, as from a nuclear reaction.

ra•di•o fre•quen•cy *n.* A frequency which is above 15,000 cycles per second that is used in radio transmission.

rad•ish *n.* The edible root of the radish plant.

ra•di•um *n.* A radioactive metallic element symbolized by Ra.

ra•di•us *n.* A line from the center of a circle to its surface or circumference. **radii, radiuses** *pl.*

ra•don *n.* A heavy, colorless, radioactive gaseous element symbolized by Rn.

raf•fle *n.* A game of chance; a lottery in which one buys chances to win something.

raft *n.* A floating structure made from logs or planks.

raft•er *n.* A timber of a roof which slopes.

rag *n.* A useless cloth sometimes used for cleaning purposes.

rag•a•muf•fin *n.* A child who is unkempt.

rage *n.* Violent anger.

rag•ged *adj.* To be torn or ripped.

rag•weed *n.* A type of plant whose pollen can cause hay fever.

raid *n.* A sudden invasion or seizure.

rail *n.* A horizontal bar of metal, wood, or other strong material supported at both ends or at intervals; the steel bars used to support a track on a railroad.

rail•ing *n.* A barrier of wood.

rain *n.* The condensed water from atmospheric vapor, which falls to earth in the form of drops.

rain•bow *n.* An arc containing bands of colors of the spectrum formed opposite the sun and reflecting the sun's rays.

rain•coat *n.* A water-resistant or waterproof coat.

raise *v.* To cause to move upward; to build; to make greater in size, price, or amount; to increase the status; to grow.

rai•sin *n.* A dried grape.

rake *n.* A tool with a long handle at the end and a set of teeth at the other end used to gather leaves and other matter; a slope or incline. **rake** *v.*

ral•ly *v.* To call together for a purpose. *n.* A rapid recovery, as from depression, exhaustion, or any setback; a meeting whose purpose is to rouse or create support.

RAM *abbr.* Random access memory.

ram *n.* A male sheep; an implement used to drive or crush by impact; to cram or force into place.

ram•ble *v.* To stroll or walk without a special destination in mind; to talk without a sequence of ideas.

ram•bunc•tious *adj.* Rough or boisterous. **rambunctiousness** *n.*

ramp *n.* An incline which connects two different levels.

ram•pant *adj.* Exceeding or growing without control; wild in actions; standing on the hind legs and elevating both forelegs.

ram-rod *n.* A metal rod used to drive or plunge the charge into a muzzle-loading gun or pistol; the rod used for cleaning the barrels of a rifle or other firearm.

ram•shack•le *adj.* Likely to fall apart from poor construction or maintenance.

ranch *n.* A large establishment for raising cattle, sheep, or other livestock; a large farm that specializes in a certain crop or animals.

ran•cid *adj.* Having a rank taste or smell.

ran•dom *adj.* Done or made in a way that has no specific pattern or purpose.

range *n.* An area of activity; a tract of land over which animals such as cattle and horses graze; an extended line or row especially of mountains; an open area for shooting at a target; large cooking stove with burners and oven. *v.* to arrange in a certain order; to extend or proceed in a particular direction.

rank *n.* A degree of official position or status. *v.* To place in order, class, or rank.

ran•sack *v.* To search or plunder through every part of something.

ran•som *n.* The price demanded or paid for the release of a kidnapped person; the payment for the release of a person or property detained.

rant *v.* To talk in a wild, loud way.

rap•id *adj.* Having great speed; completed quickly or in a short time.

ra•pi•er *n.* A long, slender, straight sword with two edges.

rap•port *n.* A harmonious relationship.

rapt *adj.* Deeply absorbed or carried away with something and not noticing anything else; engrossed. **raptness** *n.*, **raptly** *adv.*

rare *adj.* Scarce; infrequent; held in high esteem or admiration because of infrequency.

ras•cal *n.* A person full of mischief; a dishonest person.

rash *adj.* Acting without consideration or caution. *n.* A skin irritation or eruption.

rasp *n.* A file with course raised and pointed projections. *v.* To scrape or rub with a course file; to utter something in a rough, grating voice. **rasper** *n.*

rasp•ber•ry *n.* A small edible fruit, red or black in color and having many small seeds.

rasp•y *adj.* Grating; irritable.

rat *n.* A rodent similar to the mouse, but having a longer tail.

ratch•et *n.* A mechanism consisting of a pawl that allows a wheel or bar to move in one direction only.

rate *n.* The measure of something to a fixed unit; the degree of value; a fixed ratio or amount. *v.* To appraise. **rating** *n.*

rath•er *adv.* Preferably; with more reason or justice; more accurate or precise.

rat•i•fy *v.* To approve something in an official way. **ratification** *n.*

rat•ing *n.* A relative evaluation or estimate of something.

ra•ti•o *n.* The relationship between two things in amount, size, degree, expressed as a proportion.

ra•tion *n.* A fixed portion or share. *v.* To provide or allot in portions. **rationing** *n.*

ra•tio•nal *adj.* Having the faculty of reasoning; being of sound mind.

rat•tle *v.* To make a series of rapid, sharp noises in quick succession; to talk rapidly; chatter. *n.* A baby's toy made to rattle when shaken.

rat•tled *adj.* To be in a state of confusion; broken down; worn; lacking composure; demonstrating or indicating a loss of control and composure.

rat•tler *n.* A rattlesnake; a venomous snake which has a series of horny, modified joints which make a rattling sound when moved.

rau•cous *adj.* Loud and rowdy; having a rough hoarse sound; disorderly. **raucously** *adv.*, **raucousness** *n.*

rav•age *v.* To bring on heavy destruction; devastate.

rave *v.* To speak incoherently; to speak with enthusiasm. *n.* The act of raving.

ra•ven *n.* A large bird, with shiny black feathers. *adj.* Of or relating to the glossy sheen or color of the raven.

ra•vine *n.* A deep gorge with steep sides in the earth's surface, usually created by flowing water.

raw *adj.* Uncooked; in natural condition; not processed; inexperienced; damp, sharp, or chilly.

ray *n.* A thin line of radiation or light; a small trace or amount; one of several lines coming from a point.

ray•on *n.* A synthetic cellulose yarn; any fabric made from such yarn.

ra•zor *n.* A sharp cutting instrument used especially for shaving.

reach *v.* To stretch out; to be able to grasp. *n.* The act of stretching out.

re•act *v.* To act in response to; to undergo a chemical change; to experience a chemical reaction.

read *v.* To visually go over something as a book, and to understand its meaning; to learn or be informed.

read•y *adj.* Prepared for use or action; quick or prompt; willing.

real *adj.* Something existing; genuine; true.

re•al•ism *n.* Concern or interest with actual fads and things as they really are.

re•al•i•ty *n., pl.* **-ties** The fact or state of being real or genuine; an actual situation or event.

re•al•ize *v.* To understand correctly; to make real.

re•al•ly *adv.* Actually; truly; indeed.

realm *n.* A scope or field of any power or influence.

ream *n.* A quantity of paper containing 500 sheets.

reap *v.* To harvest a crop with a sickle or other implement.

rear *n.* The back. *adj.* Of or at the rear. *v.* To raise up on the hind legs; to raise as an animal or child.

rea•son *n.* A statement given to confirm or justify a belief, promise, or excuse; the ability to decide things, to obtain ideas, to think clearly, and to make logical and rational choices and decisions. *v.* To discuss something logically; reasoning.

re•bate *n.* A deduction allowed on items sold; a discount; money which is returned to the purchaser from the original payment. *v.* To return part of the payment. rebater n.

re•bel *v.* To refuse allegiance; to resist any authority; to react with violence. *n.* One who opposes authority.

re•bel•lious *adj.* Engaged in rebellion; relating to a rebel or rebellion.

re•bound *v.* To spring back; to recover from a setback or frustration. *n.* Recoil.

re•buff *v.* To refuse abruptly; to snub.

re•build *v.* To make extensive repairs to something; to reconstruct; remodel.

re•call *v.* To order or summon to return; to ask for something to be returned, so that defects can be fixed or repaired; to remember; to recollect.

re•cant *v.* To formally admit that a previously held belief was wrong by making public confession.

re•cap *v.* To replace the cap; to retread an old tire; to review or summarize something; to recapitulate.

re•cede *v.* To move back; as floodwater; to withdraw from an agreement.

re•ceipt *n.* The written acknowledgment of something received.

re•ceive *v.* To take or get something; to greet customers or guests; to accept as true or correct.

re•cent *adj.* Happening at a time just before the present.

re•cep•ta•cle *n.* Anything which serves as a container; an electrical outlet designed to receive a plug.

re•cep•tion *n.* The act or manner of receiving something; a formal entertainment of guests, as a wedding reception.

re•cep•tion•ist *n.* An employee who greets callers and answers the telephone for a business.

re•cep•tive *adj.* Able to receive; open to

suggestion or persuasion; positively inclined to agree. **receptiveness, receptivity** n.

re·cess n. A break in the normal routine; a depression or niche in a smooth surface.

re·ces·sion n. The act of receding; withdrawal; a period or time of reduced economic activity.

re·ces·sion·al n. The exiting of the participants in a formal ceremony.

rec·i·pe n. The directions and a list of ingredients for preparing food.

re·cip·ro·cate v. To give and return mutually, one gift or favor for another.

re·cite v. To repeat from memory; to give an account of something in detail.

reck·less adj. State of being careless and rash when doing something.

reck·on v. To calculate; to compute; to estimate; to consider; to assume.

reck·on·ing n. The act of calculation or counting.

re·claim v. To redeem; to reform; to recall; to change to a more desirable condition or state.

rec·la·ma·tion n. The state of being reclaimed.

re·cline v. To assume a prone position.

rec·luse n. A person who chooses to live in seclusion.

rec·og·nize v. To experience or identify something or someone as having been known previously; to appreciate.

re·coil v. To fall back or to rebound.

rec·om·mend v. To suggest to another as desirable; advise.

rec·om·pense v. To reward with something for a service.

rec·on·cile v. To restore a friendship after an estrangement.

re·con·nais·sance n. An observation of territory such as that of the enemy.

re·con·noi·ter v. To survey a region.

re·con·sid·er v. To think about again with a view to changing a previous action or decision. **reconsideration** n.

re·cord v. To write down for future use or permanent reference; to preserve sound on a tape or disk for replay; a phonograph record.

re·count v. To tell the facts; narrate or describe in detail; to count again. n. A second count to check the results of the first count.

re·coup v. To be reimbursed; to recover.

re·course n. A turning to or an appeal for help.

re·cov·er v. To regain something which was lost; to be restored to good health.

rec·re·ant adj. Cowardly; unfaithful. **recreant** n.

rec·re·a·tion n. Refreshment of body and mind; a pleasurable occupation or exercise.

re·cruit v. To enlist someone for military or naval purposes; to look for someone as for a service or employment. n. A newly enlisted person.

rec·tal adj. Referring to the rectum of the body.

rec·tan·gle n. A parallelogram with all right angles.

rec·ti·fy v. To make correct; to purify by repeated distillations; to make an alternating current a direct current.

rec·ti·lin·e·ar adj. Made up of or indicated by straight lines; bounded by straight lines.

rec·ti·tude n. Rightness in principles and conduct; correctness.

rec·tor n. A member of the clergy in charge of a parish; a priest in charge of a congregation, church, or parish; the principal or head of a school or of a college.

rec·tum n. The lower terminal portion of the large intestine connecting the colon and anus.

re·cum·bent adj. Lying down or reclining.

re·cu·per·ate v. To regain strength or to regain one's health; to recover from a financial loss. **recuperation** n., **recuperative** adj.

re·cur v. To happen, to return, or to appear again. **recurrence, recurrent** adj.

re·dress v. To put something right.

red tape n. Routines which are rigid and

271

may cause a delay in a process; bureaucratic requirements.

re•duce *v.* To decrease; lessen in number, degree, or amount; to put into order; to lower in rank; to lose weight by dieting.

re•dun•dant *adj.* Exceeding what is necessary; repetitive; intentionally or inadvertently duplicative.

red•wood *n.* A tree found in California which is very tall and wide.

reed *n.* Tall grass with a slender stem, which grows in wet areas; a thin tongue of wood, metal, cane, or plastic; placed in the mouthpiece of an instrument to produce sounds by vibrating.

reef *n.* A chain of rocks, coral, or sand at or near the surface of the water.

reek *v.* To emit vapor or smoke; to give off a strong offensive odor.

reel *n.* A device which revolves on an axis, used for winding up or letting out fishing line, rope, or other string-like material.

re•en•ter *v.* To enter a room or area again.

re•fer *v.* To direct for treatment, information, or help.

ref•er•ee *n.* A person who supervises a game, making sure all the rules are followed.

ref•er•ence *n.* The act of referring someone to someplace or to something.

ref•er•en•dum *n.* A public vote on an item for final approval or for rejection.

ref•er•ent *n.* That which is referred to, such as a person.

re•fill *v.* To fill something again.

re•fine *v.* To purify by removing unwanted substances or material; to improve.

re•fin•er•y *n.* A place or location used for the purpose of refining products, such as sugar.

re•fin•ish *v.* The act of putting a new surface onto something, such as wood.

re•flect *v.* To throw back rays of light from a surface; to give an image, as from a mirror; to ponder or think carefully.

re•flec•tor *n.* Something which is able to reflect things, such as light.

re•flex *adj.* Turning, casting, or bending backward. *n.* An involuntary reaction of the nervous system to a stimulus.

re•for•est *v.* To replant a forest.

re•form *v.* To reconstruct, make over, or change something for the better; improve; to abandon or give up evil ways.

re•frac•tion *n.* The state of being refracted or deflected.

re•frac•to•ry *adj.* Unmanageable; obstinate; difficult to melt; resistant to heat. *n.* Something which does not change significantly when exposed to high temperatures; a kiln or furnace.

re•frain *v.* To hold back.

re•fresh *v.* To freshen something again.

re•fresh•ment *n.* Something which will refresh, such as a cold drink or snack.

re•frig•er•ate *v.* To chill; to preserve food by chilling; to place in a refrigerator.

re•frig•er•a•tor *n.* A box-like piece of equipment which chills food and other matter.

ref•uge *n.* Shelter or protection from harm; any place one may turn for relief or help.

ref•u•gee *n.* A person who flees to find safety; especially from a homeland.

re•fund *v.* To return or pay back; to reimburse.

re•fur•bish *v.* To make clean; to renovate.

re•fus•al *n.* The denial of something which is demanded.

re•fuse *v.* To decline; to reject; to deny.

ref•use *n.* Rubbish; trash.

re•fute *v.* To overthrow or to disprove with the use of evidence.

re•gain *v.* To recover; to reach again.

re•gal *adj.* Of or appropriate for royalty.

re•gard *v.* To look upon closely; to consider; to have great affection for. *n.* Careful attention or thought; esteem or affection. *pl.* Greetings of good wishes.

re•gard•less *adj.* State of being careless or showing no regard toward something or someone.

re•gat•ta *n.* A boat race.

re•gen•cy *n.* The jurisdiction or office of a regent.

re•gen•er•ate *v.* To reform spiritually or

morally; to make or create anew; to refresh or restore.

re•gent *n.* One who rules and acts as a ruler during the absence of a sovereign, or when the ruler is under age.

reg•ime *n.* Governmental power, usually controlled by other than the citizenry.

reg•i•men *n.* A routine or repetitive treatment or practice; habit or common schedule; therapy.

reg•i•ment *n.* A military unit of ground troops which is composed of several battalions.

re•gion *n.* An administrative, political, social, or geographical area.

re•gress *v.* To return to a previous state or condition. **regression** *n.*

re•gret *v.* To feel disappointed or distressed about. *n.* A sense of loss or expression of grief; a feeling of sorrow.

reg•u•lar *adj.* Usual; normal; conforming to set principles or procedures.

re•gur•gi•tate *v.* To pour something forth; to vomit; to repeat what has been said.

re•ha•bil•i•tate *v.* To restore to a former state, by education and therapy.

re•hears•al *n.* The act of practicing for a performance.

reign *n.* The time when the monarch rules over an area.

re•im•burse *v.* To repay.

rein•deer *n.* A large deer found in northern regions, both sexes having antlers.

re•in•force *v.* To support; to strengthen with additional people or equipment.

re•it•er•ate *v.* To say or do something over and over again; to utter the basic sense again.

re•ject *v.* To refuse; to discard as useless.

re•joice *v.* To fill with joy; to be filled with joy.

re•late *v.* To tell the events of; to narrate; to bring into natural association.

re•lat•ed *adj.* To be in the same family; connected to each other by blood or by marriage.

re•la•tion•ship *n.* A connection by blood or family; kinship; friendship; a natural association.

rel•a•tive *adj.* Relevant; connected; considered in comparison or relationship to other. *n.* A member of one's family.

re•lax *v.* To make loose or lax; to relieve something from effort or strain; to become less formal or less reserved.

re•lease *v.* To set free from confinement; to unfasten; to free; to relinquish a claim on something.

re•lief *n.* Anything which decreases or lessens anxiety, pain, discomfort, or other unpleasant conditions or feelings.

re•lig•ion *n.* An organized system of beliefs, rites, and celebrations centered on a supernatural being; belief pursued with devotion. **religious** *adj.*

re•main *v.* To continue without change; to stay after the departure of others.

re•main•der *n.* Something left over.

rem•e•dy *n.* A therapy or medicine which relieves pain; something which corrects an error or fault. *v.* To cure or relieve.

re•mem•ber *v.* To bring back or recall to the mind; to retain in the mind carefully.

re•mind *v.* To cause or help to remember.

rem•i•nis•cence *n.* The practice or process of recalling the past.

re•mit *v.* To send money as payment for goods; to forgive, as a crime or sin; to slacken, make less violent, or less intense.

re•move *v.* To get rid of; to extract; to dismiss from office; to change one's business or residence.

ren•e•gade *n.* A person who rejects one allegiance for another; an outlaw; a traitor.

re•new *v.* To make new or nearly new by restoring; to resume.

ren•o•vate *v.,* To return or to restore to a good condition.

re•nown *n.* The quality of being widely honored.

rent *n.* The payment made for the use of another's property. *v.* To obtain occupancy in exchange for payment.

re•pair *v.* To restore to good or usable condition; to renew; refresh.

re•pay *v.* To pay back money; to do

something in return.

re•peat *v.* To utter something again; to do an action again.

re•pel *v.* To discourage; to force away; to create aversion.

re•pent *v.* To feel regret for something which has occurred; to change one's sinful way.

rep•e•ti•tion *n.* The act of doing something over and over again.

re•place *v.* To return something to its previous place.

re•plen•ish *v.* To add to something; to replace what has gone or been used.

rep•li•ca *n.* A reproduction or copy.

re•ply *v.* To give an answer.

re•port *n.* A detailed account; usually in a formal way. *v.* To tell about.

re•port card *n.* The report of a student's progress.

re•pos•sess *v.* To restore ownership.

rep•re•hend *v.* To show or express disapproval of.

rep•re•sent *v.* To stand for something; to serve as the official representative for.

rep•re•sent•a•tive *n.* A person or thing serving as an example or type. *adj.* Of or relating to government by representation; typical.

re•press *v.* To restrain; hold back; to remove from the conscious mind.

re•prieve *v.* To postpone punishment; to provide temporary relief.

rep•ri•mand *v.* To censure severely; rebuke.

re•pro•duce *v.* To produce an image or copy; to produce an offspring; to recreate.

rep•tile *n.* A cold-blooded, egg-laying vertebrate.

re•pub•lic *n.* A political unit or state where representatives are elected to exercise the power.

re•pulse *v.* To repel or drive back; to repel or reject rudely. **repulsive** *adj.*

rep•u•ta•ble *adj.* Honorable; in possession of a good reputation; reliable and professional.

re•pu•ta•tion *n.* The commonly held evaluation of a person's character.

re•quest *v.* To ask for something.

re•quire *v.* To demand or insist upon.

req•ui•site *adj.* Absolutely needed; necessary.

req•ui•si•tion *n.* A demand or a request.

re•sale *n.* The act of selling something again.

res•cue *v.* To free from danger.

re•search *n.* A scientific or scholarly investigation.

re•sem•ble *v.* To have similarity to something.

re•sent *v.* To feel angry about.

res•er•va•tion *n.* The act of keeping something back.

re•serve *v.* To save for a special reason; to set apart; to retain; to put off.

res•er•voir *n.* A body of water stored for the future; large reserve; a supply.

re•side *v.* To dwell permanently; to exist as a quality or attribute.

re•sign *v.* To give up; to submit to something as being unavoidable; to quit.

res•in *n.* A substance from certain plants and trees used in varnishes and lacquers.

re•sist *v.* To work against or actively oppose; to withstand.

res•o•lute *adj.* Coming from or characterized by determination.

re•solve *v.* To make a firm decision on something; to solve.

re•sort *v.* To fall back upon. *n.* A place, or recreation, for rest, and for a vacation.

re•sound *v.* To be filled with echoing sounds; to reverberate; to ring or sound loudly.

re•source *n.* A source of aid or support which can be drawn upon if needed.

re•spect *v.* To show consideration or esteem for; to relate to. *n.* Courtesy or considerate treatment.

res•pi•ra•tion *n.* The process or act of inhaling and exhaling.

re•spond *v.* To answer or reply; to act when prompted by something or someone.

re•sponse *n.* A reply; the act of replying.

re•spon•si•ble *adj.* Trustworthy; in charge; having authority. **responsibility** *n.*

rest *n.* A cessation of all work, activity, or motion. *v.* To stop work.

res•tau•rant *n.* A place which serves meals to the public.

res•ti•tu•tion *n.* The act of restoring something to its rightful owner; compensation for injury, loss, or damage.

res•tive *adj.* Nervous or impatient because of a delay.

re•store *v.* To bring back to a former condition.

re•strict *v.* To confine within limits. **restriction** *n.*

re•sult *v.* To happen or exist in a particular way. *n.* The consequence of an action, course, or operation.

re•sume *v.* To start again after an interruption.

res•u•me *n.* A summary of one's personal history, background, work, and education.

re•sus•ci•tate *v.* To return to life; to revive.

re•tail *n.* The sale of goods or commodities to the public. *v.* To sell to the consumer.

re•tain *v.* To hold in one's possession; to remember; to employ someone.

re•tard *v.* To delay or slow the progress of.

re•tar•da•tion *n.* A condition in which mental development is slow or delayed; a condition of mental slowness.

re•ten•tion *n.* The act or condition of being retained.

ret•i•na *n.* The light-sensitive membrane lining the inner eyeball connected by the optic nerve to the brain.

re•tire *v.* To depart for rest; to remove oneself from the daily routine of working. **retirement** *n.*

re•trace *v.* To go back over.

re•treat *n.* The act of withdrawing from danger; a time of study and meditation in a quiet; isolated location.

re•trieve *v.* To regain; to find something and carry it back.

ret•ro•spect *n.* A review of things in the past. **retrospective** *adj.*

re•turn *v.* To come back to an earlier condition; to reciprocate. *n.* The act of sending, bringing, or coming back.

re•turns *n.* A yield or profit from investments; a report on the results of an election.

re•un•ion *n.* The coming together of a group which has been separated for a period of time.

re•veal *v.* To disclose; to expose.

rev•el *v.* To take great delight in.

rev•e•la•tion *n.* An act of or something revealed; a manifestation of divine truth.

re•venge *v.* To impose injury in return for injury received.

re•verse *adj.* Turned backward in position. *n.* The opposite of something; change or turn to the opposite direction; to transpose or exchange the positions of.

re•vert *v.* To return to a former practice or belief.

re•view *v.* To study or look over something again; to give a report on. *n.* A study which gives a critical estimate of something.

re•vise *v.* To look over something again with the intention of improving or correcting it.

re•viv•al *n.* The act or condition or reviving; the return of a film or play which was formerly presented, a meeting whose purpose is religious reawakening.

re•vive *v.* To restore, refresh, or recall; to return to consciousness or life.

re•voke *v.* To nullify or make void by recalling.

re•volt *v.* To try to overthrow authority; to fill with disgust.

rev•o•lu•tion *n.* The act or state of orbital motion around a point; the abrupt overthrow of a government; a sudden change in a system.

re•volve *v.* To move around a central point; to spin; to rotate.

re•vue *n.* A musical show consisting of song, dances, skits, and other similar entertainment.

rhi·noc·er·os *n.* A very large mammal with one or two upright horns on the snout.

rhu·barb *n.* A garden plant with large leaves and edible stalks used for pies.

rhyme *n.* A word or verse whose terminal sound corresponds with another.

rhy·thm *n.* Music, speech, or movements characterized by equal or regularly alternating beats.

rib *n.* One of a series of curved bones enclosed in the chest of man and animals.

rib·bon *n.* A narrow band or strip of fabric.

rice *n.* A cereal grass grown extensively in warm climates.

rich *adj.* Having great wealth; of great value; satisfying and pleasing in voice, color, tone, or other qualities.

rid *v.* To make free from anything objectionable.

rid·dle *v.* To perforate with numerous holes. *n.* A puzzling problem or question which requires a clever solution.

ride *v.* To travel in a vehicle or on an animal. **rider** *n.*

ridge *n.* A long, narrow crest; a horizontal line formed where two sloping surfaces meet.

rid·i·cule *n.* Actions or words intended to make a person or thing the object of mockery.

ri·dic·u·lous *adj.* Causing derision or

right an·gle *n.* An angle of 90 degrees; an angle with two sides perpendicular to each other.

rig·id *adj.* Not bending; inflexible; severe; stern.

rig·or *n.* The condition of being rigid or stiff; stiffness of temper; harshness.

rind *n.* A tough outer layer which may be peeled off.

ring *n.* A circular mark, line, or object; a small circular band worn on a finger. *v.* To make a clear resonant sound.

rink *n.* A smooth area covered with ice used for ice-skating.

rinse *v.* To wash lightly with water. *n.* A hair coloring or conditioning solution.

ri·ot *n.* A turbulent public disturbance.

rip *v.* To tear apart violently; to move violently or quickly. *n.* A torn place.

rip·cord *n.* A cord which, when pulled, releases a parachute from its pack.

ripe *adj.* Fully developed or aged, mature.

rip·ple *v.* To cause to form small waves on the surface of water; to waver gently.

rise *v.* To move from a lower position to a higher one; to extend upward; to meet a challenge. *n.* The act of going up or rising; an elevation in condition or rank. **riser** *n.*

risk *n.* A chance of suffering or encountering harm or loss.

rite *n.* A formal religious ceremony; any

more objects.

roach *n.* A European freshwater fish; cockroach.

road *n.* A public highway used for vehicles, people, and animals; a path or course.

road block *n.* An obstruction in a road, which prevents passage.

roam *v.* To travel aimlessly.

roar *v.* To utter a deep prolonged sound of excitement; to laugh loudly.

roast *v.* To cook meat by using dry heat in an oven. *n.* A cut of meat.

rob *v.* To take property unlawfully from another person. **robber** *n.*, **robbery** *n.*

robe *n.* A long loose garment usually worn over night clothes; a long flowing garment worn on ceremonial occasions.

rob•in *n.* A large North American bird with a black head and reddish breast.

ro•bot *n.* A machine capable of performing human duties.

ro•bust *adj.* Full of strength and health; rich; vigorous.

rock *n.* A hard naturally formed material.

rock•er *n.* A curved piece, usually of wood, on which a cradle or chair rocks.

rock•et *n.* A device propelled with the thrust from a gaseous combustion. *v.* To move rapidly.

rode *v.* Past tense of *ride*.

ro•dent *n.* A mammal, such as a rat, mouse, or beaver having large incisors used for gnawing.

ro•de•o *n.* A public show, contest, or demonstration of ranching skills.

rogue *n.* A scoundrel or dishonest person; an innocent or playful person.

roll *v.* To move in any direction by turning over and over; to sway or rock from side to side, as a ship; to make a deep prolonged sound, as thunder. *n.* A list of names.

roll•er *n.* A cylinder for crushing, smoothing or rolling something.

ro•mance *n.* A love affair characterized by ideals of devotion and purity; a fictitious story filled with extravagant adventures.

romp *v.* To play or frolic in a carefree way.

rook•ie *n.* An untrained person; a novice or inexperienced person.

room *n.* A section or area of a building set off by partitions or walls. *v.* To occupy or live in a room.

roost *n.* A place or perch on which birds sleep or rest.

root *n.* The part of a plant which grows in the ground. *v.* To search or rummage for something.

rope *n.* A heavy cord of twisted fiber.

ro•sa•ry *n.* A string of beads for counting prayers; a series of prayers.

rose *n.* A shrub or climbing vine having sharp prickly stems and variously colored fragrant flowers.

ros•ter *n.* A list of names.

ro•tate *v.* To turn on an axis; to alternate something in sequence.

rot•ten *adj.* Decomposed, morally corrupt; very bad.

ro•tund *adj.* Plump; rounded.

rouge *n.* A cosmetic coloring for the cheeks.

rough *adj.* Having an uneven surface; violent or harsh. *n.* The part of a golf course with tall grass.

round *adj.* Curved; circular; spherical. *v.* To become round; to surround.

rouse *v.* To awaken or stir up.

route *n.* A course of travel. *v.* To send in a certain direction.

rout•er *n.* In computers, a distribution device allowing connections among several networks via a system of electronic channels.

rou•tine *n.* Activities done regularly. *adj.* Ordinary.

rove *v.* To wander over a wide area.

row *n.* A number of things positioned next to each other; a continuous line. *v.* To propel a boat with oars.

roy•al *adj.* Relating to a king or queen.

roy•al•ty *n.* Monarchs and or their families; a payment to someone for the use of copyright or services.

rub *v.* To move over a surface with friction and pressure; to cause to become worn or frayed.

rub•ber *n.* A resinous elastic material obtained from tropical plants or produced synthetically.

rub•bish *n.* Worthless trash; nonsense.

rub•ble *n.* The pieces of broken material or stones.

ru•by *n.* A deep-red precious stone.

rud•der *n.* A broad, flat, hinged device attached to the stern of a boat, used for steering.

rud•dy *adj.* Red in color or hue.

rude *adj.* Discourteous; offensively blunt.

ruff *n.* A stiff collar which has pleats in it.

ruf•fi•an *n.* A lawless, rowdy person.

ruf•fle *n.* A pleated strip or frill; a decorative band. *v.* To disturb or destroy the smoothness.

rug *n.* A heavy textile fabric used to cover a floor.

rug•ged *adj.* Strong; rough; having an uneven or rough surface.

ru•in *n.* Total destruction. *v.* To destroy. **ruination** *n.*

rule *n.* Controlling power; an authoritative direction or statement. *v.* To have control over; to be in command.

rum *n.* A type of liquor made from molasses and distilled.

rum•ble *v.* To make a heavy, continuous sound. *n.* A long, deep rolling sound.

rum•mage *v.* To look or search thoroughly by digging or turning things over; to ransack.

ru•mor *n.* An uncertain truth circulated from one person to another; gossip. *v.* To spread by rumor.

run *v.* To hurry busily from place to place; to move quickly in such a way that both feet leave the ground for a portion of each step; to be a candidate seeking an office; to drain or discharge.

run•down *adj.* The state of being worn down.

rung *n.* A bar or board which forms a step of a ladder.

rup•ture *n.* A state of being broken; the act of bursting.

ru•ral *adj.* Pertaining to the country.

rush *v.* To move quickly; to hurry; to be in a hurry.

rust *n.* Ferric oxide which forms a coating on iron material exposed to moisture and oxygen.

rus•tic *adj.* Characteristic of country life. *n.* A simple person. **rustically** *adv.*

rus•tle *v.* To move making soft sounds.

ruth•less *adj.* Merciless.

rye *n.* A cultivated cereal grass whose seeds are used to make flour and whiskey.

S

S, s The nineteenth letter of the English alphabet.

sa•ber *n.* A lightweight sword.

sa•ber-toothed ti•ger *n.* A type of extinct cat which was characterized by the great development of the upper canines.

sa•ble *n.* A carnivorous mammal having soft, black or dark fur.

sab•o•tage *n.* An act of destruction, intended to obstruct production of war material by the opposing side.

sack *n.* A strong bag for holding articles; dismissal from a position or job; sleeping bag or bed.

sack out *v.* To go or to get into bed.

sack race *n.* Type of race where the contestants jump inside a sack to the finish line.

sac•ra•ment *n.* A formal Christian rite performed in a church, as a baptism. The consecrated bread and wine of the Eucharist; the Lord's Supper.

sa•cred *adj.* Dedicated to worship; holy.

sac•ri•fice *n.* The practice of offering something, as an animal's life, to a deity. *v.* To give up something of value for something else.

sac•ri•lege *n.* A technical violation of what is sacred because it is consecrated to God.

sad *adj.* Marked by sorrow; unhappy; causing sorrow; deplorable.

sad•dle *n.* A seat for a rider, as on the back of a horse or bicycle. *v.* To put a saddle on; to load down; to burden.

sad•dle•bag *n.* A cover pouch put across the back of the horse.

sad•dler *n.* A person who makes or sells saddles.

sa•fa•ri *n.* A trip or journey; a hunting expedition in Africa.

safe *adj.* Secure from danger, harm, or evil; not likely to cause harm. *n.* A strong metal container used to protect and store important documents or money.

safe•guard *n.* A precautionary measure.

safe•ty *n.* A condition of being safe from injury or hurt.

safe•ty pin *n.* A type of pin with a clasp that has a guard to cover its point.

sag *v.* To droop; to sink from pressure or weight; to lose strength.

sa•ga *n.* A long heroic story.

sage *n.* A person recognized for judgment and wisdom.

said *v.* Past tense of *say*.

sail *n.* A strong fabric used to catch the wind and cause a ship to move *v.* To travel on a sailing vessel.

sail•boat *n.* A boat propelled with a sail.

sail•cloth *n.* A type of canvas used for boat sails.

sail•er *n.* A boat which has specified sailing qualities.

sail•fish *n.* A type of fish that has a large dorsal fin.

sail•ing *n.* The skill of managing a ship.

sail•or *n.* The person that sails a boat or a ship.

saint *n.* A person of great purity who has been officially recognized as such by the Roman Catholic Church. **saintly** *adj.*

sake *n.* Motive or reason for doing something.

sal•ad *n.* A dish usually made of green vegetables, fruit, or meat tossed with dressing.

sal•ad dres•sing *n.* A type of dressing used for the flavoring of a salad.

sal•a•man•der *n.* A lizard-like amphibian with porous, scaleless skin.

sa•la•mi *n.* A spiced sausage made of beef and pork.

sa•la•ry *n.* A set compensation paid on a regular basis for services rendered. **salaried** *adj.*

sale *n.* An exchange of goods for a price; disposal of items at reduced prices.

sales *adj.* Pertaining to selling.

sales•clerk *n.* A person who sells in a store.

sales tax *n.* A tax placed on the sale of goods.

sa•li•va *n.* Tasteless fluid secreted in the mouth which aids in digestion.

salm•on *n.* A large game fish with pinkish flesh.

sa•lon *n.* A large drawing room; a business establishment pertaining to fashion.

sa•loon *n.* A place where alcoholic drinks are sold; a barroom.

salt *n.* A white crystalline solid, mainly sodium chloride, found in the earth and sea water, used as a preservative and a seasoning. **salty** *adj.*

sal•tine *n.* A crisp cracker sprinkled with salt.

salt lake *n.* A lake that has become salty.

salt marsh *n.* An area of flat land subject to the overflow of salt water.

salt•shak•er *n.* A type of container used for the purpose of sprinkling salt onto foods.

salt•wa•ter *adj.* Seawater.

sal•u•ta•ry *adj.* Wholesome; healthful.

sal•u•ta•tion *n.* An expression; a greeting of good will, as used to open a letter.

sal•u•ta•tor•i•an *n.* A student who usually has the second highest rank in the class.

sa•lute *v.* To show honor to a superior officer by raising the right hand to the forehead. *n.* An act of respect or greeting.

sal•vage *n.* The act of rescuing a ship, its cargo, or its crew; property which has been saved. *v.* To save from destruction.

sal•va•tion *n.* The means which effect salvation; deliverance from the effects of sin.

salve *n.* A medicated ointment used to soothe the pain of a burn or wound.

sa•mar•i•tan *n.* A person who is ready to help others in need.

sam•ba *n.* A type of Brazilian dance.

same *adj.* Identical; exactly alike; similar; not changing. *pron.* The very same one or thing.

sam•ple *n.* A portion which represents the whole. *v.* To try a little.

sam•pler *n.* A person who collects or examines samples; a sewing student's practice samples, often in designs, letters, or other decorative forms.

sam•pling *n.* A small section, part, or portion collected as a sample or analysis.

sam•u•rai *n.* The warrior aristocracy of Japan.

san•a•to•ri•um *n.* An institution for treating chronic diseases.

sanc•ti•fy *v.* To make holy.

sanc•tion *n.* Permission from a person of authority; a penalty to ensure compliance. *v.* To officially approve an action.

sanc•ti•ty *n.* The state of being holy.

sanc•tu•ar•y *n.* A sacred, holy place, as the part of a church, where services are held; a safe place; a refuge.

sand *n.* Fine grains of disintegrated rock found in deserts and on beaches. *v.* To smooth or polish with sandpaper.

san•dal *n.* A shoe fastened to the foot by straps attached to the sole.

sand•bag *n.* A sand-filled bag.

sand•bar *n.* A sand ridge which has been built by currents of the water.

sand•blast *n.* A stream of sand projected by steam used for cleaning.

sand•box *n.* A receptacle that contains loose sand.

sand dol•lar *n.* A flat circular sea urchin that lives in shallow water on the sandy bottom.

sand•er *n.* A person who sands; a device for sanding.

sand flea *n.* A type of flea that may be found on the sand.

sand fly *n.* A type of small biting fly that has two wings.

sand•pa•per *n.* A type of paper covered on one side with sand used for the purpose of smoothing rough edges.

sand•pile *n.* A large pile of sand that children can play in.

sand•pip•er *n.* A small shore bird having a long soft-tipped bill.

sand•stone *n.* A type of sedimentary rock.

sand•storm *n.* A storm in the desert that can drive clouds of sand in front of it.

sand trap *n.* A hazard on the golf course filled with sand.

sand•wich *n.* Two or more slices of bread between which a filling, such as cheese or meat, is placed.

sand•y *adj.* Containing or consisting of sand.

sane *adj.* Having a healthy, sound mind; showing good judgment.

san•i•tar•y *adj.* Free from bacteria or filth which endanger health.

san•i•ta•tion *n.* The process of making something sanitary.

san•i•tize *v.* To make sanitary; to make clean or free of germs.

san•i•ty *n.* The state of being sane.

sank *v.* Past tense of *sink*.

sap *n.* The liquid which flows or circulates through plants and trees. *v.* To weaken or wear away gradually.

sap•phire *n.* A clear, deep blue gem, used in jewelry.

sar•casm *n.* An insulting or mocking statement or remark.

sar•dine *n.* A small edible fish of the herring family, often canned in oil.

sash *n.* A band worn over the shoulder or around the waist.

sas•sa•fras *n.* The dried root of a North American tree, used as flavoring.

sat•el•lite *n.* A natural or man-made object which orbits a celestial body.

sat•in *n.* A smooth, shiny fabric made of silk, nylon, or rayon, having a glossy face and dull back.

sat•ire *n.* The use of mockery, sarcasm, or humor in a literary work to ridicule or attack human vice.

sat•is•fac•tion *n.* Anything which brings about a happy feeling; the fulfillment of a need, appetite, or desire; a source of gratification.

sat•is•fy *v.* To fulfill; to give assurance to.

sat•u•rate *v.* To make completely wet; to soak or load to capacity.

sauce *n.* A liquid or dressing served as an accompaniment to food.

sau•cer *n.* A small shallow dish for holding a cup.

sau•er•kraut *n.* Shredded and salted cabbage cooked in its own juices until tender and sour.

sau•na *n.* A steam bath in which one is subjected to heat produced by water poured over heated rocks.

sau•sage *n.* Chopped meat, usually pork, highly seasoned, stuffed into a casing and cooked.

save *v.* To rescue from danger, loss, or harm; to prevent loss or waste; to keep for another time in the future; to be delivered from sin.

sav•ior *n.* One who saves.

sa•vor *n.* The taste or smell of something. *v.* To have a particular smell; to enjoy.

saw *n.* A tool with a sharp metal blade edged with teeth-like points for cutting. *v.* Past tense of see; to cut with a saw.

sax•o•phone *n.* A brass wind instrument having finger keys and a reed mouthpiece.

say *v.* To speak aloud; to express oneself in words; to indicate; to show. *n.* The chance to speak; the right to make a decision.

scab *n.* The stiff, crusty covering which forms over a healing wound.

scaf•fold *n.* A temporary support of metal or wood erected for workers who are building or working on a large structure.

scaf•fold•ing *n.* The system of scaffolds.

scald *v.* To burn with steam or a hot liquid; to heat a liquid to a temperature just under boiling.

scale *n.* A flat plate which covers certain animals, especially fish and reptiles; a device for weighing; a series of marks indicating the relationship between a map or model and the actual dimensions.

sca•lene *adj.* Having three sides not equal in their lengths.

scal•lion *n.* A type of onion that forms a thick basal part but without a bulb.

scalp *n.* The skin which covers the top of the human head where hair normally grows. *v.* To remove the scalp from.

scal•pel *n.* A small, straight knife with a narrow, pointed blade, used in surgery.

scamp•er *v.* To run playfully about.

scam•pi *n.* A type of large shrimp prepared with a garlic sauce.

scan *v.* To examine all parts closely; to look at quickly; to analyze the rhythm of a poem.

scan•dal *n.* Something which brings disgrace when exposed to the public; gossip.

scan•dal•ous *adj.* Being offensive to morality.

scan•ner *n.* The device for sensing recorded data.

scant *adj.* Not plentiful or abundant; inadequate.

scar *n.* A permanent mark which remains on the skin after a sore has healed.

scarce *adj.* Not common or plentiful.

scare *v.* To become scared or to frighten someone suddenly.

scare•crow *n.* A human figure usually placed in a garden for the purpose of scaring off animals and preventing them from eating what is being grown.

scared *adj.* The state of fear one may be thrown into.

scarf *n.* A wide piece of cloth worn around the head, neck, and shoulders for warmth.

scar•let *n.* A bright or vivid red.

scar•y *adj.* Able to scare; frightening, sinister, or surprising.

sca•thing *adj.* To be bitterly severe.

scat•ter *v.* To spread around; to distribute in different directions.

sca•venge *v.* To salvage something from being discarded; to take away from an area.

scav•en•ger *n.* An animal, as a vulture, which feeds on decaying or dead animals or plant matter.

scene *n.* A view; the time and place where an event occurs; a public display of temper; a part of a play.

scen•er•y *n.* Printed scenes or other accessories used with a play.

sce•nic *adj.* Pertaining to natural scenery.

scent *n.* A smell; an odor. *v.* To smell; to give something a scent.

scent•ed *adj.* To have a smell or a scent.

scep•ter *n.* A rod or staff carried by a king as a sign of authority.

sched•ule *n.* A list or written chart which shows the times at which events will happen, including specified deadlines.

scheme *n.* A plan of action; an orderly combination of related parts; a secret plot.

schnau•zer *n.* A type of dog that has a long head, small ears, and a wiry coat.

schol•ar *n.* A student with a strong interest in learning.

schol•ar•ly *adj.* Suitable to learned persons.

schol•ar•ship *n.* A grant given to a student to enable them to go to school.

school *n.* A place for teaching and learning; a group of persons devoted to similar principles.

school board *n.* The board of people in charge of schools.

school•book *n.* A textbook used for the schoolwork done in schools.

school bus *n.* A vehicle used to take children to and from school.

school•ing *n.* The instruction given in school.

school•room *n.* A classroom used for teaching.

school•work *n.* The lessons done in school.

sci•ence *n.* The study and explanation of natural phenomena in an orderly way.

sci-fi *adj.* Pertaining to science fiction.

scis•sors *pl. n.* A cutting tool consisting of two blades joined and pivoted so that the edges are close to each other.

scoff *n.* The expression of derision or scorn.

scold *v.* To accuse or reprimand harshly.

scoop *n.* A small, shovel-like tool. *v.* To lift up or out.

scoot *v.* To go suddenly and quickly.

scoot•er *n.* Type of child's foot-operated toy consisting of a board mounted between two wheels.

scope *n.* The range or extent of one's actions; the space to function or operate in.

scorch *v.* To burn slightly, changing the color and taste of something; to parch with heat.

scorched *adj.* Discolored by scorching.

score *n.* A numerical record of total points won in a game or other contest; the result of an examination; a grouping of twenty items; a written musical composition which indicates the part to be performed by each person; a groove made with a pointed tool. *v.* To achieve or win; to arrange a musical score for.

score•board *n.* A board used to display the score of a game.

scorn *n.* Contempt; disdain. *v.* To treat with scorn.

scorn•ful *adj.* Being full of scorn.

scor•pi•on *n.* An arachnid having an upright tail tipped with a poisonous sting.

scoun•drel *n.* A villain or a robber.

scour *v.* To clean by rubbing with an abrasive agent; to clean thoroughly.

scout *v.* To observe activities in order to obtain information. *n.* A person whose job is to obtain information; a member of the Boy Scouts or Girl Scouts.

scout•ing *n.* The action of one who scouts.

scowl *v.* To have an angry look; to frown.

scrab•ble *v.* To scratch about frantically, as if searching for something.

scram•ble *v.* To move with panic.

scrap *n.* A small section or piece. *v.* To throw away waste.

scrap•book *n.* A book for collecting various paper items or other flat objects.

scrape *v.* To rub a surface with a sharp object in order to clean.

scrap heap *n.* A large pile of metal which has been discarded.

scratch *v.* To mark or make a slight cut on; to mark with the fingernails. *n.* The mark made by scratching; a harsh, unpleasant sound.

scratch pa•per *n.* The paper used just to take notes; disposable tablets.

scratch•y *adj.* Marked with scratches.

scrawl *n.* To write or draw quickly and often illegibly.

scraw•ny *adj.* Very thin; skinny.

scream *v.* To utter a long, sharp cry, as of fear or pain. *n.* A long piercing cry.

screech *v.* To make a shrill, harsh noise.

screech owl *n.* A type of owl that has a tuft of feathers on its head, with a distinctive sound.

screen *n.* A movable object used to keep something from view, to divide, or to decorate; a flat reflecting surface on which a picture is projected. *v.* To keep from view.

screen•ing *n.* A metal mesh that may be used to cover a window.

screw *n.* A metal piece that resembles a nail, having a spiral thread used for fastening things together; a propeller on a ship. *v.* To join by twisting.

screw•driv•er *n.* A type of tool used for turning screws.

scrib•ble *v.* To write without thought or care to penmanship.

scribe *n.* A person whose profession is to copy documents and manuscripts.

script *n.* The written text of a play.

scrip•ture *n.* A sacred writing.

scroll *n.* A roll of parchment or similar material used in place of paper.

scrooge *n.* A person who is miserly.

scrub *v.* To clean something by rubbing. *slang* To cancel.

scruff *n.* The region on the back of the neck.

scru•ti•nize *v.* To look at or to examine something very carefully.

scu•ba *n.* An acronym for self-contained underwater breathing apparatus; an apparatus used by divers for underwater breathing.

scu•ba di•ver *n.* A person who swims under the water with the use of scuba gear.

scuff *v.* To drag or scrape the feet while walking. *n.* A rough spot.

scuf•fle *v.* To struggle in a confused manner.

sculpt *v.* To carve; to make a sculpture.

sculp•tor *n.* A person who creates statues from clay, marble, or other material.

sculp•ture *n.* The art of processing a hard or soft material into another form, such as a statue; the result of this act.

scum *n.* A thin layer of waste matter floating on top of a liquid.

scur•ry *v.* To move quickly; to scamper.

scythe *n.* A tool with a long handle and curved, single-edged blade, used for cutting hay, grain and grass.

sea *n.* The body of salt water which covers most of the earth; a large body of salt water.

sea•coast *n.* Land that borders the sea.

seal *n.* A device having a raised emblem, displaying word or symbol, used to certify a signature or the authenticity of a document; a tight closure which secures; a large aquatic mammal with a sleek body and large flippers; the fur or pelt of a seal.

sea lev•el *n.* The level of the sea's surface, used as a standard reference point in measuring the height of land or the depth of the sea.

seam *n.* The line formed at the joint of two pieces of material.

sear *v.* To wither or dry up; to shrivel; to burn or scorch.

search *v.* To look over carefully; to find something; to probe. **searcher** *n.*

sea•son *n.* One of the four parts of the year: spring, summer, fall or autumn, and winter; a time marked by particular activities or celebrations. *v.* To add flavorings or spices; to add interest or enjoyment.

seat *n.* A place or spot, as a chair, stool, or bench, on which to sit; the part of the body used for sitting; the buttocks.

se•cede *v.* To withdraw from an organization or group.

se•clude *v.* To isolate; to keep apart.

sec•ond *n.* A unit of time equal to 1/60 of a minute; a very short period of time; an object which does not meet first class standards.

sec•on•dar•y *adj.* Not being first in importance; inferior; pertaining to a secondary school; high school.

se•cret *n.* Knowledge kept from others; a mystery.

sec•re•tar•y *n.* A person hired to write and keep records for an executive or an organization; the head of a government department. **secretarial** *adj.*

sec•tion *n.* A part or division of something; a separate part. *v.* To divide or separate into sections.

sec•tor *n.* An area or zone in which a military unit operates; the part of a circle bounded by two radii and the arc they cut.

se•cure *adj.* Safe and free from doubt or fear; sturdy or strong; not likely to fail. *v.* To tie down, fasten, lock, or otherwise protect from risk or harm; to ensure.

se•cu•ri•ty *n.* The state of being safe and free from danger or risk; protection; an object given to assure the fulfillment of an obligation.

see *v.* To have the power of sight; to understand; to experience; to imagine; to predict.

seed *n.* A fertilized plant ovule with an embryo, capable of producing an offspring. *v.* To plant seeds; to remove the seeds from.

seek *v.* To search for; to try to reach; to attempt.

seem *v.* To appear to be; to have the look of.

see•saw *n.* A board supported in the center which allows children to alternate being up and down.

seg•ment *n.* Any of the parts into which a thing is divided.

sel•dom *adv.* Not often.

se•lect *v.* To choose from a large group; to make a choice.

self *n.* The complete and essential being of a person; personal interest, advantage or welfare. **selves** *pl.*

sell *v.* To exchange a product or service for money; to offer for sale.

se•mes•ter *n.* One of two periods of time in which a school year is divided.

sem•i•co•lon *n.* A punctuation mark, used to separate clauses, having a degree of separation stronger than a comma but less than a period.

send *v.* To cause something to be conveyed from one place to another; to dispatch.

sen•ior *adj.* Of higher office or rank; referring to the last year of high school or college. *n.* One who is older or of higher rank.

sense *n.* Sensation; feeling; the physical ability which allows a person to be aware of things around him; the five senses: taste, smell, touch, sight, and hearing. *v.* To feel through the senses; to have a feeling about.

sen•tence *n.* A series of words arranged to express a complete thought; a prison term for a person, decided by a judge or jury. *v.* To set the terms of punishment.

sep•a•rate *v.* To divide or keep apart by placing a barrier between; to go in different directions; to set apart from others. *adj.* Single; individual.

se•ri•ous *adj.* Sober; grave; not trivial; important.

ser•mon *n.* A message or speech delivered by a clergyman during a religious service.

ser•pent *n.* A snake.

ser•vant *n.* One employed to care for someone or his property.

serve *v.* To take care of; to wait on; to prepare and supply; to complete a term of duty; to act in a certain capacity; to start the play in some sports.

serv•er *n.* In computers, an electronic program or device designed to deliver information as a service to clients.

serv•ice *n.* Help given to others; a religious gathering; the military; a set of dishes or utensils. *v.* To repair; to furnish a service to something or someone.

set *v.* To put or place; to cause to do; to regulate; to adjust; to arrange; to place in a frame or mounting; to go below the horizon; to establish or fix. *n.* A group of things which belong together; a piece of equipment made up of many pieces; a young plant. *adj.* Established; ready.

set•ting *n.* The act of putting something somewhere; the scenery for a show or other production; the place where a novel, play, or other fictional work takes place.

set•tle *v.* To arrange or put in order; to restore calm or tranquillity to; to come to an agreement on something; to resolve a problem or argument; to establish in a new home or business.

sev•er•al *adj.* More than one or two, but not many; separate.

se•vere *adj.* Strict; stern; hard; not fancy; extremely painful; intense.

sew *v.* To fasten or fix; to make stitches with thread and needle.

sew•age *n.* The solid waste material carried away by a sewer.

sew•er *n.* A conduit or drain pipe used to carry away waste.

sex *n.* One of two divisions, male and female, into which most living things are grouped; sexual intercourse.

shab•by *adj.* Worn-out; ragged.

shack *n.* A small, poorly built building.

shade *n.* A shadow that will gather with the coming of darkness; a comparative darkness due to the interception of the rays of the sun by an object.

shad•ow *n.* An area from which light is blocked; a shaded area. *v.* To cast or throw a shadow on.

sha•dy *adj.* Being sheltered or protected from the rays of the sun.

shaft *n.* A long, narrow part of something; a beam or ray of light; a long, narrow underground passage; a tunnel; a vertical opening in a building for an elevator.

shag•gy *adj.* Covered with long, matted, or coarse hair.

shake *v.* To move or to cause a back and forth or up and down motion; to tremble; to clasp hands with another, as to welcome or say farewell; to upset or disturb.

shall *v. Will* in the first person future tense, used with the pronouns *I* or *we* to express future tense; with other nouns or pronouns to indicate promise, determination, or a command.

shal•low *adj.* Not deep; lacking intellectual depth.

shame *n.* A painful feeling of embarrassment or disgrace brought on by doing something wrong; dishonor; disgrace; a disappointment.

sham•poo *n.* A soap used to cleanse the hair and scalp; a liquid preparation used to clean upholstery and rugs.

sham•rock *n.* A form of clover with three leaflets on a single stem; regarded as the national flower and emblem of Ireland.

sha•pa•ble *adj.* To be capable of being shaped.

shape *n.* The outline or configuration of something; the condition of something; the finished form in which something may appear. *v.* To cause to take a particular form.

shape•less *adj.* Having no real or definite shape.

share *n.* A part or portion given to or by one person; one of equal parts, as the capital stock in a corporation.

share•ware *n.* In computers, software distributed without charge on a trial basis, in expectation of fair payment to the author by eventual users.

shark *n.* A large marine fish which eats other fish and is dangerous to man; a greedy, crafty, person.

sharp *adj.* Having a thin edge or a fine point; capable of piercing or cutting; clever; quick-witted; intense; painful.

sharp•en *v.* To make something sharp.

shat•ter *v.* To burst suddenly into pieces.

shave *v.* To remove a thin layer; to cut body hair, as the beard, by using a razor; to come close to.

she *pron.* A female previously indicated by name.

shed *v.* To pour out or cause to pour; to throw off without penetrating; to cast off or leave behind. *n.* A small building for shelter or storage.

sheep *n.* A cud-chewing thick-fleeced mammal, domesticated for meat and wool; a meek or timid person. **sheep** *pl.*

sheep dog *n.* A type of dog raised for herding or watching over sheep.

sheep•herd•er *n.* A person who is in charge of a herd of sheep; a shepherd.

sheer *adj.* Very thin; almost transparent; complete; absolute; very steep, almost perpendicular.

sheet *n.* A large piece of cloth for covering a bed; a single piece of paper; a continuous, thin piece of anything.

shelf *n.* A flat piece of wood, metal, plastic, or other rigid material attached to a wall or within another structure, used to hold or store things. **shelves** *pl.*

shell *n.* The hard outer covering of certain organisms; something light and hollow which resembles a shell; the framework of a building under construction; a case containing explosives fired from a gun.

shel•ter *n.* Something which gives protection or cover. *v.* To give protection.

shelve *v.* To put aside; to place on a shelf.

shep•herd *n.* A person who takes care of a flock of sheep; a person who takes care of others.

sher•bet *n.* A sweet frozen dessert made with fruit juices, milk or water, egg white, and gelatin.

sher•iff *n.* A high ranking law-enforcement officer.

shield *n.* A piece of protective metal or wood held in front of the body; anything which serves to conceal or protect; a badge or emblem.

shift *n.* A group of people who work together; a woman's loose-fitting dress. *v.* To change direction or place; to change or move the gears in an automobile.

shine *v.* To give off light; to direct light; to make bright or glossy; to polish shoes. *n.* Brightness.

shin•er *n.* A black eye.

shin•gle *n.* A thin piece of material, as asbestos, used to cover a roof or side of a

house. *v.* To apply shingles to.

ship *n.* A large vessel for deep-water travel or transport. *v.* To send or transport.

ship•ment *n.* The process of shipping goods from one port to another.

ship•wreck *n.* The loss of a ship; destruction; ruin.

shirt *n.* A garment worn on the upper part of the body.

shiv•er *v.* To tremble or shake with excitement or chill.

shock *n.* A sudden blow or violent impact; an unexpected, sudden upset of mental or emotional balance; a serious weakening of the body caused by the loss of blood pressure or sudden injury. *v.* To strike with great surprise, disgust, or outrage; to give an electric shock.

shoe *n.* An outer cover for a foot; the part of a brake which presses against the drum or wheel to slow or stop the motion. *v.* To put on shoes.

shoe•lace *n.* A string used to fasten a shoe.

shoot *v.* To kill or wound with a missile, as a bullet, fired from a weapon; to discharge or throw rapidly; to push forward or begin to grow by germinating.

shoot•ing star *n.* A meteor that appears in the sky as a temporary streak of light.

shop *n.* A small business or small retail store; a place where certain goods are produced. *v.* To visit a store in order to examine or buy things.

shop•keep•er *n.* A person who runs a store.

shop•lift *v.* To take something from a store without paying for it.

shop•ping cen•ter *n.* A group of stores gathered in one area for easier access.

shore *n.* The land bordering a body of water.

shore•front *n.* The land located along a shore.

shore•line *n.* A line or location where a body of water and the shore meet.

short *adj.* Having little height or length; less than normal in distance, time, or other qualities; less than the needed amount.

short•age *n.* A lack in the amount needed.

short•cut *n.* A type of route more direct than the one usually taken.

shorts *n.* Underpants or outer-pants which end at the knee or above.

shot *n.* The discharging of a gun, rocket, or other device; an attempt; a try; an injection; a photograph.

should *v.* Past tense of *shall*, used to express obligation, duty, or expectation.

shoul•der *n.* The part of the body located between the neck and upper arm; the side of the road. *v.* To use the shoulder to push or carry something; to take upon oneself.

should•n't *contr.* Should not.

shout *v.* To yell. *n.* A loud cry.

shove *v.* To push something or someone in a manner that may be rough.

shov•el *n.* A tool with a long handle and a scoop, used for picking up material or for digging. *v.* To move, dig, or scoop up with a shovel; to push or move large amounts rapidly.

show *v.* To put within sight; to point out; to explain; to put on display. *n.* A display; a movie, play or similar entertainment.

show•er *n.* A short period of rain; a party with gifts given in honor of someone; a bath with water spraying down on the bather. *v.* To take a shower; to be extremely generous.

shred *n.* A narrow strip or torn fragment; a small amount *v.* To rip, tear, or cut into shreds.

shrew *n.* A small mouse-like mammal, having a narrow, pointed snout.

shrimp *n.* A small, edible shellfish.

shrink *v.* To make or become less or smaller; to pull back from; to flinch.

shrub *n.* A woody plant which grows close to the ground and has several stems beginning at its base.

shrug *v.* To raise the shoulders briefly to indicate indifference.

shud•der *v.* To tremble uncontrollably, as from fear.

shuf•fle *v.* To drag or slide the feet; to mix together in a haphazard fashion; to rearrange or change the order of cards.

shut *v.* To move a door, drawer, or other object to close an opening; to block an entrance; to lock up; to cease or halt operations.

shut•tle *n.* A device used to move thread in weaving; a vehicle, as a train or plane, which travels back and forth from one location to another.

shy *adj.* Bashful; timid; easily frightened. *v.* To move suddenly from fear.

sib•ling *n.* One of two or more children from the same parents.

sick *adj.* In poor health; ill; nauseated.

sick•le *n.* A tool with a curved blade attached to a handle, used for cutting grass or grain.

sick•ly *adj.* Somewhat unwell.

side *n.* A surface between the front and back or top and bottom of an object; either surface of a flat object; an opinion or point of view the opposite of another. *v.* To take a stand and support the opinion of a particular side.

side•burns *n.* The short side-whiskers worn by the man on the side of his face.

side•walk *n.* A type of paved walk used by pedestrians at the side of the street.

siege *n.* The action of surrounding a town or port in order to capture it; a prolonged sickness.

sift *v.* To separate coarse particles from small or fine ones by passing through a sieve.

sigh *v.* To exhale a long, deep breath, usually when tired or sad.

sight *n.* The ability to see with the eyes; the range or distance one can see; a view; a device on a firearm used to guide the aim.

sign *n.* A piece of paper, wood, metal, etc., with information written on it; a gesture that tells or means something. *v.* To write one's name on.

sig•nal *n.* A sign which gives a warning; the image or sound sent by television or radio.

sig•na•ture *n.* The name of a person,

written by that person; a distinctive mark which indicates identity.

sig·ni·fy *v.* To express or make known by a sign; to indicate. **significant** *adj.*

sign lan·guage *n.* A means of communicating by using hand gestures; the language of deaf people.

sign·post *n.* A type of post that bears signs on it for the use of giving directions.

si·lence *n.* The state or quality of being silent; quiet. *v.* To make quiet.

si·lent *adj.* Making no sound; not speaking; mute; unable to speak.

silk *n.* A soft, thread-like fiber spun by silkworms; thread or fabric made from silk.

sil·ly *adj.* Foolish; lacking good sense, seriousness, or substance.

si·lo *n.* A tall, cylindrical structure for storing food for farm animals; an underground shelter for guided missiles.

silt *n.* A deposit of soil and sediment that may have been caused by a river.

sil·ver *n.* A soft, white metallic element used in tableware, jewelry, and coins, symbolized by *Ag. adj.* Of the color silver.

sil·ver·smith *n.* A person who makes goods and articles out of silver.

sim·i·lar *adj.* Almost the same, but not identical.

sim·i·le *n.* A part of speech used for the purpose of comparing two things often unalike.

sim·mer *v.* To cook just below boiling; to be near the point of breaking, as with emotion.

sim·ple *adj.* Easy to do or understand; not complicated; ordinary; not showy; lacking intelligence or education.

sim·plic·i·ty *n.* The state of being easy to understand; naturalness; sincerity.

sim·pli·fy *v.* To make easy or simple. **simplification** *n.*

sim·u·late *v.* To have the appearance, effect, or form of; to act in imitation of.

si·mul·ta·ne·ous *adj.* Occurring at exactly the same time.

sin *n.* The breaking of a religious law or a law of God. *v.* To do something morally wrong.

since *adv.* At a time before the present. *prep.* During the time later than; continuously from the time when something occurs.

sin·cere *adj.* Honest; genuine; true.

sin·cer·i·ty *n.* The state of being sincere.

sine *n.* A function in trigonometry.

sing *v.* To use the voice to make musical tones; to make a humming or whistling sound.

sin·gle *adj.* Of or referring to only one; separate; individual; unmarried. *n.* A separate, individual person or item; a dollar bill.

sin·gu·lar *adj.* Separate; one; extraordinary; denoting a single unit, thing or person.

sin·is·ter *adj.* Evil or causing evil.

sink *v.* To submerge beneath a surface; to go down slowly; to become less forceful or weaker. *n.* A basin for holding water connected to a drain.

sink·er *n.* A weight used for the purpose of sinking a fishing line into the water.

sink·hole *n.* A type of hollow depression where drainage is able to collect.

si·nus *n.* A body cavity; one of eight air spaces in the bones of the face which drain into the nasal cavity. **sinuses** *pl.*

sip *v.* To drink in small amounts.

si·phon *n.* A tube through which liquid from one container can be drawn into another by forced air pressure.

sir *n.* A respectful term used when addressing a man.

sire *n.* A man who has rank and authority.

si·ren *n.* A whistle which makes a loud wailing noise, as a warning or signal; a seductive woman.

sir·loin *n.* The cut of meat from the hindquarter.

sis·ter *n.* A female having the same parents as another; a woman in membership with others.

sis·ter·hood *n.* The state of being a sister.

sis·ter·ly *adj.* Related to being a sister.

sit *v.* To rest the body with the weight on

the buttocks; to cover eggs for hatching; to pose for a portrait.

site *n.* A location of planned buildings.

sit•ting *n.* An act of one who sits; a photography session.

sit•ting duck *n.* A defenseless target.

sit•u•a•tion *n.* The way in which something or someone is placed within its surroundings.

size *n.* The measurement or dimensions of something.

siz•zle *v.* To make a hissing sound, as of fat frying.

skate *n.* A device with rollers which attaches to the shoe and allows one to glide over ice or roll over a wooden or cement surface.

skate•board *n.* A narrow piece of wood with wheels attached.

ska•ter *n.* A person who is able to skate.

skat•ing *n.* The action or the art of gliding on skates.

skel•e•tal *adj.* Pertaining to or relating to the skeleton.

skel•e•ton *n.* The framework of bones that protects and supports the soft tissues and organs.

skep•tic *n.* A person who doubts or questions.

sketch *n.* A rough drawing or outline; a brief literary composition.

sketch•book *n.* A kind of book used for the purpose of sketching things.

skew *v.* To turn or slant. *n.* A slant.

skew•er *n.* A piece of metal used as a pin for the purpose of fastening foods together in order to broil them on a grill.

ski *n.* One of a pair of long, narrow pieces of wood worn on the feet for gliding over snow or water. *v.* To travel on skis. **skis** *pl.*

ski boot *n.* A type of rigid boot attached to the ski and used to hold the ski on the foot.

skid *v.* To slide to the side of the road; to slide along without rotating.

ski•ing *n.* The sport of jumping and moving on skis.

ski jump *n.* The jump made by someone who is wearing skis; a large steep ramp used for the sport of ski jumping.

ski lift *n.* A type of conveyor used to bring the skiers to the top of the hill that they will ski back down.

skill *n.* Ability gained through practice; expertise.

skilled *adj.* To have acquired a skill for something.

skil•let *n.* A type of footed pot used for cooking foods on the hearth; a frying pan.

skill•ful *adj.* Displaying a skill.

skim *v.* To remove the top layer; to remove floating matter; to read over material quickly; to travel over lightly and quickly.

skin *n.* The tough, outside covering of man and some animals; the outside layer of a vegetable or fruit; the fur or pelt of an animal.

skink *v.* To serve something like a drink.

skink•er *n.* A person who serves liquor.

skin•ny *adj.* Lacking a sufficient amount of flesh on the body, making one look thin.

skin•tight *adj.* Closely fitted to one's body.

skip *v.* To move in light jumps or leaps; to go from one place to another, missing what is between.

skirt *n.* A piece of clothing that extends down from the waist. *v.* To extend along the boundary; to avoid the issue.

ski-run *n.* The trail used for skiing.

skit *n.* A type of humorous story.

skit•tish *adj.* Easily frightened; nervous; jumpy.

skull *n.* The bony part of the skeleton which protects the brain.

skunk *n.* A black mammal with white streaks down its back, which sprays an unpleasant smelling liquid when annoyed or frightened.

sky *n.* The upper atmosphere above the earth; the celestial regions. **skies** *pl.*

sky•div•ing *n.* The sport of jumping out of an airplane while it is flying in the air.

sky•lark *n.* A type of lark, large in size and especially noted for its song.

sky•light *n.* A large window in the ceiling

289

of a building.

sky•line *n.* The outline of a building or other very large object against the sky.

sky•scrap•er *n.* A type of building which is very tall and therefore seems to scrape the sky.

sky•writ•ing *n.* Writing formed in the sky with the use of smoke.

slab *n.* A thick piece or slice.

slack *adj.* Not taut or tense; sluggish; lacking in strength. *v.* To make slack. *n.* A part of something which hangs loose.

slack•er *n.* One who shirks an obligation.

slacks *n.* Long pants or trousers.

slain *v.* Past perfect tense of *slay*.

sla•lom *n.* A type of skiing where the skier zig-zags down the hill between upright obstacles such as flags.

slam *v.* To shut with force; to strike with a loud impact. *n.* A loud noise produced by an impact.

slang *n.* Informal language that contains made-up words or common words used in a different or uncommon way.

slant *v.* To lie in an oblique position; to slope; to report on something giving only one viewpoint. *n.* An incline or slope.

slap *n.* A sharp blow with an open hand.

slash *v.* To cut with a fast sweeping stroke; to reduce or limit greatly. *n.* A long cut.

slate *n.* A fine grained rock that splits into thin layers, often used as a writing surface or roofing material.

slaugh•ter *v.* To kill livestock for food; to kill in great numbers.

slave *n.* A person held against his will and made to work for another.

slave dri•ver *n.* A person who is the supervisor of slaves.

slave•hold•er *n.* A person who is the owner of the slaves.

slay *v.* To kill or to destroy something in a violent manner.

sled *n.* A vehicle with runners, used to travel on snow or ice.

sled dog *n.* A type of dog trained to pull a sledge.

sledge *n.* A kind of vehicle pulled by dogs, that has low runners and is used for transporting loads over the snow.

sledge•ham•mer *n.* A type of hammer which is very heavy and must be wielded with both hands.

sleek *adj.* Smooth and shiny; neat and trim.

sleep *n.* A natural state of rest for the mind and body. *v.* To rest in sleep.

sleep•ing bag *n.* A cloth-lined bag used for sleeping.

sleep•walk•er *n.* A person who is able to walk while still asleep.

sleep•y *adj.* Pertaining to sleep.

sleet *n.* Rain, partially frozen.

sleeve *n.* The part of a garment which covers the arm; a case for something.

sleigh *n.* A vehicle on runners usually pulled over ice and snow by horses.

sleigh bell *n.* A type of bell attached to a sleigh.

slen•der *adj.* Slim; inadequate in amount.

slept *v.* Past tense of *sleep*.

slice *n.* A thin cut; a portion or share; in golf, a ball in flight that curves off to the right of its target. *v.* To cut into slices.

slick *adj.* Smooth and slippery; quick; clever; attractive for the present time but without quality or depth. *n.* Water with a thin layer of oil floating on top.

slick•er *n.* A raincoat made of yellow oilcloth.

slide *v.* To move smoothly across a surface without losing contact. *n.* The act of sliding; a slanted smooth surface usually found on playgrounds; a transparent picture which can be projected on a screen; a small glass plate for examining specimens under a microscope.

slight *adj.* Minor in degree; unimportant. *v.* To ignore.

slim *adj.* Slender; meager; not much.

slime *n.* A wet, slippery substance.

sling *n.* A piece of material, as leather, or a strap which secures something; a piece of fabric worn around the neck used to support an injured hand or arm; a weapon made of a strap, used to throw a stone.

sling·shot *n.* A type of v-shaped device which has an elastic band and is used to propel objects such as rocks through the air.

slip *v.* To move in a smooth, quiet way; to fail or lose one's balance. *n.* The action of slipping; the place between two piers used for docking a boat; a woman's undergarment; a small piece of paper; a portion of a plant used for grafting.

slip·knot *n.* A type of knot that will slip along the rope of which it is made.

slip·per·y *adj.* To cause something to slip.

slip up *v.* Make a blunder or mistake.

slit *v.* To cut a slit into something. *n.* A narrow opening or cut into something.

slith·er *v.* To slide or slip in an indirect manner; to move like a snake.

sliv·er *n.* A thin, narrow piece of something that has been broken off.

slob *n.* One who is slovenly.

slob·ber *v.* To dribble from the mouth.

slo·gan *n.* A phrase used to express the aims of a cause.

slop *n.* A tasteless liquid food.

slope *v.* To slant upward or downward. *n.* An upward or downward incline.

slop·py *adj.* Wet, muddy, or slippery, as in weather conditions; careless, unkempt, or disheveled in appearance.

slot *n.* A narrow, thin groove or opening.

sloth *n.* Laziness; a slow mammal found in South America.

slov·en·ly *adj.* Untidy, as in one's personal appearance.

slow *adj.* Moving at a low rate of speed; requiring more time than usual; not lively; sluggish; not interesting. *adv.* At less speed; in a slow manner; slowly.

slug *n.* A slow animal related to the snail; a bullet or a lump of metal. *v.* To strike forcefully with the fist or a heavy object.

slug·gish *adj.* Slow to respond to a treatment or to a stimulation.

slum *n.* A crowded urban neighborhood marked by poverty.

slum·ber *v.* To sleep; to doze.

slum·ber par·ty *n.* A type of overnight gathering, usually at someone's house.

slump *v.* To fall or sink suddenly.

slush *n.* Melting snow; snow that is partially melted.

sly *adj.* Cunning; clever; sneaky.

smack *v.* To slap; to press and open the lips with a sharp noise. *n.* The act or noise of slapping something.

small *adj.* Little in size, quantity, or extent; unimportant.

small in·tes·tines *n.* The section of the intestines located between the colon and the stomach.

smart *adj.* Intelligent; clever.

smash *v.* To break into small pieces; to move forward violently, as to shatter; to ruin. *n.* The act or sound of crashing. *adj.* Outstanding.

smear *v.* To spread or cover with a sticky, oily, or moist substance.

smell *v.* To notice an odor by means of the olfactory sense organs. *n.* An odor; the ability to perceive an odor; the scent of something.

smel·ly *adj.* Having a smell or odor.

smile *n.* A grin; a facial expression in which the corners of the mouth turn upward, indicating pleasure.

smirk *v.* To smile in a conceited way.

smith *n.* One who repairs or shapes metal.

smith·y *n.* The place where a smith works.

smock *n.* A loose-fitting garment worn to protect one's clothes while working.

smog *n.* A mixture of smoke and fog.

smoke *n.* A cloud of vapor released into the air when something is burning. *v.* To preserve or flavor meat by exposing it to smoke.

smoke·house *n.* A place or building where meat and fish are cured by using smoke.

smoke jum·per *n.* A type of fire fighter who parachutes to the area of a fire that may have become hard to reach by land.

smoke·stack *n.* The chimney from which gases and smoke are discharged.

smooth *adj.* Not irregular; flat; without lumps, as in gravy; without obstructions or impediments. *adv.* Evenly. *v.* To make less difficult; to remove obstructions; to illegally without paying duty fees.

smug·ly *adv.* Done in a smug manner.

snack *n.* A small amount of food taken between meals.

snack bar *n.* An eating place for the public that serves snacks at a counter.

snag *n.* A stump or part of a tree partly hidden under the surface of water; a pull in a piece of fabric. *v.* To tear on a rough place.

snail *n.* A type of gastropod mollusk that can live in a spiral shell.

snail-paced *adj.* To be moving at a slow pace.

snake *n.* Any of a large variety of scaly reptiles, having a long tapering body.

snake·bite *n.* A bite of a snake on the skin.

snake charm·er *n.* A person who exhibits powers to charm a snake.

snake pit *n.* A place of complete disorder.

snake·skin *n.* Leather prepared from the skin of a snake.

snap *v.* To break suddenly with a sharp, quick sound; to fly off under tension; to snatch something suddenly.

snap·dra·gon *n.* A type of plant having white, yellow, or crimson flowers.

snap·per *n.* A type of carnivorous fish

sneak·y *adj.* Marked by snittiness.

sneer *v.* To express scorn by the look on one's face.

sneeze *v.* To expel air from the nose suddenly and without control.

sniff *v.* To inhale through the nose in short breaths.

snip *v.* To cut off in small pieces and with quick strokes. *n.* A small piece.

snipe *n.* A bird with a long bill which lives in marshy places. *v.* To shoot at people from a hidden position.

snip·pet *n.* A small part or thing.

snips *n.* A type of hand shears that can be used for cutting metal.

snob *n.* A person who considers himself better than anyone else and who looks down on those he sees as his inferiors.

snooze *v.* To sleep for a short time.

snore *v.* To breathe with a harsh noise while sleeping.

snor·kel *n.* A tube that extends above the water, used for breathing while swimming face down.

snort *v.* To force air through the nostrils with a loud, harsh noise.

snout *n.* The nose of an animal.

snow *n.* Vapor that forms crystals in cold air and falls to the ground in white flakes.

snow•man *n.* A figure made out of snow usually resembling a man or woman.

snow•mo•bile *n.* A type of vehicle used to travel on the snow.

snow•plow *n.* A machine used for removing the snow from a driving or walking area.

snow•shoe *n.* A type of shoe used to travel on top of the snow.

snow•storm *n.* A storm made up of snow.

snow tire *n.* A type of tire used by a car when there is snow on the street in order to get better traction.

snow•y *adj.* Covered by snow.

snub *v.* To treat with contempt or in an unfriendly way. **snub** *n.*

snug *adj.* Warm, pleasant, comfortable.

snug•gle *v.* To curl up to someone in an affectionate manner.

so *adv.* To a degree or extent as a result; likewise; also; indeed. *conj.* In order that; therefore.

soak *v.* To be thoroughly wet; to penetrate.

soap *n.* A cleansing agent made of an alkali and fat, and used for washing. *v.* To rub with soap.

soap•box *n.* A platform used by an informal orator.

soar *v.* To glide or fly high without any noticeable movement; to rise higher than usual.

sob *v.* To weep with short, quick gasps.

so•ber *adj.* Not drunk or intoxicated; serious; solemn; quiet.

soc•cer *n.* A game in which two teams of eleven men each try to kick a ball into the opposing team's goal.

so•cia•ble *adj.* Capable of friendly social relations; enjoying the company of others.

so•cial *adj.* Having to do with people living in groups; enjoying friendly companionship with others. *n.* An informal party or gathering.

so•cial•ism *n.* A system in which people as a whole, and not individuals, control and own all property.

so•ci•e•ty *n.* People working together for a common purpose; companionship.

so•ci•ol•o•gy *n.* The study of society and the development of human society. **sociologic**, **sociological** *adj.*

sock *n.* A short covering for the foot, ankle, and lower part of the leg; a hard blow.

sock•et *n.* A hollow opening into which something is fitted.

so•da *n.* Sodium carbonate; a flavored, carbonated drink.

sod•den *adj.* Completely saturated; very wet.

so•di•um *n.* A metallic element symbolized by Na.

so•fa *n.* An upholstered couch with arms and a back.

soft *adj.* Not stiff or hard; not glaring or harsh; mild or pleasant; gentle in sound.

soft•ball *n.* A game played on a smaller diamond than baseball, with a larger, softer ball.

soft•ware *n.* In computer science, data, as routines, programs and languages, essential to the operation of computers.

sog•gy *adj.* Saturated with a liquid or moisture.

sol•ace *n.* Comfort in a time of trouble, grief, or misfortune. **solacer** *n.*

so•lar *adj.* Relating to or connected with the sun; utilizing the sun for power or light; measured by the earth's movement around the sun.

sol•ar sys•tem *n.* The sun and the planets, asteroids, and comets that orbit it.

sol•dier *n.* An enlisted person who serves in the military.

sole *n.* The bottom of a foot or shoe; single, the only one; a flat fish.

sol•emn *adj.* Very serious; characterized by dignity; sacred.

so•lic•it *v.* To try to obtain; to ask earnestly; to beg or entice a person persistently. **solicitation** *n.*

sol•id *adj.* Having a definite firm shape and volume; having no crevices; not hollow; having height, weight and length; without interruption; reliable, sound and upstanding. *n.* A solid substance.

sol·i·taire *n.* A single gemstone set by itself; a card game played by one person.

sol·i·tude *n.* The act of being alone or secluded; isolation.

so·lo *n.* A musical composition written for and performed by one single person or played by one instrument.

sol·stice *n.* Either of the two times in a twelve month period at which the sun reaches an extreme north or south position.

sol·u·ble *adj.* Capable of being dissolved; able to be solved or explained.

solve *v.* To find the answer to.

som·ber *adj.* Dark; gloomy; melancholy.

some *adj.* Being an indefinite number or quantity; unspecified. *pron.* An undetermined or indefinite quantity. *adv.* An approximate degree.

some·bod·y *n.* A person unknown.

some·day *adv.* At an unspecified future time.

some·how *adv.* In a way.

som·er·sault *n.* The act or acrobatic stunt in which one rolls the body in a complete circle, with heels over head.

son *n.* The male child of a man or woman.

so·na·ta *n.* An instrumental composition with movements contrasting in tempo and mood but related in key.

song *n.* A piece of poetry put to music; the act or sound of singing.

son·ic *adj.* Pertaining to sound or the speed of sound.

son·net *n.* A poem made up of fourteen lines.

soon *adv.* In a short time; in the near future; quickly.

soot *n.* The black powder generated by incomplete combustion of a fuel.

soothe *v.* To make comfortable; to calm.

soph·o·more *n.* A second year college or high school student.

so·pran·o *n.* The highest female singing voice.

sor·cer·y *n.* The use of supernatural powers.

sor·did *adj.* Filthy; very dirty; morally corrupt.

sore *adj.* Tender or painful to the touch, as an injured part of the body; severe or extreme. *n.* A place on the body which has been bruised, inflamed, or injured in some way. **sorely** *adv.*

so·ror·i·ty *n.* A social organization for women.

sor·row *n.* Anguish; mental suffering; an expression of grief. **sorrowful** *adj.*, **sorrowfully** *adv.*

sor·ry *adj.* Feeling or showing sympathy or regret; worthless.

sort *n.* A collection of things having common attributes or similar qualities. *v.* To arrange according to class, kind, or size.

souf·flé *n.* A fluffy dish made of egg yolks, whipped egg whites, and other ingredients, served as a main dish or sweetened as a dessert.

soul *n.* The spirit in man believed to be separate from the body and the source of a person's emotional, spiritual, and moral nature.

sound *n.* A sensation received by the ears from air, water, noise, and other sources. *v.* To make a sound; to make noise. *adj.* Free from flaw, injury, disease, or damage.

soup *n.* A liquid food made by boiling meat and/or vegetables, in water.

sour *adj.* Sharp to the taste; acid; unpleasant; disagreeable. *v.* To become sour or spoiled. **sourly** *adv.*

source *n.* Any point of origin or beginning; the beginning or place of origin of a stream or river.

south *n.* The direction opposite of north. *adv.* To or towards the south.

sou·ve·nir *n.* An item kept as a remembrance of something or someplace.

sov·er·eign *n.* A ruler with supreme power; a monarch. *adj.* Possessing supreme jurisdiction or authority.

sow *v.* To scatter or throw seeds on the ground for growth. *n.* A female pig.

space *n.* The unlimited area in all directions in which events occur and have relative direction; an interval of time; the area beyond the earth's atmosphere.

spade *n.* A tool with a flat blade used for digging, heavier than a shovel.

spa•ghet•ti *n.* Pasta made in long, thin pieces.

spam *n.* In computers, unwanted commercial messages sent electronically to a large mailing list without solicitation. *v.* To engage in such practice.

span *n.* The extent of space from the end of the thumb to the end of the little finger of a spread hand; the section between two limits or supports. *v.* To extend across.

spank *v.* To strike or slap the buttocks with an open hand as a means of punishment.

spare *v.* To refrain from injuring, harming or destroying; to refrain from using; to do without. *n.* An extra, as a spare tire.

spark *n.* A glowing or incandescent particle, as one released from a piece of burning wood. *v.* To give off sparks.

spar•row *n.* A small bird with grayish or brown plumage.

sparse *adj.* Scant; thinly distributed. **sparsely** *adv.,* **sparsity** *n.*

spasm *n.* An involuntary muscle contraction.

spat•u•la *n.* A kitchen utensil with a flexible blade for mixing soft substances.

spawn *n.* The eggs of fish or other water animals, as oysters or frogs. *v.* To lay eggs.

speak *v.* To utter words; to express a thought in words.

speak•er *n.* A person who speaks, usually before an audience.

spear *n.* A weapon with a long shaft and a sharply pointed head. *v.* To strike, pierce, or stab with a spear.

spear•mint *n.* A mint plant yielding an aromatic oil used as a flavoring.

spe•cial•ist *n.* A person who devotes his practice to one particular field.

spe•cial•ize *v.* To focus one's efforts or interests in one field of activity or study.

spec•i•men *n.* A sample; a representative of a particular thing.

spec•ta•cle *n.* A public display of something unusual. *pl.* Eyeglasses.

spec•trum *n.* The band of colors produced when light is passed through a prism or other means, separating the light into different wave lengths; any range or comprehensive variety.

spec•u•late *v.* To reflect and think deeply; to take a chance on a business venture in hopes of making a large profit.

speech *n.* The ability, manner, or act of speaking; a talk before the public.

speed *n.* Rate of action or movement; quickness; rapid motion.

spell *v.* To say out loud or write in proper order the letters which make up a word; to relieve. *n.* The state of being controlled by magic; a short period of time; a time or period of illness; an attack.

spend *v.* To give out; to use up; to pay; to exhaust.

sphere *n.* A round object with all points the same distance from a given point; globe, ball, or other rounded object. **spherical** *adj.* **spherically** *adv.*

spice *n.* A pungently aromatic plant used as flavoring in food, such as nutmeg, cinnamon, or pepper. **spice** *v.,* **spicy** *adj.*

spi•der *n.* An eight-legged arachnid with a body divided into two parts, spinning webs as a means of capturing and holding its prey.

spike *n.* A large, thick nail; a pointed metal piece on the sole of a shoe to prevent slipping, as on a sports shoe.

spill *v.* To allow or cause something to flow or run out of something.

spin *v.* To draw out fibers and twist into thread; to run something around and around; to revolve.

spin•ach *n.* A widely cultivated plant with dark green leaves, used in salads.

spine *n.* The spinal column; the backbone; the back of a bound book.

spir•it *n.* The vital essence of man, considered divine in origin; the part of a human being characterized by personality and self-consciousness; the mind; the Holy Ghost; the creative power of God; a supernatural being, as a ghost or angel.

spite *n.* Hatred or malicious bitterness; a grudge. **spiteful** *adj.*, **spitefully** *adv.*

splash *v.* To spatter a liquid; to wet or soil with liquid; to make a splash. **splash** *n.*, **splashy** *adj.*

spleen *n.* A highly vascular, flattened organ which filters and stores blood, located below the diaphragm.

splice *v.* To join together by wearing, overlapping, and binding the ends. **splice** *n.*

splint *n.* A device used to hold a fractured or injured limb in the proper position for healing. **splint** *v.*

spoil *v.* To destroy the value, quality, or usefulness; to overindulge as to harm the character.

spoke *n.* One of the rods that serve to connect and support the rim of a wheel. *v.* Past tense of *speak*.

sponge *n.* Any of a number of marine creatures with a soft, porous skeleton which soaks up liquid. *v.* To clean with a sponge.

spon·ta·ne·ous *adj.* Done from one's own impulse without apparent cause.

spook *n.* A ghost. *v.* To scare or frighten. **spooky** *adj.*

spoon *n.* An eating or cooking utensil; a shiny metallic fishing lure.

spo·rad·ic *adj.* Occurring occasionally or at irregular intervals. **sporadically** *adv.*

sport *n.* An interesting diversion; a particular game or physical activity with set rules; a person who leads a fast life

sprawler *n.*

spray *n.* A liquid dispersed in a fine mist or droplets. **sprayer** *n.*

spread *v.* To unfold or open fully; to apply or distribute over an area; to force apart; to extend or expand.

spree *n.* An excessive indulgence in an activity; a binge.

spright·ly *adj.* Vivacious, lively.

sprint *n.* A short, fast race. **sprinter** *n.*

sprung *v.* Past perfect tense of *spring*.

spry *adj.* Quick; brisk; energetic.

spur *n.* A sharp, projecting device worn on a rider's boot, used to nudge a horse.

spy *n.* A secret agent who obtains information; one who watches other people secretly.

squab·ble *v.* To engage in a petty argument.

squad *n.* A small group organized to perform a specific job.

squad·ron *n.* A type of naval unit that has two or more divisions.

squal·id *adj.* Marked by degradation, poverty, or neglect.

squall *v.* To cry out. *n.* A brief but violent wind storm at sea.

squan·der *v.* To spend extravagantly or wastefully.

square *n.* A parallelogram with four equal sides; an implement having a T or L shape used to measure right angles; in math, to multiply a number by itself.

square root *n.* A number which when

squaw *n.* A Native American woman.

squeak *v.* To utter a sharp, penetrating sound. **squeak** *n.*, **squeaky** *adj.*

squeal *v.* To produce or to make a shrill cry. **squealer** *n.*

squeam•ish *adj.* Easily shocked or nauseated. **squeamishly** *adv.*

squeeze *v.* To press together; to extract by using pressure. *n.* An instance of squeezing for pleasure; a hug.

squid *n.* A type of ten-armed cephalopod with a tapered body.

squint *v.* To view something through partly closed eyes; to close the eyes in this manner. **squint** *n.*

squire *n.* An old-fashioned title for a rural justice of the peace, lawyer, or judge; a man who escorts a woman; a young man who ranks just below a knight. **squire** *v.*

squirm *v.* To twist the body in a wiggling motion.

squir•rel *n.* A rodent with gray or brown fur, having a long bushy tail and dark eyes.

squirt *v.* To eject in a thin stream or jet; to wet with a squirt. *n.* The act of squirting.

squish•y *adj.* Soft and damp.

sta•bi•lize *v.* To make firm; to keep from changing.

sta•ble *n.* A building for lodging and feeding horses or other farm animals. *adj.* Standing firm and resisting change.

stac•ca•to *adj.* Marked by sharp emphasis.

stack *n.* A large pile of straw or hay; any systematic heap or pile; a chimney. *v.* To fix cards so as to cheat.

sta•di•um *n.* A large structure for holding athletic events or other large gatherings.

staff *n.* A pole or rod used for a specific purpose; the people employed to assist in the day-to-day affairs of running a business, organization, or government; a group of people on an executive or advisory board; the horizontal lines on which notes are written. **staff** *v.*, **staffs**, **staves** *pl.*

stag *n.* The adult male of various animals; a man who attends a social gathering without a woman companion.

stag•ger *v.* To walk unsteadily; to totter.

stag•nant *adj.* Not flowing; standing still; foul from not moving; inactive.

stair *n.* A step or a series of steps.

stair•case *n.* A series or a flight of steps that connect one level to another.

stake *n.* A bet placed on a game of chance; a sharpened piece of wood for driving into the ground. **stake** *v.*

stale *adj.* Having lost freshness; deteriorated; lacking in interest; dull; inactive.

stale•mate *n.* A position in chess when a player cannot move without placing his king in check.

stalk *n.* The main axis of a plant. *v.* To approach in a stealthy manner.

stall *n.* An enclosure in a barn, used as a place to feed and confine animals; a sudden loss of power in an engine; a booth used to display and sell. *v.* To try to put off doing something; to delay.

stal•lion *n.* An uncastrated, fully grown male horse.

sta•men *n.* The pollen-producing organs of a flower.

stam•i•na *n.* Physical or moral endurance.

stam•mer *v.* To make involuntary halts or repetitions of a sound or syllable while speaking. **stammerer** *n.*

stamp *v.* To put the foot down with force; to imprint or impress with a die, mark, or design. *n.* The act of stamping; the impression or pattern made by a stamp; a postage stamp.

stam•pede *n.* A sudden rush of panic, as of a herd of horses or cattle. *v.* To cause a stampede.

stance *n.* The posture or position of a standing person or animal.

stand *v.* To be placed in or maintain an erect or upright position; to take an upright position; to remain unchanged; to maintain a conviction; to resist. *n.* The act of standing; a device on which something rests; a booth for selling items.

stand•ard *n.* A model which stands for or is accepted as a basis for comparison. **standard** *adj.*

stand•ing *n.* A status, reputation, or

achievement; a measure of esteem. *adj.* Unchanging; stationary; not moving.

sta•ple *n.* A principle commodity grown in an area; a major element; a metal fastener designed to hold materials such as cloth or paper. **stapler** *n.*

star *n.* A self-luminous body that is a source of light; any of the celestial bodies that can be seen in the night sky; a symbol having five or six points and resembling a star; a famous celebrity.

starch *n.* Nutrient carbohydrates found in foods such as rice and potatoes. *v.* To stiffen clothing by using starch.

stare *v.* To look with an intent, direct gaze. **stare, starer** *n.*

stark *adj.* Bare; total; complete; forbidding in appearance.

star•tle *v.* To cause a sudden surprise; to shock. **startle** *n.*

starve *v.* To suffer or die from not having food; to suffer from the need of food, love, or other necessities.

state *n.* A situation, mode, or condition of something; a nation; the governing power or authority of; one of the subdivisions or areas of a federal government. *v.* To make known verbally.

stat•ic *adj.* Not moving. *n.* A random noise heard on a radio.

sta•tion *n.* The place where someone or something is directed to stand; a scheduled stopping place; the place from which radio and television programs are broadcast.

sta•tion•ar•y *adj.* Not movable; unchanging.

sta•tion•er•y *n.* Writing paper and envelopes.

sta•tis•tic *n.* An estimate using an average or mean on the basis of a sample taken; numerical data.

stat•ue *n.* A form sculpted from wood, clay, metal, or stone.

stay *v.* To remain; to pause; to maintain a position; to halt or stop; to postpone or delay an execution. *n.* A short visit.

stead *n.* The position, place, or job of another.

stead•fast *adj.* Not changing or moving; firm in purpose; true.

stead•y *adj.* Firmly placed, fixed or set; not changing; constant; uninterrupted.

steal *v.* To take another person's property; to move in a sly way; to move secretly.

steam *n.* Water in the form of vapor; the visible mist into which vapor is condensed by cooling. **steamy** *adj.*

steel *n.* A various mixture of iron, carbon, and other elements; a strong material that can be shaped when heated. **steely** *adj.*

stem *n.* The main stalk of a plant; the main part of a word to which prefixes and suffixes may be added. *v.* To stop or retard the progress or flow of something.

sten•cil *n.* A form cut into a sheet of material, as cardboard or plastic, so that when ink or paint is applied, the pattern will reproduce on paper or another material.

step *n.* A single completed movement in walking, dancing, or running; the distance of such a step; the part of a ladder that one places the feet on.

ster•e•o•type *n.* A conventional opinion or belief; a metal printing plate.

ster•ile *adj.* Free from microorganisms; sanitary; unable to reproduce.

ster•ling *n.* An alloy of 92.5% silver and another metal, such as copper.

stern *adj.* Inflexible; harsh. *n.* The rear of a boat or ship. **sternly** *adv.*

ster•num *n.* A long, flat bone located in the chest wall, connecting the collarbones and the cartilage of the first seven pairs of ribs.

steth•o•scope *n.* An instrument used to listen to the internal sounds of the body.

stew *v.* To cook slowly; to simmer; to boil; to worry. *n.* A dish of stewed meat and potatoes.

stew•ard *n.* A manager of another's financial affairs; a person responsible for maintaining household affairs; a male attendant on an airplane or ship; a flight attendant.

stick *n.* A slender piece of wood; a club,

rod, or walking stick. *v.* To put a hole in something; to pierce; to cling; to become jammed.

stiff *adj.* Not flexible; not easily bent; awkward.

sti•fle *v.* To suffocate; to cut off; to suppress; to keep back.

stig•ma *n.* A mark of disgrace.

still *adj.* Silent; calm; peaceful; until now or another time. **still** *v.*, **stillness** *n.*

stim•u•lant *n.* An agent which arouses or accelerates physiological activity.

stim•u•late *v.* To excite to a heightened activity; to quicken. **stimulation** *n.*

stim•u•lus *n.* Something that excites to action.

sting *v.* To prick with something sharp; to feel or cause to feel a smarting pain; to cause or feel sharp pain, either physical or mental. *n.* The act of stinging; the injury or pain caused by the stinger of a bee or wasp. **stinger** *n.*

stin•gy *adj.* Not giving freely; cheap.

stink *v.* To give off a foul odor that is highly offensive.

stip•u•late *v.* To settle something by agreement; to establish conditions of agreement; to lay out conditions. **stipulation** *n.*

stir *v.* To mix a substance by moving round and round; to agitate or provoke.

stir•rup *n.* A loop extending from a horse's saddle, used to support the rider's foot.

stitch *n.* In sewing, a single loop formed by a needle and thread; the section of loop of thread, as in sewing. *v.* To join with a stitch.

stock *n.* A supply of goods kept on hand; animals living on a farm; a share in ownership, as in a company or corporation; the raw material or the base used to make something. *v.* To provide with stock. *adj.* Regular, common, or typical.

stock•ing *n.* A knitted covering for the foot.

stock•y *adj.* Short and plump; built sturdily.

stom•ach *n.* The organ into which food passes from the esophagus; one of the primary organs of digestion. *v.* To tolerate or stand; to put up with.

stone *n.* Rock; compacted earth or mineral matter; a gem or jewel; the seed or pit of certain fruits.

stool *n.* A seat without a backrest and arms; a small version of this on which to rest the feet; a bowel movement.

stoop *v.* To bend the body forward and downward from the waist. *n.* A porch attached to a house.

stop *v.* To cease; to halt; to refrain from moving, operating, or acting; to block or obstruct; to visit for a short time. *n.* A location where a bus, train, or other means of mass transportation may pick up or drop off passengers.

stor•age *n.* The act of storing or keeping; in computers, the part of a computer in which all information is held; the memory.

store *n.* A business offering merchandise for sale; a supply to be used in the future. *v.* To supply; to accumulate.

stork *n.* A large, wading bird.

storm *n.* An atmospheric condition marked by strong winds with rain, sleet, hail, or snow. *v.* To charge or attack with a powerful force. **stormy** *adj.*

sto•ry *n.* A narration of a fictional tale or account; a lie; a level in a building or house.

stout *adj.* Strong; sturdy; substantial; courageous. **stoutly** *adv.*

stove *n.* An apparatus in which oil, electricity, gas, or other fuels are consumed to provide the heat for cooking.

stow *v.* To pack or put away.

strad•dle *v.* To sit or stand with the legs on either side of something; to favor both sides of an issue. **straddler** *n.*

straight *adj.* Being without bends, angles, or curves; upright; erect; honest; undiluted; unmodified. *n.* In poker, a numerical sequence of five cards not of the same suit.

strain *v.* To stretch beyond a proper limit, to injure by putting forth too much effort;

to pass through a sieve to separate small particles from larger ones.

strait *n.* A narrow passageway which connects two bodies of water.

strange *adj.* Not previously known or experienced; odd; peculiar; alien.

stran•ger *n.* A person unknown; a newcomer.

stran•gle *v.* To kill by choking.

strap *n.* A long, narrow strip of leather or other material used to secure objects.

strat•e•gy *n.* The skillful planning and managing of an activity.

straw *n.* A stalk of dried, threshed grain; a slender, plastic or paper straw used to suck up a liquid. *adj.* Yellowish brown.

straw•ber•ry *n.* A low plant with white flowers and red fruit; the fruit of this plant.

stray *v.* To roam or wander. *n.* A lost or wandering animal or person. **strayer** *n.*

stream *n.* A small body of flowing water; a steady or continuous succession or procession. *v.* To flow in or like a stream.

street *n.* A public thoroughfare in a town or city with buildings on either or both sides.

strength *n.* The quality of being strong; power in general; degree of concentrated potency.

stren•u•ous *adj.* Necessitating or characterized by vigorous effort or exertion. **strenuously** *adv.*

stress *n.* Special significance; an emphasis given to a specific syllable, word, action, or plan; strain or pressure.

stretch *v.* To extend fully; to extend forcibly beyond proper limits; to prolong. *n.* The state or act of stretching.

strick•en *adj.* Suffering, as from an emotion, illness, or trouble.

to stop working as a protest against something or in favor of rules or demands presented to an employer. **strike** *n.*

string *n.* A strip of thin twine, wire, or catgut used on stringed musical instruments; a series of ads, items, or events.

strin•gent *adj.* Of or relating to strict requirements; marked by obstructions or scarcity.

strip *v.* To take off the outer covering; to divest or pull rank; to remove one's clothes; to rob.

stripe *n.* A streak, band, or strip of a different color or texture; a piece of material or cloth worn on the sleeve of a uniform to indicate rank, award, or service.

stroke *n.* The movement of striking; a sudden action with a powerful effect; a single movement made by the hand or as if by a brush or pen; a sudden interruption of the blood supply to the brain. *v.* To pass the hand over gently.

stroll *v.* To walk in a slow, leisurely way.

strong *adj.* Exerting or possessing physical power; durable; difficult to break. **strongly** *adv.*

struc•ture *n.* A construction made up of a combination of related parts. **structural** *adj.*

strug•gle *v.* To put forth effort against opposition.

stub *n.* A short, projecting part; the short end of something after the main part has been removed or used.

stub•born *adj.* Inflexible; difficult to control, handle, or manage.

stuc•co *n.* Fine plaster used to coat exterior walls and to decorate interior walls.

stud *n.* An upright post, as in a building frame, to which sheets of wallboard or paneling are fastened; a small removable

stud•y *n., pl.* **-ies** The process of applying the mind to acquire knowledge.

stum•ble *v.* To trip and nearly fall over something; to come upon unexpectedly.

stump *n.* The part of a tree which remains after the top is cut down. *v.* To puzzle or be puzzled; to walk heavily; to campaign.

stun *v.* To render senseless by or as if by a blow.

stu•pen•dous *adj.* Astonishing or highly impressive.

stu•pid *adj.* Slow in apprehension or understanding. **stupidity** *n.*

stur•dy *adj.* Possessing robust strength and health. **sturdily** *adv.*

stut•ter *v.* To speak with involuntary repetitions of sound.

sty *n.* An inflammation of the edge of an eyelid.

style *n.* A method, manner, or way of performing, speaking, or clothing; elegance, grace, or excellence in performance or appearance. **stylish** *adj.*

suave *adj.* Ingratiating; smoothly pleasant in manner.

sub•con•scious *adj.* Below the level of consciousness.

sub•due *v.* To bring under control by influence, training, persuasion or force.

sub•ject *n.* The word in a sentence that defines a person or thing; a person who is under the control of another's governing power. *v.* To subdue or gain control over. **subjection** *n.*

sub•ject•ive *adj.* Taking place within, relating to or preceding from an individual's emotions or mind. **subjectively** *adv.*, **subjectivity** *n.*

sub•ma•rine *adj.* Operating or existing beneath the surface of the sea. *n.* A ship that travels underwater.

sub•merge *v.* To plunge under the surface of the water.

sub•mit *v.* To give into or surrender to another's authority. **submission** *n.*

sub•or•di•nate *adj.* Being of lower class or rank; minor; inferior.

sub•poe•na *n.* A legal document requiring a person to appear in court for testimony.

sub•se•quent *adj.* Following in time, place, or order.

sub•side *v.* To move to a lower level or sink; to become less intense.

sub•sist *v.* To have continued existence.

sub•soil *n.* The layer of earth that comes after the surface soil.

sub•stance *n.* Matter or material of which anything consists.

sub•sti•tute *n.* Something or someone that takes the place of another.

sub•ter•ra•ne•an *adj.* Located, situated, or operating underground.

sub•ti•tle *n.* An explanatory title, as in a document, book, etc.; a written translation that appears at the bottom of a foreign motion picture screen.

sub•tract *v.* To deduct or take away from.

sub•urb *n.* A residential community near a large city. **suburban** *adj.*

sub•way *n.* An underground electrically powered train.

suc•ceed *v.* To accomplish what is attempted; to come next or to follow.

suc•cess *n.* Achievement of something intended or desired; attaining wealth, fame, or prosperity.

suc•ces•sion *n.* The act or process of following in order; sequence; series; the order, sequence or act by which something changes hands.

such *adj.* Of this or that kind or thing; a great degree or extent in quality. *pron.* Of a particular degree or kind; a person or thing of such.

suck *v.* To pull liquid in the mouth by means of a vacuum created by the lips and tongue. *n.* The action of sucking.

su•crose *n.* Sugar obtained from the sugar beet or sugar cane.

suc•tion *n.* The process or act of sucking.

sud•den *adj.* Happening very quickly without warning or notice; sharp; abrupt; marked by haste. **suddenly** *adv.*, **suddenness** *n.*

suede *n.* Leather with a napped finish.

su•et *n.* The hard fat around the kidney and loins of sheep.

suf•fer *v.* To feel pain or distress; to sustain injury, loss, or damage. **sufferer** *n.*

suf•fi•cient *adj.* As much as is needed or desired. **sufficiency** *n.*, **sufficiently** *adv.*

suf•fix *n.* A form affixed to the end of a word.

suf•fo•cate *v.* To kill by depriving something or someone of oxygen. **suffocation** *n.*

sug•ar *n.* A sweet, water-soluble, crystalline carbohydrate. *slang* A nickname.

sug•gest *v.* To give an idea for action or consideration; to imply, hint or intimate.

sug•ges•tion *n.* The act of suggesting; a slight insinuation; hint.

su•i•cide *n.* The act of taking one's own life. **suicidal** *adj.*

suit *n.* A set of articles, as clothing, to be used or worn together; in cards, one of the four sets: spades, hearts, clubs, and diamonds that make up a deck. *v.* To meet the requirements of; to satisfy.

sul•fur or **sul•phur** *n.* A light, yellow, nonmetallic element occurring naturally in both combined and free form, used in making matches, gunpowder and medicines.

sulk *v.*, To be sullenly silent.

sul•len *adj.* Ill-humored; melancholy; gloomy; depressing.

sul•try *adj.* Hot and humid.

sum *n.* The result obtained by adding; the whole amount, quantity, or number; summary.

sum•ma•ry *n.* The sum or substance; a statement covering the main points. **summarily** *adv.*

sum•mer *n.* The warmest of the four seasons, following spring and coming before autumn. **summery** *adj.*

sum•mit *n.* The top and highest point, degree, or level.

sum•mons *n.* An order or command to perform a duty; a notice to appear at a certain place.

sun *n.* The star around which other planets of the solar system orbit; the energy, light, and heat emitted by the sun; sunshine.

sun•down *n.* The time of day the sun sets.

sunk•en *adj.* Submerged or deeply depressed in.

su•per *adj.* Exceeding a norm; in excessive intensity or degree; surpassing most others; superior in rank, status or position; excellent.

su•perb *adj.* Of first-rate quality.

su•per•fi•cial *adj.* Pertaining to a surface; concerned only with what is not necessarily real.

su•pe•ri•or *adj.* Of higher rank, grade, or dignity. *n.* A person who surpasses another in rank or excellence. **superiority** *n.*, **superiorly** *adv.*

su•per•nat•u•ral *adj.* Beyond the natural world; pertaining to a divine power. **supernaturally** *adv.*

su•per•sede *v.* To take the place of; to set aside.

su•per•sti•tion *n.* A belief founded, despite evidence that it is irrational; a belief, resulting from faith in magic or chance. **superstitious** *adj.*

su•per•vise *v.* To have charge in directing the work of other people. **supervision**, **supervisor** *n.*

sup•per *n.* The evening meal of the day.

sup•ple•ment *n.* A part that compensates for what is lacking.

sup•ply *v.* To provide with what is needed; to make available. **supplier** *n.*

sup•port *v.* To bear or hold the weight of; to tolerate; to give assistance or approval.

sup•pose *v.* To think or assume as true; to consider probable. **supposed** *adj.*, **supposedly** *adv.*

sup•press *v.* To put an end to something by force; to choose to ignore; to remove to a lower, subconscious level.

su•preme *adj.* Of the highest authority, rank, or power.

sure *adj.* Firm and sturdy; being impossible to doubt; inevitable; not liable to fail. **surer, surest** *adj.*, **surely** *adv.*

surf *n.* The swell of the sea that breaks upon the shore. *v.* To ride on the crest of a wave; in computers, to browse randomly on an internet system.

sur•face *n.* The exterior or outside boundary of something; outward appearance.

surge *v.* To increase suddenly. *n.* A large swell of water:

sur•geon *n.* A physician who practices surgery.

sur•ger•y *n.* The branch of medicine in which physical deformity or disease is treated by an operative procedure.

sur•mount *v.* To overcome; to be at the top.

sur•name *n.* A person's family's last name.

sur•pass *v.* To go beyond the limits of; to be greater than. **surpassingly** *adv.*

sur•plus *n.* An amount beyond what is needed.

sur•prise *v.* To come upon unexpectedly or suddenly; to cause to feel amazed or astonished. **surprise, surpriser** *n.*, **surprisingly** *adv.*

sur•ren•der *v.* To give up or yield possession or power. *n.* The act of surrendering.

sur•ro•gate *n.* A person who puts himself in the place of another. **surrogate** *v.*

sur•round *v.* To extend around all edges of something; to enclose or shut in.

sur•veil•lance *n.* Close observation kept over an activity or person, especially as a suspect.

sur•vey *v.* To examine in detail; to determine area, boundaries, or position and elevation of a section of the earth's surface. **surveyor** *n.*

sur•vive *v.* To continue to exist; to outlast; to outlive. **surviving** *adj.*, **survival, survivor** *n.*

su•shi *n.* A Japanese dish of thin slices of fresh, raw fish.

sus•pect *v.* To have doubt or distrust; to have a suspicion or inkling of someone or something. **suspect** *n.*

sus•pend *v.* To bar from a privilege for a certain time, as a means of punishment; to hang so as to allow free movement.

sus•pense *n.* The feeling of being insecure or undecided, resulting from uncertainty.

sus•pi•cion *n.* The instance of suspecting something wrong without proof. **suspicious** *adj.*, **suspiciously** *adv.*

sus•tain *v.* To hold up and keep from falling; to suffer or undergo an injury.

su•ture *n.* The stitching together or joining the edges of an incision or cut.

swab *n.* A small stick with a wad of cotton on both ends, used to apply medication. **swab** *v.*

swad•dle *v.* To wrap closely, using a long strip of flannel or linen.

swal•low *v.* To cause food to pass from the mouth to the stomach; to retract or take back, as words spoken. *n.* The act of swallowing.

swan *n.* A mostly pure white bird having a long neck and heavy body.

swap *v.* To trade something for something in return. **swap** *n.*

swarm *n.* A large number of insects, as bees; a large group of persons or things. **swarm** *v.*, **swarmer** *n.*

swat *v.* To hit with a sharp blow.

sway *v.* To move or swing from right to left or side to side; to exert influence or control.

swear *v.* To make an affirmation under oath. **swearer** *n.*

sweat *v.* To excrete a salty moisture from the pores of the skin; to perspire.

sweat gland *n.* One of the tubular glands that secrete sweat externally through pores.

sweat•er *n.* A knitted or crocheted garment with or without sleeves attached.

sweep *v.* To touch very lightly; to remove or clear away with a brush or broom; to move with an even action.

sweet *adj.* Having a sugary, agreeable flavor; arousing pleasant emotions; *n.* A beloved or dear person.

swell *v.* To increase in size or bulk; to grow in volume. *n.* The process, effect, or act of swelling; a continuous wave that is long and billowing. *adj.* Fine; excellent; smart.

swel•ter *v.* To suffer from extreme heat.

swerve *v.* To turn aside from the regular course.

swift *adj.* Moving with great speed; accomplished or occurring quickly. **swiftly** *adv.*, **swiftness** *n.*

swim *v.* To move oneself through water by moving parts of the body.

swin•dle *v.* To cheat out of property or money; to practice fraud. **swindle**, **swindler** *n.*

swine *n.* A hoofed mammal with a snout, related to pigs and hogs; a low, despicable person. **swinish** *adj.*

swing *v.* To move freely back and forth; to hang or to be suspended. *n.* The act of a swing; a seat that hangs from chains or ropes; in music, jazz played by a larger band and developed by using simple harmonic patterns. **swinger** *n.*

swirl *v.* To move with a whirling, rotating motion. **swirl** *n.*, **swirly** *adj.*

switch *n.* A small, thin, flexible stick, twig or rod; in electronics, a device for opening or closing an electric circuit. *v.* To shift to another train track; to exchange.

sword *n.* A weapon with a long, pointed cutting blade.

syc•a•more *n.* A North American tree used widely for shade.

sy•co•phant *n.* A self-seeking flatterer.

syl•la•ble *n.* A word or part of one that consists of a single vocal impulse, usually consisting of one or more vowels or consonants.

syl•la•bus *n.* An outline of a course of study.

syl•van *adj.* Living or located in the woods.

sym•bi•o•sis *n.* The living together in close union of two dissimilar organisms.

sym•bol *n.* Something that stands for or represents something else. **symbolic**, **symbolical** *adj.*, **symbolically** *adv.*

sym•met•ri•cal *adj.* Involving symmetry. **symmetricalness** *n.*

sym•me•try *n.* Balance in form, size, and position of parts on two sides of an axis.

sym•pa•thet•ic *adj.* Having or showing kindness or sympathy for others. **sympathetically** *adv.*

sym•pa•thize *v.* To respond to someone or something with sympathy.

sym•pa•thy *n.* Mutual understanding or affection during a time of sadness or loss.

sym•pho•ny *n.* A large orchestra with wind, percussion and string sections. **symphonic** *adj.*

sym•po•si•um *n.* A gathering or meeting where several specialists give short speeches on a topic or on subjects related.

symp•tom *n.* A sign of change in a body's functions or appearance.

symp•tom•at•ic *adj.* Having the characteristics of a particular disease but arising from something else.

syn•chro•nize *v.* To operate or take place at the same time.

syn•chro•nous *adj.* Existing at precisely the same time.

syn•chro•scope *n.* A device for showing the two associated machines are working in synchronism with one another.

syn•co•pate *v.* To shorten words by omitting sounds of the letters in the middle of the word; to shift the accents in a musical composition. **syncopation** *n.*

syn•di•cate *n.* An organization set up to carry out business transactions; a company that sells materials for simultaneous publication at a number of different locations. **syndication** *n.*

syn•drome *n.* A set of concurrent symptoms that indicate or characterize a disorder or disease.

syn•o•nym *n.* A word that means the same or nearly the same as another. **synonymous** *adj.*, **synonymy** *n.*

syn•op•sis *n.* A shortened statement or narrative. **synopses** *pl.*

syn•os•to•sis *n.* The joining or the union of bones which are separate to form a single bone.

syn•the•sis *n.* A production of a substance by the joining of chemical elements. **syntheses** *pl.*

syn•the•size *v.* To produce or to make with synthesis.

syn•thet•ic *adj.* Involving synthesis. **synthetically** *adv.*

syph•i•lis *n.* An infectious venereal disease transmittable by direct contact and usually progressing in severity.

sy•ringe *n.* A medical instrument used to inject or draw fluids from the body.

syr•up *n.* A sticky, thick, sweet liquid, used as a topping for food.

sys•tem *n.* A method or way of doing something; the human body or related parts of the body that perform vital functions; an orderly arrangement. **systematic** *adj.*, **systematically** *adv.*

sys•to•le *n.* The regular rhythmic contraction of the heart that pumps blood through the aorta and pulmonary artery. **systolic** *adj.*

T

T, t The twentieth letter of the English alphabet.

tab *n.* A strip, flap, or small loop that projects from something.

tab•er•na•cle *n.* A portable shelter or structure used by the Jews during their journey out of Egypt; a place of worship.

ta•ble *n.* An article of furniture having a flat top, supported by legs; a collection of related signs, values, or items. *v.* To put off or postpone.

tab•u•lar *adj.* Pertaining to or arranged in a table or list.

ta•chom•e•ter *n.* An instrument for measuring velocity and speed.

tac•it *adj.* Understood; expressed or implied nonverbally; implicit. **tacitly** *adv.*, **tacitness** *n.*

tack *n.* A small, short nail with a flat head; a sewing stitch used to hold something temporarily; the changing of a sailboat from one direction to another. *v.* To change the direction in which a sailboat is going.

tack•le *n.* Equipment used for fishing or other sports; an apparatus of ropes and pulley blocks for pulling and hoisting heavy loads. **tackled** *v.*, **tackler** *n.*

tack•y *adj.* Slightly sticky; shabby; lacking style or good taste; flashy.

ta•co *n.* A type of Mexican or Spanish food made of a tortilla folded over with a filling inside.

tact *n.* Having the ability to avoid what would disturb someone. **tactful, tactless** *adj.*, **tactfully, tactlessly** *adv.*, **tactfulness, tactlessness** *n.*

tac•tic *n.* A way or method of working toward a goal; the art of using strategy to gain military objectives or other goals. **tactical** *adj.*, **tactician** *n.*

tad *n.* A small boy; an insignificant degree or amount.

tad•pole *n.* The early stage in the growth of a frog or toad during which it breathes by external gills, has a long tail, and lives in the water; a polliwog.

taf•fe•ta *n.* A stiff, smooth fabric of rayon, nylon, or silk.

tag *n.* A piece of plastic, metal, paper, or other material that is attached to something in order to identify it; a children's game of running and tagging.

tail *n.* The posterior extremity, extending from the end or back of an animal. *pl.* The opposite side of a coin from heads.

tai•lor *n.* One whose profession is making, mending, and altering clothing.

taint *v.* To spoil, contaminate, or pollute. *n.* A blemish or stain.

take *v.* To seize or capture; to get possession of; to receive, swallow, absorb, or accept willingly; to attack and surmount; to choose or pick. *n.* The process of acquiring; the total receipts at an event.

talc *n.* A soft, fine-grained, smooth mineral used in making talcum powder.

tale *n.* A story or recital of relating events that may or may not be true; a malicious or false story; gossip.

tal•ent *n.* The aptitude, disposition, or

characteristic ability of a person.

talk *v.* To communicate by words or speech; to engage in chatter or gossip. *n.* A speech or lecture.

tall *adj.* Of greater than average height; of a designated or specified height; imaginary.

tal·low *n.* Hard fat rendered from sheep or cattle, used to make candles, lubricants, and soap. **tallow** *adj.*

tal·ly *n.* A record or counting of money, amounts, or scores. *v.* To agree with; to reckon or figure a score; to count.

tal·on *n.* A long, curved claw found on birds or animals. **taloned** *adj.*

tam·bou·rine *n.* A percussion instrument made of a small drum with jingling metal disks around the rim.

tame *adj.* Not wild or ferocious; domesticated or manageable. *v.* To make docile or calm. **tamely** *adv.*, **tamer** *n.*

tam·per *v.* To change, meddle, or alter something; to use corrupt measures to scheme.

tan *v.* To cure a hide into leather by using chemicals. *n.* A brownish skin tone caused by exposure to the sun.

tan·dem *n.* Any arrangement that involves two or more things, animals, or persons arranged one behind the other; a bicycle built for two.

tang *n.* A sharp, distinct taste or smell; a slender shank that projects from a tool and connects to a handle. **tangy** *adv.*

tan·gent *n.* A line that touches a curved line but does not intersect or cross it; a sudden change to another course.

tan·ger·ine *n.* A small citrus fruit with an easily peeled orange skin, resembling an orange.

tan·gi·ble *adj.* Capable of being appreciated or felt by the sense of touch; capable of being realized.

tan·gle *v.* To mix, twist, or unite in a confused manner making separation difficult.

tan·go *n.* A ballroom dance with long, gliding steps. **tango** *v.*

tank *n.* A large container for holding or storing a gas or liquid. **tankful** *n.*

tan·ta·lize *v.* To tease or tempt by holding or keeping something just out of one's reach. **tantalizing** *adj.*

tan·ta·lum *n.* A metallic element symbolized by Ta.

tan·trum *n.* A fit; an outburst or a rage.

tap *v.* To strike repeatedly, usually while making a small noise; to strike or touch gently; to make secret contact with something; in medicine, to remove fluids from the body. **tapper** *n.*

tape *n.* A narrow strip of woven fabric; a string or ribbon stretched across the finish line of a race.

ta·per *n.* A very slender candle. *v.* To become gradually smaller or thinner at one end.

tap·es·try *n.* A thick fabric woven with designs and figures.

tap·i·o·ca *n.* A bead-like substance used for thickening and for puddings.

tar·dy *adj.* Late; not on time. **tardily** *adv.*, **tardiness** *n.*

tar·get *n.* An object marked to shoot at; an aim or goal.

tar·iff *n.* Duty or tax on merchandise coming into or going out of a country.

tar·nish *v.* To become discolored or dull; to lose luster; to spoil.

tar·ot *n.* A set of 22 major and 56 minor cards used for fortune-telling, each card showing a virtue, an elemental force, or a vice.

tar·pau·lin *n.* A sheet of waterproof canvas used as a protective covering.

tart *adj.* Sour; biting in tone or meaning.

task *n.* A bit of work, usually assigned by another; a job.

taste *n.* The ability to sense or determine flavor in the mouth; a personal liking or disliking. *v.* To test or sense flavors in the mouth.

tat·tle *v.* To reveal the secrets of another by gossiping. **tattler** *n.*

tat·too *n.* A permanent design or mark made on the skin by pricking and inserting an indelible dye. **tattoo** *v.*, **tattooer** *n.*

taught *v.* Past tense of *teach*.

taut *adj.* Tight; emotionally strained. **taut·ly** *adv.*, **tautness** *n.*

tau·tol·o·gy *n.* Redundancy; a statement which is an unnecessary repetition of the same idea; a pattern of logic that seems to prove but is in fact a restatement of the premise.

tav·ern *n.* An inn; an establishment or business licensed to sell alcoholic drinks.

tax *n.* A payment imposed and collected from individuals or businesses by the government.

tax·i *v.* To move along the ground or water surface on its own power before taking off.

tax·i·cab *n.* A vehicle for carrying passengers for money.

tax·i·der·my *n.* The art or profession of preparing, stuffing, and mounting animal skins. **taxidermist** *n.*

tea *n.* A small tree or bush which grows where the climate is very hot and damp; a drink made by steeping the dried leaves of this shrub in boiling water.

teach *v.* To communicate skill or knowledge; to give instruction or insight. **teacher** *n.*

team *n.* Two or more players on one side in a game; a group of people trained or organized to work together; two or more animals harnessed to the same implement.

tear *v.* To become divided into pieces; to separate; to rip into parts or pieces; to move fast; to rush. *n.* A rip or torn place.

tear *n.* A fluid secreted by the eye to moisten and cleanse.

tease *v.* To make fun of; to bother; to annoy; to tantalize. *n.* A person who teases. **teaser** *n.*, **teasingly** *adv.*

tech·ne·ti·um *n.* A metallic element symbolized Tc.

tech·ni·cal *adj.* Expert; derived or relating to technique; relating to industry or mechanics.

tech·nique *n.* A technical procedure or method of doing something.

tech·nol·o·gy *n.* The application of scientific knowledge to serve man in industry, commerce, medicine and other fields.

te·di·ous *adj.* Boring; taking a long time. **tedium** *n.*

tee *n.* A peg used to hold a golf ball on the first stroke toward a hole; a peg used to support a football during a field goal attempt. **tee** *v.*

teem *v.* To abound; to be full of; to swarm or crowd.

teens *pl. n.* The ages between 13 and 19; the years of one's life between 13 and 19.

teeth *pl. n.* The plural of *tooth*.

tel·e·gram *n.* A message sent or received by telegraph. **telegram** *v.*

tel·e·graph *n.* A system for communicating; a transmission sent by wire or radio. *v.* To send messages by electricity over wire. **telegrapher, telegraphist** *n.*, **telegraphic** *adj.*

te·lep·a·thy *n.* Communication by means of mental processes rather than ordinary means. **telepathic** *adj.*

tel·e·phone *n.* A system or device for transmitting conversations by wire. **telephone** *v.*, **telephoner** *n.*

tel·e·scope *n.* An instrument which contains a lens system which makes distant objects appear larger and nearer. **telescopic** *adj.*

tel·e·vi·sion *n.* Reception and transmission of images on a screen with sound; the device that reproduces television sounds and images.

tell *v.* To relate or describe; to command or order. **tellable, telling** *adj.*, **teller** *n.*

tel·lu·ri·um *n.* An element symbolized by Te.

tel·net *n.* In computers, a protocol allowing users to log in and access files from any terminal.

tem·per *n.* The state of one's feelings. *v.* To modify something, making it flexible or hard.

tem·per·a·ment *n.* Personality; a characteristic way of thinking, reacting, or behaving. **temperamental** *adj.*

tem·per·ance *n.* Moderation; restraint; moderation or abstinence from drinking alcoholic beverages.

tem·per·ate *adj*. Avoiding extremes; moderate.

tem·per·a·ture *n*. A measure of heat or cold in relation to the body or environment; an elevation in body temperature above the normal 98.6 degrees Fahrenheit.

tem·pest *n*. A severe storm, usually with snow, hail, rain, or sleet.

tem·ple *n*. A place of worship; the flat area on either side of the forehead.

tem·po *n*. The rate of speed at which a musical composition is to be played.

tem·po·rar·y *adj*. Lasting for a limited amount of time; not permanent.

tempt *n*. To encourage or draw into a foolish or wrong course of action; to lure. **temptation, tempter** *n*.

te·na·cious *adj*. Persistent; stubborn. **tenacity** *n*.

ten·ant *n*. A person who pays rent to occupy another's property.

tend *v*. To be inclined or disposed; to be directed; to look after.

ten·den·cy *n*. A disposition to act or behave in a particular way; a particular direction, mode, outcome, or direction.

ten·der *adj*. Fragile; soft; not hard or tough; painful or sore when touched. *n*. Something offered as a formal bid or offer; compassionate; a supply ship. *v*. To make an offer to buy or purchase; to present as a resignation.

ten·der·loin *n*. A cut of tender pork or beef.

ten·don *n*. A band of tough, fibrous tissues that connect a muscle and bone.

ten·dril *n*. A thread-like part of a climbing plant which attaches itself to a support. **tendrilled** *adj*.

ten·nis *n*. A sport played with a ball and racket by 2 or 4 people on a rectangular court.

ten·or *n*. An adult male singing voice, above a baritone.

tense *adj*. Taut or stretched tightly; nervous; under strain.

ten·sion *n*. The condition of stretching or the state of being stretched.

tent *n*. A portable shelter made by stretching material over a supporting framework.

ten·ta·cle *n*. A long, unjointed, flexible body part that projects from certain invertebrates, as the octopus.

ten·ta·tive *adj*. Experimental; subject to change; not definite. **tentatively** *adv*.

ten·ure *n*. The right, state, or period of holding something, as an office or property. **tenured** *adj*.

te·pee *n*. A conical tent made of hides or bark used by some of the Indians of North America.

tep·id *adj*. Lukewarm; neither hot nor cold.

ter·bi·um *n*. A metallic element of the rare-earth group symbolized by Tb.

term *n*. A phrase or word; a limited time or duration; a phrase having a precise meaning.

ter·mi·nal *adj*. Of, forming, or located at the end; final. *n*. A station at the end of a bus line, railway, or airline; in computers, the end location of the information network, where electronic signals can be encoded or decoded into readable text; a worksite dedicated to such activity, usually consisting of computer, monitor, and keyboard.

ter·mi·nate *v*. To bring to a conclusion or end; to finish. **termination** *n*.

ter·mite *n*. The winged or wingless insect which lives in large colonies feeding on wood.

ter·race *n*. An open balcony or porch; a level piece of land that is higher than the surrounding area; a row of houses built on a sloping or raised site.

ter·ra cot·ta *n*. A hard, baked clay used in ceramic pottery.

ter·rain *n*. The surface of an area, as land.

ter·ra·pin *n*. An edible turtle of North America, living in both fresh and salt water.

ter·res·tri·al *adj*. Something earthly; not heavenly; growing or living on land.

ter·ri·ble *adj.* Causing fear or terror; intense; extreme; horrid; difficult. **terribly** *adv.*, **terribleness** *n.*

ter·ri·er *n.* A very active small dog, originally bred by hunters to dig for burrowing game, now kept as a family pet.

ter·rif·ic *adj.* Terrifying; excellent; causing amazement.

ter·ri·fy *v.* To fill with fear or terror; to frighten. **terrified, terrifying** *adj.*

ter·ri·to·ry *n.* An area, usually of great size, which is controlled by a particular government; a district or area assigned to one person or group.

ter·ror *n.* Extreme fear.

ter·ror·ism *n.* The state of being terrorized or the act of terrorizing; the use of intimidation to attain one's goals or to advance one's cause.

ter·ror·ist *n.* One who causes terror.

terse *adj.* Brief; using as few words as possible without loss of force or clearness. **tersely** *adj.*, **terseness** *n.*

test *n.* An examination or evaluation of something or someone; an examination to determine one's knowledge, skill, intelligence or other qualities.

tes·ta·ment *n.* A legal document which states how one's personal property is to be distributed upon his death.

tes·ti·fy *v.* To give evidence while under oath; to serve as proof. **testifier** *n.*

tes·ti·mo·ny *n.* A solemn affirmation made under oath; an outward expression of a religious experience.

tes·tis *n.* The sperm producing gland of the male. **testes** *pl.*

test tube *n.* A thin glass tube closed at one end, used in biology and chemistry.

test-tube ba·by *n.* A baby conceived outside of a mother's womb by fertilizing an egg removed from the mother and then returning the fertilized egg to the mother's womb.

tet·a·nus *n.* An often fatal disease marked by muscular spasms, commonly known as lockjaw.

teth·er *n.* A rope or chain which fastens an animal to something but allows limited freedom to wander within its range.

text *n.* The actual wording of an author's work; the main part or body of a book. **textual** *adj.*, **textually** *adv.*

tex·tile *n.* A cloth made by weaving; yarn or fiber for making cloth. **textile** *adj.*

tex·ture *n.* The look, surface, or feel of something; the basic makeup. **textural** *adj.*, **texturally** *adv.*

than *conj.* In comparison with or to something.

thank *v.* To express one's gratitude; to credit.

thank·ful *adj.* Feeling or showing gratitude; grateful. **thankfully** *adv.*, **thankfulness** *n.*

that *adj.* The person or thing present or being mentioned. *conj.* Used to introduce a clause stating what is said. **those** *pl.*

thatch *n.* Grass, straw, or similar material used to make a roof. *v.* To overlay or cover with thatch.

thaw *v.* To change from a frozen state to a liquid or soft state; to grow warmer; to melt.

the *art.* Used before nouns and noun phrases as a determiner, designating particular persons or things. *adv.* Used to modify words in the comparative degree; by so much; by that much.

the·a·ter or **the·a·tre** *n.* A building adapted to present dramas, motion pictures, plays, or other performances; a performance.

the·at·ri·cal *adj.* Extravagant; designed for show, display, or effect.

theft *n.* The act of stealing; larceny.

their *adj.* or *pron.* The possessive case of *they*; belonging to two or more things or beings previously named.

the·ism *n.* The belief in the existence of God. **theist** *n.*, **theistic** *adj.*

them *pron.* The objective case of *they*.

theme *n.* The topic or subject of something; in music, a short melody of a musical composition. **thematic** *adj.*

them·selves *pron.* Them or they; a form

of the third person plural pronoun.

then *adv.* At that time; soon or immediately. *adj.* Being or acting in or belonging to or at that time.

the·oc·ra·cy *n.* Government by God or by clergymen who think of themselves as representatives of God. **theocrat** *n.*, **theocratic** *adj.*

the·ol·o·gy *n.* The religious study of the nature of God, beliefs, practices, and ideas. **theologian** *n.*

the·o·rize *v.* To analyze theories. **theoretician, theorist** *n.*

the·o·ry *n.* A general principle or explanation which covers the known facts; an offered opinion which may possibly, but not positively, be true.

ther·a·py *n.* The treatment of certain diseases; treatment intended to remedy an undesirable condition. **therapist** *n.*

there *adv.* In, at, or about that place; toward, into, or to. **thereabouts, thereafter, thereby, therefore, therefrom, therein** *adv.*

ther·mal *adj.* Having to do with or producing heat.

ther·mom·e·ter *n.* A glass tube containing mercury which rises and falls with temperature changes.

ther·mo·plas·tic *adj.* Pliable and soft when heated or warm but hard when cooled. **thermoplastic** *n.*

ther·mo·stat *n.* A device that automatically responds to temperature changes and activates equipment such as air conditioners and furnaces to adjust the temperature to correspond with the setting on the device.

the·sau·rus *n.* A book which contains synonyms and antonyms.

these *pron.* The plural of *this.*

the·sis *n.* A formal argument or idea; a paper written by a student that develops an idea or point of view. **theses** *pl.*

they *pron.* The two or more beings just mentioned.

thick *adj.* Having a heavy or dense consistency; having a considerable extent or depth from one surface to its opposite.

thief *n.* A person who steals.

thim·ble *n.* A small cap-like protection for the finger, worn while sewing.

thin *adj.* Having very little depth or extent from one side or surface to the other; not fat; slender.

thing *n.* Something not recognized or named; an idea, conception, or utterance; a material or real object.

things *n. pl.* One's belongings.

think *v.* To exercise thought; to use the mind, to reason and work out in the mind; to visualize.

thirst *n.* An uncomfortably dry feeling in the throat and mouth accompanied by an urgent desire for liquids. **thirsty** *adj.*

this *pron.* The person or thing that is near, present, or just mentioned; the one under discussion. **these** *pl.*

this·tle *n.* A prickly plant usually producing a purplish or yellowish flower.

thith·er *adv.* To that place; there; on the farthest side.

thong *n.* A narrow strip of leather used for binding.

tho·rax *n.* The section or part of the human body between the neck and abdomen, supported by the ribs and breastbone. **thoracic** *adj.*

tho·ri·um *n.* A radioactive metallic element symbolized by Th.

thorn *n.* A sharp, pointed, woody projection on a plant stem.

thor·ough *adj.* Complete; intensive; accurate; very careful; absolute.

those *adj.* The plural of *that.*

though *adv.* Nevertheless; in spite of.

thought *n.* The process, act, or power of thinking; a possibility; an idea.

thou·sand *n.* The cardinal number equal to 10 x 100.

thread *n.* A thin cord of cotton or other fiber; the ridge going around a bolt, nut or screw. *v.* To pass a thread through, as to thread a needle.

threat *n.* An expression or warning of intent to do harm; anything holding a possible source of danger. **threaten** *v.*, **threatener** *n.*, **threateningly** *adv.*

threw *v.* Past tense of *throw*.

thrift *n.* The careful use of money and other resources. **thriftily** *adv.*, **thriftiness** *n.*, **thrifty** *adj.*

thrill *n.* A feeling of sudden intense excitement, fear, or joy.

thrive *v.* To prosper; to be healthy; to do well in a position.

throat *n.* The front section or part of the neck containing passages for food and air.

throt•tle *n.* The valve which controls the flow of fuel to an engine. *v.* To control the speed or fuel with a throttle.

through *prep.* From the beginning to the end; in one side and out the opposite side; finished.

throw *v.* To toss or fling through the air with a motion of the arm; to hurl with force.

thrust *v.* To push; to shove with sudden or vigorous force. *n.* A sudden stab or push.

thumb *n.* The short first digit of the hand; the part of the glove that fits over the thumb. *v.* To browse through something quickly.

thun•der *n.* The loud explosive sound made as air is suddenly expanded by heat and then quickly contracted again.

thwart *v.* To prevent from happening; to prevent from doing something. *n.* A seat positioned crosswise in a boat.

thy *adj.* Pertaining to oneself; your.

thyme *n.* An aromatic mint herb whose leaves are used in cooking.

thy•roid *adj.* Pertaining to the thyroid gland. *n.* The gland in the neck of man that produces hormones which regulate food use and body growth.

tick *n.* One of a series of rhythmical tapping sounds made by a clock; a small bloodsucking parasite, many of which are carriers of disease.

tick•et *n.* A printed slip of paper or cardboard allowing its holder to enter a specified event or to enjoy a privilege.

tick•le *v.* To stroke lightly so as to cause laughter; to amuse or delight.

tid•al wave *n.* An enormous rise of destructive ocean water caused by a storm or earthquake.

tid•bit *n.* A choice bit of food, news, or gossip.

tide *n.* The rise and fall of the surface level of the ocean which occurs twice a day due to the gravitational pull of the sun and moon on the earth.

ti•dy *adj.* Well arranged; neat; orderly.

tie *v.* To secure or bind with a rope, line, cord or other similar material; to make secure or fasten with a rope; to make a bow or knot in; to match an opponent's score. *n.* A string, rope, cord or other material used to join parts or hold something in place; a necktie; a beam that gives structural support; [with *railroad*] a device, as timber, laid crosswise to support train tracks.

tier *n.* A layer or row placed one above the other.

ti•ger *n.* A large carnivorous cat having tawny fur with black stripes.

tight *adj.* Set closely together; bound or securely firm; not loose; taut; difficult. **tighten** *v.*

tile *n.* A thin, hard, flat piece of plastic, asphalt, baked clay, or stone used to cover walls, floors, and roofs. *v.* To cover with tile.

till *prep.* Until; unless or before. *v.* To cultivate; to plow. *n.* A small cash register or drawer for holding money.

tilt *v.* To tip, as by raising one end. *n.* The state of tilting or being tilted.

tim•ber *n.* Wood prepared for building; a finished piece of wood or plank.

time *n.* A continuous period measured by clocks, watches, and calendars; the period or moment in which something happens.

tim•id *adj.* Lacking self-confidence; shy.

tin *n.* A white, soft, malleable metallic element, symbolized by *Sn*; a container made of tin.

tinc•ture *n.* A tinge of color; an alcohol solution of some medicinal substance. *v.*

To tint.

tin•der *n.* A readily combustible substance or material used for kindling.

tin•gle *v.* To feel a stinging or prickling sensation. **tingle** *n.*, **tingly** *adj.*

tin•ny *adj.* Pertaining to or composed of tin.

tin•sel *n.* Thin strips of glittering material used for decorations.

tint *n.* A slight amount or trace of color. *v.* To color.

ti•ny *adj.* Minute; very small.

tip *v.* To slant from the horizontal or vertical. *n.* Extra money given as an acknowledgment of a service; a helpful hint.

ti•rade *n.* A long, violent speech or outpouring, as of censure.

tire *v.* To become or make weary; to be fatigued; to become bored. *n.* The outer covering for a wheel, usually made of rubber.

tire•less *adj.* Untiring. **tirelessly** *adv.*

tis•sue *n.* Similar cells and their products developed by plants and animals; a soft, absorbent piece of paper, consisting of two layers.

ti•ta•ni•um *n.* A metallic element symbolized by Ti.

tithe *n.* A tenth of one's income given voluntarily for the support of a church. **tithe** *v.*, **tither** *n.*

ti•tle *n.* An identifying name of a book, poem, play, or other creative work; a name or mark of distinction indicating a rank or an office; in law, the evidence giving legal right of possession or control.

to *prep.* Toward, opposite or near; in contact with; as far as; used as a function word indicating an action, movement, or condition suggestive of movement; indicating correspondence, dissimilarity, similarity, or proportion.

toad *n.* A tailless amphibian, resembling the frog but without teeth in the upper jaw and having a rougher, drier skin.

toast *v.* To heat and brown over a fire or in a toaster. *n.* Sliced bread browned in a toaster. **toasty** *adj.*, **toaster** *n.*

to•bac•co *n.* A suspected carcinogenic tropical American plant containing nicotine, whose leaves are chewed and smoked.

to•bog•gan *n.* A long sled-like vehicle without runners, having long thin boards curved upwards at the forward end. **tobogganist** *n.*, **toboggan** *v.*

to•day *adv.* On or during the present day. *n.* The present time, period, or day.

toe *n.* One of the extensions from the front part of a foot; the part of a stocking, boot or shoe that covers the toes.

to•geth•er *adv.* In or into one group, mass, or body; regarded jointly; in time with what is happening or going on. **togetherness** *n.*

toil *v.* To labor very hard and continuously. *n.* A difficult task. **toilsome** *adj.*

toi•let *n.* A porcelain apparatus with a flushing device, used as a means of disposing body wastes.

to•ken *n.* A keepsake; a symbol of authority or identity; a piece of imprinted metal used in place of money. *adj.* Done as a pledge or indication.

tol•er•ate *v.* To put up with; to recognize and respect the opinions and rights of others; to endure; to suffer.

toll *n.* A fixed charge for travel across a bridge or along a road. *v.* To sound a bell in repeated single, slow tones.

tom *n.* A male turkey or cat.

tom•a•hawk *n.* An ax used as a weapon or tool by Native Americans.

to•ma•to *n.* A garden plant cultivated for its edible fruit; the fruit of such a plant.

tomb *n.* A vault for burying the dead; a grave.

to•mor•row *n.* The day after the present day. *adv.* On the day following today.

ton *n.* A measurement of weight equal to 2,000 pounds.

tone *n.* A vocal or musical sound that has a distinct pitch, loudness, quality, and duration; the condition of the body and muscles when at rest.

tongue *n.* The muscular organ attached to

the floor of the mouth, used in tasting, chewing, and speaking; anything shaped like a tongue, as the material under the laces or buckles of a shoe.

to•night *n.* This night; the night of this day; the night that is coming. *adv.* On or during the present or coming night.

too *adv.* Also; as well; more than is needed.

tool *n.* An implement used to perform a task; anything needed to do one's work. *v.* To make or shape with a tool. **tooling** *n.*

tooth *n.* One of the hard, white structures rooted in the jaw and used for chewing and biting; the small, notched, projecting part of any object, such as a gear, comb or saw. **toothed, toothless** *adj.*, **teeth** *pl.*

top *n.* The highest part or surface of anything; a covering or lid; the aboveground part of a rooted plant; the highest degree; a toy having a symmetric body with a tapered end upon which it spins.

torch *n.* A stick of resinous wood which is burned to give light; any portable device which produces hot flame.

tor•ment *n.* Extreme mental anguish or physical pain; a source of trouble or pain. *v.* To cause terrible pain; to pester, harass, or annoy.

tor•na•do *n.* A whirling, violent windstorm accompanied by a funnel-shaped cloud that travels a narrow path over land; a whirlwind; a cyclone.

tor•rent *n.* A swift, violent stream; a raging flood. **torrential** *adj*

tor•rid *adj.* Parched and dried by the heat.

tor•toise *n.* A turtle that lives on the land; a person or thing regarded as slow.

tor•ture *n.* The infliction of intense pain as punishment; something causing anguish or pain. *v.* To subject or cause intense suffering; to wrench or twist out of shape.

toss *v.* To fling or throw about continuously; to throw up in the air.

tot *n.* A young child; a toddler.

to•tal *n.* The whole amount or sum; the entire quantity. *adj.* Absolute; complete.

touch *v.* To allow a part of the body, as the hands, to feel or come into contact with; to hit or tap lightly; to eat or drink; to join; to come next to; to have an effect on; to move emotionally. *n.* An instance or act of touching; the feeling, fact, or act of touching or being touched; a trace; a tiny amount.

tough *adj.* Resilient and strong enough to withstand great strain without breaking or tearing; strong; hardy; very difficult; difficult to cut or chew. *n.* An unruly person; a thug.

tour *n.* A trip with visits to points of interest; a journey; a period or length of service at a single place or job. **tourism, tourist** *n.*

tour•na•ment *n.* A contest involving competitors for a title or championship.

tour•ni•quet *n.* A device used to temporarily stop the flow of blood through an artery.

tow *v.* To drag or pull, as by a chain or rope. *n.* The act of being pulled; a rope or line for pulling or dragging; coarse, broken flax, hemp, or jute fiber prepared for spinning.

to•ward *prep.* In the direction of; just before; somewhat before; regarding; with respect to.

tow•el *n.* An absorbent piece of cloth used for drying or wiping. **towel** *v.*

tow•er *n.* A very tall building or structure; a skyscraper; a place of security or defense.

town *n.* A collection of houses and other buildings larger than a village and smaller than a city.

toy *n.* An object designed for the enjoyment of children; any object having little value or importance; a small trinket; a bauble; a dog of a very small breed. *v.* To amuse or entertain oneself.

trace *n.* A visible mark or sign of a thing, person, or event; something left by some past agent or event. *v.* To follow the course or track of; to copy by drawing over the lines visible through a sheet of transparent paper.

track *n.* A mark, as a footprint, left by the passage of anything; a regular course; a set of rails on which a train runs; a circular or oval course for racing. *v.* To follow a trail of footprints.

trac·tor *n.* A diesel or gasoline-powered vehicle used in farming to pull another piece of machinery.

trade *n.* A business or occupation; skilled labor; a craft; an instance of selling or buying; a swap. **trade** *v.*, **tradable** *adj.*, **trader** *n.*

tra·di·tion *n.* The doctrines, knowledge, practices, and customs passed down from one generation to another. **traditional** *adj.*

traf·fic *n.* The passage or movement of vehicles; trading, buying and selling; the signals handled by a communications system. **trafficker** *n.*

trag·e·dy *n.* An extremely sad or fatal event or course of events; a story, play, or other literary work which arouses terror or pity by a series of misfortunes or sad events.

trail *v.* To draw, drag, or stream along behind; to follow in the tracks of; to follow slowly behind or in the rear; to let hang so as to touch the ground. *n.* Something that hangs or follows along behind; a rough path through woods.

trail·er *n.* One who trails; a large vehicle that transports objects and is pulled by another vehicle.

train *n.* The part of a long gown that trails behind the wearer; a long moving line of vehicles or persons; a group of railroad cars. *v.* To instruct so as to make skillful or capable of doing something; to aim; to direct. **trainee, trainer** *n.*

trait *n.* A quality or distinguishing feature, such as one's character.

trai·tor *n.* A person who betrays one's country, a cause, or another's confidence.

tra·jec·to·ry *n.* The curved line or path of a moving object.

tram·mel *n.* A long, large net used to catch birds or fish; something that impedes movement.

tramp *v.* To plod or walk with a heavy step.

n. A homeless person or vagrant who travels about aimlessly.

tram·po·line *n.* A flexible stretched canvas device on which an athlete or acrobat may perform.

trance *n.* A stupor, daze, mental state, or condition, such as produced by drugs or hypnosis.

tran·quil *adj.* Very calm, quiet, and free from disturbance. **tranquillity** *n.*, **tranquilly** *adv.*, **tranquilize** *v.*

trans·fer *v.* To remove, shift, or carry from one position to another. **transferable** *adj.*

trans·form *v.* To change or alter completely in nature, form or function.

trans·late *v.* To change from one language to another while retaining the original meaning; to explain.

trans·lu·cent *adj.* Diffusing and admitting light but not allowing a clear view.

trans·mis·sion *n.* The act or state of transmitting; in mechanics, the gears and associated parts of an engine which transmit power to the driving wheels of an automobile or other vehicle.

trans·mit *v.* To dispatch or convey from one thing, person, or place to another. **transmissible, transmittable** *adj.*, **transmitter** *n.*

trans·par·ent *adj.* Admitting light so that images and objects can be clearly viewed; easy to understand; obvious.

trans·port *v.* To carry or move from one place to another. *n.* A vessel or ship used to carry military supplies and troops; the act of transporting. **transportation** *n.*

trap *n.* A device for holding or catching animals; a device which hurls clay pigeons, disks, or balls into the air to be fired upon by sportsmen; anything which deliberately catches or stops people or things. *v.* To catch in a trap; to place in an embarrassing position.

tra·peze *n.* A short horizontal bar suspended by two ropes, used for acrobatic exercise or stunts.

trau·ma *n.* A severe wound caused by a

sudden physical injury; an emotional shock causing substantial damage to a person's psychological development.

tra·vail *n.* Strenuous mental or physical exertion; labor in childbirth. *v.* To undergo the sudden sharp pain of childbirth.

trav·el *v.* To journey or move from one place to another. *n.* The process or act of traveling. **traveler** *n.*

tray *n.* A flat container having a low rim used for carrying, holding, or displaying something.

treach·er·ous *adj.* Disloyal; deceptive; unreliable. **treachery** *n.*

tread *v.* To walk along, on, or over; to trample. *n.* The act or manner of treading; the part of a wheel which comes into contact with the ground.

trea·son *n.* Violation of one's allegiance to a sovereign or country, as giving or selling state secrets to another country or attempting to overthrow the government. **treasonous** *adj.*

treas·ure *n.* Hidden riches; something regarded as valuable. *v.* To save and accumulate for future use; to value.

treas·ur·er *n.* A person having charge and responsibilities for funds.

treas·ur·y *n.* A place where public or private funds are kept.

treat *v.* To behave or act toward, to regard in a given manner; to provide entertainment or food for another at one's own expense or cost. *n.* A pleasant surprise; something enjoyable which was unexpected. **treatable** *adj.,* **treatment** *n.*

tree *n.* A tall woody plant, usually having a single trunk of considerable height; a diagram resembling a tree, as one used to show family descent.

trem·ble *v.* To shake involuntarily, as with fear or from cold; to feel anxiety.

tre·men·dous *adj.* Extremely huge; vast.

trem·or *n.* A quick, shaking movement; any continued and involuntary trembling or quavering of the body.

trench *n.* A ditch; a long, narrow excavation in the ground. *v.* To cut deep furrows for protection.

trend *n.* A general inclination, direction, or course; a fad, *v.* To have or take a specified direction. **trendsetter** *n.*

tres·pass *v.* To infringe upon another's property; in law, to invade the rights, property, or privacy of another.

tri·al *n.* In law, the examination and hearing of a case before a court of law in order to determine the case; an attempt or effort; an experimental treatment or action to determine a result.

tri·an·gle *n.* A plane figure bounded by three sides and having three angles. **triangular** *adj.,* **triangularity** *n.*

tribe *n.* A group of people composed of several villages, districts, or other groups which share a common language, culture, and name.

trick *n.* An action meant to fool, as a scheme; a prank; a feat of magic. *v.* To deceive or cheat. **tricky** *adj.,* **trickery** *n.*

trick·le *v.* To flow in droplets or a small stream.

tri·cy·cle *n.* A small vehicle having three wheels, propelled by pedals.

tried *adj.* Tested and proven reliable or useful.

tri·fle *n.* Something of little value or importance; a dessert made with cake, jelly, wine, and custard. *v.* To use or treat without proper concern.

trig·ger *n.* A lever pulled to fire a gun; a device used to release or start an action. *v.* To start.

trim *v.* To cut off small amounts in order to make neater; to decorate. *adj.* Neat.

trin·ket *n.* A small piece of jewelry.

tri·o *n.* A set or group of three.

trip *n.* Travel from one place to another; a journey; a loss of balance. *v.* To stumble.

trip·le *adj.* Having three parts. *v.* To multiply by three.

trip·let *n.* One of three born at the same time.

trip·li·cate *n.* A group of three identical things.

tri·pod *n.* A three-legged stand or frame.

trop•ic *n.* Either of two imaginary parallel lines which constitute the Torrid Zone. *pl.* The very warm region of the earth's surface between the Tropic of Cancer and the Tropic of Capricorn. **tropical** *adj.*

trot *n.* The gait of a horse or other four-footed animal, between a walk and a run, in which the hind leg and opposite front leg move at about the same time.

trou•ble *n.* Danger; affliction; need; distress; an effort; physical pain, disease or malfunction. *v.* To bother; to worry; to be bothered; to be worried.

truce *n.* An agreement to stop fighting; a cease-fire.

truck *n.* An automotive vehicle used to carry heavy loads; any of various devices with wheels designed to move loads; garden vegetables for sale. **trucker** *n.*

trudge *v.* To walk heavily; to plod.

true *adj.* In accordance with reality or fact; not false; real; loyal; faithful.

trunk *n.* The main part of a tree; the human body, excluding the head, arms and legs; a sturdy box for packing clothing, as for travel or storage; the long snout of an elephant.

trust *n.* Confidence or faith in a person or thing; care or charge; the confidence or arrangement by which property is managed and held for the good or benefit of another person. *v.* To have confidence or faith in; to believe; to expect; to entrust; to depend on.

truth *n.* The facts corresponding with actu-

pass something through. **tubal** *adj.*

tug *v.* To strain and pull vigorously. *n.* A hard pull; a strong force.

tum•ble *v.* To fall or cause to fall; to perform acrobatic rolls, somersaults, and similar maneuvers; to mix up; to turn over and over. **tumbler** *n.*

tum•ble•down *adj.* Ramshackle; in need of repair.

tu•mor *n.* A swelling on or in any part of the body; an abnormal growth.

tu•na *n.* Any of several large food fish.

tun•dra *n.* A treeless area in the arctic regions having a subsoil which is permanently frozen.

tune *n.* A melody which is simple and easy to remember; agreement; harmony. *v.* To adjust. **tunable** *adj.*, **tunably** *adv.*, **tuner** *n.*

tun•nel *n.* An underground or underwater passageway. **tunnel** *v.*

tur•bine *n.* A motor having one or more rotary units mounted on a shaft, which are turned by the force of gas or a liquid.

tur•bu•lent *adj.* Marked by a violent disturbance.

turf *n.* A layer of earth with its dense growth of grass and matted roots.

tur•key *n.* A large game bird of North America, having a bare head and extensible tail; the meat of this bird.

tur•moil *n.* A state of confusion or commotion.

turn *v.* To move or cause to move around a center point; to revolve or rotate; to transform or change; to move so that the bottom side of something becomes the top and the top becomes the bottom; to strain or sprain.

turn•o•ver *n.* The process or act of turning over; an upset; a change or reversal; the number of times merchandise is bought, sold, and restocked in a certain period of time; a piece of pastry made by putting a filling on one half of the dough and turning the other half over to enclose the filling.

tur•quoise *n.* A blue-green gemstone; a light bluish-green color. **turquoise** *adj.*

tur•tle *n.* A scaly-skinned animal having a soft body covered with a hard shell into which the head, legs, and tail can be retracted.

tusk *n.* A long, curved tooth, as of an elephant or walrus.

tus•sle *n.* A hard fight or struggle with a problem or person.

tu•tor *n.* A person who teaches another person privately. *v.* To teach, coach, or instruct privately.

tux•e•do A semiformal dress suit worn by men.

twice *adv.* Double; two times.

twig *n.* A small branch which grows from a larger branch on a tree.

twi•light *n.* The soft light of the sky between sunset and complete darkness.

twin *n.* One of two persons born at the same time to the same mother; one of two similar persons or things. *adj.* Having two similar or identical parts.

twine *v.* To weave or twist together. *n.* A strong cord or thread made by twisting many threads together.

twinge *n.* A sudden, sharp pain; a brief emotional or mental pang.

twin•kle *v.* To gleam or shine with quick flashes; to sparkle.

twirl *v.* To rotate or cause to turn around and around.

twist *v.* To wind two or more pieces of thread, twine, or other materials together to make a single strand; to curve; to bend, to distort or change the meaning of; to injure and wrench.

twist•er *n.* A tornado; a cyclone; one that twists. In baseball, a ball batted or thrown in a twisting, spinning motion.

twit *v.* To tease about a mistake. *n.* A taunting reproach.

twitch *v.* To move or cause to move with a jerky movement. *n.* A sudden tug.

twit•ter *v.* To utter a series of chirping sounds; to chatter nervously.

two•bit *adj.* Insignificant.

two bits *n.* Twenty-five cents.

two-faced *adj.* Double-dealing.

two•fold *n.* Being double; as much or as many.

two•time *v.* To be unfaithful to.

ty•coon *n. slang* A business person of wealth and power.

tyke *n.* A small child.

type *n.* A class or group of persons or things; letters, numbers, and other symbols typewritten on paper or another surface; in printing, the piece of plastic, metal, or wood having the character or characters that are printed; a model or example of. *v.* To identify according to some sort of classification; to typewrite.

typ•i•cal *adj.* Exhibiting the characteristics of a certain class or group.

typ•i•fy *v.* To be characteristic or typical of; to show all the traits or qualities of.

typ•ist *n.* The operator of a typewriter.

ty•rant *n.* An absolute, unjust, or cruel ruler; one who exercises power, authority, or control unfairly.

U

U, u The twenty-first letter of the English alphabet.

ud•der *n.* The milk-producing organ pouch of some female animals, having two or more teats.

ug•ly *adj.* Offensive; unpleasant to look at.

u•ku•le•le *n.* A small, four-stringed musical instrument, originally from Hawaii.

ul•cer *n.* A festering, inflamed sore on a mucous membrane or on the skin that results in the destruction of the tissue. **ulceration** *n.*, **ulcerate** *v.*

ul•ti•mate *adj.* Final; ending; most extreme. **ultimately** *adv.*

ul•ti•ma•tum *n.* A final demand, proposal, or choice, as in negotiating.

ul•tra•vi•o•let *adj.* Producing radiation having wave-lengths just shorter than those of visible light and longer than those of X rays. **ultraviolet** *n.*

um•brel•la *n.* A collapsible frame covered with plastic or cloth, held above the head as protection from sun or rain.

um•pire *n.* In sports, the person who rules on plays. *v.* To act as an umpire.

un•a•ble *adj.* Not having the capabilities.

u•nan•i•mous *adj.* Agreed to completely; based on the agreement of all.

un•a•void•a•ble *adj.* Inevitable; unstoppable. **unavoidably** *adv.*

un•a•ware *adj.* Not realizing.

un•bear•a•ble *adj.* Not possible to endure; intolerable. **unbearably** *adv.*

un•be•liev•a•ble *adj.* Incredible; hard to accept; not to be believed.

un•cer•tain *adj.* Doubtful; not sure; not known; hard to predict.

un•changed *adj.* Having nothing new or different.

un•cle *n.* The brother of one's mother or father; the husband of an aunt.

un•com•fort•a•ble *adj.* Disturbed; not at ease physically or mentally; causing discomfort. **uncomfortably** *adv.*

un•com•mon *adj.* Rare; odd; unusual. **uncommonly** *adv.*

un•con•di•tion•al *adj.* Without conditions or limits. **unconditionally** *adv.*

un•con•scious *adj.* Not mentally aware; done without thought; not on purpose.

un•con•sti•tu•tion•al *adj.* Contrary to the constitution of a state or country.

un•cov•er *v.* To remove the cover from something; to disclose. **uncovered** *adj.*

un•de•cid•ed *adj.* Unsettled; having made no firm decision; open to change.

un•der *prep.* Below, in place or position; in a place lower than another; less in degree,

number, or other quality; inferior in rank, quality, or character.

un•der•brush *n.* Small bushes, vines, and plants that grow under tall trees.

un•der•grad•u•ate *n.* A college or university student studying for a bachelor's degree.

un•der•line *v.* To draw a line directly under something.

un•der•neath *adv.* Beneath or below; on the under side; lower. *prep.* Under; below.

un•der•pass *n.* A road or walk that goes under another.

un•der•stand *v.* To comprehend; to realize; to know the feelings and thoughts of. **understanding** *v.*

un•der•stand•a•ble *adj.* Able to sympathize or comprehend.

un•der•stood *adj.* Agreed upon by all.

un•der•take *v.* To set about to do a task; to pledge oneself to a certain job; to attempt. **undertaking** *n.*

un•der•tak•er *n.* A person who prepares the dead for burial.

un•der•wa•ter *adj.* Occurring, happening or used beneath the surface of the water.

un•de•sir•a•ble *adj.* Offensive; not wanted. **undesirably** *adv.*

un•do *v.* To cancel; to reverse; to loosen or unfasten; to open a package.

un•done *adj.* Not finished; unfastened; ruined.

un•eas•y *adj.* Feeling or causing distress or discomfort; embarrassed; uncertain. **uneasily** *adv.*, **uneasiness** *n.*

un•em•ployed *adj.* Without a job; without work. **unemployment** *n.*

un•e•qual *adj.* Not even; not fair; not of the same size or time; lacking sufficient ability. **unequaled** *adj.*

un•e•ven *adj.* Not equal; varying in consistency or form; not balanced.

un•ex•pect•ed *adj.* Surprising; happening without warning. **unexpectedly** *adv.*

un•fair *adj.* Not honest; marked by a lack of justice. **unfairness** *n.*

un•faith•ful *adj.* Breaking a promise or agreement; without loyalty.

• •

un•fa•mil•iar *adj.* Not knowing; strange; foreign. **unfamiliarity** *n.*

un•fit *adj.* Not suitable; not qualified; in poor body or mental health.

un•fold *v.* To open up the folds of and lay flat; to reveal gradually.

un•for•get•ta•ble *adj.* Impossible or hard to forget; memorable.

un•for•tu•nate *adj.* Causing or having bad luck, damage, or harm. *n.* A person who has no luck.

un•grate•ful *adj.* Not thankful; showing no appreciation. **ungratefully** *adv.*

un•hap•py *adj.* Sad; without laughter or joy; not satisfied or pleased. **unhappily** *adv.*, **unhappiness** *n.*

un•heard *adj.* Not heard; not listened to.

u•ni•corn *n.* A mythical animal resembling a horse, with a horn in the center of its forehead.

u•ni•cy•cle *n.* A one-wheeled vehicle with pedals.

un•i•den•ti•fied fly•ing ob•ject *n.* A flying object that cannot be explained or identified, abbreviated as *UFO*.

u•ni•form *n.* Identical clothing worn by the members of a group to distinguish them. **uniformly** *adv.*

u•ni•fy *v.* To come together as one; to unite. **unifier** *n.*

un•in•hab•it•ed *adj.* Not lived in; empty.

un•in•ter•est•ed *adj.* Having no interest or concern in; not interested.

un•ion *n.* The act of joining together of two or more groups or things; a group of countries or states joined under one government; a marriage; an organized body of employees who work together to upgrade their working conditions and wages.

u•nique *adj.* Unlike any other; sole. **uniqueness** *n.*, **uniquely** *adv.*

u•nit *n.* Any one of several parts regarded as a whole; an exact quantity that is used as a standard of measurement; a special section or part of a machine.

u•nite *v.* To join or come together for a common purpose.

u•ni•ty *n.* The fact or state of being one; accord; agreement; harmony.

u•ni•ver•sal *adj.* Having to do with the world or the universe in its entirety.

u•ni•verse *n.* The world, stars, planets, space, and all that is contained.

u•ni•ver•si•ty *n.* An educational institution offering undergraduate and graduate degrees in a variety of academic areas.

un•just *adj.* Not fair; lacking justice or fairness. **unjustly** *adv.*

un•kempt *adj.* Poorly groomed; messy; untidy.

un•kind *adj.* Harsh; lacking in sympathy, concern, or understanding.

un•known *adj.* Strange; unidentified; not known; not familiar or famous.

un•like *prep.* Dissimilar; not alike; not equal in strength or quantity; not usual.

un•lim•it•ed *adj.* Having no boundaries.

un•load *v.* To take or remove the load; to unburden; to dispose or get rid of by selling in volume.

un•lock *v.* To open, release, or unfasten a lock; open with a key.

un•luck•y *adj.* Unfortunate; having bad luck; disappointing or unsuitable.

un•manned *adj.* Designed to operate or be operated without a crew of people.

un•mis•tak•a•ble *adj.* Very clear and evident; understood; obvious.

un•nat•u•ral *adj.* Abnormal or unusual; strange; artificial. **unnaturally** *adv.*

un•nec•es•sar•y *adj.* Not needed; not appropriate. **unnecessarily** *adv.*

un•nerve *v.* To frighten; to upset. **unnervingly** *adv.*

un•num•bered *adj.* Countless; too great to be counted; not organized by number; lacking serial arrangement.

un•oc•cu•pied *adj.* Empty; not occupied.

un•pack *v.* To remove articles out of suitcases, boxes, or other storage places.

un•pleas•ant *adj.* Not agreeable; not pleasant. **unpleasantness** *n.*

un•pop•u•lar *adj.* Not approved or liked. **unpopularity** *n.*

un•pre•dict•a•ble *adj.* Not capable of being foretold; not reliable.

unpredictably *adj.*

un•pre•pared *adj.* Not equipped or ready.

un•pro•fes•sion•al *adj.* Contrary to the standards of a profession; having no professional status.

un•prof•it•a•ble *adj.* Showing or giving no profit; serving no purpose.

un•qual•i•fied *adj.* Lacking the proper qualifications; unreserved.

un•rav•el *v.* To separate threads; to solve; to clarify; to come apart.

un•real *adj.* Having no substance or reality.

un•rea•son•a•ble *adj.* Not according to reason; exceeding all reasonable limits.

un•re•li•a•ble *adj.* Unable to be trusted; not dependable.

un•re•served *adj.* Done or given without reserve; unlimited.

un•re•strained *adj.* Not held back, forced, or affected.

un•ru•ly *adj.* Disorderly; difficult to subdue or control.

un•sat•is•fac•to•ry *adj.* Unacceptable; not pleasing.

un•screw *v.* To loosen; to unfasten by removing screws.

un•scru•pu•lous *adj.* Without morals, guiding principles, or rules.

un•seat *v.* To cause to lose one's seat; to force out of office.

un•sel•fish *adj.* Willing to share; thinking of another's well-being before one's own. **unselfishly** *adv.*, **unselfishness** *n.*

un•set•tle *v.* To cause to be upset or excited; to disturb. **unsettled, unsettling** *adj.*

un•sheathe *v.* To draw a sword from a sheath or other case

un•sight•ly *adj.* Not pleasant to look at; ugly.

un•skilled *adj.* Having no skills or training in a given kind of work.

un•skill•ful *adj.* Lacking in proficiency; done without skill; awkward or amateurish in execution. **unskillfully** *adv.*, **unskillfulness** *n.*

un•sound *adj.* Having defects; not solidly made; unhealthy in body or mind.

unsoundly *adv.*, **unsoundness** *n.*

un•speak•a•ble *adj.* Of or relating to something which cannot be expressed or described; ineffable; incapable of articulation. **unspeakably** *adv.*

un•sta•ble *adj.* Not steady or firmly fixed; having the tendency to fluctuate or change.

un•stead•y *adj.* Not secure; unstable; variable. **unsteadily** *adv.*

un•sub•stan•tial *adj.* Lacking strength, weight, or solidity; unreal; absent of physical reality.

un•suit•a•ble *adj.* Unfitting; not suitable; not appropriate.

un•tan•gle *v.* To free from entanglements.

un•thank•ful *adj.* Ungrateful; not expressing or experiencing gratitude.

un•think•a•ble *adj.* Unimaginable; beyond the limits of one's capabilities; not within possibility.

un•ti•dy *adj.* Messy; showing a lack of tidiness. **untidily** *adv.*, **untidiness** *n.*

un•tie *v.* To unfasten or loosen; to free from a restraint or bond.

un•til *prep.* Up to the time of. *conj.* To the time when; to the degree or place.

un•time•ly *adj.* Premature; before the expected time; outside the orderly arrangement of planned events. **untimeliness** *n.*

un•told *adj.* Not revealed; not told; inexpressible; cannot be described or revealed.

un•touch•a•ble *adj.* Incapable of being touched, obtained or reached; beyond the consequences of one's actions; not punishable or responsible.

un•true *adj.* Not true; contrary to the truth; not faithful; disloyal.

un•truth *n.* Something which is not true; the state of being false.

un•used *adj.* Not put to use; never having been used.

un•u•su•al *adj.* Not usual; uncommon. **unusually** *adv.*, **unusualness** *n.*

un•ut•ter•a•ble *adj.* Incapable of being described or expressed; unpronounceable; ineffable. **unutterably** *adv.*

un•veil *v.* To remove a veil from; to uncover; to reveal,

un•war•y *adj.* Not cautious or careful; careless.

un•whole•some *adj.* Unhealthy; morally corrupt or harmful.

un•will•ing *adj.* Reluctant; not willing. **unwillingly** *adv.*, **unwillingness** *n.*

un•wind *v.* To undo or reverse the winding of; to untangle; to relax or release pressure or tension.

un•wise *adj.* Lacking good judgment or common sense; carelessly thought out; incompletely or incorrectly calculated. **unwisely** *adv.*

un•wor•thy *adj.* Not deserving; not becoming or befitting; lacking merit or worth; shameful. **unworthiness** *n.*

up *adv.* From a lower position to a higher one; on, in, or to a higher level, position, or place; to a greater degree or amount; in or into a specific action or an excited state.

up•beat *n.* The relatively unaccented beat preceding the downbeat. *adj.* Optimistic; happy; positive and encouraging in tone.

up•bring•ing *n.* The process of teaching and rearing a child; the collective experiences of childhood.

up•com•ing *adj.* About to take place or appear; in the near future; not yet occurring; anticipated.

up•date *v.* To revise or bring up to date; to modernize. **update** *n.*

up•draft *n.* An upward current of air.

up•grade *v.* To increase the grade, rank, or standard of. *n.* An upward slope.

up•hill *adv.* Up an incline. *adj.* Hard to accomplish; going up a hill or incline.

up•hol•ster *v.* To cover furniture with fabric covering, cushions, and padding. **upholsterer**, **upholstery** *n.*

up•keep *n.* The cost and work needed to keep something in good condition.

up•land *n.* A piece of land which is elevated or higher than the land around it.

up•lift *v.* To raise or lift up; to improve the social, economic, and moral level of a group or of a society; to encourage or

make positive.

up•on *prep.* On.

up•per *adj.* Higher in status, position or location. *n.* The part of a shoe to which the sole is attached.

up•per case *n.* The large or capital case of letters.

up•stairs *adv.* Up one or more flights of stairs. *adj.* Situated on the upper floor.

up•stand•ing *adj.* Straightforward; honest; upright.

up•tight *adv.* Nervous, tense, or anxious.

up-to-date *adj.* Most current or recent; appropriate to the present time; contemporary.

up•town *adj.* Toward or in the upper part of town; indicating class, wealth, or social status. **uptown** *adj.*

up•ward *adv.* From a lower position to or toward a higher one. *adj.* Directed toward a higher position. **upwardly** *adv.*

ur•ban *adj.* Pertaining to a city or having characteristics of a city; living or being in a city. **urbanite** *n.*, **urbanize** *v.*

urge *v.* To encourage, push, or drive; to recommend persistently and strongly. *n.* An influence, impulse, or force.

ur•gent *adj.* Requiring immediate attention. **urgency** *n.*, **urgently** *adv.*

u•rine *n.* In mammals, the yellowish fluid waste produced by the kidneys.

us•a•ble or **use•a•ble** *adj.* Fit or capable of being used. **usability** *n.*

us•age *n.* The way or act of using something; the way words are used.

u•su•al *adj.* Ordinary or common; regular; customary.

u•su•al•ly *adv.*, **usualness** *n.*

u•surp *v.* To take over by force without authority. usurpation, usurper n.

u•ten•sil *n.* A tool, implement, or container, especially one for the kitchen

u•ter•us *n.* An organ of female mammals within which young develop and grow before birth. **uterine** *adj.*

u•til•i•ty *n.* The state or quality of being useful; a company which offers a public service, as water, heat, or electricity.

u•ti•lize *v.* To make or put to use.

ut•ter *v.* To say or express verbally; to speak. *adj.* Absolute; complete.

ut•ter•ance *n.* A statement; a vocal sound; any of several speech acts by which persons communicate abstractions; the act of voicing in a language.

ut•ter•ly *adv.* Absolutely; completely; without reservation or limitation.

u•vu•la *n.* The fleshy projection which hangs above the back of the tongue.

V

V, v The twenty-second letter of the English alphabet; the Roman numeral for 5.

va•cant *adj.* Empty; not occupied; without expression.

va•cate *v.* To leave; to cease to occupy.

va•ca•tion *n.* A period of time away from work for pleasure, relaxation, or rest.

vac•ci•nate *v.* To inject with a vaccine so as to produce immunity to an infectious disease. **vaccination** *n.*

vac•cine *n.* A solution of weakened or killed microorganisms, as bacteria or viruses, injected into the body to produce immunity to a disease.

vac•u•um *n.* A space absolutely empty; a void; a vacuum cleaner.

vag•a•bond *n.* A homeless person who wanders from place to place; a tramp.

va•gar•y *n.* An eccentric or capricious action or idea. **vagarious** *adj.*

va•gi•na *n.* The canal or passage extending from the uterus to the external opening of the female reproductive system.

vag•i•ni•tis *n.* An inflammation of the vagina.

va•grant *n.* A person who wanders from place to place. *adj.* Roaming from one area to another without a job. **vagrancy** *n.*

vague *adj.* Not clearly expressed; not sharp or definite. **vaguely** *adv.*

vain *adj.* Conceited; lacking worth or substance; having too much pride in oneself.

val•ance *n.* A decorative drapery across the top of a window.

vale *n.* A valley, especially a small green pasture surrounded by hills.

val•e•dic•to•ri•an *n.* The student ranking highest in a graduating class, who delivers a speech at the commencement.

val•en•tine *n.* A card or gift sent to one's sweetheart on Valentine's Day, February 14th.

val•et *n.* A man who takes care of another man's clothes and other personal needs; a hotel employee who attends to personal services for guests.

val•iant *adj.* Brave; exhibiting valor. **valiance, valor** *n.*

val•id *adj.* Founded on facts or truth.

val•ley *n.* Low land between ranges of hills or mountains.

val•u•a•ble *adj.* Of great value or importance; having a high monetary value.

valve *n.* The movable mechanism which opens and closes to control the flow of a substance through a pipe or other passageway.

va•moose *v.* To leave in a hurry.

vam•pire *n.* In folklore, an undead buried person believed to rise from the grave at night to suck the blood of sleeping persons; a person who preys on others.

vam•pire bat *n.* A tropical bat that feeds on the blood of living mammals.

van *n.* A large closed wagon or truck.

van•dal•ism *n.* The malicious anonymous defacement or destruction of private or public property.

vane *n.* A metal device that turns in the direction the wind is blowing; a thin rigid blade of an electric fan, propeller, or windmill.

va•nil•la *n.* A flavoring extract used in cooking, baking, and cold desserts, prepared from the vanilla bean.

van•ish *v.* To disappear suddenly; to drop out of sight; to go out of existence.

van•i•ty *n.* Conceit; extreme pride in one's ability, possessions, or appearance;

hopelessness of effort.

van•tage *n.* A superior position; an advantage.

va•por *n.* Moisture or smoke suspended in air, as mist or fog.

var•i•a•ble *adj.* Changeable; tending to vary; inconstant. *n.* A quantity or thing which can vary.

var•i•ance *n.* The state or act of varying; difference; conflict.

var•i•a•tion *n.* The result or process of varying; the degree or extent of varying; a different form of a given theme, with modifications in rhythm, key, or melody.

var•ie•gat•ed *adj.* Having marks of different colors. **variegate** *v.*, **variegation** *n.*

va•ri•e•ty *n.* The state or character of being varied or various; a number of different kinds; an assortment.

var•i•ous *adj.* Of different kinds.

var•mint *n.* A troublesome animal, especially one that preys on livestock or crops in cultivated areas; an obnoxious person.

var•nish *n.* A solution used to coat or cover a surface with a hard, transparent, shiny film. *v.* To put varnish on.

var•si•ty *n.* The best team representing a college, university, or school.

var•y *v.* To change; to make or become different; to be different; to make different kinds.

vas•cu•lar *adj.* Having to do with vessels circulating fluids, as blood.

va•sec•to•my *n.* Method of male sterilization involving the surgical excision of a part of the tube which conveys semen.

vast *adj.* Very large or great in size. **vastly** *adv.*, **vastness** *n.*

vault *n.* An arched structure that forms a ceiling or roof; a room for storage and safekeeping, as in a bank, usually made of steel; a burial chamber. *v.* To supply or construct with a vault; to jump or leap with the aid of a pole.

veg•e•ta•ble *n.* A plant, as green beans or lettuce, raised for the edible part.

veg•e•tar•i•an *n.* A person whose diet does not include meat from animals. *adj.* Consuming only plant products. vegetarianism n.

veg•e•ta•tion *n.* Plants or plant life which grows from the soil.

ve•hi•cle *n.* A motorized device for transporting goods, equipment, or passengers; any means by which something is transferred, expressed, or applied.

veil *n.* A piece of transparent cloth worn on the head or face for concealment or protection; anything that conceals from view. *v.* To cover or conceal.

vein *n.* A vessel which transports blood back to the heart after passing through the body; one of the branching support tubes of an insect's wing; a long wavy, irregularly colored streak, as in marble, or wood.

ve•lour *n.* A soft velvet-like woven cloth having a short, thick nap.

vel•vet *n.* A fabric made of rayon, cotton, or silk, having a smooth, dense pile. **velvety** *adj.*

ven•det•ta *n.* A fight or feud between blood related persons, involving revenge killings; a lifelong commitment to retaliate for a real or imaginary wrongdoing.

ven•dor *n.* A person who sells, as a peddler; an authorized middle agent between manufacturer and retailer. **vending** *adj.*

ven•er•a•ble *adj.* Meriting or worthy of respect by reason of dignity, position, or age; valued through tradition. **veneration** *n.*

ve•ne•re•al dis•ease *n.* A contagious disease, as syphilis or gonorrhea, which is typically acquired through sexual intercourse.

ve•ne•tian blind *n.* A window blind having thin, horizontal slats which can be adjusted to desired angles so as to vary the amount of light admitted.

ven•i•son *n.* The edible flesh of a deer.

ven•om *n.* A poisonous substance secreted by some animals, as scorpions or snakes, usually transmitted through a bite or sting. **venomous** *adj.*

ve•nous *adj.* Of or relating to veins;

ven·ture n. A course of action involving risk, chance, or danger, especially a business investment. v. To take a risk.

ven·ue n. The place where a crime or other cause of legal action occurs; the locale of a gathering or public event; the surrounding circumstances that alter an activity.

verb n. The part of speech which expresses action, existence, or occurrence.

ver·bal adj. Expressed in speech; expressed orally; not written; relating to or derived from a verb. n. An adjective, noun, or other word based on a verb and retains some characteristics of a verb. **verbally** adv., **verbalize** v.

ver·ba·tim adv. Word for word; without paraphrase or condensation of expression.

ver·be·na n. An American garden plant having variously colored flower clusters.

verge n. The extreme edge or rim; margin; the point beyond which something begins. v. To border on.

ver·min n. A destructive, annoying animal harmful to one's health.

ver·sa·tile adj. Having the capabilities of doing many different things; having many functions or uses. **versatility** n.

verse n. Writing that has a rhyme; poetry; a subdivision of a poem or chapter of the Bible.

ver·sion n. An account or description told from a particular point of view; a translation from another language, especially a translation of the Bible; a form or particular point of view; a condition in which an organ, such as the uterus, is turned; man-

base; the point at which two lines meet to form an angle. **vertices** pl.

ver·ti·cal adj. In a straight up-and-down direction; being perpendicular to the plane of the horizon or to a primary axis; upright. **vertically** adv.

ver·y adv. To a high or great degree; truly; absolutely; exactly; actually; in actual fact.

ves·sel n. A hollow or concave utensil, as a bottle, kettle, container, or jar; a hollow craft designed for navigation on water, one larger than a rowboat.

vest n. A sleeveless garment open or fastening in front, worn over a shirt.

ves·tige n. A trace or visible sign of something that no longer exists; an attenuated remnant. **vestigial** adj., **vestigially** adv.

ves·try n. A room in a church used for meetings and classes; a priest's or minister's work office.

vet·er·an n. A person with a long record or experience in a certain field; one who has served in the military.

vet·er·i·nar·i·an n. One who is trained and authorized to give medical treatment to animals. **veterinary** adj.

ve·to n. The power of a government executive, as the president or a governor, to reject a bill passed by the legislature. v. To reject a bill passed by the legislature.

vi·a prep. By way of; by means of.

vi·al n. A small, closed container used especially for liquids; a test tube.

vi·a·duct n. A bridge, resting on a series of arches, carrying a road or railroad.

vi·brate v. To move or make move back

and forth or up and down. **vibration** n.

vi·car·i·ous adj. Undergoing or serving in the place of someone or something else; experienced through sympathetic or imaginative participation in the experience of another.

vice n. An immoral habit or practice; evil conduct; second in command.

vi·ce ver·sa adv. With the order or meaning of something reversed.

vi·chys·soise n. A soup made from potatoes, chicken stock, and cream, flavored with leeks or onions and usually served cold.

vi·cin·i·ty n. The surrounding area or district; the state of being near in relationship or space.

vi·cious adj. Dangerously aggressive; having the quality of immorality.

vic·tim n. A person who is harmed or killed by another; a living creature slain and offered as sacrifice; one harmed by circumstance or condition. **victimize** v.

vic·tor n. A person who conquers; the winner.

vic·to·ri·ous adj. Being the winner in a contest.

vic·to·ry n. A defeat of those on the opposite side.

vid·e·o adj. Being, related to, or used in the reception or transmission of television; a videotape.

view n. The act of examining or seeing; a judgment or opinion; the range or extent of one's sight; something kept in sight. v. To watch or look at attentively; to consider.

vig·il n. A watch with prayers kept on the night before a religious feast; a period of surveillance.

vig·or n. Energy or physical strength; intensity of effect or action.

vile adj. Morally disgusting, miserable, and unpleasant. **vilely** adv., **vileness** n.

vil·la n. A luxurious home in the country; a country estate.

vil·lage n. An incorporated settlement, usually smaller than a town. **villager** n.

vil·lain n. An evil or wicked person; a criminal; an uncouth person.

vin·ai·grette n. A small ornamental bottle with a perforated top, used for holding an aromatic preparation such as smelling salts.

vin·di·cate v. To clear of suspicion; to set free; to provide a defense or justification for. **vindication** n.

vin·dic·tive adj. Showing or possessing a desire for revenge; spiteful.

vine n. A plant whose stem needs support as it climbs or clings to a surface.

vin·e·gar n. A tart, sour liquid derived from cider or wine.

vin·tage n. The grapes or wine produced from a particular district in one season.

vi·nyl n. A variety of shiny plastics, simulating leather, often used for clothing and for covering furniture.

vi·o·la n. A stringed instrument, slightly larger and deeper in tone than a violin.

vi·o·late v. To break the law or a rule; to disrupt or disturb a person's privacy.

vi·o·lence n. Physical force or activity used to cause harm, damage, or abuse.

vi·o·let n. A small, low-growing plant with blue, purple, or white flowers; a purplish-blue color.

vi·o·lin n. A small stringed instrument, played with a bow.

vi·per n. A poisonous snake; an evil or treacherous person.

vir·gin n. A person who has never had sexual intercourse. adj. In an unchanged or natural state, as an untimbered forest.

vir·ile adj. Having the qualities and nature of a man; capable of sexual performance in the male. **virility** n.

vir·tue n. Morality, goodness or uprightness; a special type of goodness. **virtuous** adj., **virtuously** adv.

vi·rus n. Any of a variety of microscopic organisms which cause diseases; in computers, a program that automatically distributes itself along the web of online devices, usually malicious in nature.

vi·sa n. An official authorization giving

permission on a passport to enter a specific country.

vis•cid *adj*. Sticky; having an adhesive quality.

vise *n*. A tool in carpentry and metalwork having two jaws to hold things in position.

vis•i•bil•i•ty *n*. The degree or state of being visible; the distance that one is able to see clearly.

vis•i•ble *adj*. Apparent; exposed to view.

vi•sion *n*. The power of sight; the ability to see; an image created in the imagination; a supernatural appearance.

vis•it *v*. To journey to or come to see a person or place. *n*. A professional or social call. **visitor, visitation** *n*.

vi•sor *n*. A brim on the front of a hat which protects the eyes.

vi•su•al *adj*. Visible; relating to sight.

vi•tal *adj*. Essential to life; very important. **vitally** *adv*.

vi•ta•min *n*. Any of various substances found in foods that are essential to good health.

vit•re•ous *adj*. Related to or similar to glass.

vit•ri•fy *v*. To convert into glass or a substance similar to glass, by heat and fusion.

vi•va•cious *adj*. Filled with vitality or animation; lively. **vivaciously** *adv*.

viv•i•fy *v*. To give life to. **vivification** *n*.

viv•id *adj*. Bright; brilliant; intense; having clear, lively, bright colors. **vividly** *adv*.

vo•cab•u•lar•y *n*. A list or group of words and phrases, usually in alphabetical order; all the words that a person uses or understands.

vo•cal *adj*. Of or related to the voice; uttered by the voice; to speak freely.

vo•ca•tion *n*. A career, occupation, or profession.

vo•cif•er•ate *v*. To utter or cry out loudly; to shout. **vociferation** *n*., **vociferous** *adj*.

vod•ka *n*. A colorless liquor of neutral spirits distilled from fermented rye or wheat mash.

vogue *n*. The leading style or fashion; pop-

ularity. **vogue** *adj*.

voile *n*. A fine, soft, sheer fabric used for making light clothing and curtains.

volt•age *n*. The amount of electrical power, given in terms of volts.

vol•ume *n*. The capacity or amount of space or room; a book; a quantity; the loudness of a sound.

vol•un•tar•y *adj*. Done cooperatively or willingly; from one's own choice.

vol•un•teer *n*. One who offers himself for a service of his own free will. *v*. To offer voluntarily.

vo•lup•tu•ous *adj*. Full of pleasure; delighting the senses; sensuous; luxury. voluptuousness n.

vo•ra•cious *adj*. Having a large appetite; insatiable. **voraciously** *adv*.

vote *n*. The expression of one's choice by voice, by raising one's hand, or by secret ballot. *v*. To express one's views. **voteless** *adj*., **voter** *n*.

vo•tive *adj*. Performed in fulfillment of a vow or in devotion.

vouch *v*. To verify or support as true; to guarantee. **voucher** *n*.

vow *n*. A solemn pledge or promise, especially one made to God; a marriage vow.

vow•el *n*. A sound of speech made by voicing the flow of breath within the mouth; a letter representing a vowel, as *a, e, i, o, u,* and sometimes *y*.

voy•age *n*. A long trip or journey.

vul•gar *adj*. Showing poor manners; crude; immoral or indecent. **vulgarity** *n*.

vul•ner•a•ble *adj*. Open to injury or attack. **vulnerability** *n*., **vulnerably** *adv*.

W

W, w The twenty-third letter of the English alphabet.

wad *n*. A small crumpled mass or bundle; a soft plug used to hold shot or gunpowder charge in place.

wade *v*. To walk through a substance as mud or water which hampers one's steps.

wa•fer *n.* A small, thin, crisp cracker, cookie, or candy.

waf•fle *n.* Pancake batter cooked in a waffle iron.

wag *v.* To move quickly from side to side or up and down. *n.* A playful, witty person. **waggish** *adj.*

wage *n.* A payment of money for labor or services. *v.* To conduct.

wa•ger *v.* To make a bet. **wager** *n.*

wag•on *n.* A four-wheeled vehicle used to transport goods; a station wagon; a child's four-wheeled cart with a long handle.

wail *n.* A loud, mournful cry or weep. *v.* To make such a sound.

waist *n.* The narrow part of the body between the thorax and hips; the middle part or section of something narrower than the rest.

wait•er *n.* A person who serves food at a restaurant.

wake *v.* To come to consciousness, as from sleep. *n.* A vigil for a dead body; the surface turbulence caused by a vessel moving through water.

walk *v.* To move on foot over a surface; to pass over, go on, or go through by walking; in baseball, to advance to first base after four balls have been pitched. **walker** *n.*

wall *n.* A vertical structure to separate or enclose an area. *v.* To provide or close up, as with a wall.

wal•la•by *n.* A small or medium-sized marsupial related to the kangaroo and found in Australia.

wal•let *n.* A flat folding case for carrying paper money.

wal•lop *n.* A powerful blow; an impact.

wall•pa•per *n.* Decorative paper for walls, usually having a colorful pattern.

wal•nut *n.* An edible nut with a hard, light-brown shell; the tree on which this nut grows.

wal•rus *n.* A large marine mammal of the seal family, having flippers, tusks, and a tough hide.

waltz *n.* A ballroom dance in 3/4 time; music for a waltz. *v.* To dance a waltz; to advance successfully and easily.

wam•pum *n.* Polished shells, once used as currency by North American Indians.

wand *n.* A slender rod used by a magician.

wan•der *v.* To travel about aimlessly; to roam; to stray. **wanderer** *n.*

wane *v.* To decrease in size or extent; to decrease gradually.

wan•gle *v.* To resort to devious methods in order to obtain something wanted. **wangler** *n.*

want *v.* To wish for or desire; to need; to lack, to fail to possess a required amount; to hunt in order to apprehend. *n.* The state of lacking a required or usual amount.

war *n.* An armed conflict among states or nations; a state of discord; the science of military techniques or procedures.

ward *n.* A section in a hospital for certain patients requiring similar treatment; a person under protection or surveillance.

ware•house *n.* A large building used to store merchandise. *v.* To store or accumulate in large quantities for future distribution.

wares *pl. n.* Manufactured items of the same general kind; items or goods for sale.

warm *adj.* Moderate heat; neither hot nor cold; comfortably established; marked by a strong feeling; having pleasant feelings.

warn *v.* To give notice or inform beforehand; to call to one's attention; to alert.

warp *v.* To become bent out of shape; to deviate from a proper course. *n.* The condition of being twisted or bent; threads running down the length of a fabric.

war•rant *n.* A written authorization giving the holder legal power to search, seize, or arrest. *v.* To provide a reason; to give proof **warrantable** *adj.*, **warrantor** *n.*

war•ri•or *n.* One who fights in a war or battle.

war•y *adj.* Marked by caution; alert to danger.

wash *v.* To cleanse by the use of water; to remove dirt; to move or deposit as if by the force of water. *n.* A process or instance of ver an ocean or lake.

•ter ta•ble *n.* The upper limit of the ortion of the ground completely saturat- d with water.

•ter•tight *adj.* Closed or sealed so ghtly that no water can enter; leaving no nance for evasion.

•ter•way *n.* A navigable body of water; channel for water.

•ter•y *adj.* Containing water; diluted; cking effectiveness. **wateriness** *n.*

tt *n.* A unit of electrical power repre- nted by current of one ampere, produced y the electromotive force of one volt.

ve *v.* To move back and forth or up and own; to motion with the hand. *n.* A vell or moving ridge of water; a curve or url, as in the hair.

•ver *v.* To sway unsteadily; to move ack and forth; to weaken in force.

x *n.* A natural yellowish substance made y bees, solid when cold and easily melted r softened when heated. **waxy** *adj.*

y *n.* A manner of doing something; a ndency or characteristic; a habit or cus- mary manner of acting or living; a direc- on; freedom to do as one chooses.

y•far•er *n.* A person who travels on ot.

y•lay *v.* To attack by ambush.

y•ward *adj.* Unruly; unpredictable.

pron. First person plural of *I*, used to fer to the person speaking and one or ore other people.

ak *adj.* Having little energy or strength;

another person.

wear *v.* To have on or put something on the body; to display. *n.* The act of wearing out or using up; the act of wearing.

wea•ry *adj.* Exhausted; tired, feeling fatigued. *v.* To make or become tired; to become fatigued. **wearily** *adv.,* **weariness** *n.*

wea•sel *n.* A mammal with a long tail and short legs; a sly, sneaky person.

weath•er *n.* The condition of the air or atmosphere in terms of humidity, temperature, and similar features. *v.* To become worn by the actions of weather; to survive.

weave *v.* To make a basket, cloth, or other item by interlacing threads or other strands of material.

web *n.* A cobweb; a piece of interlacing material which forms a woven structure; something constructed as an entanglement; a thin membrane that joins the toes of certain water birds.

wed *v.* To take as a spouse; to marry.

we'd *contr.* We had; we should.

wed•ding *n.* A marriage ceremony; an act of joining together in close association.

wedge *n.* A tapered, triangular piece of wood or metal used to split logs, to add leverage, and to hold something open or ajar. *v.* To force or make something fit.

wed•lock *n.* Marriage; the state of being married.

weed *n.* An unwanted plant which interferes with the growth of grass, vegetables, or flowers.

week *n.* A period of seven days, beginning with Sunday and ending with Saturday; the time or days normally spent at school or work.

week•day *n.* Any day of the week except Saturday or Sunday.

week•end *n.* The end of the week from the period of Friday evening through Sunday evening.

weep *v.* To shed tears; to express sorrow, joy, or emotion by shedding tears; to cry.

wee•vil *n.* A small beetle having a downward curving snout, which damages plants.

weigh *v.* To determine the heaviness of an object by using a scale; to consider carefully in one's mind; to be of a particular weight; to oppress or burden.

weight *n.* The amount that something weighs; heaviness; a heavy object used to hold or pull something down; an overpowering force; the quality of a garment for a particular season. *v.* To make heavy.

weight•less *adj.* Lacking the pull of gravity; having little weight.

weight•y *adj.* Burdensome; important.

weird *adj.* Having an extraordinary or strange character.

wel•come *v.* To extend warm hospitality; to accept gladly. *adj.* Received warmly. *n.* A greeting upon one's arrival.

weld *v.* To unite metallic parts by applying heat and sometimes pressure, allowing the metals to bond together. *n.* A joint formed by welding.

wel•fare *n.* The state of doing well; governmental aid to help the disabled or disadvantaged.

well *n.* A hole in the ground which contains a supply of water; a shaft in the ground through which gas and oil are obtained. *adj.* Being in good health; in an agreeable state.

we'll *contr.* We will; we shall.

well-be•ing *n.* The state of being healthy, happy, or prosperous.

well-done *adj.* Completely cooked; done properly.

well-groomed *adj.* Clean, neat; properly cared for.

well-known *adj.* Widely known; famous or notorious; commonly acknowledged as true.

well-man•nered *adj.* Polite; having good manners.

well-mean•ing *adj.* Having good intentions.

well-to-do *adj.* Having more than enough wealth; modestly comfortable in social status.

welsh *v.* To cheat by avoiding a payment

to someone; to neglect an obligation.
welsher *n.*

welt *n.* A strip between the sole and upper part of a shoe; a slight swelling on the body, usually caused by a blow to the area.

wel·ter·weight *n.* A boxer weighing between 136 and 147 pounds.

went *v.* Past tense of *go.*

wept *v.* Past tense of *weep.*

were *v.* Plural past tense of *to be;* conditional voice of *to be.*

we're *contr.* We are.

were·n't *contr.* Were not.

west *n.* The direction of the setting sun; the direction to the left of a person facing north.

whale *n.* A very large mammal resembling a fish which lives in salt water.

wharf *n.* A pier or platform at the edge of water where ships can load and unload.

what *pron.* Which one; which things; which type or kind. *adv.* In which way. *adj.* Which particular one.

what·ev·er *pron.* Everything or anything. *adj.* No matter what.

what's *contr.* What is.

wheat *n.* A grain ground into flour, used to make breads and similar foods.

wheel *n.* A circular disk which turns on an axle; an apparatus having the same principles of a wheel; something which resembles the motion or shape of a wheel. *v.* To move on or as if by wheels; to turn around a central axis; to rotate, pivot, or turn around.

wheel·bar·row *n.* A vehicle having one wheel, used to transport small loads.

wheel·chair *n.* A mobile chair for disabled persons.

wheeze *v.* To breathe with a hoarse whistling sound. *n.* A high whistling sound.

whelk *v.* Any of various large water snails, sometimes edible.

when *adv.* At what time; at which time. *pron.* What or which time. *conj.* While; at the time that; although.

whence *adv.* From what source or place;

from which.

when·ev·er *adv.* At any time; when. *conj.* At whatever time.

where *adv.* At or in what direction or place.

where·a·bouts *n.* The approximate location; one's present geographical place. *adv.* Near, at, or in a particular location.

where·as *conj.* It being true or the fact; on the contrary.

where·by *conj.* Through or by which.

wher·ev·er *adv.* In any situation or place.

wheth·er *conj.* Indicating a choice; alternative possibilities; either.

whet·stone *n.* A stone used to sharpen scissors, knives, and other implements.

whew *interj.* Used to express relief; or tiredness.

which *pron.* What one or ones; the one previously; whatever one or ones; whichever. *adj.* What one; any one of.

which·ev·er *pron.* Any; no matter which or what.

whiff *n.* A slight puff; a light current of air; a slight breath or odor.

while *n.* A length or period of time. *conj.* During the time that; even though; at the same time; although.

whim *n.* A sudden desire or impulse.

whim·per *v.* To make a weak, soft crying sound. **whimper** *n.*

whim·si·cal *adj.* Impulsive; erratic; light and spontaneous. **whimsically** *adv.,*

whine *v.* To make a squealing, plaintive sound; to complain in an irritating, childish fashion.

whin·ny *v.* To neigh in a soft gentle way.

whip *v.* To spank repeatedly with a rod or stick; to punish by whipping. *n.* A flexible stick or rod used to herd or beat animals; a dessert made by whipping ingredients; the utensil used to do so.

whip·lash *n.* An injury to the spine or neck caused by a sudden jerking motion of the head.

whip·poor·will *n.* A brownish nocturnal bird of North America.

whir *v.* To move with a low purring sound.

whirl *v.* To rotate or move in circles; to twirl; to move, drive, or go very fast. *n.* A rapid whirling motion. **whirler** *n.*

whirl·pool *n.* A circular current of water.

whirl·wind *n.* A violently whirling mass of air; a tornado.

whirl·y·bird *n.* A helicopter.

whisk *v.* To move with a sweeping motion; to move quickly or lightly. *n.* A sweeping movement; a utensil used in cooking; to stir.

whisk·er *n.* The hair that grows on a man's face; the long hair near the mouth of dogs, cats, and other animals. *pl.* A man's beard.

whis·key *n.* An alcoholic beverage distilled from rye, barley, or corn.

whis·per *v.* To speak in a very low tone; to tell in secret. *n.* A low rustling sound; the act of whispering.

whis·tle *v.* To make a clear shrill sound by blowing air through the teeth, through puckered lips, or through a special instrument. *n.* A device used to make a whistling sound. **whistler** *n.*

white *n.* The color opposite of black; the part of something white or light in color, as an egg or the eyeball; a member of the Caucasian group of people. *adj.* Having a light color; pale; pure; without sin.

white·cap *n.* A wave having a top of white foam.

white-col·lar *adj.* Relating to an employee whose job does not require manual labor.

white·wash *n.* A mixture made of lime and other ingredients and used for whitening fences and exterior walls. *v.* To cover up a problem; to pronounce someone as being innocent without really investigating.

whith·er *adv.* To what state, place, or circumstance; wherever.

whit·tle *v.* To cut or carve off small shavings from wood with a knife; to remove or reduce gradually. **whittler** *n.*

whiz *v.* To make a whirring or buzzing sound, a projectile passing at a high rate of speed through the air; a person having notable expertise, as with a computer.

who *pron.* Which or what certain individual, person, or group; referring to a person previously mentioned.

who'd *contr.* Who would; who had.

who·ev·er *pron.* Whatever person; all or any persons.

whole *adj.* Complete; having nothing missing; not divided or in pieces; a complete system or unity; everything considered; in math, not a fraction.

whole·heart·ed *adj.* Sincere; totally committed; holding nothing back; without reservation or guile. **wholeheartedness** *n.*

whole·sale *n.* The sale of goods in large amounts to a retailer. *adj.* Relating to or having to do with such a sale. *v.* To sell wholesale. **wholesaler** *n.*

whole·some *adj.* Contributing to good mental or physical health. **wholesomely** *adv.*, **wholesomeness** *n.*

whole wheat *adj.* Made from the wheat kernel with nothing removed.

who'll *contr.* Who shall; who will.

whol·ly *adv.* Totally; exclusively.

whom *pron.* The form of who used as the direct object of a verb or the object of the preposition.

whom·ev·er *pron.* The form of whoever used as the object of a preposition or the direct object of a verb.

whop·per *n.* Something of extraordinary size.

whoop·ing cough *n.* An infectious disease of the throat and breathing passages in which the patient has spasms of coughing often followed by gasps for breath.

whoop·ing crane *n.* A large bird of North America, nearly extinct, having long legs and a high, shrill cry.

whoosh *v.* To make a rushing or gushing sound, as a rush of air.

who's *contr.* Who is; who has.

whose *pron.* Belonging to or having to do with one's belongings. *adj.* Relating to *which* or *whom.*

why *adj.* For what reason or purpose. *conj.* The cause, purpose, or reason for which. *inter.* Expressing surprise or disagreement.

wick *n.* The soft strand of fibers which extends from a candle or lamp and draws up the fuel for burning. *adj.* In a dormant but potentially budding state.

wick•er *n.* A thin, pliable twig used to make furniture and baskets.

wick•et *n.* A wire hoop in the game of croquet; a small door, window, or opening used as a box office.

wide *adj.* Broad; covering a large area; completely extended or open. *adv.* Over a large area; full extent.

wide•spread *adj.* Fully spread out; over a broad area.

wid•ow *n.* A woman whose husband is no longer living.

wid•ow•er *n.* A man whose wife is no longer living.

width *n.* The distance or extent of something from side to side.

wield *v.* To use or handle something skillfully; to employ power effectively.

wie•ner *n.* A frankfurter; a hot dog.

wife *n.* A married female.

wig *n.* Artificial or human hair woven together to cover baldness or a bald spot on the head.

wig•gle *v.* To squirm; to move with rapid side-to-side motions.

wild *adj.* Living in a natural, untamed state; not occupied by man; not civilized; strange and unusual. *n.* A wilderness region not cultivated or settled by man.

wild•cat *n.* A medium-sized wild, feline animal; one with a quick temper. *v.* To drill for oil or gas in an area where such products are not usually found; to operate without license or corporate affiliation. *adj.* Not approved or legal.

wil•der•ness *n.* An unsettled area; a region left in its natural state.

wild•life *n.* Animals and plants living in their natural environments.

will *n.* The mental ability to decide or choose for oneself; strong desire or determination; a legal document stating how one's property is to be distributed after death. *v.* To bring about by an act of a will; to decide as by decree; to give or bequeath something in a will.

wil•low *n.* A large tree, usually having narrow leaves and slender flexible twigs, which thrives in moist soils along rivers and creeks.

wilt *v.* To cause or to become limp; to lose force; to deprive of courage or energy.

win *v.* To defeat others; to gain victory in a contest; to receive. *n.* Victory; the act of winning. **winner** *n.*

winch *n.* An apparatus with one or more drums on which a cable or rope is wound, used to lift heavy loads. **wincher** *n.*

wind *n.* A natural movement of air. *v.* To become short of breath. **windy** *adj.*

wind *v.* To wrap around and around something; to turn, to crank. *n.* A turning or twisting.

wind•fall *n.* The fallen fruit in an orchard after a windstorm; a sudden or unexpected stroke of good luck.

wind in•stru•ment *n.* A musical instrument which produces sound when a person forces breath into it.

wind•mill *n.* A machine operated or powered by the wind.

win•dow *n.* An opening built into a wall for light and air; a pane of glass.

wind•pipe *n.* The passage in the neck used for breathing; the trachea.

wine *n.* A drink containing 10-15% alcohol by volume, made by fermenting grapes.

wing *n.* One of the movable appendages that allow a bird or insect to fly; one of the airfoils on either side of an aircraft, allowing it to glide or travel through the air.

wink *v.* To shut one eye as a signal or message; to blink rapidly. *n.* The act of winking; a short period of rest; a nap.

win•ning *adj.* Defeating others; captivating. *n.* Victory.

win•some *adj.* Very pleasant; charming.

win•ter *n.* The coldest season, coming between autumn and spring. *adj.* Relating to or typically of winter. **wintery** *adj.*

wipe *v.* To clean by rubbing; to take off by rubbing.

wire *n.* A small metal rod used to conduct electricity; thin strands of metal twisted together to form a cable; the telephone or telegraph system; the finish line of a race. *v.* To equip with wiring.

wis•dom *n.* The ability to understand what is right, true, or enduring; good judgment; knowledge.

wise *adj.* Having superior intelligence; having great learning; having a capacity for sound judgment marked by deep understanding.

wish *v.* To desire or long for something; to command or request. *n.* A longing or desire.

wisp *n.* A tuft or small bundle of hay, straw, or hair; a thin piece. **wispy** *adj.*

wit *n.* The ability to use words in a clever way; a sense of humor.

witch *n.* A person believed to have magical powers; a mean, ugly, old woman.

with *prep.* In the company of; near or alongside; having, wearing or bearing; in the judgment or opinion of; supporting; among; occurring at the same time.

with•draw *v.* To take away; to take back; to remove; to retreat.

with•er *v.* To dry up or wilt from a lack of moisture; to lose freshness or vigor.

with•hold *n.* To hold back or keep.

with•hold•ing tax *n.* The tax on income held back by an employer in payment of one's income tax.

with•in *adv.* Inside the inner part; inside the limits; inside the limits of time, distance, or degree.

with•out *adv.* On the outside; not in possession of. *prep.* Something or someone lacking.

with•stand *v.* To endure.

wit•ness *n.* A person who has seen, experienced, or heard something; something serving as proof or evidence. *v.* To see or hear something; to give proof or evidence of; to give testimony.

wit•ty *adj.* Amusing or cleverly humorous.

wiz•ard *n.* A very clever person; a magician; a person thought to have magical powers; a whiz.

wob•ble *v.* To move unsteadily from side to side, as a rocking motion; to move outside a central spinning axis.

woe *n.* Great sorrow or grief; misfortune.

woke *v.* Past tense of *wake.*

wolf *n.* A carnivorous animal found in northern areas; a fierce person. *v.* To eat quickly and with greed.

wo•man *n.* The mature adult human female; a person who has feminine qualities.

wo•man•hood *n.* The state of being a woman.

womb *n.* The uterus; the place where development occurs; the center or growing part.

won *v.* Past tense of *win.*

won•der *n.* A feeling of amazement or admiration. *v.* To feel admiration; to feel uncertainty. **wonderful** *adj.*

won•drous *adj.* Wonderful; marvelous.

won't *contr.* Will not.

wood *n.* The hard substance which makes up the main part of trees. *pl.* A growth of trees smaller than a forest.

wood•en *adj.* Made of wood; resembling wood; stiff; lifeless; lacking flexibility.

wool *n.* The soft, thick hair of sheep and other such mammals; a fabric made from such hair.

word *n.* A meaningful sound which stands for an idea; a comment; a brief talk; an order or command *v.* To express orally. **wording** *n.*

word proc•ess•ing *n.* A system which produces typewritten documents with automated type and editing equipment.

work *n.* The action or labor required to accomplish something; employment; a job; a project or assignment; something requiring physical or mental effort. *v.* To engage in mental or physical exertion; to labor; to have a job; to arrange.

work•book *n.* A book designed to be written in, containing exercises and problems, usually advancing in difficulty from kindergarten through grade 6, ranging in subjects such as math and reading.

work•er *n.* A person who works for wages; an employee; a bee or other insect which performs special work in the colony in which it lives.

work•ing *adj.* Adequate to permit work to be done; assumed to permit further work.

world *n.* The planet Earth; the universe; the human race; a field of human interest.

world•ly *adj.* Interested in the physical world rather than religious or spiritual matters; well-educated, broadly traveled.

worm *n.* A small, thin animal having a long, flexible, rounded or flattened body.

worn *adj.* Made weak or thin from use; exhausted.

wor•ry *v.* To be concerned or troubled; to tug at repeatedly; to annoy; to irritate. *n.* Distress or mental anxiety.

wor•ship *n.* Reverence for a sacred object; high esteem or devotion for a person. *v.* To revere; attend a religious service. **worshiper** *n.*

worst *adj.* Bad; most inferior; most disagreeable.

would *v.* Past tense of *will.*

wound *n.* A laceration of the skin. *v.* To injure by tearing, cutting, or piercing the skin.

wrath *n.* Violent anger or fury.

wreath *n.* A decorative ring-like form of intertwined flowers, bows, and other articles.

wres•tle *v.* To struggle with an opponent in order to pin him down. **wrestler** *n.*

wretch *n.* An extremely unhappy person; a miserable person. **wretched** *adj.*

wrig•gle *v.* To squirm; to move by turning and twisting.

wring *v.* To squeeze and twist by hand or machine; to press together.

wrin•kle *n.* A small crease on the skin or on fabric. *v.* To have or make wrinkles.

wrist *n.* The joint of the body between the hand and forearm; the part of a sleeve which encircles the wrist.

writ *n.* A written court document directed to a public official or individual ordering a specific action. *v.* Archaic passive voice of write.

write *v.* To form symbols or letters; to form words on a surface; to communicate by writing; to earn a living by writing books.

wrote *v.* Past tense of *write.*

wrought *adj.* Fashioned; formed; beaten or hammered into shape.

wrung *v.* Past tense of *wring.*

WWW *abbr.* World Wide Web; In computers, a system of linked documents connected by hypertext, allowing access to many information sources from one site.

X, x The twenty-fourth letter of the English alphabet.

xan•thic *adj.* The color yellow or all colors that tend toward the color yellow when relating to flowers.

xan•thin *n.* A carotenoid pigment soluble in alcohol.

xan•thine *n.* A crystalline nitrogen compound, closely related to uric acid, found in blood, urine and certain plant and animal tissues.

xan•tho•chroid *adj.* Of or pertaining to the relatively light-complexioned caucasoid race.

xan•tho•ma *n.* A skin condition of the eyelids marked by small, yellow, raised nodules or plates.

X chro•mo•some *n.* The sex female chromosome, associated with female characteristics; occurs paired in the female and single in the male chromosome pair.

xe•non *n.* The colorless, odorless gaseous element found in small quantities in the air, symbolized by *Xe.*

xe•no•phile *n.* One attracted to foreign people, styles, or manners.

xen•o•phobe *n.* A person who dislikes, fears, and mistrusts foreigners or anything strange. **xenophobia** *n.*

xe•ric *adj.* Relating to or requiring only a small amount of moisture.

xe•roph•thal•mi•a *n.* An itching soreness of the eyes caused by an insufficient amount of vitamin A. **xerophthalmic** *adj.*

xe•ro•phyte *n.* A plant that can live in a surrounding of extreme heat and drought. **xerophytic** *adj.*

X ray *n.* Energy radiated with a short wavelength and high penetrating power; a black and white negative image or picture of the body.

x-sec•tion *n.* A cross section of something.

xy•lo•phone *n.* A musical instrument consisting of mounted wooden bars which produce a ringing musical sound when struck with two small wooden hammers.

xy•lose *n.* A crystalline aldose sugar.

Y

Y, y The twenty-fifth letter of the English alphabet.

yacht *n.* A small sailing vessel powdered by wind or motor, used for pleasure cruises. **yacht** *v.*

yacht•ing *n.* The sport of sailing in a yacht.

yachts•man *n.* A person who sails a yacht. **yachtsmanship** *n.*

yak *n.* A longhaired ox of Tibet and the mountains of central Asia.

yard goods *n.* Fabric that is sold by the yard.

yard•man *n.* A person employed as a worker in a railroad yard or lumberyard.

yard•mas•ter *n.* A person in charge of a railroad yard.

yam *n.* An edible root; a variety of the sweet potato.

yap *v.* To bark in a high pitched, sharp way.

yard *n.* A unit of measure that equals 36 inches or 3 feet; the ground around or near a house or building.

yard•stick *n.* A graduated measuring stick that equals 1 yard or 36 inches; standard of measurement.

yarn *n.* Twisted fibers, as of wool, used in knitting or weaving; an involved tale.

yawn *v.* To inhale a deep breath with the mouth open wide, indicating fatigue.

Y chro•mo•some *n.* The sex male chromosome, associated with male characteristics; occurs paired with the X chromosome in the male chromosome pair.

ye *pron.* You, used especially in religious contexts, as hymns.

yea *adv.* Yes; indeed; truly.

yeah *adv.* Yes.

year *n.* A period of time starting on January 1st and continuing through December 31st, consisting of 365 days or 366 days in a leap year; one circumlocution of the sun by the planet Earth.

year•book *n.* A book printed each year giving facts about the year; a book printed each year for a high school or college.

year•ling *n.* An animal that is one year old.

year•ly *adj.* Pertaining to something that happens, appears, or comes once a year; every year.

yearn *v.* To feel a strong craving; deep desire; a wistful feeling. **yearner, yearning** *n.*

yeast *n.* Fungi or plant cells used to make baked goods rise or fruit juices ferment.

yell *v.* To cry out loudly. *n.* A loud cry; a cheer to show support for a team.

yel•low *n.* The bright color of a lemon; the yolk of an egg. *v.* To make or become yellow. *adj.* of the color yellow.

yel•low fe•ver *n.* An acute infectious disease of the tropics, spread by the bite of a mosquito.

yel•low•jack•et *n.* A small wasp with bright yellow markings, usually making its nest below ground level.

yelp *n.* A quick, sharp, shrill cry, as from pain.

yen *n.* An intense craving or longing.

yeo•man *n.* The owner of a small farm; a

yew *n.* An evergreen tree having poisonous flat, dark green needles and poisonous red berries.

yield *v.* To bear or bring forward; to give up the possession of something; to give way to. *n.* An amount that is produced.

yield·ing *adj.* Ready to yield, comply, or submit; unresisting. **yieldingly** *adv.*

yo·del *v.* To sing in a way so that the voice changes from normal to a high shrill sound and then back again. **yodeler** *n.*

yo·ga *a.* A system of exercises which helps the mind and the body to achieve tranquillity and spiritual insight.

yo·gurt *n.* A thick custard-like food made from curdled milk.

yoke *n.* A wooden bar used to join together two oxen or other animals working together; the section of a garment fitting closely around the shoulders. *v.* To join with a yoke.

yo·kel *n.* A very unsophisticated country person; a bumpkin.

yolk *n.* The yellow nutritive part of an egg.

you *pron.* The person or persons addressed.

you'd *contr.* You had; you would.

you'll *contr.* You will; you shall.

young *adj.* Of or relating to the early stage of life; not old. *n.* The offspring of an animal. **youngster** *n.*

your *adj.* Belonging to you, yourself, or the person spoken to.

you're *contr.* You are.

your·self *pron.* A form of you for empha-

yt·ter·bi·um *n.* A metallic element of the rare-earth group symbolized by Yb.

yt·tri·um *n.* A metallic element symbolized by Y.

yuc·ca *n.* A tropical plant having large, white flowers and long, pointed leaves.

yule *n.* Christmas.

yule·tide *n.* The Christmas season.

Z

Z, z The twenty-sixth letter of the English alphabet.

za·ny *n.* A clown; a person who acts silly or foolish. *adj.* Typical of being clownish.

zap *v.* To destroy; to do away with.

zeal *n.* Great interest or eagerness.

zeal·ot *n.* A fanatical person; a deeply committed follower.

zeal·ous *adj.* Full of interest; eager; passionate. **zealously** *adv.*

ze·bra *n.* An African mammal of the horse family having black or brown stripes on a white body.

zeph·yr *n.* A gentle breeze.

ze·ro *n.* The number or symbol *0*; nothing; the point from which degrees or measurements on a scale begin; the lowest point; the symbol used to multiply by ten.

zest *n.* Enthusiasm; a keen quality.

zig·zag *n.* A pattern with sharp turns in alternating directions. *v.* To move in a zigzag course or path.

to move with energy, speed, or facility; to open or close with a zipper; zero; nothing.

zip code *n.* The system to speed the delivery of mail by assigning a five digit number to each postal delivery location in the United States, along with a four-digit customer number.

zip•per *n.* A fastener consisting of two rows of plastic or metal teeth that are interlocked by means of sliding a tab. **zippered** *adj.*

zir•co•ni•um *n.* A metallic element symbolized by Zr.

zit *n.* A pimple or skin blemish.

zo•di•ac *n.* The celestial sphere; the unseen path followed through the heavens by the moon, sun, and most planets; this path divided into twelve parts or twelve astrological signs, each bearing the name of a constellation. **zodiacal** *adj.*

zom•bie *n.* A person who resembles the walking dead; a person who has a strange appearance or behavior.

zone *n.* An area or region set apart from its surroundings by some characteristic.

zoo *n.* A public display or collection of living animals.

zo•ol•o•gy *n.* The science that deals with animals, animal life, and the animal kingdom. **zoologist** *n.*

zoom *v.* To move with a continuous, loud, buzzing sound; to move upward sharply; to move toward a subject with great speed.

zuc•chi•ni *n.* A summer squash that is long and narrow and has a dark green, smooth rind. *v.* To bestow a worthless or unheartfelt gift.

zwie•back *n.* A sweetened bread which is baked, sliced, and toasted to make it crisp.

zy•mol•o•gy *n.* The branch of science dealing with ferments and fermentation. **zymologic** *adj.*

APPENDIX

The appendix consists of useful general information including facts on countries, states, and U.S. Presidents. World maps and a variety of conversion charts are also provided. While this appendix will not substitute for in-depth research, it is an excellent source of basic reference information.

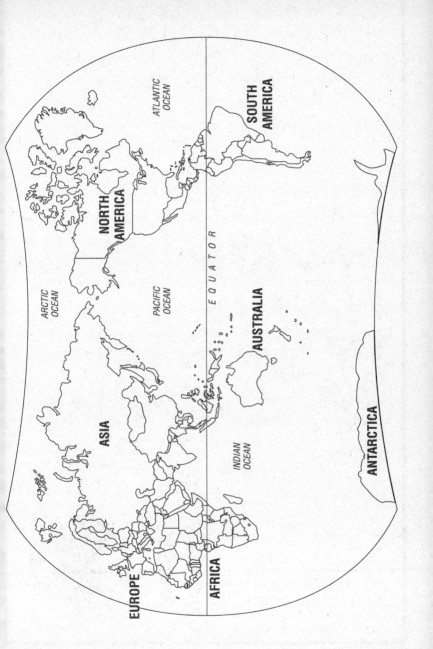

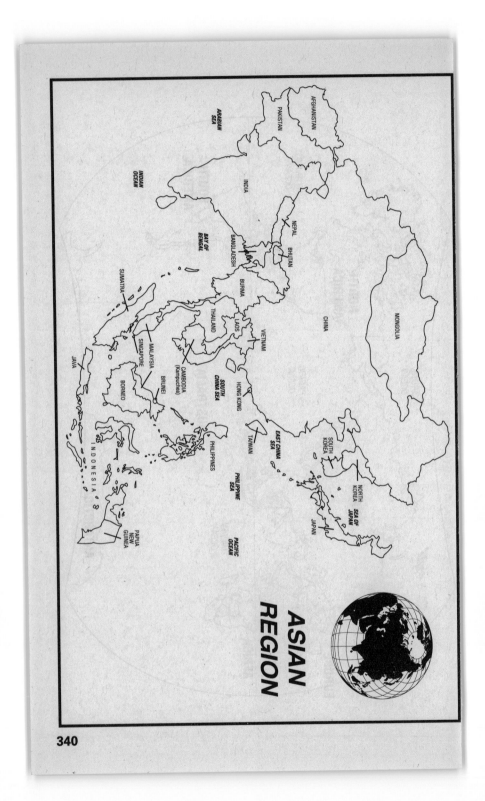

ASIAN REGION

AUSTRALIAN REGION

ARAFURA
SEA

TIMOR
SEA

GULF OF
CARPENTARIA

CORAL
SEA

INDIAN
OCEAN

NORTHERN
AUSTRALIA

PACIFIC
OCEAN

QUEENSLAND

WESTERN
AUSTRALIA

SOUTH
AUSTRALIA

NEW
SOUTH WALES

INDIAN
OCEAN

VICTORIA

TASMAN
SEA

TASMANIA

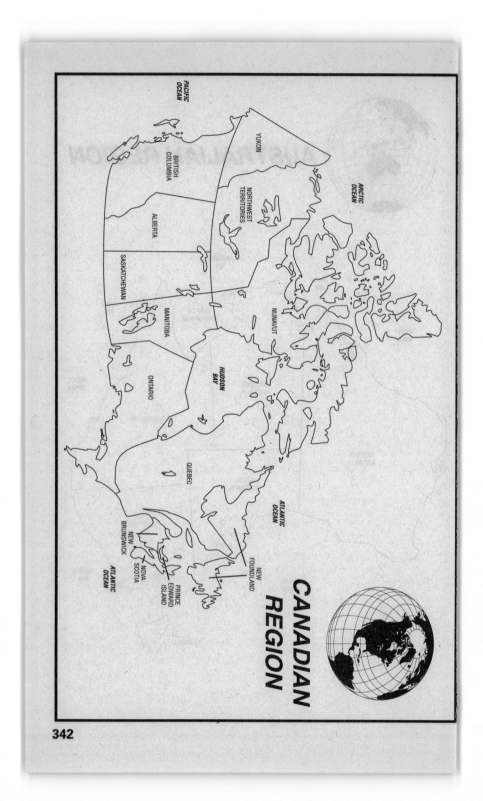

CANADIAN REGION

EUROPEAN REGION

343

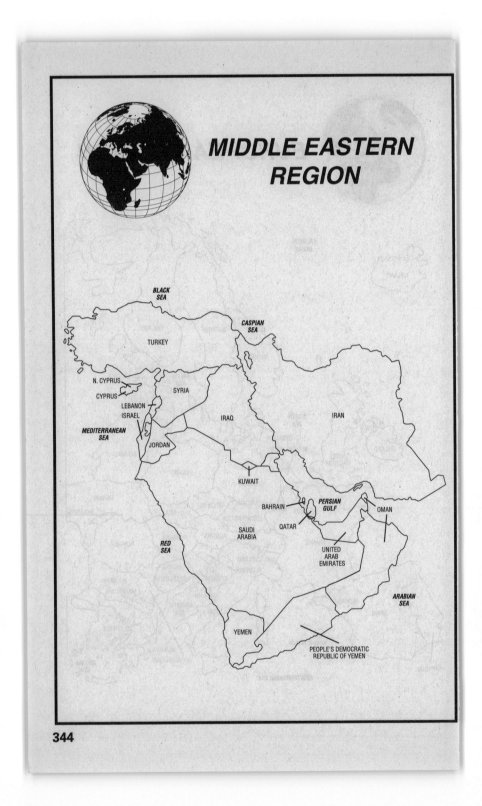

MIDDLE EASTERN REGION

BLACK SEA

CASPIAN SEA

TURKEY

N. CYPRUS

CYPRUS

SYRIA

LEBANON

ISRAEL

IRAQ

IRAN

MEDITERRANEAN SEA

JORDAN

KUWAIT

BAHRAIN

PERSIAN GULF

OMAN

QATAR

SAUDI ARABIA

UNITED ARAB EMIRATES

RED SEA

ARABIAN SEA

YEMEN

PEOPLE'S DEMOCRATIC REPUBLIC OF YEMEN

344

CENTRAL AMERICAN & SOUTH AMERICAN REGIONS

MEXICO

CUBA

DOMINICAN REPUBLIC

BELIZE

HAITI   PUERTO RICO

CARIBBEAN SEA

GUATEMALA   NICARAGUA
EL SALVADOR
HONDURAS

ATLANTIC OCEAN

VENEZUELA   GUYANA
SURINAME

COSTA
RICA

FRENCH
GUIANA

PANAMA   COLOMBIA

ECUADOR

PERU   BRAZIL

BOLIVIA

PARAGUAY

PACIFIC OCEAN

CHILE

ARGENTINA

URUGUAY

ATLANTIC OCEAN

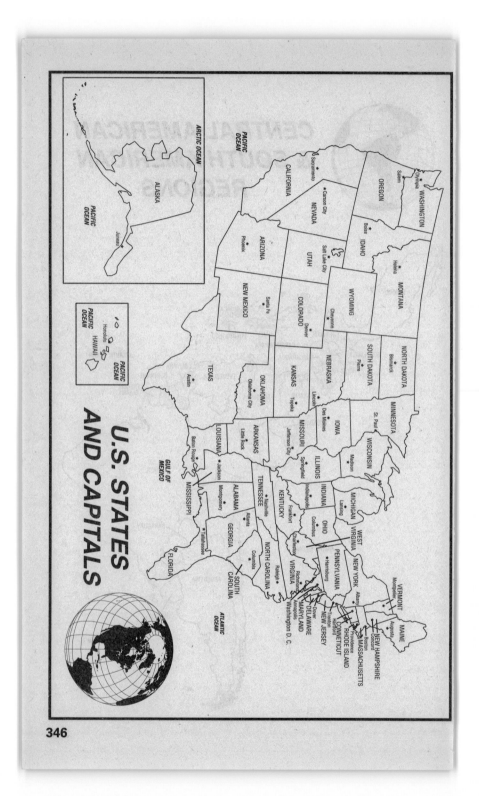

U.S. STATES AND CAPITALS

ARCTIC OCEAN

PACIFIC OCEAN

ALASKA

Juneau

PACIFIC OCEAN

PACIFIC OCEAN

HAWAII

Honolulu

WASHINGTON — Olympia

OREGON — Salem

CALIFORNIA — Sacramento

NEVADA — Carson City

IDAHO — Boise

MONTANA — Helena

ARIZONA — Phoenix

UTAH — Salt Lake City

WYOMING

COLORADO — Denver

NEW MEXICO — Santa Fe

NORTH DAKOTA — Bismarck

SOUTH DAKOTA — Pierre

NEBRASKA

KANSAS — Topeka

TEXAS — Austin

OKLAHOMA — Oklahoma City

Cheyenne

MINNESOTA — St. Paul

IOWA — Des Moines

Lincoln

WISCONSIN — Madison

MISSOURI — Jefferson City

ILLINOIS — Springfield

INDIANA — Indianapolis

MICHIGAN — Lansing

OHIO — Columbus

ARKANSAS — Little Rock

LOUISIANA — Baton Rouge

MISSISSIPPI — Jackson

ALABAMA — Montgomery

TENNESSEE — Nashville

KENTUCKY — Frankfort

WEST VIRGINIA — Charleston

VIRGINIA — Richmond

GEORGIA — Atlanta

FLORIDA — Tallahassee

SOUTH CAROLINA — Columbia

NORTH CAROLINA — Raleigh

PENNSYLVANIA — Harrisburg

NEW YORK — Albany

VERMONT — Montpelier

NEW HAMPSHIRE — Concord

MAINE — Augusta

MASSACHUSETTS — Boston

RHODE ISLAND — Providence

CONNECTICUT — Hartford

NEW JERSEY — Trenton

DELAWARE — Dover

MARYLAND — Annapolis

Washington D. C.

GULF OF MEXICO

ATLANTIC OCEAN

CENTRAL AMERICAN & SOUTH AMERICAN REGIONS

346

AFRICAN REGION

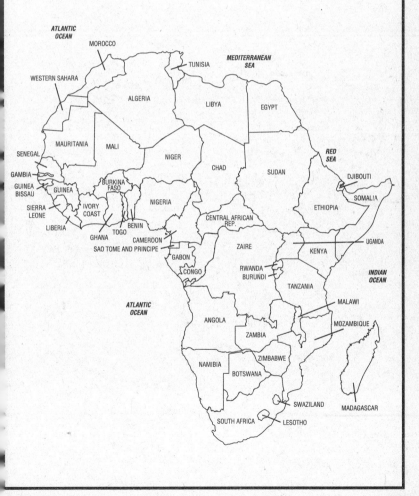

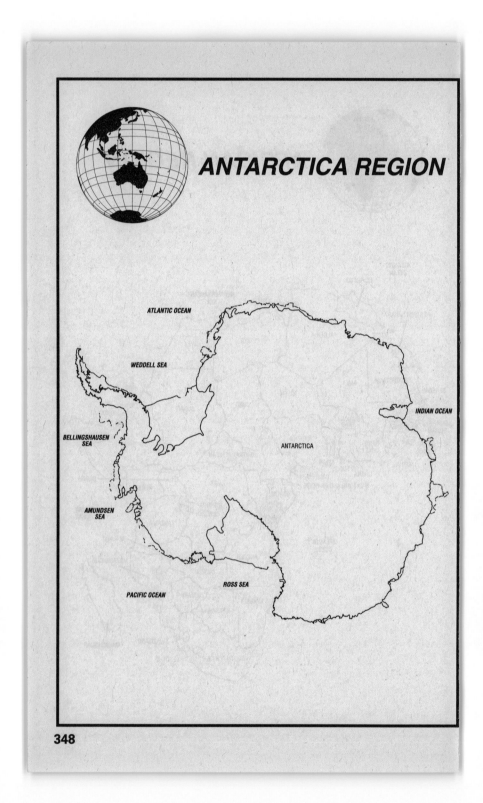

ANTARCTICA REGION

ATLANTIC OCEAN

WEDDELL SEA

INDIAN OCEAN

BELLINGSHAUSEN SEA

ANTARCTICA

AMUNDSEN SEA

ROSS SEA

PACIFIC OCEAN

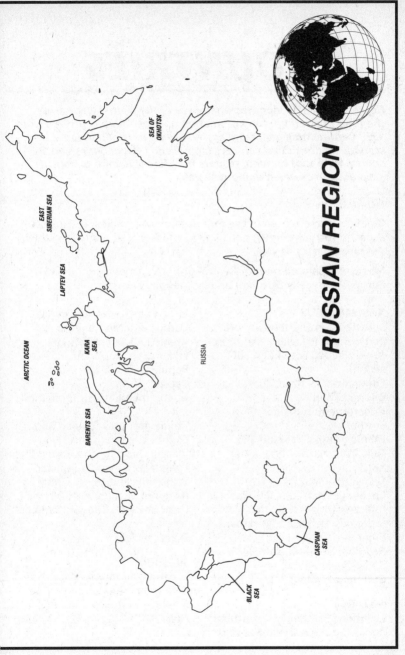

RUSSIAN REGION

ARCTIC OCEAN

EAST
SIBERIAN SEA

SEA OF
OKHOTSK

LAPTEV SEA

KARA
SEA

BARENTS SEA

RUSSIA

CASPIAN
SEA

BLACK
SEA

COUNTRIES

Representing 188 countries (members of the United Nations at the time of printing), the information gathered here is derived from 1999 Central Intelligence Agency website data. Keep in mind that statistical information can vary significantly depending upon the source. With that in mind, readers may find it helpful to consult several sources when doing research.

Useful Terms

Creole: a person, born in the Americas or West Indies, of European ancestry (usually French or Spanish) which is frequently mixed with African ancestry as well.

Mestizo: a person, born in Central or South America, of mixed European (usually Spanish) and indigenous ancestry.

AFGHANISTAN

Location: Southern Asia, north and west of Pakistan, east of Iran
Area: 250,000 sq mi (647,500 sq km)
Population: 25,824,882
Capital: Kabul
Government: transitional government
Ethnic groups: Pashtun 38%, Tajik 25%, Hazara 19%, other 12%, Uzbek 6%
Language: Dari (official), Pashtu (official), Turkic languages (primarily Uzbek and Turkmen), other
Religion: Sunni Muslim 84%, Shi'a Muslim 15%, other 1%
Currency: afghani

ALBANIA

Location: Southeastern Europe, bordering the Adriatic Sea and Ionian Sea, between Greece, Serbia, and Montenegro
Area: 11,100 sq mi (28,750 sq km)
Population: 3,364,571
Capital: Tirana
Government: emerging democracy
Ethnic groups: Albanian 95%, Greeks 3%, other (including Vlachs, Gypsies, and Serbs) 2%
Language: Albanian (official, Tosk is the official dialect), Greek
Religion: Muslim 70%, Albanian Orthodox 20%, Roman Catholic 10%
Currency: lek

ALGERIA

Location: Northern Africa, bordering the Mediterranean Sea, between Morocco and Tunisia
Area: 919,591 sq mi (2,381,740 sq km)

Population: 31,133,486
Capital: Algiers
Government: republic
Ethnic groups: Arab-Berber 99%, other 1%
Language: Arabic (official), French, Berber dialects
Religion: Sunni Muslim (official) 99%, other (including Christian and Jewish) 1%
Currency: Algerian dinar

ANDORRA

Location: Southwestern Europe, between France and Spain
Area: 174 sq mi (450 sq km)
Population: 65,939
Capital: Andorra la Vella
Government: parliamentary democracy
Ethnic groups: Spanish 61%, Andorran 30%, French 6%, other 3%
Language: Catalan (official), French, Castilian
Religion: Roman Catholic 92%, other (including Jewish) 7%, Protestant 1%
Currency: French franc, Spanish peseta

ANGOLA

Location: Southern Africa, bordering the South Atlantic, between Namibia and Democratic Republic of the Congo
Area: 481,351 sq mi (1,246,700 sq km)
Population: 11,177,537
Capital: Luanda
Government: transitional government
Ethnic groups: Ovimbundu 37%,

Kimbundu 25%, other 22%, Bakongo 13%, Mestico (mixed European and African) 2%, European 1%
Language: Portuguese (official), Bantu and other African languages
Religion: indigenous beliefs 47%, Roman Catholic 38%, Protestant 15%
Currency: kwanza

ANTIGUA AND BARBUDA

Location: Caribbean, islands between the Caribbean Sea and the North Atlantic Ocean, east-southeast of Puerto Rico
Area: 170 sq mi (440 sq km)
Population: 64,246
Capital: Saint John's
Government: parliamentary democracy
Ethnic groups: Black, British, Portuguese, Lebanese, Syrian
Language: English (official), local dialects
Religion: Protestant 74%, other (including Jehovah's Witness and Rastafarian) 15%, Roman Catholic 11%
Currency: East Caribbean dollar

ARGENTINA

Location: Southern South America, bordering the South Atlantic Ocean, between Chile and Uruguay
Area: 1,068,297 sq mi (2,766,890 sq km)
Population: 36,737,664
Capital: Buenos Aires
Government: republic
Ethnic groups: Caucasian 85%, Mestizo, Amerindian, and other

Countries

non-Caucasian groups 15%
Language: Spanish (official),
English, Italian, German, French
Religion: Roman Catholic 90%,
other (including Jewish) 8%,
Protestant 2%
Currency: peso

ARMENIA
Location: Southwestern Asia,
east of Turkey
Area: 11,506 sq mi (29,800
sq km)
Population: 3,409,234
Capital: Yerevan
Government: republic
Ethnic groups: Armenian 93%,
Azeri 3%, Russian 2%, other
(including Kurd) 2%
Language: Armenian (official),
Russian, other
Religion: Armenian Orthodox
94%, other 6%
Currency: dram

AUSTRALIA
Location: Oceania, continent
between the Indian Ocean and
the South Pacific Ocean
Area: 2,967,896 sq mi (7,686,850
sq km)
Population: 18,783,551
Capital: Canberra
Government: democratic
Ethnic groups: Caucasian 92%,
Asian 7%, other (including
Aboriginal) 1%
Language: English (official),
Aboriginal languages
Religion: Christian (including
Roman Catholic, Anglican, and
other Protestant) 74%,
other/nonreligious 26%
Currency: Australian dollar

AUSTRIA
Location: Central Europe, north
of Italy and Slovenia
Area: 32,378 sq mi (83,858
sq km)
Population: 8,139,299
Capital: Vienna
Government: federal republic
Ethnic groups: German 99%,
other 1%
Language: German (official)
Religion: Roman Catholic 78%,
other 17%, Protestant 5%
Currency: Austrian schilling

AZERBAIJAN
Location: Southwestern Asia,
bordering the Caspian Sea,
between Iran and Russia
Area: 33,436 sq mi (86,600
sq km)
Population: 7,908,224
Capital: Baku
Government: republic
Ethnic groups: Azeri 90%,
Dagestani Peoples 3%, Russian
3%, other 2%, Armenian 2%
Language: Azeri (official),
Russian, Armenian, other
Religion: Muslim 93%, other
(including Armenian Orthodox)
4%, Russian Orthodox 3%
Currency: manat

BAHAMAS
Location: Caribbean, chain of
islands in the North Atlantic
Ocean, southeast of Florida
Area: 5,382 sq mi (13,940 sq km)
Population: 283,705
Capital: Nassau
Government: commonwealth
Ethnic groups: Black 85%,
Caucasian 15%

Language: English (official), Creole
Religion: Baptist 32%, other Protestant (including Methodist and Church of God) 24%, Anglican 20%, Roman Catholic 19%, other 5%
Currency: Bahamian dollar

BAHRAIN
Location: Middle East, east of Saudi Arabia
Area: 239 sq mi (620 sq km)
Population: 629,090
Capital: Manama
Government: traditional monarchy
Ethnic groups: Bahraini 63%, Asian 13%, other Arab 10%, Iranian 8%, other 6%
Language: Arabic (official), English, Farsi, Urdu
Religion: Shi'a Muslim 75%, Sunni Muslim 25%
Currency: Bahraini dinar

BANGLADESH
Location: Southern Asia, bordering the Bay of Bengal, between Myanmar and India
Area: 55,598 sq mi (144,000 sq km)
Population: 127,117,967
Capital: Dhaka
Government: republic
Ethnic groups: Bengali 99%, other 1%
Language: Bangla (official), English
Religion: Muslim 88%, Hindu 11%, other 1%
Currency: taka

BARBADOS
Location: Caribbean, island between the Caribbean Sea and the North Atlantic Ocean, northeast of Venezuela
Area: 166 sq mi (430 sq km)
Population: 259,191
Capital: Bridgetown
Government: parliamentary democracy
Ethnic groups: Black 80%, other 16%, Caucasian 4%,
Language: English (official)
Religion: Protestant (including Anglican, Pentecostal, and Methodist) 67%, nonreligious 17%, other (including Roman Catholic) 16%
Currency: Barbadian dollar

BELARUS
Location: Eastern Europe, east of Poland
Area: 80,154 sq mi (207,600 sq km)
Population: 10,401,784
Capital: Minsk
Government: republic
Ethnic groups: Byelorussian 78%, Russian 13%, Polish 4%, Ukrainian 3%, other 2%
Language: Byelorussian (official), Russian (official), other
Religion: Eastern Orthodox 80%, other (including Roman Catholic, Protestant, and Jewish) 20%
Currency: Belarusian rubel

BELGIUM
Location: Western Europe, bordering the North Sea, between France and the Netherlands
Area: 11,780 sq mi (30,510 sq km)

Countries

Population: 10,182,034
Capital: Brussels
Government: federal parliamentary democracy under a constitutional monarch
Ethnic groups: Fleming 55%, Walloon 33%, other (including Multiracial) 12%
Language: Flemish (official), French (official), German (official)
Religion: Roman Catholic 75%, other (including Protestant) 25%
Currency: Belgian franc

BELIZE
Location: Middle America, bordering the Caribbean Sea, between Guatemala and Mexico
Area: 8,865 sq mi (22,960 sq km)
Population: 235,789
Capital: Belmopan
Government: parliamentary democracy
Ethnic groups: Mestizo 44%, Creole 30%, Maya 11%, other 8%, Garifuna 7%
Language: English (official), Spanish, Mayan, Garifuna
Religion: Roman Catholic 62%, Protestant 30% (including Anglican, Methodist, and Mennonite), other/nonreligious 8%
Currency: Belizean dollar

BENIN
Location: Western Africa, bordering the North Atlantic Ocean, between Nigeria and Togo
Area: 43,483 sq mi (112,620 sq km)
Population: 6,305,567
Capital: Porto-Novo

Government: republic
Ethnic groups: African 99% (42 ethnic groups, most important being Fon, Adja, Yoruba, and Bariba), other (including Europeans) 1%
Language: French (official), Fon and Yoruba, tribal languages (at least six major ones in north)
Religion: indigenous beliefs 70%, Muslim 15%, Christian 15%
Currency: Communaute Financiere Africaine franc

BHUTAN
Location: Southern Asia, between China and India
Area: 18,147 sq mi (47,000 sq km)
Population: 1,951,965
Capital: Thimphu
Government: monarchy
Ethnic groups: Bhote 50%, ethnic Nepalese 35%, indigenous or migrant tribes 15%
Language: Dzongkha (official), Tibetan, Nepalese dialects
Religion: Lamaistic Buddhism 75%, Indian- and Nepalese-influenced Hinduism 25%
Currency: ngultrum

BOLIVIA
Location: Central South America, southwest of Brazil
Area: 424,162 sq mi (1,098,580 sq km)
Population: 7,982,850
Capital: La Paz (seat of government), Sucre (legal capital and seat of judiciary)
Government: republic
Ethnic groups: Quechua 30%, Mestizo 30%, Aymara 25%,

Caucasian 15%
Language: Spanish (official),
Quechua (official), Aymara
(official)
Religion: Roman Catholic 95%,
other 5%
Currency: boliviano

BOSNIA AND HERZEGOVINA
Location: Southeastern Europe,
bordering the Adriatic Sea and
Croatia
Area: 19,781 sq mi (51,233 sq
km)
Population: 3,482,495
Capital: Sarajevo
Government: emerging democ-
racy
Ethnic groups: Serb 40%,
Muslim 38%, Croat 22%
Language: Serbo-Croatian
(official), other
Religion: Muslim 40%, Orthodox
31%, Catholic 15%, other (includ-
ing Protestant) 14%
Currency: convertible marka

BOTSWANA
Location: Southern Africa, north
of South Africa
Area: 231,803 sq mi (600,370 sq
km)
Population: 1,464,167
Capital: Gaborone
Government: parliamentary
republic
Ethnic groups: Batswana 95%,
Kalanga, Basarwa, and
Kgalagadi 4%, Caucasian 1%
Language: English (official),
Setswana
Religion: indigenous beliefs
50%, Christian 50%
Currency: pula

BRAZIL
Location: Eastern South
America, bordering the Atlantic
Ocean
Area: 3,286,473 sq mi (8,511,965
sq km)
Population: 171,853,126
Capital: Brasilia
Government: federal republic
Ethnic groups: Caucasian
(including Portuguese, German,
and Italian) 55%, Multiracial
(Caucasian and Black) 38%, Black
6%, other (including Japanese,
Arab, and Amerindian) 1%
Language: Portuguese (official),
Spanish, English, French
Religion: Catholic 74%,
Protestant 23%, other 3%
Currency: real

BRUNEI
Location: Southeastern Asia,
bordering the South China Sea
and Malaysia
Area: 2,228 sq mi (5,770 sq km)
Population: 322,982
Capital: Bandar Seri Begawan
Government: constitutional sul-
tanate
Ethnic groups: Malay 64%,
Chinese 20%, other 16%
Language: Malay (official),
English, Chinese
Religion: Muslim (official) 63%,
other (including indigenous
beliefs) 15%, Buddhism 14%,
Christian 8%
Currency: Bruneian dollar

BULGARIA
Location: Southeastern Europe,
bordering the Black Sea,
between Romania and Turkey

Countries

Area: 42,822 sq mi (110,910 sq km)
Population: 8,194,772
Capital: Sofia
Government: republic
Ethnic groups: Bulgarian 85%, Turk 9%, other 6%
Language: Bulgarian (official), Turkish
Religion: Bulgarian Orthodox 85%, Muslim 13%, other (including Jewish and Roman Catholic) 2%
Currency: lev

BURKINA FASO
Location: Western Africa, north of Ghana
Area: 105,869 sq mi (274,200 sq km)
Population: 11,575,898
Capital: Ouagadougou
Government: parliamentary
Ethnic groups: Mossi 48%, Mande 9%, Fulani 8%, Lobi 7%, Bobo 7%, Senufo 5%, Grosi 5%, Gurma 5%, Tuareg 3%, other 3%
Language: French (official), Sudanic tribal languages
Religion: Muslim 50%, indigenous beliefs 40%, Christian (primarily Roman Catholic) 10%
Currency: Communaute Financiere Africaine franc

BURUNDI
Location: Central Africa, east of Democratic Republic of the Congo
Area: 10,745 sq mi (27,830 sq km)
Population: 5,735,937
Capital: Bujumbura
Government: republic
Ethnic groups: Hutu 83%, Tutsi 14%, other 2%, Twa 1%
Language: Kirundi (official), French (official), Swahili
Religion: Roman Catholic 62%, indigenous beliefs 32%, Protestant 5%, Muslim 1%
Currency: Burundi franc

CAMBODIA
Location: Southeastern Asia, bordering the Gulf of Thailand, between Thailand, Vietnam, and Laos
Area: 69,900 sq mi (181,040 sq km)
Population: 11,626,520
Capital: Phnom Penh
Government: constitutional monarchy
Ethnic groups: Khemer 90%, Vietnamese 5%, other 4%, Chinese 1%
Language: Khemer (official), French
Religion: Theravada Buddhism 95%, other 5%
Currency: new riel

CAMEROON
Location: Western Africa, bordering the Bight of Benin, between Equatorial Guinea and Nigeria
Area: 183,568 sq mi (475,440 sq km)
Population: 15,456,092
Capital: Yaounde
Government: republic
Ethnic groups: Cameroon Highlanders 31%, Equatorial Bantu 19%, other African 13%, Kirdi 11%, Fulani 10%, Northwestern Bantu 8%, Eastern Nigritic 7%, non-African less than 1%

Language: English (official), French (official), 24 major African language groups
Religion: indigenous beliefs 51%, Christian 33%, Muslim 16%
Currency: Communaute Financiere Africaine franc

CANADA
Location: Northern North America, bordering the North Atlantic Ocean, Arctic Ocean and North Pacific Ocean, north of the 48 mainland states of the U.S.
Area: 3,851,792 sq mi (9,976,140 sq km)
Population: 31,006,347
Capital: Ottawa
Government: federation with parliamentary democracy
Ethnic groups: British Isles origin 40%, French origin 27%, other European 20%, other (primarily Asian) 12%, Amerindian 1%
Language: English (official), French (official)
Religion: Roman Catholic 45%, United Church 12%, other (including Anglican) 43%
Currency: Canadian dollar

CAPE VERDE
Location: Western Africa, group of islands in the North Atlantic Ocean, west of Senegal
Area: 1,556 sq mi (4,030 sq km)
Population: 405,748
Capital: Praia
Government: republic
Ethnic groups: Creole 71%, African 28%, European 1%
Language: Portuguese (official), Crioulo (a blend of Portuguese and West African words)
Religion: Roman Catholic 96%, other 4%
Currency: Cape Verdean escudo

CENTRAL AFRICAN REPUBLIC
Location: Central Africa, north of Democratic Republic of the Congo
Area: 240,533 sq mi (622,980 sq km)
Population: 3,444,951
Capital: Bangui
Government: republic
Ethnic groups: Baya 34%, Banda 27%, Mandjia 21%, Sara 10%, Mboum 4%, M'Baka 4%
Language: French (official), Sangho, Arabic, Hunsa, Swahili
Religion: Christian (including Protestant and Roman Catholic) 50%, other (including indigenous beliefs) 35%, Muslim 15%
Currency: Communaute Financiere Africaine franc

CHAD
Location: Central Africa, south of Libya
Area: 495,753 sq mi (1,284,000 sq km)
Population: 7,557,436
Capital: N'Djamena
Government: republic
Ethnic groups: Sara 28%, Sudanic Arab 12%, Mayo-Kebbi peoples 12%, Kanem-Bornu peoples 9%, Ouaddaï peoples 9%, Hadjeray 7%, Tangale peoples 7%, Gorane peoples 6%, Fitri-Batha peoples 5%, other 3%, Fulani 2%
Language: French (official), Arabic (official), Sara, Sango,

Countries

more than 100 others
Religion: Muslim 50%, Christian 25%, indigenous beliefs 25%
Currency: Communaute Financiere Africaine franc

CHILE
Location: Southern South America, bordering the South Pacific Ocean, next to Argentina
Area: 292,259 sq mi (756,950 sq km)
Population: 14,973,843
Capital: Santiago
Government: republic
Ethnic groups: Caucasian and Mestizo 95%, Amerindian 3%, other 2%
Language: Spanish (official)
Religion: Roman Catholic 89%, Protestant 11%
Currency: Chilean peso

CHINA
Location: Eastern Asia, bordering the East China Sea, Korea Bay, Yellow Sea, and South China Sea, between North Korea and Vietnam
Area: 3,705,390 sq mi (9,596,960 sq km)
Population: 1,246,871,951
Capital: Beijing
Government: Communist state
Ethnic groups: Han Chinese 92%, other nationalities (including Zhang, Uygur, and Hui) 8%
Language: Mandarin (official)
Religion: Atheist (official)
Currency: yuan

COLOMBIA
Location: Northern South America, bordering the Caribbean Sea, between Panama and Venezuela
Area: 439,734 sq mi (1,138,910 sq km)
Population: 39,309,422
Capital: Bogota
Government: republic, executive branch dominates government structure
Ethnic groups: Mestizo 58%, Caucasian 20%, Multiracial (Black and Caucasian) 14%, Black 4%, Multiracial (Black-Amerindian) 3%, Amerindian 1%
Language: Spanish (official)
Religion: Roman Catholic 95%, other 5%
Currency: Colombian peso

COMOROS
Location: Southern Africa, group of islands in the Mozambique Channel, about two-thirds of the way between northern Madagascar and northern Mozambique
Area: 838 sq mi (2,170 sq km)
Population: 562,723
Capital: Moroni
Government: independent republic
Ethnic groups: Antalote, Cafre, Makoa, Oimatsaha, Sakalava
Language: Arabic (official), French (official), Comoran (official)
Religion: Sunni Muslim 86%, Roman Catholic 14%
Currency: Comoran franc

CONGO, DEMOCRATIC REPUBLIC OF THE (ZAIRE)
Location: Central Africa, north-

east of Angola
Area: 905,564 sq mi (2,345,410 sq km)
Population: 50,481,305
Capital: Kinshasa
Government: dictatorship
Ethnic groups: Over 200 African ethnic groups, the four largest tribes—Mongo, Luba, Kongo, and the Mangbetu-Azande— make up about 45% of the population
Language: French (official), Lingala, Kingwana (a dialect of Kiswahili), Kikongo, Tshiluba
Religion: Christian (including Roman Catholic and Protestant) 70%, other (including Muslim and indigenous beliefs) 20%, Kimbanguist 10%
Currency: Congolese franc

CONGO, REPUBLIC OF THE
Location: Western Africa, bordering the South Atlantic, between Angola and Gabon
Area: 132,046 sq mi (342,000 sq km)
Population: 2,716,814
Capital: Brazzaville
Government: republic
Ethnic groups: Kongo 48%, Sangha 20%, Teke 17%, M'Bochi 12%, other 3%
Language: French (official), Lingala and Monokutuba, many local languages and dialects
Religion: Christian 50%, indigenous religion 48%, Muslim 2%
Currency: Communaute Financiere Africaine franc

COSTA RICA
Location: Middle America, bordering both the Caribbean Sea and the North Pacific Ocean, between Nicaragua and Panama
Area: 19,730 sq mi (51,100 sq km)
Population: 3,674,490
Capital: San Jose
Government: democratic republic
Ethnic groups: Caucasian and Mestizo 96%, Black 2%, Amerindian 1%, Chinese 1%
Language: Spanish (official)
Religion: Roman Catholic 80%, Protestant 15%, other 5%
Currency: Costa Rican colon

COTE d'IVOIRE
Location: Western Africa, bordering the North Atlantic Ocean, between Ghana and Liberia
Area: 124,502 sq mi (322,460 sq km)
Population: 15,818,068
Capital: Yamoussoukro
Government: republic
Ethnic groups: Baoule 23%, Africans from other countries 19%, Bete 18%, Senoufou 15%, Malinke 11%, other 10%, Lebanese 2%, non-Africans 2%
Language: French (official), 60 native dialects with Dioula the most widely spoken
Religion: Muslim 60%, Christian 22%, indigenous 18%
Currency: Communaute Financiere Africaine franc

CROATIA
Location: Southeastern Europe, bordering the Adriatic Sea,

359

Language: Serbo-Croatian (official), other
Religion: Catholic 77%, other (including Muslim) 12%, Orthodox 11%
Currency: Croatian kuna

CUBA

Location: Caribbean, island between the Caribbean Sea and the North Atlantic Ocean, south of Florida
Area: 42,803 sq mi (110,860 sq km)
Population: 11,096,395
Capital: Havana
Government: Communist state
Ethnic groups: Multiracial (Black and Caucasian) 51%, Caucasian 37%, Black 11%, Chinese 1%
Language: Spanish (official)
Religion: Atheist (official) 58%, Roman Catholic 40%, Protestant 2%
Currency: Cuban peso

CYPRUS

Location: Middle East, island

Cypriot pound, Turkish Cypriot area: Turkish lira

CZECH REPUBLIC

Location: Central Europe, southeast of Germany
Area: 30,387 sq mi (78,703 sq km)
Population: 10,280,513
Capital: Prague
Government: parliamentary democracy
Ethnic groups: Czech 94%, Slovak 3%, Polish 1%, German 1%, other 1%
Language: Czech (official), Slovak
Religion: Christian (including Roman Catholic and Protestant) 43%, Atheist 40%, other (including Orthodox) 17%
Currency: koruna

DENMARK

Location: Northern Europe, bordering the Baltic Sea and the North Sea, on a peninsula north of Germany
Area: 16,639 sq mi (43,094

Eskimo, Faroese, German
Language: Danish (official),
Faroese, Greenlandic, German
Religion: Evangelical Lutheran
91%, other 7%, other Protestant
and Roman Catholic 2%
Currency: Danish krone

DJIBOUTI
Location: Eastern Africa, border-
ing the Gulf of Aden and the Red
Sea, between Eritrea and
Somalia
Area: 8,494 sq mi (22,000 sq km)
Population: 447,439
Capital: Djibouti
Government: republic
Ethnic groups: Somali 60%, Afar
35%, other (including French,
Arab, and Ethiopian) 5%
Language: French (official),
Arabic (official), Somali, Afar
Religion: Muslim 94%,
Christian 6%
Currency: Djiboutian franc

DOMINICA
Location: Caribbean, island
between the Caribbean Sea and
the North Atlantic Ocean, about
one-half of the way from Puerto
Rico to Trinidad and Tobago
Area: 290 sq mi (750 sq km)
Population: 64,881
Capital: Roseau
Government: parliamentary
democracy
Ethnic groups: Black 89%,
Multiracial (Black and Caucasian)
7%, Carib Amerindian 2%,
other 2%
Language: English (official),
French patois
Religion: Roman Catholic 77%,

Protestant (including Methodist,
Pentecostal, and Seventh-Day
Adventist) 15%, other/nonreli-
gious 8%
Currency: East Caribbean dollar

DOMINICAN REPUBLIC
Location: Caribbean, eastern
two-thirds of the island of
Hispaniola, east of Haiti
Area: 18,815 sq mi (48,730
sq km)
Population: 8,129,734
Capital: Santo Domingo
Government: republic
Ethnic groups: Multiracial (Black
and Caucasian) 73%, Caucasian
16%, Black 11%
Language: Spanish (official)
Religion: Roman Catholic 95%,
other 5%
Currency: Dominican peso

ECUADOR
Location: Western South
America, bordering the Pacific
Ocean at the Equator, between
Colombia and Peru
Area: 109,483 sq mi (283,560
sq km)
Population: 12,562,496
Capital: Quito
Government: republic
Ethnic groups: Mestizo 55%,
Amerindian 25%, Spanish 10%,
Black 10%
Language: Spanish (official),
Amerindian languages (particu-
larly Quechua)
Religion: Roman Catholic 95%,
other 5%
Currency: sucre

Countries

EGYPT
Location: Northern Africa, bordering the Mediterranean Sea, between Libya and the Gaza Strip
Area: 386,660 sq mi (1,001,450 sq km)
Population: 67,273,906
Capital: Cairo
Government: republic
Ethnic groups: Eastern Hamitic stock (including Egyptians, Bedouins, and Berbers) 99%, other (including Greek, Nubian, and Armenian) 1%
Language: Arabic (official), English, French
Religion: Muslim (primarily Sunni) 94%, other (including Coptic Christian) 6%
Currency: Egyptian pound

EL SALVADOR
Location: Middle America, bordering the North Pacific Ocean, between Guatemala and Honduras
Area: 8,124 sq mi (21,040 sq km)
Population: 5,839,079
Capital: San Salvador
Government: republic
Ethnic groups: Mestizo 94%, Amerindian 5%, Caucasian 1%
Language: Spanish (official), Nahua
Religion: Roman Catholic 78%, Protestant 17%, other 5%
Currency: Salvadoran colon

EQUATORIAL GUINEA
Location: Western Africa, bordering the Bight of Biafra, between Cameroon and Gabon
Area: 10,830 sq mi (28,050 sq km)
Population: 465,746
Capital: Malabo
Government: republic in transition to multiparty democracy
Ethnic groups: Fang 83%, Bubi 10%, Ndowe 4%, Annobonés 2%, other 1%
Language: Spanish (official), French (official), Fang, Bubi
Religion: Christian 89%, indigenous beliefs 5%, other (including Atheist, Muslim, and nonreligious) 6%
Currency: Communaute Financiere Africaine franc

ERITREA
Location: Eastern Africa, bordering the Red Sea, between Djibouti and Sudan
Area: 46,842 sq mi (121,320 sq km)
Population: 3,984,723
Capital: Asmara
Government: transitional government
Ethnic groups: Tigrinya 50%, Tigre and Kunama 40%, Afar 4%, Saho 3%, other 3%
Language: Afar, Amharic, Arabic, Tigre and Kunama, Tigrinya
Religion: Muslim, Coptic Christian, Roman Catholic, Protestant
Currency: nafka

ESTONIA
Location: Eastern Europe, bordering the Baltic Sea and Gulf of Finland, between Latvia and Russia
Area: 17,462 sq mi (45,226 sq km)

Countries

Population: 1,408,523
Capital: Tallinn
Government: parliamentary democracy
Ethnic groups: Estonian 65%, Russian 28%, Ukrainian 3%, other 2%, Byelorussian 2%
Language: Estonian (official), Russian, Ukrainian, English, Finnish, other
Religion: other 66%, Estonian Orthodox 20%, Lutheran 14%
Currency: Estonian kroon

ETHIOPIA
Location: Eastern Africa, west of Somalia
Area: 435,184 sq mi (1,127,127 sq km)
Population: 59,680,383
Capital: Addis Ababa
Government: federal republic
Ethnic groups: Oromo 40%, Amhara and Tigrean 32%, Sidamo 9%, Shankella 6%, Somali 6%, Afar 4%, Gurage 2%, other 1%
Language: Amharic (official), Tigrinya, Orominga
Religion: Muslim 45%–50%, Ethiopian Orthodox 35%–40%, other (including indigenous beliefs) 15%–20%
Currency: birr

FIJI
Location: Oceania, island group in the South Pacific Ocean, about two-thirds of the way from Hawaii to New Zealand
Area: 7,054 sq mi (18,270 sq km)
Population: 812,918
Capital: Suva
Government: republic
Ethnic groups: Fijian 51%, Indian 44%, other (including European, other Pacific Islanders, and overseas Chinese) 5%
Language: English (official), Fijian, Hindustani
Religion: Christian 52%, Hindu 38%, other (including Muslim) 10%
Currency: Fijian dollar

FINLAND
Location: Northern Europe, bordering the Baltic Sea, Gulf of Bothnia, and Gulf of Finland, between Sweden and Russia
Area: 130,127 sq mi (337,030 sq km)
Population: 5,158,372
Capital: Helsinki
Government: republic
Ethnic groups: Finn 93%, Swede 6%, other 1%
Language: Finnish (official), Swedish (official)
Religion: Evangelical Lutheran 89%, other/nonreligious 10%, Greek Orthodox 1%
Currency: markka or Finmark

FRANCE
Location: Western Europe, bordering the Bay of Biscay and English Channel, between Italy and Spain
Area: 211,208 sq mi (547,030 sq km)
Population: 58,978,172
Capital: Paris
Government: republic
Ethnic groups: Celtic/ Latin stock, Slavic, North African, Indochinese, Basque
Language: French (official)

Countries

Religion: Christian (including Roman Catholic and Protestant) 92%, unaffiliated 6%, other (including Jewish and Muslim) 2%
Currency: French franc

GABON
Location: Western Africa, bordering the Atlantic Ocean at the Equator, between Republic of the Congo and Equatorial Guinea
Area: 103,347 sq mi (267,670 sq km)
Population: 1,225,853
Capital: Libreville
Government: republic, multiparty presidential regime
Ethnic groups: Fang, Eshira, Bapounou, Bateke, other Africans, Europeans
Language: French (official), Fang, Myene, Bateke, Bapounou/Eschira, Bandjabi
Religion: Christian 80%, indigenous beliefs 19%, Muslim 1%
Currency: Communaute Financiere Africaine franc

GAMBIA
Location: Western Africa, bordering the North Atlantic Ocean and Senegal
Area: 4,363 sq mi (11,300 sq km)
Population: 1,336,320
Capital: Banjul
Government: republic under multiparty democratic rule
Ethnic groups: African (including Mandinka, Fula, and Wolof) 99%, non-African 1%
Language: English (official), Mandinka, Wolof, Fula

Religion: Muslim 90%, Christian 9%, indigenous beliefs 1%
Currency: dalasi

GEORGIA
Location: Southwestern Asia, bordering the Black Sea, between Turkey and Russia
Area: 26,911 sq mi (69,700 sq km)
Population: 5,066,499
Capital: Tbilisi
Government: republic
Ethnic groups: Georgian 70%, Armenian 8%, Russian 6%, Azeri 6%, other 5%, Ossetian 3%, Abkhaz 2%
Language: Georgian (official), Russian, Armenian, Azeri, other
Religion: Georgian Orthodox and Russian Orthodox 75%, Muslim 11%, other (including Armenian Apostolic and unknown) 14%
Currency: lari

GERMANY
Location: Central Europe, between the Netherlands and Poland, south of Denmark
Area: 137,803 sq mi (356,910 sq km)
Population: 82,087,361
Capital: Berlin
Government: federal republic
Ethnic groups: German 92%, other 5%, Turkish 2%, Italians 1%
Language: German (official)
Religion: Protestant 38%, Roman Catholic 34%, other (including Muslim and unaffiliated) 28%
Currency: deutsche mark

Countries

GHANA

Location: Western Africa, bordering the Gulf of Guinea, between Cote d'Ivoire and Togo
Area: 92,100 sq mi (238,540 sq km)
Population: 18,887,626
Capital: Accra
Government: constitutional democracy
Ethnic groups: Akan 44%, Moshi-Dagomba 16%, Ewe 13%, Ga 8%, other 1%
Language: English (official), African languages (including Akan, Moshi-Dagomba, and Ewe)
Religion: indigenous beliefs 38%, other (including Christian) 32%, Muslim 30%
Currency: new cedi

GREECE

Location: Southern Europe, bordering the Aegean Sea, Ionian Sea, and the Mediterranean Sea, between Albania and Turkey
Area: 50,942 sq mi (131,940 sq km)
Population: 10,707,135
Capital: Athens
Government: parliamentary republic
Ethnic groups: Greek 98%, other 2%
Language: Greek (official), English, French
Religion: Greek Orthodox 98%, Muslim 1%, other 1%
Currency: drachma

GRENADA

Location: Caribbean, island between the Caribbean Sea and Atlantic Ocean, north of Trinidad and Tobago
Area: 131 sq mi (340 sq km)
Population: 97,008
Capital: Saint George's
Government: parliamentary democracy
Ethnic groups: Black 85%, Multiracial (Black and Caucasian) 11%, other 4%
Language: English (official), French patois
Religion: Roman Catholic 53%, other Protestant 33%, Anglican 14%
Currency: East Caribbean dollar

GUATEMALA

Location: Middle America, bordering the Caribbean Sea, between El Salvador and Mexico
Area: 42,042 sq mi (108,890 sq km)
Population: 12,335,580
Capital: Guatemala
Government: republic
Ethnic groups: Mestizo 56%, Amerindian or predominantly Amerindian 44%
Language: Spanish, Amerindian languages
Religion: Roman Catholic, Protestant, traditional Mayan
Currency: quetzal

GUINEA

Location: Western Africa, bordering the North Atlantic Ocean, between Guinea-Bissau and Sierra Leone
Area: 94,927 sq mi (245,860 sq km)
Population: 7,538,953
Capital: Conakry

Countries

Government: republic
Ethnic groups: Peuhl 40%,
Malinke 30%, Soussou 20%,
other tribes 10%
Language: French (official), tribal
languages
Religion: Muslim 85%, Christian
8%, indigenous beliefs 7%
Currency: Guinean franc

GUINEA-BISSAU
Location: Western Africa, border-
ing the North Atlantic Ocean,
between Guinea and Senegal
Area: 13,946 sq mi (36,120
sq km)
Population: 1,234,555
Capital: Bissau
Government: republic
Ethnic groups: Balanta 27%,
Fulani 23%, other 17%, Malinke
12%, Mandyako 11%, Pepel 10%
Language: Portuguese (official),
Crioulo, African languages
Religion: indigenous beliefs
50%, Muslim 45%, Christian 5%
Currency: Communaute
Financiere Africaine franc

GUYANA
Location: Northern South
America, bordering the North
Atlantic Ocean, between
Suriname and Venezuela
Area: 83,000 sq mi (214,970
sq km)
Population: 705,156
Capital: Georgetown
Government: republic
Ethnic groups: East Indian 49%,
Black 32%, Multiracial (Black and
Caucasian) 12%, Amerindian 6%,
Caucasian and Chinese 1%
Language: English (official),
Amerindian dialects
Religion: Christian 57%, Hindu
33%, other (including Muslim)
10%
Currency: Guyanese dollar

HAITI
Location: Caribbean, western
one-third of the island of
Hispaniola, west of the
Dominican Republic
Area: 10,714 sq mi (27,750 sq km)
Population: 6,884,264
Capital: Port-au-Prince
Government: republic
Ethnic groups: Black 95%,
Multiracial (Black and Caucasian)
and Caucasian 5%
Language: French (official),
Creole (official)
Religion: Roman Catholic 80%,
Protestant (including Baptist,
Pentecostal, and Adventist) 16%,
other/nonreligious 4%
Currency: gourde

HONDURAS
Location: Middle America, bor-
dering the Caribbean Sea,
between El Salvador and
Nicaragua
Area: 43,278 sq mi (112,090
sq km)
Population: 5,997,327
Capital: Tegucigalpa
Government: republic
Ethnic groups: Mestizo 90%,
Amerindian 7%, Black 2%,
Caucasian 1%
Language: Spanish (official),
Amerindian dialects
Religion: Roman Catholic 97%,
other 3%
Currency: lempira

HUNGARY
Location: Central Europe, north-west of Romania
Area: 35,919 sq mi (93,030 sq km)
Population: 10,186,372
Capital: Budapest
Government: republic
Ethnic groups: Hungarian 90%, Romani (Gypsy) 4%, German 3%, Serb 2%, other 1%
Language: Hungarian (official), other
Religion: Roman Catholic 68%, Calvinist 20%, other (including Atheist and Lutheran) 12%
Currency: forint

ICELAND
Location: Northern Europe, island between the Greenland Sea and the North Atlantic Ocean, northwest of the United Kingdom
Area: 39,768 sq mi (103,000 sq km)
Population: 272,512
Capital: Reykjavik
Government: constitutional republic
Ethnic groups: homogeneous mixture of Norwegian and Celtic stock
Language: Icelandic (official)
Religion: Evangelical Lutheran 96%, other Protestant and Roman Catholic 3%, none 1%
Currency: Icelandic krona

INDIA
Location: Southern Asia, bordering the Arabian Sea and the Bay of Bengal, between Myanmar and Pakistan
Area: 1,269,340 sq mi (3,287,590 sq km)
Population: 1,000,848,550
Capital: New Delhi
Government: federal republic
Ethnic groups: Indo-Aryan 72%, Dravidian 25%, Mongoloid and other 3%
Language: Hindi (official), English (official), 14 official regional languages, other
Religion: Hindu 80%, Muslim 14%, other (including Christian, Sikh, and Buddhist) 6%
Currency: Indian rupee

INDONESIA
Location: Southeastern Asia, group of islands between the Indian Ocean and the Pacific Ocean
Area: 741,097 sq mi (1,919,440 sq km)
Population: 216,108,345
Capital: Jakarta
Government: republic
Ethnic groups: Javanese 45%, other 26%, Sundanese 14%, Madurese 8%, coastal Malays 7%
Language: Bahasa Indonesia (official), English, Dutch, local dialects
Religion: Muslim 88%, Protestant 5%, other (including Roman Catholic, Hindu, and Buddhist) 7%
Currency: Indonesian rupiah

IRAN
Location: Southwestern Asia, bordering the Gulf of Oman, the Persian Gulf, and the Caspian Sea, between Iraq and Pakistan

2%, other 1%
Language: Persian and Persian dialects (official), Turkic and Turkic dialects, Kurdish, Luri, Balochi, Arabic, Turkish, other
Religion: Shi'a Muslim 89%, Sunni Muslim 10%, other (including Zoroastrian, Jewish, and Christian) 1%
Currency: Iranian rials

IRAQ

Location: Southwestern Asia, bordering the Persian Gulf, between Iran and Kuwait
Area: 168,754 sq mi (437,072 sq km)
Population: 22,427,150
Capital: Baghdad
Government: republic
Ethnic groups: Arab 75%–80%, Kurdish 15%–20%, other (including Turkoman and Assyrian) 5%
Language: Arabic (official), Kurdish
Religion: Shi'a Muslim 60%–65%, Sunni Muslim 32%–37%, other (including Christian) 3%
Currency: Iraqi dinar

IRELAND

Location: Western Europe, island

Anglican 3%, other 5%
Currency: Irish pound

ISRAEL

Location: Southwestern Asia, bordering the Mediterranean Sea, between Egypt and Lebanon
Area: 8,019 sq mi (20,770 sq km)
Population: 5,749,760
Capital: Jerusalem
Government: republic
Ethnic groups: Jewish (including European/American-born, Israeli-born, and African-born) 80%, non-Jewish 20% (primarily Arab)
Language: Hebrew (official), Arabic, English
Religion: Judaism 80%, Islam 15%, other (including Christian) 5%
Currency: new Israeli shekel

ITALY

Location: Southern Europe, peninsula extending into the central Mediterranean Sea, northeast of Tunisia
Area: 116,305 sq mi (301,230 sq km)
Population: 56,735,130
Capital: Rome
Government: republic

Slovene, and Albanian
Language: Italian (official),
German, French, Slovene
Religion: Roman Catholic 98%,
other 2%
Currency: Italian lira (Lit)

JAMAICA
Location: Caribbean, island in
the Caribbean Sea, south of
Cuba
Area: 4,243 sq mi (10,990 sq km)
Population: 2,652,443
Capital: Kingston
Government: parliamentary
democracy
Ethnic groups: Black 90%,
Multiracial (Black and Caucasian)
7%, other 2%, East Indian 1%
Language: English (official),
Creole
Religion: Protestant 61%, other
(including indigenous beliefs)
35%, Roman Catholic 4%
Currency: Jamaican dollar

JAPAN
Location: Eastern Asia, island
chain between the North Pacific
Ocean and the Sea of Japan,
east of the Korean Peninsula
Area: 145,882 sq mi (377,835 sq
km)
Population: 126,182,077
Capital: Tokyo
Government: constitutional
monarchy
Ethnic groups: Japanese 99%,
other 1%
Language: Japanese (official)
Religion: Shinto 51%, Buddhism
38%, other 11%
Currency: yen

JORDAN
Location: Southwestern Asia,
northwest of Saudi Arabia
Area: 34,445 sq mi (89,213 sq
km)
Population: 4,561,147
Capital: Amman
Government: constitutional
monarchy
Ethnic groups: Arab 98%,
Circassian 1%, Armenian 1%
Language: Arabic (official),
English
Religion: Sunni Muslim 96%,
Christian 4%
Currency: Jordanian dinar

KAZAKHSTAN
Location: Central Asia, northwest
of China
Area: 1,049,150 sq mi (2,717,300
sq km)
Population: 16,824,825
Capital: Astana
Government: republic
Ethnic groups: Kazakh (Qazaq)
46%, Russian 35%, other 7%,
Ukrainian 5%, German 3%,
Uzbek 2%, Tatar 2%
Language: Russian (official),
Kazakh (official)
Religion: Muslim 47%, Russian
Orthodox 44%, other (including
Protestant) 9%
Currency: Kazakhstani tenge

KENYA
Location: Eastern Africa, border-
ing the Indian Ocean, between
Somalia and Tanzania
Area: 224,961 sq mi (582,650
sq km)
Population: 28,808,658
Capital: Nairobi

Countries

Government: republic
Ethnic groups: Kikuyu 22%, Luhya 14%, Luo 13%, Kalenjin 12%, Kamba 11%, other (including Asian, European, and Arab) 16%, Kisii 6%, Meru 6%
Language: English (official), Swahili (official), numerous indigenous languages
Religion: Christian (including Protestant and Roman Catholic) 66%, indigenous beliefs 26%, other (including Muslim) 8%
Currency: Kenyan shilling

KIRIBATI

Location: Oceania, group of islands in the Pacific Ocean, about one-half of the way from Hawaii to Australia
Area: 277 sq mi (717 sq km)
Population: 85,501
Capital: Tarawa
Government: republic
Ethnic groups: Micronesian
Language: English (official), Gilbertese
Religion: Roman Catholic 53%, Protestant 41%, other (including Seventh-Day Adventist, Baha'i, and Church of God) 6%
Currency: Australian dollar

KOREA, NORTH

Location: Eastern Asia, northern half of the Korean Peninsula bordering the Korea Bay and the Sea of Japan, between China and South Korea
Area: 46,541 sq mi (120,540 sq km)
Population: 21,386,109
Capital: P'yongyang
Government: Communist state, one-man dictatorship
Ethnic groups: Korean
Language: Korean (official)
Religion: Atheist or nonreligious 68%, indigenous beliefs 16%, other (including Ch'ondogyo and Buddhist) 16%
Currency: North Korean won

KOREA, SOUTH

Location: Eastern Asia, southern half of the Korean Peninsula bordering the Sea of Japan and the Yellow Sea
Area: 38,023 sq mi (98,480 sq km)
Population: 46,884,800
Capital: Seoul
Government: republic
Ethnic groups: Korean
Language: Korean (official)
Religion: other/nonreligious 50%, Buddhism 23%, Christian (including Protestant and Roman Catholic) 27%
Currency: South Korean won

KUWAIT

Location: Southwestern Asia, bordering the Persian Gulf, between Iraq and Saudi Arabia
Area: 6,880 sq mi (17,820 sq km)
Population: 1,991,115
Capital: Kuwait
Government: nominal constitutional monarchy
Ethnic groups: Kuwaiti 45%, other Arab 35%, South Asian 9%, other 7%, Iranian 4%
Language: Arabic (official), English
Religion: Sunni Muslim 45%, Shi'a Muslim 40%, other (including Christian, Hindu, and

Parsi) 15%
Currency: Kuwaiti dinar

KYRGYZSTAN
Location: Central Asia, west of China
Area: 76,641 sq mi (198,500 sq km)
Population: 4,546,055
Capital: Bishkek
Government: republic
Ethnic groups: Kirghiz 52%, Russian 18%, Uzbek 13%, other 12%, Ukrainian 3%, German 2%
Language: Kirghiz (official), Russian (official)
Religion: Muslim 75%, Russian Orthodox 20%, other 5%
Currency: Kyrgyzstani som

LAOS
Location: Southeastern Asia, northeast of Thailand, west of Vietnam
Area: 91,429 sq mi (236,800 sq km)
Population: 5,407,453
Capital: Vientiane
Government: Communist state
Ethnic groups: Lao Loum 68%, Lao Theung 22%, Lao Soung (including the Hmong and the Yao) 9%, ethnic Vietnamese/Chinese 1%
Language: Lao (official), French, English,
Religion: Buddhist 60%, other (including indigenous beliefs) 40%
Currency: new kip

LATVIA
Location: Eastern Europe, bordering the Baltic Sea, between Estonia and Lithuania
Area: 24,938 sq mi (64,589 sq km)
Population: 2,353,874
Capital: Riga
Government: parliamentary democracy
Ethnic groups: Latvian 57%, Russian 30%, Byelorussian 4%, other 3%, Ukrainian 3%, Polish 3%
Language: Lettish (official), Lithuanian, Russian
Religion: other/nonreligious 60%, Christian (including Protestant, Roman Catholic, and Russian Orthodox) 40%
Currency: Latvian lat

LEBANON
Location: Southwestern Asia, bordering the Mediterranean Sea, between Israel and Syria
Area: 4,015 sq mi (10,400 sq km)
Population: 3,562,699
Capital: Beirut
Government: republic
Ethnic groups: Arab 95%, Armenian 4%, other 1%
Language: Arabic (official), French, English, Armenian
Religion: Islam 70%, Christian 30%
Currency: Lebanese pound

LESOTHO
Location: Southern Africa, an enclave of South Africa
Area: 11,718 sq mi (30,350 sq km)
Population: 2,128,950
Capital: Maseru
Government: parliamentary constitutional monarchy

Leone
Area: 43,000 sq mi (111,370 sq km)
Population: 2,923,725
Capital: Monrovia
Government: republic
Ethnic groups: indigenous African tribes 95%, Americo-Liberians 3%, other 2%
Language: English (official), tribal languages
Religion: indigenous beliefs 70%, Muslim 20%, Christian 10%
Currency: Liberian dollar

LIBYA

Location: Northern Africa, bordering the Mediterranean Sea, between Egypt and Tunisia
Area: 679,359 sq mi (1,759,540 sq km)
Population: 4,992,838
Capital: Tripoli
Government: Islamic Arabic Socialist "Mass-State"
Ethnic groups: Arab-Berber 97%, other 3%
Language: Arabic (official), Italian, English
Religion: Sunni Muslim 97%, other 3%
Currency: Libyan dinar

Religion: Roman Catholic 80%, Protestant 7%, other 13%
Currency: Swiss franc, franken, franco

LITHUANIA

Location: Eastern Europe, bordering the Baltic Sea, between Latvia and Russia
Area: 25,174 sq mi (65,200 sq km)
Population: 3,584,966
Capital: Vilnius
Government: parliamentary democracy
Ethnic groups: Lithuanian 81%, Russian 9%, Polish 7%, other 2%, Byelorussian 1%
Language: Lithuanian (official), Polish, Russian
Religion: Roman Catholic 79%, other (including Russian Orthodox and Lutheran) 21%
Currency: Lithuanian litas

LUXEMBOURG

Location: Western Europe, between France and Germany
Area: 998 sq mi (2,586 sq km)
Population: 429,080
Capital: Luxemborg
Government: constitutional

monarchy
Ethnic groups: Celtic base (with
French and German blend),
Portuguese, Italian, and
European
Language: Luxembourgian,
German, French, English
Religion: Roman Catholic 97%,
Protestant and Jewish 3%
Currency: Luxembourg franc

MACEDONIA
Location: Southeastern Europe,
north of Greece
Area: 9,781 sq mi (25,333 sq km)
Population: 2,022,604
Capital: Skopje
Government: emerging democ-
racy
Ethnic groups: Macedonian 66%,
Albanian 23%, Turkish 4%,
Gypsies 3%, Serb 2%, other 2%
Language: Macedonian (official),
Albanian, Turkish, Serbo-
Croatian, other
Religion: Eastern Orthodox 67%,
Muslim 30%, other 3%
Currency: Macedonian denar

MADAGASCAR
Location: Southern Africa, island
in the Indian Ocean, east of
Mozambique
Area: 226,656 sq mi (587,040
sq km)
Population: 14,873,387
Capital: Antananarivo
Government: republic
Ethnic groups: Malayo-
Indonesian, Cotiers, French,
Indian, Creole, Comoran
Language: French (official),
Malagasy (official)
Religion: indigenous beliefs

52%, Christian 41%, Muslim 7%
Currency: Malagasy franc

MALAWI
Location: Southern Africa, east
of Zambia
Area: 45,745 sq mi (118,480
sq km)
Population: 10,000,416
Capital: Lilongwe
Government: multiparty democ-
racy
Ethnic groups: Chewa, Nyanja,
Tumbuko, Yao, Lomwe, Sena,
Tonga, Ngoni, Ngonde, Asian,
European
Language: English (official),
Chichewa (official)
Religion: Protestant 55%, Roman
Catholic 20%, Muslim 20%,
other 5%
Currency: Malawian kwacha

MALAYSIA
Location: Southeastern Asia,
peninsula and northern one-third
of the island of Borneo, south of
Vietnam
Area: 127,317 sq mi (329,750 sq
km)
Population: 21,376,066
Capital: Kuala Lumpur
Government: constitutional
monarchy
Ethnic groups: Malay and other
indigenous 58%, Chinese 26%,
other 9%, Indian 7%,
Language: Bahasa Melayu (offi-
cial), English, Chinese dialects,
Indian languages
Religion: Muslim 53%, Buddhist
17%, other (including Hindu and
Christian) 30%
Currency: ringgit

Countries

MALDIVES
Location: Southern Asia, group of atolls in the Indian Ocean, south-southwest of India
Area: 116 sq mi (300 sq km)
Population: 300,220
Capital: Male
Government: republic
Ethnic groups: Sinhalese, Dravidian, Arab, African
Language: Maldivian Divehi (official), English
Religion: Sunni Muslim 100%
Currency: rufiyaa

MALI
Location: Western Africa, south-west of Algeria
Area: 395,367 sq mi (1,240,000 sq km)
Population: 10,429,124
Capital: Bamako
Government: republic
Ethnic groups: Mande (including Bambara, Malinke, and Sarakole) 50%, Peul 17%, Voltaic 12%, Tuareg and Moor 10%, Songhai 6%, other 5%
Language: French (official), Bambara, numerous African languages
Religion: Muslim 90%, indigenous beliefs 9%, Christian 1%
Currency: Communaute Financiere Africaine franc

MALTA
Location: Southern Europe, islands in the Mediterranean Sea, south of Italy
Area: 124 sq mi (320 sq km)
Population: 381,603
Capital: Valletta
Government: parliamentary democracy
Ethnic groups: Maltese
Language: Maltese (official), English (official)
Religion: Roman Catholic 98%, other 2%
Currency: Maltese lira

MARSHALL ISLANDS
Location: Oceania, group of atolls and reefs in the North Pacific Ocean, about one-half of the way from Hawaii to Papua New Guinea
Area: 70 sq mi (181.3 sq km)
Population: 65,507
Capital: Majuro
Government: republic
Ethnic groups: Micronesian
Language: English (official), Marshallese, Japanese
Religion: Christian (including Protestant and Roman Catholic) 70%, Mormon 3%, other (including Jehovah's Witness) 27%
Currency: United States dollar

MAURITANIA
Location: Northern Africa, bordering the North Atlantic Ocean, between Senegal and Western Sahara
Area: 397,954 sq mi (1,030,700 sq km)
Population: 2,581,738
Capital: Nouakchott
Government: republic
Ethnic groups: Multiracial (predominantly Maur and Black) 40%, Maur 30%, Black 30%
Language: Hasaniya Arabic (official), Wolof (official)
Religion: Muslim 100%
Currency: ouguiya

MAURITIUS

Location: Southern Africa, island in the Indian Ocean, east of Madagascar
Area: 718 sq mi (1,860 sq km)
Population: 1,182,212
Capital: Port Louis
Government: parliamentary democracy
Ethnic groups: Indo-Mauritian 68%, Creole 27%, Sino-Mauritian 3%, Franco-Mauritian 2%
Language: English (official), Creole, French, Hindi, Urdu, Hakka, Bojpoori
Religion: Hindu 52%, Roman Catholic 26%, other (including Muslim) 20%, Protestant 2%
Currency: Mauritian rupee

MEXICO

Location: Middle America, bordering the Caribbean Sea and the Gulf of Mexico, between Guatemala and the U.S.
Area: 761,602 sq mi (1,972,550 sq km)
Population: 100,294,036
Capital: Mexico
Government: federal republic
Ethnic groups: Mestizo 60%, Amerindian or predominantly Amerindian 30%, Caucasian 9%, other 1%
Language: Spanish (official), Mayan dialects
Religion: Roman Catholic 89%, Protestant 6%, other 5%
Currency: New Mexican peso

MICRONESIA

Location: Oceania, island group in the North Pacific Ocean, about three-quarters of the way from Hawaii to Indonesia
Area: 271 sq mi (702 sq km)
Population: 131,500
Capital: Palikir
Government: republic
Ethnic groups: nine ethnic Micronesian and Polynesian groups
Language: English (official), Trukese, Pohnpeian, Yapese, Kosrean
Religion: Roman Catholic 50%, Protestant 47%, other 3%
Currency: United States dollar

MOLDOVA

Location: Eastern Europe, northeast of Romania
Area: 13,067 sq mi (33,843 sq km)
Population: 4,460,838
Capital: Chisinau
Government: republic
Ethnic groups: Moldavian and Romanian 65%, Ukrainian 14%, Russian 13%, Gagauz 4%, Bulgarian 2%, Jewish 2%
Language: Moldovan (official), Russian
Religion: Eastern Orthodox 96%, Jewish 2%, other 2%
Currency: Moldovan leu

MONACO

Location: Western Europe, bordering the Mediterranean Sea, on the southern coast of France, near the border with Italy
Area: .8 sq mi (1.95 sq km)
Population: 32,149
Capital: Monaco
Government: constitutional monarchy
Ethnic groups: French 47%, other

Area: 604,247 sq mi (1,565,000 sq km)
Population: 2,617,379
Capital: Ulaanbaatar
Government: republic
Ethnic groups: Mongol 90%, Kazakh 4%, Chinese 2%, Russian 2%, other 2%
Language: Khalkha Mongol (official), Turkic, Russian, Chinese
Religion: Buddhist 96%, Muslim 4%
Currency: tughrik

MOROCCO

Location: Northern Africa, bordering the North Atlantic Ocean and the Mediterranean Sea, between Algeria and Western Sahara
Area: 172,413 sq mi (446,550 sq km)
Population: 29,661,636
Capital: Rabat
Government: constitutional monarchy
Ethnic groups: Arab-Berber 99%,

groups 99%, other 1%
Language: Portuguese (official), indigenous dialects
Religion: indigenous beliefs 50%, Christian 30%, Muslim 20%
Currency: metical

MYANMAR (BURMA)

Location: Southeastern Asia, bordering the Andaman Sea and the Bay of Bengal, between Bangladesh and Thailand
Area: 261,969 sq mi (678,500 sq km)
Population: 48,081,302
Capital: Rangoon (regime refers to the capital as Yangon)
Government: military regime
Ethnic groups: Burman 68%, Shan 9%, Karen 7%, other 5%, Rakhine 4%, Chinese 3%, Mon 2%, Indian 2%
Language: Burmese (official)
Religion: Buddhist 89%, other (including Muslim and indigenous beliefs) 7%,
Baptist 3%, Roman Catholic 1%

Africa
Area: 318,694 sq mi (825,418 sq km)
Population: 1,648,270
Capital: Windhoek
Government: republic
Ethnic groups: Ovambo 51%, other 16%, Nama 13%, Kavangos 10%, Herero 8%, San 2%
Language: German, English (official), Afrikaans, indigenous languages
Religion: Christian (including Lutheran) 80%, indigenous religions 20%
Currency: Namibian dollar

NAURU
Location: Oceania, island in the South Pacific Ocean, south of the Marshall Islands
Area: 8 sq mi (21 sq km)
Population: 10,605
Capital: government offices in Yaren District
Government: republic
Ethnic groups: Nauruan 58%, other Pacific Islander 26%, Chinese 8%, European 8%
Language: Nauruan (official), English
Religion: Protestant 67%, Roman Catholic 33%
Currency: Australian dollar

NEPAL
Location: Southern Asia, between China and India
Area: 54,363 sq mi (140,800 sq km)
Population: 24,302,653
Capital: Kathmandu
Government: parliamentary democracy
Ethnic groups: Newars, Indians, Tibetans, Gurungs, Magars, Tamangs, Bhotias, Rais, Limbus, Sherpas
Language: Nepali (official), many dialects
Religion: Hindu 87%, Buddhist 8%, other (including Muslim) 5%
Currency: Nepalese rupee

NETHERLANDS, THE
Location: Western Europe, bordering the North Sea, between Belgium and Germany
Area: 16,036 sq mi (41,532 sq km)
Population: 15,807,641
Capital: Amsterdam, The Hague is the seat of government
Government: constitutional monarchy
Ethnic groups: Dutch 94%, other (including Moroccans and Turks) 6%
Language: Dutch (official), other
Religion: Christian (including Roman Catholic and Protestant) 59%, Muslim 3%, other (including unaffiliated) 38%
Currency: Netherlands guilder, gulden, florin

NEW ZEALAND
Location: Oceania, islands in the South Pacific Ocean, southeast of Australia
Area: 103,737 sq mi (268,680 sq km)
Population: 3,662,265
Capital: Wellington
Government: parliamentary democracy
Ethnic groups: European 75%,

377

Countries

Maori 10%, other (including Asian) 12%, Pacific Islander 3%
Language: English (official), Maori
Religion: other/nonreligious 44%, Christian (including Presbyterian and Roman Catholic) 31%, Anglican 21%, Methodist 4%
Currency: New Zealand dollar

NICARAGUA
Location: Middle America, bordering both the Caribbean Sea and the North Pacific Ocean, between Costa Rica and Honduras
Area: 49,998 sq mi (129,494 sq km)
Population: 4,717,132
Capital: Managua
Government: republic
Ethnic groups: Mestizo 69%, Caucasian 17%, Black 9%, Amerindian 5%
Language: Spanish (official)
Religion: Roman Catholic 95%, Protestant 5%
Currency: gold cordoba

NIGER
Location: Western Africa, southeast of Algeria
Area: 489,189 sq mi (1,267,000 sq km)
Population: 9,962,242
Capital: Niamey
Government: republic
Ethnic groups: Hausa 56%, Djerma 22%, Fula 9%, Tuareg 8%, Beri Beri 4%, Arab, Toubou, and Gourmantche 1%
Language: French (official), Hausa, Djerma

Religion: Muslim 89%, indigenous beliefs 11%
Currency: Communaute Financiere Africaine franc

NIGERIA
Location: Western Africa, bordering the Gulf of Guinea, between Benin and Cameroon
Area: 356,668 sq mi (923,770 sq km)
Population: 113,828,587
Capital: Abuja
Government: republic transitioning from military to civilian rule
Ethnic groups: Hausa, Fulani, Yoruba, Ibo, Ijaw, Kanuri, Ibibio, Tiv
Language: English (official), Hausa, Yoruba, Ibo, Fulani
Religion: Muslim 50%, Christian 40%, indigenous beliefs 10%
Currency: naira

NORWAY
Location: Northern Europe, bordering the North Sea and the North Atlantic Ocean, west of Sweden
Area: 125,181 sq mi (324,220 sq km)
Population: 4,438,547
Capital: Oslo
Government: constitutional monarchy
Ethnic groups: Germanic (including Nordic, Alpine, and Baltic), Lapps
Language: Norwegian (official)
Religion: Evangelical Lutheran 88%, other Christian 4%, other/nonreligious 8%
Currency: Norwegian krone

OMAN

Location: Southwestern Asia, bordering the Arabian Sea, Gulf of Oman, and Persian Gulf, between Yemen and United Arab Emirates
Area: 82,031 sq mi (212,460 sq km)
Population: 2,446,645
Capital: Muscat
Government: monarchy
Ethnic groups: Omani Arab 74%, Indian 13%, Bangladeshi 4%, other 4%, Pakistani 3%, Egyptian 2%
Language: Arabic (official), English
Religion: Muslim 88%, Hindu 7%, other (including Christian) 5%
Currency: Omani rial

PAKISTAN

Location: Southern Asia, bordering the Arabian Sea, between India on the east and Iran and Afghanistan on the west and China in the north
Area: 310,402 sq mi (803,940 sq km)
Population: 138,123,359
Capital: Islamabad
Government: federal republic
Ethnic groups: Punjabi, Sindhi, Pashtun, Baloch, Muhajir
Language: Punjabi, Sindhi, Siraiki, Pashtu, Urdu (official), English (official), Burushaski, Balochi, Hindko, Brahui, and other
Religion: Sunni Muslim 77%, Shi'a Muslim 20%, other (including Christian and Hindu) 3%

Currency: Pakistani rupee

PALAU

Location: Oceania, group of islands in the North Pacific Ocean, southeast of the Philippines
Area: 177 sq mi (458 sq km)
Population: 18,467
Capital: Koror
Government: constitutional government in free association with the U.S.
Ethnic groups: Polynesian, Malayan, and Melanesian
Language: English (official), Palauan, Sonsorolese, Angaur, Japanese, Tobi (all official within certain states)
Religion: Christian (including Roman Catholic and Protestant) 63%, Modekngei 27%, other 10%
Currency: United States dollar

PANAMA

Location: Middle America, bordering both the Caribbean Sea and the North Pacific Ocean, between Colombia and Costa Rica
Area: 30,193 sq mi (78,200 sq km)
Population: 2,778,526
Capital: Panama
Government: constitutional republic
Ethnic groups: Mestizo 70%, Amerindian and Multiracial (West Indian) 14%, Caucasian 10%, Amerindian 6%
Language: Spanish (official), English
Religion: Roman Catholic 85%, Protestant 15%

Countries

Currency: balboa

PAPUA NEW GUINEA
Location: Southeastern Asia, group of islands including the eastern half of the island of New Guinea, east of Indonesia
Area: 178,703 sq mi (462,840 sq km)
Population: 4,705,126
Capital: Port Moresby
Government: parliamentary democracy
Ethnic groups: English (official), Motu, many indigenous dialects
Religion: Christian (including Protestant and Roman Catholic) 92%, Anglican 5%, indigenous beliefs 3%
Currency: kina

PARAGUAY
Location: Central South America, northeast of Argentina
Area: 157,046 sq mi (406,750 sq km)
Population: 5,434,095
Capital: Asuncion
Government: republic
Ethnic groups: Mestizo (Mixed Spanish and Amerindian) 95%, Caucasian and Amerindian 5%
Language: Spanish (official), Guarani
Religion: Roman Catholic 89%, Protestant 5%, other 6%
Currency: guarani

PERU
Location: Western South America, bordering the South Pacific Ocean, between Chile and Ecuador
Area: 496,224 sq mi (1,285,220 sq km)
Population: 26,624,582
Capital: Lima
Government: republic
Ethnic groups: Amerindian 45%, Mestizo 37%, Caucasian 15%, other (including Black, Japanese, and Chinese) 3%
Language: Spanish (official), Quechua (official), Aymara
Religion: Roman Catholic 93%, Protestant 6%, other 1%
Currency: nuevo sol

PHILIPPINES
Location: Southeastern Asia, group of islands between the Philippine Sea and the South China Sea, east of Vietnam
Area: 115,830 sq mi (300,000 sq km)
Population: 79,345,812
Capital: Manila
Government: republic
Ethnic groups: Christian Malay 92%, Muslim Malay 4%, other 3%, Chinese 1%
Language: Pilipino (official), English (official)
Religion: Roman Catholic 83%, Protestant 9%, Muslim 5%, other (including Buddhist) 3%
Currency: Philippine peso

POLAND
Location: Central Europe, east of Germany
Area: 120,727 sq mi (312,683 sq km)
Population: 38,608,929
Capital: Warsaw
Government: democratic state
Ethnic groups: Polish 98%, German 1%, other 1%

Language: Polish (official)
Religion: Roman Catholic 95%, other (including Eastern Orthodox and Protestant) 5%
Currency: zloty

PORTUGAL
Location: Southwestern Europe, bordering the North Atlantic Ocean, west of Spain
Area: 35,672 sq mi (92,391 sq km)
Population: 9,918,040
Capital: Lisbon
Government: parliamentary democracy
Ethnic groups: homogeneous Mediterranean stock, African
Language: Portuguese (official)
Religion: Roman Catholic 97%, Protestant denominations 1%, other 2%
Currency: Portuguese escudo

QATAR
Location: Southwestern Asia, peninsula bordering the Persian Gulf and Saudi Arabia
Area: 4,416 sq mi (11,437 sq km)
Population: 723,542
Capital: Doha
Government: traditional monarchy
Ethnic groups: Arab 40%, Pakistani 18%, Indian 18%, other 14%, Iranian 10%
Language: Arabic (official), English
Religion: Muslim 95%, other 5%
Currency: Qatari riyal

ROMANIA
Location: Southeastern Europe, bordering the Black Sea, between Bulgaria and Ukraine
Area: 91,699 sq mi (237,500 sq km)
Population: 22,334,312
Capital: Bucharest
Government: republic
Ethnic groups: Romanian 89%, Hungarian 9%, other 2%
Language: Romanian (official), Hungarian, German
Religion: Romanian Orthodox 70%, unaffiliated 18%, Roman Catholic 6%, Protestant 6%
Currency: leu

RUSSIA
Location: Northern Asia, bordering the Arctic Ocean, between Europe and the North Pacific Ocean
Area: 6,592,741 sq mi (17,075,200 sq km)
Population: 146,393,569
Capital: Moscow
Government: federation
Ethnic groups: Russian 82%, other 8%, Tatar 4%, Ukrainian 3%, Chuvash 1%, Bashkir 1%, Byelorussian 1%
Language: Russian (official), many others
Religion: other/nonreligious 74%, Russian Orthodox 16%, Muslim 10%
Currency: ruble

RWANDA
Location: Central Africa, east of Democratic Republic of the Congo
Area: 10,170 sq mi (26,340 sq km)
Population: 8,154,933
Capital: Kigali

Countries

Government: republic, multiparty presidential system
Ethnic groups: Hutu 80%, Tutsi 19%, Twa 1%
Language: Kinyarwanda (official), French (official), English (official)
Religion: Roman Catholic 65%, other (including indigenous beliefs and Muslim) 26%, Protestant 9%
Currency: Rwandan franc

SAINT KITTS AND NEVIS
Location: Caribbean, islands in the Caribbean Sea, about one-third of the way from Puerto Rico to Trinidad and Tobago
Area: 104 sq mi (269 sq km)
Population: 42,838
Capital: Basseterre
Government: constitutional monarchy
Ethnic groups: Black 95%, other 5%
Language: English (official)
Religion: Protestant 85%, Roman Catholic 7%, other 8%
Currency: East Caribbean dollar

SAINT LUCIA
Location: Caribbean, island between the Caribbean Sea and North Atlantic Ocean, north of Trinidad and Tobago
Area: 239 sq mi (620 sq km)
Population: 154,020
Capital: Castries
Government: constitutional monarchy
Ethnic groups: Black 90%, Multiracial (Black and Caucasian) 6%, East Indian 3%, Caucasian 1%

Language: English (official), French patois
Religion: Roman Catholic 90%, Protestant 7%, Anglican 3%
Currency: East Caribbean dollar

SAINT VINCENT AND THE GRENADINES
Location: Caribbean, islands in the Caribbean Sea, north of Trinidad and Tobago
Area: 131 sq mi (340 sq km)
Population: 120,519
Capital: Kingstown
Government: constitutional monarchy
Ethnic groups: Black 82%, Multiracial (Black and Caucasian) 14%, other 4%
Language: English (official), French patois
Religion: Protestant (including Anglican, Pentecostal, and Methodist) 57%, other/nonreligious 33%
Currency: East Caribbean dollar

SAMOA (FORMERLY WESTERN SAMOA)
Location: Oceania, group of islands in the South Pacific Ocean, about one-half of the way from Hawaii to New Zealand
Area: 1,104 sq mi (2,860 sq km)
Population: 229,979
Capital: Apia
Government: constitutional monarchy
Ethnic groups: Samoan 93%, Euronesians 7%
Language: Samoan (official), English (official)
Religion: Christian 100%

Currency: tala

SAN MARINO
Location: Southern Europe, an enclave in central Italy
Area: 23 sq mi (60 sq km)
Population: 25,061
Capital: San Marino
Government: republic
Ethnic groups: Sammarinese 83%, Italian 12%, other 5%
Language: Italian (official)
Religion: Roman Catholic 95%, other 5%
Currency: Italian lira

SAO TOME AND PRINCIPE
Location: Western Africa, islands straddling the Equator in the Gulf of Guinea, west of Gabon
Area: 386 sq mi (1,000 sq km)
Population: 154,878
Capital: Sao Tome
Government: republic
Ethnic groups: Mestico (Portuguese-African), Angolan, Mozambican
Language: Portuguese (official)
Religion: Roman Catholic 81%, other (including Protestant) 19%
Currency: dobra

SAUDI ARABIA
Location: Southwestern Asia, bordering the Persian Gulf and the Red Sea, north of Yemen
Area: 756,981 sq mi (1,960,582 sq km)
Population: 21,504,613
Capital: Riyadh
Government: monarchy
Ethnic groups: Arab 90%, Afro-Asian 10%
Language: Arabic (official)
Religion: Muslim 100%
Currency: Saudi riyal

SENEGAL
Location: Western Africa, bordering the North Atlantic Ocean, between Guinea-Bissau and Mauritania
Area: 75,749 sq mi (196,190 sq km)
Population: 10,051,930
Capital: Dakar
Government: republic under multiparty democratic rule
Ethnic groups: Wolof 43%, Pular 24%, Serer 15%, other 9%, Diola 4%, Mandink 3%, Soninke 1%, European and Lebanese 1%
Language: French (official), Wolof, Pulaar, Diola, Mandingo
Religion: Muslim 92%, indigenous beliefs 6%, Christian (primarily Roman Catholic) 2%
Currency: Communaute Financiere Africaine franc

SEYCHELLES
Location: Eastern Africa, group of islands in the Indian Ocean, northeast of Madagascar
Area: 176 sq mi (455 sq km)
Population: 79,164
Capital: Victoria
Government: republic
Ethnic groups: Seychellois (mixture of Asian, African, and European stock)
Language: English (official), French (official), Creole
Religion: Roman Catholic 90%, Anglican 8%, other 2%
Currency: Seychelles rupee

Countries

SIERRA LEONE
Location: Western Africa, bordering the North Atlantic Ocean, between Guinea and Liberia
Area: 27,699 sq mi (71,740 sq km)
Population: 5,296,651
Capital: Freetown
Government: constitutional democracy
Ethnic groups: Mende 35%, Temne 32%, Limba 8%, Kono 5%, Bullom-Sherbo 4%, Fulani 4%, Kuranko 4%, Yalunka 3%, other 3%, Kissi 2%
Language: English (official), Mende, Temne, Krio
Religion: Muslim 60%, indigenous beliefs 30%, Christian 10%
Currency: leone

SINGAPORE
Location: Southeastern Asia, islands between Malaysia and Indonesia
Area: 250 sq mi (647.5 sq km)
Population: 3,531,600
Capital: Singapore
Government: republic within commonwealth
Ethnic groups: Chinese 76%, Malay 15%, Indian 6%, other 3%
Language: Chinese (official), Malay (official), Tamil (official), English (official)
Religion: other (including Muslim, Christian, and Hindu) 46%, Buddhist 32%, Taoist 22%
Currency: Singapore dollar

SLOVAKIA
Location: Central Europe, south of Poland
Area: 18,859 sq mi (48,845 sq km)
Population: 5,396,193
Capital: Bratislava
Government: parliamentary democracy
Ethnic groups: Slovak 86%, Hungarian 11%, Romani (Gypsy) 2%, Czech 1%
Language: Slovak (official), Hungarian
Religion: Roman Catholic 60%, other (including Atheist) 28%, Protestant 8%, Orthodox 4%
Currency: koruna

SLOVENIA
Location: Southeastern Europe, eastern Alps bordering the Adriatic Sea, between Austria and Croatia
Area: 7,821 sq mi (20,256 sq km)
Population: 1,970,570
Capital: Ljubljana
Government: parliamentary democratic republic
Ethnic groups: Slovene 91%, Croat 3%, other 3%, Serb 2%, Muslim 1%
Language: Slovenian (official), Serbo-Croatian, other
Religion: Roman Catholic 71%, other (including Atheist, Lutheran, and Muslim) 29%
Currency: tolar

SOLOMON ISLANDS
Location: Oceania, group of islands in the South Pacific Ocean, east of Papua New Guinea
Area: 10,985 sq mi (28,450 sq km)
Population: 455,429
Capital: Honiara
Government: parliamentary

democracy
Ethnic groups: Melanesian 93%,
Polynesian 4%, Micronesian 2%,
European 1%
Language: English (official),
Melanesian, Polynesian
Religion: Anglican 34%, Roman
Catholic 19%, other (including
other Protestant and indigenous
beliefs) 19%, Baptist 17%, United
(Methodist/Presbyterian) 11%,
Currency: Solomon Islands
dollar

SOMALIA
Location: Eastern Africa, border-
ing the Gulf of Aden and the
Indian Ocean, east of Ethiopia
Area: 246,201 sq mi (637,660
sq km)
Population: 7,140,643
Capital: Mogadishu
Government: none
Ethnic groups: Somali 98%,
Bantu 1%, other 1%
Language: Somali (official),
Arabic, Italian, English
Religion: Sunni Muslim 100%
Currency: Somali shilling

SOUTH AFRICA
Location: Southern Africa, at the
southern tip of the continent of
Africa
Area: 471,008 sq mi (1,219,912
sq km)
Population: 43,426,386
Capital: Pretoria (administrative),
Cape Town (legislative),
Bloemfontein (judicial)
Government: republic
Ethnic groups: Black 75%,
Caucasian 14%, Multiracial
(Black and Caucasian) 9%,

Indian 2%
Language: Afrikaans, English,
Ndebele, Pedi, Sotho, Swazi,
Tsonga, Tswana, Venda, Xhosa,
Zulu (all official)
Religion: Christian 67%, indige-
nous and indigenous beliefs
30%, other (including Hindu,
Muslim, and nonreligious) 3%
Currency: rand

SPAIN
Location: Southwestern Europe,
bordering the Bay of Biscay,
Mediterranean Sea, North
Atlantic Ocean, and Pyrenees
Mountains, southwest of France
Area: 194,884 sq mi (504,750
sq km)
Population: 39,167,744
Capital: Madrid
Government: parliamentary
monarchy
Ethnic groups: composite of
Mediterranean and Nordic stock
Language: Castilian Spanish
(official), Catalan, Galician,
Basque
Religion: Roman Catholic 99%,
other 1%
Currency: peseta

SRI LANKA
Location: Southern Asia, island
in the Indian Ocean, south of
India
Area: 25,332 sq mi (65,610
sq km)
Population: 19,144,875
Capital: Colombo
Government: republic
Ethnic groups: Sinhalese 74%,
Tamil 18%, Moor 7%, Burgher,
Malay, and Vedda 1%

Countries

Language: Sinhala (official),
Tamil 18%
Religion: Buddhist 69%, other
(including Christian and Muslim)
16%, Hindu 15%
Currency: Sri Lankan rupee

SUDAN
Location: Northern Africa, bor-
dering the Red Sea, between
Egypt and Eritrea
Area: 967,494 sq mi (2,505,810
sq km)
Population: 34,475,690
Capital: Khartoum
Government: transitional
Ethnic groups: Sudanese Arab
49%, other 12%, Dinka 12%,
Nuba 8%, Beja 6%, Nuer 5%,
Azande 3%, Bari 3%, Fur 2%
Language: Arabic (official),
Nubian, Ta Bedawie
Religion: Sunni Muslim 70%,
indigenous beliefs 25%,
Christian 5%
Currency: Sudanese pound

SURINAME
Location: Northern South
America, bordering the North
Atlantic Ocean, between French
Guiana and Guyana
Area: 63,039 sq mi (163,270
sq km)
Population: 431,156
Capital: Paramaribo
Government: republic
Ethnic groups: Creole 35%, Indo-
Pakistani 33%, Javanese 16%,
Bush Negro 10%, Amerindian
3%, other 3%
Language: Dutch (official),
English, Sranang Tongo,
Hindustani, Javanese

Religion: Hindu 27%, Protestant
25%, Roman Catholic 23%,
Muslim 20%, other (including
indigenous beliefs) 5%
Currency: Surinamese guilder,
gulden, or florin

SWAZILAND
Location: Southern Africa,
between Mozambique and
South Africa
Area: 6,703 sq mi (17,360 sq km)
Population: 985,335
Capital: Mbabane (administra-
tive), Lobamba (legislative)
Government: monarchy, inde-
pendent member of
Commonwealth
Ethnic groups: African 97%,
European 3%
Language: English (official),
siSwati (official)
Religion: Christian 60%, indige-
nous beliefs 40%
Currency: lilangeni

SWEDEN
Location: Northern Europe, bor-
dering the Baltic Sea, Gulf of
Bothnia, Kattegat, and
Skagerrak, between Finland and
Norway
Area: 173,731 sq mi (449,964
sq km)
Population: 8,911,296
Capital: Stockholm
Government: constitutional
monarchy
Ethnic groups: Swedish 89%,
other 6%, Finnish 2%,
Yugoslavian 1%, Iranian 1%,
Bosnian 1%
Language: Swedish (official)
Religion: Evangelical Lutheran

94%, other 4%, Roman
Catholic 2%
Currency: Swedish krona

SYRIA
Location: Southwestern Asia,
bordering the Mediterranean
Sea, between Lebanon and
Turkey
Area: 71,498 sq mi (185,180 sq
km)
Population: 17,213,871
Capital: Damascus
Government: republic under
military regime
Ethnic groups: Arab 90%, Kurds,
Armenians, and other 10%
Language: Arabic (official),
Kurdish, Armenian
Religion: Sunni Muslim 74%,
Alawite, Druze, and other
Muslim sects 16%, Christian
(various sects) 10%
Currency: Syrian pound

TAJIKISTAN
Location: Central Asia, west of
China
Area: 55,251 sq mi (143,100
sq km)
Population: 6,102,854
Capital: Dushanbe
Government: republic
Ethnic groups: Tajik 65%, Uzbek
25%, other 7%, Russian 3%
Language: Tajik (official), Russian
Religion: Sunni Muslim 80%,
other (including Russian
Orthodox) 15%, Shi'a Muslim 5%
Currency: Tajikistani ruble

TANZANIA
Location: Eastern Africa, bordering the Indian Ocean, between

Kenya and Mozambique
Area: 364,900 sq mi (945,090
sq km)
Population: 31,270,820
Capital: Dar es Salaam
Government: republic
Ethnic groups: African 99%,
other 1%
Language: Swahili (official),
English (official), many local lan-
guages
Religion: Christian 45%, Muslim
35%, indigenous beliefs 20%
Currency: Tanzanian shilling

THAILAND
Location: Southeastern Asia,
bordering the Andaman Sea and
the Gulf of Thailand, southeast
of Myanmar
Area: 198,456 sq mi (514,000
sq km)
Population: 60,609,046
Capital: Bangkok
Government: constitutional
monarchy
Ethnic groups: Thai 75%,
Chinese 14%, other 11%
Language: Thai (official), English
Religion: Buddhism 95%,
Muslim 4%, other 1%
Currency: baht

TOGO
Location: Western Africa, border-
ing the Bight of Benin, between
Benin and Ghana
Area: 21,927 sq mi (56,790
sq km)
Population: 5,081,413
Capital: Lome
Government: republic under
transition to multiparty demo-
cratic rule

Countries

•••

Ethnic groups: native African (37 tribes, largest are Ewe, Mina, and Kabre) 99%, European and Syrian-Lebanese less than 1%
Language: French (official), Ewe, Mina, Kabye, Dagomba
Religion: indigenous beliefs 70%, Christian 20%, Muslim 10%
Currency: Communaute Financiere Africaine franc

TONGA
Location: Oceania, group of islands in the South Pacific Ocean, about two-thirds of the way from Hawaii to New Zealand
Area: 289 sq mi (748 sq km)
Population: 109,082
Capital: Nuku'alofa
Government: hereditary constitutional monarchy
Ethnic groups: Polynesian, Europeans
Language: Tongan (official), English (official)
Religion: Free Wesleyan 41%, Roman Catholic 16%, other (including Mormon) 43%
Currency: pa'anga

TRINIDAD AND TOBAGO
Location: Caribbean, islands between the Caribbean Sea and the North Atlantic Ocean, northeast of Venezuela
Area: 1,981 sq mi (5,130 sq km)
Population: 1,102,096
Capital: Port-of-Spain
Government: parliamentary democracy
Ethnic groups: East Indian 40%, Black 40%, Multiracial (Black and Caucasian) 14%, other 4%, Caucasian 1%, Chinese 1%
Language: English (official), Hindi, French, Spanish
Religion: Roman Catholic 32%, Hindu 24%, Anglican 15%, other Protestant 14%, other 9%, Muslim 6%
Currency: Trinidad and Tobago dollar

TUNISIA
Location: Northern Africa, bordering the Mediterranean Sea, between Algeria and Libya
Area: 63,170 sq mi (163,610 sq km)
Population: 9,513,603
Capital: Tunis
Government: republic
Ethnic groups: Arab 98%, European 1%, Jewish and other 1%
Language: Arabic (official), French
Religion: Muslim 98%, Christian 1%, other (including Jewish) 1%
Currency: Tunisian dinar

TURKEY
Location: Southwestern Asia, bordering the Black Sea, between Bulgaria and Georgia, between Greece and Syria
Area: 301,382 sq mi (780,580 sq km)
Population: 65,599,206
Capital: Ankara
Government: republican parliamentary democracy
Ethnic groups: Turkish 80%, Kurdish 20%
Language: Turkish (official), Kurdish, Arabic
Religion: Muslim 100% (primari-

ly Sunni)
Currency: Turkish lira

TURKMENISTAN
Location: Central Asia, bordering the Caspian Sea, between Iran and Kazakhstan
Area: 188,456 sq mi (488,100 sq km)
Population: 4,366,383
Capital: Ashgabat
Government: republio
Ethnic groups: Turkmen 77%, Uzbek 9%, Russian 7%, other 5%, Kazakh 2%
Language: Turkmen (official), Russian, Uzbek, other
Religion: Muslim 89%, Eastern Orthodox 9%, unknown 2%
Currency: Turkmen manat

UGANDA
Location: Eastern Africa, west of Kenya
Area: 91,135 sq mi (236,040 sq km)
Population: 22,804,973
Capital: Kampala
Government: republic
Ethnic groups: other 23%, Baganda 17%, Karamojong 12%, Basogo 8%, Iteso 8%, Langi 6%, Rwanda 6%, Bagisu 5%, Acholi 4%, Lugbara 4%, Bunyoro 3%, Batobo 3%, non-African (European, Asian, Arab) 1%
Language: English (official), Luganda, Swahili
Religion: Christian 65%, indigenous beliefs 19%, other (including Muslim) 16%
Currency: Ugandan shilling

UKRAINE
Location: Eastern Europe, bordering the Black Sea, between Poland and Russia
Area: 233,089 sq mi (603,700 sq km)
Population: 49,811,174
Capital: Kiev
Government: republic
Ethnic groups: Ukrainian 73%, Russian 22%, other 4%, Jewish 1%
Language: Ukrainian (official), Russian, Romanian, Polish, Hungarian
Religion: Ukrainian Orthodox 61%, other (including Protestant, Roman Catholic, and Jewish) 32%, Ukrainian Catholic 7%
Currency: hryvna

UNITED ARAB EMIRATES
Location: Southwestern Asia, bordering the Gulf of Oman and the Persian Gulf, between Oman and Saudi Arabia
Area: 32,000 sq mi (82,880 sq km)
Population: 2,344,402
Capital: Abu Dhabi
Government: federation of emirates
Ethnic groups: South Asian 50%, other Arab and Iranian 23%, Emiri 19%, other (including Westerners and East Asians) 8%
Language: Arabic (official), Persian, English, Hindi, Urdu
Religion: Muslim 96%, other (including Christian and Hindu) 4%
Currency: Emirian dirham

Countries

UNITED KINGDOM
Location: Western Europe, islands between the North Atlantic Ocean and the North Sea, northwest of France
Area: 94,525 sq mi (244,820 sq km)
Population: 59,113,439
Capital: London
Government: constitutional monarchy
Ethnic groups: Caucasian 94%, Asian Indian 2%, other 2%, Pakistani 1%, Black 1%,
Language: English (official), Welsh, Scottish, Gaelic
Religion: Anglican 44%, Muslim 17%, Presbyterian 14%, other (including Hindu, Sikh, and Jewish) 12%, Roman Catholic 10%, Methodist 3%
Currency: British pound

UNITED STATES OF AMERICA
Location: North America, bordering both the North Atlantic Ocean and the North Pacific Ocean, between Canada and Mexico
Area: 3,717,796 sq mi (9,629,091 sq km)
Population: 272,639,608
Capital: Washington, DC
Government: federal republic, strong democratic tradition
Ethnic groups: Caucasian 72%, African-American 12%, Latino 11%, Asian 4%, Amerindian 1%
Language: English, Spanish
Religion: Protestant 56%, Roman Catholic 28%, other/nonreligious 14%, Jewish 2%
Currency: United States dollar

URUGUAY
Location: Southern South America, bordering the South Atlantic Ocean, between Argentina and Brazil
Area: 68,039 sq mi (176,220 sq km)
Population: 3,308,523
Capital: Montevideo
Government: republic
Ethnic groups: Caucasian 88%, Mestizo 8%, Black 4%
Language: Spanish (official)
Religion: Roman Catholic 66%, Protestant 2%, other/nonreligious 30%, Jewish 2%
Currency: Uruguayan peso

UZBEKISTAN
Location: Central Asia, north of Afghanistan
Area: 172,741 sq mi (447,400 sq km)
Population: 24,102,473
Capital: Tashkent
Government: republic
Ethnic groups: Uzbek 80%, Russian 6%, Tajik 5%, Kazakh 3%, Karakalpak 3%, other 2%, Tatar 1%
Language: Uzbek (official), Russian, Tajik, other
Religion: Muslim 88% (primarily Sunni), Eastern Orthodox 9%, other 3%
Currency: Uzbekistani som

VANUATU
Location: Oceania, group of islands in the South Pacific Ocean, about three-quarters of the way from Hawaii to Australia
Area: 5,699 sq mi (14,760 sq km)
Population: 189,036

Capital: Port-Vila
Government: republic
Ethnic groups: Ni-Vanuatu 98%, other 2%
Language: English (official), French (official), Bislama (official)
Religion: Presbyterian 37%, Anglican 15%, Catholic 15%, other 15%, indigenous beliefs 8%, Seventh-Day Adventist 6%, Church of Christ 4%
Currency: vatu

VENEZUELA

Location: Northern South America, bordering the Caribbean Sea and the North Atlantic Ocean, between Colombia and Guyana
Area: 352,143 sq mi (912,050 sq km)
Population: 23,203,466
Capital: Caracas
Government: republic
Ethnic groups: Mestizo 67%, Caucasian (including Spanish, Portuguese, and Italian) 21%, Black 10%, Amerindian 2%
Language: Spanish (official), numerous indigenous dialects
Religion: Roman Catholic 93%, other 7%
Currency: bolivar

VIETNAM

Location: Southeastern Asia, bordering the Gulf of Thailand, Gulf of Tonkin, and South China Sea, alongside China, Laos, and Cambodia
Area: 127,243 sq mi (329,560 sq km)
Population: 77,311,210
Capital: Hanoi
Government: Communist state
Ethnic groups: Vietnamese 87%, other 4%, Tho 2%, Chinese 2%, Tai 2%, Khmer 1%, Muong 1%, Nung 1%
Language: Vietnamese (official), Chinese, English, French, Khmer, tribal languages
Religion: Buddhist, Taoist, Roman Catholic, indigenous beliefs, Islam, Protestant, Cao Dai, Hoa Hao
Currency: new dong

YEMEN

Location: Southwestern Asia, bordering the Arabian Sea, Gulf of Aden, and Red Sea, between Oman and Saudi Arabia
Area: 203,849 sq mi (527,970 sq km)
Population: 16,942,230
Capital: Sanaa
Government: republic
Ethnic groups: predominantly Arab, some Afro-Arab, South Asian
Language: Arabic (official)
Religion: Muslim (including Sunni and Shi'a) 99%, other (including Jewish, Christian, and Hindu) 1%
Currency: Yemeni rial

YUGOSLAVIA

Location: Southeastern Europe, present-day Yugoslavia consists of the republics of Serbia and Montenegro
Area: 39,500 sq mi (102,305 sq km)
Population: 11,206,847
Capital: Belgrade (Serbia),

Countries

Podgorica (Montenegro)
Government: republic
Ethnic groups: Serbian 63%, Albanian 17%, Montenegrin 5%, other 4%, Yugoslav 3%, Hungarian 3%, Muslim 3%, Romani (Gypsy) 1%, Croat 1%
Language: Serbo-Croatian (official), Albanian
Religion: Orthodox 64%, Muslim 19%, other (including Roman Catholic) 17%
Currency: New Dinar

ZAMBIA

Location: Southern Africa, east of Angola
Area: 290,583 sq mi (752,610 sq km)
Population: 9,663,535
Capital: Lusaka
Government: republic
Ethnic groups: African 99%, European 1%
Language: English (official), indigenous
Religion: Christian 50%-75%, Muslim and Hindu 24%-49%, indigenous beliefs 1%
Currency: Zambian kwacha

ZIMBABWE

Location: Southern Africa, northeast of Botswana
Area: 150,803 sq mi (390,580 sq km)
Population: 11,163,160
Capital: Harare
Government: parliamentary democracy
Ethnic groups: Shona 71%, Ndebele 16%, other 12%, Caucasian 1%
Language: English (official), Shona, Sindebele
Religion: Christian-indigenous mix 50%, Christian 25%, indigenous beliefs 24%, other (including Muslim) 1%
Currency: Zimbabwean dollar

THE UNITED STATES DECLARATION OF INDEPENDENCE

IN CONGRESS, July 4, 1776

The Unanimous Declaration of the Thirteen United States of America

When in the course of human events, it becomes necessary for one people to dissolve the political bands which have connected them with another, and to assume among the powers of the earth, the separate and equal station to which the laws of Nature and of Nature's God entitle them, a decent respect to the opinions of mankind requires that they should declare the causes which impel them to the separation.

We hold these truths to be self-evident, that all men are created equal, that they are endowed by their Creator with certain unalienable rights, that among these are life, liberty and the pursuit of happiness. That to secure these rights, governments are instituted among men, deriving their just powers from the consent of the governed,—That whenever any form of government becomes destructive of these ends, it is the right of the people to alter or to abolish it, and to institute new government, laying its foundation on such principles and organizing its powers in such form, as to them shall seem most likely to effect their safety and happiness. Prudence, indeed, will dictate that governments long established should not be changed for light and transient causes; and accordingly all experience hath shown, that mankind are more disposed to suffer, while evils are sufferable, than to right themselves by abolishing the forms to which they are accustomed. But when a long train of abuses and usurpations, pursuing invariably the same object evinces a design to reduce them under absolute despotism, it is their right, it is their duty, to throw off such government, and to provide new guards for their future security.—Such has been the patient sufferance of these Colonies; and such is now the necessity which constrains them to alter their former systems of government. The history of the present King of Great Britain is a history of repeated injuries and usurpations, all having in direct object the establishment of an absolute tyranny over these States. To prove this, let facts be submitted to a candid world.

He has refused his assent to laws, the most wholesome and necessary for the public good.

The Declaration of Independence

He has forbidden his Governors to pass laws of immediate and pressing importance, unless suspended in their operation till his assent should be obtained; and when so suspended, he has utterly neglected to attend to them.

He has refused to pass other laws for the accommodation of large districts of people, unless those people would relinquish the right of representation in the legislature, a right inestimable to them and formidable to tyrants only.

He has called together legislative bodies at places unusual, uncomfortable, and distant from the depository of their public records, for the sole purpose of fatiguing them into compliance with his measures.

He has dissolved Representative Houses repeatedly, for opposing with manly firmness his invasions on the rights of the people.

He has refused for a long time, after such dissolutions, to cause others to be elected; whereby the legislative powers, incapable of annihilation, have returned to the people at large for their exercise; the State remaining in the mean time exposed to all the dangers of invasion from without, and convulsions within.

He has endeavored to prevent the population of these States; for that purpose obstructing the laws for naturalization of foreigners; refusing to pass others to encourage their migration hither, and raising the conditions of new appropriations of lands.

He has obstructed the administration of justice, by refusing his assent to laws for establishing judiciary powers.

He has made judges dependent on his will alone, for the tenure of their offices, and the amount and payment of their salaries.

He has erected a multitude of new offices, and sent hither swarms of officers to harrass our people, and eat out their substance.

He has kept among us, in times of peace, standing armies without the consent of our legislatures.

He has affected to render the military independent of and superior to the civil power.

He has combined with others to subject us to a jurisdiction foreign to our constitution, and unacknowledged by our laws; giving his assent to their acts of pretended legislation:

For quartering large bodies of armed troops among us:

For protecting them, by a mock trial, from punishment for any murders which they should commit on the inhabitants of these States:

For cutting off our trade with all parts of the world:

For imposing taxes on us without our consent:

The Declaration of Independence

For depriving us in many cases, of the benefits of trial by jury:

For transporting us beyond seas to be tried for pretended offenses:

For abolishing the free system of English laws in a neighboring province, establishing therein an arbitrary government, and enlarging its boundaries so as to render it at once an example and fit instrument for introducing the same absolute rule into these Colonies:

For taking away our charters, abolishing our most valuable laws, and altering fundamentally the forms of our governments:

For suspending our own legislatures, and declaring themselves invested with power to legislate for us in all cases whatsoever.

He has abdicated government here, by declaring us out of his protection and waging war against us.

He has plundered our seas, ravaged our coasts, burnt our towns, and destroyed the lives of our people.

He is at this time transporting large armies of foreign mercenaries to complete the works of death, desolation and tyranny, already begun with circumstances of cruelty and perfidy scarcely paralleled in the most barbarous ages, and totally unworthy of the head of a civilized nation.

He has constrained our fellow citizens taken captive on the high seas to bear arms against their country, to become the executioners of their friends and brethren, or to fall themselves by their hands.

He has excited domestic insurrections amongst us, and has endeavored to bring on the inhabitants of our frontiers, the merciless Indian savages, whose known rule of warfare, is an undistinguished destruction of all ages, sexes and conditions.

In every stage of these oppressions we have petitioned for redress in the most humble terms: Our repeated petitions have been answered only by repeated injury. A prince, whose character is thus marked by every act which may define a tyrant, is unfit to be the ruler of a free people.

Nor have we been wanting in attentions to our British brethren. We have warned them from time to time of attempts by their legislature to extend an unwarrantable jurisdiction over us. We have reminded them of the circumstances of our emigration and settlement here. We have appealed to their native justice and magnanimity, and we have conjured them by the ties of our common kindred to disavow these usurpations, which, would inevitably interrupt our connections and correspondence. They too have been deaf to the voice of justice and of consanguinity. We must, therefore, acquiesce in the necessity which denounces our separation, and hold them, as we hold the rest of mankind, enemies in war, in peace friends.

The Declaration of Independence

WE THEREFORE, the Representatives of the United States of America, in General Congress, Assembled, appealing to the Supreme Judge of the world for the rectitude of our intentions, do, in the name, and by authority of the good people of these Colonies, solemnly publish and declare that these United Colonies are, and of right ought to be FREE AND INDEPENDENT STATES; that they are absolved from all allegiance to the British Crown, and that all political connection between them and the State of Great Britain, is and ought to be totally dissolved; and that as free and independent States, they have full power to levy war, conclude peace, contract alliances, establish commerce, and to do all other acts and things which independent States may of right do.

And for the support of this Declaration, with a firm reliance on the protection of Divine Providence, we mutually pledge to each other our lives, our fortunes and our sacred honor.

CONSTITUTION OF THE UNITED STATES

The items in italics are not part of the original text but are widely used today for clarification.

Constitution of the United States [1787]
Preamble
We the People of the United States, in Order to form a more perfect Union, establish Justice, insure domestic Tranquility, provide for the common defense, promote the general Welfare, and secure the Blessings of Liberty to ourselves and our Posterity, do ordain and establish this Constitution for the United States of America.
Article I: *The Legislative Branch*
Section 1
All legislative Powers herein granted shall be vested in a Congress of the United States, which shall consist of a Senate and House of Representatives.
Section 2
Clause 1: The House of Representatives shall be composed of Members chosen every second Year by the People of the several States, and the Electors in each State shall have the Qualifications requisite for Electors of the most numerous Branch of the State Legislature.
Clause 2: No Person shall be a Representative who shall not have attained to the Age of twenty-five Years, and been seven Years a Citizen of the United States, and who shall not, when elected, be an Inhabitant of that State in which he shall be chosen.
Clause 3: Representatives and direct Taxes shall be apportioned among the several States which may be included within this Union, according to their respective Numbers, which shall be determined by adding to the whole Number of free Persons, including those bound to Service for a Term of Years, and excluding Indians not taxed, three-fifths of all other Persons. The actual Enumeration shall be made within three Years after the first Meeting of the Congress of the United States, and within every subsequent Term of ten Years, in such Manner as they shall by Law direct. The Number of Representatives shall not exceed one for every thirty Thousand, but each State shall have at Least one Representative; and until such

Constitution of the United States

enumeration shall be made, the State of New Hampshire shall be entitled to choose three, Massachusetts eight, Rhode Island and Providence Plantations one, Connecticut five, New York six, New Jersey four, Pennsylvania eight, Delaware one, Maryland six, Virginia ten, North Carolina five, South Carolina five, and Georgia three.

Clause 4: When vacancies happen in the Representation from any State, the Executive Authority thereof shall issue Writs of Election to fill such Vacancies.

Clause 5: The House of Representatives shall choose their Speaker and other Officers; and shall have the sole Power of Impeachment.

Section 3

Clause 1: The Senate of the United States shall be composed of two Senators from each State, chosen by the Legislature thereof, for six Years; and each Senator shall have one Vote.

Clause 2: Immediately after they shall be assembled in Consequence of the first Election, they shall be divided as equally as may be into three Classes. The Seats of the Senators of the first Class shall be vacated at the Expiration of the second Year, of the second Class at the Expiration of the fourth Year, and of the third Class at the Expiration of the sixth Year, so that one-third may be chosen every second Year; and if Vacancies happen by Resignation, or otherwise, during the Recess of the Legislature of any State, the Executive thereof may make temporary Appointments until the next Meeting of the Legislature, which shall then fill such Vacancies.

Clause 3: No Person shall be a Senator who shall not have attained to the Age of thirty Years, and been nine Years a Citizen of the United States, and who shall not, when elected, be an Inhabitant of that State for which he shall be chosen.

Clause 4: The Vice President of the United States shall be President of the Senate, but shall have no Vote, unless they be equally divided.

Clause 5: The Senate shall choose their other Officers, and also a President pro tempore, in the Absence of the Vice President, or when he shall exercise the Office of President of the United States.

Clause 6: The Senate shall have the sole Power to try all Impeachments. When sitting for that Purpose, they shall be on Oath or Affirmation. When the President of the United States is tried, the Chief Justice shall preside: And no Person shall be convicted without the Concurrence of two-thirds of the Members present.

Clause 7: Judgment in Cases of Impeachment shall not extend further than to removal from Office, and disqualification to hold and enjoy any Office of honor, Trust or Profit under the United States: but the Party convicted shall nevertheless be liable and subject to Indictment, Trial, Judgment and Punishment, according to Law.

Section 4

Clause 1: The Times, Places and Manner of holding Elections for

Constitution of the United States

Senators and Representatives, shall be prescribed in each State by the Legislature thereof; but the Congress may at any time by Law make or alter such Regulations, except as to the Places of choosing Senators.

Clause 2: The Congress shall assemble at least once in every Year, and such Meeting shall be on the first Monday in December, unless they shall by Law appoint a different Day.

Section 5

Clause 1: Each House shall be the Judge of the Elections, Returns and Qualifications of its own Members, and a Majority of each shall constitute a Quorum to do Business; but a smaller Number may adjourn from day to day, and may be authorized to compel the Attendance of absent Members, in such Manner, and under such Penalties as each House may provide.

Clause 2: Each House may determine the Rules of its Proceedings, punish its Members for disorderly Behavior, and, with the Concurrence of two-thirds, expel a Member.

Clause 3: Each House shall keep a Journal of its Proceedings, and from time to time publish the same, excepting such Parts as may in their Judgment require Secrecy; and the Yeas and Nays of the Members of either House on any question shall, at the Desire of one-fifth of those Present, be entered on the Journal.

Clause 4: Neither House, during the Session of Congress, shall, without the Consent of the other, adjourn for more than three days, nor to any other Place than that in which the two Houses shall be sitting.

Section 6

Clause 1: The Senators and Representatives shall receive a Compensation for their Services, to be ascertained by Law, and paid out of the Treasury of the United States. They shall in all Cases, except Treason, Felony and Breach of the Peace, be privileged from Arrest during their Attendance at the Session of their respective Houses, and in going to and returning from the same; and for any Speech or Debate in either House, they shall not be questioned in any other Place.

Clause 2: No Senator or Representative shall, during the Time for which he was elected, be appointed to any civil Office under the Authority of the United States, which shall have been created, or the Emoluments whereof shall have been increased during such time; and no Person holding any Office under the United States, shall be a Member of either House during his Continuance in Office.

Section 7

Clause 1: All Bills for raising Revenue shall originate in the House of Representatives; but the Senate may propose or concur with Amendments as on other Bills.

Constitution of the United States

Clause 2: Every Bill which shall have passed the House of Representatives and the Senate, shall, before it becomes a Law, be presented to the President of the United States; If he approve he shall sign it, but if not he shall return it, with his Objections to that House in which it shall have originated, who shall enter the Objections at large on their Journal, and proceed to reconsider it. If after such Reconsideration two-thirds of that House shall agree to pass the Bill, it shall be sent, together with the Objections, to the other House, by which it shall likewise be reconsidered, and if approved by two-thirds of that House, it shall become a Law. But in all such Cases the Votes of both Houses shall be determined by yeas and Nays, and the Names of the Persons voting for and against the Bill shall be entered on the Journal of each House respectively. If any Bill shall not be returned by the President within ten Days (Sundays excepted) after it shall have been presented to him, the Same shall be a Law, in like Manner as if he had signed it, unless the Congress by their Adjournment prevent its Return, in which Case it shall not be a Law.

Clause 3: Every Order, Resolution, or Vote to which the Concurrence of the Senate and House of Representatives may be necessary (except on a question of Adjournment) shall be presented to the President of the United States; and before the Same shall take Effect, shall be approved by him, or being disapproved by him, shall be repassed by two-thirds of the Senate and House of Representatives, according to the Rules and Limitations prescribed in the Case of a Bill.

Section 8

Clause 1: The Congress shall have Power To lay and collect Taxes, Duties, Imposts and Excises, to pay the Debts and provide for the common Defense and general Welfare of the United States; but all Duties, Imposts and Excises shall be uniform throughout the United States;

Clause 2: To borrow Money on the credit of the United States;

Clause 3: To regulate Commerce with foreign Nations, and among the several States, and with the Indian Tribes;

Clause 4: To establish a uniform Rule of Naturalization, and uniform Laws on the subject of Bankruptcies throughout the United States;

Clause 5: To coin Money, regulate the Value thereof, and of foreign Coin, and fix the Standard of Weights and Measures;

Clause 6: To provide for the Punishment of counterfeiting the Securities and current Coin of the United States;

Clause 7: To establish Post Offices and post Roads;

Clause 8: To promote the Progress of Science and useful Arts, by securing for limited Times to Authors and Inventors the exclusive Right to their respective Writings and Discoveries;

Clause 9: To constitute Tribunals inferior to the supreme Court;

Clause 10: To define and punish Piracies and Felonies committed on the high Seas, and Offences against the Law of Nations;

Clause 11: To declare War, grant Letters of Marque and Reprisal, and make Rules concerning Captures on Land and Water;

Clause 12: To raise and support Armies, but no Appropriation of Money to that Use shall be for a longer Term than two Years;

Clause 13: To provide and maintain a Navy;

Clause 14: To make Rules for the Government and Regulation of the land and naval Forces;

Clause 15: To provide for calling forth the Militia to execute the Laws of the Union, suppress Insurrections and repel Invasions;

Clause 16: To provide for organizing, arming, and disciplining, the Militia, and for governing such Part of them as may be employed in the Service of the United States, reserving to the States respectively, the Appointment of the Officers, and the Authority of training the Militia according to the discipline prescribed by Congress;

Clause 17: To exercise exclusive Legislation in all Cases whatsoever, over such District (not exceeding ten Miles square) as may, by Cession of particular States, and the Acceptance of Congress, become the Seat of the Government of the United States, and to exercise like Authority over all Places purchased by the Consent of the Legislature of the State in which the Same shall be, for the Erection of Forts, Magazines, Arsenals, dock-Yards, and other needful Buildings;—And

Clause 18: To make all Laws which shall be necessary and proper for carrying into Execution the foregoing Powers, and all other Powers vested by this Constitution in the Government of the United States, or in any Department or Officer thereof.

Section 9

Clause 1: The Migration or Importation of such Persons as any of the States now existing shall think proper to admit, shall not be prohibited by the Congress prior to the Year one thousand eight hundred and eight, but a Tax or duty may be imposed on such Importation, not exceeding ten dollars for each Person.

Clause 2: The Privilege of the Writ of Habeas Corpus shall not be suspended, unless when in Cases of Rebellion or Invasion the public Safety may require it.

Clause 3: No Bill of Attainder or ex post facto Law shall be passed.

Clause 4: No Capitation, or other direct, Tax shall be laid, unless in Proportion to the Census or Enumeration herein before directed to be taken.

Clause 5: No Tax or Duty shall be laid on Articles exported from any State.

Clause 6: No Preference shall be given by any Regulation of

Constitution of the United States

Commerce or Revenue to the Ports of one State over those of another: nor shall Vessels bound to, or from, one State, be obliged to enter, clear, or pay Duties in another.

Clause 7: No Money shall be drawn from the Treasury, but in Consequence of Appropriations made by Law; and a regular Statement and Account of the Receipts and Expenditures of all public Money shall be published from time to time.

Clause 8: No Title of Nobility shall be granted by the United States: And no Person holding any Office of Profit or Trust under them, shall, without the Consent of the Congress, accept of any present, Emolument, Office, or Title, of any kind whatever, from any King, Prince, or foreign State.

Section 10

Clause 1: No State shall enter into any Treaty, Alliance, or Confederation; grant Letters of Marque and Reprisal; coin Money; emit Bills of Credit; make any Thing but gold and silver Coin a Tender in Payment of Debts; pass any Bill of Attainder, ex post facto Law, or Law impairing the Obligation of Contracts, or grant any Title of Nobility.

Clause 2: No State shall, without the Consent of the Congress, lay any Imposts or Duties on Imports or Exports, except what may be absolutely necessary for executing its inspection Laws: and the net Produce of all Duties and Imposts, laid by any State on Imports or Exports, shall be for the Use of the Treasury of the United States; and all such Laws shall be subject to the Revision and Control of the Congress.

Clause 3: No State shall, without the Consent of Congress, lay any Duty of Tonnage, keep Troops, or Ships of War in time of Peace, enter into any Agreement or Compact with another State, or with a foreign Power, or engage in War, unless actually invaded, or in such imminent Danger as will not admit of delay.

Article II: *The Executive Branch*
Section 1

Clause 1: The executive Power shall be vested in a President of the United States of America. He shall hold his Office during the Term of four Years, and, together with the Vice President, chosen for the same Term, be elected, as follows:

Clause 2: Each State shall appoint, in such Manner as the Legislature thereof may direct, a Number of Electors, equal to the whole Number of Senators and Representatives to which the State may be entitled in the Congress: but no Senator or Representative, or Person holding an Office of Trust or Profit under the United States, shall be appointed an Elector.

Clause 3: The Electors shall meet in their respective States, and vote by Ballot for two Persons, of whom one at least shall not be an Inhabitant of the same State with themselves. And they shall make a List of all the Persons voted for, and of the Number of Votes for each; which List they shall sign and certify, and transmit sealed to the Seat of the Government of the United States, directed to the President of the Senate. The President of the Senate shall, in the Presence of the Senate and House of Representatives, open all the Certificates, and the Votes shall then be counted. The Person having the greatest Number of Votes shall be the President, if such Number be a Majority of the whole Number of Electors appointed; and if there be more than one who have such Majority, and have an equal Number of Votes, then the House of Representatives shall immediately choose by Ballot one of them for President; and if no Person have a Majority, then from the five highest on the List the said House shall in like Manner choose the President. But in choosing the President, the Votes shall be taken by States, the Representation from each State having one Vote; A quorum for this Purpose shall consist of a Member or Members from two-thirds of the States, and a Majority of all the States shall be necessary to a Choice. In every Case, after the Choice of the President, the Person having the greatest Number of Votes of the Electors shall be the Vice President. But if there should remain two or more who have equal Votes, the Senate shall choose from them by Ballot the Vice President.

Clause 4: The Congress may determine the Time of choosing the Electors, and the Day on which they shall give their Votes; which Day shall be the same throughout the United States.

Clause 5: No Person except a natural born Citizen, or a Citizen of the United States, at the time of the Adoption of this Constitution, shall be eligible to the Office of President; neither shall any Person be eligible to that Office who shall not have attained to the Age of thirty-five Years, and been fourteen Years a Resident within the United States.

Clause 6: In Case of the Removal of the President from Office, or of his Death, Resignation, or Inability to discharge the Powers and Duties of the said Office, the Same shall devolve on the Vice President, and the Congress may by Law provide for the Case of Removal, Death, Resignation or Inability, both of the President and Vice President, declaring what Officer shall then act as President, and such Officer shall act accordingly, until the Disability be removed, or a President shall be elected.

Clause 7: The President shall, at stated Times, receive for his Services, a Compensation, which shall neither be increased nor diminished during the Period for which he shall have been elected, and he shall not receive within that Period any other Emolument

Constitution of the United States

from the United States, or any of them.

Clause 8: Before he enter on the Execution of his Office, he shall take the following Oath or Affirmation:—"I do solemnly swear (or affirm) that I will faithfully execute the Office of President of the United States, and will to the best of my Ability, preserve, protect and defend the Constitution of the United States."

Section 2

Clause 1: The President shall be Commander in Chief of the Army and Navy of the United States, and of the Militia of the several States, when called into the actual Service of the United States; he may require the Opinion, in writing, of the principal Officer in each of the executive Departments, upon any Subject relating to the Duties of their respective Offices, and he shall have Power to grant Reprieves and Pardons for Offenses against the United States, except in Cases of Impeachment.

Clause 2: He shall have Power, by and with the Advice and Consent of the Senate, to make Treaties, provided two-thirds of the Senators present concur; and he shall nominate, and by and with the Advice and Consent of the Senate, shall appoint Ambassadors, other public Ministers and Consuls, Judges of the supreme Court, and all other Officers of the United States, whose Appointments are not herein otherwise provided for, and which shall be established by Law: but the Congress may by Law vest the Appointment of such inferior Officers, as they think proper, in the President alone, in the Courts of Law, or in the Heads of Departments.

Clause 3: The President shall have Power to fill up all Vacancies that may happen during the Recess of the Senate, by granting Commissions which shall expire at the End of their next Session.

Section 3

He shall from time to time give to the Congress Information of the State of the Union, and recommend to their consideration such Measures as he shall judge necessary and expedient; he may, on extraordinary Occasions, convene both Houses, or either of them, and in Case of Disagreement between them, with Respect to the Time of Adjournment, he may adjourn them to such Time as he shall think proper; he shall receive Ambassadors and other public Ministers; he shall take Care that the Laws be faithfully executed, and shall Commission all the Officers of the United States.

Section 4

The President, Vice President and all civil Officers of the United States, shall be removed from Office on Impeachment for, and Conviction of, Treason, Bribery, or other high Crimes and Misdemeanors.

Article III: *The Judicial Branch*
Section 1
The judicial Power of the United States, shall be vested in one supreme Court, and in such inferior Courts as the Congress may from time to time ordain and establish. The Judges, both of the supreme and inferior Courts, shall hold their Offices during good Behavior, and shall, at stated Times, receive for their Services, a Compensation, which shall not be diminished during their Continuance in Office.

Section 2
Clause 1: The judicial Power shall extend to all Cases, in Law and Equity, arising under this Constitution, the Laws of the United States, and Treaties made, or which shall be made, under their Authority;—to all Cases affecting Ambassadors, other public Ministers and Consuls;—to all Cases of admiralty and maritime Jurisdiction;—to Controversies to which the United States shall be a Party;—to Controversies between two or more States;—between a State and Citizens of another State;—between Citizens of different States,—between Citizens of the same State claiming Lands under Grants of different States, and between a State, or the Citizens thereof, and foreign States, Citizens or Subjects.

Clause 2: In all Cases affecting Ambassadors, other public Ministers and Consuls, and those in which a State shall be Party, the supreme Court shall have original Jurisdiction. In all the other Cases before mentioned, the supreme Court shall have appellate Jurisdiction, both as to Law and Fact, with such Exceptions, and under such Regulations as the Congress shall make.

Clause 3: The Trial of all Crimes, except in Cases of Impeachment, shall be by Jury; and such Trial shall be held in the State where the said Crimes shall have been committed; but when not committed within any State, the Trial shall be at such Place or Places as the Congress may by Law have directed.

Section 3
Clause 1: Treason against the United States, shall consist only in levying War against them, or in adhering to their Enemies, giving them Aid and Comfort. No Person shall be convicted of Treason unless on the Testimony of two Witnesses to the same overt Act, or on Confession in open Court.

Clause 2: The Congress shall have Power to declare the Punishment of Treason, but no Attainder of Treason shall work Corruption of Blood, or Forfeiture except during the Life of the Person attainted.

Article IV: *The States*
Section 1
Full Faith and Credit shall be given in each State to the public Acts,

Clause 3: No Person held to Service or Labor in one State, under the Laws thereof, escaping into another, shall, in Consequence of any Law or Regulation therein, be discharged from such Service or Labour, but shall be delivered up on Claim of the Party to whom such Service or Labor may be due.

Section 3

Clause 1: New States may be admitted by the Congress into this Union; but no new State shall be formed or erected within the Jurisdiction of any other State; nor any State be formed by the Junction of two or more States, or Parts of States, without the Consent of the Legislatures of the States concerned as well as of the Congress.

Clause 2: The Congress shall have Power to dispose of and make all needful Rules and Regulations respecting the Territory or other Property belonging to the United States; and nothing in this Constitution shall be so construed as to Prejudice any Claims of the United States, or of any particular State.

Section 4

The United States shall guarantee to every State in this Union a Republican Form of Government, and shall protect each of them against Invasion; and on Application of the Legislature, or of the Executive (when the Legislature cannot be convened) against domestic Violence.

Provided that no Amendment which may be made prior to the Year One thousand eight hundred and eight shall in any Manner affect the first and fourth Clauses in the Ninth Section of the first Article; and that no State, without its Consent, shall be deprived of its equal Suffrage in the Senate.

Article VI: *Legal Status of the Constitution*
Clause 1: All Debts contracted and Engagements entered into, before the Adoption of this Constitution, shall be as valid against the United States under this Constitution, as under the Confederation.
Clause 2: This Constitution, and the Laws of the United States which shall be made in Pursuance thereof; and all Treaties made, or which shall be made, under the Authority of the United States, shall be the supreme Law of the Land; and the Judges in every State shall be bound thereby, any Thing in the Constitution or Laws of any State to the Contrary notwithstanding.
Clause 3: The Senators and Representatives before mentioned, and the Members of the several State Legislatures, and all executive and judicial Officers, both of the United States and of the several States, shall be bound by Oath or Affirmation, to support this Constitution; but no religious Test shall ever be required as a Qualification to any Office or public Trust under the United States.

Article VII: *Signatures*
The Ratification of the Conventions of nine States, shall be sufficient for the Establishment of this Constitution between the States so ratifying the Same.
Done in Convention by the Unanimous Consent of the States present the Seventeenth Day of September in the Year of our Lord one thousand seven hundred and Eighty seven and of the Independence of the United States of America the Twelfth IN WITNESS whereof We have hereunto subscribed our Names.

The Bill of Rights
Amendments I–X (Adopted 1791)
Amendment I
Congress shall make no law respecting an establishment of religion, or prohibiting the free exercise thereof; or abridging the freedom of speech, or of the press; or the right of the people peaceably to assemble, and to petition the Government for a redress of grievances.
Amendment II
A well-regulated Militia, being necessary to the security of a free State, the right of the people to keep and bear arms, shall not be infringed.

Constitution of the United States

Amendment III

No Soldier shall, in time of peace be quartered in any house, without the consent of the Owner, nor in time of war, but in a manner to be prescribed by law.

Amendment IV

The right of the people to be secure in their persons, houses, papers, and effects, against unreasonable searches and seizures, shall not be violated, and no Warrants shall issue, but upon probable cause, supported by Oath or affirmation, and particularly describing the place to be searched, and the persons or things to be seized.

Amendment V

No person shall be held to answer for a capital, or otherwise infamous crime, unless on a presentment or indictment of a Grand Jury, except in cases arising in the land or naval forces, or in the Militia, when in actual service in time of War or public danger; nor shall any person be subject for the same offense to be twice put in jeopardy of life or limb; nor shall be compelled in any criminal case to be a witness against himself, nor be deprived of life, liberty, or property, without due process of law; nor shall private property be taken for public use, without just compensation.

Amendment VI

In all criminal prosecutions, the accused shall enjoy the right to a speedy and public trial, by an impartial jury of the State and district wherein the crime shall have been committed, which district shall have been previously ascertained by law, and to be informed of the nature and cause of the accusation; to be confronted with the witnesses against him; to have compulsory process for obtaining Witnesses in his favor, and to have the assistance of counsel for his defense.

Amendment VII

In Suits at common law, where the value in controversy shall exceed twenty dollars, the right of trial by jury shall be preserved, and no fact tried by a jury, shall be otherwise reexamined in any Court of the United States, than according to the rules of the common law.

Amendment VIII

Excessive bail shall not be required, nor excessive fines imposed, nor cruel and unusual punishments inflicted.

Amendment IX

The enumeration in the Constitution, of certain rights, shall not be construed to deny or disparage others retained by the people.

Amendment X

The powers not delegated to the United States by the Constitution, nor prohibited by it to the States, are reserved to the States respectively, or to the people.

Constitution of the United States

Amendments 11–27
Adopted 1798–1992
Amendment XI (1795)

The Judicial power of the United States shall not be construed to extend to any suit in law or equity, commenced or prosecuted against one of the United States by Citizens of another State, or by Citizens or Subjects of any Foreign State.

Amendment XII (1804)

The electors shall meet in their respective states and vote by ballot for President and Vice President, one of whom, at least, shall not be an inhabitant of the same state with themselves; they shall name in their ballots the person voted for as President, and in distinct ballots the person voted for as Vice President, and they shall make distinct lists of all persons voted for as President, and of all persons voted for as Vice President, and of the number of votes for each, which lists they shall sign and certify, and transmit sealed to the seat of the government of the United States, directed to the President of the Senate;—The President of the Senate shall, in the presence of the Senate and House of Representatives, open all the certificates and the votes shall then be counted;—The person having the greatest number of votes for President, shall be the President, if such number be a majority of the whole number of Electors appointed; and if no person have such majority, then from the persons having the highest numbers not exceeding three on the list of those voted for as President, the House of Representatives shall choose immediately, by ballot, the President. But in choosing the President, the votes shall be taken by states, the representation from each state having one vote; a quorum for this purpose shall consist of a member or members from two-thirds of the states, and a majority of all the states shall be necessary to a choice. And if the House of Representatives shall not choose a President whenever the right of choice shall devolve upon them, before the fourth day of March next following, then the Vice President shall act as President, as in the case of the death or other constitutional disability of the President. The person having the greatest number of votes as Vice President, shall be the Vice President, if such number be a majority of the whole number of Electors appointed, and if no person have a majority, then from the two highest numbers on the list, the Senate shall choose the Vice President; a quorum for the purpose shall consist of two-thirds of the whole number of Senators, and a majority of the whole number shall be necessary to a choice. But no person constitutionally ineligible to the office of President shall be eligible to that of Vice President of the United States.

Constitution of the United States

Amendment XIII (1865)

Section 1. Neither slavery nor involuntary servitude, except as a punishment for crime whereof the party shall have been duly convicted, shall exist within the United States, or any place subject to their jurisdiction.

Section 2. Congress shall have power to enforce this article by appropriate legislation.

Amendment XIV (1868)

Section 1. All persons born or naturalized in the United States, and subject to the jurisdiction thereof, are citizens of the United States and of the State wherein they reside. No state shall make or enforce any law which shall abridge the privileges or immunities of citizens of the United States; nor shall any State deprive any person of life, liberty, or property, without due process of law; nor deny to any person within its jurisdiction the equal protection of the laws.

Section 2. Representatives shall be apportioned among the several states according to their respective numbers, counting the whole number of persons in each state, excluding Indians not taxed. But when the right to vote at any election for the choice of electors for President and Vice President of the United States, Representatives in Congress, the Executive and Judicial officers of a State, or the members of the Legislature thereof, is denied to any of the male inhabitants of such State, being twenty-one years of age, and citizens of the United States, or in any way abridged, except for participation in rebellion, or other crime, the basis of representation therein shall be reduced in the proportion which the number of such male citizens shall bear to the whole number of male citizens twenty-one years of age in such State.

Section 3. No person shall be a Senator or Representative in Congress, or elector of President and Vice President, or hold any office, civil or military, under the United States, or under any State, who, having previously taken an oath, as a member of Congress, or as an officer of the United States, or as a member of any State legislature, or as an executive or judicial officer of any State, to support the Constitution of the United States, shall have engaged in insurrection or rebellion against the same, or given aid or comfort to the enemies thereof. But Congress may by a vote of two-thirds of each House, remove such disability.

Section 4. The validity of the public debt of the United States, authorized by law, including debts incurred for payment of pensions and bounties for services in suppressing insurrection or rebellion, shall not be questioned. But neither the United States nor any State shall assume or pay any debt or obligation incurred in aid of insurrection or rebellion against the United States, or any claim for the loss or emancipation of any slave; but all such debts, obligations

Constitution of the United States

and claims shall be held illegal and void.

Section 5. The Congress shall have power to enforce, by appropriate legislation, the provisions of this article.

Amendment XV (1870)

Section 1. The right of citizens of the United States to vote shall not be denied or abridged by the United States or by any State on account of race, color, or previous condition of servitude.

Section 2. The Congress shall have power to enforce this article by appropriate legislation.

Amendment XVI (1913)

The Congress shall have power to lay and collect taxes on incomes, from whatever source derived, without apportionment among the several states, and without regard to any census or enumeration.

Amendment XVII (1913)

The Senate of the United States shall be composed of two Senators from each State, elected by the people thereof, for six years; and each Senator shall have one vote. The electors in each State shall have the qualifications requisite for electors of the most numerous branch of the State legislatures.

When vacancies happen in the representation of any State in the Senate, the executive authority of such State shall issue writs of election to fill such vacancies: *Provided,* That the legislature of any State may empower the executive thereof to make temporary appointments until the people fill the vacancies by election as the legislature may direct.

This amendment shall not be so construed as to affect the election or term of any Senator chosen before it becomes valid as part of the Constitution.

Amendment XVIII (1919)

Section 1. After one year from the ratification of this article the manufacture, sale, or transportation of intoxicating liquors within, the importation thereof into, or the exportation thereof from the United States and all territory subject to the jurisdiction thereof for beverage purposes is hereby prohibited.

Section 2. The Congress and the several States shall have concurrent power to enforce this article by appropriate legislation.

Section 3. This article shall be inoperative unless it shall have been ratified as an amendment to the Constitution by the legislatures of the several States, as provided in the Constitution, within seven years from the date of the submission hereof to the states by the Congress.

Amendment XIX (1920)

The right of citizens of the United States to vote shall not be denied or abridged by the United States or by any State on account of sex. Congress shall have power to enforce this article by appropriate

Constitution of the United States

legislation.

Amendment XX (1933)

Section 1. The terms of the President and Vice President shall end at noon on the 20th day of January, and the terms of Senators and Representatives at noon on the 3d day of January, of the years in which such terms would have ended if this article had not been ratified; and the terms of their successors shall then begin.

Section 2. The Congress shall assemble at least once in every year, and such meeting shall begin at noon on the 3d day of January, unless they shall by law appoint a different day.

Section 3. If, at the time fixed for the beginning of the term of the President, the President elect shall have died, the Vice President elect shall become President. If a President shall not have been chosen before the time fixed for the beginning of his term, or if the President elect shall have failed to qualify, then the Vice President elect shall act as President until a President shall have qualified; and the Congress may by law provide for the case wherein neither a President elect nor a Vice President elect shall have qualified, declaring who shall then act as President, or the manner in which one who is to act shall be selected, and such person shall act accordingly until a President or Vice President shall have qualified.

Section 4. The Congress may by law provide for the case of the death of any of the persons from whom the House of Representatives may choose a President whenever the right of choice shall have devolved upon them, and for the case of the death of any of the persons from whom the Senate may choose a Vice President whenever the right of choice shall have devolved upon them.

Section 5. Sections 1 and 2 shall take effect on the 15th day of October following the ratification of this article.

Section 6. This article shall be inoperative unless it shall have been ratified as an amendment to the Constitution by the legislatures of three-fourths of the several states within seven years from the date of its submission.

Amendment XXI (1933)

Section 1. The eighteenth article of amendment to the Constitution of the United States is hereby repealed.

Section 2. The transportation or importation into any State, Territory, or possession of the United States for delivery or use therein of intoxicating liquors, in violation of the laws thereof, is hereby prohibited.

Section 3. This article shall be inoperative unless it shall have been ratified as an amendment to the Constitution by conventions in the several States, as provided in the Constitution, within seven years from the date of the submission hereof to the States by the

Congress.
Amendment XXII (1951)
Section 1. No person shall be elected to the office of the President more than twice, and no person who has held the office of President, or acted as President, for more than two years of a term to which some other person was elected President shall be elected to the office of the President more than once. But this article shall not apply to any person holding the office of President when this article was proposed by the Congress, and shall not prevent any person who may be holding the office of President, or acting as President, during the term within which this article becomes operative from holding the office of President or acting as President during the remainder of such term.
Section 2. This article shall be inoperative unless it shall have been ratified as an amendment to the Constitution by the legislatures of three-fourths of the several states within seven years from the date of its submission to the States by the Congress.
Amendment XXIII (1961)
Section 1. The District constituting the seat of Government of the United States shall appoint in such manner as the Congress may direct:
A number of electors of President and Vice President equal to the whole number of Senators and Representatives in Congress to which the District would be entitled if it were a state, but in no event more than the least populous State; they shall be in addition to those appointed by the States, but they shall be considered, for the purposes of the election of President and Vice President, to be electors appointed by a State; and they shall meet in the District and perform such duties as provided by the twelfth article of amendment.
Section 2. The Congress shall have power to enforce this article by appropriate legislation.
Amendment XXIV (1964)
Section 1. The right of citizens of the United States to vote in any primary or other election for President or Vice President, for electors for President or Vice President, or for Senator or Representative in Congress, shall not be denied or abridged by the United States or any state by reason of failure to pay any poll tax or other tax.
Section 2. The Congress shall have power to enforce this article by appropriate legislation.
Amendment XXV (1967)
Section 1. In case of the removal of the President from office or of his death or resignation, the Vice President shall become President.
Section 2. Whenever there is a vacancy in the office of the Vice President, the President shall nominate a Vice President who shall

Constitution of the United States

take office upon confirmation by a majority vote of both Houses of Congress.

Section 3. Whenever the President transmits to the President pro tempore of the Senate and the Speaker of the House of Representatives his written declaration that he is unable to discharge the powers and duties of his office, and until he transmits to them a written declaration to the contrary, such powers and duties shall be discharged by the Vice President as Acting President.

Section 4. Whenever the Vice President and a majority of either the principal officers of the executive departments or of such other body as Congress may by law provide, transmit to the President pro tempore of the Senate and the Speaker of the House of Representatives their written declaration that the President is unable to discharge the powers and duties of his office, the Vice President shall immediately assume the powers and duties of the office as Acting President.

Thereafter, when the President transmits to the President pro tempore of the Senate and the Speaker of the House of Representatives his written declaration that no inability exists, he shall resume the powers and duties of his office unless the Vice President and a majority of either the principal officers of the executive department or of such other body as Congress may by law provide, transmit within four days to the President pro tempore of the Senate and the Speaker of the House of Representatives their written declaration that the President is unable to discharge the powers and duties of his office. Thereupon Congress shall decide the issue, assembling within forty-eight hours for that purpose if not in session. If the Congress, within twenty-one days after receipt of the latter written declaration, or, if Congress is not in session, within twenty-one days after Congress is required to assemble, determines by two-thirds vote of both Houses that the President is unable to discharge the powers and duties of his office, the Vice President shall continue to discharge the same as Acting President; otherwise, the President shall resume the powers and duties of his office.

Amendment XXVI (1971)

Section 1. The right of citizens of the United States, who are 18 years of age or older, to vote shall not be denied or abridged by the United States or any state on account of age.

Section 2. The Congress shall have power to enforce this article by appropriate legislation.

Amendment XXVII (1992)

No law varying the compensation for the services of the Senators and Representatives shall take effect until an election of Representatives shall have intervened.

STATES

Information on the 50 United States was gathered from the 2000 edition of the World Almanac and Book of Facts and other sources.

ALABAMA
Capital. Montgomery
Area: 52,237 sq mi (135,294 sq km)
Population: (1998) 4,351,999
An East South Central state on the Gulf of Mexico. At the time of European settlement, Alabama was inhabited by peoples including the Creek, Cherokee, Chickasaw, and Alabama. The Spanish explored the land in the 1500s, but the first settlement in 1702 was French. The area changed hands several times, belonging to the British, Spanish, Native Americans, and the U.S. before being admitted into the union on December 14, 1819. Alabama seceded in 1861 but was readmitted in 1868. The region is comprised of hills in the north and coastal plain in the south. It experiences long hot summers and mild winters. Chief manufactured products are paper and chemicals. Chief crops are cotton and greenhouse products.

ALASKA
Capital: Juneau
Area: 615,230 sq mi (1,593,446 sq km)
Population: (1998) 614,010
A state in the Northwest corner of North America, bordered by Canada. At the time of European settlement, Alaska was inhabited by the Tlingit–Haida, Athabascan, Aleut, and Inuit peoples. Russians explored and settled there in the 1700s. The U.S. purchased Alaska from Russia in 1867. In 1896, gold was discovered there and a gold rush resulted. Alaska became a state on January 3, 1959. The climate in the southern and central regions is moist but in the north is very dry. Alaska experiences extended summer days and winter nights. Chief manufactured products are food and petroleum. Chief crops are greenhouse products, barley, and oats. Tourism and fishing are also important industries.

States

ARIZONA
Capital: Phoenix
Area: 114,006 sq mi (295,276 sq km)
Population: (1998) 4,668,631

A Southwest state on the Mexican border. At the time of European settlement, Arizona was inhabited by peoples including the Pueblo, Hohokam, Apache, and Navajo. The Spaniard Coronado explored the area in 1540. Settlements began in the 1700s. Spain ceded the land to Mexico in 1821, who ceded it to the U.S. in 1848. Arizona became a state on February 14, 1912. The Colorado Plateau in the north contains the Grand Canyon. The Mexican Highlands run northwest to southeast. The Sonoran Desert is in the southwest. Arizona is clear and dry but has winter snows in the high central areas. Chief manufactured products are electrical equipment and transportation equipment. Chief crops are cotton and lettuce. Tourism and construction are also important industries.

ARKANSAS
Capital: Little Rock
Area: 53,182 sq mi (137,741 sq km)
Population: (1998) 2,538,303

A South Central state. At the time of European settlement, Arkansas was inhabited by peoples including the Quapaw, Caddo, Osage, and Cherokee. The land was explored in the 1500 and 1600s and first settled in 1686 by France. The U.S. bought the area from France as part of the Louisiana Purchase in 1803. Arkansas was admitted into the union on June 15, 1836. It seceded in 1861 but was readmitted after the Civil War. Arkansas' regions include an eastern delta and prairie, southern lowlands and forests, and northwestern highlands, which include the Ozark Plateaus. The state has long hot summers and mild winters. Chief manufactured products are food and paper. Chief crops are rice, soybeans, and cotton.

CALIFORNIA
Capital: Sacramento
Area: 158,869 sq mi (411,471 sq km)
Population: (1998) 32,666,550

A Pacific state bordering the Pacific Ocean. At the time of European settlement, California was inhabited by peoples including the Hupa, Maidu, Quechan, and Pomo. California was explored by Spain in the 1500s and settled in 1769. U.S. traders took control from Mexico in 1848, the same year that the gold rush began. California was admitted into the union on September 9, 1850. California has mountains in the east and north and on the coast. It has a central valley and southern desert basins. The climate is moderate along the coast but extreme in the interior. Chief manufactured products are electrical equipment and machinery. Chief products are milk, cream, and grapes. Livestock and tourism are also important industries.

COLORADO
Capital: Denver
Area: 104,100 sq mi (269,619 sq km)
Population: (1998) 3,970,971
A West Central state. At the time of European settlement, Colorado was inhabited by peoples including the Ute, Pawnee, Cheyenne, and Arapaho. The area was sold to the U.S. by France as part of the Louisiana Purchase (1803). It became a state on August 1, 1876. Gold discovered in 1858 caused a population boom, which led to disputes between settlers and Native Americans. Colorado experiences low humidity, seasonal temperatures, and alpine conditions in the mountains. Plains in the east lead to a plateau in the center and the Rocky Mountains in the west. Chief manufactured products are scientific instruments and machinery. Chief crops are corn and wheat. Livestock and construction are also important industries.

CONNECTICUT
Capital: Hartford
Area: 5,544 sq mi (14,359 sq km)
Population: (1998) 3,274,069
A New England state bordering the Atlantic Ocean. At the time of European settlement, Connecticut was inhabited by peoples including the Mohegan, Pequot, Niantic, and Paugusset. Dutch and British settlers colonized the area in the 1600s. Connecticut fought in the American Revolution and became the fifth state on January 9, 1788. Connecticut has warm humid summers and cold winters. It has a northwestern upland called the Berkshires, a central lowland, and a hilly eastern upland. Chief manufactured products are transportation equipment and machinery. Chief crops are nursery stock, Christmas trees, and mushrooms.

DELAWARE
Capital: Dover
Area: 2,396 sq mi (6,206 sq km)
Population: (1998) 743,603
A peninsula on the Atlantic Ocean in the Northeast. At the time of European settlement, Delaware was inhabited by the Lenape and

Nanticoke peoples. The Dutch established a settlement in 1631, but it was destroyed during fighting with Native Americans. They settled again in 1651 but lost the land to the British in 1664. Delaware was part of Pennsylvania from 1682–1704. Delaware became the first state by ratifying the Constitution on December 7, 1787. Delaware has a moderate climate. Its northern piedmont slopes into a sea-level plain. Chief manufactured products are chemicals, food, and transportation equipment. Chief crops are soybeans, potatoes, and corn.

FLORIDA
Capital: Tallahassee
Area: 59,928 sq mi (155,214 sq km)
Population: (1998) 14,915,980
A peninsula in the South between the Atlantic Ocean and Gulf of Mexico. At the time of European settlement, Florida was inhabited by peoples including the Timucua, Apalachee, Calusa, and Seminole. The French and Spanish formed settlements in the 1500s. Spain and Britain owned the land before Spain ceded it to the U.S. in 1819. It became a state on March 3, 1845. Florida seceded in 1861 but was readmitted in 1868. The state consists of flat land and rolling hills. Its climate is subtropical in the north and tropical in the south. Chief manufactured products are food and electrical equipment. Chief crops are citrus fruits, vegetables, and melons. Tourism is also an important industry.

GEORGIA
Capital: Atlanta
Area: 58,977 sq mi (152,750 sq km)
Population: (1998) 7,652,207
A South Atlantic state on the Atlantic Ocean. At the time of European settlement, Georgia was inhabited by the Creek and Cherokee peoples. The land was settled by the Spanish in 1566 and the British in 1733. Georgia fought in the American Revolution and became the fourth state on January 2, 1788. Georgia removed its Cherokee population from 1832–38, resulting in the famous Trail of Tears. The state seceded in 1861 but was readmitted in 1870. Its climate is controlled by air masses that are maritime in summer and polar in winter. The state has the Blue Ridge Mountains in the north and northeast, piedmont in the center, and coastal plains in the east. Chief manufactured products are food and textiles. Chief crops are peanuts and cotton.

HAWAII

Capital: Honolulu
Area: 6,459 sq mi (16,729 sq km)
Population: (1998) 1,193,001

Islands in the North Pacific Ocean, 2397 miles southwest of San Francisco, California. At the time of European exploration, Hawaii was inhabited by Polynesian peoples. They remained after the 1778 visit of British captain James Cook. Hawaii became a republic in 1894 and a U.S. territory in 1898. The Japanese attack on Pearl Harbor in 1941 brought the U.S. into WWII. Hawaii was admitted into the union on August 21, 1959. The state has a subtropical climate. Its islands are the tops of a chain of submerged volcanic mountains. Chief manufactured product is food. Chief crops are sugar, pineapples, and macadamia nuts. Tourism and defense are also important industries.

IDAHO

Capital: Boise
Area: 83,574 sq mi (216,457 sq km)
Population: (1998) 1,228,684

A Mountain state in the Northwest bordering Canada. At the time of European settlement, Idaho was inhabited by peoples including the Shoshone, Northern Paiute, Bannock, and Nez Percé. It was explored by Lewis and Clark during their 1804–06 expedition, then settled by fur traders and missionaries. An 1860 gold rush increased the population and the fighting between settlers and Native Americans. Idaho became a state on July 3, 1890. Idaho has southern plains, central mountains and canyons, and northern subalpine conditions. Idaho is colder and drier in its southeastern areas. Chief manufactured products are electrical equipment, food, and wood. Chief crops are potatoes, peas, and dry beans.

ILLINOIS

Capital: Springfield
Area: 57,918 sq mi (150,008 sq km)
Population: (1998) 12,045,326

An East North Central state touching Lake Michigan. At the time of European settlement, Illinois was inhabited by peoples including the Peoria, Cahokia, Kaskaskia, and Tamoroa. Many of these groups joined to form the Illinois Confederacy. Illinois was settled by fur traders and French explorers in the late 1600s. France ceded the region to Britain in 1763, who lost it to the U.S. in 1778. On December 3, 1818, Illinois entered the union. Railroads and industries increased its population throughout the 1800 and 1900s. The climate is temperate, hot in summer and snowy in winter. Its plains are supplemented by hills only in the south. Chief manufactured products are food, machinery, and chemicals. Chief crops are corn, soybeans, and wheat.

INDIANA
Capital: Indianapolis
Area: 36,420 sq mi (94,328 sq km)
Population: (1998) 5,899,195

An East North Central state touching Lake Michigan. At the time of European settlement, Indiana was inhabited by peoples including the Miami, Kickapoo, Wea, and Shawnee. French traders built a post from 1731–32 and were followed by explorers. Britain obtained the area in 1763 but lost it to the U.S. after the American Revolution. Fighting between U.S. forces and Native Americans ended with the defeat of Tecumseh's Indian Confederation in 1811. Indiana became a state on December 11, 1816. Its temperate climate has four seasons. The state consists of southern hills, central plains, and northern flatlands. Chief manufactured products are transportation equipment, primary metals, and chemicals. Chief crops are corn, soybeans, and wheat.

IOWA
Capital: Des Moines
Area: 56,276 sq mi (145,755 sq km)
Population: (1998) 2,862,447

A West North Central state. At the time of European settlement, Iowa was inhabited by peoples including the Iowa, Ottawa, Omaha, and Sioux. The land was claimed by French explorers in 1673. It changed hands several times before France sold it to the U.S. as part of the Louisiana Purchase (1803). Settlers forced Native Americans to leave in the mid-1800s. Iowa became a state on December 28, 1846. It supported the Union during the Civil War. A watershed in Iowa runs northwest to southeast. The north has especially rich soil. The climate is humid and continental. Chief manufactured products are food, machinery, and electrical equipment. Chief crops are silage, corn, and soybeans. Livestock is also an important industry.

KANSAS
Capital: Topeka
Area: 82,282 sq mi (213,110 sq km)
Population: (1998) 2,629,067

A West North Central state. At the time of European settlement, Kansas was inhabited by the Wichita, Pawnee, Kansa, and Osage peoples. The region was settled in the 1600 and 1700s by the Spanish and French. France sold it to the U.S. as part of the Louisiana Purchase (1803). Native Americans were sent to Kansas from other areas in 1830. Violence between pro- and antislavery settlers surrounded the state's admission into the union—as a free state—on January 29, 1861. Kansas has a temperate but continental climate. Plains in the east and west surround a central prairie and hills. Chief manufactured products are transportation equipment and food. Chief crop is wheat. Livestock, especially cattle, is also an important industry.

KENTUCKY
Capital: Frankfort
Area: 40,411 sq mi (104,664 sq km)
Population: (1998) 3,936,499

An East South Central state. At the time of European settlement, Kentucky was inhabited by the Shawnee, Iroquois, Delaware, and Cherokee peoples. American pioneers explored the region in 1750–51 and settled in 1774. Daniel Boone's well-known Wilderness Trail was blazed in 1775. On June 1, 1792, Kentucky was admitted to the union. Kentucky was a Union state during the Civil War, but many Kentuckians were sympathetic to the Confederate cause. The state has a moderate climate. It features mountains in the east, hills in the north, and coal fields in the west. Chief manufactured products are transportation equipment, chemicals, and machinery. Chief crops are tobacco, corn, and soybeans.

LOUISIANA
Capital: Baton Rouge
Area: 49,651 sq mi (128,596 sq km)
Population: (1998) 4,368,967

A West South Central state on the Gulf of Mexico. At the time of European settlement, Louisiana was inhabited by peoples including the Caddo, Tunica, Choctaw, and Chitimacha. La Salle claimed the area for France in 1682. It changed hands several times before France sold it to the U.S. as part of the Louisiana Purchase (1803). Louisiana aided the U.S. during the American Revolution and was admitted into the union on April 30, 1812. The state has a subtropical climate. It consists of lowlands, marshes, and a flood plain surrounding the Mississippi River. Chief manufactured products are chemicals, transportation equipment, and petroleum. Chief crops are soybeans and sugarcane. Tourism is also an important industry.

MAINE
Capital: Augusta
Area: 33,741 sq mi (87,389 sq km)
Population: (1998) 1,244,250
A New England state on the Atlantic Ocean. At the time of European settlement, Maine was inhabited by the Abenaki, Etchemin, Penobscot, and Passamaquoddy peoples. Experts believe John and Sebastian Cabot explored Maine from 1498–99. English colonists settled successfully in the 1620s. Settlers aided in the American Revolution. Maine, which had been part of Massachusetts, became its own state on March 15, 1820. The southern coast has sandy beaches, while the northern coast has rocky peninsulas and fjords. Climate in the north is harsher than in the south. The Appalachian Mountains blanket the state. Chief manufactured products are paper and wood. Chief crops are potatoes and aquaculture. Timber and fishing are also important industries.

MARYLAND
Capital: Annapolis
Area: 12,297 sq mi (31,849 sq km)
Population: (1998) 5,134,808
A South Atlantic state on the Atlantic Ocean. At the time of European settlement, Maryland was inhabited by the Nanticoke, Choptank, Portobago, and Susquehannock peoples. Maryland was visited by French explorer Verrazano in the early 1500s, mapped by British Captain John Smith in 1608, and granted to Cecilius Calvert, Lord Baltimore by King Charles I in 1632. Maryland fought in the American Revolution and became the seventh state on April 28, 1788. Maryland fought for the Union in the Civil War but held slaves. The climate is continental in the west, humid in the east. The land consists of eastern coastal plains and western plateaus and mountains. Chief manufactured products are chemicals and food. Chief crops are greenhouse products.

MASSACHUSETTS
Capital: Boston
Area: 9,241 sq mi (23,934 sq km)
Population: (1998) 6,147,132

A New England state on the Atlantic Ocean. At the time of European settlement, Massachusetts was inhabited by peoples including the Nauset, Massachusett, Nipmuc, and Pocumtuc. The area was initially settled by two British groups: the Pilgrims in 1620 and the Puritans in 1630. The colonists won King Philip's War, 1675–76, ending conflicts with Native Americans. Massachusetts was instrumental in the American Revolution and became the sixth state on February 6, 1788. The region has a temperate climate. It consists of a jagged coast, uplands, and hills. Chief manufactured products are scientific instruments and electrical equipment. Chief crops are cranberries and greenhouse products.

MICHIGAN
Capital: Lansing
Area: 96,705 sq mi (250,466 sq km)
Population: (1998) 9,817,242

An East North Central state bordering Lakes Superior, Michigan, Huron, and Erie. At the time of European settlement, Michigan was inhabited by peoples including the Chippewa, Potawatomi, Ottawa, and Wyandot. The French were exploring the area by 1616 and settling by 1668. Britain seized their settlements in 1763. The U.S. obtained Michigan through the Treaty of Paris (1783), but the British did not leave until 1813. The population increased after the 1825 opening of the Erie Canal. Michigan entered the union on January 26, 1837. The state's Lower Peninsula is hilly, while its Upper Peninsula is swampy with some rugged areas. The Lower Peninsula experiences defined seasons. The Upper Peninsula is colder. Chief manufactured products are transportation equipment and machinery. Chief crops are corn and wheat.

MINNESOTA
Capital: St. Paul
Area: 86,943 sq mi (225,182 sq km)
Population: (1998) 4,725,419

A West North Central state bordering Canada and Lake Superior. At the time of European settlement, Minnesota was inhabited by the Sioux people. French traders and explorers claimed the region in the mid-1600s. The U.S. gained the area east of the Mississippi River, which was owned by Britain, after the American Revolution, and the

States

rest of the state as part of the Louisiana Purchase (1803). On May 11, 1858, Minnesota was admitted into the union. About half of the state is comprised of central hills and the lake region. The northern part of the state lies in a storm belt from the Great Lakes, while the western part lies in the Great Plains. Chief manufactured products are food and machinery. Chief crops are corn and soybeans. Mining is also an important industry.

MISSISSIPPI
Capital: Jackson
Area: 48,286 sq mi (125,061 sq km)
Population: (1998) 2,752,092
An East South Central state on the Gulf of Mexico. At the time of European settlement, Mississippi was inhabited by peoples including the Choctaw, Chickasaw, and Natchez. Though the region was explored in 1540 by Spain's de Soto, it was claimed for France in 1682 by La Salle and settled by the French in 1699. In 1763, Britain obtained the area. The U.S. acquired Mississippi after the American Revolution. The area became a state on December 10, 1817. It seced-ed in 1861 but was readmitted in 1870. The climate in Mississippi is semi-tropical. It has a long growing season, ample rainfall, and mod-erate temperatures. It consists of a fertile delta, a western alluvial plain, northern hills, and coastal plains. Chief manufactured prod-ucts are petroleum, food, and wood. Chief crops are cotton and rice. Warehousing and distribution are also important industries.

MISSOURI
Capital: Jefferson City
Area: 69,709 sq mi (180,546 sq km)
Population: (1998) 5,438,559
A West North Central state. At the time of European settlement, Missouri was inhabited by peoples including the Sauk, Fox, Osage, and Missouri. Spaniard de Soto visited in 1541. French hunters and miners settled around 1735. The land was ceded to Spain, then returned to France before its sale to the U.S. as part of the Louisiana Purchase (1803). Lewis and Clark traversed the state during their 1804–06 expedition. Settlers had displaced the Native Americans by 1836. Missouri became a state on August 10, 1821. It fought for the Union in the Civil War but had divided loyalties. North of the Missouri River are plains and prairie, to the south are rough hills. The climate is continental. Chief manufactured products are trans-portation equipment, chemicals, and food. Chief crops are soybeans and corn. Livestock is also an important industry.

MONTANA
Capital: Helena
Area: 147,046 sq mi (380,849 sq km)
Population: (1998) 880,453
A Mountain state on the Canadian border. At the time of European settlement, Montana was inhabited by peoples including the Blackfoot, Crow, Assinboine, and Kalispel. French explorers visited the land in 1742. The U.S. bought part of it as part of the Louisiana Purchase (1803) and obtained the rest through Lewis and Clark's 1804–06 expedition. Trading posts were established in the early 1800s. Gold, railroads, and mining attracted settlers, who battled the Native Americans for decades. Montana was admitted into the union on November 8, 1889. Montana's climate is cold and continental, with little humidity. The Rocky Mountains are in the west, and the Great Plains are in the east. Chief manufactured products are wood, refined petroleum, and food. Chief crops are wheat and barley. Timber and mining are also important industries.

NEBRASKA
Capital: Lincoln
Area: 77,358 sq mi (20,0357 sq km)
Population: (1998) 1,662,719
A West North Central state. At the time of European settlement, Nebraska was inhabited by peoples including the Pawnee, Ponca, Omaha, and Oto. Spanish and French explorers visited Nebraska before the U.S. obtained it in the Louisiana Purchase (1803). Lewis and Clark explored it during their 1804–06 expedition. The region was reserved for Native Americans, but they were gradually forced onto reservations by settlers who came as early as 1823. Civil War veterans settled under the Homestead Act (1862). Nebraska was admitted into the union on March 1, 1867. Its climate is semi-arid and continental. Its land consists of the Great Plains and hills. Chief manufactured products are food and machinery. Chief crop is corn. Livestock is also an important industry.

NEVADA
Capital: Carson City
Area: 110,567 sq mi (286,369 sq km)
Population: (1998) 1,746,898
A Mountain state. At the time of European settlement, Nevada was inhabited by peoples including the Shoshone, Paiute, Bannock, and Washoe. The Spanish explored Nevada in 1776. Trappers and traders arrived from 1825–27. The U.S. acquired Nevada in 1848 at the end of

the Mexican War. The land, first settled in 1849, attracted many settlers when gold and silver were discovered. It became a state on
October 31, 1864. The climate is arid. The northern area is blanketed
by mountains, the southern area by the Mojave Desert. Chief manufactured products are printed materials, food, and concrete. Chief
crops are hay and alfalfa seed. Mining, gaming, and tourism are also
important industries.

NEW HAMPSHIRE

Capital: Concord
Area: 9,283 sq mi (24,043 sq km)
Population: (1998) 1,185,048
A New England state bordering Canada and the Atlantic Ocean. At
the time of European settlement, New Hampshire was inhabited by
the Penacook and Abenaki peoples. England's Martin Pring and
France's Champlain explored in 1603 and 1605, respectively. The first
settlement followed in 1623. Rogers' Rangers, British frontier scouts,
ended conflicts with Native Americans by 1759. New Hampshire
fought in the American Revolution, adopted a state constitution in
1776, and became the ninth state on June 21, 1788. The land consists
of hills and mountains except at the coast. It has snowy winters and
cool summers with little humidity. Chief manufactured products are
machinery and electrical equipment. Chief crops are dairy and
greenhouse products. Tourism is also an important industry.

NEW JERSEY

Capital: Trenton
Area: 8,215 sq mi (21,277 sq km)
Population: (1998) 8,115,011
A Middle Atlantic state on the Atlantic Ocean. At the time of
European settlement, New Jersey was inhabited by the Lenape people. Verrazano explored the land for France in 1524 and Hudson for
Britain in 1609. Settlers followed in 1660. New Jersey fought in the
American Revolution and was admitted into the union on December
18, 1787 as the third state. Highlands are in the far north, piedmont
is in the north central area, and coastal plain covers the south. The
climate is moderate but extreme between the northeast and southwest. Chief manufactured products are chemicals, printed materials,
and food. Chief crops are greenhouse products and tomatoes.
Pharmaceuticals and telecommunications are also important
industries.

NEW MEXICO
Capital: Santa Fe
Area: 121,598 sq mi (314,939 sq km)
Population: (1998) 1,736,931
A Southwest state on the Mexican border. At the time of European settlement, New Mexico was inhabited by peoples including the Pueblo, Navajo, Apache, and Ute. Franciscan Marcos de Niza and an unnamed slave explored the land in 1539. The first settlement was established in 1598. Settlers fought with the Native Americans but also traded with them, especially after trade began on the Santa Fe Trail in 1821. The U.S. took the area from Mexico in 1846. Conflicts prevented New Mexico from achieving statehood until January 6, 1912. The state is dry and consists of Great Plains in the east, Rocky Mountains in the center, and a plateau in the west. Chief manufactured products are electrical equipment, scientific instruments, and food. Chief crops are hay, onions, and chilies.

NEW YORK
Capital: Albany
Area: 53,989 sq mi (139,832 sq km)
Population: (1998) 18,175,301
A Middle Atlantic state bordering Canada, Lake Ontario, and the Atlantic Ocean. At the time of European settlement, New York was inhabited by peoples including the Mahican, Wappinger, Oneida, and Cayuga. British explorer Hudson and French explorer Champlain visited in 1609. The first settlement, in 1624, was Dutch. New York fought in the American Revolution and became the eleventh state on July 26, 1788. The Erie Canal, completed in 1825, boosted the state's economy. New York has a variable climate. It consists of the Adirondack Mountains in the northeast, coastal plain in the southeast, and the Catskill Mountains in the west. Chief manufactured products are printed materials, scientific instruments, and chemicals. Chief crops are apples, grapes, and strawberries.

NORTH CAROLINA
Capital: Raleigh
Area: 52,672 sq mi (136,420 sq km)
Population: (1998) 7,546,493
A South Atlantic state on the Atlantic Ocean. At the time of European settlement, North Carolina was inhabited by peoples including the Cherokee, Hatteras, Catawba, and Tuscarora. Britain's Sir Walter Raleigh established the first U.S. settlements in 1585 and 1587. Both failed. Virginians settled successfully around 1660. North Carolina

fought in the American Revolution and became the twelfth state on November 21, 1789. It seceded in 1861 but was readmitted in 1868. Its climate is sub-tropical in the east, continental in the center, and variable in the west. Its land consists of eastern coastal plains, central hills, and the western Appalachian Mountains. Chief manufactured products are chemicals, tobacco, and textiles. Chief crops are tobacco and cotton.

NORTH DAKOTA
Capital: Bismarck
Area: 70,704 sq mi (183,123 sq km)
Population: (1998) 638,244
A West North Central state on the Canadian border. At the time of European settlement, North Dakota was inhabited by peoples including the Sioux, Mandan, Arikara, and Hidatsa. French explorers first visited the region in 1738. The U.S. acquired part of the area from France as part of the Louisiana Purchase (1803) and the rest from Britain in 1818. Lewis and Clark explored the land during their 1804–06 expedition. North and South Dakota, which had been a united Dakota, divided and became states on November 2, 1889. The region is generally low-lying and is drained by the Missouri and Red Rivers. It experiences a wide range of temperatures. Chief manufactured products are food and machinery. Chief crops are wheat, barley, rye, oats, sunflowers, and flaxseed. Livestock, especially cattle, is also an important industry.

OHIO
Capital: Columbus
Area: 44,828 sq mi (116,105 sq km)
Population: (1998) 11,209,493
An East North Central state bordering Lake Erie. At the time of European settlement, Ohio was inhabited by the Wyandot, Lenape, Miami, and Shawnee peoples. France claimed the area in 1682 as a result of La Salle's 1669 visit. Traders entered around 1730. France ceded the land to Britain in 1763. British settlers battled the French and Native Americans relentlessly until the Treaty of Paris (1783). The U.S. acquired Ohio after the American Revolution. The first settlement was in 1788. Fighting with Native Americans ended completely in 1794. Ohio entered the union on March 1, 1803. The state has a temperate but variable climate. It consists of plains throughout and a plateau in the east. Chief manufactured products are transportation equipment and machinery. Chief crops are corn and hay.

OKLAHOMA
Capital: Oklahoma City
Area: 69,903 sq mi (181,049 sq km)
Population: (1998) 3,346,713
A West South Central state. At the time of European settlement, Oklahoma was inhabited by peoples including the Arapaho, Kiowa, Wichita, and Caddo. Spain's Coronado arrived in 1541. French traders entered in the 1500 and 1600s. The U.S. bought Oklahoma as part of the Louisiana Purchase (1803) and reserved it for Native Americans. Homesteading began in 1889. The land received by each settler was determined by lotteries or by runs (races to be the first to claim a piece of land). Oklahoma entered the union on November 16, 1907. The land consists of western plains and small eastern mountains. The temperate climate is humid in the east and dry in the west. Chief manufactured products are machinery, electrical equipment, rubber, and plastic. and mineral and energy exploration and production. Chief crops are wheat and cotton. Livestock and energy production are also important industries.

OREGON
Capital: Salem
Area: 97,132 sq mi (251,572 sq km)
Population: (1998) 3,281,974
A Pacific state on the Pacific Ocean. At the time of European settlement, Oregon was inhabited by peoples including the Chinook, Cayuse, Modoc, and Nez Percé. Lewis and Clark explored the land during their 1804–06 expedition. Traders arrived in 1811, settlers in 1834. Beginning in 1843, the Oregon Trail brought many to the area. Oregon entered the union on February 14, 1859. The state is comprised of coastal mountains, the eastern Cascade Mountains, a plateau east of the Cascades, and a southern valley. The coast is mild and humid. The interior is continental and dry. Chief manufactured products are wood, electrical equipment, and food. Chief crops are greenhouse products, hay, and wheat. Electronics and lumber are also important industries.

PENNSYLVANIA
Capital: Harrisburg
Area: 46,058 sq mi (119,290 sq km)
Population: (1998) 12,001,451
A Middle Atlantic state touching Lake Erie. At the time of European settlement, Pennsylvania was inhabited by peoples including the Lenape, Shawnee, Susquehannocks, and Erie. Swedish settlements

established in 1643 were taken by the Dutch, then by the British, then given to William Penn in 1681. During the American Revolution, Philadelphia was the colonies' capital and the signing place of the Declaration of Independence (1776) and the Constitution (1787). Pennsylvania became the second state on December 12, 1787. It fought for the Union in the Civil War. The Allegheny Mountains run southwest to northeast. Piedmont and coast plains are in the southeast, plateaus are in the north and west. The state has a continental climate. Chief manufactured products are chemicals, food, and electrical equipment. Chief crops are corn and hay.

RHODE ISLAND
Capital: Providence
Area: 1,231 sq mi (3,188 sq km)
Population: (1998) 988,480
A New England state on the Atlantic Ocean. At the time of European settlement, Rhode Island was inhabited by the Narragansett, Niantic, Nipmuc, and Wampanoag peoples. Verrazano explored for France in 1524. Roger Williams, banished from the Massachusetts Bay Colony, established the first settlement in 1636. Settlers fought the Native Americans in King Philip's War; conflicts ended by 1675. Rhode Island fought in the American Revolution and became the thirteenth state on May 29, 1790. The state consists of eastern lowlands and western uplands. Its climate is variable. Chief manufactured products are jewelry and silverware. Chief crops are nursery products and vegetables. Fishing is also an important industry.

SOUTH CAROLINA
Capital: Columbia
Area: 31,189 sq mi (80,780 sq km)
Population: (1998) 3,835,962
A South Atlantic state on the Atlantic Ocean. At the time of European settlement, South Carolina was inhabited by peoples including the Cherokee, Catawba, Muskogean, and Yamasee. English settlers first colonized the area in 1670. South Carolina fought in the American Revolution and became the eighth state on May 23, 1788. The state was the first to secede, in 1860, igniting the Civil War. It was readmitted in 1868. The state is humid and subtropical, although the mountains are cooler and receive more precipitation. South Carolina consists of the Blue Ridge Mountains in the northwest, piedmont in the north central area, and coastal plains in the south and east. Chief manufactured products are chemicals, textiles, and machinery. Chief crops are tobacco and cotton. Tourism is also an important industry.

SOUTH DAKOTA
Capital: Pierre
Area: 77,121 sq mi (199,743 sq km)
Population: (1998) 738,171

A West North Central state. At the time of European settlement, South Dakota was inhabited by peoples including the Mandan, Hidatsa, Arikara, and Sioux. The area was visited by the French Verendrye brothers from 1742–43. The U.S. acquired it as part of the Louisiana Purchase (1803). Lewis and Clark explored during their 1804–06 expedition. The first trading post was established in 1817, and settlements grew after gold was discovered in 1874. South Dakota entered the union on November 2, 1889, the year that the Great Sioux Agreement relegated Native Americans to reservations. South Dakota has extreme temperatures and is humid and windy. Prairie is in the east, Great Plains in the west, and Black Hills in the southwest. Chief manufactured products are machinery, food, and scientific instruments. Chief crop is corn. Livestock is also an important industry.

TENNESSEE
Capital: Nashville
Area: 42,146 sq mi (109,158 sq km)
Population: (1998) 5,430,621

An East South Central state. At the time of European settlement, Tennessee was inhabited by the Creek, Yuchi, Cherokee, and Chickasaw peoples. Spanish explorers visited the area in 1541. English and French traders and explorers arrived in the late 1600s. In 1769, Virginians established the first settlement. Tennessee helped fight in the American Revolution. It entered the union on June 1, 1796. The state seceded in 1861 but its loyalties were divided. It was readmitted in 1866. Tennessee's humid climate is continental in the north, subtropical in the south. The Great Smoky Mountains cover the east, plateaus the interior, and Gulf Coast Plains the west. Chief manufactured products are chemicals, transportation equipment, and food. Chief crops are tobacco and cotton.

TEXAS
Capital: Austin
Area: 267,277 sq mi (692,247 sq km)
Population: (1998) 19,759,614

A Southwest state bordering Mexico and the Gulf of Mexico. At the time of European settlement, Texas was inhabited by peoples including the Coahuiltecan, Karankawa, Caddo, and Comanche peoples.

States

Spain explored the area in 1541 and settled in 1682. Texas was part of Mexico until it rebelled in 1835. In 1836, Texas defeated Mexico and established the Republic of Texas. This government existed until December 29, 1845, when Texas became a state. Texas' climate is variable. Gulf Coast Plains are in the south and east, Great Plains in the north, and the Trans-Pecos basin and range in the east. Chief manufactured products are chemicals, electrical equipment, and food. Chief crop is cotton. Livestock, especially cattle, and oil and gas extraction are also important industries.

UTAH

Capital: Salt Lake City
Area: 84,904 sq mi (219901 sq km)
Population: (1998) 2,099,758

A Middle Rocky Mountain state. At the time of European settlement, Utah was inhabited by the Ute, Gosiute, Paiute, and Shoshone peoples. Spanish missionaries visited Utah in 1776 and were followed by traders. Mormons established the first settlements in 1847. The U.S. made Utah a territory in 1850. The Union and Pacific Railroads, which met in Utah, brought economic growth. On January 4, 1896, Utah was admitted into the union. Utah's arid climate is warm in the southwest and alpine in the northeast. The Great Basin is in the west, the Great Salt Lake and flats are in the northwest, the Rocky Mountains are in the northeast, and plateaus are in the southeast. Chief manufactured products are transportation equipment, food, and primary metals. Chief crops are hay and corn.

VERMONT

Capital: Montpelier
Area: 9,615 sq mi (24,903 sq km)
Population: (1998) 590,883

A New England state on the Canadian border. At the time of European settlement, Vermont was inhabited by the Abenaki, Mahican, Penacook, and Iroquois peoples. Champlain, a French explorer, arrived in 1609. The first settlement was established in 1724. Vermont helped with the American Revolution and the War of 1812. It entered the union on March 4, 1791. The Green Mountains run north to south through the state. It experiences an extreme range of temperatures. Chief manufactured products are electrical equipment and printed materials. Chief crops are dairy products, apples, and maple syrup. Tourism is also an important industry.

VIRGINIA

Capital: Richmond
Area: 42,326 sq mi (109,624 sq km)
Population: (1998) 6,791,345

A South Atlantic state on the Atlantic Ocean. At the time of European settlement, Virginia was inhabited by peoples including the Cherokee, Susquehanna, Powhatan, and Monacan. English settlers established a colony in 1607. Virginia was instrumental in the American Revolution. It became the tenth state on June 25, 1788. Virginia seceded in 1861. Richmond was the capital of the Confederacy. Virginia was readmitted to the union in 1870. The state has a mild climate. It consists of the Appalachian Mountains in the west, piedmont in the center, and coastal plains in the east. Chief manufactured products are chemicals, tobacco, and food. Chief crops are tobacco and grain corn.

WASHINGTON

Capital: Olympia
Area: 70,637 sq mi (182,950 sq km)
Population: (1998) 5,689,263

A Pacific state bordering Canada and the Pacific Ocean. At the time of European settlement, Washington was inhabited by peoples including the Yakima, Cayuse, Spokane, and Chinook. Explorers sighted the area in the late 1700s. Lewis and Clark explored during their 1804–06 expedition. In 1810 and 1811, trading posts were established by Canada and the U.S. In 1848, Washington became part of the Oregon Territory. The 1855 discovery of gold attracted settlers. Washington was admitted into the union on November 11, 1889. The state consists of the Olympic Mountains in the northwest, the Columbia Basin in the center, and Cascade Mountains in the east. Its climate is mild. Chief manufactured products are transportation equipment, food, and machinery. Chief crop is apples. Lumber and aerospace technology are also important industries.

WEST VIRGINIA

Capital: Charleston
Area: 24,231 sq mi (62,758 sq km)
Population: (1998) 1,811,156

An East Central state. At the time of European settlement, West Virginia was inhabited by the Iroquois, Cherokee, and Shawnee peoples. British explorers visited in 1671. Subsequent U.S. explorers included George Washington in 1753 and Daniel Boone. West Virginia, which was part of Virginia, was generally ruled by the eastern part of the state. When Virginia seceded in 1861, the western area created its own state, becoming West Virginia on June 20, 1863. West Virginia consists of hills and mountains, especially in the western Allegheny Plateau. Its climate is humid continental. Chief manufactured products are chemicals and primary metals. Chief crops are apples and peaches. Mining is also an important industry.

WISCONSIN
Capital: Madison
Area: 65,499 sq mi (169,642 sq km)
Population: (1998) 5,223,500
An East North Central state bordering Lakes Michigan and Superior. At the time of European settlement, Wisconsin was inhabited by the Dakota, Menominee, and Winnebago peoples. French explorer Nicolet arrived in 1634. The area was passed to Britain in 1763, then to the U.S. after the American Revolution. Hostilities between settlers and Native Americans increased as more people arrived in Wisconsin. Railroads were active by 1851. Wisconsin fought for the Union in the Civil War. The state has long, cold winters and short, warm summers. It has northern plains and highlands, central plains, western uplands, and eastern ridges and lowlands. Chief manufactured products are machinery, food, and paper. Chief crop is corn. Dairy production is also an important industry.

WYOMING
Capital: Cheyenne
Area: 97,818 sq mi (253,349 sq km)
Population: (1998) 480,907
A Mountain state. At the time of European settlement, Wyoming was inhabited by peoples including the Shoshone, Crow, Sioux, and Arapaho. French Verendrye brothers arrived in 1743. Colter of the U.S. visited Yellowstone in 1807–08. The 1820s brought traders and trappers. The Union Pacific Railroad (1868) and Forts Laramie and Bridger brought settlers and economic growth. In 1869, the territory was the first to allow women's suffrage. Wyoming became a state on July 10, 1890. Its climate is semi-arid. The state consists of the Continental Divide running northwest to southeast, central deserts and basins, and eastern Great Plains and Rocky Mountain foothills. Chief manufactured products are chemicals and petroleum. Chief crop is wheat. Oil, gas, and mineral extraction are also important industries.

UNITED STATES PRESIDENTS

Information on the United States presidents was gathered from the 2000 edition of the World Almanac and Book of Facts and other sources.

Washington, George (1732–99)
1st U.S. president (1789–97). A Virginia Federalist, Washington was a surveyor and commander of Virginia's troops during the French and Indian War. He was a member of the Continental Congress before being named commander of the Continental Army in 1775. His leadership was instrumental during the American Revolution. Washington was unanimously chosen as president at the 1787 federal convention. He was unanimously elected to a second term but declined a third.

Adams, John (1735–1826)
2nd U.S. president (1797–1801). Born in Massachusetts, Adams was a Federalist and served on the Continental Congress and the Declaration of Independence drafting committee. Adams was elected vice president in 1789 and 1792 before winning the presidency. While president, he faced public and partisan division concerning the French Revolution and was criticized for supporting the Alien and Sedition Acts (1798). Adams was defeated in the 1800 election. He authored books about government and law before and after his presidential term.

Jefferson, Thomas (1743–1826)
3rd U.S. president (1801–09). A Democrat-Republican from Virginia. Before becoming president, Jefferson's political positions included the Continental Congress, governor of Virginia, U.S. secretary of state, and vice president. He drafted and signed the Declaration of Independence in 1776. Jefferson was elected president by the U.S. House of Representatives because of a tie in the electoral college. While president, he purchased Louisiana from France and sent Lewis and Clark to explore the new land. Jefferson founded the University of Virginia in 1819.

United States Presidents

Madison, James (1751–1836)
4th U.S. president (1809–17). A Democrat-Republican from Virginia. Madison served on the Continental Congress. His leadership in the Constitutional Convention (1787) earned him the title "father of the Constitution." Madison was one of the writers of the Federalist Papers, was a member of the U.S. House of Representatives, and was secretary of state before being elected president. During his presidency, the U.S. fought and won the War of 1812.

Monroe, James (1758–1831)
5th U.S. president (1817–25). Monroe, a Democrat-Republican from Virginia, served as a soldier and officer in the American Revolution. He practiced law and was a member of the Continental Congress and the U.S. Senate, a foreign minister, governor of Virginia, and negotiator of the Louisiana Purchase. While president, Monroe cancelled Spain's debt to the U.S. in return for Florida, made legal the Missouri Compromise, and announced the Monroe Doctrine. His presidency is called the "era of good feeling" because peace existed among various government sectors.

Adams, John Q. (1767–1848)
6th U.S. president (1825–29). A Democrat-Republican from Massachusetts, Adams served as minister to several foreign nations and in the U.S. Senate in the late 1700s. In 1811, he declined appointment to the U.S. Supreme Court. Adams helped negotiate the 1814 Treaty of Ghent. As secretary of state, Adams was the architect of the 1823 Monroe Doctrine. After serving two terms as president, Adams was elected to Congress in 1831, where he served until his death.

Jackson, Andrew (1767–1845)
7th U.S. president (1829–37). A lawyer and Democrat from South Carolina, Jackson was a member of the U.S. House of Representatives and the U.S. Senate before commanding the Tennessee militia in battle against Native Americans in Florida and Louisiana. Jackson served as governor of the Florida territory. He entered the Democratic presidential race unsuccessfully in 1824 but was elected president in the following two elections. During Jackson's presidency, the national debt was paid and westward expansion increased.

Van Buren, Martin (1782–1862)
8th U.S. president (1837–41). Van Buren, a lawyer and Democrat from New York, served as governor of New York, U.S. secretary of state, and vice president before his election to the presidency. Van Buren's first year in office was also the beginning of the country's first major depression, the Panic of 1837. The crisis was not caused by Van Buren, but by the failure of Congress to limit the sale of public land. People speculated in land so much that their loans were not backed by gold or silver. Van Buren created the independent treasury, which protected government funds but probably prevented his reelection. Van Buren unsuccessfully ran for president in 1840 and 1848.

Harrison, William H. (1773–1841)
9th U.S. president (1841). A Whig from Virginia, Harrison spent decades in the military, entering as a soldier and advancing to major general as he led forces against Native Americans and the British. Especially important was his leadership in the Battle of Tippecanoe Creek in 1811. Harrison began his political career in the U.S. House of Representatives. He then served as minister to Colombia. After running for president unsuccessfully in 1836, Harrison won in 1840 with the slogan "Tippecanoe and Tyler too," alluding to his military history and his running mate, John Tyler. After serving only one month as president, Harrison died of pneumonia.

Tyler, John (1790–1862)
10th U.S. president (1841–45). A lawyer and Whig from Virginia, Tyler was in the U.S. House of Representatives and the U.S. Senate and was governor of Virginia. As William H. Harrison's running mate in the 1840 election, Tyler was elected vice president. He became president in 1841 upon Harrison's death. While president, Tyler established the U.S. Weather Bureau, signed the Preemption Act of 1841, and annexed Texas. Democrats renominated Tyler for the 1844 election, but he withdrew because Polk was the official Democratic candidate.

Polk, James K. (1795–1849)
11th U.S. president (1845–49). Polk, a Democrat, was born in North Carolina but lived in Tennessee and served two years as the governor of Tennessee. As president, Polk negotiated the Oregon boundary with Britain, fought and won the Mexican War (1846-48), and annexed much of the southwest and California. Polk did not seek reelection. He died a few weeks after leaving office.

United States Presidents

Taylor, Zachary (1784–1850)
12th U.S. president (1849–50). A Whig from Virginia, Taylor served in the military, advancing to brevetted major general. He fought Native Americans in the Northwest and South, the War of 1812, and the Mexican War, in which his forces defeated Mexican troops at Buena Vista even though they were outnumbered 4-1. Taylor was nominated for president and elected because of his military fame. In the year before his death in office, Taylor struggled to admit California and New Mexico to the union amid slavery disputes.

Fillmore, Millard (1800–74)
13th U.S. president (1850–53). A lawyer and a Whig from New York, Fillmore began his career in federal politics as a member of the U.S. House of Representatives and as vice president. He became president upon Taylor's death in 1850. As president, Fillmore addressed the slavery issue through the Compromise of 1850 and signed the Fugitive Slave Law. Because neither expansionists nor slaveholders were pleased with Fillmore's policies, he was not renominated in 1852. Fillmore ran again in 1856 but was unsuccessful.

Pierce, Franklin (1804–69)
14th U.S. president (1853–57). A lawyer and Democrat from New Hampshire, Pierce served in the U.S. House of Representatives and in the U.S. Senate. He fought in the Mexican War, advancing to brigadier general. As president, Pierce passed the Kansas-Nebraska Act (1854), which allowed popular vote in those two states to determine their position on slavery. He also purchased land from Mexico (Gadsden Purchase) and created the U.S. Court of Claims. Pierce was not renominated in the 1856 election.

Buchanan, James (1791–1868)
15th U.S. president (1857–61). Buchanan was a Democrat from Pennsylvania. He served in the U.S. House of Representatives and the U.S. Senate, spent terms as minister to Russia and Britain, and helped draft the Ostend Manifesto, which stated that the U.S. would be right in taking Cuba from Spain if their refusal to sell it continued. As president, Buchanan denied that states had a right to secede, and he tried to pacify secessionists. Though inconsistent, he supported popular sovereignty of states to decide their stance on slavery. Buchanan was not renominated in the 1860 election.

United States Presidents

Lincoln, Abraham (1809–65)

16th U.S. president (1861–65). A lawyer and Republican, Lincoln was born in Kentucky but spent most of his life in Indiana. He was a member of the U.S. House of Representatives and impressed the public during his 1858 campaign for the U.S. Senate. Lincoln lost the Senate race but was elected president two years later. Lincoln was president during the Civil War. The highlights of his years leading the Union are the Emancipation Proclamation (1863) and the Gettysburg Address (1863). Lincoln was reelected in 1864 but was assassinated only one month after the beginning of his second term and only five days after the surrender of General Lee and the Confederates.

Johnson, Andrew (1808–75)

17th U.S. president (1865–69). Johnson was born in North Carolina but lived in Tennessee. He was a tailor before serving in the U.S. House of Representatives, as governor of Tennessee, and in the U.S. Senate. He led Tennessee's Union troops in the Civil War and advanced to the rank of brigadier general. Though a Democrat, Johnson became a Republican vice president in 1864. He became president upon Lincoln's death. Because Johnson disagreed with Congress about aspects of Reconstruction, he was impeached in 1868. Though acquitted in the Senate trial, he was not renominated in the 1868 election. In 1874, Johnson was elected to the U.S. Senate.

Grant, Ulysses S. (1822–85)

18th U.S. president (1869–77). A Republican from Ohio, Grant served as an officer in the Mexican and Civil Wars. During the latter, he commanded troops most notably at Fort Henry, Fort Donelson, Shiloh, Vicksburg, and Chattanooga, advancing to General of the U.S. Army. Grant received General Lee's surrender in 1865. During Grant's first term as president, he signed the 15th Amendment and an amnesty bill. His second term was marred by corruption in both the Treasury Department and the Indian Service and by speculators' attempts to control the gold market. Upon retirement, Grant toured the world and published his memoirs.

Hayes, Rutherford B. (1822–93)

19th U.S. president (1877–81). Hayes, a lawyer and Republican from Ohio, served in the Civil War, advancing to the rank of brevetted major general. Hayes served in the U.S. House of Representatives and as governor of Ohio before winning the presidential nomination in 1876. Some of the electoral votes were disputed, but an electoral commission awarded all the disputed votes to Hayes, giving him victory over Samuel J. Tilden. As president, Hayes removed all federal troops from the South and tried to promote civil service reform. He retired after one term.

Garfield, James A. (1831–81)
20th U.S. president (1881). A Republican from Ohio, Garfield was a teacher and college administrator before rising to major general of volunteers in the Civil War. Prior to running for president, Garfield served in the U.S. House of Representatives and the U.S. Senate. Garfield was shot only a few months after his inauguration. He died two months later.

Arthur, Chester A. (1830–86)
21st U.S. president (1881–85). Arthur, a Republican from Vermont, was at times a teacher, a lawyer, and collector of the Port of New York. He became vice president in 1881 but assumed the presidency that same year upon Garfield's death. As president, he encouraged civil service reforms and opposed the high tariffs passed in 1883. He was not renominated in the 1884 election.

Cleveland, Grover (1837-1908)
22nd and 24th U.S. president (1885–89 and 1893–97). Cleveland was a lawyer and Democrat born in New Jersey but raised in New York. After serving as governor of New York, he won the 1884 presidential election. During this term, Cleveland reformed the civil service and prevented the collection of undeserved pensions. Though he was defeated in the 1888 election, he was elected again in 1892. Inflation and monetary instability were of primary concern during his second term. Cleveland repealed the 1890 Sherman Act but could not completely solve the currency problems. He was not renominated in the 1896 election.

Harrison, Benjamin (1833–1901)
23rd U.S. president (1889–93). Harrison, a Republican from Ohio, was a soldier and an officer in the Civil War. He was elected to the Senate, then to the presidency. As president, Harrison brought six states into the union and signed several pieces of legislation, including the Sherman Antitrust Act. Harrison was defeated in the 1892 election.

McKinley, William (1843–1901)
25th U.S. president (1897–1901). McKinley was a lawyer, a brevetted major in the Civil War, and a Republican from Ohio. He served in the U.S. House of Representatives, where he structured the McKinley Tariff of 1890, and as governor of Ohio before being elected president in 1896. As president, McKinley continued to advocate protective tariffs and opposed free silver. During his term, many territories were annexed, some as a result of the Spanish-American War (1898). McKinley was shot in September 1901 and died nine days later.

Roosevelt, Theodore (1858–1919)
26th U.S. president (1901–09). After Roosevelt, a Republican from New York, served as secretary of the navy in the Spanish-American War, he organized the Rough Riders, a volunteer cavalry he led in Cuba. Roosevelt was governor of New York and vice president before assuming the presidency upon McKinley's death. As president, he acquired the Panama Canal Zone and began construction of the canal, won the Nobel Peace Prize for helping end the Russo-Japanese War (1906), signed the Pure Food and Drug Act (1906), and worked to dissolve trusts. Roosevelt sought the presidency in 1912 and in 1916, arguing for U.S. involvement in WWI. He authored over 40 books.

Taft, William H. (1857–1930)
27th U.S. president (1909–13). Taft was a lawyer, judge, and Republican from Ohio. He was the first governor of the U.S. controlled Phillipines and U.S. secretary of war. While president, he championed antitrust legislation and established the Department of Labor, but his popularity declined because of his tariff policies. After losing the 1912 presidential election, Taft took positions as a law professor at Yale and Chief Justice of the U.S. Supreme Court.

Wilson, Woodrow (1856–1924)
28th U.S. president (1913–21). A Democrat from Virginia, Wilson was a college professor, president of Princeton University, and governor of New Jersey. As president, Wilson's "New Freedom" domestic policies resulted in the 17th, 18th, and 19th Amendments. Wilson also signed the Clayton Antitrust Act (1914) and instituted the Federal Reserve and the Federal Trade Commission. He championed neutrality in WWI but eventually entered the war and guided subsequent peace proceedings. His "Fourteen Points" plan won him the Nobel Peace Prize in 1919. He suffered a stroke in 1919 and was an invalid

for many months. He authored several books before his terms as president.

Harding, Warren G. (1865–1923)
29th U.S. president (1921–23). Harding, a newspaper editor and Republican from Ohio, served as lieutenant governor of Ohio and in the U.S. Senate before he was elected president. As president, Harding championed protective tariffs and opposed high income taxes and the League of Nations. Corrupt officials who had been appointed by Harding marred his administration. Harding died in office while on a speaking tour.

Coolidge, Calvin (1872–1933)
30th U.S. president (1923–29). Coolidge, a lawyer and Republican from Vermont, served terms as lieutenant governor and governor of Massachusetts. Elected vice president in 1920, he became president upon Harding's death and was elected to another term in 1924. As president, Coolidge opposed the League of Nations, reduced the national debt, and twice vetoed a bill to aid farmers. Although the Republican Party wanted to renominate Coolidge, he chose not to run in the 1928 election.

Hoover, Herbert C. (1874–1964)
31st U.S. president (1929–33). A mining engineer and Republican from Iowa, Hoover served in many foreign and social service positions, including Chairman of the American Relief Committee in London and the Commission for Relief in Belgium, and secretary of commerce. Hoover was president during the 1929 stock market crash and part of the Great Depression. Hoover established a few programs to combat the crises, but because he opposed aid through federal bureaucracy, he did not do enough to provide relief. He was defeated in the 1932 election. He wrote a book while serving as secretary of commerce.

Roosevelt, Franklin D. (1882–1945)
32nd U.S. president (1933–45). A lawyer and Democrat from New York, Roosevelt was secretary of the navy and ran for vice president. After being afflicted with polio in 1921, which left his legs paralyzed, he served as governor of New York. During Roosevelt's presidency, he combated the Great Depression through fireside chats, "New Deal" reforms, and organizations such as the Civilian Conservation Corps, the Tennessee Valley Authority, and the Public Works Administration. He met with leaders of the Allied powers fighting

WWII and established a lend-lease program to help them. Roosevelt is the only president who was elected to third and fourth terms. He died in office of a cerebral hemorrhage.

Truman, Harry S. (1884–1972)
33rd U.S. president (1945–53). A Democrat from Missouri, Truman was an artillery officer in WWI and a judge. He served in the U.S. Senate and as vice president, assumed the presidency upon Roosevelt's death, and was elected in 1948. In 1945, Truman ordered the atomic bombing of Japan that ended the war. He championed a policy of containment against the Soviet Union, announcing the Truman Doctrine to aid nations threatened by Communism. Truman established the CIA, increased Social Security, and involved the U.S. in the Korean War (1950).

Eisenhower, Dwight D. (1890–1969)
34th U.S. president (1953–61). Eisenhower, a Republican from Texas, was an officer in WWI, rising to the rank of General of the U.S. Army and Commander in Chief of all allied forces in Europe. He planned the takeover of Germany and led troops into battle. After the war, Eisenhower served as chief of staff of the U.S. Army, president of Columbia University, and commander of NATO forces in Europe. As president, Eisenhower ended the Korean War, used troops to support the integration of schools, and ended diplomacy with Cuba. Eisenhower published two books, one written before his presidential terms and one written after.

Kennedy, John F. (1917–63)
35th U.S. president (1961–63). A Democrat from Massachusetts, Kennedy served in WWII as a naval commander. He was a member of the U.S. House of Representatives and became the youngest president and the only Roman Catholic president. Kennedy's term was marred by the Bay of Pigs disaster, in which anti-Castro Cubans invaded Cuba but failed to complete their mission. Kennedy succeeded in forcing the Soviet Union to remove missiles from Cuba and in keeping troops in Berlin to prevent the spread of Communism. He championed civil rights, space exploration, and improved medical care for the elderly. Kennedy was shot and killed while riding in a motorcade in Dallas, Texas.

United States Presidents

Johnson, Lyndon B. (1908–73)

36th U.S. president (1963–69). A Democrat from Texas, Johnson served in the U.S. House of Representatives and the U.S. Senate, where he was influential and held several important positions. Elected vice president in 1960, Johnson became president upon Kennedy's death. His presidency is noted for "Great Society" reforms and increased U.S. involvement in Vietnam. Because of national and partisan conflict over involvement in Vietnam, Johnson declined renomination in the 1968 election.

Nixon, Richard M. (1913–94)

37th U.S. president (1969–74). Nixon, a Republican from California, served in WWII, was a member of the U.S. House of Representatives and the U.S. Senate, and served as vice president. Nixon was defeated in both the 1960 presidential election and in the race for governor of California. In 1968, Nixon was elected president. He became the first president to visit China, appointed four Supreme Court Justices, and began withdrawing troops from Vietnam after achieving a cease-fire. After his reelection, Nixon was nearly impeached for charges surrounding the burglary of Democratic Party headquarters. The "Watergate Scandal," as it was called, prompted Nixon's resignation.

Ford, Gerald R. (1913–   )

38th U.S. president (1974–77). A lawyer and Republican, Ford was born in Nebraska but grew up in Michigan. He served in WWII as a lieutenant commander of the navy. Ford spent 25 years in the U.S. House of Representatives before President Nixon selected him to replace resigned Vice President Spiro Agnew. Ford became president the following year, upon Nixon's resignation. After pardoning Nixon, a controversial decision, Ford successfully fought inflation, unsuccessfully combated unemployment, and championed détente (an easing of tension among nations). Ford lost the 1976 presidential election by a narrow margin.

Carter, James E. (1924–   )

39th U.S. president (1977–81). Carter, a Democrat from Georgia, served in the navy and studied nuclear physics before he was elected governor of Georgia. After winning the presidential election in 1976, Carter pardoned Vietnam draft evaders and played a crucial role in the peace talks between Israel and Egypt. Efforts to negotiate the release of hostages in Iran consumed the latter half of his term. Carter was criticized for his handling of the economy and foreign policy, causing his defeat in the 1980 election. After Carter left office, his humanitarian and conflict mediation efforts as president were recognized.

Reagan, Ronald W. (1911–   )

40th U.S. president (1981–89). Reagan, a Republican from Illinois, worked as a sports announcer and actor. He was governor of California before winning the presidency in 1980. Reagan instituted supply-side economics, which called for cutting taxes and government programs but resulted in high budget deficits. He also promoted Social Security and tax reforms. In 1981, Reagan was wounded in an assassination attempt. During Reagan's second term, he struggled to contain Communism. His administration was criticized for the sale of weapons to Iran in exchange for hostages and the use of money to aid rebels in Nicaragua.

Bush, George H. W. (1924–   )

41st U.S. president (1989–93). Bush, a Republican, was born in Massachusetts but grew up in Connecticut. After serving as a navy pilot in WWII, he moved to Texas, where he was elected to the U.S. House of Representatives. He spent eight years as vice president. As president, Bush raised taxes to combat budget deficits. He also supported democratization in the Soviet Union, which dissolved in 1991, and in Eastern Europe. Bush used force in 1989 to overthrow Panama's dictator and again in The Persian Gulf War of 1991. His popularity was quelled by a recession that began in late 1991 and cost him the 1992 election.

Clinton, William J. (1946–   )

42nd U.S. president (1993–2001). A lawyer and Democrat from Arkansas, Clinton taught at the University of Arkansas and was governor of Arkansas. As president, Clinton improved relations with Russia and China. He was able to persuade Congress to accept the North American Free Trade Agreement but not his health-care reforms. Clinton was reelected despite possible involvement in the Whitewater real estate scandal. He was impeached by the U.S. House of Representatives in 1998, as a result of another scandal over court testimony, but was acquitted by the Senate. In 1999, Clinton used force to remove Serbian troops from Kosovo. Clinton remained popular despite scandals, perhaps owing to a strong economy.

WEIGHTS AND MEASURES

ENGLISH

Length

12 inches	= 1 foot
3 feet	= 1 yard
220 yards	= 1 furlong
8 furlongs	= 1 mile
5280 feet	= 1 mile
1760 yards	= 1 mile

Area

144 square inches	= 1 square foot
9 square feet	= 1 square yard
4840 square yards	= 1 acre
640 acres	= 1 square mile
1 square mile	= 1 section
36 sections	= 1 township

Volume

1728 cubic inches	= 1 cubic foot
27 cubic feet	= 1 cubic yard

Capacity (Dry)

2 pints	= 1 quart
8 quarts	= 1 peck
4 pecks	= 1 bushel

Capacity (Liquid)

16 fluid ounces	= 1 pint
4 gills	= 1 pint
2 pints	= 1 quart
4 quarts	= 1 gallon (8 pints)

Mass

437.5 grains	= 1 ounce
16 ounces	= 1 pound (7000 grains)
14 pounds	= 1 stone
100 pounds	= 1 hundredweight [cwt]
20 cwt	= 1 ton (2000 pounds)

Troy Weights

24 grains	= 1 pennyweight
20 pennyweights	= 1 ounce (480 grains)
12 ounces	= 1 pound (5760 grains)

Measures

60 minims	= 1 fluid dram
8 fluid drams	= 1 fluid ounce
16 fluid ounces	= 1 pint

Apothecaries' Weights

20 grains	= 1 scruple
3 scruples	= 1 dram
8 drams	= 1 ounce (480 grains)
12 ounces	= 1 pound (5760 grains)

METRIC

Length

1 millimeter	= 1000 micrometers
1 centimeter	= 10 millimeters
1 meter	= 1000 millimeters
1 meter	= 100 centimeters
1 kilometer	= 1000 meters

Area

1 square centimeter	= 100 square millimeters
1 square meter	= 10,000 square centimeters
1 square meter	= 1,000,000 square millimeters
1 square kilometer	= 1,000,000 square meters

Volume

1 milliliter	= 1 cubic centimeter
1 liter	= 1000 milliliters
1 liter	= 0.001 cubic meter

Mass

1 gram	= 1000 milligrams
1 kilogram	= 1000 grams
1 metric ton	= 1,000 kilograms

Weights & Measures

APPROXIMATE CONVERSIONS FROM ENGLISH TO METRIC

Symbol	When You Know	Multiply by	To Find	Symbol
LENGTH				
in	inches	2.5	centimeters	cm
ft	feet	30	centimeters	cm
yd	yards	0.9	meters	m
mi	miles	1.6	kilometers	km
AREA				
in^2	square inches	6.5	square centimeters	cm^2
ft^2	square feet	0.09	square meters	m^2
yd^2	square yards	0.8	square meters	m^2
mi^2	square miles	2.6	square kilometers	km^2
	acres	0.4	hectares	ha
MASS				
oz	ounces	28	grams	g
lb	pounds	0.45	kilograms	kg
	short tons (2000 lb)	0.9	metric ton	t
VOLUME				
tsp	teaspoons	5	milliliters	mL
Tbsp	tablespoons	15	milliliters	mL
in^3	cubic inches	16	milliliters	mL
fl oz	fluid ounces	30	milliliters	mL
c	cups	0.24	liters	L
pt	pints	0.47	liters	L
qt	quarts	0.95	liters	L
gal	gallons	3.8	liters	L
ft^3	cubic feet	0.03	cubic meters	m^3
yd^3	cubic yards	0.76	cubic meters	m^3
TEMPERATURE (exact)				
°F	Fahrenheit	subtract 32 and multiply by 5/9	Celsius	°C

APPROXIMATE CONVERSIONS FROM METRIC TO ENGLISH

Symbol	When You Know	Multiply by	To Find	Symbol
LENGTH				
mm	millimeters	0.04	inches	in
cm	centimeters	0.4	inches	in
m	meters	3.3	feet	ft
m	meters	1.1	yards	yd
km	kilometers	0.6	miles	mi
AREA				
cm^2	square centimeters	0.16	square inches	in^2
m^2	square meters	1.2	square yards	yd^2
km^2	square kilometers	0.4	square miles	mi^2
ha	hectares (10,000 m2)	2.5	acres	
MASS				
g	grams	0.035	ounces	oz
kg	kilograms	2.2	pounds	lb
t	metric ton (1,000 kg)	1.1	short tons	t

Weights & Measures

VOLUME

mL	milliliters	0.03	fluid ounces	fl oz
mL	milliliters	0.06	cubic inches	in^3
L	liters	2.1	pints	pt
L	liters	1.06	quarts	qt
L	liters	0.26	gallons	gal
m^3	cubic meters	35	cubic feet	ft^3
m^3	cubic meters	1.3	cubic yards	yd^3

TEMPERATURE (exact)

°C	Celsius	subtract 9/5 and add 32	Fahrenheit	°F

COOKING CONVERSIONS

A few grains/pinch/dash, etc. (dry)	=	Less than 1/8 tsp
A dash (liquid)	=	A few drops
3 teaspoons	=	1 tablespoon
1/2 tablespoon	=	1-1/2 teaspoons
1 tablespoon	=	3 teaspoons
2 tablespoons	=	1 fluid ounce
4 tablespoons	=	1/4 cup
5-1/3 tablespoons	=	1/3 cup
8 tablespoons	=	1/2 cup
8 tablespoons	=	4 fluid ounces
10-2/3 tablespoons	=	2/3 cup
12 tablespoons	=	3/4 cup
16 tablespoons	=	1 cup
16 tablespoons	=	8 fluid ounces
1/8 cup	=	2 tablespoons
1/4 cup	=	4 tablespoons
1/4 cup	=	2 fluid ounces
1/3 cup	=	5 tablespoons plus 1 teaspoon
1/2 cup	=	8 tablespoons
1 cup	=	16 tablespoons
1 cup	=	8 fluid ounces
1 cup	=	1/2 pint
2 cups	=	1 pint
2 pints	=	1 quart
4 quarts (liquid)	=	1 gallon
8 quarts (dry)	=	1 peck
4 pecks (dry)	=	1 bushel
1 kilogram	=	approximately 2 pounds
1 liter	=	approximately 4 cups or 1 quart
1 cup	=	275 milliliters
1 pint	=	550 milliliters
1 quart	=	900 milliliters